ORGANIZATIONAL ANALYSIS

Essential Readings

ORGANIZATIONAL ANALYSIS

Essential Readings

David Knights

Hugh Willmott

SOUTH-WESTERN
CENGAGE Learning

Australia • Brazil • Japan • Korea • Mexico • Singapore • Spain • United Kingdom • United States

SOUTH-WESTERN
CENGAGE Learning™

Organizational Analysis: Essential Readings
David Knights and Hugh Willmott

Publishing Director: Linden Harris

Publisher: Thomas Rennie

Editorial Assistant: Charlotte Green

Content Project Editor: Lucy Arthy

Senior Production Controller: Paul Herbert

Marketing Manager: Amanda Cheung

Typesetter: KnowledgeWorks Global, India

Cover design: Adam Renvoize

© 2011, Cengage Learning EMEA

For product information and technology assistance, contact **emea.info@cengage.com**.

For permission to use material from this text or product, and for permission queries, email **clsuk.permissions@cengage.com.**

The Author has asserted the right under the Copyright, Designs and Patents Act 1988 to be identified as Author of this Work.

British Library Cataloguing-in-Publication Data
A catalogue record for this book is available from the British Library.

ISBN: 978-1-4080-2017-3

Cengage Learning EMEA
Cheriton House, North Way, Andover, Hampshire, SP10 5BE. United Kingdom

Cengage Learning products are represented in Canada by Nelson Education Ltd.

For your lifelong learning solutions, visit
www.cengage.co.uk

Purchase your next print book, e-book or e-chapter at
www.CengageBrain.com

Printed by RR Donnelley, China
1 2 3 4 5 6 7 8 9 10 – 13 12 11

To our families

BRIEF CONTENTS

CONTENTS

About the Authors

David Knights is Research Professor at the Bristol Business School and a Visiting Professor at Gothenburg School of Business, Economics and Law. He is a founding and continuing editor of the journal *Gender, Work and Organisation*. He is also the founder and continuing director of the Financial Services Research Forum that funds academic research and engages in critical debate with practitioners on this sector. He has published widely in the field of management and organization analysis and is a member of the editorial boards of several international journals.

Hugh Willmott is Research Professor at the Cardiff Business School. He has previously held appointments at the Universities of Cambridge, Manchester and Aston, and visiting appointments at the Universities of Copenhagen, Lund and Cranfield. His books include *Making Quality Critical*, *The Re-engineering Revolution*, *Managing Knowledge*, *Management Lives*, *Studying Management Critically* and *Fragmenting Work*. He has published widely in social science and management journals and currently is a member of the editorial boards of the *Academy of Management Review*, *Organization Studies*, *Journal of Management Studies and an Associated Editor of Organization*.

ACKNOWLEDGEMENTS

Geraldine Lyons who first agreed that this would be a valuable contribution and Tom Rennie and Charlotte Green who carried it through to completion.

GENERAL INTRODUCTION

This Reader is intended as an accompaniment to the use of a range of textbooks (an indicative list is provided in the references below) that are currently used in courses taught across the field of organization studies. Courses in this area assume a variety of names but have in common the study of work organizations, including the analysis of structures, exploration of processes, and the examination of aspects of behaviour. The 16 sections cover the main areas included in organization studies courses, such as Leadership and Strategy as well as some emergent areas such as Consumption, Environment and Globalization. The selected texts have been shortened to make them more readily digestible and user-friendly.

The extracts collected in the 16 sections are intended for use in smaller group sessions where topics presented in lectures are the focus of student discussions and debates. Each section comprises three to seven extracts and is prefaced by an *Introduction* by the editors. The Introduction to each section presents a brief orientation to the extracts and provides relevant background to prepare students for their study. Additionally, each section includes a short set of *Discussion Questions* to stimulate reflection and class interaction as well as a list of *Recommended Further Reading*s to assist private study and the preparation of coursework assignments.

Textbooks aim to be comprehensive in scope but they do not provide substantial reference to the sources – books and articles – that are distilled within them. In this respect, textbooks provide comprehensive breadth but necessarily lack depth and detail. By supplementing textbook study with the use of this Reader, it is intended that students will be better placed to:

- develop insight into some of the original books and articles summarized in textbooks;
- expand their capacity to examine the original sources and subject them to critical scrutiny;

- discuss the topics by reference to a shared core of reading provided by the extracts.

The extracts are intended to reflect the significant shifts within the field of organization studies that have occurred during the past decade and more. Although some elements of the field remain comparatively unaffected, the main change has been a broadening out of the topics studied and a pluralization of approaches engaged in their study. Symptomatic of this shift and also giving additional impetus to it was the publication of Burrell and Morgan's *Sociological Paradigms and Organizational Analysis* (1979). In registering and opening up field, this book (hereafter shortened to *Paradigms*) revealed how the study of organizations had relied implicitly if not explicitly on a wide range of competing perspectives – that is, 'paradigms' – that had previously not been fully acknowledged.

At the centre of *Paradigms* is the proposition that there are four very different approaches to the study of organizations. The dominant or mainstream, 'functionalist' approach that presumes activities interdependently function to maintain organizational stability. However, there are three other perspectives: radical structuralist that presumes conflict as a major source of organizational change, interpretive approaches that see organizations as negotiated entities, and radical humanism that is concerned with freeing humans from unnecessary organizational constraints and oppressions. While largely ignored by the mainstream, each of these perspectives has a legitimate right to be heard and, indeed, to be given equivalent attention. This Reader attempts to address this imbalance in the literature by giving priority to extracts that are of a non-mainstream character on topics that are normally covered in post-introductory courses.

During the 1980s and 1990s, the field of organization studies expanded beyond the mainstream, 'functionalist' approach, with textbooks appearing that were either based in (e.g. Clegg and Dunkerley's *Organization, Class and Control*, Routledge, 1980), or took more adequate account of (e.g. Thompson and McHugh's *Work Organizations*, Palgrave Macmillan 1990), one or more of the three neglected approaches. An edited textbook (Knights and Willmott, *Introducing Organization Behaviour and Management*, 2006) incorporates both by presenting key elements and assumptions of mainstream thinking prior to offering a digest of more critical and reflexive approaches. This expansion of alternatives to the mainstream has also been reflected in a number of journals dedicated to research in the field; especially, *Organization Studies, Organization Science, Journal of Management Inquiry, Organization and Ephemera*.

A common feature of these textbooks and journals is the accommodation or promotion of a more critical and reflexive approach: critical in the sense that the core, functionalist assumptions of mainstream texts is challenged; and reflexive in the sense that they appreciate how knowledge of organizations is founded upon *particular* sets of assumptions that define a distinctive approach or perspective.

A feature of this Reader is the extraction of the main contribution of each of the selections rather than their full reproduction. This has made it possible to include many more selections without the Reader becoming exceedingly long or placing a largely unproductive burden upon student readers. In this respect, our concern has been to respond constructively to what, throughout our comparatively long academic careers, we have experienced as the low pain threshold of many students to reading dense and dry academic texts (see Knights and Willmott, 1999). We would rather that students read a number of comparatively brief extracts than despair and give up at the prospect of reading something many times their length. In preparing the readings, we have endeavoured to identify their main contribution.

Our hope is that by making short extracts from journal articles and books available to students, it will enable them to acquire the skills, confidence and stamina to move on to reading full articles and research monographs. From this it will be deduced that we have some sympathy with students' frustrations with academic articles and books, which are necessarily written to satisfy academic reviewers and peers, and not to reach a wider audience of students and others. It is hardly surprising, then, that students often question the point of consulting original sources or reading more widely. In the absence of anything briefer and more digestible, students are tempted to rely upon the Internet or even more dubious sources, despite lecturers seeking to discourage this. Our brief summaries of the extracts in the Introduction to each section are intended to facilitate study by rendering academic materials more student-friendly in this area of critical organization studies.

In addition to a majority of extracts that are broadly representative of current critical thinking within organizational analysis, we have included some more seasoned texts that have acquired something of a classical status (e.g. Sennett and Cobb, 1977; Burawoy, 1979; Zuboff, 1988). Needless to say, our choice of readings has had to be highly selective. It has also been constrained by the high costs of permissions demanded by book and journal publishers. For this reason but also because of our general contribution to critical management thinking, an extract from one of our own single or multiple-authored publications has been included in each section. For students who are studying organization studies by using *Introducing Organization Behaviour and Management*, we believe that their inclusion facilitates a degree of continuity and imparts a less impersonal and intangible flavour to the Reader. For students who are not familiar with our textbook, use of this Reader may be of help in digesting its contents and appreciating their relevance. The design of the Reader is, however, intended to complement the use of a wide range of (critically oriented) textbooks (an indicative list is presented below). For that reason we direct students to texts other than our own by providing a list of recommended readings at the end of each section.

References

Burawoy, M. (1979) *Manufacturing Consent*. Chicago: The University of Chicago Press.

Sennett, R. and Cobb, J. (1977) *The Hidden Injuries of Class*. Cambridge University Press.

Zuboff, S. (1988) *In the Age of the Smart Machine: The Future of Work and Power*, New York: Basic Books.

Indicative List of Critically-Oriented Textbooks

Burrell, G. and Morgan, G. (1979) *Sociological Paradigms and Organizational Analysis*, London: Heinemann.

Clegg, S.R. and Dunkerley, D. (1980) *Organization, Class and Control*, London: Routledge.

Clegg, S.R., Pitsis, T. and Kornberger, M. (2008) *Managing and Organizations: An Introduction to Theory and Practice*, 2nd ed., London: Sage.

Fulop, L., Linstead, S. and Lilley, S. (2004) *Management and Organization: A Critical Text*, London: Macmillan Palgrave.

Grey, C. (2008) *A Very Short Fairly Interesting and Reasonably Cheap Book About Studying Organizations,* 2nd ed., London: Sage.

Knights, D. and Willmott, H.C. (1999) *Management Lives: Power and Identity in Work Organisations*, London: Sage.

Knights, D. and Willmott, H.C. (2006) *Introducing Organizational Behaviour and Management*, 4th ed., London: Cengage Learning.

Jackson, N. and Carter, P. (2004) *Rethinking Organizational Behaviour: A Poststructuralist Framework*, 2nd ed., London: Prentice-Hall.

Sennett, R. and Cobb, J. (1977) *The Hidden Injuries of Class*, Cambridge University Press.

Thompson, P. and McHugh, D. (2009) *Work Organizations: A Critical Approach*, London: Palgrave Macmillan.

Wilson, F.M. (2003) *Organizational Behaviour and Gender*, Gower: Ashgate.

ORGANIZATION THEORY

CHAPTER 1

READINGS

Clegg, S.R. and Hardy, C. (1999) 'Introduction' in *Studying Organizations*. Edited by Clegg, S.R. and Hardy, C. London: Sage, pp. 1–4.

Silverman, D. (1975) 'Accounts of Organizations: Organizational "Structures" and the Accounting Process' in *Processing People: Cases in Organizational Behaviour*. Edited by John B. MoKinlay. London; New York, Holt, Rinehart and Winston, pp. 294–299.

Willmott, H. (2003) 'Organization Theory as Critical Science?' in *The Oxford Handbook of Organization Theory*. Edited by Haridimos Tsoukas and Christian Knudsen. Oxford University Press, pp. 89, 90, 94–96, 98–99, 100–101, 107–108.

INTRODUCTION

'Organization theory' comprises numerous ways of making sense of 'organizations' founded upon diverse assumptions about their nature and characteristics. It may be presupposed, for example, that organizations are well-defined, harmonious entities; or that they are composed of multiple – occupational, departmental or work group – cultures; or that they form contradictory unities embodying conflicting principles or interests held together by relations of domination and exploitation. These are some of the perspectives or 'conversations' (Clegg and Hardy, Reading 1.1) that make up organization theory.

As you read this text, you are continuously invoking some 'theory' of what 'organization' is. However sketchy or sophisticated, this is what enables you to attribute meaning to the term, or concept, 'organization'. The meaning may be provisional but, without it, it becomes impossible to proceed. It is precisely these provisional understandings that are embraced or questioned by different theories of organization. When assessing the plausibility of competing theories of organization, it is therefore relevant to ask whether their attraction or implausibility is mainly attributable to our own, often implicit and minimally examined, theories about 'organization'.

'Theories' are not the exclusive preserve of academics or intellectuals. We all employ 'theories' to navigate, or muddle, our way through the world. 'Theory' is a grandiose term for characterizing ways of making sense that aspire to be more explicit and rigorous than everyday ways of making sense. There is, then, nothing especially disconcerting or daunting about '(organization) theory' – except, perhaps, a mystique that surrounds the idea of 'theory' as something exotic and inaccessible. Theory is actually very familiar to us. Theory, in the form of 'common sense thinking' for example, enables us, and perhaps even compels us, to act in the world and thereby make the world (e.g. organizations) the way it is. Our theories contribute to guiding and justifying our actions. Our sense of how the world is, including the reality of organization(s), depends upon which theory we engage or, perhaps more plausibly, how we are engaged by the theories to which we more or less consciously subscribe.

Much organization theory trades off common sense ideas that were taken up and refined by managers and administrators. Such theories are founded often upon mechanistic or organic metaphors that represent organizations as the human equivalent of machines or bodies that operate according to a functionalist logic. Contingency theory and organizational ecology, for example, are founded upon an organic analogy (see Reading 1.1). Theories that resonate with practitioners' presuppositions have an immediate plausibility and appeal. But they are also limited in their awareness and grasp of other theories which challenge, rather than reinforce and elaborate, received wisdom. Nonetheless, the 'face validity' of common sense theories which rely upon mechanistic or organic metaphors may lend an air of authority to everyday thinking. Even when theories do not directly guide action, they may act to rationalize and legitimize current organizational practices. It is therefore worth asking whether received wisdom is challenged or reproduced by particular theories of organization.

To the extent that theories guide actions, they are also involved in producing the realities that they seek to examine. Instead of thinking of theory as knowledge that approximates to some aspects of our world, it is instructive to consider how (dominant) theory produces a (meaningful) sense of the world. It invites us to see, and act upon, the world in a particular way. Such theory is powerful – it exerts control over how we act as well as how we think. A manager who subscribes to a (functionalist) theory that portrays organizations as unitary, rational, goal-achieving entities, for example, is likely to be predisposed to designing or redesigning structures and procedures in ways that are assumed to better fulfil this vision. This is regardless of whether individuals and groups within the organization share the manager's vision. Efforts to apply a theory will, frequently, result in unintended as well as planned changes of practice. Other members of an organization, guided by their own distinctive preferences and associated theories, may act in ways that contradict, subvert or frustrate, the intentions and related theories of the manager.

A basic insight here is that what seems plausible as a theory is often closely related to the position (e.g. 'manager' or 'worker') with which a person identifies. A 'professional' manager may be more inclined to believe in the idea of organizations as rational, goal-achieving entities, and strive to make this a reality. And the manager may well retain this idea even as they continuously face 'problems' (e.g. 'irrational' behaviour) that place in question the adequacy or generalizability of the presuppositions underpinning the manager's theory. In effect, the belief that employees should act 'rationally' – that is, according to what the manager's theory considers is 'rational' – inhibits or overrides the pressure to review the plausibility of the theory.

Our readings identify central strands of conventional wisdom and commend a variety of alternative ways of developing organization theory. In their overview of organization theory, **Stewart Clegg and Cynthia Hardy** (Reading 1.1) counterpose a dominant 'functionalist' theory of organization, in which consensus and coherence is assumed, to other broad traditions of organization theory. Notably, they draw attention to theories that are concerned to appreciate how different actors and groups within organizations account for their reality in diverse ways; or, alternatively, highlight the significance of broader politico-economic struggles for understanding how a (precarious) sense of unity or at least compliance is accomplished within relations of domination and exploitation. Specifically, they point to the intervention of David Silverman (see also Reading 1.2) who, in *The Theory of Organizations*, 'opened a Pandora's box, releasing actors as opposed to systems ... [and] ... plural definitions rather than the singular definition around organizational goals' (Clegg and Hardy, in this volume, p. 4). Clegg and Hardy also usefully note the emergence of an increased ('postmodern') awareness of how accounts of 'organization' are inescapably the products of particular intellectual frameworks, rather than the objective reports of impartial observers. This awareness, they suggest, opens up the possibility of making more informed choices. But it is perhaps also relevant to reflect upon how the very idea of choice as well as the process of choosing exemplifies a particular (powerful) way of framing the development and application of organization theory.

In 'Accounts of organizations', **David Silverman** (Reading 1.2) takes up the argument that theories of organization are deeply and unselfconsciously embedded in common sense thinking. He points out how our use of the concept 'organization' carries with it many tacit and unexamined understandings – or frameworks or interpretive procedures – about what an 'organization' 'is'. If we accept that the meaning or reality of organizations relies heavily upon how we commonsensically account for them, then it makes sense, he argues, to examine these accounting processes. This necessitates a turning away from theories and research instruments that assume the possibility of mirroring or capturing aspects of an 'out there' reality. It also presents an alternative to studies that attempt to capture or reflect the meanings ascribed to organizations by different members of work organizations. Following the argument developed by ethnomethodologists, such as Harold Garfinkel and Egon Bittner, Silverman questions whether these meanings can be captured any more readily or adequately than the ostensibly 'objective' features of organizations (e.g. 'specialization' or 'formalization'). A less commonsensical, and more rigorous, approach to the study of organizational realities, Silverman contends, requires the directing of attention to the methodical procedures through which organizational members and observers impute meanings, as contrasted to contents of accounts of organization – whether these accounts articulate the values of a particular subculture or the degree of specialization in a population of organizations, as indicated by responses to a survey, for example. The basic argument, then, is that 'the 'sensible' nature of such accounts derives not from the phenomena to which they refer but from the way in which the account makes available the features of some phenomenon and display its rational properties ... the accounting process is itself a worthwhile topic of investigation' (Silverman, 1975: 300).

Hugh Willmott (Reading 1.3) applies a critical theoretic framework based upon Habermas's theory of cognitive interests to classify different forms of organization theorizing. These are located within traditions of empirical-analytic, historical-hermeneutic and critical science. Habermas's framework provides an insightful way of differentiating between forms of knowledge and also offers a basis for reflecting upon continuities and discontinuities between modernist and postmodernist versions of critical thinking. Specifically, it invites reflection on how truth claims are warranted by reference to a universal foundation that can validate knowledge, as contrasted to the operation of discourses that value and facilitate the production of distinctive traditions of enquiry. Both the conversations to which Clegg and Hardy refer and the idea that diverse discourses, including Habermas's three traditions of scientific enquiry, resonate with Silverman's view that the plurality of perspectives comprising organization theory are not plausibly regarded as correctives to each other. As Silverman puts it, there is no universally agreed 'basis for doubting lay or professional accounts of social phenomena – although that is not to say that participants or practitioners may not doubt some accounts from within their paradigm of knowledge' (Silverman, 1973: 300).

READING 1.1 | # Studying Organizations

By Stewart R. Clegg and Cynthia Hardy

Three decades ago, an 'orthodox consensus' (Atkinson, 1971) seemed to be emerging in organization theory concerning the role of functionalism, by which we mean an approach premised on assumptions concerning the unitary and orderly nature of organizations. Functionalist research emphasizes consensus and coherence rather than conflict, dissensus and the operations of power. The key concept is that of the organization as a 'system' which is functionally effective if it achieves explicit goals formally defined through rational decision-making. Management's task, according to this view, is to define and achieve these goals; the researcher's task is to collect objective data concerning the way in which the organization functions around goal orientation and maintenance. Typically, the research method follows the normal science model, in which the nature of organizational reality is represented and expressed through a formal research design; quantitative data facilitate validation, reliability, and replicability; a steady accumulation and building of empirically

generated knowledge derives from a limited number of theoretical assumptions.

Different theoretical approaches, such as population ecology, organizational economics, contingency theory, among others, have evolved under the dual umbrella of functionalism and normal science, both of which remain driving forces in organization studies today. Meanwhile, a plethora of alternative approaches emerged, which directly challenge the supremacy of functionalism and normal science. Marsden and Townley (Chapter 17) call these approaches 'contra' science since they aim at critiquing and replacing the assumptions, approaches, and methods of normal science. One important trigger of these alternative approaches in the British content was the publication or David Silverman's (1971) *The Theory of Organizations* whose interpretative emphasis countered the functionalist view. It opened a Pandora's box releasing actors as opposed to systems; social construction as opposed to social determinism; interpretative understanding as opposed to a

READING 1.1	**Studying Organizations**
	By Stewart R. Clegg and Cynthia Hardy

logic of causal explanation; plural definitions of situations rather than the singular definition articulated around organizational goals. In the USA, Karl Weick's (1969) book *The Social Psychology of Organizing* provided another impetus for alternative work by focusing attention on the processes of organizing, rather than those entities called organizations, using similar phenomenological resources to Silverman (1971). The publication of Braverman's (1974) study of 'the labour process' brought the concerns of Marxist thinking on to the organization studies agenda, reinforcing concerns with conflict, power and resistance (Clegg and Dunkerley 1980; Littler 1982; Burawoy 1979; Knights and Willmott 1990). The framework offered by Burrell and Morgan (1979) in *Sociological Paradigms and Organizational Analysis* identified functionalist, interpretativist, radical humanist and radical structuralist paradigms. It provided a sense-making device to account for and locate these new approaches, as well as carving out legitimate spaces in which they could flourish.

Elsewhere, in the broader realms of social theory, a radical change in social and political thought was taking place under the rubric of 'postmodernism' (Laclau 1988). ...

Building on the pioneering work of intellectuals like Lyotard (1984), postmodern critiques coalesced around an antipathy to 'modernist' tendencies emphasizing grand narrative; the notion of totality; and essentialism.

The object of early postmodernist critiques clearly was Marxism. Here was a master narrative *par excellence,* the sweep of class struggle delivering a teleological 'end of history' in communist society; few categories could be more 'totalizing' than the notion of the 'mode of production', which was the key to explaining all social change everywhere. At the core of this theoretical project was 'class struggle', the essential fulcrum on which social and economic development occurred; individuals were visible only in so far as they were bearers of identities that their class position either ascribed, in which case their consciousness was 'authentic', or denied, in the case of 'false' consciousness.

Postmodern approaches challenge and invert each one of these assumptions: no grand narrative marks the unfolding of human histories. They are histories, not history: one must attend to local, fragmented specificities, the narratives of everyday lives. Any pattern that is constituted can only be a series of assumptions framed in and by a historical context. ...

For example, no necessarily essential social attributes characterize 'men' or 'women'. Instead the subjectivity of those labelled as such is culturally and historically variable and specific.

As the status of the subject is challenged so, too, is that of the researcher. No longer all-knowing, all-seeing, objective or omnipotent, the researcher is forced to re-examine, in a reflexive mode, his or her relation to the research process and the 'knowledge' it produces. No longer a disinterested observer, acutely aware of the social and historical positioning of all subjects and the particular intellectual frameworks through which they are rendered visible, the researcher can only produce knowledge already embedded in the power of those very frameworks. No privileged position exists from which analysis might arbitrate.

What are Organization Studies?

These changes have major implications for our understanding of what organization studies constitute. Gone is the certainty, if it ever existed, about what organizations are; gone, too, is the certainty about how they should be studied, the place of the researcher, the role of methodology, the nature of theory. Defining organization studies today is by no means an easy task. Our approach is to conceptualize organization studies as a series of conversations, in particular those of organization studies researchers who help to constitute organizations through terms derived from paradigms, methods and assumptions, themselves derived from earlier conversations.

But what are these conversations, what are they about and why do they exist? We believe they are evolving conversations, with emergent vocabularies and grammars, and with various degrees of discontinuity. Sometimes they are marked by voices from the centre of analysis and practice, sometimes they seem to come from left field, out of the blue. They reflect, reproduce and refute both the traditions of discourse that have shaped the study of organizations and the practices in which members of organizations engage. They relate to *organizations* as empirical objects, to *organization* as social process,

READING 1.1   **Studying Organizations** *continued*

By Stewart R. Clegg and Cynthia Hardy

and to the intersections and gaps between and within them.

Let us explain by starting with a premise: *organizations* are empirical objects. By this we mean that we see something when we see an organization, but each of us may see something different. For instance, we can refer to the World Bank as an 'organization', one with specific resources and capacities; with rules that constitute it; with a boundedness that defines it more or less loosely; with a history; with employees, clients, victims and other interested agents. These boundaries, these rules, this history, these agents must be enacted and interpreted, however, if they are to form a basis for action. For example, a rule has to be represented as something enforceable and obligatory before it means anything, and it may mean nothing or it may mean many things, to members and their experience of everyday organizational life.

As researchers, we participate in these enactment and interpretation processes. We choose what empirical sense we wish to make of organizations by deciding how we wish to represent them in our work. Representation, by any device, always involves a choice concerning what aspects of the 'organization' we wish to represent and how we will represent it. For example, some see organizations as characterized by dimensions like formalization, standardization and routinization; others as exhibiting variation, selection, retention and competition; or incurring transaction costs; or distinguished by institutionalised cultures, or whatever. We would say that to the extent that organizations achieve representation in particular terms, they always do so as an effect of theoretical privileges afforded by certain ways of seeing, certain terms of discourse, and their conversational enactment. At the same time, these terms of representation are already ways of not seeing, ways of not addressing other conversational enactments, and hence, ways of not acknowledging other possible attributes of organizations.

How aspects of organizations are represented, the means of representation, the features deemed salient, those features glossed and those features ignored, are not attributes or the organization. They are an effect or the reciprocal interaction of multiple conversations: those that are professionally organized,

through journals, research agendas, citations and networks; those that take place in the empirical world of organizations. The dynamics or reciprocity in this mutual interaction can vary some conversations of practice inform those of the profession; some professional talk dominates practice; some practical and professional conversations sustain each other; others talk past, miss and ignore each other.

Consider, again, the example of the World Bank: it shows that there is no artificial separation between the conversations in, of and around organizations. It is not the case that one discourse belongs to science and another to everyday life, that one can inform or reform the other in some determinate way. 'The World Bank' implies conversations lodged within diverse discourses with different emphases about, among other things, the scientific efficacy and adequacy of various models of economic and social development. The strategies of science are integral to its strategies of organization but its strategies of organization are more than merely this one restricted conversation. There are also the conversations that constitute the work of the members of the organization, conversations which implicate formal disciplinary knowledges, such as 'marketing', 'research and development', and all those other terms that provide a lexicon of 'management'. Such conversations and their associated practices arrange the organizational arena as a contested terrain – one where scenes are configured, agencies enrolled, interests translated, and work accomplished, a space in which the empirical object is constituted. Such conversations, derived from the disciplines, as well as from more local knowledges and their reciprocal interaction, shape the object, the *organization*.

So, whether located in the organization of an academic specialism such as ours, or applied in the constitution of actions that become the analytical subject of such specialisms, the insights of conversation, as a public phenomenon, something intersubjective and shared, involve *organizing* as a social process. By this we refer to the embeddedness of organizing within distinct local practice, of language, of culture, of ethnicity, of gender. There is always someone who speaks and engages in conversation in order for a conversation to occur. These individuals

Studying Organizations

By Stewart R. Clegg and Cynthia Hardy

have identities that are implicated in what is said, or not said. Speech is never disembodied – there is always a subject who speaks, even behind the most reifying organization theorist or desiccated bureaucrat.

Organizations are thus, sites of situated social action more or less open both to explicitly organized and formal disciplinary knowledges such as marketing, production, and so on, and also to conversational practices embedded in the broad social fabric, such as gender, ethnic and other culturally defined social relations, themselves potential subjects for formally organized disciplinary knowledges, such as anthropology, sociology, or, even organization studies. Similarly, this volume is a collection of voices involved in the analysis of organizations, as real objects, where the 'reality' of these objects is constituted through diverse conversations of the analysts and the analysands, where both practices are embedded socially in ways of being, ways of organizing.

With this conceptualization of organization studies, one can strive for reflexivity, by which we allude to ways of seeing which act back on and reflect existing ways of seeing. For instance, feminism is both a social movement and an intellectually organized discourse with many conversations contained within it. The conversations inform each arena: sometimes they constitute aspects of the other arena, and they can be used to reveal lacunae in that 'other' arena represented. Many research possibilities reside in these reflexive relations. For example, in studying organization concerned with equal employment opportunity, one might want to address its impact from within feminist discourse; or one might want to address the impact of equal employment opportunity legislation on the further bureaucratisation of the human resource management function within a sample of organizations; or one might be interested in the politics of implementation. None is a more 'correct' analysis than any other: they are different possibilities. Like any good conversation, the dialectic is reflexive, interlocutive and oriented, not to ultimate agreement, but to the possibilities of understanding of, and action within, these contested terrains. Contestation occurs not only in the scenes of action in organizations as empirical objects, for example around gender

relations, but also in the conflicting interpretations of these scenes afforded by different theoretical, as well as 'lay' or 'practical', conversations. Where desired, this contestation and associated reflexivity generate difference, although frequently, both theorists and practitioners have a practical interest in closure, not in the continual iteration of further choice. Practical foreclosure does not resolve reflexivity: it suspends it, until the next dissenting interpretation.

Readers are interpreters: to read is an active, sense-making process. Through texts such as this the reader has an opportunity to rethink his or her own conversational practices as an organization member. The dialectic moves to that between text and the reader: readers make (and change the) sense of words and make their own representations, a theme to which we return in the concluding chapter. Ultimately, the text is important for what the reader gives to it, not in how its various authors use it to reaffirm their own subjectivity. Through their particular reading, readers will find ways to employ aspects that enable them to speak for themselves in terms of their choosing.

References

Braverman, H. (1974) *Labor and Monopoly Capital*. New York: Monthly Review Press.

Burawoy, M. (1979) *Manufacturing Consent*. Chicago: University of Chicago Press.

Burrell, G. and Morgan, G. (1979) *Sociological Paradigms and Organizational Analysis*. London: Heinemann.

Clegg, S.R. and Dunkerley, D. (1980) *Organization, Class and Control*. London: Routledge and Kegan Paul.

Knights, D. and Willmott, H.C. (1990) *Labour Process Theory*. London: Academy.

Laclau, E. (1988) 'Politics and the limits of modernity' in A. Ross (ed.), *Universal Abandon: The politics of postmodernism*. Minneapolis: University of Minnesota Press. Pp. 63–82.

Littler, C. (1982) *The Labour Process in Capitalist Societies*. London: Tavistock.

Lyotard, J. (1984) *The Postmodern Condition*. Manchester: Manchester University Press.

Silverman, D. (1971) *The Theory of Organizations: Sociological Framework*. London: Heinemann.

Weick, K. (1969) *The Social Psychology of Organizing*. Reading, MA: Addison-Wesley.

READING 1.2 **Accounts of Organizations: Organizational "Structures" and the Accounting Process**

By David Silverman

... The concepts of 'organization' and 'bureaucracy' are firmly grounded in the 'natural attitude'. Within that attitude (whose main features were discussed earlier), such concepts refer to lay schemes of interpretation whereby the 'sensible' and 'rational' nature of activities is provided for and recognized, i.e. whereby activities are constituted as observable reportable phenomena. The concept of 'organization' thus provides the possibility of one kind of account, which, like other accounts, makes available the features of a non-problematic social world.

It will be recognized at once that this kind of argument is entirely unlike the manner in which the logic of the sociology of organizations has developed. In this section an attempt will be made to show that the latter relies on a particular reading of the Weberian concept of bureaucracy: a reading which it is by no means clear that Weber himself would have supported.

Almost uniformly in the literature on 'organizations', Weber's ideal-type of bureaucracy is, albeit implicitly, taken to refer to the intrinsic features of some visible object. It is as if Weber were offering to the world a painting of some object, say a table, and the question that should be correctly addressed to his portrayal should be: 'has he got it right?', i.e. has he captured the intrinsic features which make a thing a 'bureaucracy?' On this basis, subsequent writers point to studies which note: the existence of 'informal' patterns to which Weber's conceptualization does not refer and of internal inefficiencies and 'dysfunctions' in bureaucracy. As a consequence, the concepts of bureaucracy and organization have been reformulated and distinctions between 'formal' and 'informal' patterns of activities have been instituted. The picture of 'bureaucracy' has, then, been altered with the aim of establishing a better correspondence between it and the 'object' to which it purportedly refers.

Yet Weber's whole conception of the social sciences was based on a differentiation between the character of physical and social relations. As is well known, he was concerned in his empirical work to emphasize the uniquely meaningful character of

social life and to produce interpretations of social action in terms of their subjective meaning. Weber makes an attempt, then, to base his ideal-types on interlinked patterns of meaning which define the character of social phenomena; as he says, ideal-types must be judged in terms of their 'adequacy on the level of meaning'. Furthermore, as many writers on bureaucracy apparently ignore, Weber's own analysis arose in the context of a study of the bases on which authority is claimed to be (and recognized as) 'legitimate'. For Weber, then, the sense of labelling activities 'bureaucratic' arises within a rational-legal system of authority which provides a means of justifying (legitimating) a course of action by an appeal to the sanctity of enacted rules. In the sequence below, for instance, he implies that social life proceeds on the basis of interpretive procedures which specify what may be taken to be the case rather than upon what, in some ontological sense, is 'really so':

> 'Obedience' will be taken to mean that the action of the person obeying follows in essentials such a course that the content of the command may be taken to have become the basis of action for its own sake. Furthermore, the fact that it is so taken is referable only to the formal obligation, without regard to the actor's own attitude to the value or lack of value of the content of the command as such (Weber, 1964: 327).

The issue here, clearly, is that social objects become recognized by imputing motives to parties and inferring regularities in their activities. In this sense alone do social phenomena have 'intrinsic' features or possess ontological status. However, Weber's sociology does not provide for an analysis of the common sense practices through which both participants and observers come to impute social meanings (this is a point which will be returned to shortly).

If the sociologist's knowledge of organizations is contrasted with that of the lay participants in organizations, a difference and a similarity can be viewed. First, the layman manages without 'precise' or

Source: Reproduced with kind permission by Prof. David Silverman and Prof. John McKinlay from 'Accounts of Organizations: Organizational "Structures" and the Accounting Process', in Processing People: Cases in Organisational Behaviour © 1975 Holt, Rinehart and Winston.

READING 1.2

Accounts of Organizations: Organizational "Structures" and the Accounting Process

By David Silverman

'complete' definitions of 'bureaucracy' and 'organization'. Second, like the sociologist, the layman is committed to the existence of 'bureaucracy' as a 'natural fact', as an object 'out there' in the world – like the atmosphere or, indeed, a table. Sociologists, then, cannot make claims to possess sole knowledge of organizations and bureaucracies. Yet this is damaging to their pretensions in ways which do not threaten the natural scientist. While the latter can justifiably dismiss lay conceptions of natural regularities (e.g. movements of the stars, meteorological events), social regularities are preconstituted by lay conceptions. For, through the categories of natural language, laymen have predefined social structures, including bureaucracies. On the basis of their interpretive procedures, 'bureaucracy' thus comes to stand as a depiction of the intrinsic features of an object. To apply the concept is, then, to give evidence of membership of a language-community in which the definition of 'certain' activities in this way 'make sense'. Its use does *not* refer to the intrinsic features of some available object-structures or relations are not, in themselves, 'really' bureaucratic (or otherwise) – for both the recognition of social relations (as the product of underlying structures) and their display (as bureaucratic) depend upon interpretive practices which provide ways of attending to the world. The conventional sociological treatment of 'organizations' and 'bureaucracy' thus trades upon such practices in its task of producing 'sensible' and 'rational' descriptions. It is worth repeating a passage in which Wittgenstein captures this precisely:

> One thinks that one is tracing the outline of the thing's nature over and over again, and one is merely tracing round the frame through which we look at it.

It is possible, however, to treat 'bureaucracy' not as, in itself, an object, but as a language-category which provides for the object-like qualities of an activity. Rather than seeking clearer specifications of what bureaucracy 'really means' or attempting to formulate 'operational definitions', the object of investigation becomes the manner in which a concept of bureaucracy is called upon, usually as a tacit resource, to display and to acknowledge the 'sense' of actions. For, as suggested earlier, laymen do not worry themselves over much about scientific

definitions of bureaucracy; nor, indeed, do they probably use the term frequently in the course of natural conversation. Rather, in carrying out their routine business, competent members bring off comprehensible talk and action by relying on taken-for-granted knowledge of social structures (including organizational structures). The reader has only to think of the truncated conversations that regularly pass between himself and 'office-holders' (post office clerks, sales assistants, bus drivers) to realize the manner in which the encoding and decoding of such talk relies on a sense of social structures which includes knowledge of bureaucratic 'routines'. Such knowledge is typically tacit: as Garfinkel has shown, to ask the other party to spell out the assumptions on which their talk proceeds is simply to invite disruption.

In a paper called 'The Concept of Organization', Bittner develops an alternative posture parallel to that implied here. The central feature of organizational analysis, as he sets it, is a reliance on common sense knowledge of the world. For instance, post-Weberian sociologists have distinguished between 'formal organization' (programmatic constructions that prospectively define conduct) and 'informal structures' which seem to grow spontaneously in ways not provided for in the programme. Yet laymen too account for their activities in terms of rules and so the sociologist's analysis tacitly mirrors common sense. Bittner (1965) comments:

> In general, there is nothing wrong with borrowing a common sense concept for the purposes of sociological enquiry. Up to a certain point it is, indeed, unavoidable. The warrant for this procedure is the sociologists interest in exploring the common sense perspective. The point at which the use of common sense concepts becomes a transgression is where such concepts *are expected to do the analytical work of theoretical concepts*. When the actor is treated as a permanent auxiliary to the enterprise of sociological enquiry at the same time he is the object of the enquiry, there arise ambiguities that defy clarification.

By tacitly relying on actors' theories of the world, the student of organizations confuses, then, the use of the social world as a *topic* of enquiry with its

Accounts of Organizations: Organizational "Structures" and the Accounting Process *continued*

By David Silverman

employment as an unacknowledged *resource* in developing explanations and theories.

Despite his commitment to a sociology of meaning, Max Weber, according to Bittner, relied on everyday knowledge of 'bureaucracy' to produce his ideal-type. Rather than analyse the common sense presuppositions of his theory, he offers a truncated account of bureaucracy which glosses how competent actors make sense of 'rules', 'offices', and 'hierarchies' in the context of actual social scenes. This attempt to develop 'refined' operational definitions of bureaucracy, as well as analyses of interactions which trade upon what-everyone-knows about organizational structures, necessarily involves what Bittner calls a 'theoretical shortcut'. The alternative is to consider the methods by which competent members employ everyday knowledge of bureaucracy to provide for the 'sensible' and 'rational' nature of their encounters and the outcomes which these produce:

> ... the formal organizational designs are schemes of interpretation that competent and entitled users can invoke in yet unknown ways whenever it suits their purposes. The varieties of ways in which the scheme can be invoked for information, direction, justification, and so on, without incurring the risk of sanction, constitute the scheme's methodical use (Bittner, 1965).

In itself, then, bureaucracy has neither an intrinsic meaning nor is it the determinant of actions – it does not have this kind of ontological status. Rather the concept of bureaucracy exists in and through the socially sanctioned occasions of its use. Thus sociologists who point to differences in the rule-governed nature of 'formal' and 'informal' practices, mirror everyday accounting activities which also routinely seek to depict the 'sense' of 'what is happening'. The issue for analysis is rather the interpretive procedures and socially organized activities which provide for the sense of 'some-thing' having happened – for instance, by laying claim to the rule-governed character of events.

To conclude this section of the chapter, reference will be made to some materials gathered in the course of research on a large public sector organization. One routine activity in which senior members of the organization engage is the selection of recruits for junior administrative positions from a much greater number of applicants. A three man Selection Board interviews each candidate. On the occasion at which the following transcript was obtained, however, one of the members of the Board, a newcomer to the selection process, was being 'filled in' by the Chairman about the order of questioning and, more specifically, was learning that newcomers must expect to come last:

CHAIRMAN: *Bob, look, I'm going to ask you to go second. Not for any reasons of seniority ...*

BOB: *Mm.*

CHAIRMAN: *or anything like that but because he and I do so many of these things together that to a certain extent we compliment each other.*

BOB: *Mm.*

CHAIRMAN: *And therefore I want someone to be, in soccer terms, the sweeper-upper. Will you be the sweeper-upper? Do you mind?*

BOB: *Where do you want me? Second-phase possession?*

CHAIRMAN: *Will you do second-phase possession?*

BOB: *I'll be inside wing-forward.*

CHAIRMAN: *Ha, ha. ha. Right ho.*

One of the ways of inferring the sense of this exchange is by employing lay knowledge of how persons 'bring off' their talk by using it to locate their position in hierarchies. It could be argued, then, that there are grounds for identifying one talker as the senior person and the other as the junior even if that information had not otherwise been provided. First, one person introduces the new topic at the beginning of the exchange (his 'Bob, look' followed a pause in conversation) and also closes the topic ('Right ho'). Second, the same person gives an instruction to the other ('I'm going to ask you to go second'), which the latter seems to accept without questioning the authority of the speaker to give instructions. Bob is already asking 'Where do you want me' before the Chairman has asked 'Do you mind?' At the same time, the Chairman's instructions do not come over as 'pulling rank' both because this possibility is specifically excluded ('Not for reasons of seniority or anything like that') and because, rather than issue a command, the

READING 1.2	**Accounts of Organizations: Organizational "Structures" and the Accounting Process**

By David Silverman

Chairman provides rational grounds for his instruction ('but because he and I do so many of these things together ...'). The football analogy also allows his instruction to be seen in a light-hearted manner. Even so, the final politeness ('Do you mind?') hardly allows, given the fact that a senior is issuing an instruction, for the junior to refuse. As already noted, Bob complies even before he is if asked whether he 'minds' and, by continuing with the football analogy, allows the exchange to end as a joke.

By examining what makes this exchange sensible, rather than treating it as a self-evidently sensible conversation reporting on a recognizable set of events, the author has sought to show how the production and comprehension of talk always proceeds by employing a sense of social structure. Each utterance provides for a context in which it would be sensible, while the listener (or reader) makes sense of the talk by assigning it a knowable context. In this exchange, such a context is provided by the notion of 'hierarchy'. Thus the two parties talk to each other as a 'senior' and a 'junior' by displaying through their utterances the features of hierarchies. It should be stressed that hierarchies are relevant socially *only* to the extent that members attend to their existence as a relevant means for bringing off interactions. This is not, however, to engage in a solipsistic denial of the factual character of hierarchies. Rather the author is pointing out that only in and through members' activities do hierarchies acquire their facticity.

References

Weber, M. (1964) *The Theory of Social and Economic Organization*, New York: The Free Press.

Bittner, E. (1965) 'The concept of organization', *Soc. Research*, 31, 1965, 240–255.

READING 1.3	**Organization Theory as Critical Science?**

By Hugh Willmott

As knowledge production in the management disciplines has expanded in volume and increased in theoretical sophistication, doubts have grown about the coherence and viability of a conception of science that represents scientific knowledge as unified, authoritative and/or value-free. These concerns are dramatically articulated in the claim that organizational analysis comprises four incompatible and indeed hostile paradigms founded upon polarized sets of assumptions about science as well as society (Burrell and Morgan, 1979; see Willmott, 1993; see also Organization Studies, 1988) ...

Habermas's theory of cognitive interests has continuing relevance for illuminating at least three important concerns in organization studies:

- the aspiration of management knowledge to be scientific;
- the fragmentation of methodologies within organization studies;
- the scope for recognizing and combining the distinctive contributions of different forms of knowledge. ...

Knowledge and Human Interests

Three cognitive interests, Habermas contends, underpin the production of distinctive forms of knowledge (and associated types of science): a technical interest in production and control; a practical (historical-hermeneutic) interest in mutual understanding; and finally an interest in emancipation (See Table 1.3.1). Everyday human action is understood to involve combinations of these cognitive interests. For heuristic and emancipatory purposes, however, it is helpful to appreciate how human interests are constitutive of different kinds of knowledge. More particularly, the partitioning of human interests facilitates an appreciation of how the three cognitive interests – technical, practical and emancipatory and related types of

Source: Reproduced by permission of Oxford University Press from 'Organization Theory as Critical Science?', in The Oxford Handbook of Organization Theory © 2003 Oxford University Press. *www.oup.com*

READING 1.3	**Organization Theory as Critical Science?** *continued*
	By Hugh Willmott

TABLE 1.3.1 | HABERMAS' THREE KNOWLEDGE-CONSTITUTIVE INTERESTS

Cognitive Interest	Type of Science	Purpose	Focus	Orientation	Projected Outcome
Technical	Empirical-analytic	Enhance prediction and control	Identification and manipulation of variables	Calculation	Removal of irrationality within means-ends relationships
Practical	Historical-hermeneutic	Improve mutual understanding	Interpretation of symbolic communication	Appreciation	Removal of misunderstanding
Emancipatory	Critical	Development of more rational social institutions and relations	Exposure of domination and exploitation	Transformation	Removal of relations of domination and exploitation that repress without necessity

science – contribute more fully and self-consciously to the human self-formation process.

The Technical Interest

When the technical interest is engaged or articulated, it impels the production of knowledge in a way that improves the efficiency and/or effectiveness of the means of fulfilling current ends. The world is then represented as a set of given, objectified elements and processes over which human beings seek to establish and extend their control. When motivated by a 'technical' interest, these elements and processes are apprehended as independent phenomena that can be manipulated in a continuous process of design, intervention and feedback. In its scientific manifestation, the technical cognitive interest represents the world as a complex set of interdependent variables. Wage-payment systems, for example, are a typical product of such knowledge in which material and symbolic rewards are geared to the measured outputs of productive effort. It is understood that increases in productivity can, in principle, be predicted and controlled – for example, by changing the reward system, or by refining the organization of internal labour markets. Such interventions may achieve the desired results. However, from the perspective of the practical interest (see below), this is because such

interventions are consistent with the particular meanings attributed by employees to (changes in) their work, and not as a direct consequence of the redesign of their jobs. ...

The Practical Interest

The practical interest anticipates and pursues the possibility of attaining mutual understanding between people. When knowledge production is guided by this interest, the pressing concern is not to predict or control but, rather, to facilitate communication so that mutual understanding is reached, or at least advanced. This interest is termed 'practical' because *the process of making sense of the world is understood to be a precondition of any form of social action*, including the prediction and control of objectified processes (see previous section). The identification and measurement of variables, it is argued, is irremediably dependent upon 'the prior frame of reference to which they are affixed' (Habermas, 1972: 308). Knowledge guided by the practical interest addresses the question of how 'variables' are identified and operationalized in order to develop insights into the social organization of empirical-analytic knowledge production.[1] The type of science that discloses and appreciates, rather than takes for granted, such socially organized frames of reference is termed

Organization Theory as Critical Science?

By Hugh Willmott

'historical-hermeneutic' because such 'practical' knowledge necessitates the mobilisation of historically mediated processes of interpretation.

When addressing the issue of employee participation, for example, knowledge guided by a practical interest in mutual understanding might begin with the question of how employees currently make sense of their work, and then explore how such sense-making is historically and culturally embedded within a wider set of social practices, norms, and values (e.g. Gouldner 1954; Dalton 1959; Watson 1994). It may be shown how increased participation, for example, is viewed by employees in different and shifting ways – as a means of removing petty rules and/or as a more subtle form of management control. The purpose of knowledge guided by a practical knowledge is to appreciate how persons enact their situation(s), and thereby aspire to develop a better understanding of their respective orientations. ...

The Emancipatory Interest

Whereas the technical and practical interests are conceived to be endemic to human existence, the emancipatory interest is understood to be stimulated by consequences flowing from ideas and actions guided by the other two cognitive interests. This interest is provoked when, for example, employees resist techniques and lampoon ideologies that purport to 'empower' them, yet are experienced as an intensification of their work without appropriate or sufficient compensation. In elucidating the emancipatory interest, Habermas (1986) explains that:

> what I mean is an attitude which is formed in the experience of suffering from something man-made, which can be abolished and should be abolished. This is not just a contingent value-postulate: that people want to get rid of certain sufferings. No, it is something so profoundly ingrained in the structure of human societies – the calling into question, and deep-seated wish to throw off, relations which repress you without necessity – so intimately built into the reproduction of human life that I don't think it can be regarded as just a subjective attitude which may or may not guide this or that piece of scientific research. It is more (ibid: 198).

Habermas points to the experience of (unnecessary) frustration and suffering which, he contends, stimulates, yet also frustrates, a desire to 'throw off relations' that '*repress without necessity*' (my emphasis). For Habermas, critical science resonates with, and indeed is fuelled by, a desire to assert (the possibility of) greater autonomy and responsibility in the face of institutions and practices that are sensed to impede unnecessarily their contemporary expression and extension. In contrast to the 'empirical-analytic' and 'historical-hermeneutic' sciences, which each regard existing social formations and patterns of meaning as *given* objects of prediction and control or of interpretation, critical science strives to expose *the unreasoned, political basis of this givenness*. For example, instead of seeking to identify covariance between observable events (the project of empirical-analytic science) or striving to interpret the development of particular meanings (the concern of historical-hermeneutic science), critical science is concerned to reveal how patterns of behaviour and meaning are embedded in oppressive structures of domination that, potentially, are open to challenge and change. In Habermas' (1972) words, critical social science seeks:

> to determine when theoretical statements grasp invariant regularities of social action as such and when they express ideologically frozen relations of dependence that can in principle be transformed (ibid: 310).

To consider once more the case of employee participation, knowledge guided by an emancipatory interest goes beyond the 'mere' appreciation of employee orientations (e.g. towards participation) to show how these understandings are structured within relations of power and domination – relations that are potentially open to (radical) transformation that dissolve 'frozen relations of dependence' and thereby eliminate forms of socially unnecessary suffering associated with these relations. From this perspective, findings that indicate employee indifference or hostility towards a participation scheme may be interpreted as symptomatic of a structure of social and industrial relations where, historically, participation has either been excluded (e.g. by the adoption of a top-down approach to organization and job design) or introduced cynically as a means

| **Organization Theory as Critical Science?** *continued*

By Hugh Willmott

of achieving some other, often undisclosed, purpose – such as greater flexibility. Employee hostility towards, or scepticism about, participation schemes is then viewed, from the standpoint of critical science, not as evidence of worker apathy or negativity per se but, rather as indicative of institutionalized relations of dependence in which employees have been historically excluded from participation in key decisions. Precisely because such attitudes are located in a particular structure of dependency relations, they are understood to be mutable: they can be changed by transforming the structures in which such attitudes are fostered and reproduced. ...

Reflection

If it is the case that what passes for truth is historically contingent, at least until 'the ideal speech situation' has been realized rather than simply invoked as a counter-factual, then the plausibility of truth claims is conditional upon the context of their assessment, and not upon their alleged universal veracity. If this point is accepted, it then follows that even if we were to be convinced by Habermas's theory of universal pragmatics, our conviction would tell us more about the strength of our cultural receptivity to such ideas – which, of course, does not logically exclude the possibility of the theory being true – than about their veracity. In which case, forms of critical thinking that reject a Habermasian (transcendental) preoccupation with grounding truth claims become more appealing. More specifically, such scepticism enhances the appeal of approaches that attend to, and build upon, the (immanent) identification of opportunities for exposing and dissolving forms of oppression; and this is not least because they are compatible with commending Habermas's theory of cognitive interests as a *heuristic device* for appreciating the presence and potentially emancipatory contribution of different forms of science.

From a (self-critically) critical modernist perspective, postmodernist analysis may have the beneficial consequence of renewing and extending the critical strand of modernism. By prompting reflection upon assumptions and methods that are otherwise shielded from scrutiny by disciplinary complacency, blinkered self-referentiality or intellectual pride, it

may encourage deeper questioning of whether, for example, Critical Theory, and the work of Habermas especially, is excessively preoccupied with the universal justification of its own truth claims, to the neglect of exploring what can be done to challenge everyday forms of subjugation, oppression and repression by appealing to extant local understandings and traditions (Alvesson and Willmott, 1996). To this extent, at least, there is some common cause in postmodernist and critical modernist critiques of systemic modernism; (see Reading 1.1) and in this regard, it is worth quoting briefly from the (later) writings of Foucault who, though often identified with the postmodern camp, arguably straddles the critical modernism–postmodernism divide:

> the thread that may connect us with the Enlightenment is ... the permanent reactivation of an attitude – that is, of a philosophical ethos that could be described as a permanent critique of our historical era (Foucault, 1984: 42).

... *Contra* Habermas, the pursuit of freedom and equality is not, as it were, guaranteed or privileged by a foundational principle, whether its location is posited in the structure of language or in the depths of human nature. Rather, as in Laclau and Mouffe's (1985) thinking, the possibility of freedom and equality is understood to be conditional upon the development and continuing existence of discourses that attribute value to ideas of freedom and equality and the institutions that support their articulation and facilitate their realization. As Laclau and Mouffe (1990: 124) note, the absence of any apodeictic certainty that one type of society (or organization) is better than 'another' does not prevent us from reasoning politically and of preferring, for a variety of reasons, certain political positions to others. In a passage that echoes Habermas's anticipation of the ideal speech situation, without becoming encumbered by the baggage that seeks to justify it as a touchstone of objective truth, Laclau and Mouffe commend an approach to the production of knowledge and the transformation of relations that:

> tries to found itself upon the verisimilitude of its conclusions, is essentially pluralist, because it

READING 1.3	# Organization Theory as Critical Science?

By Hugh Willmott

needs to make reference to other arguments and, since the process is essentially open, these can always be contested and refuted. The logic of verisimilitude is, in this sense, essentially public and democratic (Laclau and Mouffe, 1990: 125).

From this perspective, it makes little sense to deny that methodologies favoured by critical science exert disciplinary effects that can be constraining as well as enabling – an observation that takes on board elements of the postmodernist critique of Critical Theory.

[1]This form of knowledge may also be directed at gaining a better, reflexive understanding of how its own form(s) of knowledge (e.g. about the practices of empirical-analytic science) are accomplished.

References

Alvesson, M. and Willmott, H.C. (1996) *Making Sense of Management*. London: Sage.

Burrell, G. and Morgan, G. (1979) *Sociological Paradigms and Organizational Analysis*. London: Heinemann.

Dalton, M. (1959) Men Who Manage, New York: Wiley.

Foucault, M. (1984) 'What is Enlightenment?' in Rabinow, P. (ed.), *The Foucault Reader*, Harmondsworth: Peregrine.

Gouldner, A. (1954) Patterns of Industrial Bureaucracy, Glencoe, Ill.: Free Press.

Habermas, J. (1972) *Knowledge and Human Interests*. London: Heinemann.

Habermas, J. (1986) 'Life Forms, Morality and the Task of the Philosopher'. In Dews, P. (Ed.). *Habermas; Autonomy and Solidarity*. London: Verso.

Laclau, E. and Mouffe, C. (1985) *Hegemony and Socialist Strategy: Towards a Radical Democratic Politics*. London: Verso.

Laclau, E. and Mouffe, C. (1990) 'Post-Marxism Without Apologies', in E. Laclau, *New Reflections on the Revolution of Our Time*. London: Verso, 1990.

Marsden, R. (1993) 'The Politics of Organizational Analysis'. *Organization Studies*, 14 (1): 93–124.

Organization Studies. 1988, 9, 1.

Watson, T. (1994) In Search of Management, London: Routledge.

Willmott, H.C. (1993) 'Breaking the Paradigm Mentality', *Organization Studies*, 14(5): 681–720.

Discussion Questions

1. What are the main points made by Clegg and Hardy? What relevance do they have for understanding organizations?
2. What are the similarities and differences between Silverman and Habermas's perspectives? What kind of accounts of organization are generated by these perspectives?
3. If no universal criteria can be agreed for judging claims about organization, is organization theory worthless?

Introduction Reference

Silverman, D. 1973. 'Accounts of Organisations: Organisational "Structures" and the Accounting Process', in by McKinlay, J.B. (ed). *Processing People: Cases in Organisational Behaviour*, New York: Holt, Rinehart and Winston.

Recommended Further Readings

See references accompanying the Readings plus:

Astley, W.G. (1985) 'Administrative Science as Socially Constructed Truth', *Administrative Science Quarterly*, 30(4): 497–513.

Astley, W.G. and Van de Ven, A.H. (1983) 'Central Perspectives and Debates in Organization Theory', *Administrative Science Quarterly*, 28(2): 245–273.

Benson, J.K. 'Organizations: A Dialectical View', *Administrative Science Quarterly*, 22(1): 1–21.

Hatch, M.J. with Cunliffe, A.L. *Organization Theory: Modern, Symbolic, and Postmodern Perspectives.* Oxford: Oxford University Press, 2006.

Hinings, C.R. and Greenwood, R. (2002) 'Disconnects and Consequences in Organization Theory?' *Administrative Science Quarterly*, 47, September: 411–421.

Greenwood, R., Oliver, C., Sahlin, K. and Suddaby, R. (2008) *The Sage Handbook of Organizational Institutionalism.* London: Sage.

Knights, D. (1997) 'Organization Theory in the Age of Deconstruction: Dualism, Gender and Postmodernism Revisited', *Organization Studies*, 18(1): 1–19.

Morgan, G. (1980) 'Paradigms, Metaphors, and Puzzle Solving in Organization Theory', *Administrative Science Quarterly*, 25(4): 605–622.

Seo, M. and Douglas Creed, W.E. (2002) 'Institutional Contradictions, Praxis, and Institutional Change: A Dialectical Perspective', *The Academy of Management Review*, 27(2): 222–247.

Tsoukas, H. and Knudsen, C. eds (2003) *The Oxford Book of Organization Theory: Metatheoretical Perspectives.* Oxford: Oxford University Press.

Van Maanen, J. (1995) 'Style As Theory', *Organization Science*, 6(1): 133–143.

ORGANIZING

CHAPTER 2

READINGS

Weick, K.E., Sutcliffe, K.M. and Obstfeld, D. (2005) 'Organizing and the Process of Sensemaking' in *Organization Science*, Vol. 16, No. 4: pp. 409–421.

Orlikowski, W.J. (2002) 'Knowing in Practice: Enacting a Collective Capability in Distributed Organizing' in *Organization Science*, Vol. 13, No. 3: pp. 249–273.

Knights D. and Murray, F. (1994) *Managers Divided: Organizational Politics and IT Management*. London: Wiley, pp. 29–34.

INTRODUCTION

Organizing highlights the dynamic, processual nature of reproducing and transforming forms and methods of organization, such as 'bureaucracy' and 'assembly line' or 'team' working. Even the most stable, durable, predictable organization requires that its members engage in continuous processes of negotiation over 'what is "really" happening/intended/significant' in order to enact and legitimize the realities that they continuously maintain. In doing this, they sustain a sense of meaning and develop means of rationalizing and perpetuating their activities. In short, organizational members are involved in an ongoing process of institution-building and maintenance or in developing emergent revisions or alternatives to the current form of organization.

For much of the time the process of organizing is routine and taken-for-granted. Although it is continuously enacted and therefore requires the involvement of organizational members, their participation appears to be involuntary or habitual. It is only when there is a disruption of, or challenge to, routines that their precariousness becomes evident and the active yet habitualized involvement of actors in their continuous enactment becomes fully apparent.

Karl E. Weick, Kathleen M. Sutcliffe and David Obstfeld (Reading 2.1) explore the role of sense-making in processes of organizing. Sense-making 'is central',

Weick *et al.* argue, 'because it is the primary site where meanings materialize that inform and constrain identity and action' (Reading 2.1, p. 20). What is happening in organizations is conceived to be in flux and its significance is not self-evident. Sense-making frameworks operate to interpret the flux and 'make sense of equivocal inputs' (ibid: p. 21). In effect, it is through sense-making that 'situations, organizations, and environments are talked into existence' (ibid: p. 24) which is why sense-making is considered to be central to analysing organization. The key point here is that conceiving of human activity as occurring within (an) 'organization', or as being 'organizational' does not capture the nature of the activity but, rather, places it and construes it, within a particular sense-making framework. Paying attention to 'sense-making' moves us away from conceiving of organization in terms of 'variables, nouns, quantities and structures' towards an appreciation of 'transcience, reaccomplishment, unfolding, and emergence' (ibid: p. 21). What relationship any sense-making framework bears to the phenomena that it strives to represent is difficult, and perhaps impossible, to assess as any evaluation of its accuracy will require us to invoke some other, particular sense-making framework whose credibility is open to the same questioning (see Reading 1.2). For students of sense-making, the consequence of such reflection is not to bemoan the difficulty of determining a reliable sense-making framework. Rather, it is to highlight our reliance upon sense-making, and to encourage close examination of its significance, operation and effects. In Reading 2.1, these key features of sense-making are illustrated by reference to a brief transcript of an interview with a nurse who relates her experience making sense of the health of a premature baby.

Wanda J. Orlikowski (Reading 2.2) considers the process of organizing by using an example of globally dispersed product development. Her study highlights the importance of what she terms 'organizational knowing', as contrasted with organizational knowledge and knowledge transfer, in facilitating effective sense-making in processes of product development. Attention is directed to product developers' participation the 'everyday practices' of discussion and negotiation through which they are seen to acquire the capability to work collectively in a productive manner. Orlikowski's research findings suggest that it is not so much the organizational knowledge acquired or accessed by those engaged in such activities as product development that is critical. Of greater importance is how, through interaction with colleagues, the product developers forge shared forms of sense-making (a process that is also illustrated in Reading 2.1 when describing how the second nurse holds 'both the nurse's and doctor's perspectives of the situation while identifying an account of the situation that would align the two', Reading 2.1: p. 20).

The basic idea is that knowing is deeply embodied and embedded within and through our practices. It is not something that can be reduced to codified knowledge such as that deposited in a 'knowledge management' database. As Orlikowski puts it, the collective capabilities enacted in organizing processes are reliant upon embodied, 'tacit knowledge [which] is a form of "knowing", and thus inseparable from action because it is constituted through such action' (Reading 2.2, p. 26). It is in this sense that 'knowing' is 'in practice': knowing and practice are mutually constituted. This understanding is illustrated by showing how product development work – on integrated systems software that includes 'VOS', an operating system installed on the mainframe computers of about 200 major customers around the world – was undertaken at Kappa, a large multinational organization. Orlikowski demonstrates how 'knowing in practice' involves sharing identity, interacting face to face, learning by doing and supporting participation – all of which are also seen to be fraught with difficulties and vulnerable to potentially counterproductive effects, such as 'inefficiency and risk of fragmentation'.

David Knights and Fergus Murray (Reading 2.3) focus upon the political dimension of organizing. It includes, for example, 'massaging and manipulating the reality reaching superiors' and building alliances between groups but in ways that cannot be readily identified or criticized as being 'political'. Much organizational analysis, Knights and Murray note, restricts discussion of organizational politics to overt conflict or to explaining why there has been some deviation from the pursuit or realization of official organizational goals (see Reading 1.1). So, for example, processes of organizing are seen to be shaped and subverted by forms of self-interest, including the pursuit of sectional interests by particular groups within organizations. Instead of regarding organizational politics as exceptional or marginal to processes of organizing, Knights and Murray contend that it is key to understanding the very construction of goals and the formation of interests as, for example, managers struggle to compete for scarce resources, in the form of promotion opportunities or the direction of corporate strategy. They cannot escape from the political-loading of all forms of organizing. From this perspective, an established framework of sense-making (see Reading 2.1), for example, is inherently 'political' in the sense that it provides a dominant means of 'inform(ing) and constrain(ing) identity and action' (Reading 2.1, p. 20). Establishing frameworks of sense-making is seen to be a key means of exercising power.

The naked pursuit of self-interest is, however, generally regarded as unacceptable within organizations where, in principle, managers and others are required to justify their employment by reference to corporate, rather than individual priorities. As a consequence, organizational politics are pursued through the process of representing and pursuing particular interests or goals by mobilizing the sense-making framework of formal rationality, universal interests or organizational goals. It is the very use of this framework, Knights and Murray suggest, that keeps the inherently political nature of organizing 'under wraps' so that 'the normal business of management [can] proceed' (ibid: p. 35) and anxieties can, to some extent, be allayed or rationalized by placing responsibility on the dictates of 'the organization'. Notably, the impersonal quality of 'merit' is widely deployed to justify substantial material (e.g. income, control of expenditure) and symbolic (e.g. status, access to key personnel) benefits when, routinely, the attribution of 'merit' is a highly politicized process. At the heart of organizational politics, then, is a process of concealment as political (e.g. career) goals are 'expressed through the more legitimate pursuit of formally acknowledged organizational goals' (Reading 2.3, p. 33).

READING 2.1

Organizing and the Process of Sensemaking

By Karl E. Weick, Kathleen M. Sutcliffe and David Obstfeld

Sensemaking involves the ongoing retrospective development of plausible images that rationalize what people are doing. Viewed as a significant process of organizing, sensemaking unfolds as a sequence in which people concerned with identity in the social context of other actors engage ongoing circumstances from which they extract cues and make plausible sense retrospectively, while enacting more or less order into those ongoing circumstances. Stated more compactly and more colourfully, '[S]ensemaking is a way station on the road to a consensually constructed, coordinated system of action' (Taylor and Van Every, 2000, p. 275). At that way station, circumstances are 'turned into a situation that is comprehended explicitly in words and that serves as a springboard to action' (p. 40). These images imply these important points about the question for meaning in organizational life. First, sensemaking occurs when a flow of organizational circumstances is turned into words and salient categories. Second, organizing itself is embodied in written and spoken texts. Third, reading, writing, conversing, and editing are crucial actions that serve as the media through which the invisible hand of institutions shapes conduct (Gioia et al., 1994, p. 365).

The emerging picture is one of sensemaking as a process that is ongoing, instrumental, subtle, swift, social, and easily taken for granted. The seemingly transient nature of sensemaking ('a way station') belies its central role in the determination of human behaviour. Sensemaking is central because it is the primary site where meanings materialize that inform and constrain identity and action (Mills 2003, p. 35). When we say that meanings materialize, we mean that sensemaking is, importantly, an issue of language, talk, and communication. Situations, organizations, and environments are talked into existence.

Explicit efforts at sensemaking tend to occur when the current state of the world is perceived to be different from the expected state of the world, or when there is no obvious way to engage the world. In such circumstances there is a shift from the experience of immersion in projects to a sense that the flow of action has become unintelligible in some way. To make sense of the disruption, people look first for reasons that will enable them to resume the interrupted activity and stay in action. These 'reasons' are pulled from frameworks such as institutional constraints, organizational premises, plans, expectations, acceptable justifications, and traditions inherited from predecessors. If resumption of the project is problematic, sensemaking is biased either toward identifying substitute action or toward further deliberation.

Sensemaking is about the interplay of action and interpretation rather than the influence of evaluation on choice. When action is the central focus, interpretation, not choice, is the core phenomenon (Laroche, 1995, p. 66; Lant, 2002; Weick, 1993, pp. 644–646). Scott Snook (2001) makes this clear in his analysis of the friendly fire incident over Iraq in April 1994 when two F-15 pilots shot down two friendly helicopters, killing 26 people. As Snook says, this is not an incident where F-15 pilots 'decided' to pull the trigger.

> I could have asked, 'Why did they *decide* to shoot?' However, such a framing puts us squarely on a path that leads straight back to the individual decision maker, away from potentially powerful contextual features and right back into the jaws of the fundamental attribution error. 'Why did they decide to shoot?' quickly becomes 'Why did they make the *wrong* decision?' Hence, the attribution falls squarely onto the shoulders of the decision-maker and away from the potent situation factors that influence action. Framing the individual-level puzzle as a question of meaning rather than deciding shifts the emphasis away from individual decision makers toward a point somewhere 'out there' where context and individual action overlap … Such a reframing – from decision making to sensemaking – opened *my* eyes to the possibility that, given the circumstances, even *I* could have made the same

Source: Reprinted from 'Organizing and the process of sensemaking', in Organization Science *by permission of the Institute for Operations and Research and the Management Sciences (INFORMS), 7240 Parkway Drive, Suite 300, Hanover, MD 21076 USA. INFORMS is not responsible for errors introduced in any translations of the original article.*

READING 2.1

Organizing and the Process of Sensemaking

By Karl E. Weick, Kathleen M. Sutcliffe and David Obstfeld

'dumb mistake'. This disturbing revelation, one that I was in no way looking for, underscores the importance of initially framing such senseless tragedies as 'good people struggling to make sense', rather then as 'bad ones making poor' (pp. 206–207).

To focus on sensemaking is to portray organizing as the experience of being thrown into an ongoing, unknowable, unpredictable streaming of experience in search of answers to the question, 'what's the story?' Plausible stories animate and gain their validity from subsequent activity. The language of sensemaking captures the realities of agency, flow, equivocally, transience, reaccomplishment, unfolding, and emergence, realities that are often obscured by the language of variables, nouns, qualities, and structures. Students of sensemaking understand that the order in organizational life comes just as much from the subtle, the small, the relational, the oral, the particular, the momentary as it does from the conspicuous, the large, the substantive, the written, the general, and the sustained. To work with the idea of sensemaking is to appreciate that smallness does not equate with insignificance. Small structures and short moments can have large consequences.

We take the position that the concept of sensemaking fills important gaps in organizational theory. We reaffirm important gaps in organizational theory. We reaffirm this idea and take stock of the sensemaking concept first by highlighting its distinctive features descriptively, using an extended example of paediatric nursing. Next we summarize the distinctive features of sensemaking conceptually and discuss intraorganizational evolution, instigations, plausibility, and identity. Finally, we summarize the distinctive features of sensemaking prospectively and examine future lines of work that may develop from ideas about institutions, distributed sensemaking, power, and emotion.

The Nature of Organized Sensemaking: Viewed Descriptively

Organizational sensemaking is first and foremost about the question: How does something come to be an event for organizational members? Second, sensemaking is about the question: What does an event mean? In the context of everyday life, when people confront something unintelligible and ask 'what's the story here?' their question has the force of bringing an event into existence. When people then ask 'now what should I do?' this added question has the force of bringing meaning into existence, meaning that they hope it is stable enough for them to act into the future, continue to act, and to have the sense that they remain in touch with the continuing flow of experience.

While these descriptions may help delimit sensemaking, they say little about what is organizational in all of this. The answer is that sensemaking and organization constitute one another: 'Organization is an attempt to order the intrinsic flux of human action, to channel it toward certain ends, to give it particular shape, through generalising and institutionalizing particular meanings and rules' (Tsoukas and Chia, 2002, p. 570). We need to grasp each other to understand the other. The operative emerges through sensemaking or one in which sensemaking is produced by organization.

A central theme in both organizing and sensemaking is that people organize to make sense of equivocal inputs and enact this sense back into the world to make that world more orderly. Basic moments in the process of sensemaking are illustrated in the following account, where a nurse describes what she did while caring for a baby whose condition began to deteriorate (Benner, 1994, pp. 139–140):

NURSE: *I took care of a 900-gram baby who was about 26 or 27 weeks many years ago who had been doing well for about two weeks. He had an open ductus that day. The different between the way he looked at 9am and the way he looked at 11am was very dramatic. I was at that point really concerned about what was going to happen next. There are a lot of complications of the patent ductus, not just in itself, but the fact that it causes a lot of other things. I was really concerned that the baby was starting to show symptoms of all of them.*

INTERVIEWER: *Just in that two hours?*

NURSE: *You look at this kid because you know this kid, and you know what he looked like two hours ago. It is a dramatic <u>different</u> to you, but it's hard to describe that to someone in words. You go to the* resident and say: 'Look, I'm really worried about X, Y, Z,' and they go: 'OK.' Then you wait one half hour to 40 minutes, then you go to the Fellow (the teaching physician supervising the resident) and say: 'You know, I am really worried about X, Y, X.' They say: 'We'll talk about it on rounds.'

INTERVIEWER: *What is the X, Y, Z you are worried about?*

NURSE: *The fact that the kid is more lethargic, paler, his stomach is bigger, that he is not tolerating his feedings, that his chem strip (blood test) might be a little strange. All these kinds of things. I can't remember the exact details of the case: there are clusters of things that go wrong. The baby's urine output goes down. They sound like they are in failure. This kind of stuff. Their pulses go bad, their blood pressure changes. There are a million things that go on. At this time, I had been in the unit a couple or three years.*

Sensemaking Organizes Flux

Sensemaking starts with chaos. This nurse encounters 'a million things that go on' and the ongoing potential for 'clusters of things that go wrong' – part of an almost infinite stream of events and inputs that surround any organizational actor. As Chia (2000, p. 517) puts it, we start with 'an undifferentiatied flux of fleeting sense-impressions and it is out of this brute aboriginal flux of lived experience that attention carves out and conception names'. As the case illustrates, the nurse's sensemaking does not begin de novo, but like all organizing occurs amidst a stream of *potential* antecedents and consequences. Presumably within the 24-hour period surrounding the critical noticing, the nurse slept, awoke, prepared for work, observed and tended to other babies, completed paper work and charts, drank coffee, spoke with doctors and fellow nurses, stared at an elevator door as she moved between hospital floors, and performed a variety of formal and impromptu observations. All of these activities furnish a raw flow of activity from which she may or may not extract certain cues for closer attention.

Sensemaking Starts with Noticing and Bracketing

During her routine activities, the nurse becomes aware of vital signs that are at variance with the 'normal' demeanour of a recovering baby. In response to the interruption, the nurse orients to the child and notices and brackets possible signs of trouble for closer attention. This noticing and bracketing is an incipient state of sensemaking. In this context sensemaking means basically 'inventing a new meaning (interpretation) for something that has already occurred during the organizing process, *but does not yet have a name* (italics in original), has never been recognized as a separate autonomous process, object, event' (Magala, 1997, p. 324).

The nurse's noticing and bracketing is guided by mental models she has acquired during her work, training, and life experience. Those mental models may help her recognize and guide a response to an open ductus condition or sickness more generally. Such mental models might be primed by the patient's conditions or a priori permit her to notice and make sense of those conditions (Klein *et al.*, in press). Some combination of mental models and salient cues calls her attention to this particular baby between the hours of 9 to 11 with respect to a bounded set of symptoms.

The more general point is that in the early stages of sensemaking, phenomena 'have to be forcibly carved out of the undifferentiated flux of raw experience and conceptually fixed and labelled so that they can become the common currency for communication exchanges' (Chia, 2000, p. 517). Notice that once bracketing occurs, the world is simplified.

Sensemaking is About Labelling

Sensemaking is about labelling and categorizing to stabilize the streaming of experience. Labelling works through a strategy of 'differentiation and simple-location, identification and classification, regularizing and routinization (to translate) the intractable or obdurate into a form that is more amenable to functional deployment' (Chia, 2000, p. 517). The key phrase here is 'functional deployment'. In medicine, functional deployment means imposing diagnostic labels that suggest a plausible treatment. In organizing in general, functional deployment means imposing labels on interdependent events in ways that suggest plausible acts of managing, coordinating, and distributing. Thus, the ways in which events are first envisioned immediately begins the work of organizing

Organizing and the Process of Sensemaking

By Karl E. Weick, Kathleen M. Sutcliffe and David Obstfeld

because events are bracketed and labelled in ways that predispose people to find common ground. To generate common ground, labelling ignores differences among actors and deploys cognitive representations that are able to generate recurring behaviours: 'For an activity to be said to be organized, it implied that types of behaviour in types if actors ... An organized activity provides actors with a given set of cognitive categories and a typology of actions' (Tsoukas and Chia, 2002, p. 573).

A crucial feature of these types and categories is that they have considerable plasticity. Categories have plasticity because they are socially defined, because they have to be adapted to local circumstances, and because they have a radial structure. By radial structure we mean that there a few central instances of the category, but mostly the category contains peripheral instances that have only a few of these features. This difference is potentially crucial because if people act of the basis of central prototypic cases within a category, then their action is stable; but if they act on the basis of peripheral cases that are more equivocal in meaning their action is more variable, more indeterminate, more likely to alter organizing, and more consequential for adapting (Tsoukas and Chia, 2002, p. 574).

Sensemaking is Retrospective

The nurse uses retrospect to make sense of the puzzles she observes at 11:00. She recalls 'what he looked like two hours ago. It's a dramatic difference.' Symptoms are not discovered at 11:00. Instead, symptoms are created 11:00 by looking back over earlier observations and seeing a pattern. The nurse alters the generic sensemaking recipe, 'how can I know what I think until I see what I say', into the medically more useful variant, 'how can I know what I'm seeing until I see what it was'.

Marianne Paget (1988, p. 56) has been especially sensitive to the retrospective quality of medical work as is evident in her description of mistakes in diagnosis: 'A mistake follows an act. It identifies the character of an act in its aftermath. It names it. An act, however, is not mistaken; it becomes mistaken. There is a paradox here, for seen from the inside of action, there is from the point of view of an actor, as act becomes mistaken only after it has already gone

wrong. As it is unfolding, it is not becoming mistaken at all; it is becoming.' When people bracket a portion of streaming circumstances and label them as a concern, a bad sign, a mistake, or an opportunity, the event is at an advanced stage; the label follows after and names a completed act, but the labelling itself fails to capture the dynamics of what is happening. Because mistakes and diagnoses are known in the aftermath of activity, they are fruitfully described as 'complex cognitions of the experience of now and then. They identify the too-lateness of human understanding' (Paget, 1988, pp. 96–97). So, 'the *now* of mistake collides with the *then* of acting with uncertain knowledge. *Now* represents the more exact science of hindsight, *then* the unknown future coming into being' (Paget, 1988, p. 48).

Sensemaking is About Presumption

To make sense is to connect the abstract with the concrete. In the case of medical action, 'instances of illness are concrete, idiosyncratic, and personal in their expression, and the stock of knowledge is abstract and encyclopaedic. Interpretation and experimentation engage the concrete, idiosyncratic, and personal with the abstract and impersonal' (Paget, 1988, p. 51). It is easy to miss this linkage and to portray sensemaking as more cerebral, more passive, more abstract than it typically is. Sensemaking starts with immediate actions, local context, and concrete cues, as is true for the worried nurse. She says to the resident, 'Look, I'm really worried about X,Y,Z.'

What is interesting about her concerns is that she is acting as if something is the case, which means any further action tests that hunch but may run a risk for the baby. To test a hunch is to presume the character of the illness and to update that presumptive understanding through progressive approximations: 'The [medical] work process unfolds as a series of approximations and attempts to discover an appropriate response. And because it unfolds this way, as an error-ridden activity, it required continuous attention to the patient's condition and to reparation' (Paget, 1988, p. 143).

Sensemaking is Social and Systematic

The nurse's sensemaking is influenced by a variety of social factors. These social factors might include

Organizing and the Process of Sensemaking *continued*

By Karl E. Weick, Kathleen M. Sutcliffe and David Obstfeld

previous discussions with the other nurses on duty, an offhand remark about the infant that might have been made by a parent, interaction with physicians – some of whom encourage nurses to take initiative and some who do not – or the mentoring she received yesterday.

However, it is not just the concerned nurse and her contacts that matter in this unfolding incident. Medical sensemaking is distributed across the healthcare system, and converges on the tiny patient as much through scheduling that involves cross-covering of one nurse's patients by another nurse (and through multiple brands of infusion pumps with conflicting setup protocols) as it does through the occasional appearance of the attending physician at the bedside. If knowledge about the correctness of treatment unfolds gradually, then knowledge of this unfolding sense is not located just inside the head or the nurse or physician. Instead, the locus is systemwide and is realized in stronger or weaker coordination and information distribution among interdependent healthcare workers.

Sensemaking is About Action

If the first question of sensemaking is 'what's going on here?', the second, equally important question is directly about action, as is illustrated in this case, where the nurse's emerging hunch is intertwined with the essential task of enlisting a physician to take action on the case. The talk that leads to a continual, iteratively developed, shared understanding of the diagnosis and the persuasive talk that leads to enlistment in action both illustrate the 'saying' that is so central to organizational action. In sensemaking, action, and talk are treated as cycles rather than as a linear sequence. Talk occurs both early and late, and does action, and either one can be designated as the 'starting point to the destination'. Because acting is an indistinguishable part of the swarm of flux until talk brackets it and gives it some meaning, action is not inherently any more significant than talk, but it factors centrally into any understanding of sensemaking.

Medical sensemaking is as much a matter of thinking that is acted out conversationally in the world as it is a matter of knowledge and technique applied to the world. Nurses (and physicians), like everyone else, make sense by acting thinkingly, which means that they simultaneously interpret their knowledge with

trusted frameworks, yet mistrust those very same frameworks and new interpretations. The underlying assumption in each case is that ignorance and knowledge coexist, which means that adaptive sensemaking both honours and rejects the past. What this means is that in medical work, as in all work, people face evolving disorder. There are truths of the moment that change, develop and take shape through time. It is these changes through time that progressively reveal that a seemingly correct action 'back then' is becoming an incorrect action 'now'. These changes also may signal a progression from worse to better.

Sensemaking is About Organizing Through Communication

Communication is a central component of sensemaking and organizing: 'We see communication as an ongoing process of making sense of the circumstances in which people collectively find ourselves and of the events that affect them.' The sensemaking, to the extent that it involves communication, takes place in interactive talk and draws on the resources of language in order to formulate and exchange through talk … symbolically encoded representations of these circumstances. As this occurs, a situation is talked into existence and the basis is laid for action to deal with it' (Van Every 2000, p. 58). The image of sensemaking as activity that talks events and organizations into existence which suggests that patterns of organizing are located in the actions and conversations that occur on behalf of the presumed organization and in the texts of those activities that are preserved in social structures.

We see this in the present example. As the case illustrates, the nurse's bracketed set of noticings coalesce into the impression of the baby as urgently in need of physician attention, but the nurse's choice to articulate her concerns first to a resident and then to a Fellow produces little immediate result. Her individual sensemaking has little immediate result on the organizing of care around this patient as this passage shows (Benner 1994, p. 140):

> … At this time, I had been in the unit a couple or three years. I was really starting to feel like I knew what was going on but I wasn't as good at

Organizing and the Process of Sensemaking

By Karl E. Weick, Kathleen M. Sutcliffe and David Obstfeld

throwing my weight in a situation like that. And I talked to a nurse who had more experience and I said, 'Look at this kid,' and I told her my story, and she goes: 'OK.' Rounds started shortly after that and she walks up to the Attending (Physician in charge of patient) very quietly, sidles up and says: 'You know, this kid, Jane is really worried about this kid.' She told him the story, and said: 'He reminds me about this kid, Jimmie, we had three weeks ago,' and he said: 'Oh.' Everything stops. He gets out the stethoscope and listens to the kid, examines the kid and he says: 'Call the surgeons.' (Laughter) It's that kind of thing where we knew also what had to be done. There was no time to be waiting around. He is the only one that can make that decision. It was a case we presented to other physicians who should have made the case, but didn't. We are able in two sentences to make that case to the Attending because we knew exactly what we were talking about … this particular nurse really knew exactly what she was doing. [The Attending] knew she knew what she was doing … She knew exactly what button to push with him and how to do it.

What we see here is articulation (Benner, 1994; Winter, 1987), which is defined as 'the social process by which tacit knowledge is made more explicit or usable.' To share understanding means to lift equivocal knowledge out of the tacit, private, complex, random, and past to make it explicit, public, simpler, ordered, and relevant to the situation at hand (Obstfeld, 2004). Taylor and Van Every (2000, pp. 33–44) describe a process similar to articulation: 'A situation is talked into being through the interactive exchanges of organizational members to produce a view of circumstances including people, their objects, their institutions and history, and their siting [i.e., location as a site] in a finite time and place.' This is what happens successively as the first nurse translates her concerns for the second more powerful nurse, who then rearticulates the case using terms relevant to the Attending. The second nurse absorbs the complexity of the situation (Boisot and Child, 1999) by holding both a nurse's and

doctor's perspectives of the situation while identifying an account of the situation that would align the two. What is especially interesting is that she tries to make sense of things, a complex determination that is routine in organizational life.

Summary

To summarize, this sequence highlights several distinguishing features of sensemaking, including its genesis in disruptive ambiguity, its beginnings in acts of noticing and bracketing, its mixture of retrospect and prospect, its reliance on presumptions to guide action, its embedding in interdependence, and its culmination in articulation that shades into acting thinkingly. Answers to the question 'what's the story?' emerge from retrospect, connections with past experience, and dialogue among people who act on behalf of larger social units. Answers to the question 'now what?' emerge from presumptions about the future, articulation concurrent with action, and projects that become increasingly clear as they unfold.

References

Benner, P. (1994) **The role of articulation in understanding practices and experience as sources of knowledge in clinical nursing.** J. Tully, ed. *Philosophy in an Age of Pluralism: The Philosophy of Charles Taylor in Question.* New York: Cambridge University Press, 136–155.

Boisot, M. and Child, J. (1999) **Organizations as adaptive systems in complex environments: The case of China.** *Organization Science,* 10 (3): 237–252.

Chia, R. (2000) **Discourse analysis as organizational analysis.** *Organization,* 7 (3): 513–518.

Gioia, D.A., Thomas, J.B., Clark, S.M. and Chittipeddi, K. (1994) **Symbolism and strategic change in academia: The dynamics of sensemaking and influence.** *Organization Science,* 5: 363–383.

Klein, G., Phillips, J.K., Rall, L.A. and Peluso, D.A. (In Press) **A data/frame theory of sensemaking. Unpublished manuscript.** R.R. Hoffman, ed. *Expertise Out of Context: Proc. 6th International Conf. Naturalistic Decision Making.* Mahwah, NJ: Erlbaum.

Lant, T.K. (2002) **Organizational cognition and interpretation.** J.A.C. Baum, ed., *The Blackwell Companion to Organizations.* Oxford: Blackwell, 344–362.

Laroche, H. (1995) **From decision to action in organizations: Decision-making as a social representation.** *Organization Science,* 6 (1): 62–75.

READING 2.1

Organizing and the Process of Sensemaking *continued*

By Karl E. Weick, Kathleen M. Sutcliffe and David Obstfeld

Magala, S.J. (1997) The making and unmaking of sense. *Organization Studies,* 18 (2): 317–338.

Mills, J.H. (2003) *Making Sense of Organizational Change.* London, UK: Routledge.

Obstfeld, D. (2004) **Saying more and less of what we know: The social processes of knowledge creation, innovation, and agency.** Unpublished manuscript, Irvine, CA: University of California-Irvine.

Paget, M.A. (1988) *The Unity of Mistakes.* Philadelphia, PA: Temple University Press.

Snook, S. (2001) *Friendly Fire.* Princeton, NJ: Princeton University.

Taylor, J.R. and Van Every, E.J. (2000) *The Emergent Organization: Communication as Its Site and Surface.* Mahwah, NJ: Erlbaum.

Tsoukas, H. and Chia, R. (2002) **Organizational becomings: Rethinking organizational change.** *Organization Science,* 13 (5): 567–582.

Weick, K.E. (1993) **The collapse of sensemaking in organizations: The Mann Gulch disaster.** *Administrative Science Quarterly,* 38: 628–652.

Winter, S. (1987) **Knowledge and competence as strategic assets.** D. Teece, ed. *The Competitive Challenge – Strategies for Industrial Innovation and Renewal.* Cambridge, MA: Bollinger, 159–184.

READING 2.2

Knowing in Practice: Enacting a Collective Capability in Distributed Organizing

By Wanda J. Orlikowski

With the intensification of globalization, acceleration in the rate of change, and expansion in the use of information technology, particular attention is being focused on the opportunities and difficulties associated with sharing knowledge and transferring 'best practices' within and across organizations (Leonard-Barton 1995, Brown and Duguid 1998, Davenport and Prusak 1998). Such a focus on knowledge and knowledge management is particularly acute in the context of global product development, where the development and delivery of timely and innovative products across heterogeneous cultures, locales, and markets are critical and ongoing challenges. Dealing effectively with such challenges requires more than just good ideas, strong leaders, and extensive resources; it also requires a deep competence in what may be labelled 'distributed organizing' – the capability of operating effectively across the temporal, geographic, political, and cultural boundaries routinely encountered in global operations.

What constitutes effective distributed organizing in global product development? Here, I wish to explore a possible explanation – an explanation which rests on and elaborates on the premise that effective distributed organizing is an enacted capability constituted in the everyday practices of global product development activities. Such an explanation leads away from the focus on organizational knowledge occupying much of the contemporary discourse on knowledge management, and towards a focus on organizational knowing as emerging from the ongoing and situated actions of organizational members as they engage the world. It is an explanation grounded in what it is people *do* every day to get their work done.

My focus on organizational knowing rather than knowledge is informed by the sociological work of Giddens (1984) and the anthropological studies of Lave (1998), Hutchins (1991, 1995), and Suchman (1987). In these accounts, individuals are understood to act knowledgeably as a routine part of their everyday activity. They are seen to be purposive and reflexive, continually and routinely monitoring the ongoing flow of action – their own and that of others – and the social and physical contexts in which their activities are constituted. As Giddens notes, such activities suggest an 'immense knowledgeability involved in the

Source: Reprinted from 'Knowing in Practice: Enacting a collective capability in distributed organizing', in Organization Science *by permission of the Institute for Operations and Research and the Management Sciences (INFORMS), 7240 Parkway Drive, Suite 300, Hanover, MD 21076 USA. INFORMS is not responsible for errors introduced in any translations of the original article.*

Knowing in Practice: Enacting a Collective Capability in Distributed Organizing

By Wanda J. Orlikowski

conduct of everyday life' (Giddens and Pierson 1998, p. 90). My intention here is to use the lens of organizational knowing to understand how members of global product development organizations generate and sustain knowledgeability in their distributed operations ...

A Perspective on Knowing in Practice

Both Ryle (1949) and Polanyi (1967) emphasize *knowing* in their writings. While the distinction between knowing and knowledge may seem like a subtle and inconsequential lexical shift, I believe it has substantial conceptual implications. In particular, it may lead us to miss a fundamental aspect of Schon's (1983, p. 49) observation – based on his fieldwork but informed by Ryle and Polanyi – that 'our knowing is *in* our action'. Schon examined the practice of five professions and argued that the skilful practice exhibited by the professionals did not consist of applying some a priori knowledge to a specific decision or action, but rather of a kind of knowing that was inherent in their action. As he puts it (1983, p. 49):

> When we go about the spontaneous, intuitive performance of the actions of everyday life, we show ourselves to be knowledgeable in a special way. Often we cannot say what it is that we know ... Our knowing is ordinarily tacit, implicit in our pattern of action and in our feel for the stuff with which we are dealing. It seems right to say that our knowing is *in* our action.

What is highlighted in Schon's observation is the essential role of human agency in knowledgeable performance. Maturana and Varela (1998, pp. 27, 29) similarly define knowing as 'effective action', and write that 'all doing is knowing, and all knowing is doing'. When we focus primarily on knowledge, we lose the centrality of action in knowledgeability. Schon (1983) suggests that the tendency to slip from a focus on knowing to that of knowledge is deeply rooted in our theoretical enterprise as we attempt to develop (and test) theories that make sense of (or predict) effective action. He cites the example of researchers studying how children learn to play with wooden blocks, observing that as the researchers viewed the children's actions they were 'compelled to invent a language ... [which] converted the child's *knowing*-inaction to *knowledge*-in-action' (1983, p. 59).

In a recent paper, Cook and Brown (1999) introduce the notion of knowing into the discourse on organizational knowledge, while maintaining the conventional distinction between tacit and explicit forms of knowledge. While this recognition of knowing is helpful, it nevertheless assumes that tacit knowledge is distinct and separable from knowing, and thus action. The perspective I adopt here rests on an alternative assumption – that tacit knowledge is a form of 'knowing', and thus inseparable from action because it is constituted through such action.

The primary role of action in the process of knowing is evident in Ryle's (1949) claim that knowledge is essentially a 'knowing how,' a capacity to perform or act in particular circumstances. Using an example of a boy playing chess, he suggests that the boy can be said to 'know how' to play chess if his action displays the rules of chess, even if he cannot recite them. Similarly, Polanyi (1967) points to the tacit knowing that is evident in our ability to recognize faces in a crowd or to ride bicycles even as we cannot articulate precisely how it is that we do these. Thus, we recognize the 'knowing how' (the capacity to play chess or ride a bicycle) by observing the practice (chess-playing or bicycle-riding). However, the practice has no meaning apart from the 'knowing how' that constitutes it. Remove the 'knowing how' of playing chess from the practice, and we no longer have anything recognizable as chess-playing practice. The two are inseparable as Ryle (1949, p. 32) notes:

> ... 'thinking what I am doing' does not connote 'both thinking what to do and doing it.' When I do something intelligently ... I am doing one thing and not two. My performance has a special procedure or manner, not special antecedents.

This mutual constitution of knowing and practice – while hard to conceptualize in our conventional theoretical frameworks – is a key premise underpinning Giddens' (1984) theory of structuration, Maturana and Varela's (1998) notion of autopoiesis, and Lewontin's (1995) constructionist biology. It is also effectively depicted in Escher's (1948) lithograph

Knowing in Practice: Enacting a Collective Capability in Distributed Organizing *continued*

By Wanda J. Orlikowski

FIGURE 2.2.1 | M. C. ESCHER'S 'DRAWING HANDS'

Drawing Hands (see Figure 2.2.1.), where the right hand draws the left hand even as the left hand draws the right hand.

Recent work in cognitive anthropology has reinforced the essentially mutual constitution of knowing and practice. Based on extensive field work, Lave (1988) and Hutchins (1991, 1995) have found that cognition in practice (or 'in the wild' as Hutchins evocatively puts it) is a culturally situated and ongoing social activity. In a series of studies that examined math-problem-solving activities in adults, Lave (1988) persuasively shows that competence in math is not some abstract knowledge that individuals either do or do not have, but a 'knowledge-in-practice', a situated knowing constituted by a person acting in a particular setting and engaging aspects of the self, the body, and the physical and social worlds (Lave 1988, pp. 180–181). Based on her studies, Lave writes that 'knowledge is not primarily a factual commodity or compendium of facts, nor is an expert knower an encyclopedia. Instead knowledge takes on the character of a process of knowing' (1988, p. 175). Spender (1996b, p. 64) similarly observes that: 'knowledge is less about truth and reason and more about the practice of intervening knowledgeably and purposefully in the world'.

Giddens (1984, p. 4) defines human knowledgeability as 'inherent within the ability to "go on" within the routines of social life'. Such ability to 'go on' is inseparable from human agency, where agency is the capacity of humans to 'choose to do otherwise'. Knowledgeability or knowing-in-practice is continually enacted through people's everyday activity; it does not exist 'out there' (incorporated in external objects, routines, or systems) or 'in here' (inscribed in human brains, bodies, or communities). Rather, knowing is an ongoing social accomplishment, constituted and reconstituted in everyday practice. As such, knowing cannot be understood as stable or enduring. Because it is enacted in the moment, its existence is virtual, its status provisional. Knowing how to ride a bicycle, recognize faces, play basketball, make fine flutes (Cook and Yanow 1996), or launch and recover planes on an aircraft carrier (Weick and Roberts 1993) are capabilities generated through action. They emerge from the situated and ongoing interrelationships of context (time and place), activity stream, agency (intentions, actions), and structure (normative, authoritative, and interpretive). Because these capabilities are continually generated in recurrent action, continuity is achieved and preserved as people interpret and experience their doing as 'the same' over time and across contexts (Lave 1988, p. 187). Thus, as we bicycle to work every day, we begin to take for granted that we 'know how' to ride a bicycle, and lose sight of the way in which our 'knowing how' is an active and recurrent accomplishment …

In the research study described below, I explore the globally dispersed, product development work of a large and successful multinational organization (Kappa). The empirical insights suggest a central role for practices that produce and sustain a collective and distributed knowing within the global organization. Such a focus on practices has not been central to current research on either global product development or organizational knowledge. Because it may be a valuable perspective for understanding a range of organizational activities, it is the focus of my attention here …

Knowing in Practice: Enacting a Collective Capability in Distributed Organizing

By Wanda J. Orlikowski

Sharing Identity: Knowing the Organization

A consistent challenge experienced in distributed work is maintaining coherence, commitment, and continuity across the multiple locations, priorities, and interests of the hundreds of people involved in the collaborative effort. Kappa's large size and widespread geographic dispersion ensure this challenge is faced on all VOS product development projects. Kappa members deal with this challenge by actively and recurrently producing a distinctive and shared Kappa identity with which most of them identify and through which they orient their work. This process of shared identity construction affords Kappa members a localized yet common orientation to each other and to their product development work across geographic locations and different versions of the VOS product. Thus, software engineers in, say, Holland or Spain have – and know they have – a similar orientation to software development work as do software engineers in, say, India or Australia.

This knowing about the organization and how it works is generated through the initial training and socialization workshops that all new employees participate in. It is subsequently reinforced when Kappa members appropriate the common orientation and use it to inform their everyday product development activities. Talk to any Kappa employee, and very quickly he/she will mention the 'Kappa way' as a critical element of how work is accomplished across the distributed locations of their operations. The 'Kappa way' is seen to generate the common ground on which distributed product development work is structured, and is for many a means of local and global identification within their daily activities. It is understood by Kappa members as the ongoing activity of calibrating and connecting with a set of shared values, goals, and expectations about what is important in Kappa and why ...

While the ongoing enactment of a shared identity is critical to the conduct of global product development work, it is not without risks. The 'same frame of mind' quoted above may also lead to an organizational form of groupthink with less flexibility around change. Kogut and Zander (1996, p. 515) note that shared identity 'also imposes the weighty costs of ruling out alternative ways to organize and to exploit new avenues of development'. Indeed, Kappa is currently faced with having to migrate many of its products and approaches to a new form of software development (object-oriented) utilizing a new technology platform (the Internet). This change is proving quite difficult for Kappa, given its considerable past successes with an established approach. A senior executive commented:

> The biggest challenge is changing from how we are currently working, and that feeling of security in what we are doing. With the person we have in the organization, it is quite hard to give up something that has worked now for 20 years. It is a paradox, isn't it, that people have to give up what they feel most secure about to in fact secure their future.

A shared identity has the dual nature noted by Geertz (1973) – that a *model of* reality is also a *model for* reality. In Kappa's case, ongoing enactment of a shared identity, even as it enables a particularly powerful understanding and way of acting in the world, may constrain movement away from such understanding and acting when it becomes the exclusive source of motivation, identification, attention, and action.

Interacting Face to Face: Knowing the Players in the Game

Kappa's projects typically involve the participation of hundreds of software engineers located around the world. Moreover, the participation of individuals on a project is not fixed or static, but decided through a series of work assignment contracts that are negotiated annually between a product organization and the distributed design units. There is thus a considerable social boundary to be dealt with as engineers and managers work jointly with hundreds of different people located in many different parts of the world.

Everyone I talked to within Kappa commented that one of the ways they deal with this challenge is by engaging in extensive social interaction – despite the highly distributed nature of their product

READING 2.2

Knowing in Practice: Enacting a Collective Capability in Distributed Organizing *continued*

By Wanda J. Orlikowski

development operations. Such engagement in recurrent face-to-face interaction seems particularly useful in this context because it enacts an ongoing and evolving knowing of the shifting set of players in the game, thus building and sustaining important social networks that support the doing of distributed work. It is by working with and through such social networks that Kappa members navigate and negotiate many of the challenges of working across temporal, geographic, cultural, and political boundaries.

The ongoing practice of face-to-face interaction allows Kappa members to constitute a sense of knowing their colleagues, of knowing their credibility in and commitment to specific issues, and of knowing how to collaborate with them to get things done in a globally dispersed and complex product development environment.

However, this practice of face-to-face interaction in a globally distributed organization does not come without consequences. One cost – as a project manager put it – is 'tons of travel', and the accompanying need to justify considerable travel expenses. A DU staff member gave an example of how Kappa's commitment to having people get to know each other face-to-face created a problem with Kappa's external auditor. One project had experienced a change in leadership midway through the product development effort. As soon as the new project manager took over, he went on a trip to all the development units where work on his project was being done, so that he could 'meet all the people working on the subprojects'. The auditor, however, had difficulty accepting this reason for the travel:

> This auditor kept wanting to see a report of the work done on the trip. And we tried to tell him 'No, these were not working meetings, but meetings to get to know the people.' But in his view, this was travel on company expense, and if it was on company expense, there should be a visible benefit. And we said, 'Yes, there is a visible benefit – the project manager now knows all those people.' He simply couldn't accept that the only purpose for the travel was communication.

But that's what we do, even though it's sometimes difficult to explain to outsiders.

While travel expenses are an obvious cost, what is less obvious is the physical and emotional wear and tear on Kappa members who do such extensive travel to maintain face-to-face interaction. HR managers are particularly concerned about the risk of individual burnout incurred by the toll of ongoing travel. Many VOS project members reported increased stress and decreased family time ...

Aligning Effort: Knowing How to Coordinate Across Time and Space

Kappa's products are highly complex and integrated technical systems that involve millions of lines of software code and thousands of modules. These systems need to work seamlessly with each other, reflect evolving technical standards and customer requirements, and be compatible with the previous generation of products that are still operating on customers' computers. Developing such systems successfully demands effective and ongoing coordination.

Within Kappa, such aligning of products, projects, and people across time and space is accomplished through two key activities: the consistent and widespread use of a proprietary project management model, its planning tool, and structured systems development methodology; and the annual contracting for work via standard metrics ('kilomanhours') between product organizations (POs) and local development units (DUs). Through their ongoing use of such models, tools, methodologies, contracts, and metrics, Kappa members constitute a knowing how to coordinate their global product development activities across the multiple boundaries of time, space, technology, and history that characterize Kappa's VOS product development effort.

Plans, methodologies, tools, contracts, and metrics facilitate coordination by reducing uncertainty and variability. Such use, however, can also dampen improvisation. When Kappa members use the plans, methods, and metrics to focus their attention and guide their work activities, they also inadvertently discount ideas and activities not expressible in the

READING 2.2	**Knowing in Practice: Enacting a Collective Capability in Distributed Organizing**

By Wanda J. Orlikowski

vocabulary of the plans, methods, and metrics in use. This makes Kappa vulnerable to shifts in software development paradigms. Indeed, as mentioned, such a shift is currently underway within the industry, and Kappa's dependence on its proprietary suite of project management and software development approaches is constraining its shift to a new generation of software platforms which rely on a different infrastructure (the Internet), a different programming language (Java), and different software development methodologies (object-oriented, agent-based, and parallel development). One project manager commented about Kappa's current project management model:

> I think it helps us, but the drawback is that the limit has been hit now of the capacity of that model. And our model is not today suitable for the future. It is what we call here a waterfall model of software development. It is sequential. But what we need now is a new model and a new methodology for parallel development.

Learning by Doing: Knowing How to Develop Capabilities

Given the nature of Kappa's technically complex products and strongly competitive environment, Kappa managers want to stay on the leading edge of product development so as to retain and increase their customer base and highly skilled and marketable high-tech employees. Kappa accomplishes this through three primary activities: investing in individuals and their ongoing skill development, mentoring individuals and creating opportunities for their advancement, and rewarding developers' effort. Through engaging in such activities, Kappa members recurrently enact a knowing how to develop capabilities which generates a steady supply of skills and capabilities for both the individuals themselves as well as the particular units for which they work. It also ensures that Kappa's product development work is conducted by people with strong and up-to-date skill sets.

Kappa invests extensively in its employees. One brochure handed out to new recruits describes their careers at Kappa as a 'Lifetime of Competence Development', and employees are told that they will develop 'capacities' in three areas: 'technical/professional competence' (skills in computing, Kappa's suite of technical products, as well as the specialized language, methodology, and platform used in the development of those products), 'business competence' (skills in project management, customer orientation, and the strategic issues of Kappa's current and future marketplace), and 'human competence' (skills in intercultural communication, negotiation, and proficiency in the English language).

My interviews suggest that these descriptions about the development of 'individual capacities' are not simply ideological rhetoric. A senior executive commented about the organization's HR activities:

> We pay a lot for competence development. Not only in training, but also in overseas assignments. It is our life, so we believe in paying a lot for it. We invest in the individual. And we need that to balance out that we are not the highest payer. We do not pay as well as some of our competitors, especially in the United States where they buy loyalty with options and things like that. We build loyalty through investing in the people. We have a different culture.

Investing in the individual was not just an espoused principle, but actively enacted through what people did (or did not do) every day. For instance, one senior executive noted that there was no policy within Kappa to lay off employees:

> In Kappa, we don't have the mentality to hire and fire. We care for our employees quite a bit. We are not just seeing them as producers, but they are people we also want to care for.

This commitment to employees is widely acknowledged by Kappa members, as a software engineer noted:

> Here I know I have job security ... Kappa is a good company ... They don't treat you like they do in [name of competitor], where you can be kicked out the next day ...

READING 2.2

Knowing in Practice: Enacting a Collective Capability in Distributed Organizing *continued*

By Wanda J. Orlikowski

While Kappa has traditionally succeeded in recruiting and retaining skilled individuals by investing in them, it remains an open question whether this strategy will work equally effectively in the new Internet-based technological environment and the opportunities proffered by an entrepreneurial business context.

Supporting Participation: Knowing How to Innovate

Producing technically complex products, while essential, is not sufficient for success in the fast-paced and competitive environment in which Kappa operates. The products also have to be innovative. Generating and sustaining a high level of innovativeness in product development is a significant challenge for any organization; it is even more so in the case of a highly distributed organization such as Kappa with its multiple constituencies, priorities, and interests.

This challenge is addressed within Kappa through the deliberate dispersion of product development activities to geographically distributed parts of the world, accompanied by the active integration of the distributed expertise and experience through ongoing project participation and overseas work assignments. These three activities are seen by Kappa members to significantly foster innovation and creativity.

Through the variety of activities that allow them to work inclusively with, within, and across geographic locations and cultural differences, Kappa members constitute a knowing how to innovate by leveraging the global dispersion and diversity of the organization. However, this also has its downside, in that the effort to be inclusive runs the risk of fragmentation, time delays, and conflict over priorities. A senior executive observed:

> The fundamental thing about the design organizations is that they are located in different places. And as much as it is very nice to have these organizations that are diverse, they also sometimes pull in different directions. And the big challenge is to bring them together.

A project manager noted the temporal cost of making decisions in a diverse and dispersed organization:

> There's a lot of negotiation and discussion, so it takes time before the decisions are made. And I think it can take sometimes longer to make decisions in the project.

Kappa members strongly believe that their dispersed organization and its attendant diversity is an invaluable strength. To date, these benefits appear to outweigh the costs of inefficiency and risk of fragmentation. Nevertheless, as the industry experiences a technological shift and competition increases, it is unclear whether the negative consequences of extensive dispersion and diversity will remain a controllable consequence of doing globally distributed product development work.

There is currently considerable interest in facilitating knowledge sharing across communities through the use of various intermediaries such as boundary objects (Star 1989, Henderson 1991, Carlile 1998), translators and knowledge brokers (Brown and Duguid 1998), boundary practices (Wenger 1998), and cross-community communication forums (Boland and Tenkasi 1995). Such intermediaries – whether humans or artifacts – are seen as necessary because these scholars view knowledge, particularly know-how, as 'embedded in' or 'stuck to' particular situated practices. A focus on organizational knowing, however, suggests that the notion of stickiness, at least as it applies to 'knowing how', may need revision. The 'knowing how' that is constituted in practice is not effectively understood as 'stuck' in or to that practice. That would be like saying that the words of this sentence are 'stuck' to it, when in fact they constitute it. Instead, I have proposed that 'knowing how' and practice are mutually constitutive. Thus, sharing 'knowing how' cannot be seen as a problem of knowledge transfer or a process of disembedding 'sticky' knowledge from one community of practice and embedding it in another – with or without the mediating help of boundary objects, boundary practices, brokers, or forums. Rather, sharing 'knowing how' can be seen as a process of enabling others to learn the practice that entails the 'knowing how'. It is a process of helping others develop the ability to enact – in a variety of contexts and conditions – the knowing in practice …

| READING 2.2 | **Knowing in Practice: Enacting a Collective Capability in Distributed Organizing** |

By Wanda J. Orlikowski

References

Boland, R. J. and Tenkasi, R. V. 1995. **Perspective making and perspective taking: In communities of knowing.** *Organ. Sci.* 6 350–372.

Brown, J. S. and Duguid, P. 1998. **Organizing knowledge.** *California Management Rev.* 40(3) 90–111.

Carlile, P. 1998. **From transfer to transformation: Working through knowledge boundaries in product development.** Working paper, Cambridge, MA: MIT Center for Innovation in Product Development.

Cook, S. D. N. and Brown, J. S. 1999. **Bridging epistemologies: The generative dance between organizational knowledge and organizational knowing.** *Organ. Sci.* 10(4) 381–400.

Cook, S. D. and Yanow, D. 1996. **Culture and organizational learning.** M. D. Cohen and L. S. Sproull, eds. *Organizational Learning.* Thousand Oaks, CA: Sage Publications.

Davenport, T. H. and Prusak, L. 1998. *Working Knowledge: How Organizations Manage What They Know.* Boston, MA: Harvard Business School Press.

Geertz, C. 1973. *The Interpretation of Cultures.* New York: Basic Books.

Giddens, A. 1984. *The Constitution of Society: Outline of the Theory of Structure.* Berkeley, CA: University of California Press.

Giddens, A. and Pierson, C. 1998. *Conversations with Anthony Giddens: Making Sense of Modernity.* Stanford, CA: Stanford University Press.

Henderson, K. 1991. **Flexible sketches and inflexible databases: Visual communication, conscription devices, and boundary objects in design engineering.** *Sci., Tech., Human Values* 16(4) 448–473.

Hutchins, E. 1991. **Organizing work by adaptation.** *Organ. Sci.* 2 14–39.

Kogut, B. and Zander, U. 1996. **What firms do? Coordination, identity, and learning.** *Organ. Sci.* 7 502–518.

Lave, J. 1988. *Cognition in Practice.* Cambridge, UK: Cambridge University Press.

Leonard-Barton, D. 1995. *Wellsprings of Knowledge: Building and Sustaining the Sources of Innovation.* Boston, MA: Harvard Business School Press.

Lewontin, R. 1995. **Genes, environment, and organisms.** R. Silvers, ed. *Hidden Histories of Science.* New York: New York Review of Books Publishers.

Maturana, H. R. and Varela, F. J. 1998. *The Tree of Knowledge: The Biological Roots of Human Understanding,* revised ed. Boston, MA: Shambhala Publications.

Polanyi, M. 1967. *The Tacit Dimension.* New York: Doubleday.

Ryle, G. 1949. *The Concept of Mind.* London, UK: Hutcheson.

Schon, D. A. 1983. *The Reflective Practitioner.* New York: Basic Books.

Spender, A. 1996b. **Organizational knowledge, learning, and memory: Three concepts in search of a theory.** *J. Organ. Change* 9 63–78.

Star, S. L. 1989. **The structure of ill-structured solutions: Boundary objects and heterogeneous distributed problem solving.** M. Huhns and L. Gasser, eds. *Readings in Distributed Artificial Intelligence.* Menlo Park, CA: Morgan Kaufman.

Suchman, L. A. 1987. *Plans and Situated Actions: The Problem of Human Machine Communication.* Cambridge, UK: University of Cambridge Press.

Weick, K.E. and Roberts, K. 1993. **Collective mind in organizations: Heedful interrelating on flight decks.** *Admin. Sci. Quart.* 38 357–381.

| READING 2.3 | **Managers Divided: Organizational Politics and IT Management** |

By David Knights and Fergus Murray

A recent review (Drory and Romm, 1990) of writing on organizational politics (OP) suggests that two themes emerge from the broad and diverse literature in the field. These are:

1. that OP in some sense is divergent from and antithetical to formal organizational goals. This suggests that there are formal organization goals that are in danger of being subverted by OP.

Managers Divided: Organizational Politics and IT Management *continued*

By David Knights and Fergus Murray

2. that OP tends to be associated with conflict in organizations.

In many approaches to OP there is an assumption that not only does OP tend to subvert formal organization goals but also that OP is in opposition to the rational goals of organizations (Pfeffer, 1981; Pettigrew, 1973). As such OP is about the pursuit of self-interest or the pursuit of functional managerial interests in opposition to organizational goals.

It is our view that far from representing an exception to organizational process, OP is at the centre of events and practices in organizations. Indeed, it is through OP as an ongoing social process that organizations and their 'interests' and 'goals' are constructed. As such, we would argue that it is impossible and misleading to separate off the albeit problematic pursuit of self or sectional interests from those of the organization itself. Rather, it is through the construction, negotiation and reappraisal of self, collective and organizational interests that the fragile reality of an organization is sustained, reproduced and changed.

This is not to say that the construction of organizational reality takes place in a vacuum and can therefore be turned into any reality. Paraphrasing Marx, men and women make history but not under circumstances of their own choosing. Clearly, organizational realities are constructed, reproduced and changed within historically and spatially specific conditions of possibility (Bhaskar 1989, Marsden 1993). These both constrain and open up choices to organizations.

We argue, then, that OP is a process that stands at the centre of contemporary organizations. This process is highly structured and takes place within strongly delimited conditions of possibility. As such, it is not an anarchic 'free-for-all' but is instead played out within a complex set of conditions of possibility that include formal and informal rules and accepted customs.

The central motor of OP is the struggle of individuals and collectives to achieve and reproduce a sense of material and symbolic security in the world. Within management, in particular, this struggle centres around the individual pursuit of career and the symbolic and material achievements of success. The pursuit of career and success is a process that takes place in competitive conditions that vary in their intensity over time and place.

However, while placing the pursuit of career in the boiler room of OP we are not suggesting that such pursuits and 'organizational goals' are necessarily antithetical. As we have already indicated, career pursuits are not independent of the constitution and reproduction of organizational goals and, as such, can be productive as well as unproductive in relation to their achievement. In most circumstances, disruptive political behaviour is a consequence of previous exercises of power that have failed to secure the appropriate support from others. Here grievances may well result in individuals or groups denying consent to the official goals of the organization. But while such behaviour may be seen as disruptive of the current goals, invariably and especially where the discontent is in anyway shared by a significant minority, there will be attempts to build a nucleus of support for alternative ways of achieving current, or a new set of, goals. The point that needs to be noted is that organizational goals and the politics of their achievement and/or transformation is the site of career practices in pursuit of material and symbolic security.

Nevertheless, even though there is not necessarily a tension between the pursuit of career goals and formally defined organizational goals it seems that the rules of the OP game prohibit too-explicit a display of these career goals. Instead, they remain concealed behind, though expressed through, the more legitimate pursuit of formally acknowledged organizational goals. Clearly, then, career development is sublimated, and often even lost from view, in the pursuit of ever-changing formal organizational goals and strategies.

It is largely for this reason, we would argue, that theorists like Pettigrew (1973) treat the politics within organizations as somehow aberrant, deviant and perhaps even subversive. What is happening is that the researcher identifies with those at the top of the official hierarchy whose interests often are to eradicate or anihilate the political ambitions of their subordinates partly as a way of protecting their own position and privilege. For while revolution may be a rarity, many examples of rebellion occur in organizations where

READING 2.3

Managers Divided: Organizational Politics and IT Management

By David Knights and Fergus Murray

those rising to the top actually displace the current regime. But even when political ambition is no more than a contest between equals for elevation in the career hierarchy, the basis of that competition has always to be couched in the language and collective values of the organization as a whole. While everyone knows that individual career ambitions lie behind these various organizational practices, for the 'good' of the organization and the standing and legitimacy of management in general, there has to be a pretence that it is not so.

Consequently, career competition is extremely complicated and takes place in small and hidden ways more often than in large and public disputes and battles. For example, successful managers develop an acute sense for creating an image of themselves as successful on a day to day basis. This includes treating superiors in a particular way, in putting on displays of competence for selected audiences, and massaging and manipulating the reality reaching superiors in such a way that it conveys a message of controlled competence, efficiency and innovation (Mills, 1951; Dalton, 1959; Burns & Stalker, 1962; Jackall, 1988).

It also involves complex alliances of managers within and between particular functions and departments. Thus, for example, managers from the same function may team up to convey a particular symbolic message of success to their senior executives, or they may seek allies in other functions to fight off challenges for their share of corporate resources.

The process of organizational politics, and the vast array of individual and collective strategies it involves, is necessarily driven through with a central paradox. For a great deal of managerial practice constructs a reality of its own activity that denies the *political* quality of that practice.

Neither managers nor many writers on management like to examine the fragile and precarious character of a conflictually negotiated order. Instead, a huge effort is made to give organizations the appearance that they really do run to clear formal procedures in pursuit of goals that are rationally derived from their 'objective' operating conditions. As such, we might say that *management is the political process of constructing a reality of management that denies its inherent politicality.*

Writing over thirty years ago, Burns (1961: 260) commented on this paradox as follows:

> The problem is no one regards himself as a politician, or as acting politically, except of course on occasions when he [sic] is led into accounts of successful intrigue and manoeuvring when he bolsters his self-esteem and reputation by projecting the whole affair into the safe social context of a game or joke.

Given their importance to the 'making' or 'breaking' of managerial careers, what might be termed metaphorically as the 'killing fields' (see Jackal, 1988) of politics are clearly disturbing and threatening to managerial identities. One way, then, of coping with the anxiety and insecurity they engender is to discount their seriousness through joking or to deny the existence of organizational politics altogether.

There are a number of other reasons for denying or obfuscating the politics in organizational life. Apart from protecting the organization and senior management against the fear that subordinate rebellion and even revolution are a distinct possibility, the very sense of what it is to be a manager is torn by a series of conflicting beliefs that an explicit acknowledgement of organizational politics only brings to the surface. On the one hand, fed by the meritocratic values of western democracies, managers will have some faith, however limited, in the merit based nature of reward, and even when disillusioned, they will tend to act *as if* strategy is the expression of 'real' organizational interests and that their organization is run by formal rules and procedures. On the other hand, they are aware that the whole process of management is a vast political game of intrigue, skulduggery, backroom deals, and career carve-ups. Only by elevating the formally rational and meritocratic aspects of organizations can the political and career competition be kept sufficiently 'under wraps' for the 'normal' business of management to proceed.

But a moment's thought reveals how a meritocratic system of rewards is an ideal that is unattainable if only because judgements of merit could never be so 'objective' as to be uncontestable. Insofar as all judgements of merit are tied to interpretations of one

Managers Divided: Organizational Politics and IT Management *continued*

By David Knights and Fergus Murray

or more superordinates, it is obvious that those with career ambitions will pursue various strategies to secure a favourable judgement even though success in such endeavours will often be related to their skill in obscuring what they are doing.

Despite much evidence to the contrary, meritocratic beliefs have the upper hand over views about political competition and intrigue. This is not surprising given the strength of rationalistic interpretations of management practice within academic discourses (see Marsden, 1993) and the interest that managers have in promoting an image of themselves as rational and disinterested technocrats worthy of the power-infused privileges invested in them. But neither set of beliefs can be taken at face value since they are as much accounts of events as rationalisations of success and failure. If one is successful then it will always be rationalised as a result of merit whereas failure can be designated as due to the highly political nature of decisions or unfortunate external circumstances.

Perhaps another reason for obscuring the political character of organizational life is that its acknowledgement would only serve to intensify the existential and organizational insecurity prevalent in all organizations. By subscribing to a myth of orderly and rational decision making, the inherent uncertainty of management and its potential to generate unintended and sometimes uncontrollable consequences is hidden. It is carefully laid to rest behind a durable façade of bureaucratic stability and fair play. In this way anxiety is controlled and managers do not have to confront the uncertainty of their lives; nor do they have to become conscious of the ways in which they may prostitute themselves and their sense of integrity in order to make the right political moves. Instead, this can be blamed on the dictates of 'the organization' and removed from the realm of personal choice and responsibility. There is little doubt, however, that the devious and concealed character of the political conditions and consequences of organizational behaviour also generates anxiety and insecurity that cannot easily be released or shared without suffering career disadvantage.

As we have implied, all this political activity takes place within an apparently co-operative set of collective managerial practices that constitute the co-ordination and control of organizational activity. These practices are not only precarious because of pressures from outside but the co-operative veneer is continuously threatened by individualistic strivings to attain or retain a privileged access to comparatively scarce material and symbolic resources that grant security and status. This tension between co-operation and competition is reflected in, and reinforced by, the growing technical division of labour that separates employees into routine, specialist and managerial functions each of which give differential access to organizational resources.

Overall the general intent of managerial action can be described as an individual and collective struggle characterized by co-operation, competition and conflict to secure a share of the material (e.g., income, control over expenditure) and symbolic (e.g., status, access to important projects or committees) resources organizationally available. This struggle for scarce material and symbolic resources reflects and reinforces stratifying practices that are anticipated to maintain or enhance individual security and socially valued identities, both internal and external to the organization.

The political process of organizational life, then, is fundamental to the striving of managers to create a sense of themselves that is coherent, manageable and convincing to significant others both inside and outside of the organization.

The conditions under which managers labour to 'bring off' this deep sense of self are not generally of their own choosing, in that the individual manager confronts them as a given reality. That is, managers enter a national and local arena in which what it is to be a manager, what we here call the *subjectivity of management*, is already predefined. In other words, the idea of a particular sort of management, behaviour, attitudes and norms is established and treated as 'natural', such that deviation from certain routinized practices would be heavily sanctioned. The manager moving into this context has to come to terms with these normalized modes of behaviour (Foucault, 1977), and indeed will probably have displayed a capacity to do this prior to securing a managerial status. It may be possible to effect small local changes in

| READING 2.3 | **Managers Divided: Organizational Politics and IT Management** |

By David Knights and Fergus Murray

management practice, but mere survival will involve the replication of existing practices to a greater or lesser extent.

References

Bhaskar, R (1989) *Reclaiming Reality: A Critical Introduction to Contemporary Philosophy*. London: Verso.

Burns, T (1977) *The BBC: Public Institution and Private World*. London: Macmillan.

Burns T and Stalker G. M (1961) *The Management of Innovation*. London: Pergamon.

Dalton, M. (1959) *Men Who Manage*. New York: Wiley.

Drory, A. and Romm, T. (1990) 'The Definition of Organizational Politics: A Review', *Human Relations* 43 11: 1133–1154.

Foucault, M. (1977) *Discipline and Punish*. Harmondsworth: Penguin.

Jackall, R. (1988) *Moral Mazes: The World of Corporate Managers*. New York: Oxford University Press.

Marsden, R. (1993) 'The politics of organizational analysis', *Organization Studies*, 14 1: 93–124.

Mills C. Wright (1956) *White Collar*. New York: OUP.

Pettigrew, A. (1973) *The Politics of Organizational Decision Making*. London: Tavistock.

Pfeffer, J (1981) *Power in Organizations*. Boston, MA: Pitman.

Discussion Questions

1. What difference does it make to refer to 'organizing' rather than 'organization'?
2. Is organization always 'in the making'? If so, how can continuity be accounted for?
3. How do Knights and Murray connect processes of organizing to 'organizational politics'?

Recommended Further Readings

See references accompanying the Readings plus:

Clegg, S.R., Kornberger, M. and Rhodes, C. (2007), Learning/Becoming/Organizing, *Organization* 12(2): 147–167.

Chia, R. (2003), 'Essai: Time, Duration and Simultaneity: Rethinking Process and Change in Organizational Analysis', *Organization Studies* 23(6): 863–868.

Dibben, M.R. and Munroe, I. (2003), 'Applying Process Thought', *Organization Studies* 32(2): 183–195.

Elger, T. (1975), 'Industrial Organizations: A Processual Perspective' in McKinlay, J.B., (ed.) *Processing People: Cases in Organizational Behaviour*, New York: Holt, Rinehart and Winston.

Langley, A. (2007), 'Process Thinking in Strategic Organization', *Strategic Organization* 5(3): 271–282 Also available at

Langley, A. and Truax, J. (1994), 'A Process Study of New Technology Adoption in Smaller Manufacturing Firms', *Journal of Management Studies* 31(5): 619–652.

McCabe, D. (2010), 'Strategy-as-Power: Ambiguity, Contradiction and the Exercise of Power in a UK Building Society', *Organization*, 17(2): 151–176.

Pettigrew, A. (1997), 'What is Processual Analysis?', *Scandinavian Journal of Management* 13(4): 337–348.

Tsoukas, H. and Chia, R. 'On Organizational Becoming: Rethinking Organizational Change', *Organization Science*, 13(5): 567–582.

Weick, K. (2000), 'Emergent Change as a Universal in Organizations' in Beer, M. and Nohria, N. (eds.) *Breaking the Code of Change*, Harvard Business School Press.

Winter, M., Smith, C., Cooke-Daviies, T. and Cicmil, S. (2006), 'The importance of "process" in Rethinking Project Management: The story of a UK Government-funded research network', *International Journal of Project Management*, 24(8): 650–662.

MANAGING

READINGS

Alvesson, M. and Willmott, H. (1996) 'Introducing Critical Theory to Management: Management in Critical Perspective' in *Making Sense of Management*, London: Sage. pp. 10–11, 30–32.

Jackall, R. (1988) *Moral Mazes: The World of Corporate Managers,* Oxford: Oxford University Press, pp. 12, 76–77.

Watson, T.J. (1996) 'How do Managers Think? Identity, Morality and Pragmatism in Managerial Theory and Practice' in *Management Learning*, Vol. 27, No. 3: 323–341.

Willmott, H. (1997) 'Rethinking Management and Managerial Work: Capitalism, Control and Subjectivity' in *Human Relations*, Vol. 50, No. 11: pp. 1329–1330, 1334–1335,1347–1348, 1354.

INTRODUCTION

'Managing' is pervasive in modern society – as a practice and as an ideology. As an activity reserved for managers, managing occurs in all work organizations where there is a hierarchical division of labour involving a dedication of certain responsibilities and tasks to individuals or groups who are charged with 'managing' the work of others. In this context, the *practice* of managing is widely portrayed as a universal, technical activity that comprises planning, decision-making, budgeting, etc. In a way that parallels the functionalist conception of organization 'structure' (see Introduction to section on Organization theory), the functions ascribed to 'managers' are represented as neutral means of securing particular ends; and the division of 'managers' (those who design) and 'managed' (those who execute the designs of others) forms a key part of this functionalist conception of organization. Specialization is viewed as a technical matter of maximizing efficiency, not a political matter of securing control of institutionalized disparities of material and symbolic reward. This brings us to a consideration of managing as an ideology.

As an *ideology*, 'managing', and the division of labour associated with it, is commended as an efficient and effective way of getting things done. In the sphere of work, difficulties and shortcomings are routinely diagnosed as a product of inadequate managerial skills for which the preferred solution is more or better management. They are not widely interpreted as symptomatic of social and material differences and distances between organizational members that systematically impede communication, stimulate the pursuit of self-interest and limit effort. Indeed, the ideological appeal of managerialist thinking has led to its extensive adoption to address problems across a wide range of spheres that encompass personal relationships, leisure and even death.

Most accounts of managing take for granted the legitimacy of management and, as a consequence, are preoccupied with specifying or elaborating the functions or role that managers play (Mintzberg, 1973) or identifying the characteristics (e.g. political skills) or processes (e.g. networking) that supposedly define or identify the most effective managers (Kotter, 1982). **Mats Alvesson and Hugh Willmott** (Reading 3.1) contend that these accounts abstract the activity of managing from the political economic contexts of its formation and development. When managing is represented as a technical function, the work of managers is portrayed as comprising neutral sets of roles, skills and competences that are seemingly neutral, functional and unequivocally valuable, rather than as work that is plagued by tensions, conflict and contestation that arise from being embedded within relations of domination and exploitation.

Alvesson and Willmott note how studies of managerial work that deviate from the conventional wisdom have been inspired by a number of intellectual traditions. These range from those which attend to the significance of 'informal' and extra-corporate relationships and networks (e.g. Dalton, 1956) to those that place managerial work in a wider historical context where its universality and neutrality becomes difficult to sustain (see also Reading 3.4). An important impetus for studies that address the historical context was Braverman's *Labor and Monopoly Capital* (1974) which Clegg and Hardy (see section on Organization theory) also flag up as a key contribution to the study of management and organization. Ostensibly about labour and capital, it focused most closely upon management strategies. At the heart of work organizations in capitalist enterprises, he argues, is an imperative to render labour more productive for the *sectional* purpose of securing and amassing the accumulation of capital. The functions performed by managers, Braverman contends, are principally politico-economic ones – in the sense that managers are hired to devise strategies and work processes that ensure labour's profitable subordination to capital, rather than for any purpose that could be characterized as universal or neutral. From this perspective, managing is indelibly coloured and compromised by an imperative to control labour in ways that secure its productive collaboration in the further enrichment and domination of the holders of capital. This perspective is illuminating in its appreciation of how managing occurs within a wider political economy which the sense making of managers routinely reproduces. A limitation of this view is its tendency to reduce the complexities and equivocalities of managerial work and decision-making to managers' pursuit of the interests of capital, as if these interests themselves, and the means of their realization, are not themselves subject to contestation and negotiation by managers who develop their own agendas and priorities.

Given the centrality and importance attached to 'managing', it is remarkable how little research has been devoted to the study of the people whose activities exemplify 'managing' – people who, by and large, have also produced and shaped dominant conceptions of its nature and value. In-depth studies of the practice of managing can be counted on the fingers of one hand. There have been numerous accounts of other employees and occupations, including research into shopfloor work; and there have been a number of excellent studies that touch upon certain aspects of managing (e.g. Gouldner, 1954; Kunda, 1992; Smith, 1999, Alvesson, 1996). But few studies focus directly and in detail upon what managers do (e.g. Dalton, 1956; Watson, 1994) by relying upon ethnographic methods – notably participant observation – each of which relies heavily upon participant observation to access and explore the 'insides' of managerial work.

The position of comparative privilege occupied by managers offers possible explanation of the dearth of studies of managerial work. Managers may permit other employees in their organizations to be studied – perhaps in the expectation that something might be learned that would enable them to manage their staff more effectively. As subjects of research, managers may willingly provide interviews in which they can control the information made available to researchers. They may even be prepared to convey their opinion scandidly when sufficient trust has been established, or when they are confident or arrogant enough to express their views without a PR filter or gloss. In general, however, managers are uninterested in, if not hostile to, being observed directly and closely; and, as gatekeepers of the access to a close study of their activities sought by researchers, managers are in a position to enforce this disinterest. This helps to explain why detailed research into the practices of managing (and organizing) is so scarce, and why many accounts of managerial and executive work are bland and self-serving as they generally take the form of heroic success stories where the performance of an organization is attributed to a few charismatic or exceptionally capable senior managers.

Robert Jackall (Reading 3.2) identifies managers as 'the principal carriers of the bureaucratic ethic in our era'. Notably, in recent years managers have been recruited into public sector organizations to instal and numerous bureaucratic mechanisms – in the form of contract, performance measurement and quality management. At the same time, Jackall suggests that managing is not what it seems as managerial decision-making is frequently cloaked in the vocabulary of rationality in order to appear legitimate (see also the extract from Knights and Murray in the Organizing section. Jackall's study shows how junior and middle managers tend to take their lead from senior executives who, it is understood, assess the loyalty of subordinates by the degree of their conformity to a prescribed code of behaviour. To put this another way, they are inclined to favour those who mirror their own sense of values and priorities. A recurrent issue for managers is that the behaviour of subordinates is inherently unpredictable and difficult to control. While claiming and appearing to execute the plans set out by their superordinates, subordinates may pursue their own objectives (e.g. rapid career advancement) in ways that are damaging, in the longer term, to priorities such as cost control, reputation building or profitable growth; and this problem may be exacerbated rather than mitigated by the introduction of performance-related incentives. Perversely, perhaps, it is pressure to demonstrate conformity to corporate objectives which reduces the likelihood of subordinates volunteering or communicating information that endangers their own career prospects even if its disclosure is important for attaining such objectives.

Tony Watson (Reading 3.3) points to the struggles experienced by managers who grapple with tensions between their principles and pressures to be pragmatic. His research indicates that, in practice, theories about managing tended to be sidelined in favour of what managers had found to be effective or, at least, have become routinized in their day-to-day experiences of managing. General theories – what Argyris and Schon (1974) characterize as espoused theories – were generally unused in practice because managers did not find themselves at liberty to follow their prescriptions. Instead, as captives of an established ethos and custom-and-practice within their organizations, they tended to ignore or compromise such theories, as well as their personal principles, in favour of something that kept their sense of managerial identity intact. In Watson's words, managers occupy a social position 'where they are expected to be fully "in control" ... to be in full possession of all "the facts" ... to "be men" – strong, confident, masculine individuals who can "hack it"'(p. 339). But, of course, this is a super-human expectation that even the most confident and aggressive of managers cannot possibly fulfil so that, at best, bravado substitutes for competence. The pressures can be especially acute for female managers when finding themselves under pressure either to deny their femininity or to use it to reinforce rather than subvert the masculinity of 'normal' managing. Watson's managers found themselves caught in a double bind which they routinely reproduced as they diluted or disregarded their preferred theories and associated styles (e.g. listening and paying attention to people) in order to maintain their sense of being in control (which they did by concealing their vulnerabilities by imposing their will upon others).

Hugh Willmott (Reading 3.4) picks up the theme of unpredictability and recalcitrance identified in Readings 3.2 and 3.3 when he contends that they are not universal, inevitable phenomena occasioned by the difficulties in containing chance events or reining in the capacity of human beings to act in a self-interested or 'headstrong' manner. Recalcitrance and associated uncertainties are also historical phenomena that arise when societies and organizations are established upon contradictory principles – for example, when employees are urged to use initiative and be self-determining, yet are simultaneously required to be consistent and predictable. Rules and procedures are introduced in an effort to standardize unproductive and errant behaviour. But the opposing pressure to exercise discretion in response to changing or unforeseen circumstances, such as market volatility, results in notions of loyalty, commitment, trust and shared values being invoked in an effort to transform uncertainty into control. Both the development and elaboration of rules and procedures and expanded scope for exercising discretion present further opportunities for pursuing lines of action guided by preferences and loyalties that at least partially escape the colonizing reach of the corporation and may even, perversely, be fuelled by it. The position of many managers is complicated by their own status as employees or wage labour, a status that can lead them to give priority to their own personal values, family and career objectives (e.g. expansion that is not accompanied by profitability) in directions that diverge from the preferences of capital (e.g. lay-offs of management in order to recover or improve profitability). This is why it is relevant to complement recognition of how managers experience and interpret their activity (see Weick *et al.*, Organizing section) with an appreciation of the politico-economic contexts of managerial work as it is through this activity that the contexts are themselves reproduced and transformed. These interpretations, including an identification with notions of 'professionalism' and 'loyalty', may incline managers to consent to, rather than resist, practices and objectives that are in tension with their personal values or preferences.

READING 3.1

Introducing Critical Theory to Management: Management in Critical Perspective

By Mats Alvesson and Hugh Willmott

Amid the confusion and uncertainty about what management is, there has been a tendency to privilege one meaning as a universal process that comprises a number of technical functions. Central to this formulation is the understanding that management is a distinctive component of all complex systems, and that it is rational to allocate this activity to those who are deemed to be experts. However, a moment's reflection makes it obvious that the technical functions of management do not exist, and indeed can never exist, in a social or historical vacuum. As Child (1969: 16) has noted, the meaning and activity of management is 'intimately bound up with the *social* situation of the managing group' (emphasis added). If this is so, then technical conceptions of management, which are blind to this 'situation', are actually expressions of the particular circumstances in which the theory and practice of management develops.

Hales (1993) situates the development of management in the context of the guardians of private capital and the growth of the modern state. He observes how

> 'the separation of management is an outgrowth of disparities in socio-economic power, the acquisition or ignition of work processes by private capital or the state, and the desire for control which flows from that: hence the contested nature of that separation' (ibid.: 6 and 8).

Management is thus understood, or theorized, as a product of the historical context in which it emerges, takes shape and then increasingly gives shape to its context. Hales relates the separation of management, as a function and status group, to its role in maintaining, developing and controlling forms of work organization that pre-serve disparities of socio-economic power within the private and public sectors. In practice,

the work of managers, Hales suggests, is not a neutral, technical activity precisely because disparities of ownership, income and opportunity demand, as a precondition of the coordination of employee effort, the exercise of control to stimulate effort and contain dissent.

In all societies, whether primitive or advanced, capitalist or socialist, productive progresses are coordinated or 'managed'. The issue, then, is not whether management will continue to exist as an activity. Rather, the critical issue is the *kind* of management there will be; and, most crucially, whether the theory and practice of management will continue to normalize and exploit social divisions and be driven by the priorities of elites, or whether it will because more democratically accountable to a majority of citizens, producers and consumers.

Beyond the Understanding of Management as a Technical Activity

When management is represented as a technical activity, a blind eye is turned to the *social relations* through which managerial work is accomplished and upon which it ultimately depends (Whittington, 1992). This blindness reflects and reinforces the understanding that problems of management can be adequately diagnosed and remedied by developing more efficient and effective means of technical control. Problems (e.g. unemployment, pollution) that are fundamentally *social* and political in organization come to be interpreted as amenable to *technical* solutions. However, when instrumental forms of reasoning alone are deemed to be relevant and legitimate resources for advancing the science of management (Willmott, 1995b), our understanding of management is unnecessarily and dangerously restricted in its capacity to address the escalating social and ecological problems of the modern world (see Lipietz,

READING 3.1

Introducing Critical Theory to Management: Management in Critical Perspective *continued*

By Mats Alvesson and Hugh Willmott

1992). What Burris (1993: 179) has argued in relation to the use of new communication technologies is equally applicable to the other areas and specialisms of management. Namely, that the design and implementation of new systems is to become more democratic 'with the social and political factors receiving as much attention as technical ones' (ibid.), it cannot be assumed that all problems are amenable to a 'technical fix' within the status quo or that technical experts alone possess the expertise to devise and implement effective solutions.

Blindness to the social media of management also restricts awareness of how the human difficulties and challenges associated with organizing everyday tasks are compounded whenever major divisions – manifest in differences of values, objectives and resources – exist between those involved in accomplishing such tasks. Where there are divisions – of class, gender, ethnicity, etc. – between managers and managed, everyday difficulties of securing cooperation are magnified. Whenever communication between managers and managed is impeded and distorted by institutionalized forms of domination (e.g. patriarchy), cooperation is conditional and precarious.

Managers are not unaware of the pressures and contradictions of their work. They frequently feel frustrated and abused by the system which they supposedly control, and they frequently bemoan the difficulties encountered in gaining unequivocal cooperation and commitment from their colleagues as well as from their staff (Watson, 1994). However, received wisdom provides them with minimal insight into these problems. Management education and training routinely encourages managers to privilege the claims of technical, instrumental reason (see above) though it excludes exposure to ideas that, potentially, are highly relevant for making sense of the pressures and contractions of their work. Conventional representations of management may furnish managers with a comforting sense of their own 'impartiality', 'professionalism' and functional importance. But conventional wisdom marginalizes, or trivializes, the politics of managerial work. Managers are thus prevented from gaining a more critical perspective on their involvement, as key players (and victims), in the development of 'a continually refined administration of human beings [in which]

science, technology, industry and administration interlock in a circular process' (Habermas, 1974: 254) ...

'Progressive' Conceptions of Management and the Extension of Technology

The conventional criticism of classical conceptions of management is that they fail to recognize how, in practice, management decision making is 'bounded' by limited information and pressures to reach 'closure' before all options can be thoroughly scrutinized and evaluated (March and Simon, 1958). This criticism usefully draws attention to the practicalities of managerial work in which the process of reaching optimal decisions is impeded or 'bounded' by 'realities' that will not wait for the optimal solution to be found. Empirically, Mintzberg's (1973) study of managerial work presents a picture of executives rapidly moving from one activity to another, with little time for planning or to carefully assemble and evaluate relevant information to 'satisfice' in response to immediate pressures rather than 'optimize', having weighed the alternative courses of action.

The adequacy of this understanding of the limits of managerial rationality has been challenged by those who argue that, in addition to universal limitations of information gathering and processing, decision making is invariably guided and restricted by managers' particular allegiances, preoccupations and hunches (Pettigrew, 1973; Kakabadse, 1983; Yates, 1985). It is these hunches, proven recipes and 'biases', and not just their limited capacity to process information or the commercial pressures upon them to reach closure, that lead managers to deviate from the formal, rationalist logic of classical management theory. Decision making, Child (1972: 16) concludes, 'is an essentially political process in which constraints and opportunities *are functions of the power exercised by decision-makers in the light of ideological values*' (emphasis added). Studies that pay attention to the politics of organizational decision making and the conditioning of managerial work by ideological values provide a valuable counterbalance to the over-rationalized textbook image of management. Under their influence, a new generation of researchers (e.g. Pfeffer, 1981b; Pettigrew, 1985a) and management gurus (e.g. Pascales, 1991) have focussed upon

Introducing Critical Theory to Management: Management in Critical Perspective

By Mats Alvesson and Hugh Willmott

the micropolitics of management decision making. Received wisdom is also now beginning to assimilate the understanding that managerial behaviour is mediated by organizational, sectoral, and societal cultures and contexts (Whitley, 1993).

Yet, despite this broadening of our understanding, 'progressive' research monographs, guru handbooks and academic textbooks continue to be written as if the question of 'management for what?' were either self-evident or of little practical consequence. In effect, academics who have drawn attention to the micropolitics of managerial decision making have criticized established, over-rationalized wisdom for being *imperfectly* managerial: if only other managers would learn to become more aware of the role of values in shaping their perceptions, and/or appreciate the nature and significance of organizational politics, they would then operate more effectively as many current difficulties and dysfunctions could be lessened, if not avoided (Kotter, 1982). Or, as Pettigrew (1985b: 314–16) has expressed this view,

> Changing business strategies has to involve a process of ideological and political change that eventually releases a new concept of strategy that is culturally acceptable within a newly appreciated context ... In the broadest sense, this means, prescriptively, that step one in a change process should be improve and build upon any natural processes of change by tackling questions such as how existing processes can be speeded up, how the conditions that determine people's interpretations of situations can be altered, and how contexts can be mobilized toward legitimate problems and solutions along the way to move the organization additively *[sic]* in a different strategic direction.

So-called processual accounts of managerial work and organizational change, such as those produced by Pettigrew, begin to pay attention to what he terms 'ideological and political change'. However, all too often attention is focussed upon the ideological and political dimensions of organizing simply as a means of *smoothing* the process of top-down change. Established priorities and values are assumed to be

legitimate. The insights of social science into the context and dynamics of organizational change are not prized for their capacity to stimulate a debate upon the legitimacy of current priorities. Instead, social science is identified as a neutral technology for minimizing conflict associated with managers' decisions to take 'a different strategic direction'. In such 'progressive' accounts of management and organization, precious little consideration is given to the merits, or rationality, of the 'ends' of management.[1] Prescriptively, their more or less overt emphasis is upon *supplementing* and revising established means and recipes of management control (e.g. bureaucratic rules and procedures) with *the strategic reengineering of employee norms and values* in line with the 'new concept of strategy' and the 'legitimate problems and solutions' – as identified by top management or their consultants and legitimized by academics. In this process, a technocratic ideology of management is effectively reinforced, not challenged (Willmott, 1993a).

Any theory or practice that takes for granted the ends and legitimacy of expert rule, and thereby suppresses the claims of more democratic forms of governance is, in this sense, technocratic (see Burris, 1993). Taylor's Scientific Management is an obvious example. But the contemporary rise of more 'participantive' and 'humanistic' techniques as embraced by the gurus of Excellence and Total Quality Management, though seemingly encouraging a weakening of the divisions between managers and managed, are not necessarily any less technocratic. On the contrary, ideologies associated with the strengthening of corporate culture (e.g. Theory Z, Ouchi, 1981) can portend a more totalizing means of managerial control (Willmott, 1993a) that aims to induce an internalization of norms and values selected by senior managers (Deal and Kennedy, 1982; Kilmann *et al.*, 1985).

Culturist means of control have been studied in depth by Kunda (1992) in his research of Tech, a company celebrated by mainstream commentators for its creativity and progressive, people-orientated style of management. The following excerpt is illustrative of how employees at Tech are surrounded by, and continuously subjected to, Tech Culture:

READING 3.1

Introducing Critical Theory to Management: Management in Critical Perspective *continued*

By Mats Alvesson and Hugh Willmott

Tom O'Brien has been around the company for a while; like many others, he has definite ideas about 'Tech Culture' ... But, as he is constantly reminded, so does the company. When he arrives at work, he encounters evidence of the company point of view at every turn ... Inside the building where he works, just beyond the security desk, a large television monitor is playing a videotape of a recent speech by Sam Miller (the founder and president). As Tom walks by, he hears the familiar voice discuss 'our goals, our values, and the way we do things' ... As he sits down in his office space, Tom switches on his terminal ... On his technet mail he notices among the many communications another announcement of the afternoon events; a memo titled, 'How Others See Our Values', reviewing excerpts on Tech Culture from recent managerial best sellers ... In his mail, he finds *Techknowledge,* one of the company's newsletters. On the cover is a big picture of Sam Miller against the background of a giant slogan – 'We Are One'. He also finds an order form for company publications, including Ellen Cohen's 'Culture Operating Manual' ... The day has hardly begun, yet Tom is already surrounded by 'the culture', the ever-present signs of the company's explicit concern with its employees' state of mind (and heart). (ibid.: 50–2)

This passage conveys the idea of Tech as an institution in which employees are continuously bombarded with positive images of the company and the reinforcement of corporate messages about what is expected from them. However, as our earlier discussion of the wilfulness of human beings suggested, employees are not necessarily submissive participants in processes of corporate brainwashing. Unlike the automatons portrayed in Orwell's *Nineteen Eighty-four* or Huxley's *Brave New World*, Tech employees bring alternative values and priorities to their work. Through processes of distancing and irony, Tech employees were able to expose and deflate the use of high sounding corporate rhetoric. On the other hand, Kunda's study also discloses a darker side of Tech's corporate culture: it could readily accommodate and exploit a degree of values and expectations (see also Filby and Willmott, 1988) – by encouraging employees to interpret the tolerated ridiculing of Tech ideology as a confirmation of the company's ostensibly liberal ethos. The most pervasive and insidious effect of Tech culture was its repressive tolerance (Marcuse, 1964). This, Kunda suggests, was more effective in stifling and neutralizing organized forms of resistance than the imposition of a more coercive, heavy-handed approach: 'in the name of humanism, enlightenment and progress, the engineers of Tech culture elicit the intense efforts of employees not by stirring theory experiential life, but, if anything, by degrading and perhaps destroying it' (Kunda, 1992: 224–5). Kunda usefully points out how modern ideologies – humanism, enlightenment and progress – are routinely mobilized at Tech, and often in subliminal ways, to legitimize the demands of the company upon its employees. Yet, despite the potency of Tech culture, the frustration and psychological degradation experience by Tech employees prompted many of them to develop and amplify countervailing images of this seemingly benevolent organization ...

[1]For example, in business schools, the inclusion of electives in 'business ethics' or the espousal of (pseudo) 'democratic styles' of managing tends to exemplify rather than challenge the acquisition and application of abstract techniques and idealized prescriptions.

References

Burris, B. (1993) *Technocracy at Work*. Albany, NY: State University of New York Press.

Child, J. (1969) *British Management Thought*. London: Allen and Unwin.

Child, J. (1972) 'Organizational structure, environment and performance: the role of strategic choice', *Sociology*. 6: 1–22.

Deal, T. and Kennedy, A. (1982) *Corporate Cultures; The Rites and Rituatls of Corporate Life*. New York: Addison-Wesley.

Filby, I. and Willmott, H.C. (1988) 'Ideologies and contradictions in a public relations department: the seduction and impotence of living myth', *Organization Studies*, 9(3): 335–49.

| READING 3.1 | **Introducing Critical Theory to Management: Management in Critical Perspective** |

By Mats Alvesson and Hugh Willmott

Habermas, J. (1974) *Theory and Practice*. London: Heinemann.

Hales, C. (1993) *Managing Through Organization*. London: Routledge.

Kakabadse, A. (1983) *The Politics of Management*. Aldershot: Gower.

Kilmann, R.H., Saxton, M.J. and Serpa, R. (1985) *Gaining Control of the Corporate Culture*. San Francisco, CA: Jossey-Bass.

Kotter, J.P. (1982) *The General Managers*. New York: Free Press.

Kunda, G. (1992) *Engineering Culture. Control and Commitment in a High-Tech Corporation*. Philadelphia, PA: Temple University Press.

Lipietz, A. (1992) *Towards a New Economic Order: Postfordism, Ecology and Democracy*. Cambridge: Polity Press.

March, J. and Simon, H. (1958) *Organizations*. New York: John Wiley.

Marcuse, H. (1964) *One-dimensional Man: Studies in the Ideology of Advanced Industrial Society*. Boston, MA: Beacon Press.

Mintzberg, H. (1973) *The Nature of Managerial Work*. New York: Harper and Row.

Ouchi, W. (1981) *Theory Z: How American Business Can Meet the Japanese Challenge*. New York: Addison-Wesley.

Pascale, R.T. (1992) *Managing on the Edge: How Successful Companies use Conflict to Stay Ahead*. Harmondsworth: Penguin.

Pettigrew, A. (1973) *The Politics of Organizational Decision-making*. London: Tavistock.

Pettigrew, A. (1985a) *The Awaking Giant: Continuity and Change at ICI*. Oxford: Blackwell.

Pettigrew, A. (1985b) 'Examining change in long-term context of culture and politics', in J.M. Pennings (ed.), *Organizational Strategy and Change*. San Francisco, CA: Josse-Bass.

Pfeffer, J. (1981b) 'Management as symbolic action; the creation and maintenance of organizational paradigms', in L.L. Cummings and B.M. Straw (eds.), *Research in Organizational Behaviour*. 3: 1–52.

Watson, T. (1994) *In Search of Management*. London: Routledge

Whitley, R. (1993) *Business Systems in East Asia*. London: Sage.

Whittington, R. (1992) 'Putting Giddens into action: social systems and managerial agency', *Journal of Management Studies*. 29(6): 693–712.

Willmott, H.C. (1993a) 'Strength is ignorance; slavery is freedom: managing culture in modern organizations', *Journal of Management Studies*. 30(4): 515–52.

| READING 3.2 | **Moral Mazes: The World of Corporate Managers** |

By Robert Jackall

Although managers only constitute 9.9 percent of the US labour force (in 1980), they are nonetheless the quintessential bureaucratic work group in our society. Until and unless they reach the pinnacles of their administrative hierarchies, managers not only fashion bureaucratic rules but they are also bound by them. They not only implement rational procedures and plans, often in an attempt to control irrational forces, but they are also affected by the methodical rationality that they, their peers, and their superiors put in place. Often, too, they are affected by the irrationalities that rational efforts generate. They are not only bosses, but bossed; they are not only the beneficiaries of the privileges and power that authority in bureaucracies bestow, but in most cases they are also subordinates who want to climb higher. If they do struggle to the top of their organizations, they become not just the stuff of legend and the models for the ambitious below them, but also the objects of gossip, rumour, envy, resentment, and fear. Whether they stay at the middle or reach the top, managers typically are not only in the big organization but, because their administrative expertise and knowledge of bureaucratic intricacies constitutes their livelihood, they are also of the organization. Unlike public servants, they need not avow allegiance to civil service codes or to any ethic of public service. Their sole allegiances are to the very principle of organization, to the market

READING 3.2

Moral Mazes: The World of Corporate Managers *continued*

By Robert Jackall

which itself is bureaucratically organized, to the groups and individuals in their world who can demand and command their loyalties, and to themselves and their own careers.

Managers are thus the paradigm of the white-collar salaried employee. Their conservative public style and conventional demeanour hide their transforming role in our society. In my view, they are the principal carriers of the bureaucratic ethic in our era. Their pivotal institutional position as a group not only gives their decisions great reach, but also links them to other important elites. As a result, their occupational ethics and the way they come to see the world set both the frameworks and the vocabularies for a great many public issues in our society. Moreover, managers' experiences are by no means unique; indeed, they have a deep resonance with those of a great many other white-collar occupational groups, including men and women who work in the academy, in medicine, in science, and in politics. Work – bureaucratic work in particular – poses a series of intractable dilemmas that often demand compromise with traditional moral beliefs …

In bureaucratic settings, which are institutionalized paradigms of functional rationality, technique and procedure tend to become ascendant over substantive reflection about organizational goals, at least among lower and middle-level managers, where, of course, one is expected to implement policy rather than fashion it or much less criticize it. Even at higher levels of management, one sees ample evidence of an over-riding emphasis on technique rather than on critical reasoning. In Alchemy Inc., to take but one example, high-level managers were recently given a handbook called 'Procedures for Creativity in Management'. Moreover, scientific theories of decision making, often highly specified step-by-step procedures, are the staple of administrative science, business school curricula, and management consultant programs. These theories provide managers with a whole range of conceptual tools – cost/benefit analysis, risk/benefit analysis, several measures calculate capital utilization as well as profit, and so on – that purport to 'take the black magic out of management' and routinize administration. It is worth noting that even managers who are sceptical about the efficacy of such measures are among the principal consumers of such techniques and of analytical devices of every sort. In trying to come to grips with what seem at times to be incalculable, irrational forces, one must be willing to use whatever tools are at hand. Moreover, in an increasingly professionalized managerial environment, to eschew a vocabulary of rationality or the opportunity to routinize decisions when possible, can only make one vulnerable to the charge of 'managing by the seat of the pants'.

All of this, of course, is complicated by the difficulties of assessing to what extent functionally rational devices actually are used in making decisions, particularly by higher-ups. Vocabularies of rationality are always invoked to cloak decisions, particularly those that might seem impulsive when judged by other standards. The CEO of Covenant Corporation, for instance, sold the sporting goods business from one of his operating companies to the president of that company and some associates in the leveraged buyout. The sale surprised many people since at the time the business was the only profitable operation in that particular operating company and there were strong expectations for its long-term growth. Most likely, according to some managers, the corporation was just not big enough to hold two egos as large and bruising as those of the president and the CEO. However, the official reason was that sporting goods, being a consumer business, did not fit the 'strategic profile' of the corporation as a whole. Similarly, Covenant's CEO sold large tracts of land with valuable minerals at dumbfounding low prices. The CEO and his aides said that Covenant simply did not have the experience to mine these minerals efficiently, a self-evident fact from the low profit rate of the business. In all likelihood, according to a manager close to the situation, the CEO, a man with a financial bent and a ready eye for the quick paper deal, felt so uncomfortable with the exigencies of mining these minerals that he ignored the fact that the prices the corporation was getting for the minerals had been negotiated forty years earlier. Such impulsiveness and indeed, one might say from a certain perspective, irrationality, is of course, always justified in rational and reasonable terms. It is so commonplace in the corporate world that many managers expect whatever ordered processes they do erect to be subverted or overturned by executive fiat, masquerading, of

READING 3.2	**Moral Mazes: The World of Corporate Managers**

By Robert Jackall

course, as an established bureaucratic procedure or considered judgment.

Despite such capriciousness and the ambiguity it creates, many managerial decisions are routine ones based on well-established and generally agreed upon procedures. For the most part, these kinds of decisions do not pose problems for managers. But, whenever non-routine matters, or problems for which there are no specified procedures, or questions that involve evaluative judgements are at issue, managers' behaviour and perspective change markedly. In such cases, managers' essential problem is how to make things turn out the way they are supposed to, that is, as defined or expected by their bosses.

A middle-level designer in Weft Corporation's fashion business provides a rudimentary but instructive example of this dynamic at work. She says:

> You know that old saying: 'Success has many parents; failure is an orphan'? Well, that describes decision making. A lot of people don't want to make a commitment, as least publicly. This is a widespread problem. They can't make judgements. They stand around and wait for everybody else's reaction. Let me tell you a story which perfectly illustrates this. There was a [museum] collection coming, the [Arctic] collection, and there was a great deal of interest among designers in [Arctic] things. My own feeling was that it wouldn't sell but I also recognized that everybody wanted to do it. But in this case, [our] design department was spared the trouble. There was an independent designer who had access to out president and he showed him a collection of [Arctic] designs. There were two things wrong: (1) it was too early because the collection hadn't hit town yet; (2) more important, the designs themselves were *horrible*. Anyway, [the collection] was shown in a room with everything spread out on a large table. I was called down to this room which was crowded with about nine people from the company who had seen the designs. I looked at this display and instantly hated them. I was asked what I thought but before I could open my mouth, people were jumping up and down clapping the designer on the back and so on. They had already decided to do it because the president had loved it. Of course, the whole affair was a total failure. The point is that in making decisions, people look *up* and look *around*. They rely on others, not because of inexperience, but because of fear of failure. They look up and look to others before they take any plunges.

READING 3.3	**How do Managers Think? Identity, Morality and Pragmatism in Managerial Theory and Practice**

By Tony J. Watson

One of the key research questions informing the author's participant observation study, which was carried out over 12 months in the Ryland telecommunications manufacturing and development plant of ZTC, was that of the extent to which managers can be seen as operating in terms of anything which might be identified as theories. The researcher joined the management team of the company for a 12-month period, taking on a range of responsibilities including that of developing a management competences scheme for the business. In addition to the everyday participant observation fieldwork, a set of 60 'core' interviews were carried out with managers from across the whole range of functions and level (junior

Source: Reproduced with permission of Sage Publications, London, Los Angeles, New Delhi and Singapore (via Rightslink) from 'How do managers think? Identity, Morality and Pragmatism in Managerial Theory and Practice', in Management Learning © 1996 *Sage Publications.*

How do Managers Think? Identity, Morality and Pragmatism in Managerial Theory and Practice *continued*

By Tony J. Watson

managers to directors). The managers were all fully aware that their new colleague was gathering material for an academic study as well as fulfilling specific tasks. An interest in managers' 'lay theories' was only one of the many concerns of the research project, however, and this paper relates this concern to two others. The first of these is the question of how aspects of personal identity and values, as well as theories, influence managerial thoughts and actions. The second moves this concern to the broader institutional level by considering questions of culture. The company was, in part, selected for study because it was known that there were certain dissonances within its emergent culture – people spoke of the organization energetically following certain 'progressive' managerial trends whilst, at the same time, still relying on more 'old-fashioned' systems of control. It was felt that, if this were the case, then issues of personal values and morality in managerial practice and questions about 'theories of managing' would be more pertinent to individuals and thus more readily open to investigation than they would be in a more stable setting.

It was recognized from the start that 'theory' was not a concept with which managers were likely to be immediately comfortable. This was borne out by research. Yet it did prove possible to draw out certain patterns in the thinking which informed manager's actions. It was recognized that 'theories' can operate at many levels of abstraction in people's thinking and it was left to the informants themselves to indicate those factors which shaped their practice-orientated thinking (whether they be at the level of what has been learned by trial-and-error in the factory or of lessons taken from Christian gospel) – whether or not they were happy to have the label 'theory' applied to them. We can see the wariness about 'theory' which was typical of managers in the study, as well as an awareness that there are nevertheless patterns to the ideas which inform their practice, in the words of a middle-level engineering manager who, in one of the core interviews, responded to a question about whether he followed any particular theories of management in his work with the words that he had 'no

time for management theories'. Not only that, he added, but he had 'no time for any type of theory at all'. 'So you are a practical man who works without theories?' He grinned as this was put to him and he began to shake his head at the clear challenge presented by the words 'you go around doing practical things all day. You do it all by instinct. There's absolutely no thought behind anything you do.' 'I see what you are getting at', he laughed, 'Of course there is thought behind what I do.' But do not, he implored, ask for explanation of what this thought is. Although he had 'no fancy theories', he had a 'pretty good idea of how things work in factories, in business ...' This opportunity to hear a manager's account of 'how things work' was a way into learning something of how he 'theorized' his activities.

In scores of conversations like this, some in formal interviews and some in the course of everyday conversations with managers, an attempt was made to get some idea of the 'lay theories' which managers draw upon in the course of their work. This corresponds to what Argyris and Schon (1974, 1978) call 'theories in use' – ideas which can be distinguished from 'espoused theories'. Although the theories were to be brought out through conversations, it was hoped that by contextualizing this talk within an ethnographic investigation of life in an industrial plant where there was a primary emphasis on managerial practice, as opposed to the discourse of management education and development, insights into theories in use would be gained rather than statements of what might be felt to be appropriate espoused theories. But the term 'theory in use' might still be problematic in that it implies that the theoretical principles which managers might be predisposed to apply in work tend, in practice, actually to be 'used'. This may well not be the case. Indeed, this research suggests that there is not a direct relationship between what managers would talk about – what was 'in their minds' and what it can be inferred that they would *prefer to use* as theories – and what one would see them doing *in practice*.

Whatever statement of a theoretical nature managers might make in interviews and conversations

READING 3.3	**How do Managers Think? Identity, Morality and Pragmatism in Managerial Theory and Practice**

By Tony J. Watson

and however this may represent their preferred operating principles as managers, it would be naïve to assume that these were principles which would systematically, directly and regularly be used or 'applied' in deciding lines of action. It is therefore wiser to think of the managers' theories which were being sought here as ideas which *inform* their actions rather than ones which in any sense direct or cause behaviours. In the day-to-day circumstances of managerial practice, an individual's personal intuitive guidelines might well not be followed at all, for reasons which are considered later in the paper. At other times, however, the individual, when freer to pursue their own preferred lines of action, may well be said to have 'theories in use'. What is being suggested then is a third category which falls halfway between Argyris and Schon's 'espoused theory' and 'theory in use'. It is a kind of personal theory which can be seen as a *potential theory in use* because it contains the guidelines for action which managers would follow if they were allowed to. Alternatively, it can be seen as falling more on the espoused theory side because it plays a role in the individual's internal mental debates and can be voiced in certain situations, such as interviews with researchers – even if it is not then followed in the practical circumstances in which managers find themselves …

It was very rare indeed for any managers in ZTC Ryland to talk of formal management theories when discussing their personal theories, and this is in spite of the fact that a high proportion of them had been on management courses, including ones provided by university business schools. One woman, who had both a first degree in management studies and an MBA, was one of the very few to mention any academic sources whatsoever. She responded to a question about whether she had any personal theories about doing managerial work with the comment that she had 'absorbed' management theories. She said that she 'probably expounded on them to people at work when they need to understand why this happened this way or that'. But she had not 'consciously sat down and thought I'll take on Maslow's hierarchy of needs. It's all a matter of the way you think about things; the way you approach things.'

When asked whether she could put this into words, she replied: 'The thing that pops into mind is listening and paying attention to people. But to me that is a way of life.' The term 'way of life', applied as it is here at a personal level, is close to the notion of the sort of person one is. But it also draws our attention to the moral dimension – the dimensions of values – which sits alongside the concern with 'what works'.

When all the different ways in the ZTC managers spoke of their personal theories or basic management ideas are reviewed, a clear pattern emerges. Time and again there is reference to the need to listen to people, to treat them as important, unique individuals, to treat people with respect and to build relationships of trust with the people you deal with in your work. Individuals were regularly asked why they followed these guidelines. This was done to avoid the dangers of eliciting simplistic prescriptions and cosy homilies offered simply to give a positive impression of the speaker as a human being. There were often responses along the lines of 'It is just the way I am; I was brought up to be like that' or 'I have to behave that way as a Christian'. But after being asked, for example, to what extent the broad principles being outlined were ones of 'good behaviour' and to what extent they 'worked' by leading to 'better managerial outcomes', managers tended to suggest that these were effective practices as well as moral ones. A quality manager concluded his reply to a question about the assumptions which were beneath the 'operating principles' he had spoken of with the words, 'I don't have kids but I understand that if you don't have consistency you have big problems … It's a big belief of mine. So to move all this into my theory of management: respect for the individual really, communicating, consistency. OK?' Here was a clear mixing of important personal beliefs with concepts of what had effective managerial outcomes.

The accounts which ZTC managers gave of their 'theories' which underpinned their working practices typically constituted a highly integrated mixture of the principled and the pragmatic, the normative and the positive. They would say words to the effect

How do Managers Think? Identity, Morality and Pragmatism in Managerial Theory and Practice *continued*

By Tony J. Watson

that you *ought* to listen to people but you will also *get better work from people* if you do. They would suggest that it is a good thing to encourage people to develop these skills and responsibilities at work but that people will also do *a much better job* if you do this. It was argued that it is a good and *moral* thing to set up relationships of trust with the people around you but that it also *pays off*: if people trust you they will do a lot more for you, whether they are customers, suppliers, fellow managers or subordinates.

The 'lay theories' identified here are said to fall somewhere in between the notions of *theory-in-use* and *espoused theory* written about by Argyris and Schon (1974, 1978). Depending on the circumstances in which individuals find themselves, they can be seen more as sets of espoused principles or more as actual guidelines for action. The present analysis suggests that perhaps the most useful way of thinking of these personal theories is to regard them as *potential theories-in-use* because they represent the theoretical principles which would guide action were their holders free to follow them. This concept of potential theories-in-use may usefully extend the Argyris and Schon typology and help overcome one difficulty which tends to arise when it is applied. At present the typology implies, in effect, that we should differentiate between what people *say* and what they actually *do*. This all too readily encourages users of the typology to infer a level of insincerity and dishonesty when they see a difference between what people say they believe in and what they actually do. This may indeed be a reasonable inference to make. However, what the present analysis suggests is that care should be taken in jumping to such conclusions. A *claimed* theory which is not then observed to represent the set of principles followed in a claimant's practice may well be a statement of *sincere aspiration* as readily as it may be a piece of empty rhetoric intended to mislead or obfuscate ...

When looking at the reasons behind managers acting differently from what would have been expected from their reported personal 'theories', attention is drawn in this paper to factors arising from their having to cope with the imposition of strategic and operating decisions by what was sometimes call the 'top table'. However, there may be a set of much more general factors which always need to be taken into account when examining gaps arising between what managers say they believe in and what they actually do. These are factors which take us into complex matters of human subjectivity and issues of philosophical anthropology. But the experience of working and researching in ZTC Ryland suggested that such matters are highly pertinent. The closer the researcher's involvement was with the managers, the more it became apparent that a key factor in much behaviour was simply personal insecurity, basic human fragility and ordinary human angst. The managerial role puts a lot of normal and vulnerable human beings in a position where they are expected to be fully 'in control' and to be wise about human behaviour and about business. They are expected to be in full possession of all 'the facts' of situations, and in the case of the great majority of them, to 'be men' – strong, confident, masculine individuals who can 'hack it'. When secretive, aggressive and uncooperative behaviour was observed which did not fit with what individuals had claimed to be their personal values and preferred managerial styles, it often seemed to be understandable only in terms of a gap between some of the expectations which managers feel people have of them and what we might call the stresses of working in the 'real' world. This is the world of *bounded rationality* (Simon, 1957), of unpredictability and *equivocality* (Weick, 1979), of *ambiguity* (March and Olsen, 1976) and of the *paradoxes of consequences* – the tendency identified most notably by Max Weber (1968) for chosen means often to subvert the ends for which they are devised. Managers are involved in what might be called a *double control* situation (Watson, 1994); they not only have to control their own lives and destinies, like every other human being, they have to assert control of the work efforts, thoughts and activities of other people – employees, customers, colleagues, bosses and so on. To think clearly, rationally and consistently in such a work milieu is an immense challenge. And managers'

READING 3.3 | How do Managers Think? Identity, Morality and Pragmatism in Managerial Theory and Practice

By Tony J. Watson

attempts to do so present an exciting – and continuing – challenge to the academic researcher.

References

Argyris, C. and Schon, D.A. (1974) *Theory in Practice: Increasing professional effectiveness*. San Francisco, CA: Jossey-Bass.

Argyris, C. and Schon, D.A. (1978) *Organizational Learning*. New York: Addison-Wesley.

March, J.G. and Olsen, J.P. (1976) *Ambiguity and Choice in Organizations*. Oslo: Universitets Forlagtt.

Simon, H.A. (1957) 'A Behavioural Model of Rational Choice', in *Models of Man*. New York: Wiley.

Watson, T.J. (1994) 'Managing, Crafting and Researching: Words, Skill and Imagination in Shaping Management Research', *British Journal of Management*, 5(4): 889–905.

Weber, M. (1986) *Economy and Society*. New York: Bedminster Press.

Weick, K.E. (1979) *The Social Psychology of Organising*. Reading, MA: Addison-Wesley.

READING 3.4 | Rethinking Management and Managerial Work: Capitalism, Control and Subjectivity

By Hugh Willmott

How is management and the work of managers to be analysed? A bewildering range of perspectives has been proposed in answer to this question. Some approaches identify managers as executors of universal functions necessitated by industrialization and a complex division of labour (e.g., Fayol, 1949; Barnard, 1936; Drucker, 1977); others portray managers performing diverse organizational roles (e.g., Carlson, 1951; Sayles, 1964; Mintzberg, 1973). Yet others conceptualize managerial work in relation to a plurality of corporate, occupational, and 'professional' cultures associated with different levels and specialisms of management (e.g., Dalton, 1959; Pettigrew, 1973).

Locating managerial work within a plurality of cultures has the merit of appreciating its social organized, negotiated quality. This helps correct ahistorical, functionalist, and technicist representations of management by paying much closer attention to the organizational politics and processes of managerial work (e.g., Pettigrew, 1985, Pfeffer, 1981, 1981a; Burns, 1977; Kotter, 1982; Hickson *et al.*, 1986). However, such studies continue to abstract manage-

ment and managerial work from the politico-economic media through which such work is constituted and reproduced (see Meiksins, 1984; Willmott, 1987). As Thompson and McHugh (1995, p. 14) have observed, most accounts of organization and management write out of their scripts the 'many deep-rooted features of organizational life – inequality, conflict, domination and subordination and manipulation ... in favour of behavioural questions associated with efficiency or motivation'. Pettigrew's (1985) exploration of organizational change and development at ICI, for example, is largely decoupled from an appreciation of the politico-economic conditions and consequences of this change. The importance of linking 'macro' and 'micro' forms of analysis is repeatedly stressed, and even the contribution of labour process ethnographies of work is acknowledged. But, paradoxically, neither the 'micro' processes of managerial work nor the 'macro' context of their enactment is explicitly theorized.[1]

Silence about inequality, conflict, domination and subordination, and manipulation within both orthodox and more progressive accounts of management

READING 3.4

Rethinking Management and Managerial Work: Capitalism, Control and Subjectivity *continued*

By Hugh Willmott

and organization theory (see Alvesson and Willmott, 1996) 'has provided the catalyst for formulating a critical perspective on management' (Reed, 1989, p. 10). In this paper, attention is focused upon labor process theory[2] – one influential, critical perspective for analysing managerial work ...

Braverman highlights the extent to which much managerial work parallels the terms and conditions of employment experiences by other wage workers, and thus bears the '*mark of the proletarian condition*' (Braverman, 1974, p. 467, emphasis added).[3] This is a view that has been echoed by others, such as Anthony (1977) who, in the concluding chapter of *The Ideology of Work*, observes how a majority of managers:

> ... receive generous salaries but they are ... not often consulted about the design of their organization and the structure of their jobs. They are more likely to be the unwitting victims of reorganization (more and more frequently); transferred, retained or dismissed at the behest of organizational plans drawn up by distant consultants; regarded as human resources, shuffled and distributed by specialists in management development and planning ... (ibid. p. 311).

More recently, Scarborough and Burrell (1996) have suggested that middle managers are 'subject to the process of proletarianization' (ibid. p. 183) and that they experience 'greater insecurity, stress, decline in pay relative to senior management' (ibid. p. 185). From this standpoint, it is implausible to claim that '*most* managers' own substantial amounts of the organizations in which they work, and that these share holdings are 'often large' in terms of their 'potential contribution to the wealth *and income*' of the individual manager' (Eldridge *et al.*, 1991, p. 64, emphasis added). Only a small minority of managers – in effect, the elite that 'personifies capital' (Braverman, 1974, p. 311) – occupy such positions of comparative privilege, and thus 'have a *direct* material identity of interest and outlook with the shareholders of the enterprise' (Eldridge *et al.*, 1991, p. 64, emphasis added). Other, less senior managers

may aspire to such positions; they may also have similar values, at least so long as they consider themselves to have a chance of reaching senior management. However, for the vast majority of those occupying managerial positions, such aspirations are not shared, are progressively softened or remain unrealized (Goffee and Scase, 1986; see also Savage *et al.*, 1992, Chap. 4). As a Finance Director of a major manufacturing company observed in our study of 35 companies across the major sectors of the U.K. industry:

> The one thing you learn very quickly as a manager is that your loyalty is to your profession, not necessarily to your company ... if I look at my career, I've let a lot of people go who have been extremely loyal employees, you know, and really there's not an awful lot of loyalty coming the other way in the end. You know, when you say 'Sorry, I know you've been here twenty five years. Thanks a lot for all that service but I'm still going to let you go.'

Although managers have comparatively little 'space' (or inclination, it may be added) to pursue strategies that are overtly antagonistic to 'bottom-line' results, their first allegiance (in the West, at least) is likely to be to their careers, to their families, and perhaps to their 'profession', and not the the company, as Jackall (1988, p. 12) claims, or to its profits as ends in themselves; and, to this (limited) extent, they share an attitude held by many other employees ...

As sellers of labor, managers are typically and even obsessively concerned about their individual performance, job security, and career prospects. These concerns are routinely fuelled and exploited by employers and other superordinates who deploy various sticks and carrots in an effort to induce managers to suspend their personal values and priorities when these are deemed to impede or subvert corporate objectivities (Jackall, 1988). In response, managers may mobilize other values, agendas, and concerns to diffuse, resist, or circumvent pressures that are intended to make their agency more predictable and profitable (Knights & Murray, 1994). As the Manufacturing Director at one

| READING 3.4 | **Rethinking Management and Managerial Work: Capitalism, Control and Subjectivity** |

By Hugh Willmott

of our case study companies observed: in contrast to shopfloor workers who are 'so punch-drunk that if you tell them to take their clothes off they'll do it because they are so desperate for a job', middle managers are often more resistant to changing their practices and adept at circumventing pressures to do so:

> ... convincing the middle managers of change, and getting it through, is extremely difficult, extremely difficult ... they don't want to change, and any change is seen as a threat. For example, you will find a great tranche of middle management who will not use a computer, they will not, and putting these things in or changing these things is very difficult indeed.

Such are the mundane, empirical manifestations of what Burawoy (1985) terms the ideological and political dimension of work contexts. Business plans, for example, are not mindlessly constructed or implemented by managers committed or programmed to securing capitalist objectives. Rather, pressures to be responsive to such objectives are mediated and qualified by perceived opportunities for securing or advancing a melee of identity-securing concerns and values, such as the explanation of a specialist activity, speedy promotion, the chance of more challenging work of the continuation of a quiet life, etc.[4] And, of course, it is for this reason that elaborate technologies of control – audits, share ownership schemes, appraisal systems, bonus schemes, culture programs, etc. – have been devised to contain the potential risks associated with the delegation of authority to managers.[5] This conception of the nature of managerial work is now further illustrated by reference to studies of managers at work at ICI ...

In common with other employees, managers do not 'just' operate or supervise the physical and organization means of production in ways dictated by the imperatives of capitalism. Their materiality as human subjects also obliges them to struggle with the existential significance of the purposive quality of human consciousness, and not just with its contribution to productive activity. The content and organization of managerial work is shaped and reproduced by

'material subjects' who, as individualized sellers of wage labour and targets of control, are rendered anxious about their performance and career prospects; and who, like other employees, are disciplined by a variety of 'sticks' (e.g., audits) and 'carrots' (e.g., performance-related pay schemes) which are intended to secure their cooperation and trust.

The existential concern to secure a stable and acceptable sense of self-identity is not simply 'noise' which detracts from the 'signal' in capital's circuits of control. Rather, it is an inescapable medium of the signal's generation and transmission. For this reason, it is necessary to complement, qualify, and deepen an analysis of the embeddedness of managerial work in the contradictory operation of capitalism with an appreciation of how the management of these contradictions is mediated by concerns to secure or enhance a sense of self-identity. How this might be done has been illustrated by reinterpreting evidence drawn from existing studies of managerial work. It is hoped that, in future, research into management and textbook accounts of management will address and supplant the limitations of bourgeois analysis and orthodox labour process theory.

---

[1]With regard to the 'macro' context, Pettigrew (1985) argues that 'it is not sufficient to treat [it] either just as a descriptive background, or as an eclectic list of antecedents which somehow shape the process' (ibid. pp. 36–37). Yet, in the absence of a theory of the 'macro' conditions of action, this is precisely where his contextualist analysis ends up. With regard to the 'micro' processes, there is little more than the commonsensical thesis that, as individuals and in groups, managers develop and are guided by different rationalities as they pursue objectives that are important to them. In effect, the 'micro' is identified within interest group behaviours while the 'macro' is equated with untheorized shifts in politico-economic policy making and ideologies.

[2]Since the publication of Braverman's *Labor and Monopoly Capital* (1974), there has been a continuing debate about the adequacy of both Marx's and Braverman's conception of the capitalist labour process, aspects of which are touched upon throughout the paper. The existence of a unified, uncontested conception of labour process theory cannot therefore be assumed. What I take to be central to this perspective will become apparent as the argument of this paper unfolds (see also the Introduction to Knights & Willmott, 1990).

[3]While Braverman agrees with Marx that managers perform these functions, he attaches less importance to the distinction between 'productive' and 'unproductive' labour than to the growing

READING 3.4

Rethinking Management and Managerial Work: Capitalism, Control and Subjectivity *continued*

By Hugh Willmott

separation of conception from execution within clerical and managerial work. In this respect, Braverman's analysis bears a family resemblance to studies which characterize their class location as ambiguous or contradictory on the grounds that managerial work includes elements of both capital and labour (Carchedi, 1975; Wright, 1978). For an extended discussion of the class position of white-collar workers, see Smith & Willmott (1995).

[4]Superficially, a focus upon the actors' frame of reference and associated critique of determinism echoes Child's (1972) criticism at the failure of (structural) contingency theory to appreciate how the strategic choices exercised by decision-makers are a key factor in understanding the formation and reproduction of organisational structures. His argument is that greater attentiveness to the 'ideological values' which inform managers' strategic choices – for example, about markets, manpower, technology, and forms of work organization – 'provides a useful antidote to the sociologically unsatisfactory notion that a given organizational structure can be understood in relation to the functional imperative of "systems needs" which somehow transcend the objectives of any group of organizational members' (ibid. p. 14). However, from a labour process perspective, it is unsatisfactory to abstract the development of management values from their positioning within, and reproduction of a specifically capitalist structure of production relations, as Child (1972) is inclined to do (see Wood, 1980; Whittington, 1988). In his 'political contingency theory' (Child, 1984, p. 230 *et seq*) managerial ideologies and 'politics' are treated as variables that explain how organizational structures are determined (for an extended critique, see Alvesson & Willmott, 1996).

[5]in response to an awareness that managers – at all levels – are often resistant to changes that they perceived to challenge or devalue their self-knowledge (Goffee and Scase, 1986), intermediaries (e.g., management consultants) have emerged who aspire to reformulate the identity and project of managers as 'corporate entrepreneurs' engaged in the task of creating a new, so-called 'postbureaucratic' disciplinary matrix (Fulup, 1991; cf. Burgelman, 1983; Kanter, 1983; Peters, 1987). Though the intention of these intermediaries is to develop a new, authorities purpose and identity for (middle) management, their message frequently problematizes the very 'need' – for coherence and continuity – that aspires to fill.

References

Alvesson, M. and Willmott, H.C. (1996) *Making sense of management: A critical introduction*. London: Sage.

Anthony, P. (1977) *The ideology of work*. London: Tavistock.

Barnard, C.I. (1936) *The functions of the executive*. Cambridge, MA: Harvard University Press.

Braverman, H. (1974) *Labor and monopoly capital*. New York: Monthly Press Review.

Burawoy, M. (1985) *The politics of production*. London: Verso.

Burgelman, R.A. (1983) Corporate entrepreneurship ad strategic management: Insights from a process study. *Management science*, 29(12): 1349–1364.

Burns, T. (1977) *The BBC: Public investigation and private world*. London: Macmillan.

Carchedi, G. (1975) *On the economic identification of social classes*. London: Routledge and Kegan Paul.

Carlson, S. (1951) *Executive Behaviour*. Stockholm: Strombergs.

Child, J. (1972) Organization structure, environment and performance: The role of strategic choice. *Sociology*, 6: 1–2.

Child, J. (1984) *Organization*. London: Harper and Row.

Dalton, M. (1959) *Men who manage*. New York: John Wiley.

Drucker, P. (1977) *Management*. London: Pan.

Eldridge, J., Cressey, P. and Macinnes, J. (1991) *Industrial Sociology and economic crisis*. London: Harvest/Wheatsheaf.

Ezzamel, M., Green, C., Lilley, S. and Willmott, H.C. (1995) *Changing managers and managing change*. London: The Chartered Institute of Management Accountants.

Fulup, L. (1991) Middle managers: Victims of vanguards of the entrepreneurial movement? *Journal of Management Studies*, 28(1): 25–44.

Goffee, R. and Scase, R. (1986) Are the rewards worth the effort? Changing managerial values in the 1980s. *Personnel Review*, 15: 3–6.

Hickson, D.J., Botler, R.J., Cray, D., Mallory, G.R. and Wilson, D.C. (1986) *Top decision: Strategic decision-making in organizations*. Oxford: Blackwell.

Jackall, R. (1988) *Moral Mazes: The world of corporate managers*. Oxford University Press.

Kanter, R. (1983) *The change masters: Innovations for productivity in American corporations*. New York: Simon and Schuster.

Knights, D. and Murray, F. (1994) *Managers Divided*. London: Wiley.

Kotter, J. (1982) *The general managers*. Glencoe, IL: Free Press.

Meiksins, P. (1984) Scientific management and class relations. *Theory and Society*, 13(2): 177–210.

Mintzberg, H. (1973) *The nature of managerial work*. New York: Harper.

Peters, T. (1987) *Thriving on chaos*. London: Macmillan.

Pettigrew, A. (1973) *The politics of organizational decision making*. London: Tavistock.

Pettigrew, A. (1985) *The awakening giant: Continuity and change at ICI*. Oxford: Basil Blackwell.

Pfeffer, J. (1981) Management as symbolic action: The creation and maintenance of organizational paradigms. In L.L. Cummings and B.M. Staw (Eds.), *Reasearch in Organizational Behaviour* (Volume 3). London: JAI Press.

| READING 3.4 | **Rethinking Management and Managerial Work: Capitalism, Control and Subjectivity** |

By Hugh Willmott

Pfeffer, J. (1981a) *Power in organizations*. London: Pitman.

Reed, M. (1989) *The sociology of management*. London: Pitman

Savage, M., Barlow, J., Dickens, P. and Fielding, T. (1992) *Property, bureaucracy and culture: Middle-class formation in contemporary Britain*. London: Routledge.

Sayles, L.R. (1964) *Managerial Behaviour*. New York: McGraw-Hill.

Scarborough, H. and Burrell, G. (1996) The axeman cometh: The changing roles and knowledges of middle managers. In S. Clegg and G. Palmer (ed), *The politics of management knowledge*. London: Sage.

Thompson, P. and McHugh, D. (1995) *Work organizations* (2nd ed.). London: Macmillan.

Whittington, R. (1988) Environmental structure and theories of strategic choice. *Journal of Management Studies*, 25(6): 521–536.

Willmott, H. (1987) Studying managerial work: A critique and proposal. *Journal of Management Studies*, 24(3): 249–270.

Wood, S. (1980) Corporate strategy and organizational studies. In D. Dunkerley and G. Salaman (ed), *International yearbook of organization studies*, pp. 52–71.

Wright, E.O. (1978) *Class, crisis and the state*. London: New Left Books.

Discussion Questions

1. What insights do Jackall and Watson bring to the understanding of managing?
2. 'Managing is a demanding, complex and sometimes contradictory process'. Explain why you agree and/or disagree with this opinion.
3. How would you describe and explain the position occupied by managers in organizations?
4. What changes would be required to reduce the hypocrisy and deception involved in processes of managing?

Introduction References

Argyris, C. and Schon, D.A. (1974) *Theory in Practice: Increasing Professional Effectiveness*. San Franscico, CA: Jossey-Bass.

Braverman, H. (1974) *Labour and Monopoly Capital*, Monthly Review Press.

Collinson, D.L. and Hearn, J.R. (1996) *Men as Managers, Managers as Men: Critical Perspectives on Men, Masculinities and Managements*, London: Sage.

Dalton, M. (1959) *Men who manage*, New York: John Wiley.

Gouldner, A. 1954. *Patterns of Industrial Bureaucracy*, New York: Free Press.

Kotter, J. (1982) *The general managers*, Glencoe, IL: Free Press.

Kunda, G. (1992) *Engineering Culture. Control and Commitment in a High-Tech Corporation*, Philadelphia, PA: Temple University Press.

Mintzberg, H. (1973) *The nature of managerial work*, New York: Harper.

Smith, V. (1999), *Managing in the corporate interest: Control and resistance in an American bank*, Berkeley, CA: University of California Press.

Watson, T. (1994) *In search of management*, London: Routledge.

Recommended Further Readings

See references to all the above texts plus:

Alvesson, M. (1996), *Communication, power and organization*, Berlin: Walter de Gruyter.

Cunliffe, A.L. (2004), 'On Becoming a Critically Reflexive Practitioner', *Journal of Management Education*, 28(4): 407–426.

Hales, C. (2002), 'Why do Managers Do What They Do? Reconciling Evidence and Theory in Accounts of Managerial Work', *British Journal of Management*, 10(4): 335–350.

Hoggett, P. (1996), 'New Modes of Control in the Public Service', *Public Administration*, 74(1): 9–32.

Kanter, R.M. (1977), *Men and Women of the Corporation*, New York: Basic Books.

Knights, D. and Murray, F. (1994), *Managers Divided*, London: Wiley.

Knights, D. and Willmott, H.C. (1999), *Management Lives*, London: Sage.

Parker, M. (2004), 'Becoming Manager Or, the Werewolf Looks Anxiously in the Mirror, Checking for Unusual Facial Hair', *Management Learning*, 35(1): 45–59.

Roberts, J. (1984), 'The Moral Character of Management Practice', *Journal of Management Studies*, 21(3): 287–302.

Sims, D. (2008), 'Managerial Identity Formation in a Public Sector Professional: An Autobiographical Account', *International Journal of Public Administration*, 31(9): 988–1002.

Watson, T. (2001) *In Search of Management: Culture, Chaos and Control in Managerial Work*, London: Cengage Learning.

STRATEGY

CHAPTER 4

READINGS

Whittington, R. (2003) 'The Work of Strategizing and Organizing: For a Practice Perspective' in *Strategic Organization*, Vol. 1, No. 1: pp. 117–118, 119–123.

Chia, R. and Mackay, B. (2007) 'Post-processual Challenges for the Emerging Strategy-as-Practice Perspective: Discovering Strategy in the Logic of Practice' in *Human Relations*. Vol. 60: pp. 225–229.

Levy, D.L., Alvesson, M. and Willmott, H.C. (2003) 'Critical Approaches to Stragetic Management' in *Studying Management Critically*, London: Sage. pp. 92–110.

Knights, D. and Morgan, G. (1991) 'Corporate Strategy, Organizations and Subjectivity: A Critique' in *Organization Studies*, Vol. 2: pp. 262–265.

INTRODUCTION

The field of strategy has been dominated by thinking that conceives of strategy as an outcome of a more or less rational calculation about competitive advantage in relation to buyers, suppliers, new entrants, the availability of substitutes as well as industry competitors. According to Porter (1979: 137), 'the corporate strategist's goal is to find a position in the industry where his or her company can best defend itself against these forces or can influence them in its favour'. In rational analysis, prescription is blended with analysis in ways that elevate the rational decision-making of strategists as it pays minimal attention to the broader institutional context – such as the distinctive cultural values and organizational politics – within and through which decisions are actually made, including the values that bestow legitimacy upon rational models as a key component of top managerial ideology.

Post-rational analysis directly challenges the coherence and credibility of models that represent strategic management as a logical series of steps that proceed from information gathering, through the rational identification of a strategic position, to its systematic implementation. Post-rational analysis aspires to show how, in practice, strategic decision-making emerges from local understandings, recipes and routines, and is therefore resistant to, and subversive of, rational calculation and control. This is the focus of the 'practice' approach advocated by Whittington in Reading 4.1. In post-rational analysis, strategy is conceived as a negotiated, institutionally mediated outcome of complex processes that incorporate competing values and conflicts of interest. Such features include the contextually specific understandings and processes of bargaining (see Readings in Chapter 3) that are conceived to govern the formulation and acceptability of strategic visions and their practical implementation – features of decision-making that are unacknowledged, or treated as sources of 'noise' to be eliminated, in rational models of strategy. In Reading 4.2, Chia and Mackay draw out a number of key presuppositions that underpin research on strategy as process.

Post-rational studies of the strategy process have analysed strategy as the outcome of political bargaining processes among managerial elites (Cressey *et al.*, 1985) and have indicated how their cognitive frameworks assume and promote their sectional interests (Smircich and Stubbart, 1985). But they have tended to focus on internal struggles among managerial factions rather than with labour, on their relations with external stakeholders (e.g. major shareholders), and have abstracted their analysis from the wider historical and social contexts. Pettigrew's (1985) influential study of ICI, for example, makes direct reference to the way dominant groups are protected by the 'existing bias of the structures and cultures of an organization' (ibid: 45), and how these groups actively mobilize this socio-economic context to 'legitimize existing definitions of the core strategic concerns, to help justify new priorities, and to delegitimize other novel and threatening definitions of the organization's situation' (ibid) but it neglects the historically distinctive, politico-economic organization and contractions of the production and consumption processes that have shaped the development and direction of strategic management at ICI. As Whittington contends, 'the limits of feasible change within ICI were defined not simply by the personal competencies and organizational advantages of particular managers ... but also by evolving class structures of contemporary British society' (1992: 701).

Richard Whittington's (Reading 4.1) advocacy of a 'practice perspective' echoes the concerns of post-rational analysis as it commends a focus upon the practical business of strategizing, but with particular reference to the formal work of strategic and organizational design. His concern is to focus upon 'situated, concrete activity' (p. 64) in order to discover what strategists actually do as 'a step to creating practical wisdom' (p. 63) about the business of doing strategy. A post-rational focus upon process is maintained but its attentiveness to culture and politics tends to be displaced by a preoccupation with the identification of skills, the tools and techniques that are used, and how the products of strategizing are consumed. Even the question of how specialists work together to craft strategies, or indeed become strategists, is abstracted from the examination of culture and politics. There is an underlying assumption that practices are 'shared' (Whittington and Melin, 2002: 44), rather than contested (see Contu and Willmott, 2003). This issue is taken up in Reading 4.3.

Students of strategy processes and practices share an interest in a close-up examination of how strategy is accomplished, as contrasted with the arm's-length specification of the forces that are conceived in rational analysis to comprise an industry's structure and to condition strategists' efforts to establish a favourable position within it. Such approaches also tend to retain an understanding of strategy as a set of (processual or practical) features of the world 'out there' to be captured by analysis without much reflexive regard for how their theoretical stance is productive of the identification and representation of such features. Whittington (2003: 121, emphasis added), for example, conceives of the practice perspective as being 'concerned with finding out what strategists' and organizers' jobs *really* are'. The difficulty with this intent is that it pays no attention to, and possibly denies, the interrelationship of the subjects and objects of knowledge. It is assumed that the world 'out there' is entirely separate from, and uninfluenced by, how this world is understood or theorized by imperfect and partial perspectives developed by researchers.

In different ways, the other Readings point to limitations in the emergent strategy-as-practice approach and commend alternatives to it. In Reading 4.2, **Rober Chia and Brad Mackay** identify and then challenge four presuppositions underpinning scholarship in the strategy-as-practice perspective. The first of these is the emphasis upon the purposive activity of strategists, as contrasted with the significance of habitual, inertial routinized practices that provide consistency to the flow of actions. Second, and related, there is an attentiveness to manifest actions and accounts of actions rather than tacit understandings and propensities that are understood to be deeply embedded within practices that largely precede and escape the intentional volition or control of actors. Third, it is suggested that the attribution of strategic intent or choice to strategists may be a legacy of a particular Enlightenment tradition in which it is assumed that 'for us to perceive, act and relate to objects around us there must first be some internal mental representations in the form of an image, a map or a plan' (p. 68). Challenging the presupposition that deliberate intent is a prerequisite for practice, it is suggested that such practices may be largely habitual but then retrospectively represented as intended or strategic. Finally, these reflections are drawn together by commending a more 'radical' analysis of strategy as practice which turns away from the residual 'mentalism' and 'cognitivism' detected in the approach exemplified in Whittington's formulation (Reading 4.1).

David Levy, Mats Alvesson and Hugh Willmott (Reading 4.3) show how Critical Theory holds out the promise of revealing the taken-for-granted assumptions and ideologies as it challenges the political neutrality of mainstream strategy thinking as a tool for improving performance and effectiveness. Specifically, they apply Gramsci's analysis of contestation among social forces to consider how the strategic coordination of economic, organizational, and discursive resources operates to secure the hegemony of dominant groups, but also acts to open up spaces for resistance by labour, environmentalists, and other forces challenging the status quo. This involves a retention and a reconstruction of the concept of strategy. No longer is strategy conceived as the preserve of a managerial elite for whom academics are (self-evidently) stationed to provide more 'scientific' or 'effective' theories and recipes. Instead academics and practitioners are invited to abandon the illusion of spurious objectivity and an associated technocratic conception of effectiveness in favour of a perspective that locates 'strategic management' – its discourses and its enactments – in the interaction of forces that establish and sustain, or challenge and remove, socially divisive and ecologically destructive practices of corporations and their elites.

David Knights and Glenn Morgan (Reading 4.4) focus upon the dominance and influence of discourses on strategy as a 'way of seeing' that discipline's managerial practice as it provides a sense of 'truth' about the purpose of organizations and the work of (senior) management. Knights and Morgan invite us to shift our perspective on 'strategy'. Instead of regarding it as a descriptive label that identifies a domain of researchable objects (e.g. 'strategies', 'environments', etc.), they view it as a particular way of representing and making sense of this domain engaged by analysts and practitioners as they both construe and constitute what analysis of strategy commonsensically aspires to capture or reflect. Treating discourse simply as a sign that designates things disregards its *constitutive* force. This awareness is absent from rational and post-rational models of strategy as there is no concern to examine their contribution to defining and sustaining the phenomena that they aspire to study. Where this concern is prioritized, the analytical focus is upon the truth effects of language in ordering the world in particular ways. Instead of understanding the language that comprises the field of strategy – such as 'firms' and 'markets' – as more or less accurate (and thus impartial) descriptions of an external social reality, such terms are understood to constitute the world in a particular, partisan, politically charged way: their use exerts truth effects insofar as they become widespread and institutionalized. This approach does not seek to specify what the practices (e.g. of strategizing) are but, rather, upon how the 'group of rules' comprising a discourse operates to constitute social practices, spawns their identification as 'strategy', and renders them intelligible in particular ways – such as Porter's definition of the corporate strategist role to which we referred at the beginning of this Introduction.

| READING 4.1 | **The Work of Strategizing and Organizing: For a Practice Perspective** |

By Richard Whittington

It takes a lot of work to make a strategy or design an organization. Consider just the formal side. Data are gathered and analysed, documents are written and presentations made. There are project meetings, board meetings, conferences, workshops and away-days. Midnight oil is burnt and weekends lost. The work is expensive. It calls on senior managers, middle managers, strategic planners, organization development experts, management consultants, communications specialists and sometimes lawyers and investment bankers. And there is even more work in getting these strategies or organization designs actually implemented. The work of strategizing and organizing is a serious business.

My argument here is for the importance of this work to the merit of *Strategic Organization*. Seeing strategy and organization as achieved by the labour of highly skilled workers brings to the new journal at least six sets of research questions: briefly, where and how is the work of strategizing and organizing actually done; who does this strategizing and organizing work; what are the skills required for this work and how are they acquired; what are the common tools and techniques of strategizing and organizing; how is the work of strategizing and organizing organized itself; and finally how are the products of strategizing and organizing communicated and consumed?

READING 4.1

The Work of Strategizing and Organizing: For a Practice Perspective

By Richard Whittington

These questions are practically important. They are also in tune with the 'practice turn' in contemporary organization and social theory (Brown and Duguid, 2001; Orlikowski, 2002; Schatzki *et al.*, 2000). The next section introduces the practice perspective on strategizing and organizing, distinguishing *it* from the process tradition and making the case for starting with the formal side. I shall then return to the six questions around the who, where, how and what of strategic and organizational work. Besides offering rich opportunities in terms of research, I shall argue that these kinds of questions are particularly pressing for those of us who are workers in business schools ourselves. My closing remarks start with a personal confession; they go on to consider the implications of the practice perspective both for testing theory and for the relationship between strategy and organization.

Process and Practice in Strategizing and Organizing

We are long familiar with Weick's (1969: 44) call for organizational researchers to 'become stingy in their use of nouns, generous in their use of verbs, and extravagant in their use of gerunds'. For Weick (1969), the point of privileging verbs over nouns was to re-envisage organizations as processes rather than states. Since then, the verb form has helped establish processes of strategic decision-making and strategic change as central issues within strategy and organizational research (Garud and Van de Ven, 2002).

But my six questions at the start interpret the verbs of strategizing and organizing at another level. Brown and Duguid (2000: 95) have recently called for attention to what they call 'the internal life of process', the practices by which work is actually done. As in Orr's (1996) study of photocopying engineers, this kind of practice can be in tension with the formal processes of organizations. In practice, Orr's photocopying engineers often fix the machines despite the process, not because of it. The practice notion implies a close attention to the work done by people *inside* organizational processes.

This attention to people's actual activity follows a broader 'practice turn' in social theory since the 1980s (Bourdieu, 1990; Schatzki *et al.*, 2000). The notion of practice is interpreted in various ways, but

a common thread is an appreciation of the skill by which people make do with the resources they have in their everyday lives (de Certeau, 1984). There is a stronger focus on people than organizations, the routine as opposed to change, and situated activity rather than abstract processes. The intellectual orientation is Aristotelian, interested in the practical wisdom that gets things done as well as the detached truths of conventional science (Tsoukas and Cummings, 1997).

This practice perspective has developed in accounting (Hopwood and Miller, 1994), innovation (Dougherty, 1992), technology (Orlikowski, 2000) and learning (Brown and Duguid, 2001). In each of these spheres, the objective is to uncover how people actually get on with their work inside organizations. The concern is principally for the performance of practitioners in terms of their local effectiveness, only indirectly for the performance of organizations as wholes. Effectiveness typically involves a mastery of the routine and skilful adaptation at the edge of standard procedures. My argument is for equivalent attention to the work of strategizing and organizing ...

Six Research Questions on Strategizing and Organizing

The argument so far has been for more attention to the work involved in making strategies and designing organizations. This prompts at least six sets of questions for empirical research, each with a practical bent. On some of these questions we are already accumulating quite large bodies of research, but they come from disparate traditions, ranging from institutional theory to the study of learning. On others, we have intuitive knowledge based upon experience, but little that is hard. Framing these six questions within a practice perspective offers a common identity that may motivate research in nascent areas and give coherence where existing researchers do not yet recognize shared interests.

1. How and Where is Strategizing and Organizing Work Actually Done?

We know more about the work of strategy-making than the work of organizational design. The most

The Work of Strategizing and Organizing: For a Practice Perspective *continued*

By Richard Whittington

intimate account of organizing work remains that of General Motors' divisionalization between the wars (Chandler, 1962; Sloan, 1963; Freeland, 2000). The strategic decision-making and planning literatures do tell us a good deal about the use of analysis, information and formal procedure in strategizing (Nurt, 2001). But in concentrating on processes, these literatures still leave out the sheer labour of strategy (Whittington, 1996). The practice perspective is interested in situated, concrete activity. This is the work in boardrooms and awaydays, on phones and in front of computer screens. Only recently have researchers begun to uncover the work of boards and awaydays in action (Mezias *et al.*, 2001; Hendry and Seidl, 2003; Samra-Fredericks, 2003). The research opportunity is to discover more about how to structure and intervene effectively in this kind of situated activity, both for strategy-making and organizational design.

2. Who Does the Formal Work of Strategizing and Organizing and How Do They Get To Do It?
The practice perspective is interested in the workers of strategy and organization. Here we do have a growing body of knowledge on managerial elites and how their expertise and interests can influence the nature of business strategy and organization (Fligstein, 1990; Pettigrew, 1992). There is an increasing recognition too of the role of middle managers in strategy-making (Floyd and Lane, 2000). Management consultants are also coming under scrutiny (Kipping and Engwall, 2002). But from all this at least two things are not yet clear. First, we do not know much about how managerial elites, middle managers, consultants and all the other possible participants actually work together in making strategies and designing organizations. The division of labour in strategizing and organizing is still obscure. Given the issues at stake, this division of labour is likely to be fraught. When and how different groups of participants take a larger and more influential share are important questions. Second, we know little about how people become strategists and organizers. While there is a good deal on the formation and selection of managers in general (Gunz and Jalland, 1997), relatively unknown are the education and career paths

of the specialists in strategy and organization – corporate planners, strategy consultants, OD professionals and the like. These are questions that motivate the business school students in our classes, and we should have more to tell them.

3. What are the Skills Required for Strategizing and Organizing Work and How are they Acquired?
As we learn more about the work and workers of strategic and organizational design, so we shall know more about the skills involved. In the field of strategy at least, the emphasis is on the ability to enter strategic 'conversations': it is important the strategist can talk strategy with the senior team (Liedtka, 1998). We can imagine something similar for the organizational designer. Here there is a direct link to the 'communities of practice' approach to workplace knowledge, where legitimate participation within the community entails learning the 'proper speech' of that community (Wenger, 1998). Strategists and organizers have to be able to master the discourse of strategy and organization. While the communities of practice tradition typically emphasizes situated learning through experience and exchange, to the extent that strategy and organizing involves more general tools and discourse, then some of this learning will rely on access to external, formal sources of knowledge, for instance business schools and text books (Brown and Duguid, 2001). We do not know, however, about the balance between the formal and the experiential in the making of strategists and organizers. Again, it seems incumbent upon business school scholars to know more about the skills their students will use and how they acquire them.

4. What are the Common Tools and Techniques of Strategizing and Organizing and How are these used in Practice?
Researchers are beginning to compile inventories of common strategy and organizational tools (Rigby, 2001; Malone *et al.*, 1999). We also know from the institutionalist literature how managerial tools are diffused over time and across borders (Abrahamson, 1996; Djelic, 1998). What we know much less about is how such tools are used in action (Jarzabkowski, 2004). Orlikowski's (2000) close analysis of the use of Lotus Notes in two different offices shows

READING 4.1

The Work of Strategizing and Organizing: For a Practice Perspective

By Richard Whittington

workers' active and creative engagement with apparently standard software, demonstrating a clear distinction between 'designed technologies' and 'technologies-in-use'. The same is likely to be true for the technologies of strategy and organization. How do managers actually use such common-or-garden techniques as SWOT analyses, portfolio matrices or organization charts? The managerial cognition literature at least suggests that shared understandings of such techniques and their outputs can be problematic (Porac *et al.*, 2002). We need to know more about strategic and organizational technologies 'in-use', and to appreciate the demands they place on their users and the range of artful improvisations made in practice.

5. How is the Work of Strategizing and Organizing Organized Itself?

Making strategies and designing organizations are laborious and expensive activities, often drawing on a wide range of workers and extending over long periods of time. The work of strategy and organization needs to be organized. For strategy, we have the impression that the large central planning departments of old are now defunct. But how firms organize strategy work in the centre and periphery of contemporary organizations remains obscure (Johnson and Huff, 1998). Yet the routines, committee structures and project groups that constitute the organization of strategy-making can make a substantial difference. For instance, Jarzabkowksi and Wilson (2002) attribute part of Warwick University's relative success to the detailed practices of its planning and budgeting cycles. Blackler *et al.* (2000) show that the different organizing principles of three strategy development groups had significant impact upon the stress of strategizing work and success in getting proposals adopted. We need more research across different organizational contexts and different strategizing and organizing tasks to establish patterns for the effective organization of strategic and organizational work.

6. How are the Products of Strategizing and Organizing Communicated and Consumed?

Strategies and organizational designs must be communicated and acted upon in order to make them real. But the practice perspective emphasizes the creative, improvisatory nature of consumption as well as production (de Certeau, 1984). In the hands of their consumers – stakeholders within the organization and outside – strategies and organizational designs are precarious, indefinite products, whose interpretation is never secure. The means by which new strategies and designs are represented and communicated become critical to what is understood and implemented. For Blackler *et al.*'s (2000) strategy groups, representational technologies such as whiteboards and computer graphics were central to developing and communicating new strategies. Smith's (2001) insights into the role of textual nominalization in organizations suggests that even the lengthy reports of design, with their grandiose titles, can play an important role in coordinating people's work across time and locations, whether or not the detail is carefully read. Suggestive though this is, there remains a large research agenda here in the technologies of communicating strategic and organizational designs and the ways in which they are 'consumed' throughout the enterprise.

Acknowledgements

I would like to thank Joel Baum and Royston Greenwood for their helpful comments on an earlier draft of this essay. The usual disclaimers apply.

References

Abrahamson, E. (1996) 'Management Fashion', *Academy of Management Review* 21: 254–85.

Blacker, F., Crump, N. and McDonald, S. (2000) 'Organizing Processes in Complex Activity Networks', *Organization* 7(2): 277–300.

Bourdieu, P. (1990) *The Logic of Practice*. Cambridge: Polity.

Brown, J.S. and Duguid, P. (2000) *The Social Life of Information*. Boston, MA: Harvard University Press.

Brown, J.S. and Duguid, P. (2001) 'Knowledge and Organization: a Social-practice Perspective', *Organization Science* 12(2): 198–215.

Chandler, A.D. (1962) *Strategy and Structure: Chapters in the History of American Enterprise*. Boston, MA: MIT Press.

READING 4.1

The Work of Strategizing and Organizing: For a Practice Perspective *continued*

By Richard Whittington

De Certeau, M. (1984) *The Practice of Everyday Life.* Berkeley, CA: University of California Press.

Djelic, M.-L. (1998) *Exporting the American Model: the Post-War Transformation of European Business.* Oxford: Oxford University Press.

Dougherty, D. (1992) 'A Practice-centred Model of Organizational Renewal through Product Innovation', *Strategic Management Journal* 13, Summer Special Issue: 77–96.

Fligstein, N. (1990) *The Transformation of Corporate Control.* Cambridge, MA: Harvard University Press.

Floyd, S.W. and Lane P. (2000) 'Strategizing throughout the Organization: Management Role Conflict and Strategic Renewal', *Academy of Management Review* 25(1): 154–177.

Freeland, R.F. (2000) *The Struggle for Control of the Modern Corporation: Organizational Change at General Motors, 1924–1970.* Cambridge: Cambridge University Press.

Garud, R. and Van de Ven, A. (2002) 'Strategic Change Processes', in A. Pettigrew, H. Thomas and R. Whittington (eds) *The Handbook of Strategy and Management.* London: Sage.

Gunz, H. and Jalland, M. (1997) Managerial Careers and Business Strategies', *Academy of Management Review* 21(3): 7: 18–56.

Hendry, J. and Seidl, D. (2003) 'The Structure and Significance of Strategic Episodes: Social Systems Theory and the Practice of Strategic Change', *Journal of Management Studies* 40(1).

Hopwood, A.G. and Miller, P. (1994) *Accounting as a Social and Institutional Practice.* Cambridge: Cambridge University Press.

Jarzabkowski, P. (2004) 'Strategy as Practice: Recursiveness and Adaptiveness-in-Use', *Organization Studies,* 25(4): 529–560.

Jarzabkowski, P. and Wilson, D.C. (2002) 'Top Teams and Strategy in a UK University', *Journal of Management Studies* 39(3): 355–383.

Johnson, G. and Huff, A.S. (1998) 'Everyday Innovation/ Everyday Strategy', in G. Hamel, C.K. Prahalad, H. Thomas and D. O'Neal (eds) *Strategic Flexibility: Managing in a Turbulent Environment.* London: Wiley.

Kipping, M. and Engwall, L. (2002) *Management Consulting.* Oxford: Oxford University Press.

Liedtka, J.M. (1998) 'Strategic Thinking: Can it be Taught?', *Long Range Planning* 31(1): 120–129.

Malone, T.W., Crowston, K., Lee, J. *et al.* (1999) 'Tools for Inventing Organizations', *Management Science* 45(3): 425–443.

Mezias, J., Grinyer, P. and Guth, W.D. (2001) 'Changing Collective Cognition: a Process Model for Strategic Change', *Long Range Planning* 34(1): 71–96.

Nurt, P. (2001) 'Strategic Decision-making', in M. Hitt, R. Freeman and J. Harrison (eds) *The Blackwell Handbook of Strategic Management.* Oxford: Blackwell.

Orlikowski, W. (2000) 'Using Technology and Constituting Structures: a Practice Lens for Studying Technology in Organizations', *Organization Science* 12(4): 404–428.

Orlikowski, W. (2002) 'Knowing in Practice: Enacting a Collective Capability in Distributive Organizing', *Organization Science* 13(3).

Orr, J.E. (1996) *Talking about Machines: an Ethnography of a Modern Job.* Ithaca, NY: ILR Press.

Pettigrew, A.M. (1992) 'On Studying Managerial Elites', *Strategic Management Journal* 13: 163–182.

Porac, J.F., Ventresca, M. and Mishina, Y. (2002) 'Interorganizational Cognition and Interpretation', in J. Baum (ed.) *The Blackwell Companion to Organizations.* Oxford: Blackwell.

Rigby, D. (2001) 'Management Tools and Techniques: a Survey', *California Management Review* 43(2): 139–160. [http://metalib.cf.ac.uk:8331/INS01/icon_eng/v-sfx-1.gif]

Samra-Fredricks, D. (2003) 'Strategizing as Lived Experience and Strategists' Everyday Efforts to Shape Strategic Direction', *Journal of Management Studies* 40(1).

Schatzki, T., Knorr-Cetina, K. and von Savigny, E. (2000) *The Practice Turn in Contemporary Theory.* London: Routledge.

Sloan, A. (1963) *My Years with General Motors.* London: Sidgwick & Jackson.

Smith, D.E. (2001) 'Texts and the Ontology of Institutions and Organizations', *Studies in Culture, Organizations and Societies* 7: 158–198.

Tsoukas, H. and Cummings, S. (1997) 'Marginalization and Recovery: the Emergence of Aristotelian Themes in Organization Studies', *Organization Studies* 18(4): 655–683.

Weick, K.E. (1969) *The Social Psychology of Organizing.* Reading, MA: Addison-Wesley.

Wenger, E. (1998) *Communities of Practice: Learning, Meaning and Identity.* Cambridge: Cambridge University Press.

Whittington, R. (1996) 'Strategy as Practice', *Long Range Planning* 29: 731–735.

READING 4.2

Post-processual Challenges for the Emerging Strategy-as-Practice Perspective: Discovering Strategy in the Logic of Practice

By Robert Chia and Brad Mackay

There are several philosophical presuppositions that underpin scholarship in strategy process research and, for the most part, the strategy-as-practice perspective. In what follows, we identify four such presuppositions inherent in these accounts.

First, processes and practices are generally construed as purposeful activities *of* individuals/organizations. This 'process reducibility thesis' (Rescher, 1996: 27) deems all processes and practices to be reducible to the actions of actors and things. In this way, individual agency is given ontological primacy over activities, processes and practices and the individual is therefore assumed to be the *initiator* of such activities, processes and practices. Causal efficacy is attributed to the former. The forces of change are, therefore, not viewed as *immanent* in things and human situations but rather externally imposed by the will of conscious actors. Changes are only brought about through the active, deliberate intentions and actions of individuals. The flourishing strategy-as-practice perspective appears to subscribe to this ontological posture. For instance, Salvato suggests that organizational processes resulting in strategic variation are a consequence of '*deliberate managerial acts* leading to innovative business projects' (2003: 101, our emphasis). Similarly, Samra-Fredericks, in her very insightful study of strategizing as lived experience, focuses on a community of *six core strategists*, their talk, acts of persuasion and a number of specific decisions and outcomes (2003). In all this, however, her focus remains the actions of individuals who are taken to be the authors of strategic change. The possibility that strategic change and the directions taken may be brought about by culturally and historically shaped tendencies and dispositions acquired through social practices internalized by the actors remains relatively unexamined. In a final example, Maitlis and Lawrence, in their study of a failure in organizational strategizing, highlight the role of assigning blame for an organization's problems 'as well as (the) search for *someone* to move the process forward' (2003: 129, our emphasis). The idea that there may be an immanent logic of a situation, a 'propensity of things' (Jullien, 1999: 27) that provides an element of directionality and that moves things along in a more-or-less predictable manner; what Bourdieu (1990) calls a 'sociality of inertia', is not entertained in this explanatory schema. Such an immanent logic that gives consistency to the flow of actions that ensues is what we might begin to re-construe as the essence of strategy-as-practice.

Without the incorporation of this insight from the 'practice turn' when strategy-as-practice scholars use terms such as micro-processes or micro-practices, they refer mainly to the purposeful activities *of* conscious agents and not so much to these *trans-individual* social practices. When they do so, they remain within the realms of *methodological individualism*; the individual is viewed as a self-contained, self-motivating human agent who *acts* on its external environment. Most explanations of strategic behaviour can be traced back to this conception of individual agency; individual actions constitute practice and this produces events, situations and outcomes. However, as a number of social theorists including de Certeau have emphasized this theoretical approach to explaining social practices is unwarranted:

> The examination of ... practices does not (require nor) imply ... individuality. The social atomism ... on the basis of which groups are supposed to be formed ... play no part in this (his) study ... each individual is a locus in which an incoherent (and often contradictory) plurality of such relational determinations interact.
>
> *(de Certeau, 1984: xi)*

For practice theorists it is the internalized practices or *schemata of action* (or what Bourdieu (1990), calls *habitus*) that are the real 'authors' of everyday coping action. This kind of practical intelligence is defined by an absence of a proper locus of agency; individuality is construed as a secondary effect of primary practice. The strategy-as-practice perspective, we argue, can be better grounded theoretically by adopting such an understanding of practice.

READING 4.2

Post-processual Challenges for the Emerging Strategy-as-Practice Perspective: Discovering Strategy in the Logic of Practice *continued*

By Robert Chia and Brad Mackay

Second, and consistent with this emphasis on individualism, process theorists and strategy-as-practice researchers are particularly attentive to the explicit and articulated character of the social world, and to the manifest aspects of processes and practices. It is organizations and individuals that are seen to change so much so that change is construed as an epiphenomenon of social entities. Viewed as such, phenomena are characterized by 'descriptive fixity' (Rescher, 1996: 35): they can be linguistically captured and accurately represented through established categories, concepts and representations. The epistemology of representationalism prevails. From this perspective, it makes every sense to study strategy process and strategy practice by longitudinally tracking the actual visible activities agents engage in organizational settings, as each study reviewed here does. Archival documents, ethnographic data, interviews, observation of proceedings at meetings, and records of talk and conversation form the basis of this form of ethnography. To capture the embodied capacities, the dispositions, know-how and tacit understanding that reside within practices themselves (Schatzki, 2001), however, requires a cultivated sensitivity to the less visible but detectable propensities and tendencies of human situations intimated above. This is because practices are not so much the visible doings of actors per se, but culturally and historically transmitted *regularities* detectable through the patterns of activities actually carried out. They are 'temporarily unfolding and spatially dispersed nexus of doings and sayings' (Schatzki, 1996: 289) organized around 'shared practical understanding' (Schatzki, 2001: 2). It is the observed historically and culturally shaped regularities of such activities and not the activities themselves that constitute what is meant by strategy-as-practice. As such they imply *trans-individuality*; cultural transmission, socialization, institutionalized constraints, embodied mannerism, etc., play a crucial role in explaining human doings.

As an example of such a historically and culturally transmitted disposition, take the notion of regional speaking 'accents' transmitted and acquired unconsciously through immersion in a specific local community. The individual is constituted, defined and identified by his/her accents, predispositions and mannerisms and this may either prove to be strategically advantageous or disadvantageous depending on the inherent directionality of the situation he/she finds him/herself in. The individual is predisposed to behave in a particular manner and to react to strategic circumstances in a manner that is congruent with his/her own sense of upbringing and identity. In this way strategy and identity are intimately co-constitutive of each other. In explaining strategy-as-practice, therefore, we need to be more cognizant of how such *trans-individual* forces shape outlooks and orientations and hence predispose actors towards particular strategic choices of action. The explanation of how particular strategic practices and 'choices' are arrived at can then be moderated through this understanding.

Third, coupled with the emphasis on individualism and on the observable and manifest is an epistemological assumption regarding the essential purposefulness and intentionality of human action. This is a legacy of the Enlightenment. Descartes, in particular, emphasized that for us to perceive, act and relate to objects around us there must first be some internal mental representations in the form of an image, a map or a plan. Moreover, choice of action is a central feature of this cognitive model of human action. Actors are deemed to be conscious, deliberate, goal-directed and intentional in their actions. This is especially the case with regards to strategy-making. After all, how could a strategy be called so if it is: a) unconsciously motivated, or non-deliberately formulated; b) immanent rather than transcendent and goal-oriented; c) not explicitly articulated in some representational form and hence providing a useful and observable guide to action? As Hendry and Seidl suggest, 'We cannot escape the fact, however, that even in its routine aspects strategy is explicitly concerned with the creation of *intentional, often radical change*' (2003: 177, our emphasis) … These eminently reasonable assumptions may be overturned if we adopt a radically different set of philosophical presuppositions regarding agency and action. Deliberate intentionality is not a prerequisite for the articulation of a strategy; strategy may emerge as a consequence of the inherent

Post-processual Challenges for the Emerging Strategy-as-Practice Perspective: Discovering Strategy in the Logic of Practice

By Robert Chia and Brad Mackay

predisposition of an actor to unselfconsciously respond to external circumstances in a manner that we may *retrospectively* recognize as being consistently strategic. Such a view, as with the practice turn in social theory and philosophy puts the transmission of practices rather than agency at the centre of strategic analysis.

Finally, there is an implicit or explicit subscription by both strategy process researchers and strategy-as-practice theorists to the presuppositions of 'theoretical holism' (Dreyfus, 1991a: 5) in terms of explanatory efficacy. This posits a holistic network of intentional states, tacit belief systems and values that provide explanatory adequacy for accounting for the meaning of action. It is what inspires the rise in ethnographic studies and on the emphasis on understanding the meaning of action in context. Advocates of theoretical holism, including Pettigrew (1997), view it as being opposed to linear explanations. But this is to obviate yet another more radical possibility associated with the practice turn in philosophy and social theory; that is an alternative '*practical* holism' that eschews the primacy of mentalism, cognitivism or even intentionality in engaging with the day-to-day affairs of the world. According to this practice view, there is no need to have recourse to beliefs, values and abstract principles in order to explain social behaviour and practice. The counterfactual implications of this practical holism for the Samra-Fredericks ethnographic study, for instance, would be to treat the activities of the six core strategists and their 'beliefs, opinions, values, assumptions, feelings, perceptions, meaning and so on' (2003: 152) as secondary retrospective rationalizations, and to go beyond the talk of strategists to show how the organizational history and situation, cultural mediation, individual socialization, internalized habits, mannerisms and tendencies shape predispositions and hence the character and direction of strategic outcomes. It is this insistence on the primacy of practice over individualities that allows us to consider strategy-as-practice in a way that evades the trappings of methodological individualism.

Shifting the focus away from studying exclusively individual activities/events and situations, such as the actions, talk and work of strategic practitioners in workshops, strategy away-days and strategic episodes, for example, does not imply removing agency from the equation altogether. What it does mean is to assume a post-processual stance which: 1) places ontological primacy on practices rather than actors; 2) philosophically privileges practice-complexes rather than actors and things as the locus of analysis; and 3) makes the locus of explanation the field of practices rather than the intentions of individuals and organizations.

References

Bourdieu, P. (1990) *The logic of practice*. Cambridge: Polity Press.

De Certeau, M. (1984) *The practice of everyday life*. Berkeley, CA: University of California Press.

Dreyfus, H. (1991a) *Being-in-the-world*. Cambridge, MA: MIT Press.

Hendry, J. and Seidl, D. (2003) The structure and significance of strategic episodes: Social systems theory and the routine practices of strategic change. *Journal of Management Studies*, 40(1): 175–96.

Jullien, F. (1999) *The propensity of things: Towards a history of efficacy in China*. New York: Zone Books.

Maitlis, S. and Lawrence, T. (2003) Orchestral manoeuvres in the dark: Understanding failure in organizational strategizing. *Journal of Management Studies*, 40–1: 109–39.

Pettigrew, A. (1997) What is processual analysis? *Scandinavian Journal of Management*, 13(4): 337–48.

Rescher, N. (1996) *Process metaphysics*. New York: State University of New York Press.

Salvato, C. (2003) The role of micro-strategies in the engineering of firm evolution. *Journal of Management Studies*, 40(1): 83–108.

Samra-Fredericks, D. (2003) Strategizing as lived experience and strategists' everyday efforts to shape strategic direction. *Journal of Management Studies*, 40(1): 141–74.

Schatzki, T.R. (1996) Practices and actions: A Wittgensteinian critique of Bourdieu and Giddens. *Philosophy of the Social Sciences*, 27(3): 283–308.

Schatzki, T.R. (2001) Introduction: Practice theory. In T.R. Schatzki, K. Knorr Cetina and E. von Savigny (Eds), *The practice turn in contemporary theory*. London: Routledge, pp. 1–14.

READING 4.3

Critical Approaches to Strategic Management

By David L. Levy, Mats Alvesson and Hugh C. Willmott

Contemporary Approaches to Strategy

Contemporary approaches to strategy are hardly monotholic, though much current thinking is anchored by the work of Michael Porter and Henry Mintzberg. Mintzberg and colleagues (1998) discusses ten schools and five definitions of strategy. One of these, 'strategy as ploy', builds on the game theoretic and military heritage of strategy. It suggests that strategy can be about deceptive and unpredictable maneuvers that confuse and outflank competitors. The concept of 'ploy' implies a certain deviousness that invites critical scrutiny of underlying goals and motives. It also suggests that social contestation is more a matter of superior maneuvering than ideological or coercive domination (Abercrombie, Hill, and Turner, 1980). This 'take' on strategy implies possibilities for effective challenges by subordinate groups.

Strategy as 'position' offers a predominant conceptual framework in the field. Porter's (1980) landmark *Competitive Strategy* reinterpreted the microeconomics of industrial organization in a managerial context. Close analysis of Porter's work and subsequent developments provides considerable fuel for Critical Theorists concerned with the reproduction of hierarchical economic relations, since it highlights the contradictions between idealized myths of 'perfect competition' and the more grounded concepts of market power explored by business school strategists. Porter's work uses economic analysis of market failures to suggest how firms might seek above-normal profits in less than competitive market segments. Porter's subsequent book, *Competitive Advantage* (1985), which resonates more with the 'resource based view' of the firm (Wernerfelt, 1984), attempts to explain how a firm might actively build market barriers and sustain monopolistic structures. It was not without some justification, perhaps, that Microsoft argued in its anti-trust suit defence that it was merely pursuing the precepts of good business strategy.

Some scholars firmly established within the strategy field have critiqued the prescriptive, technocratic approach to strategy, represented by the work of Porter (1980; 1985), Andrews (1971) and Chandler (1962), for its reliance on a rational, logical, and linear model of analysis and planning. Sun Tzu's classic work on military strategy (1983), though often expressed as a series of maxims, advocates an approach that is non-linear, unpredictable, and paradoxical, commending the title 'The Art of War' rather than The Science of War (Luttwak, 1987; Quinn & Cameron, 1988). Mintzberg (1994; 1998) has been particularly prominent in arguing that the actuality of strategy is better characterized as an emergent rather than planned organizational phenomenon. Mintzberg emphasizes the recursive processes of learning, negotiation, and adaptation by which strategy is actually enacted, and suggests that the planning–implementation distinction is unsustainable (Mintzberg, 1990). Mintzberg argues that such processes are both inevitable *and* functional.

A greater attentiveness to strategy as process has been accompanied by increased appreciation of the cognitive models, or frames, which channel managers' perceptions of their environment (El Sawy and Pauchant, 1988; Whipp, Rosenfeld, and Pettigrew, 1989). Weick (1995) has argued that organizational members actively constitute and reify their environments, bringing sense and order to complex and confusing social worlds in which they are located. In turn, perceptions of the external environment shape and constitute managerial cognition and action (Daft and Weick, 1984). Institutional theory, which has become increasingly prominent in recent management thought, clearly displays a constructivist influence in its emphasis on cognitive and normative pressures in shaping field-level norms and practices (DiMaggio and Powell, 1983; Scott and Meyer, 1994). Despite an affinity of the constructivist perspective with an instrumental formulation of CT's historical hermeneutic epistemology (see Willmott, 2003), which seeks to uncover meaning rather than causation, few authors utilize a constructivist analysis of strategy to draw implications concerning broader structures of dominance and inequity. Quite the contrary, the perspective is routinely used to generate suggestions for how managers can improve the strategy process by actively changing corporate cultures and frames (Whittington, 1993). A few notable exceptions have argued that if strategy is rooted in the values and cognitive frames of

| # Critical Approaches to Strategic Management

By David L. Levy, Mats Alvesson and Hugh C. Willmott

senior managers, it is likely to reproduce their ideological frameworks and promote their sectional interests (Bourgeois and Brodwin, 1984; Smircich and Stubbart, 1985).

Understanding the strategy process is also a concern of those who view it as the outcome of political bargaining processess among managerial elites (Bower and Doz, 1979; Child, 1972; Cressey, Eldridge, and MacInnes, 1985). However, most studies of the politics of strategy focus on internal struggles among managerial factions rather than with labour or external stakeholders, and tend to abstract from wider historical and social contexts. Managers are still viewed as the only organizational actors with legitimate access to the strategy process, a form of discursive closure that trivializes the politics of strategic management. Pettigrew's (1985) influential study of ICI, for example, makes direct reference to the way dominant groups are protected by the 'existing bias of the structures and cultures of an organization' (1985: 45), and how these groups actively mobilize this socioeconomic context to 'legitimize existing definitions of the core strategic concerns, to help justify new priorities, and to delegitimize other novel and threatening definitions of the organization's situation' (1985: 45). Nevertheless, Pettigrew neglects the historically distinctive, politico-economic organization and contradictions of the production and consumption processes that have shaped the development and direction of strategic management at ICI. As Whittington (1992: 701) contends, 'the limits of feasible change within ICI were defined not simply by the personal competencies and organizational advantages of particular managers ... but also by the evolving class structures of contemporary British society'. As with the constructivist approach, advocates of strategy-as-bargaining are also quick to jump to managerialist prescriptions. Whittington (1993), for example, proposes mechanisms to ensure that the strategy process remains objective rather than being captured by a particular management faction; moreover, he suggests that managers can draw from broader, less visible sources of power, such as 'the political resources of the state, the network resources of ethnicity, or, if male, the patriarchal resources of masculinity' (ibid: 38). In such thinking, the extra-organizational conditions and forces neglected by Mintzberg and others are identified as potentially decisive weapons in the arsenal of strategic management.

Critical Theory: Unmasking and Deconstructing Strategy

A basic limitation of much processual analysis is that little account is taken of how managers come to assume and maintain a monopoly of what has become institutionalized as 'strategic' decision-making responsibility. Nor, relatedly, is there concern to explore how managers' practical reasoning about corporate strategy is conditioned by, and contributes to, the constitution of politico-economic structures that extend well beyond the boundaries of any particular organization. Yet, mainstream strategy talk is not innocent. It is a powerful rhetorical device that frames issues in particular ways and augments instrumental reason; it operates to bestow expertise and rewards upon those who are 'strategists'; and its military connotations reinforce a patriarchal orientation to the organization of work.

Shrivastava's (1986) landmark critique analysed the strategy field using five operational criteria, derived from Giddens (1979). These indicate its ideological nature: the factual underdetermination of action norms; universalization of sectional interests; denial of conflict and contradiction; normative idealization of sectional goals; and the naturalization of the status quo. Shrivastava concluded that strategic management was undeniably ideological, and that strategic discourse helped legitimize existing power structures and resource inequalities. Drawing from Habermas, Shrivastava sought emancipation in the 'acquisition of communicative competence by all subjects that allows them to participate in discourse aimed at liberation from constraints on interaction' (p. 373). He also called on researchers 'to generate less ideologically value-laden and more universal knowledge about strategic management of organizations' (p. 374).

While Shrivastava's faith in the possibility of universal, objective knowledge betrays his modernist leanings, more recent critical contributions display a more postmodern sensibility. Abandoning the search for objective truth or for autonomous subjects who could potentially recognize their 'real' interests, postmodern critiques are concerned with the constitutive power of strategic discourse. Knights and Morgan (1991: 252), for example, see 'corporate strategy as a set of discourses and practices which transform managers and employees alike into subjects who secure their sense of purpose and reality by

Critical Approaches to Strategic Management *continued*

By David L. Levy, Mats Alvesson and Hugh C. Willmott

formulating, evaluating and conducting strategy'. Managers cannot stand outside of ideology to impose their strategems on unwitting workers. Rather, they too are entangled in discursive webs. Strategy constructs a myth of commonality of organizational purpose by positing lofty and unattainable aspirations (Harfield, 1998). The invocation of military metaphors, for example, brands competitors as 'enemies' to be defeated, and mobilizes maximum effort from the rank and file who are exhorted to sacrifice individual needs to the greater glory of the corporation.

While projecting solidarity of purpose and the universality of the interests of senior managers and stockholders, the discourse of strategy legitimates organizational hierarchy with differential influence and rewards. The importance attached to strategy also implies that employees who work outside of what is identified as the strategic core of an organization make a lesser contribution and therefore cannot be expected to participate, even marginally, in decisions for which others are responsible. It also provides a rationale for differentiating the pay and conditions of 'core' and 'peripheral' employees. The need to assert the status of an elite group of 'strategic managers' is perhaps particularly acute in advanced economies where manual labor is declining and traditional divisions between task execution and conception are loosened up. According to Stoney (1998: 4):

> In the strategic management model, responsibility for corporate level decision-making rests with a core or strategic elite who are discharged from the day-to-day responsibilities of operational activities, these being devolved to the lowest possible level of control. Undistracted by operational matters and line responsibility, the elite, often an 'executive board', is left free to concentrate on strategic thinking and decision-making.

The strong top-down model of strategic management draws upon the picture of the general drawing up a battle plan and then ordering the troops to carry it through. This image stands in a relation of (unresolved) tension to recent contributions to strategic management that have emphasized the core competence associated with employees. The literature on core competence and organizational learning acknowledges the significance of the skills and knowledge, much of it tacit, embodied and distributed throughout the organization on the one hand, yet assumes that top management can and should control it. As mentioned by Scarbrough (1998: 225), champions of a core competence approach treat the firm as the command and control mechanism beloved of the traditional planning school. The strategic management literature, focusing on the leadership role of top management, is typically oriented toward aspirant top managers. However, very few people are, or will ever become, top managers responsible for corporate strategies. Perhaps, then, the value and appeal of strategic management as a field of instruction lies elsewhere, in its ideological appeal to students and employees who are encouraged to adopt a top management perspective and engage in grandiose fantasies about sitting down with corporate elites to discuss strategy and direct the resources of major companies (see Knights and Morgan, 1991). It is far less gratifying to imagine oneself as a low-level manager working on mundane operational issues. Similar motives may guide academics interested in researching and teaching in the field.

The privileged status of 'strategy' is apparent in the promotional efforts of management consultants. One computer consultancy company claiming to integrate strategic and IT perspectives was, upon closer scrutiny, lacking competence in projects with any advanced strategic component. In retrospect, a senior manager described this talk of strategy as 'a sales trick', designed to keep customers and employees happy while the latter really were doing programming and 'getting the bucks in' (Alvesson, 2000). In a large R&D company, mid-level managers described themselves as 'occupied with the larger picture' and with 'strategies', even though they were far from the market, had no overall business responsibility, and were supposed to work strictly within a segment of an overall product development process (Alvesson and Sveningsson, 2003).

Strategic discourse constitutes not only strategists but also 'the problems for which it claims to be a solution' (Knights & Morgan, 1991: 255). In doing so, it contributes toward an instrumental, techno-

READING 4.3 | Critical Approaches to Strategic Management

By David L. Levy, Mats Alvesson and Hugh C. Willmott

cratic orientation in corporate life that emphasizes efficiency and competitiveness over consideration of environmental or social values. Moreover, problems worthy of strategic management are found in widening circles of social and economic life. Stoney (1998) has described the increasing pervasiveness of strategic management in the British public sector under the guise of concerns for efficiency and accountability. Although advocates of strategic management in the public sector claim that it professionalizes and depoliticizes government services, Stoney contends that 'it represents a deliberate attempt to change the very nature of local government in a manner which conformed to a specific set of interests: the interests of capital' (ibid: 13). For local authorities competing to attract mobile capital, the language of strategy 'instills potential investors with confidence that "rational" economic strategy can be pursued locally without fear of political and bureaucratic hindrance and without the uncertainty and reversals in policy that used to accompany changes in the political complexion of the council' (ibid: 19). Moreover, strategy in the public sector is seen to be complicit in promoting a market-based ideology in which citizens are transformed into consumers and state officials into a managerial elite: 'In this managerial transformation, the traditional public sector themes of collectivism, welfare and civic duty have become unfashionable' (ibid).

While Critical Theory offers considerable insight into the ideological and constitutive role of strategic discourse in reproducing organizational and societal relations of power, it is somewhat limited by the lack of concern with the 'truth of strategy' (Knights and Morgan, 1991: 252). Almost all the critical writing on strategy, including the three articles in the July 1998 special issue of the *Electronic Journal of Radical Organization Theory* (EJROT), draw primarily from Critical Theorists of the Frankfurt School and from postmodern scholars to critique strategy as ideology and discourse. While it is generally acknowledged that strategic discourse has effects in broader economic and power relations, making it difficult to disentangle the material and ideological dimensions (Smircich and Stubbart, 1985), much critical writing implies that 'it is not the *practices* of strategic man-

agement which require urgent investigation', as Booth (1998) puts it in the introduction to the aforementioned special issue of EJROT.

It is tempting to be dismissive of the instrumental value of strategy, even on its own terms. Many maxims of strategy appear to be faddish aphorisms, which are likely to prove poor guides for action. We have seen trends toward conglomerate acquisitions in the 1970s followed by admonitions to 'stick to your knitting' in the 1980s (Peters and Waterman, 1982). Enthusiasm for elaborate and detailed strategic planning waned in the 1980s as General Electric led the way in dismantling its planning system. Mintzberg (1994) provides anecdotal evidence of the failure of planning, and reviews numerous empirical studies that failed to find a financial payoff from strategic planning. Many simple models, such as the growth-share matrix, have gone through cycles of popularity and disillusionment (Seeger, 1984). SWOT (Strengths, Weaknesses, Opportunities, and Threats) analysis, a cornerstone of the strategic planning process, is frequently undertaken but seemingly rarely carried through in the development of strategies (Hill and Westbrook, 1997). Pfeffer (1994) compared five highly successful US companies with Porter's framework for strategic positioning and found that none of the companies followed the prescribed recipe.

Nevertheless, the 'truth' of strategy does have import when we take seriously the agency of corporate and state actors in privileging and protecting economic and political advantage. An interest in the discourse of strategic management should not necessarily just focus on its ideological effects and the consequences for managers constituting themselves as 'strategists' but should also investigate the substantive effects of the subjects acting according to the strategic management precepts. Mintzberg (1990) criticizes the approach to strategic management taken by MBA education. He argues that it produces people with analytical skills and a great faith in running business from a distance, but with very limited knowledge of how companies actually work and create value. Their approach, Mintzberg argues, overemphasizes financial criteria and underplays productive corporate development, having harmful effects on

READING 4.3 | **Critical Approaches to Strategic Management** *continued*

By David L. Levy, Mats Alvesson and Hugh C. Willmott

the economy in the long run. Sveningsson (1999) has shown how strategic management knowledge 'colonized' the thinking and acting of senior managers in the Swedish newspaper industry and led to the transformation of newspapers into parts of conglomerates. A joint focus on managerial subjectivity and substantial effects is perhaps to be recommended (see Ezzamel and Willmottt, 2002). A different form of strategic analysis could usefully inform appropriate action by progressive social forces concerned with social contests and emancipation, as well as assisting the development of more democratic organizational forms engaged in market competition such as co-ops and collectives. The following section explores the relevance of Gramsci's work to outline an approach to strategy that pays attention to the political economy of strategic practice and considers the hegemonic alignment of ideological, political, and economic issues.

Strategy as Power: a Significance of Hegemony

Gramsci's conception of hegemony provides a point of departure for a critical approach that emphasizes the interaction of material and discursive practices, structures, and strategems in establishing and sustaining corporate dominance and legitimacy in the face of challenges from social actors and economic rivals (Gramsci, 1971; Sassoon, 1987, 2000). This perspective refocuses attention on the content and goals of strategy as it draws attention to the political nature of strategic practice.

In corporations 'strategy' is practised to improve market and technological positioning, sustain social legitimacy, discipline labour, influence government policy and, not least, we have suggested, aggrandize the architects and purveyors of strategy. In a broad sense, all strategy is political. Strategy-as-power operates through the dialectical interplay of 'structure' and 'agency'. Power inheres in the specific configurations of economic, ideological, and organizational forces that regulate, stabilize, and constitute social worlds and identities, and which form the terrain for strategic contestation; power is also exercised by agents attempting to shape – establish and resist – these configurations. Through this process, agency is attributed to actions to which strategic intent is ascribed.

Gramsci's perspective on power and ideology addresses some of the theoretical problems related to the treatment of agency and strategy in Critical Theory and poststructuralism. Critical Theorists explain consent to oppressive structures of capitalism in terms of ideological domination. Disadvantaged groups come to accept and reproduce their position of subordination as they uncritically accept ruling ideas. Abercrombie and colleagues (1980), amongst others, have criticized this 'dominant ideology thesis' on the grounds that it accords too little agency to the dominated 'dupes', and too much intent to the dominant class, as well as too little modesty to intellectuals who presume to know the 'real interests' of others. The CT concept of ideology is viewed as overly monolithic and functionalist. It also requires people seeking emancipation to turn to Critical Theory intellectuals who, along with ruling elites, ostensibly stand outside the dominant culture and ideology. From a Gramscian standpoint, poststructuralist conceptions of power embedded in pervasive discourse are also problematic when discursive disciplinary power is understood to pervade every societal nook and cranny. In such interpretations of postructuralist analysis, agents are seen to have little room to resist or evade the constitutive power of discourses.

Hall (1986) argues that the Gramscian notion of hegemony finds some viable ground between the structural determination of ideas of crude Marxism and the fluid, endless slippage of meaning explored in some versions of poststructural analysis. Hegemony refers to a historically specific alignment of economic, political and ideological forces that coordinates major social groups into a dominant alliance. Hall argues that ideology can be understood as the articulation of meaning, temporarily fixed and loosely coupled to economic and political structures. Securing a relatively stable hegemonic bloc requires material payoffs, political compromises, and the projection of moral and intellectual leadership. Hegemony is never total and complete, however, and dissent persists: the persistence of plural, overlapping and interpenetrating social and cultural forms opens up theoretical space for agency and resistance. Processes of contestation and liberation are at once fuelled by the suffering and the frustration that the

| # Critical Approaches to Strategic Management

By David L. Levy, Mats Alvesson and Hugh C. Willmott

hegemonic bloc produces, and is enabled by the capability of people to question prevailing priorities and institutionalized norms of conduct. Crucially, consent in a hegemonic system does not rely principally on colonization by dominant ideologies. Instead, it is understood, at least in part, as a strategic, contingent compliance, based on a realistic assessment of the balance of forces. This formulation avoids some of the problems associated with ideology as 'false consciousness'.

It is the complex, dynamic, and unstable nature of hegemonic formations that brings richness to Gramsci's strategic conception of power. Historical blocs rest on insecure foundations of fragmented, contradictory ideologies and uneasy alliances, providing the potential for instability, contestation, and change. Gramsci asked of social structure: 'What is this effective reality? Is it something static and immobile, or is it not rather a relation of forces in continuous motion and shift of equilibrium?' (Gramsci, 1971: 172). Understanding the dynamic relationships between the economic and ideological aspects of this complex system affords opportunities to uncover windows of opportunity and key points of leverage, but this requires careful analysis: 'It is the problem of the relations between structure and superstructure which must be accurately posed if the forces which are active in the history of a particular period are to be correctly analyzed and the relations between them determined' (Gramsci, 1971: 177). Gramsci outlined two particular forms of strategy commonly evinced in social conflicts. 'Passive revolution' describes a process of evolutionary, reformist change that, while preserving the essential aspects of social structure, entails extensive concessions by relatively weak hegemonic groups. One might formulate this form of strategy as depending heavily on the decline or disorganization of hegemonic groups, rather than the careful marshalling and application of resources by subordinate groups. The concept of 'war of position', in contrast, engages a military metaphor to suggest how subordinate groups might skillfully avoid a futile frontal assault against entrenched adversaries. The war of position constitutes a longer-term strategy, coordinated across multiple bases of power. Its intent is to gain influence in the cultural institutions of civil society, to develop organizational and economic capacity, and to exploit tensions in hegemonic coalitions in order to win new allies. As in a game of chess, power lies not just in possession of the playing pieces but in their configuration; each set of moves and counter-moves reconfigures the terrain and opens up new avenues for contestation.

This view of strategy is implicit in the literature that examines the conditions under which social movements emerge, analyze and pursue successful strategies for social change. By locating agents of change outside of dominant corporate organizational forms, social movement theory offers a potentially more radical approach to resistance and change than progressive forms of 'participative strategy', with their attendant dangers of being co-opted as pseudo-participation. As McAdam, McCarthy and Zald (1996) argue, effective social movements exploit historically specific political opportunities, develop organizational and material resources, and frame issues discursively in ways which challenge hegemonic thinking yet resonate sufficiently with extant cultural forms to mobilize broad support. Ganz (2000), for example, claims that the UFW succeeded in organizing California farmworkers where the AFL-CIO failed due to strategic capacity, not just because of a favorable opportunity structure or the possession of adequate resources. Strategic capacity in this case study comprised a diverse, well-networked leadership, and an organizational form that encouraged accountability, diverse perspectives, and explicit strategy-making. Cress and Snow (2000), in a study of fifteen homeless social movement organizations, found that outcomes were influenced by organizational, tactical, political, and framing variables. The coordination of strategy across multiple bases of power indicates a largely unacknowledged intellectual affinity with the Gramscian concept of hegemony.

Traditional market-oriented strategies also have political dimensions. As Porter's Five Forces analysis indicates, the primary goal of strategy is to increase a firm's bargaining leverage over its competitors, potential entrants, suppliers, and customers. The result of successful strategic practice is the weakening of competition and the concentration of economic power, an outcome which is hardly possible to separate from

READING 4.3 | **Critical Approaches to Strategic Management** *continued*

By David L. Levy, Mats Alvesson and Hugh C. Willmott

political and ideological power. Of course, companies also pursue overtly political strategies in their efforts to influence the regulatory environment. Much of the limited literature that does exist on corporate political strategy, however, adopts a managerialist rather than a critical orientation (Hillman and Hitt, 1999; Mahon, 1989; Schuler, 1996). Pfeffer and Salancik (1978), for example, have examined corporate strategies to secure advantage and reduce external dependency through control over information flows, influence over external actors, and engagement in coalition politics. Uncovering the political dimensions of apparently neutral strategic practices is, of course, a key concern of Critical Theory. Here we push further, and argue that the traditional distinction between market and political strategy is untenable. It is not just that firms need to coordinate market and nonmarket strategies to achieve economic goals (Baron, 1997). More fundamentally, markets are embedded in broader social and political structures (Callon, 1998; Granovetter, 1985) and the articulation of markets with ideological and political structures and processes enact 'circuits of power', to use Clegg's (1989) formulation. Shrivastava (1986) describes the 'continuing political battles that proactively shape the structure of competition' (ibid. 371), and emphasizes the need to analyse 'the social and material conditions within which industry production is organized, the linkages of economic production with the social and cultural elements of life, the political and regulatory context of economic production, and the influence of production and firm strategies on the industry's economic, ecological, and social environments' (ibid.).

The Gramscian approach can find purchase at the level of strategic contests within specific issue arenas. Levy and Egan (1998), for example, have examined the response of the fossil fuel industry to the prospect of climate change. Mandatory restrictions on emissions of greenhouse gases, radical technological change, and renewed environmental activism threaten oil and automobile companies with a loss of markets, more stringent regulation, and a loss of autonomy and legitimacy. The case demonstrates how companies responded to these threats to their hegemonic position with coordinated strategies in the economic, organizational and discursive realms. US-based companies in the fossil fuel sector organized a strong issue-specific industry association, challenged the scientific need for action, pointed to the high economic costs of controls, and formed alliances with unions, minorities and groups of retired people. They donated substantial amounts in political campaign contributions and have invested in shoring up markets for their traditional products. The industry has not been entirely successful in deflecting demands for change, and has drifted towards a strategy of accommodation, or 'passive revolution', in Gramsci's terms. The industry has moved toward accepting the scientific basis for emission controls, is investing substantial amounts in low-emission technologies, and has engaged in widespread public relations to portray itself and its products as green. In return, it has won broad acceptance for a flexible, market-based implementation system that preserves corporate autonomy and legitimacy. Mainstream environmental organizations and government agencies have signed on to this accommodation, offering companies renewed credibility in shaping the emerging market-based climate regime.

In recent years, companies have been deploying the discourse of social responsibility, stewardship, stakeholder management and corporate citizenship in their efforts to restore legitimacy (Levy, 1997; Luke, 1995). While some Critical Theorists might view such discursive moves as ideological distortions designed to mask the real relations of power, the Gramscian perspective interprets them as compromises that shift the terrain of contestation and create new opportunities, for example, by building external expectations of concomitant practices, and by legitimating broader managerial consideration of social and environmental goals. The difference between succumbing to ideological co-optation and an emancipatory 'war of position' is, to repeat, one of long-term strategy.

References

Abercrombie, N., Hill, S. and Turner, B.S. (1980) *The dominant ideology thesis*. London: Allen and Unwin.

Alvesson, M. (1993) Participation and pseudo-participation in a professional service company. In W. Lafferty and E. Rosentein (Eds.), *International handbook of participation in organizations* (Vol. 3,). Oxford: Oxford University Press.

READING 4.3	# Critical Approaches to Strategic Management

By David L. Levy, Mats Alvesson and Hugh C. Willmott

Alvesson, M. (2000) *Ledning av kunskapsföretag*. 3rd ed. (Management of Knowledge-Intensive Companies). Stockholm: Norstedts.

Alvesson, M. and Sveningsson, S. (2003) The good visions, bad micro-management and ugly ambiguity: Contradictions of (non)leadership in a knowledge intensive setting. *Organization Studies*.

Alvesson, M. and Willmott, H. (1996) *Making sense of management. A critical introduction*. London: Sage.

Andrews, K.R. (1971) *The concept of corporate strategy*. Homewood, Illinois: Irwin.

Baron, D.P. (1997) Integrated strategy, trade policy and global competition. *Californian Management Review*, 39(2): 145–69.

Booth, C. (1998) Critical approches to strategy: an introduction to the special competition. *Electronic Journal of Radical Organization Theory*, 4(1).

Bower, J.L. and Doz, Y. (1979) Strategy formulation: A social and political process. In D.E. Schendel and C.W. Hofer. (Eds.), *Strategic management* (pp. 152–166). Boston, Mass: Little, Brown.

Callon, M. (1998) *The laws of the markets*. Oxford: Blackwell.

Chandler, A.D. (1962) *Strategy and structure: Chapters in the history of the American indstrial enterprise*. Cambridge, Mass.: MIT Press.

Child, J. (1972) 'Organizational structure, environment, and performance: the role of strategic choice'. *Sociology, 6*, 1–22.

Clegg, S. (1989) *Frameworks of power*. London: Sage.

Cress, D.M. and Snow, D.A. (2000) 'The outcomes of homeless mobilization: the influence of organization, disruption, political mediation, and framing'. *American Journal of Sociology*.

Cressey, P., Eldridge, J. and MacInnes, J. (1985) *Just managing: authority and democracy in industry*. Milton Keynes: Open University Press.

Daft, R.L. and Weick, K.E. (1984) 'Toward a model of organizations as interpretation systems'. *Academy of Management Review*, 92: 284–295.

DiMaggio, P.J. and Powell, W.W. (1983) 'The iron cage revisited: institutional isomorphism and collective rationality in organizational fields'. *American Sociological Review*, 482: 147–160.

El Sawy, O.A. and Pauchant, T.C. (1988) 'Triggers, templates, and twitches in the tracking of emerging strategic issues'. *Strategic Management Journal*, 72: 455–474.

Ezzamel, M. and Willmott, H.C. (2002) 'Organizing as Discursive Practice: Beyond Rational and Processual Analyses of Strategic Management', Working Paper, Judge Institute of Management, Cambridge University, England.

Ganz, M. (2000) 'Resources and resourcefulness: strategic capacity in the unionization of California agriculture, 1959–1966'. *American Journal of Sociology*.

Gramsci, A. (1971) *Selections from the prison notebooks* (Hoare, Quintin; Nowell-Smith, Geoffrey, Trans.). New York: International Publishers.

Granovetter, M. (1985) 'Economic action and social structure: the problem of embeddedness'. *American Journal of Sociology*, 91: 481–510.

Habermas, J. (1984) *The theory of communicative action*. Cambridge: Polity Press.

Hall, S. (1986) 'Gramsci's relevance for the study of race and ethnicity'. *Journal of Communication Inquiry*, 102: 5–27.

Harfield, T. (1998) 'Strategic management and Michael Porter: a postmodern reading'. *Electronic Journal of Radical Organization Theory*, 41.

Hill, T. and Westbrook, R. (1997) 'SWOT analysis: it's time for a product recall'. *Long Range Planning*, 301: 46–52.

Hillman, A.J. and Hitt, M.A. (1999) 'Corporate political strategy formulation: a model of approach, participation, and strategy decisions'. *Academy of Management Review*, 244: 825–842.

Knights, D. and Morgan, G. (1991) 'Corporate strategy, organizations, and subjectivity: a critique'. *Organisation Studies*, 122: 251–273.

Knights, D. and Willmott, H.C. (2002) 'Autonomy as Utopia or Dystopia' in M. Parker, ed., *Utopia and Organization*, Oxford: Blackwell

Levy, D.L. (1997) 'Environmental management as political sustainability'. *Organization and Environment*, 102: 126–147.

Levy, D.L. and Egan, D. (1998) 'Capital contests: National and transnational channels of corporate influence on the climate change negotiations'. *Politics and Society*, 263: 337–361.

Luke, T.W. (1995) 'Between democratic populists and bureaucratic greens: the limits of liberal democratic responses to the environmental crisis'. *Current Perspectives in Social Theory*, 15: 245–274.

Luttwak, E.N. (1987) *Strategy: the logic of war and peace*. Cambridge, Mass.: Harvard University Press.

Mahon, J.F. (1989) 'Corporate political strategy'. *Business in the Contemporary World*, 21: 50–62.

McAdam, D., McCarthy, J. and Zald, M. (1996) *Comparative perspectives on social movements*. New York: Cambridge University Press.

Mintzberg, H. (1990) 'The design school: reconsidering the basic premise of strategic management'. *Strategic Management Journal*, 11: 171–195.

Mintzberg, H. (1994) *The rise and fall of strategic planning*. New York: The Free Press.

READING 4.3 | Critical Approaches to Strategic Management *continued*

By David L. Levy, Mats Alvesson and Hugh C. Willmott

Mintzberg, H., Ahlstrand, B. and Lampel, J. (1998) *Strategy safari: a guided tour through the wilds of strategic management*. New York: The Free Press.

Peters, T.H. and Waterman, R.H. (1982) *In search of excellence*. New York: Harper and Row.

Pettigrew, A. (1985) *The awakening giant: Continuity and change in ICI*. Oxford: Basil Blackwell.

Pfeffer, J. (1994) *Competitive advantage through people*. Boston, MA: Harvard Business School Press.

Pfeffer, J. and Salancik, G.R. (1978) *The external control of organizations: A resource dependence perspective*. New York: Harper and Row.

Porter, M.E. (1980) *Competitive strategy: techniques for analyzing industries and competitors*. New York: Free Press.

Porter, M.E. (1985) *Competitive advantage: creating and sustaining superior performance*. New York: Free Press.

Quinn, R.E. and Cameron, K.S. (1988) *Paradox and transformation: toward a theory of change in management and organization*. Cambridge, Mass.: Ballinger.

Sassoon, A.S. (1987) *Gramsci's politics*. London: Hutchinson.

Sassoon, A.S. (2000) *Gramsci and contemporary politics: Beyond pessimism of the intellect*. London: Routledge.

Scarbrough, H. (1998) Path(ological) dependency? Core competence from an organizational perspective. *British Journal of Management*, 9: 219–232.

Schuler, D. (1996) 'Corporate political strategy and foreign competition: The case of the steel industry'. *Academy of Management Journal*, 393: 720–737.

Scott, W.R. and Meyer, J.W. (Eds.). (1994) *Institutional environments and organizations*. Thousand Oaks, CA: Sage.

Seeger, J.A. (1984) 'Reversing the images of BCG's growth share matrix'. *Strategic Management Journal*, 51: 93–97.

Shrivastava, P. (1986) 'Is strategic management ideological?'. *Journal of Management*, 12: 363–377.

Smircich, L. and Stubbart, C. (1985) 'Strategic management in an enacted world'. *Academy of Management Review*, 104: 724–736.

Stoney, C. (1998) 'Lifting the lid on strategic management: A sociological narrative'. *Electronic Journal of Radical Organization Theory*, 41.

Sun Tzu. (1983) *The art of war* (Giles, Lionel, Trans.). New York: Delacorte Press.

Sveningsson, S. (1999) *Strategic Change, Power and Knowledge*. On discipline and resistance in newspaper companies (in Swedish). Lund: Lund University Press.

Weick, K. (1995) *Sensemaking in organizations*. Thousand Oaks, CA: Sage.

Wernerfelt, B. (1984) 'A resource-based view of the firm'. *Strategic Management Journal*, 5: 171–180.

Whipp, R., Rosenfeld, R. and Pettigrew, A. (1989) 'Culture and competitiveness: evidence from two mature industries'. *Journal of Management Studies*, 265: 561–589.

Whittington, R. (1992) 'Putting Giddens into action: social systems and managerial agency'. *Journal of Management Studies*, 296: 493–512.

Whittington, R. (1993) *What is strategy - and does it matter?* London: Routledge.

Willmott, H.C. (1993) 'Strength is ignorance; slavery is freedom: managing culture in modern organizations', *Journal of Management Studies*.

Willmott, H.C. (2003), 'Organization theory as critical science: The case of "new Organizational forms"' in C. Knudsen and H. Tsoukas (eds.), *Organization Theory as Science: Prospects and Limitations*, Oxford University Press.

READING 4.4 | Corporate Strategy, Organizations and Subjectivity: A Critique

By David Knights and Glenn Morgan

Strategic discourse has become dominant over the last thirty years in business schools and organizations. This was not inevitable, but the result of the accomplishment of actors committed to expanding and reproducing their own sphere of power and knowledge. In our view, this process has a number of power effects. On the one hand, it negates and devalues alternative approaches to organizations. In this sense, it

Source: Reproduced with permission of Sage Publications, London, Los Angeles, New Delhi and Singapore from 'Corporate strategy, Organizations and subjectivity: A critique', in Organization Studies © *1991 Sage Publications.*

| READING 4.4 | **Corporate Strategy, Organizations and Subjectivity: A Critique** |

By David Knights and Glenn Morgan

is a constraint that 'disables' particular actors. On the other hand, it 'empowers' other actors. For those who accept the logic of the discourse, it provides them with a subjective identity that is expanded, through participation in its reproduction. In combination, we can talk of the discourse of corporate strategy as constitutive of new social relations. We can therefore point towards a social theory of corporate strategy which is concerned with analyzing these power effects and in so doing opening up again alternatives which are currently being shut down.

In the rest of this section, we wish to consider the following power effects of corporate strategy discourse, in particular:

a.   It provides managers with a rationalization of their successes and failures;

b.   It sustains and enhances the prerogatives of management and negates alternative perspectives on organizations;

c.   It generates a sense of personal and organizational security for managers;

d.   It reflects and sustains a strong sense of gendered masculinity for male management;

e.   It demonstrates managerial rationality to colleagues, customers, competitors, government and significant others in the environment;

f.   It facilitates and legitimizes the exercise of power ...

Strategy as Rationalization of Success and Failure

Learning and subscribing to discourses on corporate strategy provides managers with a vocabulary of success and failure and a means of celebrating the former and rationalizing or re-defining the latter in terms of relative success (Knights and Murray 1990). Thus the vagaries of the market or of employees or customers become 'understandable' by reference to particular theories of corporate strategy. Failure can be explained away because some factor was insufficiently appreciated, but now it has become incorporated in the next round of business planning and so we can look forward to the future with confidence. It is characteristic of the discourse that everything is explicable

in the end. There is nothing that is in principle unknowable – just bits of the jigsaw that were not known at the right time, thus undermining the particular strategy adopted. ...

Strategy and Management Prerogatives

Managers utilize these explanatory schema together with the techniques and disciplinary methods to which they are linked, in order to construct accounts of the organization that enhance their own contribution and importance. In so doing, the symbolic and material privileges of management are readily enhanced and rendered legitimate. If we take the situation where the absence of property rights may generate crises of legitimacy for managers, the development of strategy within the corporation can have the effect of sustaining a new basis of managerial prerogative. Managers are credentialled experts with the ability to both define the problems the organization faces and the solutions it needs to adopt. They are essential to the functioning of the organization and it therefore follows that their prerogatives are secure and legitimate. Managerial hierarchies, together with inequalities of income and work conditions can be justified by reference to the expertise that managers bring to their task through their knowledge of strategic discourse.

Strategy and Personal Security

What we are suggesting is that strategic discourse becomes a means through which managers and staff come to 'know' themselves and their organizations. Much of its utility is the extent to which it generates a kind of one-dimensional organizational self-knowledge. So, for example, managers can present themselves to each other and to the organization as a whole as the *subjective* component of the discourse of strategy, i.e. the element in the model of success that 'can make a difference'. Practitioners are embedded in the discourse and reproduce it as one of the conditions of their own subjectivity. They are now constituted as 'strategic' actors both insofar as they act on behalf of the organization and, perhaps, in their own personal life outside work (see Knights and Morgan 1990 for a brief discussion of this). In this context, developing a

Corporate Strategy, Organizations and Subjectivity: A Critique *continued*

By David Knights and Glenn Morgan

strategy and a plan of action provides existential comfort for managers subjected to the precarious contingencies of market relations. This comfort comes from the sense that strategic intervention can give managers a feeling that their destiny is at least partly in their own hands. It rests on the creation of projects to which managers, like everyone else, can commit themselves in ways that relieve or obscure the 'meaningless void' (Sartre, 1966) or relativity of the amorphous world in which they reside.

Strategy and Gendered Identity

Associated with this sense of being in control of a precarious world is the link, for men at least, between strategy and an assertive, perhaps even aggressive macho, masculinity. So it is no accident that the conventional discourse on strategy is ahistorical, unreflective and dominated by conceptions of rationality and the control of externalities. Both strategy and masculine identity in contemporary society are informed by an instrumental-purposive model of action that denies its historical self-formation equally as much as it dismisses elements of experience which cannot 'readily be assimilated into rational categories' (Seidler 1989: 7). While there are other masculine managerial identities (see Morgan and Knights 1990 for an empirical examination of the contrasts between 'patriarchal paternal' and 'aggressive sales' masculine discourses), they tend to share this instrumental pursuit of control over that which is outside the self, or external to the boundaries that are seen as the locus of power. Very often in strategic discourse, for example, markets are conceptualized in terms of the degree of penetration an organization might be expected to secure and so the whole language can be seen as masculine in orientation. It could be argued, then, that strategic discourse and practice both reflects and reproduces what may be termed a 'masculinist conception of power' (Brittan, 1989).

Strategy and the External World

Strategic discourse provides a demonstration to outsiders of how the organization is apparently rational and in control of its destiny. In an era when ownership and control have become institutionally distinct, share-holders and the participants in the capital markets look to publicly available information from companies in order to construct their own investment decisions. Whilst there are some sources such as Annual Reports which are quantified, these are supplemented in the case of the large publicly quoted companies by the provision of a continual flow of information from specialist press officers and public relations experts. Because share prices are a complex product of investor demand, supply of stock, financial data and future expectations, the confidence in corporate management is an extremely important dimension. It is one that is contingent on demonstrating a control not just over product, labour and capital markets but also of managing information and, in particular, its interpretation. The latter has the potential to benefit or undermine the company's image and future prosperity in the same way as actual success in the various markets. The construction of managers as competent 'strategists' is increasingly crucial (see Slater 1989 for an analysis along these lines). This is not simply a case of 'impression management' (Goffman, 1971) for public consumption, though that is one aspect and is why companies are increasingly bringing in specialist public relations agencies to help them. It is also an image that has to be managed within specific sets of institutional relationships with financial institutions, the state and other organizations.

Strategy and Intra-Organizational Power

Since strategy is deemed so important by outsiders, it follows that those professional groups within the organization which can claim a central role and expertise in strategy will begin to exercise power over others through the development and transformation of rules and practices. Thus Armstrong (1984, 1987a, 1987b) argues that a central reason for the low status of engineers within management in Britain is that they have failed to capture any strategic functions – in other words, failed successfully to sustain the claim that their expertise is peculiarly essential to organizational success. By contrast, accountants, partly through their already existing linkages to outside bodies, institutions and the state, have secured a strategic advantage in terms of the design and development of corporate strategy.

READING 4.4	**Corporate Strategy, Organizations and Subjectivity: A Critique**

By David Knights and Glenn Morgan

References

Armstrong, Peter, (1984) 'Competition between organizational professions and the evolution of management control strategies' in *Work, employment and unemployment.* K. Thompson (ed.), 97–120. Milton Keynes: Open University Press.

Brittan, A., (1989) *Masculinity and power.* Oxford: Blackwell.

Goffman, Erving, (1971) The presentation of self in everyday life. Harmondsworth: Penguin.

Knights, David, and Fergus, Murray (1990) 'Technology and the marketing-driven firm: problems and prospects'. *PICT Policy Paper.* Oxford: ESRC Programme on Information and Communication Technology.

Knights, David, and Glenn Morgan, (1990) 'The concept of strategy in sociology'. *Sociology* 24/3: 475–483.

Knights, D. and Murray, F. (1990) 'Technology and the marketing driven firm: Problems and Prospects'. *PICT Policy Paper.* Oxford: ESCR Programme on Information and Communication Technology.

Morgan, Glenn, and David Knights, (1990) 'Gendering jobs: corporate strategy, managerial control and the dynamics of job segregation'. *Working Paper*, Financial Services Research Centre, University of Manchester Institute of Science and Technology.

Sartre, Jean-Paul, (1966) *Being and nothingness.* New York: Washington Square Press.

Seidler, Victor, (1989) *Rediscovering masculinity: reason, language and sexuality.* London: Routledge.

Slater, Don, (1989) 'Corridors of power' in *The politics of field research.* J.F. Gubrium and D. Silverman (eds.), 113–131. London: Sage.

Discussion Questions

1. What are the differences between rational and post-rational approaches to studying strategy? How do you assess their merits?
2. What are the distinctive features of the strategy-as-practice perspective?
3. In what sense is strategy contested?
4. How is it that language, such as talk of 'strategy', is constitutive of what it appears to represent?

Introduction References

Contu, A. and Willmott, H.C. (2003) Re-embedding Situatedness: The Importance of Power Relations in Situated Learning Theory, *Organization Science* 14: 283–97.

Cressey, P., Eldridge, J. and MacInnes, J. (1985) *Just Managing: Authority and Democracy in Industry.* Milton Keynes: Open University Press.

Pettigrew, A. (1985) *The Awakening Giant: Continuity and Change in ICI.* Oxford: Blackwell.

Porter, M. (1979) How Competitive Forces Shape Strategy, *Harvard Business Review*, Mar/Apr, 57(2): 37–145.

Smircich, L. and Stubbart, C. (1985) Strategic management in an enacted world. *Academy of Management Review* 10(4): 724–36.

Whittington, R. (1992) Putting Giddens into action: Social systems and managerial agency. *Journal of Management Studies* 29(6): 493–512.

Whittington, R. (2003) The work of strategizing and organizing: For a practice perspective. *Strategic Organization* 1(1): 117–125

Whittington, R. and Melin, L. (2002) The Challenge of Organizing/Strategizing. In A.M. Pettigrew, R. Whittington, L. Melin, C. Sanchez-Runde, F. Van Den Bosch, W. Ruigrok and T. Numagami (eds) *Innovative Forms of Organizing: International Perspectives*, London: Sage. pp. 35–48.

Recommended Further Readings

See references to all the above texts plus:

Ambrosini, V., Jenkins, M. and Collier, N. (eds.) (2007) *Advanced Strategic Management: A Multi-perspective Approach*, 2nd ed, London: Palgrave Macmillan.

Barry, D. and Elmes, M. (1997) 'Strategy Retold: Towards a Narrative View of Strategic Discourse', *Academy of Management Review* 22(2): 429–52.

Bloomfield, B.P., Coombes, R., Knights, D. and Littler, D. (eds) (1997) *Information Technology and Organizations: Strategies, Networks, and Integration: Strategies, Networks and Integration*, Oxford: Oxford University Press.

Ezzamel, M. and Willmott, H.C. (2008) 'Strategy as Discourse in a Global Retailer: A Supplement to Rationalist and Interpretive Accounts, *Organization Studies* 29(2): 191–217.

Jarzabkowski, P., Balogun, J. and Seidl, D. (2007) 'Strategizing: The challenges of a practice perspective', *Human Relations* 60(1): 5–27.

Johnson, G., Langley, A. Melin, L. and Whittington, R. (2007) *Strategy as Practice: Research Directions and Resources*, Cambridge: Cambridge University Press.

Levy, D.L. and Egan, D. (2003) 'A Neo-Gramscian Approach to Corporate Political Strategy: Conflict and Accommodation in the Climate Change Negotiations', *Journal of Management Studies* 40: 803–29.

Mintzberg, H., Ahlstrand, B. and Lampel, J. (1988) *Strategy Safari: A Guided Tour Through the Wilds of Strategic Management*, New York: Prentice-Hall.

Pettigrew, A. (1977) 'Strategy Formulation as a Political Process', *International Studies of Management and Organization* 7(2): 78–87.

Samra-Fredericks, D. (2003) 'Strategizing as Lived Experience and Strategists' Everyday Efforts to Shape Strategic Direction'. *Journal of Management Studies*, 40: 141–174, 2003. Also available at SSRN: http://ssrn.com/abstract=371248

Whipp, R. (1999) 'Creative Deconstruction: Strategy and Organizations' in Clegg, S.R. Hardy, C. and Nord, W.R., (eds), *Managing Organizations: Current Issues*, London: Sage.

Whittington, R. (2000) *What is Strategy and Does it Matter?* London: Cengage Learning.

ORGANIZATIONAL CHANGE AND INNOVATION

CHAPTER 5

READINGS

Burawoy, M. (1979) *Manufacturing Consent*. Chicago: The University of Chicago Press. pp. 81; 82; 85; 86; 87; 89; 94; 106–108; 110; 120.

Barker, J.R. (1993) 'Tightening the Iron Cage: Concertive Control in Self-Managing Teams' in *Administrative Science Quarterly*, Vol. 38: pp. 408–437.

Knights, D. and McCabe, D. (2003) 'Tales of the Unexpected: Strategic Management and Innovation' in *Organization and Innovation: Guru Schemes and American Dreams,* Milton Keynes: Open University Press/McGraw Hill; and 'Dreams and Designs on Strategy: A Critical Analysis of TQM and Management Control' in *Work, Employment and Society,* Vol. 12, No. 3, (September, 1998), pp. 433–456.

Munro, R. (1998) 'Belonging on the Move: Market Rhetoric and the Future as Obligatory Passage' in *Sociological Review*, Vol. 46, No. 2: pp. 208–243. Selection pp. 223–232; p. 237.

INTRODUCTION

Change management or management innovation has grown from its very small beginnings in the early part of the last century in Scientific Management and the Human Relations School. It is now a multi-million dollar business largely because of the numerous gurus that have traded their panaceas in popular books, videos and consultancy programmes. While the narratives that are produced by popular management thinkers have effects disproportionate to the substance of their ideas, it is important not to be entirely dismissive of the guru phenomenon. For it is as much a part of the field of study as the management and organizational practice that it seeks to shock and shape. So much so that a number of social scientists have sought to study the management guru as a phenomenon in itself (Huczynski, 1993; Clark and Salaman, 1996; Jackson, 1996). However in this set of readings, we focus less on the gurus and their panaceas than on empirical findings of practices that have innovative consequences despite not necessarily having had innovative intent. Consequently, in contrast to the mainstream literature that concentrates on sophisticated prescriptive techniques and innovation fashions, our selection of readings concentrates on empirical studies of workplace and managerial practices that have evolved often from 'below' rather than been imposed from 'above' or 'outside' and yet have transformed employees into a highly self-disciplined workforce.

Michael Burawoy (Reading 5.1) discovers highly innovative practices that have emerged from the shopfloor of an engineering company, as workers have devised complex games around production partly as a response to their subordination and the routine of factory life. This proves far more effective in generating consent and motivation than many of the techniques devised by gurus, consultants, or managers. Its success, however, is probably a function of it having been stimulated from 'below' but then readily endorsed from 'above'. Burawoy begins his analysis by complaining of the way that industrial sociology and organization theory have 'proceeded from the facts of consensus or social control' (1979: 12) rather than having sought to explain them. His participant observation ethnography of an engineering company that fortuitously had been studied by another doctoral student 30 years earlier (Roy, 1952), sets out to correct for this shortcoming by demonstrating how consent to the structure of authority and control is manufactured through shopfloor 'games', in which workers are drawn to participate and compete. Games around meeting output targets, for example, generate a competitive camaraderie among the workers such that the social relations of production (elsewhere often antagonistic because of the conflict between capitalist profit and employee wages) are at once obscured as they are secured. In effect, workers become so absorbed in playing the game and its outcome, or what is described as 'making out', that its origin as a response to management control and making subordination less painful or humiliating is lost. As a result, consent is generated to the very social relations of production that define the rules of the game. While it might be considered that because meeting targets ensures greater financial reward, this is the source of the consent but as a full member of the workforce, Burawoy sees playing the game itself as generating a common interest between workers and management in the outcome, and therefore the continuity of, the game. He then examines the conditions under which games are reproduced and the extent to which the dynamics of game-playing may undermine the stability it produces, thereby creating a crisis. Following Habermas (1975), he argues that a systems crisis will occur if while not threatening wages, playing the game begins to threaten profits. A legitimation crisis occurs where there is too much or too little uncertainty about the outcomes, causing workers to withdraw from the game and if they see no value in the outcomes of the game: a motivational crisis would have a similar effect.

James Barker (Reading 5.2) also focuses on teamworking as a disciplinary strategy something the author, following Tompkins and Cheney (1985) and Eccles and Nohria (1992), describes as 'concertive control'. This is where collective and peer group employee self-discipline with its own norms and sanctions effectively displaces some of the need for top-down, hierarchical systems of management control. Again it is not dissimilar from Burawoy's notion of consent being manufactured through participation in self-managed shopfloor games but, in Barker's case, the vehicle is teamworking. His research investigates how employees developed a set of normative rules around teamworking that controlled their actions much more powerfully and completely than the earlier system of bureaucratic rules. Bureaucratic control gave way to concerted control as the value consensus of the company's team workers was appropriated by managers and evolved into a system of normative rules that became increasingly rationalized. While some writers have considered employee self-discipline to be less rigid and oppressive than bureaucracy, Barker believes that the 'iron cage' (Weber) of rational control not only remains but that, under concertive control, the cage becomes ever tighter and more constraining.

David Knights and Daren McCabe (Reading 5.3) provide an ethnographic study of Total Quality Management (TQM) in which they find that, in practice, this innovation both fails yet sometimes exceeds what is expected of it. Often it fails where management are insufficiently committed to its demands because these conflict with their career concerns or are in other ways not in their political interests. Occasionally the innovations are resisted but most often it was found that employees had internalized quality concerns to a greater extent than management and then workers often exceeded what might be expected of them in relation to delivering on its content. The text selected derives from two distinct publications drawing on two distinct case studies in Qualbank and Medbank respectively. Both demonstrate levels of failure on the part of management and success where in identifying with TQM practice, employees are transformed into subjects that secure their sense of identity, meaning and reality through complying with, or consenting to, its innovation demands. In Qualbank, the Crosby approach to TQM had been adopted and the system of developing snags or suggestions for change was a central feature. However, senior management did not fully resource the programme such that large numbers of snags were sent up the line only to fall into a 'black hole'. Employees found this unacceptable and yet their internalization of the quality programme meant that they often sought to fill the vacuum left by management. Similarly Medbank developed a quality programme characterized by phrases such as 'right-first-time' and the 'customer comes first' and yet the company did not train their Head Office. Consequently, the branches were able to use the quality programme as a 'stick' to 'beat' the Head Office staff resulting in some major antagonisms and tensions. The lack of integration simply enabled the branch staff to talk quality while behaving as before with the rationale that they could not operationalize the programme when it was contradicted by policies and instructions from Head Office. Overall the excerpt demonstrates that quality programmes or any other innovation can have unintended consequences, some of which may be extremely negative but others that may be positive in securing more commitment from employees than would be anticipated.

Rolland Munro (Reading 5.4), drawing on material from an empirical case study, provides an analysis that illustrates how management manages change through strategies of inclusion and exclusion based on concepts of belonging. You either *belong* to the future of progress, autonomy, ownership, and flexibility or you are still in the past of custom, tradition, and loyalty. The latter, Munro argues, are viruses that must be expunged from the person by never letting identities settle so that they can return to traditional affiliations. Belonging must always be kept on the move, so to speak. In this sense, we can see that people's feelings of belonging are mobilized largely for instrumental ends. This may be seen as the transformation of organizations through what we have come to call a 'new managerialism' that insists on market relations being the measure of everything. So, for example, the 'internal market' is imported into the organization as a means of ensuring that everybody is accountable to everybody else. But clearly it also undermines traditional relations of belonging since if there is a failure to deliver on promises; norms of loyalty no longer restrain the switch to another provider. While this has always been in principle, although often not in practice, the rule in external market relations, it is a radical change in the management of internal organizational relations. It is not, however, without ambiguity especially where even hierarchical relations are reformulated into market relations. Munro points to three ambiguities respectively over strategy, performance measurement and core/periphery employees. Firstly, there are asymmetrical assumptions where superiors are thought to have the better knowledge; secondly, superiors can arbitrarily decide what counts as a measure of performance; and thirdly, which employees are really inside in contrast to outsiders that are merely hired labour. Resolving these ambiguities is a major resource in managing identity but the cards are stacked against those not in a position of hierarchical superiority or enjoying the role of 'purchaser' of supplies.

READING 5.1	**Manufacturing Consent**
	By Michael Burawoy

Making out … inserts the worker into the labour process as an individual rather than as a member of a class distinguished by a particular relationship to the means of production. Workers control their machines instead of being controlled by them, and this enhances their autonomy …

The significance of creating a game out of the labour process, however, extends beyond the particularities of making out. The very activity of playing a game generates consent with respect to its rules. The point is more than the obvious, but important, assertion that one cannot both play the game and at the same time question the rules. The issue is: which is logically and empirically prior, playing the game or the legitimacy of the rules? Here I am not arguing that playing the game rests on a broad consensus; on the contrary, consent rests upon – is constructed through – playing the game …

The rules, which in the case of making out present themselves in the form of a set of social relations in production, are evaluated in terms of the defined outcomes of the game – making out or not making out – and not in terms of some broader set of outcomes that are also the consequence of the game, such as the generation of profit, the reproduction of capitalist relations of production, and so forth. Therefore, to the extent that it is institutionalized – as it is in making out – the game becomes an end in itself, overshadowing, masking, and even inverting the conditions out of which it emerges. As long as workers are engaged in a game involving their relations to a machine, their subordination to the process of production becomes an object of acquiescence. Equally, incorporation into a game involving other agents of production (workers, foremen, etc.) generates an acquiescence in the *social* relations of control inscribed in the labor process, that is, the relations in production. Two consequences of game-playing have so far been delineated: first, game-playing obscures the relations of production in response to which the game is originally constructed; second, game-playing generates consent to the social relations in production that define the rules of the game.

Individual (as opposed to collective) violation of rules leads to ritual punishment, which has the effect

| **Manufacturing Consent**

By Michael Burawoy

of reinforcing these obscuring and consent-producing consequences. That is, a violation of rules has the consequence of strengthening their hold over productive activities and relations. Thus, attempts by management to squeeze a little extra out of workers frequently enhanced consensual relations on the shop floor. Operators at Allied continually complained about 'being screwed' by the company, and initially I associated this with some vague notion of exploitation. Soon I discovered that such anguish referred to the company's failure to provide the necessary conditions to play the game of making out ...

It is not so much the monetary incentive that concretely coordinates the interests of management and worker but rather the play of the game itself, which generates a common interest in the outcome and in the game's continuity. Any game that provides distinctive rewards to the players establishes a common interest among the players – whether these are representatives of capital or labor in providing for the conditions of its reproduction. Insofar as games encompass the entire labour process, the value system to which they give rise will prevail on the shop floor. Activities are evaluated and interests established as a consequence of the game. In other words, interests are not given primordially, nor are they necessarily brought to the shop floor from socialization experiences outside work. Rather, they are organized by the specific form of relations in production; in our example, interests are defined by relations to the game of making out. The day-to-day experience emerges out of the organization of work and defines the interests of the various agents of production once their basic survival – which, as far as workers are concerned, is an acceptable wage – is assured. When the labor process is organized into some form of game involving the active participation of both management and worker, the interests of both are concretely coordinated. In other work situations the labor process organizes different constellations of interests, of a kind that may render the interests of workers and management irrevocably antagonistic ...

[Games] generate power struggles and conflict with management. In denying the primordiality of interests and stressing their emergence out of the organization of work, I have come to different conclusions.

Games do, indeed, arise from worker initiatives, from the search for means of enduring subordination to the labor process, but they are regulated, coercively where necessary, by management. Once a game is established, however, it can assume a dynamics of its own, and there is no guarantee that it will continue to reproduce the conditions of its existence. On the contrary, it is possible that playing the game will tend to undermine the rules that define it ...

Or, more generally, one can ask: What are the conditions for the reproduction of games? Under what conditions will the game's own dynamics undermine the harmony it also produces and so lead to a crisis? More specifically, what are the conditions under which making out can be continually played on the shop floor? Does this game have consequences other than the production of consent and profit – consequences that continually threaten its reproduction? Does making out sow the seeds of its own destruction? ...

A game loses its ability to absorb players under any of the following three conditions: first, when uncertainty is too great and outcomes are entirely beyond the control of players; second, when uncertainty is too slight and outcomes may become completely controlled by players; third, when players are indifferent to the possible outcomes ...

While playing the game of making out never directly threatens the minimum wage, it can under certain circumstances endanger profits. I shall term this first kind of crisis *a system crisis*. A crisis of a second kind stems from workers' withdrawal from the game either because of too much or too little uncertainty in the attainment of making out *(legitimation crisis)* or because making out no longer has any value to the players *(motivational crisis)* ...

In identifying the separation of conception and execution, the expropriation of skill, or the narrowing of the scope of discretion as the broad tendency in the development of the capitalist labour process, Harry

Manufacturing Consent *continued*

By Michael Burawoy

Braverman missed the equally important parallel tendency toward the expansion of choices within those ever-narrower limits. It is the latter tendency that constitutes a basis of consent and allows the degradation of work to pursue its course without continuing crisis …

The internal labor market contributes to both the obscuring and securing of surplus value in a number of ways. First, it internalizes the features most characteristic of the external labor market – namely, the competitive individualism of 'free and equal' labourers. Second, the mobility it engenders at the point of production dissolves some of the tensions between worker and management and generates new tensions among workers. In both these ways the interests of the worker are constituted as those of one individual agent against other individuals rather than those of one class opposed to another class. On the other hand, in fostering a commitment to the enterprise by rewarding seniority, the internal labour market concretely coordinates the interests of capitalist and labourer in the generation of surplus value.

This interpretation diverges from that of Doeringer and Piore, who see the internal labor market as an adaptation to enterprise-specific skills. Although this is a by no means unimportant feature, it is difficult to square their theory with Braverman's compelling degradation thesis: the decline of enterprise-specific skills and the ease with which they are acquired. How can one reconcile the rise of internal labor markets with the increasing separation between conception and execution? Certainly Braverman makes no such attempt. Richard Edwards (see Chapter 8 Reading 8.1), borrowing from Max Weber, Michel Crozier, and Alvin Gouldner, argues that the internal labor market is part of a system of bureaucratic control that rationalized the enterprise's power by making its application more predictable and stable, and hence bureaucratic control evoked more stable and predictable behaviour from workers; that is, bureaucratic control tended to legitimize the firm's exercise of power, and translate it into authority.

Although his analysis goes beyond Doeringer and Piore, in that it focuses on control, how the exercise of power is legitimized through rules is as unclear in Edwards' writing as it is in Weber's.

By contrast, I am arguing that what is significant about rules is not that they increase stability and predictability but that they confine increased uncertainty within narrower limits. Thus, the internal labor market bases itself in a complex of rules, on the one hand, while expanding the *number* of choices on the other. Nor should these choices be belittled by saying that one boring, meaningless job is much the same as any other. The choice gains its significance from the material power it gives to workers in their attempts to resist or protect themselves from managerial domination. Workers have a very definite interest in the preservation and expansion of the internal labor market, as the most casual observation of the shop floor would demonstrate. Moreover, it is precisely that interest that draws workers into the bidding system and generates consent to its rules and the conditions they represent, namely, a labor process that is being emptied of skill …

The emerging internal state protects the managerial prerogative to fashion and direct the labor process by imposing constraints on managerial discretion and by endowing workers with rights as well as obligations …

I have shown that, in the period between 1945 and 1975, the application of force was increasingly limited to violation of rules that defined an expanding arena of consent. In doing so, I have regarded the enterprise as obscuring and securing surplus value through the organization, displacement, and repression of struggles, through the constitution and presentation of the interests of the corporation as the interests of all, and through the promotion of individualism, and I have also assumed that the obscuring and securing of surplus value can be examined independently of such external factors as the global state, markets, and the reproduction of labour power.

READING 5.2	**Tightening the Iron Cage: Concertive Control in Self-Managing Teams**
	By James R. Barker

In this paper, I provide an ethnographic account of how an organization's control system evolved in response to a managerial change from hierarchical, bureaucratic control to concertive control in the form of self-managing teams. The study investigates how the organization's members developed a system of value-based normative rules that controlled their actions more powerfully and completely than the former system. I describe the organization and its members and provide a detailed account of the dynamics that emerged as concertive control became manifest through the members' interactions. This account depicts how concertive control evolved from the value consensus of the company's team workers to a system of normative rules that became increasingly rationalized. Contrary to some proponents of such systems, concertive control did not free these workers from Weber's iron cage of rational control. Instead, the concertive system, as it became manifest in this case, appeared to draw the iron cage tighter and to constrain the organization's members more powerfully.

> I don't have to sit there and look for the boss to be around; and if the boss is not around, I can sit there and talk to my neighbor or do what I want. Now the whole team is around me and the whole team is observing what I'm doing.

'Ronald', a technical worker in a small manufacturing company, gave me this account one day while I was observing his work team. Ronald works in what contemporary writers call a post-bureaucratic organization, which is not structured as a rule-based hierarchy. He works with a team of peers who are all equally responsible for managing their own work behaviours. But Ronald described an unexpected consequence of this team-based design. With his voice concealed by work noise, Ronald told me that he felt more closely watched now than when he worked under the company's old bureaucratic system. He said that while his old supervisor might tolerate someone coming in a few minutes late, for example, his team had adopted a 'no tolerance' policy on tardiness and that members monitored their own behaviours carefully.

Ronald's comments typify life under a new form of organizational control that has prospered in the last decade as a means of avoiding the pitfalls of bureaucracy. This form, called 'concertive control', grows out of a substantial consensus about values, high-level coordination, and a degree of self-management by members or workers in an organization. This paper describes and analyses the development of concertive control after Ronald's company, 'ISE Communications', converted to self-managing (or self-directing) teams, a concertive structure that resulted in a form of control more powerful, less apparent, and more difficult to resist than that of the former bureaucracy (see Table 5.2.1). The irony of the change in this postbureaucratic organization is that, instead of loosening, the iron cage of rule-based, rational control, as Max Weber called it, actually became tighter ...

Concertive Control as a Fourth Strategy

Almost since the beginning of modern organizational study, influential theorists have argued that decentralized, participative, and more democratic systems of control offer the most viable alternatives to the bureaucracy's confining routines and rules (e.g., Follett, 1941; Lewin, 1948). This continual push toward participation and a flat organizational structure has become something of an obsession in managerial literature in the last decade or so (Eccles and Nohria, 1992). Contemporary writers have unleashed a flood of literature announcing the 'coming demise of bureaucracy and hierarchy' (Kanter, 1989: 351) and detailing the dawn of a postbureaucratic age in which control emerges not from rational rules and hierarchy but from the concertive, value-based actions of the organization's members (Soeters, 1986; Ogilvy, 1990; Parker, 1992). Characteristic of this movement are influential business consultants such as Tom Peters (1988) and Peter Drucker (1988) who have urged corporate executives to de-bureaucratize their firms and adopt more ideologically based designs drawn around unimpeded, agile authority structures that grow out of a company's consensual, normative ideology, not from its system of formal rules. By cutting out bureaucratic offices and rules, organizations can flatten hierarchies, cut costs, boost productivity, and

Source: Reproduced with permission from 'Tightening the Iron Cage: Concertive Control in Self-Managing Teams', in Administrative Science Quarterly © 1993 The Johnson School.

READING 5.2

Tightening the Iron Cage: Concertive Control in Self-Managing Teams *continued*

By James R. Barker

increase the speed with which they respond to the changing business world.

Tompkins and Cheney (1985) argued that the numerous variations these authors have offered on the postbureaucratic organization represent a new type of control, 'concertive' control — built on Edwards' three traditional control strategies (see Chapter 8 Reading 8.1). This form represents a key shift from management to the workers themselves, who collaborate to develop the means of their own control. Workers achieve concertive control by reaching a negotiated consensus on how to shape their behaviour according to a set of core values, such as the values found in a corporate vision statement. In a sense, concertive control reflects the adoption of a new substantive rationality, a new set of consensual values, by the organization and its members ...

I report on the processes of control that became manifest as a manufacturing organization changed and adapted to a concertive-based structure, in the form of a self-managing, or self-directed team design.

Self-managing Teams: An Exemplar of Concertive Control

Currently, the most popular planned organizational change to a postbureaucratic structure is the transformation of a traditional, hierarchically based organization to a flat confederation of concertively controlled self-managing teams. Xerox, General Motors, and Coors Brewing have all initiated this kind of change over the last few years. Although self-managing teams have gained much of their popularity in recent years, they are not a new phenomenon. Research and writing on the subject originally dates from Trist's study of self-regulating English coal miners in the 1950s (Trist *et al.*, 1963; Trist, 1981) and includes the Scandinavian experience with semiautonomous teams (Bolweg, 1976; Katz and Kahn, 1978) and early U.S. team experiences, most notably the Gaines Dog Food plant in Kansas (Walton, 1982; Ketchum, 1984). The contemporary version of the self-managing team concept draws on both the past experiences with teams in Europe and the U.S. and the more recent influence of Japanese-inspired quality circles in Western organizations (Sundstrom *et al.*, 1990; Sewell and Wilkinson, 1992).

Proponents of self-managing teams have described it as a radical change in the traditional managerial and authority structure of an organization (e.g., Orsbum *et al.*, 1990; Wellins, Byham, and Wilson, 1991). In line with the impulse toward postbureaucratic, concertive-based organizations, they assert that traditional management structures entail inflexible hierarchical and bureaucratic constraints that stifle creativity and innovation. These rigid organizations are top-heavy with managers and unresponsive to changing, dynamic markets, ultimately reducing their competitive viability. From the proponents' viewpoint, U.S. organizations must radically change their managerial structure by converting to worker-run teams and eliminating unneeded supervisors and other bureaucratic staff (traditional management structures). Proponents argue that self-managing teams make companies more productive and competitive by letting workers manage themselves in small, responsive, highly committed, and highly productive groups. Thus, the self-management perspective proposes a 'radical' shift from hierarchical supervision to hands-off, collaborative worker management.

This change from supervisory to participatory structures means that workers in a self-managing team will experience day-to-day work life in vastly different ways than workers in a traditional management system. Instead of being told what to do by a supervisor, self-managing workers must gather and synthesize information, act on it, and take collective responsibility for those actions. Self-managing team workers generally are organized into teams of 10 to 15 people who take on the responsibilities of their former supervisors. Top management often provides a value-based corporate vision that team members use to infer parameters and premises (norms and rules) that guide their day-to-day actions. Guided by the company's vision, the self-managing team members direct their own work and coordinate with other areas of the company.

Usually, a self-managing team is responsible for completing a specific, well-defined job function, whether in production or service industries. The team's members are cross-trained to perform any task the work requires and also have the authority and responsibility to make the essential decisions necessary to complete the function. Self-managing teams may build major appliances,

READING 5.2	**Tightening the Iron Cage: Concertive Control in Self-Managing Teams**
	By James R. Barker

TABLE 5.2.1 | MANIFEST AND LATENT CONSEQUENCES OF ISE'S EXPERIENCE WITH CONCERTIVE CONTROL

Manifest	Latent
1. Teams developed value consensus by drawing from ISE's vision statement.	1. Teams began to form a value-based substantive rationality, which led them to develop a mutually shared sense of ethical rational action at work.
2. Team members identified with their particular value consensus and developed emotional attachments to their shared values.	2. Authority transferred from ISE's old bureaucratic control system to the team's value system. The team members' human dignity became invested in submitting to this authority.
3. Teams formed behavioral norms from the values that enabled them to work effectively, thus put their values into action.	3. The teams became methodical about putting their values into action. Their values began a natural progression toward rationalization, which allowed the values and norms to be intellectually analyzable by all members.
4. Older team members expected new members to identify with the norms and values and act in accordance with these value-based norms.	4. Concertive control became nested in the team. Members themselves took on both superior and subordinate roles, monitoring and directing.
5. The teams' normative rules grew more rationalized. Team members enforced their rules with each other through peer pressure and behavioral sanctions.	5. ISE's concertive system became a powerful force of control. Since they had created it themselves, this control was seemingly natural and unapparent to the team members.
6. Teams further objectified and formalized the rules and shared these rules with each other. The work environment appeared to stabilize.	6. The teams had developed their own disciplines that merged their substantive values with a rule-based formal rationality. These disciplines enabled the teams to work efficiently and effectively. The teams controlled their work through a system of rational rules and the self-monitoring of their own individual and collective actions.

process insurance claims, assemble component parts for computers, or handle food service for a large hospital. Along with performing their work functions, members of a self-managing team set their own work schedules, order the materials they need, and do the necessary co-ordination with other groups. Besides freeing itself from some of the shackles of bureaucracy and saving the cost of low-level managers, the self-managing company also gains increased employee motivation, productivity, and commitment. The employees, in turn, become committed to the organization and its success (Orsburn *et al.*, 1990; Mumby and Stohl, 1991; Wellins, Byham, and Wilson, 1991) …

References

Bolweg, J.F. (1976) *Job Design and Industrial Democracy*, Leiden: Martinus Nijhoff.

Drucker, P. (1988) 'The coming of the new organizations', *Harvard Business Review*, Jan–Feb. 45–53.

Eccles, R.G. and Nohria, N. (1992) *Beyond the Hype: Rediscovering the Essence of Management*, Cambridge, MA: Harvard Business School Press.

Follett, M.P. (1941) Dynamic Administration: The Collected Papers of Mary Parker Follett in H.C. Metcalf and L. Urwick (eds.), London: Pitman.

Kanter, R.B. (1989) *When Giants Learn to Dance*, New York: Simon Shuster.

READING 5.2 | **Tightening the Iron Cage: Concertive Control in Self-Managing Teams** *continued*

By James R. Barker

Katz, D. and Kahn, R.L. (1978) *The Social Psychology of Organization*, New York: Wiley.

Ketchum, L.D. (1984) 'How redesigned plants really work', *National Productivity Review*, Vol. 3: 246–254.

Lewin, K. (1948) *Resolving Social Conflicts: Selected Papers on Group Dynamics*, New York: Harper & Row.

Mumby, D.K. and Stohl, C. (1991) 'Power and discourse in organizational studies: absence and the dialectics of control', *Discourse and Society*, Vol. 2: 313–322.

Ogilvy, J. (1990) 'The postmodern business', *Marketing and Research Today*, Feb: 4–20

Orsburn, J.D., Moran, L., Musselwhite, Ed and Zenger, J.H. (1990) *Self Directed Work Teams*, Homewood, IL: Irwin

Parker, M. (1992) 'Postmodern organizations or postmodern organizational theory?', *Organization Studies*, Vol. 13: 1–17.

Peters, T. (1988) *Thriving on Chaos*, New York: Knopf.

Sewell, G. and Wilkinson, B. (1992) 'Someone to watch over me: surveillance, disipline and the just-in-time labour process', *Sociology*, Vol. 26: 271–289.

Soeters, J.L. (1986) 'Excellent companies as social movements', *Journal of Management Studies*, Vol. 23: 299–312.

Sundstrom, E., De Meuse, K.P. and Futrell, D. (1990) Work teams: applications and effectiveness, *American Psychologist*, Vol. 45: 120–133.

Trist, E.L. (1981) The Evolution of Socio-Technical Systems, Occasional Paper no. 2 Toronto: Quality of Working Life Centre.

Trist, E.L., Higgin, G., Murray, H. and Pollock, A.B. (1963) *Organizational Choice*, London: Tavistock.

Walton, R.E. (1982) 'The Topeka work system' in R. Zager and M.P. Roscow (eds.) *The Innovative Organization*, New York: Pergamon, pp. 260–287.

Wellins, R.S., Byham, W.C. and Wilson, J.M. (1991) *Empowered Teams*, San Francisco: Jossey Bass.

READING 5.3 | **Tales of the Unexpected: Strategic Management and Innovation and Dreams and Designs on Strategy: A Critical Analysis of TQM and Management Control**

By David Knights and Darren McCabe

Introduction

A number of critical commentators have highlighted the gap, which often occurs between the 'rhetoric' and 'reality' of innovation. The focus tends to be upon the shortfall of management practice in relation to the claims of the quality gurus or management strategic designs and intentions. Here we identify such gaps or shortfalls but also extensions where practice often exceeds the aspirations of management. We argue that the problems facing managers when introducing innovations stem not only from the difficulties of implementation but also from flaws in their design. Equally, the failure but also, in some cases, the success of innovations is not always a function of inadequate implementation, so much as the unanticipated and unintended consequences of their implementation.

So far, critical research on quality management (e.g. Webb and Cleary, 1994; McArdle *et al.*, 1995; Tuckman, 1995) has tended to concentrate on the failure of quality programmes to live up to the expectations that the advocates have built up around them and/or on the intensification of work for employees that are often their result (Delbridge *et al.*, 1992; Sewell and Wilkinson, 1992; Parker and Slaughter, 1993). We seek here to add additional empirical support for these conclusions but wish to challenge some suggestions (Howcroft, 1992; Boaden and Dale, 1993; Zairi, Letsa and Oakland, 1993; Hunter and Beaumont, 1993) that the failure of quality is primarily one of implementation.

The second concern relates to the failure in both the literature and among practitioners to examine the unintended consequences of innovative strategies.

<table>
<tr><td>

READING 5.3

</td><td>

Tales of the Unexpected: Strategic Management and Innovation and Dreams and Designs on Strategy: A Critical Analysis of TQM and Management Control

By David Knights and Darren McCabe

</td></tr>
</table>

More particularly, there seems little recognition that although the unintended is often negative in its impact, sometimes the actions of employees far exceed the anticipated expectations or outcome of those who instigate a new initiative. Part of the reason for this neglect, it may be argued, is a paucity of empirical research that is independent of, or free of vested interests in, the prescriptions of quality initiatives. Another explanation is that when interventions appear not to work, there is a tendency to shift to some new fashionable innovation rather than investigate the reasons for failure of the one abandoned or marginalized.[1]

Qualbank

There is a demand within Qualbank that any innovation such as TQM be shown to reduce costs and this short-term expediency seems to have undermined much of the long term potential of the programme.

The intention behind TQM within this organization is to effect a culture change that entails empowering individuals to identify problems and to solve them so as to prevent areas of non-conformance and thereby improve customer service. A quality document allows us to elaborate upon the type of culture change management hope to effect, providing an indication of how the TQM discourse seeks to reconstruct employees as unquestioning TQM subjects:

> Quality improvement is a challenge facing all of **us. It is not an extra task** to do but a whole **new** way of working ... when **we** as individuals make a commitment to improve quality, **we promise** to do **everything in our power** to meet customer requirements and **continually** look for ways to improve quality. ... There is **a need to constantly ask ourselves** how **we** can **improve** things (emphasis added)

Here we can see management seeking to define TQM as a collective concern, which entails a redefinition of management-staff relations: it is a challenge facing all of 'us'.

There is an attempt to rule out any divisions or conflict between management and staff, as improve-

ment is something that 'we promise to do' and which 'we as individuals' must make a 'commitment to improve'. In doing so, management also attempts to redefine staff as individuals who no longer have interests distinct from those of the company. Such individuals are not to view TQM as an additional burden for which they must be recompensed.

... TQM is designed so as to generate snags and a culture of problem solving. In addition, there should be **a loop of feedback downwards.** A quality document described this as 'recognition', which involves showing 'appreciation of peoples' efforts and successes', where management's role is to 'give encouragement, recognition and help in resolving problems'. Nonetheless, the following comments by a Financial Services manager are typical of our observations regarding the lack of feedback within the branch network:

> If only we could get feedback on **one** snag then it would begin to seem worthwhile.

Whilst, a Cluster Customer Services Manager remarked:

> I find that we have a problem because we don't get the feedback ... Some things disappear into the black hole and we don't know quite what happens to them.

The minutes to a cluster meeting of quality sponsors on the 17th February 1994 stated that the area quality representative had 340 outstanding snags, which he is 'looking to reduce by 100 per month'. A Quality Sponsor explained that the problem with feedback is due to a lack of staff within the quality infrastructure:

> they need more people right from the top to bottom just dedicated to quality, not just trying to fit it in with the rest of your job, as it always comes second place ... at the area level its relying on the area representative to remember ... I mean when he gets snags he sticks them in the drawer most of the time

READING 5.3

Tales of the Unexpected: Strategic Management and Innovation and Dreams and Designs on Strategy: A Critical Analysis of TQM and Management Control *continued*

By David Knights and Darren McCabe

This view was confirmed by other respondents and our own observations.

TQM has begun to infiltrate the identity of organizational members in ways that management could not have anticipated. Paradoxically, these productive responses on the part of staff are a result of failures or shortcomings, not successes, in the implementation of the TQM strategy. Here we will consider ways in which the quality discourse has entered staff's identity.

A number of local initiatives have arisen to remedy the lacunas resulting from the lack of feedback both within the branches and between branches. One example of this can be seen at the Wigan branch where a quality sponsor had been asked by her manager to compile 'something' to compensate for the absence of feedback. It is important to remember that quality sponsors are only members of staff and perform full-time jobs such as cashiering. However, as either nominated or voluntary quality sponsors they are far more familiar with quality than average branch staff. The sponsor has developed a newsletter, which seeks to provide localised feedback, although this is available only within the Wigan branch. The following is an extract from a newsletter compiled by the sponsor:

> **The Quality Team would like to thank** all the people who have taken time to think of ideas that we can put forward as snags – **those are greatly appreciated. The winner of the monthly branch competition is Gwen**, whose idea was to try to cut down on paper wastage. The cluster competition was won by Leigh branch ... GOOD NEWS THOUGH – Wigan branch was snag of the month for March (emphasis added but capitals in original).

The extract reveals that the sponsor identifies herself with the 'quality team' and can be seen to 'thank' other members of staff from that perspective. It reflects how this member of staff has begun to internalize the strategic discourse of quality and, thereby, creatively correct or more accurately repair the damage done by the failure of the TQM programme to deliver on its promises of feedback.

Medbank

Medbank initially introduced TQM within its 'branches' to 'empower' staff and improve service to its customers. However, the training of branch staff in concepts such as 'right-first-time' had the unintended consequence of giving them a 'stick' with which to 'beat' Head Office. Head Office Staff were neither equipped to deal with the problems raised by the branch, nor had they been trained in quality concepts. Therefore, when Head Office staff made errors or were unable to provide support to the branches, the branch staff retorted that 'that's not right-first-time' or they asked 'how about the customer first?' Partial rather than comprehensive Quality Programmes are problematic inasmuch as they may, as here, stimulate intra-organizational frictions.

Ultimately TQM failed and the Training Manager explained that although the company introduced a comprehensive training programme, once individuals went back to the branches they simply worked in much the same way as before. Hence, TQM was never really operationalized:

> We won the Training award. I wish we'd won the war, we got our troops on, they knew what it meant, putting it into application, we weren't so good at that.

In contrast to Qualbank, Medbank did not put an infrastructure in place to ensure that quality was enacted. It was thought that quality would simply emerge but this was far from the case, as a member of the TQM training team indicated:

> I'm not sure that we actually got the message to them that this was ongoing ... I think you've really got to work hard at saying to the person who actually speaks to the customer, 'you know, this is your issue, not my issue'. I'm not that sure that, at that time, that we actually managed to do that as

| READING 5.3 | **Tales of the Unexpected: Strategic Management and Innovation and Dreams and Designs on Strategy: A Critical Analysis of TQM and Management Control** |

By David Knights and Darren McCabe

well as we could. I think some of it was seen as 'well it's management tools to get more out of us' – the staff can be cynical about these things.

Here, although management could have learned from the failings of TQM it was simply abandoned in favour of the next innovation.

Conclusion

From our research, it would appear that innovative strategies in the area of quality often begin their life as a formal scheme that originates with senior management. However, in the process of their implementation, such strategies are subjected to a variety of modifications and/or lose favour because of the failure to deliver the promised outcomes. In other circumstances, innovations may be 'driven' by managers lower in the hierarchy who have to compete for senior management commitment and resources with those fighting for alternative strategies. But no matter where they originate, or whose support is mobilized, innovations will rarely deliver precisely what was intended.

This is because the consequences of aggregated actions can never be entirely anticipated or controlled; unintended consequences are an inevitable feature of organisational life. Moreover, their negative impact can be exacerbated where managers are insensitive to or unaware of, their existence. As we have suggested, some of the problems of innovations such as TQM are evident in their design. For it is quite contradictory to deploy detailed prescription and hierarchical control methods when seeking employee empowerment and a more participative organizational culture. A partial and inconsistent implementation as well as managerial insensitivity to staff's commitment and their desire for feedback, only serves to undermine morale and enthusiasm for quality. In particular, it puts the 'poor' quality of management practice under the spotlight.

One needs to recognize that quality or reengineering initiatives are not politically neutral management techniques. Innovations are introduced into politically charged organizations where vested interest groups, relations of conflict and accommodation between labour and management, and intense pressures around cost reduction versus service quality prevail. These tensions and pressures invariably serve to constitute and reconstitute organizational forms, inequality, power relations and innovations; rendering management's planned intentions open to disruption. This is not simply to support Mintzberg's 'emergent' strategy thesis because, as should be apparent from our analysis, unintended consequences cannot always be managed or eradicated by more attentive management. Of course, a lack of awareness about the possibility of unintended consequences can result in their negative implications being exacerbated. But, by definition, the consequences of strategic innovations can never be entirely predicted. Nor can it be known in advance whether what is unintended will support, undermine or extend the objectives of management. Ultimately this produces a situation of uncertainty that may or may not be productive for the organization. This is not to argue the case for chaos (cf. Peters, 1990). Indeed, in the above cases, management have successfully restructured, closed hundreds of branches and shed thousands of jobs. They have successfully reduced their cost base but perhaps the ultimate unintended consequence is that, while innovation and rationalization has been carried out in the name of service quality, the public seems ever more disenchanted with the service provided. Moreover, the 'most important asset' of staff has often been depleted and frequently neglected.

To conclude, we have identified numerous instances where the unintended consequences of innovations serve to interrupt, disrupt or extend management strategies. For advocates of innovation, the phenomenon suggests a need for vigilance regarding the outcomes of any strategy. For the critics of quality, it suggests that management control may not be nearly as effective as they fear. Thus there are always disjunctures within management strategies that create space and opportunities for a variety of responses including outright resistance. Of course, such dynamics could lead to further

READING 5.3

Tales of the Unexpected: Strategic Management and Innovation and Dreams and Designs on Strategy: A Critical Analysis of TQM and Management Control *continued*

By David Knights and Darren McCabe

innovations that enhance management control but there is rarely a guarantee on outcomes. Our research reveals that a situation of uncertainty prevails and, whether 'planned' or 'emergent', strategies are subject to a variety of unanticipated consequences. Some of these may rupture, or generate resistance to, managerial objectives and others may take a strategy well beyond the dreams of its designers.

[1]During a period of six years studying innovations, we came across several companies switching their allegiances or priorities from one type of intervention to another without conducting an investigation or monitoring of outcomes.

References

Boaden, R.J. and Dale, B.G. (1993) 'Managing Quality Improvement in Financial Services: A Framework and Case Study' *Service Industry Journal*, Vol. 13, No. 1: Jan, pp. 13–39.

Delbridge, R., Turnbull, P. and Wilkinson, B. (1992) 'Pushing back the Frontiers: Management Control and Work Intensification Under JIT/TQM regimes' *New Technology, Work and Employment*, Vol. 7: pp. 97–106.

Howcroft, B. (1992) 'Customer Service in Selected Branches of a UK Clearing Bank' *The Service Industries Journal*, Vol. 2, No. 1: Jan, pp. 125–142.

Hunter, L. and Beaumont, P.B. (1993) 'Implementing TQM: Top Down or Bottom up?' *Industrial Relations Journal*, Vol. 24, No. 4: pp. 318–327.

McArdle, L., Rowlinson, M., Proctor, S., Hassard, J., and Forrester, P. (1995) 'Employee Empowerment or the Enhancement of Exploitation', in A. Wilkinson and H. Willmott (eds.), *Making Quality Critical*, London: Routledge.

Parker, M. and Slaughter, J. (1993) 'Should the Labour Movement buy TQM?' *Journal of Organizational Change Management*, Vol. 6, No. 4: pp. 43–56.

Peters, T. (1990) *Liberation Management*, New York: Knopf.

Sewell, G. and Wilkinson, B. (1992) 'Someone to Watch Over Me: Surveillance, Discipline and the JIT Labour Process', *Sociology*, Vol. 26, No. 2: 271–289.

Tuckman, A. (1995) 'Ideology, Quality and TQM' in A. Wilkinson and H.C. Willmott (eds.), *Making Quality Critical*, London: Routledge.

Webb, J. and Cleary, D. (1994) *Organisational Change and the Management of Expertise*, London: Routledge.

Zairi, M., Letza, S.R. and Oakland, J.S. (1993) 'Does TQM Impact on Bottom Line Results?' University of Bradford Management Centre.

READING 5.4

Belonging on the Move: Market Rhetoric and the Future as Obligatory Passage

By Rolland Munro

Abstract

Recent neglect of the concept of belonging may be traced to its subsumption under matters of locality or kinship (concepts that have left its theorizing rather static and underdeveloped), as well as to theoretical understandings which try to keep distinct a logic of belonging from a logic of the market. In reworking a sociological tradition that formerly associated the work of managers with a specific responsibility to induce conditions of belonging, at least within bureaucratic organizations, the present study examines closely the rhetoric deployed in a large private sector organization alongside its invention of 'internal' markets. Adopting a consumption perspective, the paper argues that a 'rubbishing' of the past within organizations may be being aimed at

READING 5.4

Belonging on the Move: Market Rhetoric and the Future as Obligatory Passage

By Rolland Munro

undermining aspects of members' belonging, especially matters of tradition, loyalty and custom. In so much as these aspects once offered themselves as 'resources' for managers' accounts (to themselves, their colleagues and their superiors), their effacement as resources can be understood as helping reframe accounts in ways that not only colonize the present and characterize the future, but sustain ambiguities vital to the imposition of pseudo-market relations, such as those between 'purchasers' and 'providers'.

> ... if not content with clinging to the past, he has trespassed upon the future ...
> *Emile Durkheim*

Introduction

In so far as their arrangements operate independently of markets, private and public institutions can be thought to create interior spaces – an 'inside' where people experience feelings of belonging.

Yet with the advent of 'internal markets' in the UK public sector, much of this understanding may no longer hold. Where there is no fixed inside, no areas that cannot be bought or sold and no space which is not open to market competition, there can be no permanent insiders. Through various discourses, going back to the Hawthorne experiments in the 1920s, if not well before, managers in organizations were called upon to help create and maintain conditions of belonging. For example, the early human relations work, following Lewin, suggested 'democratic leadership' produced 'feelings of loyalty and belonging' on the way to producing 'work of the highest quality' (Rose, 1990: 86). But this attention was not to last.

> The image of economic man that human relations had appeared to have laid to rest was now resurrected. It appeared that industrial workers did not, after all, seek 'social' rewards at work or look to the organization to provide a sense of belonging. (Rose, 1990: 97) ...

Belonging and the Consumption Thesis

Against the pessimism of Baudrillard's (1983) world of simulations, in which the very possibility of belonging has been nullified as a nostalgia for the real, Bauman's (1988; 1990) relating of 'self-identity' to 'consumption' seems promising, if problematic. This is a view that no longer relates belonging to community, or locality. Rather, Bauman insists on linking, through consumption, the 'free' market to belonging. Yet how could anyone *belong* to a market? Here is how Warde criticizes Bauman's reliance on the market economy:

> The abstract consumer does not belong: individual competing consumers do not belong: competition does not, in this field, generate belonging. The free consumer makes choices that are personal and instantaneous at the point of purchase. Belonging, by contrast, implies inter-personal and constrained decisions. (Warde, 1994: 70)

This comment is seductive. Even setting aside the dubious notion of 'free' consumers, one wants to agree with Warde: the orders of the market and the orders of belonging *seem* very different.

What makes Warde's position interesting, and provocative, is that he is not taking the naive position that we no longer belong. Nor is he suggesting consumers of everyday markets have become the anonymous and mobile creatures of microeconomic theory (see Miller, 1995). Rather Warde considers that there are other orders of belonging than those of Gemeinschaft (community) and Gesellschaft (society). Warde expands this point by indicating that, within the 'neo-tribe', the logic of belonging has sufficient force to keep out the logic of the market.

However, once one belongs to a consumption niche, a subculture or whatever, the logic of the market paradigm no longer prevails (Warde, 1994: 70).

At this point, Warde's aim is clear. He is attempting to save the possibility of belonging from its extinction through the twin forces of an encroachment of the market, on the one hand, and a marketization of belonging on the other. In the fragments of postmodernity, within the spaces of what Warde calls a 'subculture or whatever', it seems that there are matters that will, by definition, not be offered for sale. And it is in this context – the erosion of bureaucracy

| ## Belonging on the Move: Market Rhetoric and the Future as Obligatory Passage *continued*

By Rolland Munro

by the advent of the 'internal market' – that seems so threatening to the spaces of belonging, the neo-tribes, the 'subcultures or whatever' that make up large and small organizations.

Moving belonging to the margins, however, seems as unsatisfactory as its nullification. If we are not to be stuck with the consequences of presupposing an inalienable difference between a logic of markets and a logic of belonging, it is important to unwrap Warde's analysis. Warde is surely right to point to 'people acting in accordance with the logic of group membership regardless of cost' (70). Yet, bearing in mind the concept of cultural capital (Bourdieu, 1984), it is important not to conflate the logic of the market with the phenomenon of certain goods, variable to any particular group, being effectively debarred from sale.

Persons clearly understand how money works: they know that money can buy goods and that goods can buy money; and they further understand that goods cannot buy other goods. This is the strict logic of the market, the elimination of barter. There is, then, a discipline within the market system. Its logic cannot be flouted willy-nilly. As Bauman (1991) makes clear, consumer freedom means the orientation of one's life to *market-approved* commodities. In Bauman's view, the freedom of the market is bought at one terrible price: there is – and this is a truth for institutions as well as individuals – no freedom *from* the market. The market appears as a 'self-organizing system' in the sense that everything has the potential to be organized 'in', at least in terms of money. Other trading systems, such as barter, are effectively organized 'out'. Flexible and all encompassing though the market is often made to seem, the notion of the market system is not entirely vacuous. Barter is excluded.

In placing all as thus belonging 'inside' the market, Bauman is equally, if in a different way to Warde, keeping separate the logic of the market, consumer freedom, from the logic of belonging, what he calls the aspiration of human liberty and the management of collective life. This brings me to the main point. An appreciation of market logic need not result in it being blindly followed as 'rational'. It is critical, indeed, not to overlook the possibility of an apparent aporia in conduct: persons who are rational enough to

understand the logic of the market may still generate conditions in which it becomes irrational always to follow this logic. People can, for example, draw on their knowledge of market logic to create good organizational reasons for circumventing the market. Thus, for economists to insist that consumers blindly follow market logic, means that they unwittingly rule out the possibility that people are rational!

The logic of the market creates itself as an effect that, like any other artefact, can be deployed for other purposes. Thus, rather than leave the market passively as an 'alter', in the form defined by Cohen (1092), its systematic feature, that of excluding barter, can be co-opted, and adapted, to create or bolster a celebration of *alternative* practices. The fact that barter is *always* excluded from the free market accomplishes itself as an artefact, positively or negatively, with which to constitute membership of specific communities. For example, groupings, such as a baby-sitting circle, can be created by a more or less tacit insistence on the return of favours in kind. While local exchange trading systems (known as LETS) go further by recording debits and credits, they reject the exchange of work for more 'global' currencies; rather than using it as a lever for extracting money in the form of interest', the point of their recording of debt is to 'bind the community together' (Purdue *et al.*, 1997: 657). Similarly, a deliberate exclusion over money for particular goods might be arranged by any group through constructing, explicitly or tacitly, rules which circumvent those of the market, such as the 'gift' of papers in academic communities. As with the exchange of favours among friends, or sexual partners, it is the very 'exclusion' of money from certain exchanges that invests relations with a special significance.

It is this inversion to the 'polluting' status (Douglas, 1966) of barter, in so-called market economies, that Warde overlooks. Rules to facilitate barter – or for that matter laws that facilitate the exchange of money for money – are culturally specific. But this is also where the existence of a market economy effectively aids and helps enforce the regulation of goods for which money must not pass. Indeed, that goods can be bought for money, and that money can buy goods, offers two possibilities for surveillance by members of a group over the conduct of other members. For

| **Belonging on the Move: Market Rhetoric and the Future as Obligatory Passage**

By Rolland Munro

example, within large organizations, time can be spent with other members of the organization in ways that would have to be accounted for, if the people concerned belonged to different organizations. Or information is exchanged within the institution in ways that prohibit it from being passed 'outside'. Nevertheless, it is crucial to see that such artefacts of surveillance are *parasitic* on the market. It is the facticity of money transactions being normal, *elsewhere,* that makes possible a scrutiny over exchanges of items debarred from sale.

A second matter Warde overlooks is that analysis seeks to illuminate social conduct, not replicate it. That various groups try to keep the social separate and distinct from the economic does not entitle social theorists to follow suit. For Mary Douglas, any attempt, analytically, to make processes of belonging *de facto* separate from the mechanisms of exchange is disastrous:

> Theories of consumption which assume a puppet consumer, prey to the advertiser's wiles, or consumers jealously competing for no sane motive, lemming consumers rushing to disaster, are frivolous, even dangerous. (Douglas and Isherwood, 1980: 89)

In Douglas and Isherwood's consumption thesis, 'any choice between goods is the result of, and contributes to, culture'. Processes of belonging are integral to devices that facilitate exchange:

> The meanings conveyed along the goods channel are part and parcel of the meanings in the kinship and mythology channels. (Douglas and Isherwood, 1980: 88)

As Friedman (1990: 327) states the matter, this line of argument 'began with the recognition that goods are building blocks of life-worlds'. And this integration of belonging with exchange is not new to the 'market' economy, it is a feature of all societies. As Cohen (1982) argues that a 'sense of belonging, of what it means to belong' is constantly evoked by 'whatever comes to hand'. Perhaps a

'readiness-to-hand' and 'disposability' makes consumer goods distinctive today and, like food, supple to identity work (see also Munro, 1995; 1996).

With these two points in mind, the pitfall of framing belonging in ways that equate it with culture *minus* markets can be avoided. First, and in line with Hegel's dictum that the very act of looking back inflates a notion of progress, the newly formed group has to be given a new ground from which to look back. The new image is one of being 'in' markets. The takeover, it seems, has forced the Group to join the 'outside world':

> The contrast between pre-Goodadverts strategy to post-Goodadverts strategy basically centred around positioning in the outside world. (Group Finance Director)

By thinking of itself as 'in' markets, the image is one of the Group being ready to meet global competition, of being world-class, of now being *outward*-looking in terms of strategy. ... Quantity or quality? Cost or flexibility? Ambiguity appears to have been placed right at the core of performance measurement.

Well, not quite. Within Worldbest, for reasons already explained, interpretability will be all on the one side; the side of the 'purchaser'. So in thinking of relations between managers in the line, something else is changing. An 'internal market' is appearing at each level of the hierarchy. On the one side, the senior, as budget holder, exists as 'purchaser'; on the other side the subordinate, as budgetee, stands as 'provider'. Any feelings of persons in the hierarchy belonging to each other, in line with previous responsibilities, seem more or less abandoned. Accountability is being restaged *as if* for the 'loan' of resources by the purchaser, the provider promises to 'deliver'.

This brings me to a discussion of the third repertoire. At work within the relations discussed above is a potential inclusion and exclusion of people and, critically, exclusion will be directed most at those 'named' by their senior as failing to deliver. Thus, the third repertoire revolves around an equally 'old' control technology, that of employment practices. In that managers are hired and fired, promoted and

Belonging on the Move: Market Rhetoric and the Future as Obligatory Passage *continued*

By Rolland Munro

demoted, made visible and made invisible, people 'come and go'. As Strathern (1982: 271) remarks in the context of her analysis of class:

> Mobility has signification only if someone can arrive and depart, move between fixed points. In putting value on the mobility of individuals, by the very same token we perpetuate the hierarchy by which the movement is measured.

Since the market, even in these administrative spaces, has become as 'inside' as it is outside, *anyone* is now replaceable. And this is so for the middle managers. As subordinate, they no longer 'belong' to a superior in quite the way that could make him or her feel 'responsible'.

At any time, a superior in Worldbest can move beyond the authority relations of traditional bureaucracy. Once images of the internal market are in play, managers can also cut the figure of a 'purchaser'. The image of a market sets up a permission to drop existing ties and select a new provider. Relations are thus no longer subject to a logic of belonging, but are made inter-dependent with market criteria. Nor is it only those employees or managers who take the plunge and become 'consultants' that should be warned, it is all those who can't or won't detach themselves from the past. All those who can't see that past help given to colleagues, or past service given to superiors, is irrelevant; all those who can't 'bite the bullet' and accept that all that stuff about loyalty and tradition is just so much water under a bridge.

The complexities of this reformulation of hierarchical relations into market relations can be considered as made up of three, interrelated, parts. First, ambiguities over strategy sustain an asymmetry in assumptions that the superior has a better knowledge base. Second, there is the ambiguity being added by the creation of additional performance measures, with its asymmetrical effect of a superior deciding which measures really count. Third, ambiguity is created over which manager is really 'inside' the organization, and who is merely 'hired'.

Of course, each of these different forms of ambiguity is potentially resolvable. For example, one interpretation of the extended range of performance measures is that one variable will always 'count' more than any of the others. Here is one view:

> Certainly the budget is the heaviest weighting in performance evaluation. It focuses on cost, yes, but everything else impacts on the budgeted costs. (Plant Director.)

Repeating that the budget 'provides a key measure of success', the plant director added that 'better information can be obtained'. Yet this 'better information', as noted, is still awaiting the information systems of the future. Failing these, interpretation is still being relied upon:

> ... at the moment gut feel still plays a large part in deciding what is successful. (Production Director.)

So once again, the superior gets to decide how to read results. And this is a system which is sufficiently justifiable to offer a deferral of the performance measurement system of the future:

> I'm sceptical about having narrowly defined the objectives as it can lead to just focusing on those being measured precisely instead of tackling the real problems. (Plant Director.)

This reads like a return to the past. But it is not quite. The ability to *resolve* ambiguity is being made to run one way: as 'purchaser', interpretability is to be all on the side of the superior.

In case it be thought that these ambiguities are already in place in most organizations, it should be added that the main point here is concerned with who is able to muster ambiguity *as a resource* in identity work. Contra Cohen's (1982) theme of ambiguity being a resource, made generally available by virtue of an epistemological bar on knowledge of the meanings behind each other's expressions, there is a marked asymmetry to the availability of resources with which to *resolve* ambiguities, when needed. All the ability to resolve ambiguity lies with the senior manager, either in a role of hierarchical superior, or in a role of 'purchaser'.

| READING 5.4 | **Belonging on the Move: Market Rhetoric and the Future as Obligatory Passage** |

By Rolland Munro

Discussion

People become aware of their culture at its boundaries. This now familiar theme formed the premise for the second set of essays in Cohen's (1982) edited volume, addressing the problem of members 'belonging to the whole'. It is a theme which tied feelings of belonging closely to culture, while avoiding the more facile conflation of community with localities. Yet this conjunction of belonging with culture was a theme which met immediate opposition within itself, notably in the form of Strathern's essay on the 'real Elmdoners', whose distinctiveness placed 'little stress on cultural criteria ... and considerable stress on a sense of belonging' (1982).

Drawing on the example of Worldbest, I have explicated how the process of calling for accounts was reworked in ways that put belonging on the move. In particular, by investigating a 'rubbishing' of the past, the paper has suggested how it is *images* of the market – more than the market itself – which may be having effects. Once images are in play, they act as resources that can be drawn upon for identity-making. Images of markets do not offer themselves, therefore, as mirrors of practice, so much as they are themselves *expressive*. Arriving in the form of discourse, images set up 'permissions' for employees to draw on one form of words instead of another. The discourse effect is that one form of words registers, objectively, *as if* it is an 'argument', or 'the way forward'; while another form of words is heard by others merely as an 'excuse', or is read as the speaker being 'resistant' to change. As one form of words takes on resonance, and becomes repeated, so another 'older' form of words becomes marginalized, or silenced.

In studying *how* change is advertised in a large UK organization, I have attempted to dislodge the readily available critique of managers as concerned only with efficiency and effectiveness. I have stressed, instead, that battles over affiliation and belonging are already, and always, at work. For example, managers at Worldbest were incited to belong to the 'outside world' – a world of markets – at the very moment that markets were being created 'inside' the organization by adoption of the structure of 'purchasers' and 'providers'. Where this is so, internal markets do more than suggest themselves as a response to ruptures in 'external' markets. With careful analysis, they indicate different *configurations* of artefacts are in play and, with this, clarify the potential, both for control and for forms of resistance.

This stress on the production of subjectivities, while proceeding in very different ways, comes to some similar conclusions to that of Althusser (1971: 182):

> the individual is interpellated as a (free) subject in order that he shall submit freely to the commandments of the Subject ... [and] ... (freely) accept his subjection.

However, in pointing to an ambivalence in Althusser over the concept of interpellation, between being *either* the means of engagement with subjects *or* the mode of constitution of subjects, Krips (1994: 70) has proposed to arrest this 'equivocation' and reconceive interpellation as the process by which 'antagonisms constitute subjects and desires'. Krips continues:

> being won by *individuals* from a continuous, if fragmented, negotiation of human interaction. The very elusiveness of belonging is still underwriting the spectre of anomie stalking Western society. Even when cultural geographers examine 'place myths' (Shields, 1991), the 'social centrality' involves a 'wilful concentration which creates a node in a wider landscape of continual dispersion' (Shields, 1992: 103).

Perhaps Worldbest at the time of the study veered to an extreme, rather than is typical. In other institutions, the hospital, the council, the university, it may be more obvious that 'new' and 'old' images of organization do not replace each other. More likely, they create an *intertextuality* for the subject, a need to move skilfully between talk of the future and a ceremonial evocation of the past. Different forms of accountability provide different dangers, whose co-presence may incite someone look back to 'custom' and 'precedent', and at other times make them look to 'strategy' and 'the way forward'.

READING 5.4

Belonging on the Move: Market Rhetoric and the Future as Obligatory Passage *continued*

By Rolland Munro

References

Althusser, L. (1971), 'Ideology and ideological state apparatuses', in *Lenin and Philosophy and Other Essays*, pp. 121–186, London: New Left Books.

Baudrillard, J. (1983), *Simulations*, translated by P. Foss *et al.*, New York: Semiotext(e).

Bauman, Z. (1988), *Freedom*, Milton Keynes: Open University Press.

Bauman, Z. (1990), *Thinking Sociologically*, Oxford: Blackwell.

Bauman, Z. (1991), *Modernity and Ambivalence*, Cambridge: Polity Press.

Bourdieu, P. (1984), *Distinction: a Social Critique of the Judgement of Taste*, translated by R. Nice, London: Routledge.

Campbell, C. (1995), 'The sociology of consumption', in D. Miller, (ed.), *Acknowledging Consumption: a review of new studies*, pp. 96–126. London: Routledge.

Cohen, A.P. (ed.) (1982), *Belonging: Identity and Social Organization in British Rural Cultures*, Manchester: Manchester University Press.

Douglas, M. (1966), *Purity and Danger: An Analysis of Concepts of Pollution and Taboo*, London: Routledge and Kegan Paul.

Douglas, M. and Isherwood, B. (1980), *The World of Goods: towards an anthropology of consumption*, Harmondsworth: Penguin.

Friedman, J. (1990), 'Being in the world: globalization and localization', *Theory, Culture & Society*, Vol. 8: 311–328.

Knights, D. and Willmott, H.C. (1987), 'Organisational culture as management strategy: a critique and illustration from the financial services industry', *International Studies in Management and Organisation*, Vol. XVII, No. 3: 4–63.

Krips, H. (1994), 'Interpellation, antagonism, repetition', *Rethinking Marxism*, Vol. 7, No. 4: 59–71.

Miller, D. (1995), 'Consumption as the vanguard of history: a polemic by way of an introduction', in D. Miller, (ed.), *Acknowledging Consumption: a review of new studies*, pp. 1–57, London: Routledge.

Munro, R. (1995), 'Disposal of the meal', in D. Marshall, (ed.), *Food Choice and the Food Consumer*, pp. 313–325, Glasgow: Blackie, (1995).

Munro, R. (1996), 'The consumption view of self: extension, exchange and identity', in S. Edgell, K. Hetherington and A. Warde, (eds.), *Consumption Matters: the production and experience of consumption*, pp. 248–273, The Sociological Review Monograph. Oxford: Blackwell.

Purdue, D., Durrschmidt, J. P.Jowers and O'Doherty, R. (1997), 'DIY culture and extended milieaux; LETS, veggie boxes and festivals', *The Sociological Review*, Vol. 45, No. 4: 645–667.

Shields, R. (1991), *Places on the Margin: alternative geographies of modernity*, London: Routledge.

Shields, R. (1992), 'Individuals, consumption cultures and the fate of community' in R. Shields (ed.), *Lifestyle Shopping: the subject of consumption*, pp. 99–113, London: Routledge.

Strathern, M. (1982a), 'The place of kinship; kin, class and village status in Elmdon, Essex', in A.P. Cohen, (ed.), *Belonging: identity and social organization in British rural cultures*, pp. 72–100, Manchester: Manchester University Press.

Warde, A. (1994), 'Consumers, identity, and belonging: reflections on some theses of Zygmunt Bauman' in R. Keat, N. Whiteley, and N. Abercrombie, *The Authority of the Consumer*, pp. 58–74, London: Routledge.

Discussion Questions

1. In what ways does organizational change and innovation emerge not directly out of management designs?
2. To what extent can teamworking be seen as an organizational innovation that facilitates management control?
3. Can you provide an account of how and why people lower down the hierarchy are sometimes more committed to innovations than the managers who introduce them?
4. Do you think that a concern for identity and belonging is one of the more effective tools in managing change and innovation?

Introduction References

Eccles, R.G. and Nohria, N. (1992) *Beyond the Hype: Rediscovering the Essence of Management*, Cambridge, MA: Harvard Business School Press.

Habermas, J. (1975) *Legitimation Crisis*, Boston, MA: Beacon Press.

Roy, D. (1952) 'Restriction of Ouput in a Piecework Machine Shop' *PhD Dissertation*, University of Chicago.

Tompkins, P.K. and Cheney, G. (1985). Communication and unobtrusive control. In R. McPhee and P.K. Tompkins (eds.), *Organizational communication: Traditional themes and new directions*. Beverly Hills, CA: Sage, pp. 179–210.

Recommended Further Readings

See references above to Barker, Knights and McCabe, and Munro plus:

Argyris, C. (1992) *On Organizational Learning*, Oxford: Blackwell.

Barker, J.R. (1999) *The Discipline of Teamwork*, London: Sage.

Hammer, M. and Champy, J. (1993) '*Reengineering the Corporation: A Manifesto For Business Revolution*, London: Nicholas Brealey Publishing.

Fairhurst, G.T. (1993) 'Echoes of the vision when the rest of the organization talks total quality' *Management Communication Quarterly*, Vol. 6, No. 4: May 331–71.

Fairhurst, G.T. and Wendt, R.F. (1993) 'The Gap in Total Quality A Commentary' *Management Communication Quarterly*, Vol. 6, No. 4: 441–51.

Klimoski, R. (1994) 'A "total quality" Special Issue' *Academy of Management Review*, 19: 390–391.

Knights, D. and Willmott, H. (eds.) *The Reengineering Revolution*. Sage: London.

McCabe, D. (2000) 'Factory innovations and management machinations: the productive and repressive relations of power' *Journal of Management Studies*, Vol. 37, No. 7: 931–53.

McCabe, D., Knights, D., Kerfoot, D., Morgan, G. and Willmott, H. (1998) 'Making Sense of "Quality" – Towards a Review and Critique of Quality Initiatives in Financial Sevices' *Human Relations*, Vol. 51, No. 3: 389–411.

Watson, T.J. (1994) *In Search of Management*, London: Routledge.

HUMAN RESOURCE MANAGEMENT

CHAPTER **6**

READINGS

Legge, K. (2005) *Human Resource Management – Rhetorics and Realities.* Anniversary Edition. Basingstoke: Macmillan Press. pp. 101–31.

Kerfoot, D. and Knights, D. (1992) 'Planning for Personnel? HRM Reconsidered' in *Journal of Management Studies*, Vol. 29, No. 5: 651–68.

Townley, B. (1997) 'Foucault, Power/Knowledge, and its Relevance for Human Resource Management' in *Postmodern Management Theory*. Edited by Marta B. & Linda Smircich. Ashgate: Aldershot. pp. 515–41.

Jacques, R. (1999) 'Developing a Tactical Approach to Engaging with 'Strategic' HRM' in *Organization*, Vol. 6, No. 2: 199–222. Extracts 199–201; 216–17.

INTRODUCTION

While there has always been a function in organizations that could be described as managing the human resource, it is only in the last 20 years or so that a specialism called human resource management (HRM) has existed. It was a development partly made inevitable by the increasing size of organizations and the rise of management as agents of absentee capital owners. Paternalistic forms of management, largely adopted by owner managers who treated their employees as an extension of their families, were less convincing once there was a separation of ownership and control and when size precluded regular face-to-face interaction between senior management and staff. Personnel administration arose to fill the gap left by the impossibility of managing each employee personally. Following in the footsteps of other bureaucratic procedures for organizing activities in a uniform, equitable and standardized manner, personnel administration provided the formal means of ensuring an orderly management of employees from recruitment to displacement. This involved a variety of tasks including personnel record maintenance, employee benefits, equal opportunity, health and safety, appraisal, job evaluation, training, promotion, and retirement issues. In many companies the personnel manager was also responsible for industrial relations matters such as collective negotiation with local employee representatives or the trade union at a regional or national level. At the height of union power in the 1960s and 1970s, however, this task was often passed onto an industrial relations manager who usually had board status if the company was a public limited corporation (plc).

That industrial relations was frequently seen as too important for the personnel manager was an indication of the relatively low esteem in which the function was regarded by other managers and in the organization as a whole. Line managers would seek to appropriate those activities (e.g. selection and recruitment, promotion) that they saw as having a direct bearing on production. Perceiving the personnel department as primarily an administrative support function, the line would resist any significant managerial intervention. Sometimes viewed as the conscience of the organization because of their close association with the rights and welfare of employees, it is not surprising that personnel managers had a comparatively low status. The feminization of the function did not help to ameliorate this low status. For despite much anti-discriminatory legislation, gendered job segregation, broken careers and unequal pay have contributed to a continued inequality of opportunity between the sexes (Collinson et al., 1990) and an associated demise of occupations such as Personnel that attract a disproportionate number of women.

By the 1980s a new opportunity to enhance the role and standing of personnel management arose and the new designation human resource management (HRM) began to be adopted. A number of conditions had coincided to give the impetus to the HRM function to assert itself in a proactive fashion rather than simply administering personnel matters. Stimulated by economic deregulation, attention had shifted toward strategic planning of a company's activities within a situation of greater market competition enhanced by an ideology of entrepreneurialism. The growth and comparative cheapness of new technology had combined with the growing cost of labour to culminate in recognition that the human resource was a company's greatest asset. Consequently, the new HRM emerged not only to exploit this asset to its full potential but also to ensure that a strategy for the human resource was firmly embedded in the corporate strategy. At a stroke, HRM was both necessary in the boardroom where it had been previously conspicuous by its absence and central to strategic planning in major companies. Academics, consultants and gurus rushed onto the bandwagon of a newly elevated function to enhance its and their own material and symbolic importance. Ever since, there has been considerable debate in the literature about the actual difference between HRM and personnel management and the extent to which the HRM strategy to improve the status of the personnel function has been successful.

Karen Legge (Reading 6.1) reaches the conclusion that since there is little chance of an integration of HRM and corporate and business strategy, it might be argued that HRM is no more than a rhetorical device for elevating personnel management. It is for this reason that she spends a good deal of time asking what HRM is and how it differs from personnel management.

While Legge identifies four models of HRM, the major distinction is between the normative, the behavioural and the critical. *Normative models* may be seen to prescribe certain minimum conditions for the concept of HRM to apply. Ordinarily it suggests that HRM differs from personnel management insofar as it attempts to integrate the personnel or HR function with the strategy as defined by the senior management in the organization. Guest (1987), for example, argues that the goals of HRM are integration, employee commitment, flexibility and adaptability and quality. The *behavioural models* attempt to describe what HRM does without acknowledging that all descriptions are a selection based on certain values. They describe the various practices (e.g. recruitment, job design and training, pay and performance) and management theory perspectives (e.g. scientific management, human relations, Fordism, strategy, flexible specialisation, Just in Time, quality management) without recognizing that this helps to legitimize and reproduce them. *Critical models*, by contrast, argue that HRM is often a mask or smokescreen for what is the unacceptable face of the enterprise culture. Having presented the alternatives, Legge then takes the normative model, as presented by Guest (1987) and puts it to the test of practice, concluding that HRM, whether 'soft' (a humanistic approach) or 'hard' (a preoccupation with efficiency and measurable performance) has only been adopted in a few sites. If HRM means the integration of managing employees with strategic planning as a whole, hardly any organizations comply. Since a great deal of management is characterized by 'seat of the pants' decision-making, Legge suggests that the HRM of academic discourse is more symbolic than material and more 'rhetoric' than 'reality'.

The **Kerfoot and Knights** extract (Reading 6.2) focuses on the discrepancies between policy and practice that belie the rhetoric where HRM is seen to represent a more strategic mode of managing personnel than what went before. The argument of the article is that HRM type practices may arise and be developed in the absence of HRM policies or even when such policies seem to have little comparative effect in directing organizational change. Through an intensive empirical case study, it was found that certain HRM practices emerged at lower levels of the hierarchy and more or less by accident rather than by design. When struggling to recruit staff for transitional periods of high demand for labour because of seasonal peaks in business, a number of mature women were employed on a temporary or part time basis. These women often had lifetime experience of bringing up children and managing a home in addition to engaging in part-time work. As a result, they had developed numerous unacknowledged skills that prove extremely valuable in managing work situations and, in particular, the social complexities of teamworking. Without guidance or training, these mature women seemed often to fall naturally into an informal leadership role within the teams in which they worked. This was doubly advantageous to the company in that their implicit and therefore formally 'free' managerial skills facilitated the smooth working of teams and thus complemented the formal function of team leaders. Recognizing the value of these workers, HRM began a positive campaign to recruit them, although this policy had little relationship to the strategic planning of HRM at the executive level. Supporting Legge's analysis, this finding sits uncomfortably with the view that

HRM policy is formulated at the highest levels as an integrated strategy that supports the corporate mission.

Barbara Townley (Reading 6.3) has built a reputation around applying the insights of Michel Foucault to the HRM field and, like many of the extracts in this section, focuses more on the academic discipline of HRM than directly on its practice. She argues that the discipline of HRM is largely informed by functionalism or systems theory where the preoccupation is to identify and give scientific credibility to those features of an organization or society that may be seen to facilitate its smooth functioning and orderly stability. HRM discourses then ordinarily examine the techniques of managing the human resource with the aim of improving their efficiency and effectiveness. In short, HRM discourse is managerialist in its objective to help managers reproduce or transform the social arrangements already in place within the organization of labour so as to contribute significantly and more effectively to the organization's goals, be they profit or public service. Critical perspectives are quite rare in this field for even when a critical claim is made, texts often revert back to a managerialist attempt to prescribe how to improve HRM techniques and practices. Townley's adoption of Foucault provides an alternative where the aim is to provide an analysis of what HRM is doing in the sense of the knowledge and power it creates. The emphasis is on how the techniques 'fix' individual employees in time and space, thus transforming them into manageable objects of the power-knowledge that constitutes HRM as a practice. The discourse is then a way of rationally classifying, ordering, grading and measuring the population of employees so as to bring them within the systematic disciplinary gaze of HRM control.

Roy Jacques (Reading 6.4) questions the binary opposition between managerialists and critical theorists with respect to 'strategic' HRM. He begins by rejecting the concern that many authors (including those above) have with what HRM is, as if it had an essential nature, in favour of asking what are its effects. He believes that the concept of HRM came about because there was some rupture in the managerialist organizational hegemony due to the ineffectiveness of centralizing and rationalizing organizational resources along classical management theory lines. HRM, then, opens up the question of power relations (see section on Power, Chapter 8) since managers see that treating labour as merely a capital resource is self-defeating, but this raises the scope for critics to identify points of contradiction where interventions can reverse managerial hegemony. It is Jacques' view that while managerialists may be too preoccupied with maximizing profit, critical theorists too often deny its significance because they subscribe to an outdated concept of management versus labour. Without output and profit, there is nothing over which to negotiate in terms of dividing up the spoils more equitably. Moreover, in today's knowledge-intensive workplaces, the old divisions between managers and labour no longer hold since more and more employees are engaged in types of work that could be classified as management. Following de Certeau (1984), Jacques suggests a tactical engagement with, rather than a strategic approach to HRM since this facilitates a more productive relationship between management and labour than either managerialist or critical approaches allow.

READING 6.1 | Human Resource Management – Rhetorics and Realities

By Karen Legge

Introduction

'Personnel management' has increasingly given way to 'human resource management' (HRM) or, better still, to 'strategic human resource management'. Nor is this shift exclusively confined to those followers of fashion, the commercial management consultants. It may be charted first in the writings of US academics and managers (for example, Tichy *et al.*, 1982; Fombrun *et al.*, 1984; Beer and Specter, 1985; ...). Quickly, however, the term was taken up by both UK managers (for example, Armstrong, 1987; Fowler, 1987) and UK academics (for example, Guest, 1987; Storey, 1987 ...). By the end of the 1980s and the beginning of the 1990s the floodgates were open.

Both managers and academics, particularly in the UK, have recognized the problem of identifying clear differences between personnel management and HRM ... [but] ...

We can take two approaches. First, we can ask whether their normative models differ; secondly, whether their descriptive–behavioural models–their respective practices differ.

Similarities

First, a close comparison suggests that there are clear similarities between the two.

1. Both models emphasize the importance of integrating personnel/HRM practices with organizational goals ...
2. Both models vest personnel/HRM firmly in line management.
3. Both models ... emphasize the importance of individuals fully developing their abilities for their own personal satisfaction to make their 'best contribution' to organizational success ...
4. Both models identify placing the 'right' people into the 'right' jobs as an important means of integrating personnel/HRM practice with organizational goals, including individual development ...

So, is there any difference between the normative models of HRM and those of personnel management? One is tempted to say 'not a lot'. And, indeed,

the sharp contrasts that Guest (1987) elicits in his comparison of what he terms personnel management and human resource management 'stereotypes', in spite of his disclaimers, appear to owe much to an implicit comparison of the *descriptive* practice of personnel management with the *normative* aspirations of HRM, rather than comparing like with like ...

Differences

The differences between the normative models of personnel and human resource management are more those of meaning and emphasis than substance – but nonetheless 'real' for that.

1. First, many statements about personnel management when placed in the context of the texts from which they are derived, seem to see it as a management activity which is largely aimed at non-managers. Apart from management development (often treated as a separate activity or function), personnel management appears to be something performed on subordinates by managers rather than something that the latter experience themselves – other than as a set of rules and procedures that may constrain their freedom in managing their subordinates as they think fit. HRM, on the other hand, not only emphasizes the importance of employee development but focuses particularly on development of the management team ... This shift of emphasis appears related to two other differences.

2. The second is that while both personnel management and HRM highlight the role of line management, the focus is different. In the personnel management models, line's role is very much an expression of the view that all managers manage people, so all managers in a sense carry out 'personnel management'. It also carries the recognition that most specialist personnel work still has to be implemented within line management's departments where the workforce is physically located. In the HRM models, HRM is vested in line management as business

READING 6.1

Human Resource Management – Rhetorics and Realities *continued*

By Karen Legge

managers responsible for coordinating and directing all resources in the business unit in pursuit of bottom line results ...

3. The third difference is that most HRM models emphasize the management of the organization's culture as the central activity for senior management ... Peters and Waterman's (1982) linking of 'strong cultures' with financial success (however spurious), along with American management's fascination with the linkages between a stereotyped 'Japanese' employment culture and Japanese economic strength, has raised the development and management of an appropriate culture as the strategic or 'transformational' leadership activity, that gives direction, a sense of purpose and involvement to all organizational members. It is through an integrated and internally consistent set of HR policies in relation to recruitment, selection, training, development, rewarding and communications, that the organization's core values can best be conveyed, according to the normative HRM models. Integration, therefore, is a doubly important issue – not just integration of HRM policies with strategy, but the internal integration and consistency of HRM policies themselves to enact a coherent 'strong' culture. The normative personnel management models do not present personnel policies as senior management's instrument for reinforcing or changing organizational values in a manner consistent with preferred business strategy.

These three differences in emphasis all point to HRM, in theory being essentially a more central strategic management task than personnel management in that it is experienced by managers, as the most valued company resource to be managed, it concerns them in the achievement of business goals and it expresses senior management's preferred organizational values. From this perspective, it is not surprising that Fowler (1987, p. 3) identifies the real difference between HRM and personnel management as 'not what it is, but who is saying it' (See Jacques, Reading 6.4 for a slightly different view). In a nutshell HRM 're-presents the discovery of personnel management by

chief executives'. If this is so what factors stimulated such a belated discovery?

HRM Revisited: The Critical-Evaluative Model

It is against this backdrop, contextualizing the emergence of HRM, that a very different set of models may be introduced. Several commentators ... have recognized a puzzle. On the one hand there is much hype about the change from personnel management to HRM, on the other, little evidence that either of the HRM models already outlined are being implemented consistently or on a scale commensurate to the hype (cf. Storey, 1992b) ... It can be argued that there is little difference between *normative* models of HRM and personnel management, although there are clear contrasts between the normative models of HRM and the *descriptive–behavioural* model of personnel management. Furthermore, if we accept the contingent perspective of the 'hard' HRM model, it allows for the equation of HRM with most of the existent employee relations styles; if we accept the absolutist perspective of the 'soft' HRM model, it looks very similar to the long-established sophisticated human relations model (see also Marchington, 1992). So why all the excitement?

Sceptical commentators would take the following critical view. The importance of HRM lies not in the objective reality of its normative models and their implementation but in the phenomenological reality of its rhetoric. It should be understood as a cultural construction comprising a series of metaphors redefining the meaning of work and the way individual employees relate to their employers. Just as a metaphor gives new meaning to the familiar by relating it to the unfamiliar (and vice versa), so those that comprise HRM can give a new, managerially prescribed meaning to employment experiences that, within a pluralist perspective might be considered unpalatable.

Conclusion: HRM in Action

Having considered normative, descriptive–functional and critical–evaluative models of HRM, we now need to go on to identify what is enacted in practice – quite apart from the rhetoric considered briefly in the preceding discussion.

READING 6.1	**Human Resource Management – Rhetorics and Realities**

By Karen Legge

In looking at what HRM 'should be' two different perspectives have been identified. The one sees HRM in a contingent light – as a strategically oriented perspective on personnel management cohering with business strategy. This contingent perspective seems to owe most to the 'hard' version of the HRM model – and is the one favoured by the Michigan School (Fombrun *et al.*, 1984) in the US. The other sees HRM in absolutist terms – as a special variant of personnel management, typified by the 'mutuality' model of the Harvard School in the US, and Guest's (1991) representation of such principles in the UK. Just what the model might look like in substantive rather than categorizing terms has been succinctly summarized by Sisson (1994b, pp. 7–9) (see Figure 6.1.1).

Beliefs and Assumptions

Business and customer (internal and external) needs are main referent. Search for excellence and quality and continuous improvement are dominant values. Aim to go 'beyond contract'; emphasis on 'can-do' outlook and high energy. Widespread use of team analogy and metaphors. High levels of trust. HRM central to business strategy

Managerial Role

Top managers are highly visible and provide a vision for the future that employees can share. They also offer transformational 'leadership', setting the mission and values of the organization. Middle managers inspire, encourage, enable and facilitate change by harnessing commitment and cooperation of employees; they also see the development of employees as a primary role.

Organisation Design

'Federal', highly decentralised 'flat' organisation structures. Job design congruent with organisation structure, technology and personnel policies. 'Cross-functional' project teams and informal groups responsible for particular products or services or customers; they 'contract' contribution to organisation with jobs defined in terms of team role. Teams enjoy large measure of autonomy and there is great deal of 'task' flexibility, if not interchangeability between members

Personnel Policies

Numerical flexibility, i.e. core and periphery workforce. Time flexibility, e.g. annual hours etc. Single status, i.e. reward, etc. of core employees reflects contribution Selection—emphasis on attitudes as well as skills. Appraisal—open and participative with emphasis on two-way feedback. Training—learning, growth and development of core employees are fundamental values; lateral as well as upward career advancement with emphasis on 'general' as well as 'specific' 'employability'. Equal opportunities reward systems—individual and group performance pay; skill-based pay; profit and gain sharing; share ownership; flexible benefits package, e.g. 'cafeteria' principle. Participation and involvement—extensive use of two-way communication and Problem-solving groups.

FIGURE 6.1.1	SISSON'S MODEL OF THE HRM ORGANIZATION

READING 6.1

Human Resource Management – Rhetorics and Realities *continued*

By Karen Legge

References

Armstrong, M. (1987) 'Human resource management: a case of the emperor's new clothes:', *Personnel Management*, 19(8): 30–5.

Beer, M. and Spector, B. (1985) 'Corporate-wide transformations in human resource management', in R.E. Walton and P.R. Lawrence (eds.), *Human Resource Management Trends and Challenges*, Boston: Havard Business School Press, 219–53.

Fombrun, C., Tichy, N.M. and Devanna, M.A. (eds) (1984) *Strategic Human Resource Management*, New York: Wiley.

Guest, D.E. (1987) 'Human resource management and industrial relations', *Journal of Management Studies*, 24(5): 503–21.

Guest, D.E. (1991) 'Personnel management: the end of orthodoxy?', *British Journal of Industrial Relations*, 29(2): 149–76.

Marchington, M. (1992) *Managing the Team: A Guide to Successful Employee Involvement*, Oxford: Blackwell.

Peters, T.J. and Waterman, R.H. Jr. (1982) *In Search of Excellence, Lessons from America's Best Run Companies*, New York: Harper and Row.

Sisson, K. (1994b) 'Personnel management: paradigms, practice and prospects', in K. Sisson (ed.), *Personnel Management* (2nd edn), Oxford: Blackwell, 3–50.

Storey, J. (1987) 'Developments in the management of human resources: an interim report', *Warwick Papers in Industrial Relations*, 17, IRRU, School of Industrial and Business Studies: University of Warwick (November).

READING 6.2

Planning for Personnel? HRM Reconsidered

By Deborah Kerfoot and David Knights

Since the 1980s the discourse of human resource management (HRM) has begun to establish itself in management thinking and practice as well as within the academic and consultant literature. Claims have been made on its behalf to the effect that it represents a significant element in the current displacement of earlier adversarial systems of industrial/employment relations. Although on investigation organizational practices do not often live up to the rhetoric, HRM is portrayed as a self-conscious set of practices designed to integrate business strategy and the management of human resources. Indeed, the Chief Executive in the case study presented in this article had precisely such ideals in mind. What we have found, however, is a much greater discontinuity between policy and practice or senior management intention and organizational effects within this particular company. Despite failing to create for the personnel division a central strategic function, certain practices emerged in managing the routines of work lower down the hierarchy, which could be seen at least as having the flavour of HRM. The argument

of the article is that HRM type practices can develop in the absence of HRM policies or in the event of their comparative failure to direct organizational change.

Human Resource Management in Perspective

Contemporary managerial literatures frequently suggest that traditional practices of managing personnel are increasingly being displaced by 'human resource management' (HRM). Yet a diversity of views about the content of HRM … [see previous reading] … and an undoubted 'elasticity in the meaning of the term' (Storey, 1989, p.8) render its usage both variable and imprecise. Clearly, much of the debate about human resource management could be regarded as an outcrop of the current interest in corporate and business strategy. 'Strategic management' has assumed an overwhelming significance among practitioners as a result of being heavily promoted in the popular management literature (e.g. Peters and Waterman, 1982) and subjected to a 'hard sell' by management consultants. Academics have also contributed to the populism

Source: Reproduced with permission of Wiley-Blackwell from 'Planning for Personnel? HRM Reconsidered', in the Journal of Management Studies © *1992 Wiley and Sons Ltd.*

READING 6.2

Planning for Personnel? HRM Reconsidered

By Deborah Kerfoot and David Knights

of the concept of strategy (Knights and Morgan, 1991). From this perspective, the view is that long term corporate and business planning makes little sense independently of a strategic management of employees through HRM.

In its North American context, the genesis of HRM can be traced to the Harvard Business School MBA where HRM was established as an alternative to traditional courses in personnel management (Guest, 1990; Hendry and Pettigrew, 1990). A number of conditions appear to have stimulated the shift toward strategic thinking on personnel related matters (cf. Guest, 1990), thus contributing to the establishment of a 'new industrial relations' (Kochan *et al.*, 1986) in the US at this time. First there was an increasing problem for corporate America of world competition and in particular, the growing trade deficit in the 1970s and 1980s. Second was the specific competition stemming from Japanese industry where managements appeared to have cultivated more flexible and productive workforces. Third, and of increasing importance, was the spread of thinking on corporate strategy, growing from new ways of accounting for and calculating business expansion and development (Hoskin and MaCVE, 1986).

As some writers (Storey and Sisson, 1990) have argued, the particular conditions within which HRM emerged in mid-1980s Britain were partly responsible for the 'transformation' of the personnel function in the UK being markedly less prevalent here than in the American context. In particular, the changing climate of industrial relations following the New Right politics and economics of this period only tended to reinforce an ad hoc approach to management in UK companies ... [Despite a managerial rhetoric of managing human resources strategically, this is certainly how events unfolded in our case study where much more effective policies evolved in the lower reaches of the hierarchy] ...

The Case Study

Pensco is a medium sized mutual life insurance company, which has operated very successfully in a niche market within financial services over several decades. A variety of methods of research were adopted over a total period of three years including formal questionnaires, semi-structured in-depth interviews with managers and staff, tape recorded management meetings, documentary investigation of records on company policy and practice, historical literature and participant observation.

A central feature of the programme for 'modernizing' and 'professionalizing' Pensco had been the introduction of a corporate strategy built around a set of 'business and action plans'. Within this, the CE was committed to giving personnel a central strategic function in accordance with certain elements of his understanding of HRM ...

In order to advance the plan for an upgraded personnel division, the CE sanctioned a considerable increase in resources, which included the recruitment of a new personnel manager and a number of personnel assistants of middle ranking grade. At the same time as these developments were taking place, the CE was attempting to restructure his senior management team. He had secured the early retirement of the Assistant General Manager (AGM) of personnel, but in replacing him, another objective intervened which proved to be incompatible with the overall aim to establish personnel as a central strategic function. Some time before the CE was fully in charge, and against his better judgement, his predecessor had promoted someone (Peter) to the role of AGM in customer services. Peter subsequently failed to reach the 'high' standards of the new regime, judged by the speed of processing documents during the busy 'annual bulge' period. The CE used this failure as an excuse to replace Peter, and give him the AGM vacancy in the personnel division.

Whether this restructuring was intended to ensure the failure, which led ultimately to Peter's resignation cannot be confirmed. But the new appointment was inappropriate for Peter was a trained actuary with no expertise of, or experience in, personnel management. He also subscribed to the 'old traditions of paternalism', incongruous with the demands of the new regime ...

Team Building in Pensco

At the core of the CE's programme for corporate change was the concept of building a company-wide

READING 6.2

Planning for Personnel? HRM Reconsidered *continued*

By Deborah Kerfoot and David Knights

team. This incorporated a combination of the following three elements. The first was 'flattening' the occupational status hierarchy by means of reducing vertically the number of status demarcations ... A second element was the reorganization of clerical work practices into team-based production groups and within this, the regrouping of large numbers of low grade clerical workers into semi-self regulatory work groups, as reported on below. The third element was an attempt to introduce a management system characterized by increasing 'openness' and greater employee participation, as part of a two-way communication flow throughout the remaining levels of the company. The overall package was aimed at generating a unified company identity to facilitate the attainment of managerial objectives emerging from the corporate strategy ...

Participatory sessions were organized on a divisional basis as a result of a directive 'from the top', administered by the training section of personnel, and conducted by management in each division. Sessions involved groups of employees attending exercises in what was billed as 'participation and feedback'.

Follow-up training at the behest of the 'higher ups' was organized by a training manager in personnel who was not only doubtful of management's commitment to providing the required finance for the initiative, but who felt herself to be overworked and struggling with inadequate resources on a daily basis. Her doubts were confirmed when it shortly transpired that insufficient time, money and labour had been allocated for the bulk of the task, as was commitment from a number of staff in the training area of personnel.

Attending one of the team building communication sessions, we found that a majority of the 35 staff present were critical of the company in general terms. While this may perhaps be expected of employees, staff also complained of their enforced attendance at the meetings, given that work and unanswered telephone calls would simply pile up in their absence. Most also doubted the company's sincerity regarding the whole team building programme, and were sceptical of management's competence to fulfill the ideals that it laid down. Staff were more 'realistic' with

respect to the hierarchical nature of the employment relationship, recognizing fundamental contradictions in the idealistic image of the 'flattened' hierarchy and the company-wide team. A comment typical of these views from among numerous examples was expressed as follows:

> If I walked out of here and got hit by a bus, they could get someone else to do this job tomorrow. Everyone's dispensable ... They wouldn't like us all to get hit by the same bus at the same time. That would be very inconvenient.

Many were critical of management's attachment to a particular 'fad of the month', and of the company's failure even barely to resource many of its previous initiatives.

Despite all the talk about 'people-oriented' management, in the end what seemed to count were budgetary targets, cutting costs arid improving productivity.

> You come back, your overtime is slashed, you're understaffed because of the budget and they still want standards to be maintained. A lot of people at my level are leaving (Colin, Junior Supervisor).

Clearly there was more than a degree of scepticism about the teambuilding programme on the part of these staff but this extended also into the ranks of lower and middle management. As one of the departmental managers put it:

> They can see they're being patronized ... Making them feel part of a team when really, everyone's here to do a job of work and if you don't, certain consequences follow. In a way I feel it's cosmetic ...

... Although consistent with the company's recent commitment to strategic planning, the greater attention to team working had been the outcome of the more immediate concerns of line management to retain staff and improve productive performance. Of particular concern to management then, was the opportunity that these working arrangements provided for creating team and divisional rivalry, and competition

READING 6.2	**Planning for Personnel? HRM Reconsidered**
	By Deborah Kerfoot and David Knights

over the achievement of key performance tasks. By inducing 'ownership' of the work tasks in groups of individuals identified as teams, these changes eventually manifested themselves in increased productivity and the better retention of a labour force increasingly subject to high turnover ... For example in the company's largest division – Customer Service – staff turnover rates fell from a high of almost 50 per cent per year to around 13 per cent, whilst the increase in productivity measured by time targets for processing each document rose from 70 per cent to 95 per cent ... In the following discussion section, we explore the divergent and contrasting effectiveness of the formal 'top down' team building programme with the more informal system of teamworking.

Discussion

As has been suggested earlier, the literature has a tendency to advance a complex ideal model of HRM, which bears a questionable relationship to contemporary management and organizational practice. Neither American nor British industry has 'lived up to' the model, leading to claims or criticisms that HRM is more myth than reality. Our scepticism of this approach to understanding change in the management of organizations is based on a theoretically informed analysis of the empirical data so far presented. The changes in Pensco derive *not* directly from an ideal model of 'good' practice or even from the policy intentions of senior management, but were contingent upon a diverse range of often unconnected and uncoordinated organizational processes. Changes in traditional working arrangements were stimulated by a number of coincidental factors, sustained by managers much lower down the hierarchy, but made possible by the encouragement of a Chief Executive who was routinely circumventing his AGM of personnel in seeking to transform organizational practice.

By virtue of an element of camaraderie and self-organization, team members tended also to become more committed to achieving high standards in performing their tasks if only to outwit or outdo their neighbours in other teams. Team competitions promoted by management further reinforced this

self-discipline as members developed a greater degree of internal solidarity and team identity.

... Despite management claims of success with team building, the improved working practices and self-discipline derived much more from slowly evolving and contingent changes in team working occurring in the lower reaches of the organization. Some of these improvements were enhanced as an unintended consequence of resolving recruitment shortages by employing 'mature entrant' women; for it emerged almost accidentally that they could be employed as highly competent 'matriarchal' leaders of teams (Kerfoot and Knights, 1991/1994). This was a fortuitous rather than planned strategy but once these older women were seen not only to resolve serious staffing problems but also had a positive impact on team working, the 'mature entrant scheme' was further institutionalized as a formal personnel policy. Otherwise team working, the publicly displayed league tables and the prizes awarded to departmental managers and section leaders responsible for specific team target success, was a line management issue. ...

It is not suggested here that power was being exercised where none existed before; rather its exercise evolved to reflect ... a shift in the management of the labour resource from one where team working was a mere convenience in allocating 'batches' of work to groups, into a practice designed to stimulate a greater identification and ownership of work tasks and responsibilities. This new development is consistent with the broader concerns of the organization to provide a more competitive service to the customer, reduce staff turnover and generate a faster turnaround in the administrative processing of products. While this company in no way 'fits' the ideal model characterized in the literature, it is our view that by a combination of a series of accidents, contingent processes and management designs, certain practices that might be seen as precursors to a more fully formed HRM strategy are beginning to evolve in Pensco.

While our case study company had incorporated a plan to strengthen the strategic role of personnel so that its activities would more closely align with other elements of the corporate strategy document, conflicting political objectives obstructed its smooth

Planning for Personnel? HRM Reconsidered *continued*

By Deborah Kerfoot and David Knights

development. Nonetheless, two initiatives on 'team building' had an organizational impact, which though diverting from senior management intentions, could be seen broadly as consistent with aspects of the Chief Executive's desire to manage human resources more strategically. ...

It seems to us that there may be an alternative position worthy of further investigation. Our case study analysis suggests that certain practices, such as 'team building', may be acquiring a new emphasis. Though not leading to changes that necessarily represent an 'ideal model' of HRM, these practices nonetheless reflect and reproduce some of its important features. Changes surrounding the team building programme have certainly strengthened the degree of management control in Pensco. Team working has facilitated a greater degree of measuring and monitoring productivity and performance, and has rewarded individuals and teams accordingly. But also it has generated a degree of self-discipline that was absent before the introduction of team working. ...

[However,] working practices do not simply follow, in unilinear fashion, the lines of hierarchical power in an organization. And indeed, business plans may often be little more than elaborate rationalizations of the practices that have already evolved and are continuing to unfold in the lower reaches of the organization. Therefore, the point of our argument here is that the 'flow of change' in an organization is as much derived from the 'grassroots' as it is from senior management. While this may be seen as an 'anti-strategy' thesis, we would want to resist moving so far in that direction. For the discussions and actions that surround strategic thinking at the top of an organization clearly do filter down the hierarchy, and may well be one of the major stimuli in focusing the minds of those whose decisions and actions can make a difference in the development of working practices. Furthermore, a commitment to strategic management on the part of an organization does have considerable impact on the way that employees at all levels see themselves; in short, on their identity as competent members of the organization. Our argument is no more than that strategy, whether relating

to human resources or any other aspect of the business, does not run smoothly from design to final outcome, as might be imagined from ideal models or even the intentions of senior management. Things are much more messy as our case study has intimated. But from our perspective this is not so surprising for we would argue that HRM – like many other managerial and organizational innovations – rarely emerges as a fully formed/fledged set of practices but evolves in complex and indeterminable ways as we have suggested; accordingly, the everyday practices within organizations ought to inform the language and ideas of HRM as much as those ideas attempt to influence the practice.

References

Guest, D.E. (1990) 'Human resource management and the American dream', *Journal of Management Studies*, 27(4): 378–97.

Guest, D.E. (1991) 'Personnel management: the end of orthodoxy?' *British Journal of Industrial Relations*, 29(2): 149–76.

Hendry, C. and Pettigrew, A. (1986) 'The practice of strategic human resource management'. *Personnel Review* 15(5): 3–8.

Hoskin, K.W. and MaCVE, R.H. (1986) 'Accounting and the examination: a genealogy of disciplinary power', *Accounting, Organizations and Society*, pp. 105–36.

Kerfoot, D. and Knights, D. (1991/1994) 'The Gendered Terrains of Paternalism', in S. Wright, D. Marsden, M. Roper and E. Young (eds), *Anthropology of Organisations*, London: Routledge, pp. 124–39.

Knights, D. and Morgan, G. (1991) 'Corporate strategy, subjectivity and organisations', *Organisation Studies*, 12(2): 251–73.

Kochan, T.A., Katz, H. and McKersie, R.B. (1986) *The Transformation of American Industrial Relations*, New York: Basic Books.

Peters, T.J. and Waterman, R.H. Jr. (1982) *In Search of Excellence, Lessons from America's Best Run Companies*, New York: Harper and Row.

Storey, J. (1989) *New Perspectives on Human Resource Management*, London: Cengage Learning.

Storey, J. and Sisson, K. (1990) Limits to transformation: human resource management in the British context, *Industrial Relations Journal*, 21(1): 60–5.

| READING 6.3 | **Foucault, Power/Knowledge, and its Relevance for Human Resource Management** |

By Barbara Townley

Underlying most studies of HRM, although often remaining implicit, is what may be identified as a systems maintenance or functionalist perspective. Reflecting concerns with improvement in efficiency that derive from classical management theory, HRM is an organization mechanism through which goal achievement and survival may be promoted. Its aim is to make the organization more orderly and integrated. In HRM, connotations of goal-directed activity, inputs and outputs, stability, adaptability, and systems maintenance predominate. From this perspective HRM is the black box of production, where organizational inputs – employees – are selected, appraised, trained, developed, and remunerated to deliver the required output of labour. Within this framework HRM practices are all too frequently technique oriented, presented as the tools or instruments that enable the effective attainment of goals – an approach that behaviourist psychology has a tendency to reinforce. Research concerns are usually to make HRM practices more efficient, and they reflect the belief that knowledge of them, through the services of its handmaiden, science, will progressively be made more accurate. As such, the study of HRM stands well within a modernist, and largely positivist tradition …

Here, I wish to set aside these traditional methods of ordering and examine an alternative and, it is argued, more productive line of analysis. I do so by drawing upon the work of Michel Foucault …

HRM is presented as the *construction and production of knowledge*. It attempts to reduce the space resulting from the unspecified nature of a contract. It constitutes a discipline and a discourse, which organizes analytical space – the indeterminacy between promise and performance. HRM serves to render organizations and their participants calculable arenas, offering, through a variety of technologies, the means by which activities and individuals become knowable and governable. HRM disciplines the interior of the organization, organizing time, space, and movement within it. Through various techniques, tasks, behaviour and interactions are categorized and measured.

HRM provides measurement of both physical and subjective dimensions of labour offering a technology that renders individuals and their behaviour predictable and calculable. In so doing, HRM helps to bridge the gap between promise and performance, between labour power and labour, and it organizes labour into a productive force.

To recap the argument, the basic unit of analysis in understanding HRM was identified as the nature of exchange embodied in the employment relationship. Given the essentially indeterminate nature of this relationship, the problematic then becomes how this relational, exchange activity is organized. Foucault's concept of power–knowledge was introduced to illustrate how HRM acts to impose order on the inherently undecidable. Attempting to clarify the indeterminacy of contract requires 'effective instruments for the formation and accumulation of knowledge – methods of observations, techniques of registration, procedures for investigation and research, apparatuses of control' (Foucault, 1980: 102). The construction of knowledge in HRM operates through rules of classification, ordering, and distribution; definitions of activities; fixing of scales; and rules of procedure, which lead to the gradual emergence of a distinct HRM discourse. Associated with these practices are concepts of rationality, scientificity, measurement, grading – the language and the knowledge of the HRM specialist. Through mechanisms of registration, assessment, and classification – areas of study often neglected or dismissed as technical or administrative procedures – it becomes possible to illustrate how a body of knowledge operates to objectify those on whom it is applied. It is also in this discourse that the individual becomes located as an object of knowledge. Classification schemes, offered as techniques of simplification and clarification for the analysis of labour, both as effort and object, become inextricably tied to its disciplinary operation.

A Foucauldian perspective presents an alternative way for perceiving and ordering material. Rather than thinking in functional terms of recruitment, appraisal, remuneration, and so on, in this

Source: *Reproduced with the kind permission of Professor Barbara Townley, St Andrews University, from 'Foucault, Power/Knowledge, and its Relevance for Human Resource Management', in* Postmodern Management Theory © *1997 Ashgate Publishing.*

Foucault, Power/Knowledge, and its Relevance for Human Resource Management *continued*

By Barbara Townley

perspective an emphasis is placed on how HRM employs disciplinary practices to create knowledge and power. These practices fix individuals in conceptual and geographical space, and they order or articulate the labour process. Processes of individualization and individuation create an industrial subject who is analysable and describable. As an approach, it allows HRM to be analysed as the 'will to knowledge', that is, as a system of knowledge and modality of power. It is sufficiently detailed an approach to allow for the 'micropolitics' of power to be addressed and, by pro-

viding examples of how the concern with 'knowing' labour as a 'population' can percolate down to its effects on the individual, allows for highly individualized practices to be related to an intelligible whole. In doing so, it also provides the basis for reorienting contemporary, historical, and comparative analyses of HRM.

References

Foucault, M. (1980) *Power/Knowledge: Selected Interviews and other Writings 1972–77*, translated and edited by C. Gordon, London: Tavistock.

Developing a Tactical Approach to Engaging with 'Strategic' HRM

By Roy Jacques

From 'What is HRM?' to 'What does HRM do?'

In broad agreement with the general goals of the special issue editors, this essay will attempt to avoid either blanket acceptance or blanket condemnation of the (strategic) HRM[1] concept.[2] It will affirm the importance of critical engagement with these relationships, but will also be critical of much existing critical theory and practice. In accord with the editors' conception of HRM as a 'moving concept', it will suggest a 'tactical' approach to engagement, to facilitate thinking about the possible, sometimes conflicting, appropriations of HRM for agendas of organizational effectiveness as well as for agendas of social justice and change. This move involves putting aside the question of what HRM 'is', as though it had a discoverable essence. It is not even enough that we ask what HRM *does*. If we are to make use of the HRM concept – whether for organizational effectiveness, social equity or both – we must become more sensitive to the tactical deployment of the concept *as 'HRM' is signified in organizational relationships of power*. We must come to better understand how these relationships operate, what consequences they have and how they can be influenced.

The editors of this special issue outline three streams of HRM thinking. For purposes of this essay, I will combine the first two and speak of 'managerialist' and 'critical' perspectives on HRM. These terms are not comprehensive and they homogenize much heterogeneity of detail. My critique is applicable only to the broad boundary conditions and assumptions which have largely shaped and limited discussion of the idea of HRM to date. Work such as Hollway (1991), Townley (1994) and, hopefully, Jacques (1996) shows that my binary representation of positions is not exhaustive. At present, however, managerialist and critical enunciative positions in binary opposition to each other do constitute the main sites from which one can speak academically about HRM. This essay will call for examination of that condition for the purpose of opening up new sites for engagement.

Like most managerialist and some critical writers, I believe the emergence of HRM as a new signifier within organizational discourse is more than a smokescreen for business-as-usual. This emergence is linked with some fundamental changes in the relationships structuring work – but not in a straightforward manner. That is, there is something of value

READING 6.4	**Developing a Tactical Approach to Engaging with 'Strategic' HRM**

By Roy Jacques

here to analyse, but what is important is not necessarily what is represented as being important. *What is of paramount importance in the emergence of HRM as a signifier is that it is linked to a partial rupture in managerialist organizational hegemony. This rupture originates in the growing centrality of work done in knowledge-intensive, 'multicephalous'[3] environments in which Fayolian/Weberian/ Barnardian 'rationalization' of organizational resources becomes ineffective.* For those critical of managerialism, this represents an opportunity in that an element of organizational power has 'slipped the leash' and its control is up for grabs. For those seeking merely to organize effectively for profitability, this means engaging with questions of power long since swept under the table, questions such as 'what activities create value?' and 'who has a right to the value produced?'.

Because the HRM concept is linked to these shifts in power relations, its deployment in organizational discourse (academic and applied) can have great power for influencing values and practices in the workplace. Thus, its nominal *meanings* (which are indeed spurious) are of little consequence. The concept is important to engage with because of its *effects*. Language controls and structures possibilities for action and the signifier 'HRM' is a powerful element in the emerging language of organizing.

The danger, I fear, is that the binary opposition of managerialist and critical perspectives will prevent effectively engaging with the HRM concept *either* for profit or equity. To date, managerialist writing has treated the human more or less solely as a capital 'resource', and failed to engage the hard questions of power and voice that are increasingly necessary in order to be even instrumentally effective as a profit producer.

Similarly, but conversely, most critical writers reject out of hand the idea that the human be thought of as a capital resource. While this is admirable from a certain perspective, such romantic Humanism prevents engagement with the dominant language of the workplace in which, like it or not, 'human capital' and 'human resources' are representations of the worker one must be able to deploy in order to

interact with, and influence, the web of power relationships structuring the workplace.

In my reading of this literature, the claimed differences between HRM and more traditional personnel management seem to cluster around three themes: (1) comprehensive, as opposed to patchwork, direction of the human function in organizations; (2) linking operational HR issues to the firm's strategy and structure; (3) learning to regard expenditures on labor and worker-embodied knowledge as an investment rather than an expense – that is, viewing the human *resource* as human *capital*.

Tactical HRM: Ethics, Profits, Alliances – and Conflict

Perhaps, rather than speak of *strategic* Human Resource Management, we should be working to develop a *tactical HRM* in the sense of de Certeau (1984, leitmotif above). He reminds us that when working from a marginal position one is left to work with materials provided by the dominant discourse (such as the concept of 'human capital'). Direct opposition is not a tactical possibility because one does not have the power to overthrow. One must work from positions of tactical insinuation, traveling light and striking where momentary opportunity presents itself. Most of all, we must not expect to build victories that have temporal durability, as everything over time slides into the dominant. What is useful at one point for its critical potential becomes selectively absorbed, often quickly, in a manner that drains the critical element while retaining the appearance of tolerance to the critical (e.g. 'organizational culture', 'deconstruction' 'postmodernism')[4].

A key tool for such engagement is a deconstructive practice. By this I do not specifically mean Derridean analysis, but I do mean operating in that spirit to identify internal contradictions in systems, to exploit the conflicts and absences present in the interplay between representations, using nominally stated arguments of those with voice (i.e. the need to manage human 'resources') to create openings for those without. Destabilizing the claims of any one representation of knowledge removes the possibility of acting 'objectively.' If the polyvalence of the world can be

Developing a Tactical Approach to Engaging with 'Strategic' HRM *continued*

By Roy Jacques

maintained in 'organizational' discourse, one can argue based on this that every position is value-laden, that the deployment of HRM is unavoidably an attempt to influence relationships of power. If this can be accomplished, it is a powerful pry-bar that can be used by the marginal to penetrate into the otherwise seamless surface of the dominant truth.

Two points are important to remember because they can be used as starting points for a tactical engagement with the HRM concept.

- In post-industrial workplaces, managers must strike a Faustian bargain with the past; in order to produce profits effectively, it becomes necessary to engage in a dialogue about the production of value, which the critically engaged can extend to a dialogue about rights to that value once produced.

- Because worker attitude becomes a critical element of effective functioning, the need for top management to convince *themselves* that they have a mutually satisfying relationship with employees is being replaced by a need for top managers to convince the *employees,* creating a need for greater authenticity and mutuality in managerial dealings.

In this context, one cannot be 'strategic' about HRM in the sense propagated by the managerialist HRM literature. A synoptic connection between strategy, structure and HRM choices is a hopelessly incomplete template. In order to pursue even the instrumental project of developing humans as a resource for profit production, it will be necessary to contextualize and historicize present day practices. One would not want to sign up to fight the 'new industrial revolution' of 1920 today.

So, How Human(ist) is HRM?

None of the comments above should be interpreted to imply, as so much American writing does, that all needs can simultaneously be met and that problems of reward, dominance, marginality and incommensurable views can be made to disappear. No, these problems remain and are probably insoluble, but they can be mitigated or aggravated by our choices.

I advocate scrutiny of the changing relationships of the workplace – of which HRM is an important part – in order to minimize the degree to which the struggle over these differences is based on irrelevant assumptions and simplistic oppositions. The HRM concept is a powerful signifier. Let us think carefully and act aggressively in attempting to influence its deployment.

Above all, let us first look to the discursive constitution of both managerialist and critical perspectives on HRM, to disengage them from the Humanism that presents social reality to us in the form of opposing individuals. It may well be that a more *humane* resource management can be constructed by permitting the working subject to be *less* human, to become a 'capital' resource. It may be that following the conflicts between inter-subjective themes can help us avoid dead-end constructions of problems in terms of oppressor and oppressed individuals. It may well serve the cause of equity if, in our debates about the deployment of knowledge in organizations, the (Humanist concept of) 'man [sic] would be erased, like a face drawn in the sand at the edge of the sea' (Foucault, 1973: 387).

---

[1]Since the basic idea of HRM involves linking the human function to strategic planning, it seems to me the terms 'HRM' and 'Strategic HRM' both refer to pretty much the same object. I will use HRM throughout, but the prefix 'strategic' should be understood to be implicit.

[2]While I use the term 'concept', the more precise phrase I would use, varying from one point to the next, would be 'discursive object', or 'enunciative modality'. To be a bit more inviting to the reader who has not first studied Foucault, I chose the less technical 'concept' as being a step better that 'construct', which has all the wrong connotations.

[3]Pondy and Mitroff (1979) long ago noted that, according to Boulding's hierarchy of systems' 'open systems' (level 4), on which mainstream American organizational theory since the 1960s has been built, are simplistic representations of most organizational situations. 'Multicephalous systems' (level 8), in which knowledge, and action upon that knowledge, emerge from multiple locations rather than residing in a simple hierarchy, better describe the situations of greatest importance.

[4]Chomsky has written extensively about this phenomenon under the label of 'manufacturing consent'. Also Jaques and White (1995). In Jaques (1996), this is discussed under the label of 'procrustean revolutions'.

| READING 6.4 | **Developing a Tactical Approach to Engaging with 'Strategic' HRM** |

By Roy Jacques

References

De Certeau, M. (1984) *The Practice of Everyday Life*. Berkeley: University of California Press.

Foucault, M. (1973) *The Order of Things: An Archaeology of the Human Sciences*. New York: Random House.

Hollway, W. (1991) *Work Psychology and Organizational Behaviour*. London: Sage.

Jaques, R. (1996) *Manufacturing the Employee*. London: Sage.

Jaques, R. and White, R. (1995) 'Operationalizing the Postmodernity Construct for Efficient Organizational Change Management' [title is tongue-in-cheek], *Journal of Organizational Change Management*, 8(2): 45–71.

Pondy, L.R. and Mitroff, I.I. (1979) 'Beyond Open Systems Models of Organization', in L.L. Cummins (ed.), *Research in Organizational Behavior*, London: JAI Press, 1: 3–39.

Townley, B. (1994) *Reframing Human Resource Management*, London: Sage.

Discussion Questions

1. What are the differences between normative, behavioural, and critical models of HRM?
2. What is the difference between personnel management and human resource management?
3. Is a strategic HRM policy always possible and necessarily the most effective?
4. Is HRM concerned primarily with transforming employees into manageable subjects?

Introduction References

Collinson, D., Knights, D. and Collinson, M. (1990) *Managing to Discriminate*, London: Routledge.

De Certeau, M. (1984) *The Practice of Everyday Life*. Berkeley: University of California Press.

Guest, D.E. (1987) 'Human resource management and industrial relations', *Journal of Management Studies*, 24(5): 503–21.

Recommended Further Readings

See references accompanying the Readings plus:

Keenoy, T. (1997) 'HRMism and the Languages of Re-presentation. Review Article', *Journal of Management Studies*, 34(5): 825–41.

Storey, J. (1992) *Developments in the Managing of Human Resources*, Oxford: Blackwell.

Storey, J. (ed.) (2007) *Human Resource Management; a Critical Text*, London: Cengage Learning.

LEADERSHIP AND SYMBOLISM | CHAPTER 7

READINGS

Knights, D. and Willmott, H. (1992) 'Conceptualizing Leadership Processes: A Study of Senior Managers in a Financial Services Company' in *Journal of Management Studies*. Vol. 29, No. 6: 768–775.

Smircich, L. and Morgan, G. (1982) 'Leadership: The Management of Meaning' in *Journal of Applied Behavioural Science*. Vol. 18, No. 3: pp. 257, 258–263.

Jones, M. (1996) 'Symbols and Symbolic Behaviour: Definitions and Distinctions' in *Studying Organizational Symbolism: What, How, Why?* London: Sage. pp. 2–4.

INTRODUCTION

> ... the concept and practice of leadership, and variant forms of direction and control, are so powerfully ingrained into popular thought that the absence of leadership is often seen as an absence of organization. (Smircich and Morgan, Reading 7.3, p. 138)

Problems of organization are frequently attributed to weakness or failure of leadership. Such diagnoses largely disregard the effects of the context on organizational performance as they abstract the characteristics of individuals or groups held responsible from the benign or hostile conditions of organizational action. As attention is focused upon 'leadership', it comes to assume symbolic importance. Unsurprisingly, an abiding concern of mainstream research has been to identify features of effective leadership behaviour – in the possession of distinctive traits or successful styles. Complex and contradictory social practices of organizing and managing (see sections in the chapters on Organizing and Managing) are reduced to a set of characteristics ascribed to particular individuals almost irrespective of the conditions in which these are applied. This limitation is shared by need achievement theory (McClelland, 1961), path–goal theory (House, 1971), normative decision theory (Vroom and Yetton, 1973), cognitive resource theory (Fiedler, 1986;

Fiedler and Garcia, 1987) and transformational theory (Bass, 1985). In each case, minimal regard is paid to broader historical, political and cultural conditions of 'leadership' processes.

The state of leadership research is perverse since, as Bryman *et al.* (1988, p. 25) have argued,

> through a greater attention to contexts, it may also be possible to bring the field of leadership theory and research much closer to the needs and experiences of leaders themselves than much quantitative research on leadership has been able to accomplish.

An important challenge to the dominant paradigm of leadership research has been mounted by those who have sought to expose its basis in unexamined reasoning (*e.g.* Calder, 1977; Pfeffer, 1977). Their main argument is that research should focus upon how ideas about leadership are commonly *attributed* – by practitioners as well as researchers – to particular individuals or situations. For example, in his classic study of male youths, Whyte (1955) notes how, in this culture, leadership was attributed to the person whose behaviour conformed most closely with the values of the 'street corner society'. A focus upon processes of attribution usefully highlights how leadership qualities are contextually defined rather than naturally or universally given. When this is overlooked, researchers simply adopt and uncritically legitimize dominant views and values as they uncritically deploy or refine everyday assumptions and categories (see Reading 7.2 in the Organization theory section). Indeed, it has been suggested that the field requires analyses of leadership processes which give them 'some real meaning through deep probes into leadership activity' (Greene, 1976; Mintzberg, 1982, p. 255).

The distinct value and potency of social scientific enquiry, we suggest, resides in treating as problematical what, in everyday life as academics and practitioners, we take for granted. In this way, we may advance both self-understanding and our collective capacity to dispel the authority attached to the theory and practice of 'leadership'. In particular, it is necessary to reflect more deeply upon the relationship between our general understandings of leadership and the relations of power through which this knowledge has developed. Reflection upon the *contextual* attribution of leadership qualities serves to show us how, because power is relational, involving interdependence between more and less advantaged groups, dominant conceptions of leadership are inherently situated, precarious and provisional. Their existence depends upon the reproduction of the relations of power and, ultimately, the support of 'followers', that support their plausibility. Leadership research might usefully be reoriented to examine the processes through which dominant, common sense, symbolic identifications of leadership behaviour are sustained (or transformed).

Of approaches that study leadership as a *social* practice, institutional theory has made the most substantial contribution. At the heart of an institutional theory of leadership is the neo-Weberian understanding that 'principles of domination and cultural ties' (Biggart and Hamilton, 1987, p. 432) are more important for understanding processes of leadership than the identification of traits, styles and situational contingencies. Leadership processes are deemed to be embedded in 'cultural assumptions and "understood ideas" about the proper ways of structuring relationships amongst individuals' (Biggart and Hamilton, 1987, p. 430) – assumptions that are held by 'leaders' and 'followers' alike – rather than regarded as the expression of specific personality characteristics or contextual variables.

A limitation of institutional theory is that it tends to assume a deep consensus about 'cultural assumptions' and 'understood ideas' (Biggart and Hamilton, 1987, p. 430) or to believe that this consensus is unproblematical. Inadequate account is taken of how 'consensus' is forged within relations of domination – in the sense that followers are comparatively disadvantaged – by a comparative lack of material and symbolic resources – in formulating, let alone mounting, a challenge to those (leaders) who routinely shape and reproduce 'the proper way of structuring relationships amongst individuals' (ibid.). Instead of assuming an underlying consensus between leaders and followers, we believe that it is more plausible and instructive to understand the achievement of 'consent' from 'followers' as precarious, and often accomplished through exercises of power (see Cooper, Ezzamel and Willmott, 2008). To put this argument more directly, the cultural analysis of how meanings become shared must be complemented by a structural analysis of leadership as mediated by *relations of power*. This focus upon relations of power emphasizes interdependence rather than ownership. The seeming 'possession' of power by occupants of senior managerial positions cannot be sustained or exercised without the shared – symbolically mediated – interpretations and cooperation of 'less powerful' others. Here the symbolic dimension of leadership is important since the meanings which secure and sustain power relations have to be negotiated and can never be presumed to meet with the acceptance of others merely because they are uttered from the mouths of leaders.

David Knights and Hugh Willmott (Reading 7.1) analyse an extract from a transcript of a tape recorded meeting between top managers drawn from a longitudinal study of a medium-sized UK insurance company. Their conceptual framework combines elements of existentialism, phenomenology and structural theory to prise open the practical dynamics of social reproduction that are largely ignored in mainstream studies of leadership. Their study attends to 'live' processes that are presented in the full disclosure of the raw research data. Analytically, Knights and Willmott move beyond institutional theorists' generalized formulation of leadership as 'a relationship amongst persons embedded in a social setting at a given historic moment' (Biggart and Hamilton, 1987, p. 439) to analyse power and subjectivity as integral constituents of the social practice that is commonsensically represented as 'leadership'. Although the extract focuses on the transcript of data selected from a one-day senior executive meeting, its analysis is informed by extensive knowledge of the company's history and changing approach to management acquired during its longitudinal study. What the extract explores, and what is largely unseen in orthodox studies, is the presence of power and subjectivity in the practical accomplishment of realities to which the concept 'leadership' is routinely attributed.

Linda Smircich and Gareth Morgan (Reading 7.2) relate leadership to the management of meaning. For them, leadership involves the process of framing and defining the reality of others, and they understand leaders as those with an obligation or right to undertake such framing. Whether in formal or informal settings, leaders are seen to emerge or be identified in terms of those who are assigned, or who assume, responsibility for 'framing experience in a way that provides a viable basis for action' (p. 134). It is a process that crucially involves the formation of 'follow-ership' in the sense that others must be willing, or be incentivized or coerced into, suspending their capacity to define reality. That the 'willingness' of others is often conditional or reluctant suggests that there are frequently struggles between groups or individuals in the process of framing and 'agreeing' the situation, as illustrated in Reading 7.1. Such struggles are tempered, or at least routinely suppressed, in formal organizations where meanings and associated bases for action are compara-tively well established and institutionalized. Notably, there is generally a hierarchi-cal structure of authority relationships in which there is an expectation that those placed in senior positions will (legitimately) frame and define the – material and symbolic – realities experienced by others. That said, there is likely to be some dis-parity and tension between what is intended or expected by superordinates and what is forthcoming from their subordinates. Smircich and Morgan suggest that an important aspect of leadership is a capacity to mitigate such tensions by framing the situation in ways that retain motivation and focus.

Michael Jones (Reading 7.3) underscores the significance of the symbolic meaning of the most mundane of actions – such as the meaning conveyed to parti-cipants at a retreat who were asked to bring their own 'brown bag' lunch. The rel-evance of symbols and symbolism for leadership processes is illustrated by the case of the head of the New York City Health Administration who is seen to set out and commend a particular view, or meaning, of the agency by repeatedly using symbols associated with a particular 'perspective'. Of course, artefacts (e.g. archi-tecture, office design) and communications (e.g. emails, logos) have no inherent or fixed meaning. Rather, they are invested with meanings as they are interpreted within, and in relation to, specific contexts. Meanings are symbolic in the sense that they comprise a set of signs – language, images and associations – that render a particular activity or belief desirable, important and valuable, or unattractive in-consequential and worthless. So, for example, in a context where employees believe that managers are obsessed with cost-cutting regardless of its unintended, detrimen-tal effects, a brown bag lunch *may* reinforce this assessment and further antagonize staff whom their 'leaders' are endeavouring to win over. As Jones emphasizes, it is important to appreciate that this assessment is one 'reading', a reading that de-pends upon how activities (the retreat), expressions (the invitation) and objects (the lunch) are interpreted. Several meanings – for example, the insensitivity or in-competence of management – may be read into a communication, such as the brown bag lunch invitation. The key point is that all kinds of artefacts and activi-ties – including production technologies and other apparently 'hard' elements of or-ganizations like budgets and reports – are imbued with symbolic meaning. This extends to how people are treated in organizations – in processes of recruitment, selection and remuneration, for example – which depends upon the symbols mobi-lized in the determination of their value.

It is to be hoped that these extracts offer some helpful responses to Min-tzberg's (1982) plea for leadership research that produces 'startling insight' and 'real meaning'. This is perhaps a tall order as one person's insight is another's platitude.

READING 7.1

Conceptualizing Leadership Processes: A Study of Senior Managers in a Financial Services Company

By David Knights and Hugh Willmott

The historical and organizational context of our empirical material is that of the recent appointment of a Chief Executive who has won the support of the Board to develop a more dynamic and 'professional' approach to the management of the company in conditions of increasing competitiveness and uncertainty within the UK financial services industry (cf. Levy and Merry, 1986; Tichy and Devanna, 1986). More specifically, the data present an exchange between the Chief Executive and the Head of the Customer Service division. Their exchange relates to the corporate task, identified in the company's strategic planning document, of 'moving the management decision-making style away from centralized, consensus decision-making to an approach based more upon delegation of authority, but subject to consultation'. In response to the Chief Executive's request for comments on progress with this task, the AGM Customer Service volunteered:

AGM CUSTOMER SERVICE: *My overall feeling about it is that it isn't really working very well. I suspect that part of it is, I find anyway, that a lot of decisions have to pass through you, and I get the feeling that you are very much on overload as a result of it.*

CHIEF EXECUTIVE: *There are a number of areas where I want to make sure that things are done to my standard or in my way.*

AGM CUSTOMER SERVICE: *That will have an effect. I mean New Business is a good example, and it's causing some difficulties because people are getting two directions. They're not very different – the aims are the same, but the way of achieving them is slightly different and that's causing confusions out there, and additional work. And I think we're beginning to go through the same sort of problems with the automation of branches. And I think we do need to identify and clarify where the responsibilities are and how we're actually going to deal with that.*

CHIEF EXECUTIVE: *Branch Automation is a very good example where, with a new management coming in, I see it as very important that I impose a set of standards inside the organization that I wish to see*

adhered to. For instance, if I had been here last year, I would like to think that I would have stopped New Business because it just wasn't good enough. I don't want to see that happen again. So, in the early stages there will be a necessity for me to be directly involved … I'm going to be very intimately concerned with running the office, certainly over the next two or three years. But what I had in mind here (i.e. with regard to developing an effective new management team) is whether we are making progress in moving away from the idea of trying to sort the thing out at morning prayers every day: should we all sit round the table and take decisions or should they in fact be taken by smaller groups where there are, say, three or four people working on a project?*

AGM FINANCE: *I'm beginning to see what I call the Walter (surname of Chief Executive) way of doing things … picking on two or three or four of the top team, but not including Richard (Chief Executive) usually, and I value that because I think if you're left totally alone you'll try and make a decision that is sensible and rational to you, but it's a jolly good test to have to persuade an unreasonable person like Jim or someone like that …*

OTHER AGM (JIM): *You mean a reactionary! (huge laughter).*

AGM FINANCE: *What you're trying to do is the right thing, and so it's not so much delegated, it's half delegated, isn't it? We're not independent divisions, but it's not quite the whole table involvement.*

CHIEF EXECUTIVE: *I think it's a big test for you, actually. I've got every confidence that you will go away and get the things done that you set out to do. I've got no qualms about that. I think one of the big tests for you is to recognise the things that are sufficiently interdivisional that need involve either me or other divisional managers. And the other thing is to recognize things that are sufficiently awkward that they need to have a general manager signing them off, because they have a strategic implication. They may look mundane but they are strategic in another sense, and that is one of your tests, to work out how to read those. Branch Automation is a very good example*

Source: Reproduced with permission of Sage Publications, London, Los Angeles, New Delhi and Singapore from 'Conceptualizing Leadership Processes: A Study of Senior Managers in a Financial Services Company', in the Journal of Management Studies © 1992 Sage Publications.

READING 7.1

Conceptualizing Leadership Processes:
A Study of Senior Managers in
a Financial Services Company *continued*

By David Knights and Hugh Willmott

because on the face of it, it is just another system that is going into the office ...

AGM CUSTOMER SERVICE: *May I try ...*

CHIEF EXECUTIVE: *But in fact what it is, if I may just finish off as an illustration is that is going to permeate the company for the next ten years because it's going to control how information actually flows around the company, and that's why I want to see what's going on there, because of these really massive implications.*

AGM CUSTOMER SERVICE: *I think the point that I would like to make is that I think that one needs to distinguish between direction, which is clearly your prerogative and the more detailed decision-making, and I've felt that there's been a tendency to move down to a more detailed decision-making ...*

CHIEF EXECUTIVE: *Oh, certainly, I think the idea of being in the City office and taking everything that is going just isn't on. Not with me and my temperament. I intend to be right there and I will stay there as long as I find, taking New Business as an example, that there have been 'hot line' cases for two-and-a-half weeks and they still haven't left the office. That sort of thing will just drive me mad. And if anybody wants to get rid of me on jobs like that, there's a simple answer: just don't let me see ... (Laughter)*
Can I make one final comment and then move on to the next task. That is that it's well worth our while to try to stand back and be quite detached about these issues. If you feel that it's not working on the right basis then I think it's up to you to say so, and to be quite direct with me if that is what is concerning you: and just say, 'Bugger off and find something else to deal with'. And I am quite prepared to listen to that, and if necessary to do exactly that. But a number of my interests are quite calculated. They're not random. That's the end of it. (Without further ado, the Chief Executive immediately turned to the next element of the key tasks for the senior management team.)

As noted earlier in selecting this extract for analysis, we acknowledge our reliance upon general understandings of what constitutes 'leadership' behaviour. But our perception that the meeting involves the Chief Executive 'leading' his senior management team in a review of progress on changing their decision-making style does not require us to remain at the level of common sense when undertaking an analysis of their interaction. By interpreting the extract as an expression of the phenomenological, existential and structural dimensions of the dynamics of leadership practice, we step outside the orthodox paradigm of leadership research, where the preoccupation is in identifying effective leadership in terms of specific traits, styles or contextual contingencies.

The Phenomenological Dimension

Institutional theorists (e.g. Biggart and Hamilton, 1987; Selznick, 1957) and students of organizational symbolism (Pfeffer, 1981; Smircich and Morgan, 1982) have identified the management of meaning as a central activity of organizational actors as they develop, shape and negotiate the contents of the interpretive schemes that define their situation. It is central precisely because, as Berger and Luckmann (1966, p. 78) put it, 'the objectivity of the institutional world, however massive it may appear to the individual, is a humanly produced, constructed objectivity'. The interaction between the AGM Customer Service (hereafter CS) and the Chief Executive (hereafter CE) illustrates how social reality – in this instance, what we may typify as the reality of leadership or of management decision-making – is practically accomplished through a (contested) process of negotiation about the effectiveness (and perhaps legitimacy) of the new approach. The contention of the CS is that it 'isn't really working very well'. His interpretation of the situation is that the CE is not delegating and, as a consequence, is 'very much on overload'. The CS also claims that staff are receiving divergent instructions which are 'causing confusions out there and additional work'.

What, for the CS, is the reality of the new approach is contested by the CE. For the CE, its reality is one in which senior managers, including the CS, are failing to grasp its requirements (e.g. the strategic

READING 7.1	**Conceptualizing Leadership Processes: A Study of Senior Managers in a Financial Services Company**

By David Knights and Hugh Willmott

significance of Branch Automation) and meet its standards. For him, it is this, not an unwillingness to delegate, that compels him to intervene and, in doing so, to issue instructions that conflict with those given by other members of the senior management 'team'. Arguably, there is much at stake in such interaction. It is not simply a difference of opinion about progress on a particular corporate task. Rather, mundane interactions of this kind are expressive of contests between interpretive schemes that mediate the very production of reality. As Berger and Luckmann (1966, p. 84) have argued, forms of knowledge – such as the competing ways of knowing the world articulated by the CE and the CS – involve a *realization in the double sense of the word*. In an obvious sense, their respective knowledges allow each executive to apprehend the objectivated reality of the 'new approach'. In addition, and in a less obvious sense, it is a realization in the sense of 'ongoingly producing this reality' (Berger and Luckmann, 1966). More specifically, the knowledge or discourse that becomes dominant, or hegemonic, will constitute organizational subjects in its image insofar as it becomes accepted and institutionalized as objective truth, and internalized as subjective reality.

The CE uses the interjection of the CS as an opportunity to engage and reinforce a set of typifications through which he seeks to realize the meaning of the task of changing their approach to management decision-making. What it means, he declares, is an undertaking to move away from thrashing out problems of strategic significance on a daily basis in the 'morning prayers' meeting attended by all members of the senior management team. In its place, the strategy document requires an approach in which these problems are examined, and decisions taken, by smaller groups who liaise with the CE. Whilst professing a willingness to listen to those who have reservations about progress with the introduction of the new approach, the CE simultaneously asserts his prerogative to disregard such reservations when they are inconsistent with 'a number of his interests' which 'are quite calculated'. He is then not constrained by what might be characterized as the conservatism or

inertia associated with consensus decision-making. Instead, he is able to select the members of each project group, to guide the direction of their thinking and to monitor progress. A process of decentralized, delegated decision-making serves to strengthen the role and influence of the CE. It creates an 'inner cabinet' of senior managers who enjoy the sponsorship of the CE and reciprocate by confirming the rationality of adopting his 'way of doing things'. In this, he is positively assisted by his recent recruit, the AGM Finance, who affirms the value of the principle of delegation rather than entering into a discussion of its practical implementation. Further assistance is provided by the other AGM (Jim), a respected member of the 'old guard' approaching retirement, as he associates any questioning of 'the Walter way of doing things' with a reactionary attitude.

Through this dialogue, the task of changing the approach to management decision-making is interpreted in a way which reflects and reinforces the definition of the situation held by the CE. Indeed, the interaction itself can be seen as an exemplification of the new approach which he is seeking to introduce. The concerns of the CS about the problem of the centralization of decision-making ('a lot of decisions have to pass through you') and the confusion and additional work produced by the CE's interventions ('people are getting two directions') are reinterpreted as symptoms of the CS's own incompetence and of a more generalized failure amongst senior managers to adopt the new standards and decision-making style. Silence from the other managers in response to the CE's request for comments on progress with this task is not surprising given that the CS's attempt to question 'things' meets with a rebuke and implied criticism of his performance.

The Existential Dimension

Recognition of this dimension resonates with psychoanalytically informed studies of leadership (e.g. Kets de Vries, 1991; Kets de Vries and Miller, 1985; Zaleznik and Kets de Vries, 1975) in which attention is paid to the affective as well as the cognitive aspects of social processes. However, in these studies there is

Conceptualizing Leadership Processes: A Study of Senior Managers in a Financial Services Company *continued*

By David Knights and Hugh Willmott

a tendency simply to substitute pyschoanalytic for behavioural characteristics to identify the traits and styles of different kinds of leaders. For example, Kets de Vries and Miller (1985) draw upon ideas about narcissism to identify three types of (narcissistic) leader: reactive (bad), self-deceptive (tolerable but weak) and constructive (good). While it would be possible to apply their framework by suggesting how, in this transcript, the CE exemplifies many characteristics of the reactive leader (e.g. intolerant of criticism, humiliates opponents, use of scapegoats), our focus is upon the extent to which both the CE and the CS have invested themselves in their respective 'knowledge' of the situation.

Their interaction is clearly emotionally charged. Neither is indifferent to, or detached from, the reality of the new approach. Even though the CE's call for detachment seems to indicate his faith in, and commendation of, such a possibility, his response to the CS and his clear reluctance to open up the issue for discussion suggests that 'standing back' is acceptable so long as it is done in a way that is consistent with his conception of what 'detachment' means. Arguably, the tactics deployed to curtail and control the discussion of the new approach could be interpreted as a product of a narcissistic personality which, unable to deal with the complexity and ambiguity of social reality, routinely splits it into elements that are either ideal (all good) or persecutory (all bad). In this example, it would be quite reasonable for the CS to feel persecuted by the CE and to attribute this to his failure to confirm the CE's sense of superiority and self-sufficiency. However, this psychological reductionism fails to take adequate account of the burden of responsibility placed upon the CE and his dependence upon the performance of his fellow managers. In substantial part, his reaction arises in response to felt pressures to realize the ideals of corporate efficiency to which the strategic plans are directed.

Having said this, the exchange between the CE and the CS is fuelled by their respective vulnerabilities. On the one hand, the CE is anxious about the potential of the CS's intervention to undermine his credibility as the chief architect and implementer of

the corporate plans. On the other hand, the CS is vulnerable to the interventions of the CE in his area in a way that undermines his authority. Their interaction is motivated by this vulnerability; and their respective efforts to construct reality in a way that 'realizes' their sense of identity cannot sensibly be excluded from the analysis of their interaction. This existential dimension, in which what Giddens (1991, p. 53) terms self-identity – 'the self as reflexively understood by the person in terms of her or his biography' is either affirmed or denied in the course of the interaction.

In the event, the CS's interjection was seized by the CE as an opportunity for asserting his authority through the public humiliation of the CS. For example, before the CS has a chance to complete his response to the request for comments upon the progress on changing the approach to decision-making within the company, the CE interrupts to justify his close involvement in the running of the office. He is emphatic in his insistence that things must be done 'to my standard', thereby indicating to other managers that the quality of decision-making in their areas will not escape his critical scrutiny. Not surprisingly, perhaps, there is no ready support for the CS in his attempt to open up some discussion of progress on this key task – which suggests either that he had not taken the (politically astute) precaution of canvassing the views of his fellow managers or that any sympathizers were silenced by the force of the CE's dismissive response. Even the humorous intervention of the other AGM, a long-standing associated and past sponsor of the CS, failed to diffuse the tension of the situation or the ferocity of the CE's attack. Indeed, if anything, it backfired by implying that the CS was a fellow reactionary, an interpretation that affirmed the view of the CE's definition of the situation.

The Structural Dimension

Finally, attention to the structural dimension of leadership processes has an affinity with studies that are concerned with the position of leaders (French and Raven, 1959; French and Snyder, 1959; Frost and Stahelski, 1988; Stahelski *et al.*, 1989), which has

READING 7.1

Conceptualizing Leadership Processes: A Study of Senior Managers in a Financial Services Company

By David Knights and Hugh Willmott

been related to the strategic contingencies and dependencies associated with particular roles or functions (Hickson *et al.*, 1971; Pfeffer and Salancik, 1978). Specifically, French and Raven's (1959) typology identifies rank or hierarchical position as a source of power. The capacity to provide rewards, apply coercive sanctions, gain access to expertise and information and secure esteem amongst subordinates can each be related (but not reduced) to the occupancy of a comparatively elevated position within organizational hierarchies.

In our extract, it is relevant to connect the capacity of the CE to assert and articulate at some length his definition of the situation to his position at the apex of the organizational hierarchy. Not only does the occupancy of this position 'entitle' him to make the demand for 'things' to be done to his standards (even if his managers are unwilling or unable to comply with such demands) but it also allows him repeatedly to frustrate and override the attempts of the CS to raise issues. The course of the interaction is at once enabled and constrained by their respective positions in the hierarchy. As head of a non-democratic bureaucracy, the CE is in a position not only to allocate tasks amongst his senior managers but to assess their competence – publicly as well as privately. In the meeting from which this transcript is taken, his position enables him to chair the review of progress, to articulate his prerogative to impose standards and to terminate the discussion at will.

However, the capacity of the CE to dominate the meeting cannot be examined adequately by reference to his position within the organizational hierarchy. For the power invested in this position is itself a medium and outcome of the politico-economic structure of society in which the owners of resources (capitalists or policy-holders) appoint and seek to control employees, including managers, to secure and expand these resources. The purpose of hierarchy is not simply to achieve an efficient division and coordination of labour but to ensure that resources are deployed to facilitate growth. Arguably, it is this concern that underpins the plan to make decision-making in the company more sensitive and responsive to its strategic

significance for the organization's competitive position. Likewise, it is this politico-economic context that makes salient the CE's criticisms of the handling of the surge of New Business 'where there have been hot-line cases for two and a half weeks and they still haven't left the office'. For it resonates with the power-invested general understanding that both corporate performance and individual identity is dependent upon beating the competition, a coupling of concerns which is articulated in the CE's declaration that evidence of ineffectiveness such as that discerned in the handling of New Business will drive him mad. In this sense, the CE himself reveals his own subjugation to the discipline of the politico-economic system as he uses his position to demand a comparable level of subjugation from his fellow managers (Knights and Willmott, 1989; 1990).

References

Berger, P. and Luckmann, T. (1966) *The Social Construction of Reality*. Harmondsworth: Penguin.

Biggart, N.W. and Hamilton, G.G. (1987) 'An institutional theory of leadership'. *Journal of Applied Behavioral Science*, 23(4): 429–41.

French, J. and Raven, B.H. (1959) 'The bases of social power'. In Cartwright, D. (Ed.), *Studies in Social Power*. Ann Arbor, Mich.: Institute for Social Research.

French, J. and Snyder, R. (1959) 'Leadership and interpersonal power.' In Cartwright, D. (Ed.), *Studies in Social Power*. Ann Arbor, Mich.: Institute for Social Research.

Frost, D.E. and Stahelski, A.J. (1988) 'The systematic measurement of French and Raven's bases of social power in workgroup'. *Journal of Applied Social Psychology*, 18(5): 75–89.

Giddens, A. (1991) *Modernity and Self-Identity*. Cambridge: Polity.

Hickson, D.J., Hinings, C.R., Lee, C.A. and Pennings, J.M. (1971) 'A strategic contingencies theory of intra-organizational power'. *Administrative Science Quarterly*, 16: 216–29.

Kets de Vries, M.F.R. (1991) 'Whatever happened to the philosopher-king? The leader's addiction to *power*'. *Journal of Management Studies*, 28(4): 339–5.

Kets de Vries, M.F.R. and Miller, D. (1985) 'Narcissism and leadership: an object relations perspective'. *Human Relations*, 38(6): 583–601.

Conceptualizing Leadership Processes: A Study of Senior Managers in a Financial Services Company *continued*

By David Knights and Hugh Willmott

Knights, D. and Willmott, H.C. (1989) 'From degradation to subjugation: subjectivity and power in the labour process'. *Sociology*, 23(4): 535–58.

Levy, A. and Merry, U. (1986) *Organizational Transformation*. New York: Praeger.

Pfeffer, J. (1981) 'Management as symbolic action: the creation and maintenance of organizational paradigms'. In Cummings, L.L. and Staw, B.M. (Eds.), *Research in Organizational Behavior,* Vol. 3. Greenwich, Conn.: JAI Press.

Pfeffer, J. and Salancik, C. (1978) *The External Control of Organizations.* New York: Harper & Row.

Selznick, P. (1957) *Leadership in Administration.* New York: Harper & Row.

Smircich, L. and Morgan, C. (1982) 'Leadership: the management of meaning'. *Journal of Applied Behavioral Science,* 18(3): 257–73.

Stahelski, A.J., Frost, D.E. and Patch, M.E. (1989) 'Use of socially dependent bases of power: French and Raven's theory applied to workgroup leadership'. *Journal of Applied Social Psychology,* 19(4): 283–97.

Tichy, N.M. and Devanna, M.A. (1986) *The Transformational Leader.* New York: Wiley.

Zaleznick, A. and Kets De Vries, M.F.R. (1975) *Power and the Corporate Mind.* Boston: Houghton Mifflin.

Leadership and the Management of Meaning

By Linda Smircich and Gareth Morgan

The concept of leadership permeates and structures the theory and practice of organizations and hence the way we shape and understand the nature of organized action, and its possibilities. In fact, the concept and practice of leadership, and variant forms of direction and control, are so powerfully ingrained into popular thought that the absence of leadership is often seen as an absence of organization. Many organizations are paralysed by situations in which people appeal for direction, feeling immobilized and disorganized by the sense that they are not being led. Yet other organizations are plagued by the opposite situation characterized in organizational vernacular as one of 'all chiefs, no Indians' – the situation where the majority aspire to lead and few to follow. Thus, successful acts of organization are often seem to rest in the synchrony between the initiation of action and the appeal for direction; between the actions of leaders and the receptivity and responsiveness of followers ...

The Phenomenon of Leadership

Leadership is realized in the process whereby one or more individuals succeeds in attempting to frame and define the reality of others. Indeed, leadership situations may be conceived as those in which there exists an *obligation* or a perceived *right* on the part of certain individuals to define the reality of others.

This process is most evident in unstructured group situations where leadership emerges in a natural and spontaneous manner. After periods of interaction, unstructured leaderless groups typically evolve common modes of interpretation and shared understandings of experience that allow them to develop into a social organization (Bennis & Shepard, 1965). Individuals in groups that evolve this way attribute leadership to those members who structure experience in meaningful ways. Certain individuals, as a result of personal inclination or the emergent expectation of others, find themselves adopting or being obliged to take a leadership role by virtue of the part they play in the definition of the situation. They emerge as leaders because of their role in framing experience in a way that provides a viable basis for action, e.g., by mobilizing meaning, articulating and defining what has previously remained implicit or unsaid, by inventing images and meanings that provide a focus for

Source: Reproduced with permission of Sage Publications, London, Los Angeles, New Delhi and Singapore (via Rightslink) from 'Leadership: The Management of Meaning', in the Journal of Applied Behavioural Science © 1982 Sage Publications.

READING 7.2	# Leadership and the Management of Meaning
	By Linda Smircich and Gareth Morgan

new attention, and by consolidating, confronting, or changing prevailing wisdom (Peters, 1978; Pondy, 1976). Through these diverse means, individual actions can frame and change situations, and in so doing enact a system of shared meaning that provides a basis for organized action. The leader exists as a formal leader only when he or she achieves a situation in which an obligation, expectation, or right to frame experience is presumed, or offered and accepted by others.

Leadership, like other social phenomena, is socially constructed though interaction (Berger & Luckmann, 1966), emerging as a result of the constructions and actions of both leaders and led. It involves a complicity or process of negotiation through which certain individuals, implicitly or explicitly, surrender their power to define the nature of their experience to others. Indeed, leadership depends on the existence of individuals willing, as a result of inclination or pressure, to surrender, at least in part, the powers to shape and define their own reality. If a group situation embodies competing definitions of reality, strongly held, no clear pattern of leadership evolves. Often, such situations are characterized by struggles among those who aspire to define the situation. Such groups remain loosely coupled networks of interaction, with members often feeling that they are 'disorganized' because they do not share a common way of making sense of their experience.

Leadership lies in large part in generating a point of reference, against which a feeling of organization and direction can emerge. While in certain circumstances the leader's image of reality may be hegemonic, as in the case of charismatic or totalitarian leaders who mesmerize their followers, this is by no means always the case. For the phenomenon of leadership in being interactive is by nature dialectical. It is shaped through the interaction of at least two points of reference, i.e. of leaders and of led.

This dialectic is often the source of powerful internal tensions within leadership situations. These manifest themselves in the conflicting definitions of those who aspire to define reality and in the fact that while the leader of a group may forge a unified pattern of meaning, that very same pattern often provides a point of reference for the negotiation of leadership (Sennett, 1980). While individuals may look to a

leader to frame and concretize their reality, they may also react against, reject, or change the reality thus defined. While leadership often emerges as a result of expectations projected on the emergent leader by the led, the surrender of power involved provides the basis for negation of the situation thus created. Much of the tension in leadership situations stems from this source. Although leaders draw their power from their ability to define the reality of others, their inability to control completely provides seeds of disorganization in the organization of meaning they provide.

The emergence of leadership in unstructured situations thus points toward at least four important aspects of leadership as a phenomenon. First, leadership is essentially a social process defined through interaction. Second, leadership involves a process of defining reality in ways that are sensible to the led. Third, leadership involves a dependency relationship in which individuals surrender their powers to interpret and define reality to others.[1] Fourth, the emergence of formal leadership roles represents an additional stage of institutionalization, in which rights and obligations to define the nature of experience and activity are recognized and formalized.

Leadership in Formalized Settings

The main distinguishing feature of formal organization is that the way in which experience is to be structured and defined is built into a stock of taken for granted meanings, or 'typifications' in use (Schutz, 1967) that underlie the everyday definition and reality of the organization. In particular, a formal organization is premised upon shared meanings that define roles and authority relationships that institutionalize a pattern of leadership. In essence, formal organization truncates the leadership process observed in natural settings, concretizing its characteristics as a mode of social organization into sets of predetermined roles, relationships, and practices, providing a blueprint of how the experience of organizational members is to be structured.

Roles, for example, institutionalize the interactions and definitions that shape the reality of organizational life. Rules, conventions, and work practices present ready-made typifications through which experience is to be made sensible. Authority relationships legitimize the pattern of dependency relations that

Leadership and the Management of Meaning *continued*

By Linda Smircich and Gareth Morgan

characterize the process of leadership, specifying who is to define organizational reality, and in what circumstances. Authority relationships institutionalize a hierarchical pattern of interaction in which certain individuals are expected to define the experience of others – to lead, and others to follow. So powerful is this process of institutionalized leadership and the expectation that someone has the right and obligation to define reality, that leaders are held to account if they do not lead 'effectively'. Those expecting to be led, for example, often rationalize their own inaction or ineffectiveness by scapegoating through statements such as 'she is a poor manager' or 'he is messing things up'. On the other hand, occupancy of an authority role presents the leader in every situation with an existential dilemma – how to define and structure the element of organizational reality encountered at a given time. Formal organizations are often heavily populated by those who feel obliged to define the reality and experience of others in a way that is consistent with their idea of 'being a good leader'. To fail in this obligation is to fail in one's organizational role.

In these ways, patterns of formal organization institutionalize aspects of the leadership process within the context of a unified structure that specifies patterns of desired interaction, sense making, and dependency. As in the case of leadership as an emergent process, formal structures of organized action also contain a dialectical tension between the pattern of action and meaning that the structure seems to establish, and the tendency of individuals to reinterpret, or even react against, the structure thus defined. While submitting to the dominant pattern of meaning, individuals frequently strive to develop patterns of their own, a phenomenon well documented in studies of the so-called 'informal organization' (Roethlisberger and Dickson, 1939).

It is this inherent tension that calls for the development of a mediating form of leadership, bridging the gulf between the requirements of institutionalized structure and the natural inclinations of its human agents. It is this form of leadership that we most often recognize as leadership in informal organizations – the interpersonal process linking structure and the human beings who inhabit this structure. The person that is most easily recognized as an organizational leader is the one who rises above and beyond the

specification of formal structure to provide members of the organization with a sense that they are organized, even amidst an everyday feeling that at a detailed level everything runs the danger of falling apart.

Similarly, successful corporate leaders who give direction to the organization in a strategic sense frequently do so by providing an image or pattern of thinking in a way that has meaning for those directly involved (Quinn, 1980). This is reflected in part in Selznick's (1957) conception of leadership as involving the embodiment of organizational values and purpose. Strategic leadership, in effect, involves providing a conception and direction for organizational process that goes above and beyond what is embedded in the fabric of organization as a structure, i.e., a reified and somewhat static pattern of meaning.

Formal organization thus embodies at least two distinctive, yet complementary aspects of the phenomenon of leadership: (1) the structure of organization institutionalizes the leadership process into a network of roles, often in an overconcretized and dehumanizing form; (2) mediating or interpersonal leadership – what is most evident as leadership in action – operationalizes the principles of leadership as an emergent process within the context of the former. This is usually as a means of transcending the limitations of the former for containing the dialectical tension that it embodies, and as a means of giving the whole coherence and direction over time. These two aspects of leadership have been well recognized in leadership research (Katz and Kahn, 1966) and are frequently interpreted and studied in terms of a relationship between 'initiating structure' and 'consideration' (e.g., Stogdill, 1974) …

When leaders act they punctuate contexts in ways that provide a focus for the creation of meaning (see Figure 7.2.1). Their action isolates an element of experience, which can be interpreted in terms of the context in which it is set. Indeed, its meaning is embedded in its relationship with its context. Consider, for example, the simple situation in which someone in a leadership role loses his or her temper over the failure of an employee to complete a job on time. For the leader this action embodies a meaning that links the event to context in a significant way, e.g., 'This employee has been asking for a reprimand for a long

READING 7.2	**Leadership and the Management of Meaning**
	By Linda Smircich and Gareth Morgan

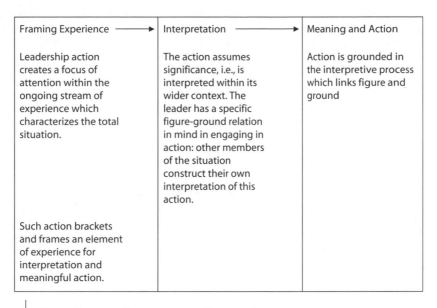

Framing Experience ⟶	Interpretation ⟶	Meaning and Action
Leadership action creates a focus of attention within the ongoing stream of experience which characterizes the total situation.	The action assumes significance, i.e., is interpreted within its wider context. The leader has a specific figure-ground relation in mind in engaging in action: other members of the situation construct their own interpretation of this action.	Action is grounded in the interpretive process which links figure and ground
Such action brackets and frames an element of experience for interpretation and meaningful action.		

FIGURE 7.2.1 | FROM FRAMING EXPERIENCE TO GUIDING ACTION

time'; 'This was an important job'; 'This office is falling apart'. For the employees in the office, the event may be interpreted in similar terms, or a range of different constructions placed upon the situation, e.g., 'Don't worry about it, he always loses his temper from time to time'; 'She's been under pressure lately because of problems at home'.

The leader's action may generate a variety of interpretations that set the basis for meaningful action. It may serve to redefine the context into a situation where the meeting of deadlines assumes greater significance, or merely serves as a brief interruption in daily routine, soon forgotten. As discussed earlier, organized situations are often characterized by complex patterns of meaning, based on rival interpretations of the situation. Different members may make sense of situations with the aid of different interpretive schemes, establishing 'counter-realities', a source of tension in the group situation that may set the basis for change of an innovative or disintegrative kind. These counter-realities underwrite much of the political activities within organizations, typified by the leader's loyal lieutenants – the 'yes men' accepting

and reinforcing the leader's definition of the situation and the 'rebels' or 'out' groups forging and sustaining alternative views.

Effective leadership depends upon the extent to which the leader's definition of the situation, e.g., 'People in this office are not working hard enough', serves as a basis for action by others. It is in this sense that effective leadership rests heavily on the framing of the experience of others, so that action can be guided by common conceptions as to what should occur. The key challenge for a leader is to manage meaning in such a way that individuals orient themselves to the achievement of desirable ends. In this endeavour the use of language, ritual, drama, stories, myths, and symbolic construction of all kinds may play an important role (Pfeffer, 1981; Pondy, Frost, Morgan and Dandridge, 1982; Smircich 1982). They constitute important tools in the management of meaning. Through words and images, symbolic actions and gestures, leaders can structure attention and evoke patterns of meaning that give them considerable control over the situation being managed. These tools can be used to forge particular kinds of

| **Leadership and the Management of Meaning** *continued*

By Linda Smircich and Gareth Morgan

figure-ground relations that serve to create appropriate modes of organized action. Leadership rests as much in these symbolic modes of action as in those instrumental modes of management, direction, and control that define the substance of the leader's formal organizational role.

[1]Bougon, M. (1980) Schemata, leadership and organizational behaviour. Doctoral dissertation, Cornell University.

References

Bennis, W.G. & Shepherd, H.A. (1965) A theory of group development. *Human Relations*, 9, 415–457.

Berger, P. & Luckmann, T. (1966) *The social construction of reality*. New York: Anchor Books.

Frost, P.J., Morgan P.J. & Pondy, L.R. (1983). In L.R. Pondy, P.J. Frost, G. Morgan, & T.C. Dandridge (Eds.), *Organizational symbolism*. Greenwich, CT: JAI Press. pp. 187–198.

Katz, D. & Kahn, R.L. (1966) *The social psychology of organizations*. New York: Wiley.

Peters, T.J. (1978) Symbols, patterns and settings: An optimistic case for getting things done. *Organizational Dynamics*, 3–22.

Pfeffer, J. (1981) Management as symbolic action: The creation and maintenance of organizational paradigms. *Research in Organizational Behavior*, 3, 1–52.

Pondy, L.R. (1976) Leadership is a language game. In M. McCall & M. Lombardo (Eds.), *Leadership: Where else can we go?* Durham, N.C.: Duke University Press.

Quinn, J.B. (1980) *Strategies for change*. New York: Irwin.

Roethlisberger, F.J. and Dickson, W.J. (1939) *Management and the worker*. Cambridge, Mass.: Harvard University Press.

Schutz, A. (1967) *Collected papers I: The problem of social reality*. (2nd ed.). The Hague: Martinus Nijhoff.

Selznick, P. (1957) *Leadership in administration*. New York: Harper & Row.

Sennett, R. (1980) *Authority*. New York: Knopf.

Smircich, L. (1982) Organizations as shared meanings. In Pondy, L.R., Frost, P., Morgan, G. and Dandridge, T. (Eds.). *Organizational symbolism*. Greenwich, Conn.: JAI Press.

Stogdill, R.M. (1974) *Handbook of leadership: A survey of theory and research*. New York: The Free Press.

| **Symbols and Symbolic Behaviour: Definitions and Distinctions**

By Michael Jones

Human beings, perhaps more than other animals, have a great propensity toward, dependency on, and responsiveness to symbols and symbolizing (e.g., Chapple and Coon, 1942, p. 481; Rose, 1962, p. 4; Rossi, 1980, p. 25; White, 1949). Cassirer (1944, p. 26) proposed that 'instead of defining man as an animal *rationale*, we should define him as an animal *symbolicum*' (quoted in Schultz, 1944, p. 75). According to Cohen (1976, p. 23), 'Symbols are objects, acts, relationships or linguistic formations that stand ambiguously for a multiplicity of meanings.' Morgan, Frost and Pondy (1983, pp. 4–5) further write that a symbol 'is a sign which denotes something much greater than itself', embodying and representing a wider pattern of meaning:

Symbols are created and recreated whenever human beings vest elements of their world with a pattern of meaning and significance which extends beyond its intrinsic content. Any object, action, event, utterance, concept or image offers itself as raw material for symbol creation, at any place, and at any time. (See also Goffman, 1959; Rose, 1962, p. 6; Rossi, 1980, p. 24; Whyte, 1961, p. 24.)

Consider this example. On becoming head of the New York City Health Services Administration, Gordon Chase called in commissioners and senior managers. He asked them what they had been up to

Symbols and Symbolic Behaviour: Definitions and Distinctions

By Michael Jones

recently. Some told him how many meetings they attended, the number of staff they had hired, the volume of memos they had written and other bureaucratic activities they had completed. 'But whom did you make healthy today (or last week, or last year)?' asked Chase. 'Did you make anybody in New York healthier – and how do you know?' Chase wished to emphasize the results of services, not the mechanics of running public agencies.

> I wanted the right perspective – I wanted my managers to be conscious of the fact that we were there to make people healthier, and not to lose sight of that fact in the daily squabblings that we all had to endure.

The agency's mission, according to Chase, was to 'make government work' by serving people and doing it well (Chase and Reveal, 1983, pp. 177–179).

To convey his conception of organizational values, Chase used language, a form of symbolization; that is, words stand for things but are not the thing themselves. In addition, Chase's questions meant something other than what they at first seemed to signify; he was not in fact soliciting a report but expressing dissatisfaction with existing assumptions and setting forth new rules for behaviour. He communicated this not through words alone but through the order of his queries, the repetition of his performance with each senior manager, and the fact that as the new head of the agency, anything he said or did in such circumstances could be considered a signal of changing values and expectations. Utterances, events, and conditions served as vehicles of symbolic communication and interaction for Chase on this occasion. The symbolic cuts through the 'noise' of all the visual, aural, and other stimuli to indicate what is important and meaningful.

Symbols and symbolic behaviour evoke emotions (Cohen, 1976, p. 23). For instance, Hirschhorn (1988, pp. 247–248) reports meeting with the representative of a research organization who had been delegated to ask him to facilitate a retreat for senior scientists. She told him that the scientists 'felt undersupported and unappreciated' and believed that the controller and president were 'nickel-and-diming' the labs to death. She thought the retreat would be a difficult one. Hirschhorn inquired about preparations and was told that everyone was being asked to bring a brown-bag lunch. 'Having heard that the major presenting complaint (the ostensible issue or problem) was "nickel-and-diming", I urged her to tell the president that it would be better to provide lunch for the retreat.' He reminded the representative that participants had to do difficult and emotional work; 'they would appreciate such a symbol of support,' he said. She hesitated, contending that the president might never agree. 'Puzzled and irritated, I realized that I was experiencing the same feelings that bothered the scientists of the company,' writes Hirschhorn. 'So the president, even before I met him and before I even had a contract, was nickel-and-diming me to death as well!' Although trained in psychodynamics, Hirschhorn was not immune to the impact of symbolism. Use of the traditional expressions 'brown bag it' and 'nickel-and-diming' immediately aroused his emotions and coloured his perceptions.

References

Cassirer, E. (1944) *An essay on man.* New Haven, CT: Yale University Press.

Chapple, E.O. and Coon, C.S. (1942) *Principles of anthropology.* New York: Holt.

Chase, G. and Reveal, E.C. (1983) *How to manage in the public sector.* Reading, MA: Addison-Wesley.

Cohen, A. (1976) *Two-dimensional man: An essay on the anthropology of power and symbolism in complex society.* Berkeley: University of California Press.

Goffman, I. (1959) *The presentation of self in everyday life.* Garden City, NY: Doubleday.

Hirschhorn, L. (1988) *The workplace within: The psychodynamics of organizational life.* Cambridge, MA: MIT Press.

Morgan, P.J., Frost, P.J. and Pondy, L.R. (1983) In L.R. Pondy, P.J. Frost, G. Morgan, and T.C. Dandridge (Eds.), Organizational symbolism. Greenwich, CT: JAI Press. pp. 187–198.

Rose, A.M. (1962) *Human behaviour and social processes: An interactionist approach.* Boston: Houghton Mifflin.

Rossi, I. (1980) Introduction. In I. Rossi (Ed.), *People in culture* (pp.1–28). New York: Praeger.

Schultz, M. (1994) *On studying organizational cultures: Diagnosis and understanding.* New York: Walter de Gruyter.

White, L.A. (1949) *The science of culture, a study of man and civilization.* New York: Farrar, Staus and Giroux.

Whyte, W.F. (1961) *Men at work.* Homewood, IL: Dorsey Press and Richard D. Irwin.

Discussion Questions

1. How is leadership understood within the three extracts?
2. It has been suggested that the key to understanding leadership is consideration of followership. What might be the basis for this suggestion and do you find it plausible?
3. '[The] occupancy of an authority role presents the leader in every situation with an existential dilemma – how to define and structure the element of organizational reality encountered at a given time' (Smircich and Morgan, Reading 7.2, p. 134). Identify and explore some examples that illustrate this point.
4. How is symbolism important to leadership?

Introduction References

Bass, B. (1985) *Leadership and Performance: Beyond Expectations*. New York: Free Press.

Biggart, N.W. and Hamilton, G.G. (1987) 'An institutional theory of leadership'. *Journal of Applied Behavioral Science* 23(4): 429–41.

Bryman, A., Bresnen, M., Beardsworth, A. and Keil, T. (1988) 'Qualitative research and the study of leadership'. *Human Relations* 41(1): 13–30.

Calder, B. (1977) 'An attribution theory of leadership'. In Staw, B.M. and Salancik, G.R. (Eds.), *New Directions in Organizational Behavior*. Malabar, Fl.: Krieger.

Cooper, D. Ezzamel, M. and Willmott, H.C. (2008) 'Examining "institutionalization": a critical theoretic perspective' in Greenwood, R., Oliver C, Suddaby R. and Sahlin-Anderson, K. (eds.), *Handbook of Organizational Institutionalism*, London: Sage.

Fielder, F.E. (1986) 'The contribution of cognitive resources and behavior to organizational performance'. *Journal of Applied Social Psychology* 16(6): 532–48.

Fielder, F.E. and Carcia, J.E. (1987) *New Approaches to Effective Leadership: Cognitive Resources and Organization Performance*. New York: Wiley.

Greene, C.N. (1976) 'Disenchantment with leadership research: some causes, recommendations and alternative directions' in Hunt, J.C. and Larson, L.L., eds., *Leadership: The Cutting Edge*, Carbondale, Ill: Southern Illinois University Press.

House, R.J. (1971) 'Path goal theory of leader effectiveness'. *Administrative Science Quarterly*, 16, 321–38.

McClelland, D. (1961) *The Achieving Society*. Princeton, N.J.: Van Nostrand.

Mintzberg, H. (1982) 'If you're not serving Bill and Barbara, then you're not serving leadership'. In Hunt, J.G., Sekaran, U. and Schriesheim, C.A. (Eds.), *Leadership: Beyond Establishment Views*. Carbondale, Ill: Southern Illinois University Press.

Pfeffer, J. (1977) 'The ambiguity of leadership'. *Academy of Management Review*, January, 104–12.

Vroom, V.H. and Yetton, P.W. (1973) *Leadership and Decision Making*. Pittsburgh: University of Pittsburgh Press.

Whyte, W.F. (1955) *Street Corner Society: The Social Structure of an Italian Slum*. Chicago: University of Chicago Press.

Recommended Further Readings

See references to all the above texts plus:

Alvesson, M. and Sveningsson, S. (2003) 'The great disappearing act: difficulties in doing "leadership"', *The Leadership Quarterly*, 14(3): 359–81.

Biggart, N.W. and Hamilton, G.G. (1987) 'An institutional theory of leadership'. *Journal of Applied Behavioral Science*, 23(4): 429–41.

Bryman, A. (1986) *Leadership and Organisation*, London: Routledge.

Bryman, A. (2004) 'Qualitative research on leadership: A critical but appreciative review', *The Leadership Quarterly*, 15(6): 729–769

Collinson, D. (2006) 'Rethinking followership: A poststructuralist analysis of follower identities', *The Leadership Quarterly*, 17(2): 179–189.

Greene, C.N. (1976) 'Disenchantment with leadership research: some causes, recommendations and alternative directions' in Hunt, J.C. and Larson, L.L.

(eds.), *Leadership: The Cutting Edge*, Carbondale, Ill.: Southern Illinois University Press.

Grint, K. (1997) *Leadership: classical, contemporary, and critical approaches,* Oxford University Press, 1997.

Grint, K. (2005) 'Problems, problems, problems: The social construction of "leadership"', *Human Relations*, 58(11): 1467–94.

Hosking, D. (1988) 'Organizing, leadership and skilful process', *Journal of Management Studies*, 25(2): 147–166.

Paul, J. (1996) 'A symbolic interactionist perspective on leadership', *Journal of Leadership & Organizational Studies*, 3(2): 82–93.

Wood, M. (2005) 'The fallacy of misplaced leadership', *Journal of Management Studies*, 42(6): 1101–1121.

POWER, CONTROL AND RESISTANCE

CHAPTER 8

READINGS

Edwards, R. (1979) *Contested Terrain: The Transformation of the Workplace in the 20th Century*. New York: Basic Books, pp. 16–18; 20–21; 51–52; 57–8.

Knights, D. and Willmott, H. (1999) *Management Lives: Power and Identity in Work Organisations*. London: Sage, pp. 95–99.

Collinson, D. (1994) 'Strategies of Resistance: Power, Knowledge and Subjectivity in the Workplace' in *Resistance and Power in Organization*, Edited by Jermier, J.M., Knights, D. and Nord, W.R. London: Routledge. pp. 25–68.

Knights, D. and Vurdubakis, T. (1994) 'Foucault, Power, Resistance and All That', in *Resistance and Power in Organizations*. Edited by Jermier, J. *et al*. London: Routledge, pp. 167–198.

INTRODUCTION

Power is a concept that is central to any analysis within the social sciences including organization theory; resistance has received rather less attention. In this section, we seek to give equal attention to both although some degree of asymmetry is unavoidable if we are to reflect the literature fairly. Probably the earliest trace of the concept of power in organization studies is in Max Weber's *Theory of Social and Economic Organization* (1947) and his analysis of bureaucracy (Albrow, 1970). Weber saw bureaucracy as a system of power in which leaders exercise control over others through a set of legal-rational rules backed up by authority and discipline and legitimated by their superior rationality (Albrow, 1970). In the hands of the father of functionalism in social theory – Talcott Parsons (1949), Weber's work was translated more in terms of authority in which power need not be exercised because an overall value consensus was presumed to prevail. Only in political science did power remain a central concept until, in the 1980s, more critical organization theorists rejected the dominant functionalist paradigm in favour of theories influenced by Marxism or, more correctly, neo-Marxism in which the exercise of managerial power was seen to be both a condition and consequence of conflicts that were theorized as ubiquitous in work organizations. Power has remained a pivotal concept in organization studies ever since but currently conceptualizations seem to have polarized between those influenced by a Marxian conflict paradigm and those drawn to Foucault's notion of it as synonymous with social relations but always linked with knowledge. Our selection of extracts draws primarily on authors subscribing to a Foucauldian perspective largely because of his notion of power in being productive as well as constraining, positive as well as negative, a property of relations rather than persons, and distributed rather than centralized in a single location either personal or institutional seems to resonate more with contemporary organizational life. We begin, however, with a classic piece that reflects the revival by Braverman of Marx's labour process theory.

Our first extract from **Richard Edwards** (Reading 8.1) begins by arguing that productive output in organizations is the outcome of a conflict or struggle between capitalists and labour as resistance to managerial control either fails or ends in some compromise whereby top-down coordination is rendered effective. Edwards defines control as the ability of capitalists or managers to secure the desired productive behaviour from labour. While there are different types of control, as we shall see, there are always three distinct elements that have to be coordinated. These are *directing* workers in the specific details of their tasks; *evaluating* the quality and quantity of their performance and intervening to maintain standards; and *disciplining* and rewarding employees to ensure co-operation and compliance with management objectives. Edwards also distinguishes three types of control as follows:

Simple control, which is more related to traditional owner-managed small enterprises and continues only on the periphery of the modern industrial system. It is based on the personal and informal exercise of power but could be entirely arbitrary and inconsistent and certainly not appropriate once an organization grew in size. Here when economic resources became more concentrated, two more formal or 'structural' approaches to managerial control displaced simple control. Concentration in larger corporations had resulted not only in difficulties in maintaining control through personal or close supervision but also in collective resistance on the part of labour. Technical control was a product of advances in technology and the growth of mass production where the machine could determine the speed and flow of the work and eventually, through collective bargaining, management could draw on the legitimacy of union leaders to help secure control of the workforce. Here the type of control merged with another – bureaucratic control – where control becomes embedded in the social relations of production. Organizations not involved in mass production, at least prior to the computer age, could not readily utilize technical controls but hierarchy, a detailed and specialized division of labour, and a career system framed in an impersonal set of rules provided the solution for large organizations of this kind. Indeed it swept through most large organizations since through its system of rules and regulations it facilitated control at a distance. If identification with the workforce was helpful this could come in the form of formal or informal union leaders who would negotiate compliance in return for wage increases each year. However, as Edwards indicates, these compromises were often long drawn out affairs in which the conflict between capital and labour was a constant threat to the smooth and profitable development of the corporation as it was to the stability and security of employment.

The extract from **David Knights and Hugh Willmott** (Reading 8.2) is included in place of the analysis of power by Steven Lukes (1974) because it provides a summary that seeks to render the ideas more intelligible through illustrating the concepts with reference to characters in popular novels related to work and organization. However, it also seeks to develop the analysis through critical reflection on its strengths and limitations. It provides a full summary of the three conceptions of power described by Lukes as follows:

Originally developed by Dahl (1961) and colleagues, a one-dimensional conception of power perceives it to exist when individuals or groups could assert their will or secure compliance in situations where there is observable conflict. By contrast, from a two-dimensional perspective advanced by Bacharach and Baratz (1970) potential conflicts are kept off the agenda so determining the conditions in advance of any explicit exercise of power. Lukes' contribution is to offer a third dimension where power is seen as not only keeping potentials for conflict off the agenda but so defining the situation for others that they internalize norms and comply even when it is against their interests. Knights and Willmott examine Lukes' analysis as a reflection of his radical humanism where power was seen to deny or restrict individual's essential autonomy. Each dimension of power can be seen as an increasingly more virulent threat to this autonomy. The authors agree with Lukes' critique of the first two dimensions of power and that his third dimension captures how socialization generates norms of compliance and conformity but they disagree with the idea that 'real interests' can be readily identified or that individual autonomy is what has to be defended. Indeed in other work, following Foucault they have demonstrated that autonomy can be extremely oppressive and as much a vice as a virtue (Knights and Willmott, 2002). Furthermore, the authors criticize Lukes' failure to acknowledge that the powerful may be victims as well as perpetrators of their own manipulations and that their compulsive desire to control is often self-defeating (see extracts on masculinity in the section on Inequality and Diversity).

David Collinson (Reading 8.3) gives more attention to the reverse of power–resistance that he believes has been neglected in empirical studies of the workplace. He argues that the history of management theory has been a focus on responding to or preventing labour resistance. Perhaps because of their success, attention of late has been more on the consent, compliance and self-discipline of subordinates and the ease with which their resistance can be outflanked. In order to demonstrate that resistance at work is still alive and well, Collinson turns to two empirical case studies to outline two distinct strategies of resistance – one through distance and the other through persistence. Both involve the use of their monopoly over certain technical and production-related knowledges. In contrast to Jackall's (1988) managers who rarely failed to pass information up the hierarchy to their bosses, shopfloor workers in the first case study restricted the flow of knowledge and information in order to appropriate both space and time for themselves so as to avoid any intensification of labour. Despite management attempts to generate a closer and more informal relationship with their shopfloor employees, workers kept their distance refusing to reciprocate in using first names, and rejecting offers of cigarettes or car lifts. This maintenance of distance and the refusal to have any responsibility for the company paradoxically simply reinforced managerial prerogative and legitimacy and left workers vulnerable to disciplinary practices and the loss of jobs when the market for their products declined. Resistance through persistence was the exact opposite for it sought to extract knowledge from management. The case study involved a woman who appeared to have suffered discrimination in relation to her promotion from a Grade 6 to a Grade 7 position when she became pregnant. Through her union representatives, the resistance took the form of extracting as much knowledge and information as possible and using this effectively to overturn an unfair decision, thus promoting equal opportunity within the company.

David Knights and Theo Vurdubakis (Reading 8.4) seek to correct some misunderstandings of the concept of power and, by implication, of resistance that they detect in recent criticisms of Foucault. Critics generally and specifically in studies of work and organization argue that Foucault fails to theorize resistance because his conception of power precludes it. They identify three problems upon which critics focus when seeking to deny any conception of resistance in Foucault. These concern respectively the problems of where resistance is to be located if power is everywhere, who are to be its agents when their subjectivity is an effect of power, and how it can be justified if resistance invariably results in just the displacement of one power regime by another. The authors go through each of these objections to suggest that they reflect commitment to a dualistic or binary conception of power and resistance where they are always seen as opposite and exclusive of one another – a view not recognizable in Foucault since he sees them as simply two sides of the same coin. Consequently, just because power is widely dispersed does not mean that it is exhaustive of social relations, thus precluding space for resistance. For Foucault power is not a stable and unitary monolith so much as a contingent, fragile and precarious arrangement within which resistance is just as likely to occur as compliance. Resistance does not have to be outside of power relations as they are not mutually exclusive and, moreover, power is often 'productive' of resistance. Similarly although we are constituted by exercises of power, this does not prevent us being agents of resistance and indeed Foucault recommends that we resist by refusing the identity that power bestows upon us. Finally, critics argue that Foucault provides no reason why we should or do resist power; they demand a universal or grand theory or a theory of rights and objective interests that Foucault refuses to provide, largely because he believes resistance cannot be examined independently of the concrete local sites in which particular struggles are embedded. At the same time, while appealing to human rights in defence of resistance to particular subjugations because that is all there is in contemporary society, Foucault also warns us to retain a sceptical eye because humanism itself is no guarantee of emancipated political outcomes and indeed, it can be oppressive in forcing us to live by its orthodoxy.

READING 8.1	**Contested Terrain: The Transformation of the Workplace in the 20th Century**

By Richard Edwards

Three Faces from the Hidden Abode

How much work gets done every hour or every day emerges as a result of the struggle between workers and capitalists.

In what follows, the system of control (in other words, the social relations of production within the firm) are thought of as a way in which three elements are coordinated:

1. Direction, or a mechanism or method by which the employer directs work tasks, specifying what needs to be done, in what order, with what degree of precision or accuracy, and in what period of time.
2. Evaluation, or a procedure whereby the employer supervises and evaluates to correct mistakes or other failures in production, to assess each worker's performance, and to identify individual workers or groups of workers who are not performing tasks adequately.
3. Discipline, or an apparatus that the employer uses to discipline and reward workers, in order to elicit cooperation and enforce compliance with the capitalist's direction of the labour process.

The Types of Control

Systems of control in the firm have undergone dramatic changes in response to changes in the firm's size, operations, and environment and in the workers' success in imposing their own goals at the workplace. The new forms did not emerge as sharp discrete discontinuities in historical evolution, but neither were they simple points in a smooth and inevitable evolution. Rather, each transformation occurred as a resolution of intensifying conflict and contradiction in the firm's operations. Pressures built up, making the old forms of control untenable ...

Simple Control

In the nineteenth century, most businesses were small and were subject to the relatively tight discipline of substantial competition in product markets. The typical firm had few resources and little energy to invest in creating more sophisticated management structures. A single entrepreneur, usually flanked by a small coterie of foremen and managers, ruled the firm. These bosses exercised power personally, intervening in the labour process often to exhort workers, bully and threaten them, reward good performance, hire and fire on the spot, favour loyal workers, and generally act as despots, benevolent or otherwise, They had a direct stake in translating labour power into labour, and they combined both incentives and sanctions in an idiosyncratic and unsystematic mix. There was little structure to the way power was exercised, and workers were often treated arbitrarily. Since workforces were small and the boss was both close and powerful, workers had limited success when they tried to oppose his [sic] rule ...

Technical and Bureaucratic Control

Near the end of the nineteenth century, the tendencies toward concentration of economic resources undermined simple control while firms' needs for control increased ... [and] ... the efficacy of simple control declined. The need for coordination appeared to increase not only with the complexity of the product but also with the scale of production.

Large firms developed methods of organization that are more formalized and more consciously contrived than simple control; they are structural forms of control. Two possibilities existed; more formal, consciously contrived controls could be embedded in either the physical structure of the labour process (producing 'technical' control) or in its social structure (producing 'bureaucratic' control). In time, employers used both, for they found that the new systems made control more institutional and hence less visible to workers, and they also provided a means for capitalists to control the 'intermediate layers', those extended lines of supervision and power.

Technical control emerged from employers' experiences in attempting to control the production (or blue-collar) operations of the firm. The assembly line came to be the classic image, but the actual application of technical control was much broader. Machinery itself directed the labour process and set the pace. For a time, employers had the best of two worlds.

| READING 8.1 | **Contested Terrain: The Transformation of the Workplace in the 20th Century** *continued* |

By Richard Edwards

Inside the firm, technical control turned the tide of conflict in their favour, reducing workers to attendants of pre-paced machinery; externally, the system strengthened the employers' hands by expanding the number of potential substitute workers. But as factory workers in the late 1930s struck back with sit-downs, their action exposed the deep dangers to employers in thus linking all workers' labour together in one technical apparatus ...

These forces have produced today a second type of work organization. Whereas simple control persists in the small firms of the industrial periphery, in large firms, especially those in the mass-production industries, work is subject to technical control. The system is mutually administered by management and (as a junior partner) unions. Jobs in the GE [General Electric] plant works fit this pattern.

There exists a third method for organizing work and it too appeared in the large firms. This system, bureaucratic control, rests on the principle of embedding control in the social structure or the social relations of the workplace. The defining feature of bureaucratic control is the institutionalization of hierarchical power. 'Rule of law' – the firm's law replaces 'rule by supervisor command' in the direction of work, the procedures for evaluating workers' perfor-

mance, and the exercise of the firm's sanctions and rewards; supervisors and workers alike become subject to the dictates of 'company policy'. Work becomes highly stratified; each job is given its distinct title and description; and impersonal rules govern promotion. 'Stick with the corporation,' the worker is told, 'and you can ascend up the ladder.' The company promises the workers a *career*.

Bureaucratic control originated in employers' attempts to subject non-production workers to more strict control, but its success impelled firms to apply the system more broadly than just to the white-collar staff. Especially in the last three decades, bureaucratic control has appeared as the organizing principle in both production and non-production jobs in many large firms, and not the least of its attractions is that the system has proven especially effective in forestalling unionism.

Shop-floor conflict inevitably became part of the struggle over the regime of monopoly capitalism because it occurred in a broader social context of sharp class tensions. And it was a crisis for monopoly capitalists, because the broader context both generalized the conflict and tended to strengthen workers. The social context thus reduced the individual employer's ability to impose solutions unilaterally on his [sic] workforce.

| READING 8.2 | **Management Lives: Power and Identity in Work Organizations** |

By David Knights and Hugh Willmott

Lukes' Three-Dimensional Model

Following Lukes (1974), we can conceptualize power relations as having three dimensions, which range from comparatively self-evident and overt forms of the exercise of power to forms of power, which are more subtle and institutionalized. These are as follows:

1. Power to secure a decision in situations where there is some observable conflict of views;

2. Power to keep issues about which there are conflicting views on or off the decision-making agenda;

3. Institutionalized power to define reality in such a way as to ensure compliance because of an internalisation of norms even against people's so-called real interests.

The first dimension comprises the observable behaviour of individuals or groups who are seen to

READING 8.2	**Management Lives: Power and Identity in Work Organizations**

By David Knights and Hugh Willmott

determine, or at least influence, the form and content of decision making – for example, the decisions made by the detectives who arrest Sherman or the decision of Abe Weiss, the district attorney to treat McCoy like anyone else who is arrested (see Appendix 1 for synopsis of *Bonfire of the Vanities*):

> How *do* we treat some hotshot from Park Avenue? Like anyone else, that's how! He gets arrested, he gets the cuffs, he gets booked, he gets fingerprinted, he waits in the pens, just like anybody down there on those streets' (Wolfe, 1988; ibid.: 544)

The second dimension concerns the often non-observable behaviour involved in keeping issues on or off the agenda – for example, behind-the-scenes negotiations between various parties (lawyers, politicians, community leaders), that eventually ensured that Sherman's crime was investigated and became high profile. If only observable behaviour and conflicts are examined, some important aspects of power are ignored. For a greater exercise of power is often involved in order to prevent a controversial issue being discussed than to influence its outcome once in the public domain of decision-making. Consider the way in which McCoy's case was placed so prominently on the agenda via the mass media. For Weiss, the equitable treatment of McCoy was not simply a matter of demonstrating the impartiality of the law but of gaining the support of the community to keep him in office. Weiss had an election coming up in five months. The trial of McCoy was a means of demonstrating to the 70% of the Bronx who were black or Latin that they were being represented: 'I think that sends a helluva good signal. It lets those people know we *represent* them and they're a part of New York City' (ibid.: 544).

This brings us directly to a consideration of Lukes' third and final dimension of power. This is attentive to how those in positions of power may so define reality as to secure the general support of others, such as those who are most disadvantaged, by the exclusion of controversial issues from the political agenda. Weiss appreciated how the media could be deployed to define reality in ways that shape perceptions, expectations and demands:

Abe Weiss was one of a long line of New York district attorneys whose careers had been based on appearing on television and announcing the latest paralysing wallop to the solar plexus of crime in the seething metropolis. Weiss, the good Captain Ahab, might be the object of jokes. But he was wired to the Power, and the Power flowed through him ... (Wolfe, 1988; ibid.: 419)

Lukes contends that the 'real interests' and potential grievances of those subjected to power are obscured or distorted by powerful individuals and groups who are able to focus their minds on concerns, such as the sensational case of Sherman McCoy, which ensure that the structure of power relations is preserved. Lukes' understanding of this third dimension of power is readily applied to Stevens [in] *The Remains of the Day* (see Appendix 1 for synopsis of this novel) where a dogged devotion to duty and an unquestioning loyalty and trust is grounded in the butler's acceptance of the idea that only members of the aristocratic elite, like Lord Darlington, are capable of making informed decisions. Musing upon the qualities of a 'great butler', Stevens reflects:

> the more one considers it, the more obvious it seems: association with a *truly* distinguished household *is* a prerequisite of greatness. A great butler can only be, surely, one who can point to his years of service and say that he has applied his talents to serving a great gentleman – and, through the latter, to serving humanity. (Ishiguro, 1989: 117)

Stevens identifies with a world-view in which his sphere of influence and responsibility is restricted to providing 'the best possible service to those great gentlemen in whose hands the destiny of civilization truly lies' (ibid.: 199). Stevens' capacity to create and sustain a household of the utmost subordination comes not from decisions made by Lord Darlington but, rather, arises from an *institutionalized* belief in, and determination to reproduce, this form of aristocratic life through the adoption of high, professional standards involving considerable personal sacrifice. Similarly, the power that eventually oppresses Sherman

Management Lives: Power and Identity in Work Organizations *continued*

By David Knights and Hugh Willmott

McCoy cannot be understood by looking at the pattern of decision making of the mayor or the commissioner of police. His difficulties are the product of a range of institutionalised power relations involving the police, local politics, community concerns and the media combined with his own preoccupations with success and status.

A question remains, however, as to whether Lukes' formulation of the third dimension provides us with any greater degree of analytical purchase on the exercises of power. By focusing upon how power may be exercised outside of specific points of conflict or decision making, it usefully draws attention to institutionalized ways of relating that cannot be convincingly ascribed to the choices made by individuals who directly influence decisions or manoeuvre, behind-the-scenes, to exclude consideration of certain issues. But Lukes still seems to subscribe to a conception of power as the property of persons who are held to be powerful and, as a result, to a (class-based) sense of power which is polarized between those who have it and those who do not. These are people who define reality in such a way as to *control meaning* so that others – such as the black and Latin population of the Bronx or Stevens the butler – are rendered powerless as they are no longer capable of recognizing, let alone expressing their own 'real interests'. Leaving aside, for a moment, who is to say what their 'real interests' are, Lukes' third dimension of power might help us to understand the situation of Stevens who, through internalizing the impersonal standards of professional service uncontaminated by subjective preferences or emotions, effectively denies himself a personal life. It might also facilitate an understanding of the traps in which Sherman McCoy falls – such as his liaison with Maria that involves him in the hit-and-run incident as he drives her back from the airport. For Sherman is trapped by a preoccupation with his own social standing and self-image that is conditioned by and sustains his sexual prowess – both a product of the masculine dominated success ethic of New York culture.

However, Lukes' analysis of power focuses on the manipulations of the powerful as if they are not themselves victims as well as perpetrators of the social practices that form the backdrop to preoccupations with success and conquest ... Conceptually, the fundamental problem with Lukes' perspective is that it assumes *a priori* knowledge of the real, objective interests of particular individuals, groups or classes in society and that these exist prior to, or independently of, power relations. We would question this and argue, following Foucault (1980), that 'interests' are as much a product of the exercise of power as its condition or underlying purpose. It is not that 'interests' pre-exist power relations, and that these relations are about articulating or expressing these interests. Rather, 'interests' are identified and pursued through relations of power. If there is no purity as it were, existing outside of power relations, the attribution of 'real' interests that somehow lurk behind 'false' interests (or consciousness) is misplaced.

This perspective leads us to appreciate how reference to 'real interests' is a discursive move in a particular game that privileges certain kinds of identity. In Lukes's case, it is the game of radical humanism in which assumptions about human nature deem the self to be essentially autonomous ... and 'power' is ascribed to actions or forces that are understood to impede or restrict this essential autonomy. Lukes' identification of the three dimensions of power can be reinterpreted in this light, with each dimension presenting a more potent and insidious threat to human autonomy ... [W]e share Lukes' concern to show that power cannot adequately be conceptualized in terms of the first and second dimensions alone. Our objection, then, is not to the claim that power is most potent in its most institutionalized forms but in the assumption that 'real interests' are self-evident or can be unproblematically recognized and that individual human autonomy is the cross upon which to take up 'arms', whether theoretical or practical, to defend them.

Appendix 1

Synopsis of Tom Wolfe, The Bonfire of the Vanities, *London: Pan Books, 1988*
Set in 1980s New York, this novel explores the fast-living, quick money, dog-eat-dog world of city

Management Lives: Power and Identity in Work Organizations

By David Knights and Hugh Willmott

slickers, petty criminals, big-time hustlers and a crumbling infrastructure that struggles to stem the tide of decadence and corruption. Published just before the Wall Street crash of 1987, it charts the rise and fall of Sherman McCoy, from highly paid bond salesman living in a lavishly furnished apartment on Park Avenue to 'professional defendant' accused of a hit-and-run, racist killing. Sherman comes from a modest background but is determined to prove himself – to become A Master of the Universe. He marries well. But he also wants, and feels he deserves, a mistress 'to allow his rogue hormones out for a romp'. Married to an aged Jewish millionaire, who had made his second fortune flying Arabs to Mecca, Maria is street-wise. It is she, Maria, who uses and manipulates Sherman, preying upon his insecurity and vanity. When collecting her from the airport, Sherman takes a wrong turn off the freeway, winds up in the Bronx, a black ghetto. Driving his Mercedes through its unfamiliar darkened streets both he and Maria feel intensely threatened. Seeking a way back on to the freeway, they found themselves blocked by an obstruction. Getting out to remove it, Sherman is approached by two black youths that ask him if he needs help. He panics and runs back to the car. Maria takes the wheel and hits one of the youths as they race away. The police detectives, Martin and Goldberg, trace the car to Sherman. A dead-beat journalist, eager to revive a flagging career, is given the story. He is happy to sensationalize the incident as a racist attack on a harmless, law-abiding black youth with a promising academic career ahead of him. Black activists capitalize upon the story for their own propaganda purposes as does the district attorney, Weiss, a man with political ambitions. Sherman becomes a political football as it is turned into a racist issue that is intended to mobilize the black vote. When the news breaks, Sherman fails to close a big financial deal as he loses his nerve and his concentration. The other youth at the scene of the accident, a hood, identifies Sherman as the driver in order to avoid having to explain away why he had stopped at the barricade and Maria had taken the wheel. When Sherman tells his employer about his position, he is immediately fired in order to protect the name of the firm. The

Master of the Universe is shown to be instantly dispensable. Not only does Sherman lose his job and his family but his becomes a 'Show Trial', with orchestrated mass demonstrations outside his apartment … *The Bonfire of the Vanities* provides dramatic and highly humorous material to illustrate our views about power …

Synopsis of K. Ishiguro, The Remains of the Day, *London: Faber & Faber, 1989*

Especially in its … film version, *The Remains of the Day* can be seen primarily as a story of romance never consummated. However, the historical, political and social terrain upon which the story unfolds contains many insights into issues that are central to our interests in this book. The novel records the historical reminiscences in 1956 of Stevens who has spent the best part of his life as head butler to a Lord Darlington. Stevens narrates the story in the first person as he takes a motoring trip some time after Darlington's death. Rationalized as a well-deserved holiday, the ostensible purpose of Stevens' journey into the west-country was to see whether it might be possible to persuade Miss Kenton to return to Darlington Hall where she had been the housekeeper in the 1930s. While this concern to re-employ Miss Kenton could and was justified to his new American master at Darlington Hall on the grounds of a depleted staff, a more fundamental motive for Stevens was to repair a part of his past. Stevens had several regrets in his life as he reached his twilight hours or what might be seen as the 'remains of the day'. One was the sheer devotion and unquestioning loyalty to his master Lord Darlington who had been vulnerable and naïve in accepting much Nazi propaganda and had used his influence in political circles to persuade the British to appease Germany in the inter-war years. While regretting his minor part in this unfolding of political events, perhaps his greatest regret was more personal in that he had failed to recognize, and more to the point, to reciprocate Miss Kenton's feelings towards him when they had worked together twenty years previously. Both regrets had come about because of a devotion to duty and the insistence that he led by

READING 8.2

Management Lives: Power and Identity in Work Organizations *continued*

By David Knights and Hugh Willmott

example in refusing to allow personal matters to intervene in the conduct of service work. At the time, of course, he believed his sacrifice was justified because he was serving a master who was engaged in such noble causes as the affairs of state about which he could not possibly have an understanding. In the event of his master having made the grossest errors of judgement in supporting a fascist Germany, the justification for a life of personal sacrifice no longer existed. The novel illustrates in graphic detail not only how this domination of work over life can smother the tiniest shoots of human sensuality but also how the legacy of an aristocratic

tradition continued to play an intricate part in British politics long after the rise of democracy ... The insights of the novel into the British aristocracy and the hierarchical relations of status distinction and deference that prevail both between and within the master and servant class are invaluable for our study of power.

References

Ishiguro, K. (1989) *Remains of the day*. London: Faber and Faber.

Wolfe, T. (1988) *The Bonfire of the Vanities*. London: Pan books.

READING 8.3

Strategies of Resistance: Power, Knowledge and Subjectivity in the Workplace

By David Collinson

The following chapter is primarily concerned to highlight two different strategies of dissent and opposition. These are illustrated below by exploring two empirical case studies drawn from completed research projects that are re-examined here in the light of a specific focus upon knowledge and resistance. First, I argue that specific forms of knowledge are a crucial resource and means through which resistance can be mobilized. Knowledge in organizations is multiple, contested and shifting. Employees may not possess detailed understandings of certain bureaucratic/political processes, but they often do monopolize other technical production-related knowledges that facilitate their oppositional practices.

Second, I argue that it is not in any simple sense merely the possession, or ownership of particular knowledges that determines consent, outflanking or resistance ... Rather, it is also the way that these knowledges are deployed in particular organizational conditions and practices. The data reveal two quite different *subjective* strategies of workplace resistance that are shaped by particular orientations to knowledge, information and to those in authority. In the first case, men workers' routine resistance practices concentrate on *restricting information* from managers. They seek to escape or to avoid the demands

of authority. I term this strategy 'resistance through distance'. The second case explores a woman's resistance to a particular managerial promotion decision. The more formalized processes of her challenge to managerial decision-making are informed by the converse strategy of *extracting information* from management. This oppositional strategy I term 'resistance through persistence'. These examples are by no means exhaustive of possible resistance strategies. What they reveal are the limited possibilities available to those who engage in resistance through distance and the greater viability and effectiveness of oppositional practices designed to render management more accountable by extracting information, monitoring practices and challenging decision-making processes.

Third, it is suggested that these arguments raise important issues about the subjectivity of subordinates in relation to power, knowledge and resistance that have tended to be neglected (see also Knights 1990; Thompson 1990; Willmott 1990, Collinson, 1992a) ... Drawing on this analysis, the chapter concludes by arguing that much of the critical literature on employee behaviour tends to overstate either consent or resistance and to separate one from the other.

READING 8.3	**Strategies of Resistance: Power, Knowledge and Subjectivity in the Workplace**

By David Collinson

The bonus scheme reinforced the widespread shopfloor view that 'management can't have what they don't pay for'. Having maximized bonus, shopfloor workers frequently refused to produce further. When negotiating times with the rate fixer, workers used their technical knowledge and engineering skills to mystify output potential. One 57-year-old turner in the machine shop illustrated workers' strategies of resistance using the bonus scheme. During his 40 years' experience in engineering he had developed many 'tricks of the trade' and shortcuts on jobs ... [H]e invariably mystified and concealed his technical knowledge and skills when negotiating a time with the rate fixer, as he revealed:

> I do 400 of these a week. I always get them to do when they're needed. The time I got for this job from the rate fixer was eight minutes. But I can do them in two. Why should I worry? It pays to know your job ... You can't tell them what you can do or else you'd be doing three men's jobs for one man's wages.

Behind the appearance of conformity that he constructed when negotiating with the rate fixer, he maintained a deeper oppositional sense of self-determination. By manipulating the rate fixer, he could accumulate what different writers have called a 'kitty' (Buroway 1979) ... This ability to mystify his potential output and to 'kid' the rate fixer, was a real source of personal pride and self-validation. It confirmed his technical skills, knowledge and experience. By restricting information, he was also able to exercise some control over his output and to avoid any intensification of his labour.

This example demonstrates how working the bonus system reinforced a very narrow, limited and defensive form of resistance ... By controlling and managing production and information in this way, workers were able to appropriate both time and space.

Paradoxically, workers' resistance through distance reinforced the legitimacy of hierarchical control, left managerial prerogative unchallenged, and increased their vulnerability to disciplinary practices. This in turn suggests that it is not merely the absolute quality of knowledge and information that significantly shapes the possibility for and effectiveness of resistance. Rather, it is the way in which this knowledge is used within particular power relations. The next case study illustrates this argument further, where far from restricting information, subordinates sought to extract it from management – an approach that proved to be both more strategic and effective.

This particular promotion case took place in the motor insurance department ... [where] ... Jane ... was a grade-six motor clerk who applied for a grade-seven vacancy. Although Jane was interviewed and seriously considered, she was unsuccessful, but was told that she was 'next in line' for a grade-seven post ... [Later] ... Jane informed the company that she was pregnant. Soon afterwards, two grade-seven vacancies were advertised. Jane applied but was not interviewed. Yet, she was totally mobile and the only person in the department who had received an 'A' for her work performance in her annual appraisal in both the previous years. Jane also knew that she was the applicant with the highest educational qualifications. A woman who was not mobile and who had been rejected outright for the October vacancy and a man who had received a warning after being criticized by clients were appointed. When Jane requested an explanation, the superintendent gave no reason for her outright rejection except that he could not support her application and refused to discuss the matter further.

At this point, Jane might have decided to resist by taking her full entitlement of statutory maternity leave and then resigning from the company. Alternatively, she could have decided to remain in employment but with a different, less committed orientation to her work and to the company. But rather than choose a strategy of resistance through distance, Jane decided to challenge management's refusal to justify their promotion decision. She sought to extract further information from them concerning their criteria and decision-making processes. This form of resistance was facilitated by the fact that as an internal candidate, Jane was familiar with the company, its practices and its management. She was also a local union representative ...

READING 8.3 **Strategies of Resistance: Power, Knowledge and Subjectivity in the Workplace** *continued*

By David Collinson

This case study reveals how during the grievance procedure managers' strategies of control, particularly through their attempts to restrict information, had the effect of reinforcing the determination of both the clerk and the union representative to persist in their resistance against this promotion decision. The superintendent's initial failure to offer any explanation for the clerk's rejection alerted her to the possibility that she was probably being unfairly treated. Her suspicions were compounded by inconsistencies and inaccuracies in the managers' formal rationalizations. Once these contradictions were exposed, the managers' continued refusal to reverse their decision and their failure to offer an adequate explanation confirmed to the clerk that behind these formal discourses, the managers' hidden concern was her pregnancy (see also Martin, 1990).

The decision to arrange a crucial meeting in the early morning appeared to both women to constitute a managerial control strategy. However, this practice had precisely the opposite effect, because it merely strengthened the clerk's resolve to resist. To be effective, the woman's resistance had to be informed, extremely persistent and determined. A central strategy was the securing of more detailed technical information from managers about their decision-making process. Using various local and strategic knowledges, the clerk and the trade union representative were then able to press for the decision eventually to be overturned. In the power struggles that ensued, specific overlapping knowledges were crucially important factors in strengthening this resistance, which in turn eventually resulted in local management being outflanked.

Oppositional practices are usually informed by strategic exercise of particular knowledges, which may be for example, technical, bureaucratic and procedural, social, regional, cultural and historical, legal, economic, strategic/political and/or about self. These knowledges should neither be understated nor overstated when examining the discursive practices of subordinates. They are likely to overlap, be somewhat indeterminate, partial and shifting and often be couched in ambiguity, uncertainty and insecurity ... Nevertheless, these various knowledges can be an important condition and consequence of resistance.

Whatever form resistance takes, however, it is always inextricably linked to organizational discipline, control and power. Resistance is rarely equal to control, neither is it necessarily successful nor fundamentally subversive in its effects (Henriques, *et al.*, 1984). Yet resistance cannot be examined as if it were separate from workplace discipline and control. Oppositional practices often draw upon the very forms of control that generate resistance in the first place. Indeed, control and resistance can be so mutually reproducing that they actually constitute one another. This is particularly likely where subordinates engage in resistance through distance ...

An important feature of the oppositional strategies examined in the foregoing case studies is the overlapping and mutually embedded character of consent, compliance and resistance. In each case, resistance was circumscribed by elements of ambiguity, consent and compliance. Even the most critical and radical workers in the engineering factory supported managerial prerogative. Although in their view this was consistent with their oppositional discourses, it simultaneously expressed an ambivalence and acceptance of the prevailing power asymmetries of the company. Resistance through distance was contained *within*, rather than *against*, the idea of hierarchy and authority.

Ostensibly, resistance through persistence in the insurance company was relatively more effective, since an unfair decision was successfully challenged and overturned, which in turn had the effect of promoting equal opportunity issues throughout the company. Yet, here again, resistance was limited. It constituted a partial challenge to, but was also paradoxically confined within the principle of, managerial prerogative. While it would be inaccurate to dismiss or reduce this resistance to some notion of 'outflanking', equally it would be inappropriate to overstate its radical intentions and/or effects. The employee's demand for meritocratic treatment in promotion can be interpreted simultaneously as an expression of both resistance to patriarchal control practices and of consent to conventional career progression and to the legitimacy of hierarchical organization. The

| READING 8.3 | **Strategies of Resistance: Power, Knowledge and Subjectivity in the Workplace** |

By David Collinson

case displays the rationality, knowledgeability and determination of those who resisted. Yet underpinning these strategic practices was a set of co-existent and partly incompatible and unresolved views about hierarchy and management. As in the engineering factory, managers were heavily criticized and attacked, but a fundamental and collective challenge to the prevailing organization of production seemed highly unlikely.

To conclude, this chapter has been concerned to highlight the analytical importance of workplace resistance and to explore some of its interconnections with knowledge, power and subjectivity. Workplace resistance remains a persistent, significant and remarkable feature of modern organizations. Subordinates do continue to resist and articulate their dissatisfaction in innumerable ways despite considerable disciplinary barriers and insecurities. As we have seen, the commodification of labour not only reflects and reinforces managerial and hierarchical control, but also intensifies extensive material and symbolic insecurity for those in subordinate positions. The ever-present possibility of losing one's job is a significant discipline and disincentive to resist or challenge managerial practices.

References

Buroway, M. (1979) *Manufacturing Consent,* Chicago: Chicago University Press.

Buroway, M. (1985) *The Politics of Production,* London: Verso.

Collinson, D.L. (1992a) *Managing the Shopfloor: Subjectivity, Masculinity and Workplace Culture,* Berlin: Walter de Gruyter.

Henriques, J., Hollway, W., Unwin, C., Vein, C., Walkderdine, V. (1984) *Changing the Subject,* London: Methuen.

Jackall, R. (1988) *Moral Mazes, The World of Corporate Managers,* Oxford University Press.

Knights, D. (1990) 'Subjectivity, Power and the Labour Process' in Knights, D. and Willmott, H. (eds) *Labour Process Theory,* London: Macmillan, pp. 297–335.

Martin, J. (1990) 'Deconstructing Organizational Taboos: The Suppression of Gender Conflict in Organizations', *Organization Science* 1(4): 339–59.

Thompson, P. (1990) 'Crawling from the Wreckage: The Labour Process and the Politics of Production', in Knights, D. and Willmott, H. (eds) *Labour Process Theory,* London: Macmillan, 95–124.

Willmott, H. (1990) 'Subjectivity and the Dialectics of Praxis: Opening the Core of Labour Process Analysis', in Knights, D. and Willmot, H. (eds) *Labour Process Theory,* London: Macmillan, pp. 336–78.

| READING 8.4 | **Foucault, Power, Resistance and All That** |

By David Knights and Theo Vurdubakis

This chapter is concerned with only one aspect of labour process theory – the way in which the introduction of Foucault into the debate has generated the kind of controversy that sustains talk of a crisis. For some (e.g. Knights and Willmott, 1989; Dandeker, 1990; Sakolsky, 1992) Foucault is seen to provide a way out of the crisis, whereas for others resort to his work is nothing but a diversion, a clear symptom of the crisis itself (e.g. Thompson, 1991; Fine, 1979; Neimark, 1990). With respect to an analysis of the labour process, much of the value or otherwise of Foucault's work would appear to hinge on what one is to make of his account (or non-account) of resistance (e.g. Tanner *et al.*, 1992). As many of the early critics (Aronowitz, 1978; Edwards, 1979; Elger, 1982; Gartman, 1983; Stark, 1980) pointed out, resistance was a theoretical lacuna in Braverman's thesis and a discourse on resistance in the labour process debate has remained limited and undeveloped ever since (cf. Buroway, 1979, 1985; Knights and Collinson, 1985; Knights and Willmott, 1986, 1990; Turner, 1989). Moreover, there is by no means a consensus within the literature as to the meaning of, or significance, which should be attributed to, resistance (see Knights and Willmott, 1990). In this context, both inside and outside the labour process debate, the absence of a Foucauldian theory of resistance provides critics with further evidence

READING 8.4

Foucault, Power, Resistance and All That *continued*

By David Knights and Theo Vurdubakis

(if evidence was needed) of the invalidity of the approach.

It is our view that most of the critiques of Foucault tend to be rooted in dualistic understandings of the relationship between various subject–object polarities such as that between the individual and society, force and consent, power and powerlessness. Within such dualistic thinking resistance is perceived as one pole in a dichotomy where it is always opposite to and outside of power. By treating power and resistance as analytical conditions of each other's possibility such that 'each constitutes for the other a kind of permanent limit, a point of reversal', Foucault (1982: 225) goes some way towards deconstructing these dualisms.

We need then to question the assumptions that render knowledge of resistance self-evident.

More precisely, these issues concern specific objections to Foucault's conception of power, which critics suggest preclude a theory or analysis of resistance. They revolve around three central questions: where is resistance to be 'located', who are its 'agents' and how can it be justified? Each of these questions, we argue, is usually asked from a dualistic perspective that presumes power to be held by the powerful and wielded over the powerless. From such a perspective, Foucault's argument that there is no position exterior to power–knowledge relations and that the latter constitute the very subjects that resist it, seemingly obliterates in a single stroke the space occupied by the agents of resistance and undermines its conventional justification. The chapter is, then, concerned to locate an analysis of resistance within the relations of power and knowledge to which Foucault draws attention; it argues, therefore, that those critiques seeking to return to the comfort of 'old certainties' regarding power and resistance are misplaced.

As has already been argued, the problem of resistance raised by critics of Foucault revolves around three questions that derive from their understanding of his conception of power.

Problems of location, agency and justifiability:

1. If one is 'never outside power', is there any social space for resistance to occupy?

2. If subjectivity is an effect of power (the 'obedient subject') who are to be the agents of resistance and how can resistance ever be subversive of power? To what kind of 'liberating agency' does it have access?

3. In the absence of a theory of rights or objective interests even assuming that an explanation of resistance is after all possible, what can be the grounds of its justification? 'Why fight?' as Habermas (1986) put it.

Space for Resistance

The 'problem' of the 'location' of, or space for, resistance has its origin in Foucault's (1984a: 94) claim that 'Relations of power are not in a position of exteriority with respect to other types of relationships ... but immanent in the latter'.

As Poulantzas sees it, the world Foucault constructs is hermetically sealed: 'For if power is already there, if every power relation is immanent in itself, why should there ever be resistance? From where would resistance come, and how would it ever be possible?' (Poulantzas 1979: 148-9). Moreover if, as Foucault claims, resistance takes place so to speak, 'within' power, then resistance can offer no escape.

In identifying the paradox in these terms one takes on board a dualistic understanding of power and resistance.

This dualistic view is implicit in for instance the making of 'externality to power' a necessary condition for resistance; that resistance must always be outside the mechanisms of power it opposes. The price for this is a certain totalization of power and resistance.

Even if we were to accept, as Foucault proposes, that the binary division between resistance and power is an unreal one, that would still not be the end of the story. For Foucault took heresy a step further by claiming that power is also 'productive' of resistance.

The elimination of resistance, in other words, is not a necessary feature of the exercise of power. Nor does resistance deprive relations of power of their opportunities to reconstruct themselves; indeed,

| # Foucault, Power, Resistance and All That

By David Knights and Theo Vurdubakis

it may stimulate technologies of power to reorganize, adapt and multiply.

For most variants of Marxism, there is a historically designated agent of resistance, for example, the proletariat (e.g. Lukacs, 1971), or the 'vanguard party' (e.g. Lenin, 1961).

The possibility of losing that subject is consequently a major stumbling block for any coherent account of resistance along these lines. Yet Foucault's insistence that power relations are constitutive of subjects entails precisely such a loss. *Who*, then, after the loss of the subject does the resisting? asks Comay (1986: 116).

Such an approach, we suggest, is not very helpful. Our disagreement with Giddens is not over the status of humans as agents of power relations but with the claimed ontological foundations of this status (Hirst and Woolley, 1982). Against the notion of a universal 'knowledgable human agent', for instance, we have Foucault's (1975) suggestion that human subjects may be bringing qualitatively different forms of knowledge into power relations. But this knowledge needs to be examined in the context of the power relations in which it was made possible and is used rather than in terms of some abstract notion of human capacity. This immediately turns attention to the differences between formal and subjugated knowledges and how these may be drawn upon in struggles within power relations.

If the various dualistic notions about resistance and power discussed above are to be rejected, then it is difficult to see why there should be any need for *an* agent of resistance to be designated in advance or independently of any context in which conflict or struggle takes place.

Justifying Resistance

The paradox of Foucault's position is aptly summarized in Habermas's (1986) 'Why fight?' question. According to Habermas, Foucault's refusal to indulge in a naturalistic metaphysics which idealizes counter-power into a prediscursive referent' while commendable in itself also undercuts the grounds of his critique. Foucault feels he cannot offer any reason 'why' one does (or should) resist power. Many of Foucault's critics (e.g. Neimark, 1990) while in agreement with Habermas's critique, tend to be less careful in their formulation of the problem accusing Foucault of all the sins in

the political spectrum from being a crypto neo-conservative to glorifying all forms of deviance.

We have already indicated that, in our view, a major part of the 'problem' lies in the unexamined totalizing assumptions that not just anti-Foucauldians but also Foucauldians (e.g. Lemert and Gillan, 1982) tend to bring into the discussion. Such assumptions are, for instance, the rhetoric of a Resistance (with a capital R) confronting Power (with a capital P) or the notion that this grand 'confrontation' can be theorized independently of the concrete sites and specific political struggles where it is embedded. These notions are in turn played out in arguments couched in binary terminology such as outside/inside (Power), resistance/non-resistance, control/consent and so forth. If power, resistance and their agents are seen as context-specific then we can have no justification for 'resistance in general'. Unless we assume *a priori* the 'evil nature' of power and the 'liberatory nature' of resistance, then there is little alternative to conducting a case by case, site by site assessment.

The precariousness of the foothold is what makes the outcome of resistance as unpredictable as the conditions that make it possible.

Rather than advocating some 'Grand Gesture of Denial', Foucault looked to the local struggles of those who 'paid' the costs of particular identity formations and subjectivities. That did not mean, however, (to stretch the economic metaphor a bit further) that some general 'balance sheet' could be drawn up: opposition arises, he argued, out of the concrete experiences of certain forms of subjection: 'opposition to the power of men over women, … of psychiatry over the mentally ill, of medicine over the population, of administration over the way we live' (Foucault, 1984b: 379), Critique, he suggested, is a necessary part of such oppositional practice.

As Keenan (1987) shows, Foucault is not just saying that we need to support human rights as well as problematize their foundations and transformation – but that this support and problematization should proceed simultaneously; that is to say, we need to remain sceptical at one and the same time precisely of those rights that we support (and perhaps campaign for), if only to avoid the kind of self-subjugation or project identification which stifles critical judgement.

READING 8.4 | Foucault, Power, Resistance and All That *continued*

By David Knights and Theo Vurdubakis

While Foucault does not provide a moral blueprint to guide us in our lives (and in this sense our attraction to Foucault is as a means of developing a more philosophically adequate sociology and not a philosophy *per se*), he suggests alternative possibilities for practice and ones that do not necessarily rely on existing formal mechanisms or ways of doing things. In this respect, he denies us the comfort of conventional orthodoxies, and this is just as well.

References

Aronowitz, S. (1978) 'Marx, Braverman and the Logic of Capitalism', *Insurgent Sociologist* 8(1): 126–46.

Buroway, M. (1979) *Manufacturing Consent*, Chicago: University of Chicago Press.

Buroway, M. (1985) *The Politics of Production*, London: Verso.

Comay, R. (1986) 'The Repressive Hypothesis: Aporias of Liberation in Foucault', *Telos* 67.

Dandeker, C. (1990) *Surveillance, Power and Modernity*, Oxford: Polity Press.

Edwards, R.C. (1979) *Contested Terrain*, London: Heinemann.

Elger, T.A. (1982) 'Braverman, Capital Accumulation and Deskilling' in S. Wood (ed.) *The Degradation of Work?* London: Hutchinson.

Fine, B. (1979) 'Struggles Against Discipline: The Theory and Politics of Michel Foucault', *Capital and Class* 9: 75–96.

Foucault, Michel (1975) *I, Pierre Riviere, Having Slaughtered My Mother, My Sister and My Brother … A Case of Parricide in the 19th Century*, New York: Pantheon.

Foucault, Michel (1982) 'The Subject and the Power', in H.F. Dreyfus and P. Rabinow *Michel Foucault: Beyond Structuralism and Hermeneutics*, Brighton, Sussex: Harvester, pp. 202–26.

Foucault, Michel (1984a) *The History of Sexuality: An Introduction*, London: Allen Lane.

Foucault, Michel (1984b) *The Foucault Reader*, edited by P. Rabinow, Harmondsworth: Penguin.

Gartman, D. (1983) 'Structuralist Marxism and the Labor Process: Where Have the Dialectics Gone', *Theory and Society* 12: 659–69.

Habermas, J. (1986) *The Philosophical Discourse of Modernity*, London: Heinemann.

Hirst, P. and Woolley, P. (1982) *Social Relations and Human Attributes*, London: Tavistock.

Keenan, J. (1987) 'Power/Knowledge: Reading Foucault on Bias', *Political Theory* 15: 5–37

Knights, D. and Collinson, D. (1985) 'Redesigning Work on the Shopfloor: A Question of Control or Consent', in D. Knights, H. Wilmott, and D. Collinson (eds) *Job Redesign: Critical Perspectives on the Labour Process*, Aldershot: Gower.

Knights, D. and Wilmott, H. editors (1986) *Gender and the Labour Process*. Aldershot: Gower.

Knights, D. and Willmot, H. (1989) 'Power and Subjectivity at Work: From Degradation to Subjugation', *Sociology*. 23(4): 475–483.

Knights, D. and Willmott, H., Eds (1990) *Labour Process Theory*. London: Macmillan.

Lemert, C.C. and Gillian, G. (1982) *Michel Foucault: Social Theory and Transgression*, New York: Columbia University Press.

Lenin, V.I. (1970) *The State and Revolution*, Moscow: Progress.

Lukacs, G. (1971) *History and Class Consciousness*, London: Merlin (first published 1923)

Neimark, M. (1990) 'The King Is Dead, Long Live the King?', *Critical Perspectives in Accounting* 1: 103–14.

Poulantzas, N. (1979) *State, Power, Socialism*, London: New Left Books.

Sakolsky, R. (1992) 'Disciplinary Power in the Labour Process', in A. Sturdy, D. Knights and H. Willmott (eds) *Skill and Consent*, London: Routledge.

Stark, A. (1980) 'Class Struggle and the Transformation of the Labour Process: A Rational Approach', *Theory and Society* 9: 89–130.

Tanner, J., Davies, S., O'Grady, B., (1992) 'Immanence Changes Everything: A Critical Comment on the Labour Process and Class Consciousness', *Sociology* 26(3): 439–54.

Thompson, P. (1991) 'The Fatal Distraction: Postmodernism and Organizational Analysis' paper delivered at the Conference on New Theories of Organisation, Keele University, 3–5 April.

Turner, S. (1989) 'Depoliticizing Power', *Social Studies of Science* 19: 533–60.

Discussion Questions

1. What are the different ways in which employees can be managed or controlled?
2. Can the powerful also be victims of power?
3. Outline some important strategies of resistance to management control.

4. Can power and resistance in organizational life simply be seen as the equivalent to force and resistance in a mechanical or physical sense?

Introduction References

Albrow, M. (1970) *Bureaucracy*, London: Palgrave Macmillan.

Bachrach, P. and Baratz, M. (1970) *Power and Poverty: Theory and Practice*, New York: Oxford University Press.

Dahl, R. (1961) *Who Governs?: Democracy and Power in an American City*, New Haven, Conn.: Yale University Press.

Jackall, R. (1988) *Moral Mazes, The World of Corporate Managers*, Oxford University Press.

Knights, D. and Willmott, H.C. (2002) 'Virtue or Vice?: Reflecting on Competing Discourses of Autonomy' in Parker, M. (editor) *Utopia and Organization*, London: Sage, pp. 59–81.

Lukes, S. (1974) *Power: A Radical View*, London: Macmillan.

Parsons, T. (1949) *The Theory and Structure of Social Action*, New York: The Free Press.

Weber, M. (1947) *Theory of Social and Economic Organization*, London: Routledge and Kegan Paul.

Recommended Further Readings

See references above to Collinson, and Knights and Vurdubakis plus:

Albrow, M. (1970) *Bureaucracy*, London: Palgrave Macmillan.

Clegg, S.R. (1989) *Frameworks of Power*, Sage.

Clegg, S.R. (1975) *Power, Rule and Domination: A Critical and Empirical Understanding of Power in Sociological Theory and Organizational Life*, London: Routledge and Kegan Paul.

Hindess, B. (1987) Rationality and the Characterisation of Modern Society', in Whimster, S. and Lash, S. (editors) *Max Weber, Rationality and Modernity*, London: Allen & Unwin, pp. 137–53.

Lukes, S. (2005) *Power: A Radical View*, London: Palgrave Macmillan.

Pfeffer, J. (1981) *Power in Organizations*, New York: Pitman.

Townley, B. (1993) 'Foucault, Power/Knowledge, and its Relevance for Human Resource Management', *Academy of Management Review*, 18(3): 518–545.

TECHNOLOGY

CHAPTER 9

READINGS

McLoughlin, I. and Harris, M. (1997) 'Introduction' in *Innovation, Organisational Change and Technology,* Edited by McLoughlin, I. and Harris, M., London: International Thompson Business Press, pp. 2–3; 6; 6–7; 9; 10; 11; 12; 13–15.

Cockburn, C. (1985/1994) 'Caught in the Wheels: The high cost of being a female cog in the male machinery of engineering' in *The Social Shaping of Technology*. Edited by MacKenzie, D. and Wajcman, J. Open University Press, pp. 55–65. Selection pp. 55–6; 58; 60.

Zuboff, S. (1988) *In the Age of the Smart Machine: The Future of Work and Power*, New York: Basic Books. Selection pp. 388; 389; 390; 391; 394–5; 401; 412; 413; 414.

Cooper, R. (1991) 'Formal Organization as Representation: Remote Control, Displacement, Abbreviation' in *Rethinking Organization*, Edited by Reed, M. & Hughes, M. London: Sage. pp. 254–5; 257 257–8; 263–4; 264–5; 266.

Knights, D., Noble, F., Vurdubakis, T. and Willmott, H. (2002) 'Allegories of Creative Destruction: Technology and Organisation in Narratives of the e-Economy' in *Virtual Society? Technology, Cyberbole, Reality*. Edited by Woolgar, S. Oxford: Oxford University Press, pp. 99–114.

INTRODUCTION

The contribution by **Ian McLoughlin and Martin Harris** (Reading 9.1) is particularly apposite in preceding the section on Innovation in this book in that their emphasis is on the role of technology in innovation. They provide a useful introduction to the technology literature within organization and set the scene in relation to innovation by tracing the history of this literature from its earliest form in the distinction between product and process innovation and the focus on markets as the driver of change and innovation. The authors continue through to the most recent actor network approaches concerning the importance of social networks in securing and mobilizing support for particular technological innovations. In the extract, however, the focus is on how much of the literature has been concerned with a debate about

159

technological determinism and how, despite critique, it tends to reappear in a host of different forms. In some senses, this focus has rendered the discourse increasingly more intellectual rather than practical and has left behind some of the earlier work on technology as a central stimulant for economic development.

These earlier economic development studies and the diffusion or innofusion ideas that followed tended to operate as if they were politically and morally neutral. Later labour process, strategic choice, social shaping and actor-network theories all consider politics and values to be central to the developments that occur and important in terms of eventual practical outcomes and market acceptability. Many of the arguments end up in an epistemological stalemate between notions about the inescapably social character of all artefacts, on the one hand, and the material limits to such relativist 'interpretive flexibility' (McLoughlin and Harris, 1997, p. 23).

Cynthia Cockburn was one of the earliest authors to pursue a gender analysis of technology well before, as a result of the computerization of society, discourses on technology became 'sexy'. In 'Caught in the wheels' (Reading 9.2), she challenges the standard equal opportunity view that women need to become more confident and assertive if they are to enter the dominantly male world of technology and science. She takes an alternative line suggesting that such a perspective might be seen to be blaming the victim and that what needs changing is the environment surrounding technological work such that women may want to enter it. She rebels against the idea that women have to become more masculine in order to hold their own in the male-dominated sectors of technology since feminine values are inimitable to technology only because of the way it has been socially constructed when dominated by men. Her solution is to advance women-only technological enterprises.

'In the age of the smart machine' (Reading 9.3), by **Shoshana Zuboff** challenges the traditional labour process view that managers use technology primarily as a means of controlling their work force. Where there is a major preoccupation with legitimizing their authority this may be the case and it usually leads to innovation being channelled towards automation that facilitates their ability to predict and control production and organizational functions. As a result there is little chance of developing the 'informating' capacity of the new technology, where knowledge is widely distributed and shared throughout the hierarchy instead of being monopolized by managers as a means of securing their identity and control. By contrast, an 'informated' organization is involved in continuous learning and the creation of meaning that is vital to the productive power of the organization. There is a not only continuous learning but a deep interdependence between strategy formulation and the development of three other domains of managerial activity – intellective skill, technology, and a social system within the organization. This involves the fluid movement of managers across these four domains. Here Zuboff was anticipating what has become known as the knowledge-intensive organization or workplace.

In 'Formal organization as representation: remote control, displacement, abbreviation' (Reading 9.4), **Robert Cooper** provides an interesting critique of transaction costs theory (Williamson, 1975) and information theory (Schotter, 1981) arguing that their analyses of the processing of information neglect a crucial element which is *representation*. Representation is important not least because it precedes information although the latter can augment or reduce its power. Organizations do not just organize information, 'they also construct the forms in which information appears' (p. 255).

Representation embodies a principle of economy and control that is reflected in the mechanisms of remoteness where symbols or extensions of the body substitute for its direct substantive engagement. This involves displacement where representation is always a substitute for, or re-presentation (e.g. a map, a balance sheet, a model) of, an event and not the event itself and abbreviation, where the complex is made simple, the big smaller, and representations condensed to the limits of their intelligibility. Micro-electronic, telephonic computing technology exemplifies each of these forms of representation but has increasingly resulted in ever more intensified abbreviations. In this extract, abbreviation is illustrated through the example of the historical development of the practical disciplines of administration and management.

'Allegories of creative destruction' (**David Knights, Faith Noble, Theo Vurdubakis, and Hugh Willmott**; Reading 9.5) critically examines narratives of hyperbole – both positive and negative – regarding virtuality as represented by e-commerce, particularly in relation to the distribution of financial services. Two kinds of narrative that the authors draw upon because they are vivid in portraying virtual forms of distribution in a particular light are the 'future shock' and the 'emperor's new clothes' stories. The former is a story that warns against ignoring what is described as the revolutionary power of virtual distribution and concludes that managers have no choice but to embrace it or suffer the dire consequences of being left behind. One consultant likened the danger to that of the English villagers in H. G. Wells' epic *The War of the Worlds* who were overpowered by the technologically superior alien invaders from Mars. As the authors argue, it is a 'Darwinian choice between adaptation and dinosaur-like extinction'. The emperor's new clothes is the exact opposite, exposing the myths surrounding the hyperbole around virtual worlds and suggesting, ironically, that there is no substance to the claims about virtuality. As in the *Wizard of Oz*, the curtain is drawn back, and the wizard's powers are exposed as little more than 'cheap tricks produced with the help of a rather ramshackle mechanical apparatus. The Wizard is a merchant of hype' (p. 110). The point about these stories is that are they not independent of the present or future state of affairs they claim merely to be describing. Rather they are significant actors in mobilizing resources and enrolling supporters to the networks respectively of virtuality or its demise. The effectiveness of their narratives will depend on whether they, and the technologies invoked in their stories meet with cultural expectations.

READING 9.1

Introduction: Understanding Innovation, Organizational Change and Technology

By Ian McLoughlin and Martin Harris

What is Technological Innovation?

Technological innovation has been defined in a number of ways ... In some usages it has been seen as almost synonymous with the term invention, or new technology-based product or production processes (e.g. Burns and Stalker, 1961). In others, following Schumpeter (1939), it is seen as a key 'milestone' in the process which begins with the invention of a new product, process or system and concludes with the diffusion of this artefact within a given population of 'users'. In the most often cited version of this view, Freeman (1982) defines 'innovation' as the

Source: Reproduced with permission of Cengage Learning EMEA Ltd from 'Introduction', in Innovation, Organizational Change and Technology © 1997 *International Thompson Business Press, now known as Cengage Learning EMEA Ltd.*

READING 9.1

Introduction: Understanding Innovation, Organizational Change and Technology *continued*

By Ian McLoughlin and Martin Harris

point of 'first commercial application of a new process or product'. Here a distinction is normally made between product and process innovation, the former involving incorporating new technology into new or existing products (or services), whereas the latter involves adopting new technology in the actual production of new products (or services). In practice, however, this distinction has proven increasingly difficult to draw and it probably makes more sense to regard them as opposite ends of a continuum rather than as mutually exclusive categories of innovation (Gattiker, 1990, p. 20).

Markets, Innovation and Expertise

Underlying this concept of technological innovation and its associated problems is the question of 'who is the mother of invention' – that is, do innovations occur as the result of a technology push or a market pull? In the popular imagination it is the former that seems to be the most convincing explanation. ... However, it has also been argued that innovation owes less to the brilliance of inventors, their organization and management, and rather more to the way the market generates demands for new products and processes. For Freeman (1982) neither of these explanations is convincing: ...

> Innovation is essentially a two-sided or coupling activity ... On the one hand, it involves the recognition of a need ... for a new product or process. On the other hand, it involves technical knowledge, which may be generally available, but may also ... [be] the result of original research activity. Experimental development and design, trial production and marketing involve a process of 'matching' the technical possibilities and the market ...

The Diffusion of Innovations: Technological Trajectories and Paradigms

Conventionally, innovation economists have been concerned with the rate of diffusion, that is the extent and pace at which an innovation, once proven a commercial success, is taken up by others in the market place.

In the past a distinction has frequently been made between incremental and radical innovations. The former implies more or less continuous marginal changes to existing products or processes. The latter involves dis-continuous events ... which produce new products or processes.

According to this view economic growth will increasingly occur around a radically new micro-electronics based 'techno-economic' paradigm. The shift is enabled by a 'bandwagon' effect whereby pioneering firms initially develop new technological innovations to produce new products or incremental innovations in existing products ...

Diffusion or Innofusion?

How realistic is it to view the process of technological innovation as concluded once a product achieves its first commercial application? This question has been raised by James Fleck (1987), who has coined the term 'innofusion' to refer to an activity where innovation occurs during the diffusion of a product or process beyond the point of first successful adoption. This idea has particular implications for concepts such as technological trajectories and technological paradigms since it suggests that much of what occurs in these respects may owe less to the 'natural' and 'inevitable' properties said to be 'inherent' in technologies and rather more to how adopting firms assimilate and apply these capabilities.

What is the Nature of Technological and Technology-Related Organizational Change?

The idea that firms are primarily driven by technological and competitive imperatives to innovate and have little choice in the matter if they wish to survive has had considerable influence ... However, the idea of an unyielding technological and commercial imperative has increasingly been viewed as problematic, in particular since it tends to evaluate the role of such things as management and worker attitudes, existing organizational structures and cultures, industrial relations and so on, in relation to their propensity to either facilitate or impede innovation.

The first problem area concerns the 'political' nature of technological change. Technological innovations are

| READING 9.1 | # Introduction: Understanding Innovation, Organizational Change and Technology |

By Ian McLoughlin and Martin Harris

seen to arise in a more or less neutral way out of the activities of inventors or professional research and development laboratories. However, critics argue that the form and direction of technological innovation should be seen as a product of the direct influence of social and political factors, not least the interests of the state and employers.

Second, those who believe in a technological imperative assume that managers play the role of unreflective 'messengers' whose task is to read the technological and commercial signals emanating from the firm's environment and take appropriate adaptive action ... However, critics argue that managers should be seen as 'creative mediators' whose decisions and choices critically influence the ways in which particular technological and market options are selected for development.

The final area of contention concerns the implicit assumption that technological innovation is inevitably of benefit to all, if not in the short term, then certainly in the long term. Employers, management, workers and unions are held to have a common interest in ensuring technological progress. However, technological innovation may be an area over which interests diverge, or where co-operation in respect of particular changes is conditional rather than given ...

Fordism and Post-Fordism
... For writers working in this tradition, technological innovation is shaped by the social and economic characteristics of capitalist societies – particularly by the need to generate profits or accumulate capital ...

Strategic Choice and Organizational Politics
... An alternative framework is provided by the notion of strategic choice (Child, 1972). The concept highlights the key role played by organizational politics and divergent stakeholder interests in shaping the organizational outcome of technological change where external factors are regarded not as determining, but rather as contextual referents for decision makers ...

The Management of Change
Despite these criticisms processual models of change have a number of advantages over more conventional understandings of the problem of change management. Dawson (1994) argues, for example, that management literature has in the past been dominated by 'one best way' organizational development models of change ... Although fitting quite neatly with ideas about managers' need to adapt their organizations to prevailing commercial and technological imperatives, such prescriptions are less helpful in circumstances – such as those described in models of post-Fordism – where market and technological change may be in perpetual transition ...

What is Technology and What Does it Do?
As we have seen, organizational sociologists have criticized those who have viewed technology as 'neutral' and as having an inevitable determining impact on organizations. This criticism is shared by a number of schools of thought, which have sought to reveal and explore the manner in which technology is 'socially shaped' ...

The Socio-Economic Shaping of Technology
The [first social shaping] approach ... [seeks] to identify factors which influence the form or content of technology, the direction of technological innovation and its ultimate social effects ... the idea that technology has 'causal effects' on society is rejected, but the idea of technological influences on the shaping of technology itself is not. A precondition of much technological innovation is in fact seen to be existing technology. Indeed, it is the development and gradual evolution of existing technological know-how, rather than 'flashes of inspiration' among inventors, which is responsible for much new technology (MacKenzie and Wacjman, 1988).

The Social Construction of Technology
The second social shaping approach ... [focuses on] the social construction of technological knowledge embodied in individual artefacts and systems ...

[T]echnological innovation involves competition and conflict between the views of relevant 'social groups' who share a particular set of understandings and meanings concerning the technology, such as designers, consumers, protestors. These groups will have different views about the most appropriate

READING 9.1

Introduction: Understanding Innovation, Organizational Change and Technology *continued*

By Ian McLoughlin and Martin Harris

design of the artefact, or even whether it is a desirable technology at all. Various technical, social, legal and moral solutions are likely to be articulated as possible ways of resolving the problem of the most appropriate form of the technology. In this context, technological artefacts can be viewed as both culturally constructed and interpreted, not only in how technology is thought of but in its design.

References

Burns, Tom and G.M. Stalker (1961) *The management of innovation*, London: Tavistock.

Child, John (1972) 'Organizational Structure, Environment and Performance: The Role of Strategic Choice', *Sociology* 6: 1–22.

Dawson, Patrick (1994) *Organizational change : a processual approach*, London: Chapman.

Fleck, J. (1987) 'Development and establishment in Artificial Intelligence', In: Bloomfield, B. (ed.) *The Question of Artificial Intelligence*, Routledge, pp. 106–164.

Freeman, C. (1982) *The economics of industrial innovation*, London: Routledge.

MacKenzie, D. and Wajcman, J., editors (1988) *The Social Shaping of Technology*, Milton Keynes: Open University Press.

Schumpeter, Joseph Alois (1939) *Business cycles*. 2 vols. New York: Martino Pub.

READING 9.2

Caught in the Wheels: The High Cost of Being a Female Cog in the Male Machinery of Engineering

By Cynthia Cockburn

Every self-respecting man knows that 'women are no good with machinery', they are 'hopeless at technical things'. After all, the facts speak for themselves. Women don't fiddle about inside TV sets, keep an oscilloscope in the garage, or aspire to fly a Tornado jet. Every self-respecting woman, however, feels there is something fishy about these facts. We know that women make good, competent and enthusiastic technicians and engineers – most of us have met one or two. Just as many women as men reach maturity with a bent for calculation, problem-solving, design and construction. Why, then, do most of us finish up using it to interpret knitting patterns and construct patchwork quilts? Have we chosen or were we pushed? And if we chose – what exactly was the choice we were offered?

I recently bought a book of encyclopedic scope on the history of machinery and technical invention. Working through the index I have given up at P (Ptolemy IV) without finding a woman among the inventors. No doubt we women too have had our technologies, but they are not in our history books. Ours are not the technologies that soared into capitalist profitability in the eighteenth and nineteenth centuries.

Anything But an Engineer

As a result, the engineering industry today is a sorry tale: 13% of total employment in Britain (1980), it affords only 7% of women's employment. And the 608,000 women in engineering firms fill the lowliest ranks. No less than 93% are employed in the low-skilled categories of clerical, operator and 'other employees', who are often canteen and cleaning workers. 'The female percentage of employment in the different occupational categories is uneven in the extreme,' says the Engineering Industry Training Board.[1]

While no less than 70% of clerical workers are women and 30% of operators, only 2% of scientists/

| **READING 9.2** | # Caught in the Wheels: The High Cost of Being a Female Cog in the Male Machinery of Engineering |

By Cynthia Cockburn

technologists are women. 2% is also the female proportion of technicians and for engineering craft occupations only around one-third of 1% are women ...

'Equal Chances'?

People concerned with equal opportunities study these statistics and seek to help women get their 'fair share'. With this in mind, the Equal Opportunities Commission, for instance, has funded several projects aiming to understand women's disadvantages in the technical field and to encourage girls into technology. It has sponsored several career-opportunities courses for young women. It has funded a project in which women are working with teachers and pupils in schools to bring girls into technical subjects ...

Most initiatives to date have been based on the philosophy that women must be 'given more confidence'. We are continuing, the argument goes, to *fail* to make our mark in occupations that are seen to be challenging and rewarding. But are women really such weeds? I would suggest that women know very well both where we are unwelcome and what we are rejecting. We are not failing, we are on strike.

Technology: Neither Neuter nor Neutral

The prevailing belief concerning technology is that it is neutral, mankind's heritage, equally available and relevant to us all. All that women have to do is to reach out and grasp it. The 'man' in mankind, however, is no slip of the tongue. Technology is far from neutral. This should not be a difficult concept to Marxists, who are, after all, used to understanding that our technology is capitalist technology and bears the marks and serves the purposes of the class that owns it. It needs only a little further broadening of the mind to understand that our industrial technology also has the imprint and the limitations that come of being both the social property and one of the formative processes of men. Industrial, commercial, military technologies, are masculine in a very historical and material sense. They cannot readily be used in a

feminine, nor even a sexless, mode. Women are not merely failing to enter technology. On the one hand we are being repelled, and on the other we are refusing.

Men's greater average physical stature and strength are often cited as a reason for men's preponderance in engineering occupations. Yet it is not self-evident that they should be all male. Many machines, from the lever to the mill, have been developed precisely to *substitute* for human physical strength. The masculinity of technology, men's proprietorial grasp of machinery, has to be seen as a product of social rather than biological history.

Women's Values

If engineering occupations have developed as a heartland of male hegemony, it is hardly surprising that female incursions into this domain don't occur easily or painlessly. What women and women's work have come to mean, both to ourselves and to men, is something quite different. It is accepting rather than defying physical and social limitations. While 'men's work' means singlemindedly pitting everything you have, in the army, in the mines, on the high seas, 'women's work' means refusing to let go of your other self. Men's work is predicated upon someone looking after them. We look after ourselves. Women's work means staying at home with sick children if need be. It means carrying human preoccupations into the job: nursing, teaching, social work. It seems as though for women more than for men the social purpose of work is important.

To emphasize this *difference* is not to say that women and men are born this way, immutable. It is to recognize that over hundreds and possibly thousands of years society has constructed gender difference, gender complementarity, and continues to confirm and elaborate it every day, in work as well as outside work. And much in the feminine gender is good. Women (and indeed many men) value it above masculinity. We do not want to have to abandon a concern with feelings and people and purpose in order to take on technology. We don't want to exchange the society of women for the society of men, to become a kind of de-sexed satellite of a male world.

In the Age of the Smart Machine: The Future of Work and Power

By Shoshana Zuboff

The traditional environment of imperative control is fatally flawed in its ability to adequately exploit the informating capacity of the new technology.

The interdependence of the three dilemmas of transformation I have described – knowledge, authority, and technique – indicates the necessary comprehensiveness of an informating strategy. The shifting grounds of knowledge invite managers to recognize the emergent demands for intellective skills and develop a learning environment in which such skills can develop. That very recognition contains a threat to managerial authority, which depends in part upon control over the organization's knowledge base. A commitment to intellective skill development is likely to be hampered when an organization's division of labor continuously replenishes the felt necessity of imperative control. Managers who must prove and defend their own legitimacy do not easily share knowledge or engage in inquiry. Workers who feel the requirements of subordination are not enthusiastic learners. New roles cannot emerge without the structures to support them.

The Division of Labour and the Division of Learning

Organizational theorists frequently have promoted a conception of organizations as "interpretation systems." The computer mediation of an organization's productive and administrative infrastructure places an even greater premium upon an organization's interpretive capabilities, as each organizational level experiences a relatively greater preponderance of abstract cues requiring interpretation. This is as true for the plant manager as for the pulp mill worker, for the banker as well as for the clerk. In each case, oral culture and the action-centered skills upon which that culture depends are gradually eroded, and perhaps finally displaced, by the incursions of explicit information and intellective skill.

As bureaucratic coordination and communication become more dependent upon mastering the electronic text, the *acting-with* skills of the white-collar body are subordinated to the demands associated with dominating increasing quantities of abstracted information. In many cases, traditional functional distinctions no longer reflect the requirements of the business. When managers increase their engagement with the electronic text, they also risk a new kind of hyperrationalisn and impersonalization, as they operate at a greater distance from employees and customers.

When the textualizing consequences of an informating technology become more comprehensive, the body's traditional role in the production process (as a source of effort and/or skill in the service of *acting-on*) is also transformed. The rigid separation of mental and material work characteristic of the industrial division of labor and vital to the preservation of a distinct managerial group (in the office as well as in the factory) becomes, not merely outmoded, but perilously dysfunctional. Earlier distinctions between white and blue "collars" collapse. Even more significant is the increased intellectual content of work tasks across organizational levels that attenuates the conventional designations of manager and managed.

The textualization process moves away from a conception of information as something that individuals collect, process, and disseminate; instead, it invites us to imagine an organization as a group of people gathered around a central core that is the electronic text. Individuals take up their relationship toward that text according to their responsibilities and their information needs. In such a scenario, work is, in large measure, the creation of meaning, and the methods of work involve the application of intellective skill to data.

Under these circumstances, work organization requires a new division of learning to support a new division of labour. The traditional system of imperative control, which was designed to maximize the relationship between commands and obedience, depended upon restricted hierarchical access to

Source: Reprinted by permission of Basic Books, a member of the Perseus Book Group, from In the Age of the Smart Machine: The Future of Work and Power © *1988 Basic Books.*

READING 9.3

In the Age of the Smart Machine: The Future of Work and Power

By Shoshana Zuboff

knowledge and nurtured the belief that those who were excluded from the organization's explicit knowledge base were intrinsically less capable of learning what it had to offer. In contrast, an informed organization is structured to promote the possibility of useful learning among all members and thus presupposes relations of equality. However, this does not mean that all members are assumed to be identical in their orientations, proclivities, and capacities; rather, the organization legitimates each member's right to learn as much as his or her temperament and talent will allow. In the traditional organization, the division of learning lent credibility to the legitimacy of imperative control. In an informated organization, the new division of learning produces experiences that encourage a synthesis of members' interests, and the flow of value-adding knowledge helps legitimate the organization as a learning community.

The informated workplace, which may no longer be a "place" at all, is an arena through which information circulates, information to which intellective effort is applied. The quality, rather than the quantity, of effort will be the source from which added value is derived. Economists may continue to measure labor productivity as if the entire world of work could be represented adequately by the assembly line, but their measures will be systematically indifferent to what is most valuable in the informated organization. A new division of learning requires another vocabulary – one of colleagues and co-learners, of exploration, experimentation, and innovation.

Managerial Activities in the Informated Organization

The activities arrayed on the responsibility rings at a greater distance from the core incorporate at least four domains of managerial activity: intellective skill development, technology development, strategy formulation, and social system development. For example, the crucial importance of the intellective skill base requires that a significant level of organizational resources be devoted to its expansion and refinement. This means that some organizational members will be involved in both higher-order analysis and conceptualization, as well as in promoting learning and skill development among those with operational responsibility. Their aim is to expand the knowledge base and to improve the effectiveness with which data is assimilated, interpreted, and responded to. They have a central role in creating an organizational environment that invites learning and in supporting those in other managerial domains to develop their talents as educators and as learners. In this domain, managers are responsible for task-related learning, for learning about learning, and for educating others in each of the other three domains.

There is considerable interdependence among these four domains of managerial activity (intellective skill development, technology development, strategy formulation, and social system development). For example, activities related to intellective skill development cannot proceed without the social system of management that helps to foster roles and relationships appropriate to a new division of learning. Activities in either of these domains will be frustrated without technological development that supports an informating strategy. Integration and learning are responsibilities that fall within each domain, because without a shared commitment to interdependence and the production of value-adding knowledge, the legitimacy of the learning community will suffer. Business outcomes such as cost, efficiency, quality, product development, customer service, productivity, et cetera, would result from coordinated initiatives across domains. Managerial work would thus be team-oriented and interdisciplinary, and would promote the fluid movement of members across these four domains of managerial activity.

When work involves a collective effort to create and communicate meaning, the dynamics of human feeling cannot be relegated to the periphery of an organization's concerns. How people feel about themselves, each other, and the organization's purposes is closely linked to their capacity to sustain the high levels of internal commitment and motivation that are demanded by the abstraction of work and the new division of learning.

READING 9.4	**Formal Organization as Representation: Remote Control, Displacement and Abbreviation**

By Robert Cooper

In recent years, organizations have come to be seen as organizers of information. An early stimulus to this way of thinking was Simon's (1955) famous criticism of the theory of rational choice: that the latter imputes to the rational actor exaggerated capacities for processing information. In reality, human rationality is severely bounded. Formal organization was seen as an instrument for solving problems specifically deriving from bounded rationality. Williamson's (1975) theory of transaction costs is one attempt to explain bounded rationality in terms of the supply of information and its effects on the organization of the market. Two factors are salient: the cost or difficulty of acquiring necessary information about the market, and the number of firms in it. If information is freely available and firms are numerous, then, because transaction costs are low, the profit advantage goes to the individual who is self-employed. On the other hand, where information is costly and where there are few firms, transaction costs become too high and it therefore pays the individual to take employment with a big firm that can control information and thus reduce transaction costs.

Extending Williamson's analysis, Schotter (1981) has reworked the relationship between rationality and organizations in the language of information theory. Information is no longer a commodity that is more or less available; it is now that which has surprise value. If an event can be predicted or is already known, it carries little or no information. Information increases with unpredictability. Schotter views organizational structures as forms of informational complexity. Past experience becomes sedimented in an organization's structures where it functions as a guide to future events. The more completely organizational structures encode information, the less unpredictability or uncertainty there is likely to be.

Williamson and Schotter both underline the boundedness of individual rationality and then go on to say that by constructing organizations, individuals extend the limits of their capacities for processing information. For Williamson, organizations augment bounded rationality by controlling the flow of information, so reducing transaction costs for individual actors. For Schotter, organizations augment the limits of rationality by encoding as much information as possible in their structures and rules. But both Williamson and Schotter overlook a fundamental and mandatory act in the processing of information: representation. Information theory begins with the construction of a representation (pattern, picture, model) of some aspect of the world (MacKay, 1969). The representation must exist before we can go on to think about information m the Williamson–Schotter sense. When Williamson, for example, talks about the effects of information on the organization of the market he is really talking about changes in a representational construct of that market. The representation comes first; information is that which augments or reduces the power of the representation. On this analysis, organizations are not merely organizers of information; they also construct the forms in which information appears.

It is this principle of economy which makes the logic of representation more fundamental to the understanding and analysis of organizations than the traditionally more limited concept of information.

Remote control underlines the economy of convenience intrinsic to representation: one may not be able to move the mountain itself but it is easy to move a model or map of it. This mobility of representation helps us to understand why paperwork of all kinds is so essential to organizations: mobility is central to control. Representation displaces the intractable and obdurate; it denies the idea of fixed location and emphasizes movement. Displacement, therefore, means mobile and non-localizable associations. It therefore becomes inappropriate to talk, for example, about the organization and its environment since this gives the impression of distinct domains separated in space and time. In terms of displacement, organizing activity is the transformation of boundary relationships which are themselves continually shifting. Again, the concept of the boundary comes into its own. The organization's inside and outside are correlative: 'No inside is conceivable … without the

READING 9.4

Formal Organization as Representation: Remote Control, Displacement and Abbreviation

By Robert Cooper

complicity of an outside on which it relies. Complicity mixed with antagonism ... No outside would be conceivable without an inside fending it off, resisting it, "reacting" to it' (Starobinski, 1975: 342). In this way, inside and outside, organization and environment, continually displace each other. But neither remote control nor displacement are thinkable without abbreviation. Abbreviation makes possible the economy of convenience that underlies representation.

It simplifies the complex, makes the big into the small, converts the delayed into the instantaneous. It works according to a principle of condensation in which as much as is needed is condensed into as little as is needed so as to enable ease and accuracy of perception and action. Through abbreviation, representations are made compact, versatile and permutable. The development of the computer in recent years perhaps best exemplifies the abbreviation process: 'The power of ten cubic meters of 1965-vintage computer can now be held in the palm of the hand. Thanks to telephone hook-up, the mini-computer presently affords us access to millions of data' (Bertin, 1983: x). In these examples, representation combines with electronics to provide increasingly powerful means of 'abbreviating' the world.

The degree to which technologies of representation contributed to the historical development of the practical disciplines of administration and management is not widely appreciated. One aspect of this development was the tendency from the seventeenth century onwards to think in terms of the economy of convenience – instant information, knowledge 'at a glance', was what administrators demanded. In effect, this required a radical restructuring of the administrative and governmental process towards strategies of abbreviation. These strategies were directed mainly to the sense of vision – for good reasons. It is known that vision is the most efficient of the sensory systems: it can take in a far wider range of information in a much shorter span of time (Bertin, 1983). For this reason, optic-friendly technologies of representation began to emerge systematically with the increasing complexity and range of administrative problems that accompanied the population explosion in Europe in the eighteenth century.[1]

Foucault (1979) tells us that the arts of administration and government in the modern sense arose out of the demographic expansion of the eighteenth century. Before this period, government was conceived on the model of the family and governors and administrators, like good fathers, viewed their roles in terms of the management of the household where the common welfare of all was uppermost and the refractory natural forces of sea and weather, so the new breed of administrators were forced to develop more effective ways of representing and thus controlling the new urban masses of the eighteenth century. Almost by definition, a human mass defies formal knowledge and representation. Any mob or mass, simply because it lacks classification and resists calculation, is 'already seditious' (Miller, 1987: 17). In this sense, the masses were remote; their sheer numbers also made them physically unmanageable. Before they could be organized and managed, the masses had to be re-presented in the form of remote control, displacement and abbreviation. No one understood this better than Jeremy Bentham.

The principle of abbreviation is 'much condensed into little'. It is the fulcrum of Bentham's theory of management. Bentham brought it to perfection in his architectural concept of the Panopticon, 'the polyvalent apparatus of surveillance, the universal optical machine of human groupings' (Miller, 1987: 3).

The whole idea of the Panoptic principle was to connect abbreviated representations – models, signs, summaries, and the like – with a many-layered imbrication of social, political, architectural and other factors in a kind of *semio-technical hierarchy* where the simplest term could represent the most complex series, where the most intricate details of institutional behaviour could be orchestrated to respond to the briefest command, the most peremptory signal.[2] Today, this programme is being dramatically advanced by means of information technology. Zuboff (1988) shows how the informating function of information technology reveals the organization as the managing of 'electronic texts' (that is, representations) in which the major aspects of the organization's work (behavioural, technical, and so on) can be centrally summarized as realtime data on terminal

| **Formal Organization as Representation: Remote Control, Displacement and Abbreviation** *continued*

By Robert Cooper

screens; and in which Bentham's criterion of 'at-a-glance' management becomes doubly instantaneous because organizational processes are represented as they actually happen.

[1]Foucault (1977) analyses a range of vision-oriented administrative technologies that were constructed or perfected during this period; for example, hierarchical observation, normalizing judgement, the examination, the Panopticon.

[2]Again, Foucault (1977: Part 3, Chapter 1) provides some details of this technique; for example, the association between 'signalization' and the 'precise system of command'.

References

Bertin, J. (1983) *Semiology of Graphics: Diagrams, Networks, Maps.* Madison, Wisconsin: University of Wisconsin Press.

Deleuze, G. (1986) *Foucault.* Minneapolis, MN: University of Minnesota Press.

Foucault, M. (1977) *Discipline and Punish: The Birth of the Prison.* London: Allen Lane.

Foucault, M. (1979) 'Governmentality', *Ideology and Consciousness,* 6: 5–21.

Hall, R.H. (1987) *Organizations: Structure and Process.* Englewood Cliffs, NJ: Prentice-Hall.

Latour, B. (1983) 'Give me a laboratory and I will raise the world', in Kn. Knorr-Cetina and M. Mulkay (eds), *Science Observed: Perspectives on the Social Study of Science.* London: Sage Publications.

Latour, B. (1988) *The Pasteurization of France.* Cambridge, MA: Harvard University Press.

Law, J. (1986) 'On the methods of long-distance control: Vessels, navigation and the Portuguese route to India', in J. Law (ed.), *Power, Action and Belief: A New Sociology of Knowledge?* London: Routledge & Kegan Paul.

McArthur, T. (1986) *Worlds of Reference: Lexicography, Learning and Language from the Clay Tablet to the Computer.* Cambridge: Cambridge University Press.

MacKay, D.M. (1969) *Information, Mechanism and Meaning.* Cambridge, MA: MIT Press.

Miller, J.-A. (1987) 'Jeremy Bentham's Panoptic device', *October,* 41: 3–29.

O'Hara, D.T. (1988) 'What was Foucault?', in J. Arac (ed.), *After Foucault: Humanistic Knowledge, Postmodern Challenges.* New Brunswick: Rutgers University Press.

Scarry, E. (1985) *The Body in Pain: The Making and Unmaking of the World.* New York: Oxford University Press.

Schotter, A. (1981) *The Economic Theory of Social Institutions.* Cambridge: Cambridge University Press.

Scott, W.R. (1987) *Organizations: Rational, Natural and Open Systems.* Englewood Cliff, NJ: Prentice-Hall.

Serres, M. (1982) *Hermes: Literature, Science, Philosophy.* Baltimore: The Johns Hopkins University Press.

Simon, H.A. (1955) 'A behavioral model of rational choice', *Quarterly Journal of Economics,* 69: 99–118.

Simon, H.A. (1957) *Models of Man.* New York: Wiley.

Starobinski, J. (1975) 'The inside and the outside', *The Hudson Review,* 28: 333–51.

Weber, M. (1947) *The Theory of Social and Economic Organization.* Glencoe, IL: Free Press.

Weick K. (1979) *The Social Psychology of Organizing.* Reading, MA: Addison-Wesley.

Williamson, O.E. (1975) *Markets and Hierarchies: Analysis and Anti-Trust Implications.* New York: Free Press.

Zipf, G.K. (1949) *Human Behavior and the Principle of Least Effort.* Reading, MA: Addison-Wesley.

Zuboff, S. (1988) *In the Age of the Smart Machine: The Future of Work and Power.* New York: Basic Books.

| **Allegories of Creative Destruction: Technology and Organization in Narratives of the E-economy**

By David Knights, Faith Noble, Theo Vurdubakis and Hugh Willmott

Of the various such narratives of the 'virtual' in general – and of b2c [business to business] e-commerce in particular – jostling for public attention and credibility, two are particularly popular and have been selected for consideration here. These can be summed up as:

1. The 'future shock' story (after Toffler, 1971), which narrates how extant forms of enterprise

Source: Reproduced with permission of Oxford University Press from 'Allegories of Creative Destruction: Technology and Organization in Narratives of the e-Economy', in Virtual Society? Technology, Cyberbole, Reality © 2009 Oxford University Press. *www.oup.com*

Allegories of Creative Destruction: Technology and Organization in Narratives of the E-economy

By David Knights, Faith Noble, Theo Vurdubakis and Hugh Willmott

and organizing are (about to be) overwhelmed by the changes wrought by the new electronic technologies. If it is to survive in the digital age, business must embrace the vision of the cyberprophets;

2. Its diametric opposite, the 'the emperor's new clothes' story in which it is explained how things are not all they seem (and where various instances of awe-inspiring technological or organisational prowess are 'exposed' as little more than cyberhype).

Hardly a complete inventory. Rather a starting point of an exploration of two particular ways in which narratives are enacted in corporate performances of the 'virtual'.

Future shocks

The one clear lesson of the Internet is you can't stand still (Tony Blair, speech at the *Knowledge 2000 Conference*, 7 March 2000).

Future Shock (Toffler, 1971) ... [is] a shorthand description for all stories of how the technology revolution is triggering fundamental changes in the social environment which threaten a wide range of firms, (e.g. intermediaries, bricks-and-mortar retailers and so on), with 'death by 1000 clicks'. (*The Economist*, 10/12/99: 23)

What follows, is an excerpt from such a story, as told by Richard M. Melnicoff senior partner in Andersen Consulting's eCommerce division:

In H. G. Wells' classic *The War of the Worlds*, an English village awakes one day to discover that it has been invaded by decidedly unpleasant beings from Mars. Panic and confusion seize the villagers as the destructive intent of the newcomers becomes clear. "All our work undone," one local cries out. "This must be the beginning of the end!" Did similar thoughts cross the minds of greeting card companies when E-greetings sent more than 250,000 digital greetings last [i.e. 1998] Christmas Day? What about all those publishers of classified ads looking on as Monster.com stomped onto the nation's desktops? And it's safe

to assume that even the titans of Wall Street were rattled last September 1, the day schwab.com scored 20 million hits ... Why do electronic commerce contenders seem so alien? And how is it that highly successful firms, pursuing some of the most carefully thought-out strategies in the world, keep getting caught off guard by them? The answer is these established organizations are still fighting to win a game that no longer exists. Most of them continue to make the assumptions, and accept the constraints, of traditional economics and strategy. But today's electronic economy – fuelled by a unique convergence of computing, communications and content technologies – is subject to an entirely new set of rules. (Melnicoff 1999: 1.)

Certain features of this story are worth noting. *The War of the Worlds* ([1898] 1971) is a narrative of reversals of fortune. Britain, the colonial power par excellence finds itself the victim of Martian colonial aggression. The English are as swiftly and ruthlessly overpowered by the technologically superior alien invaders as they themselves had overpowered native resistance in the course of colonial expansion. As indicated in Melnicoff's account, the disruptive technologies of the new 'eEconomy' are similarly envisaged as agencies of radical reversal ...

The speed of this revolution is said to be such that executives – much like the villagers in Melnicoff's allegory – have no time to reflect on developments. As the IT Director for electronic delivery channels at Barclays Bank reports: 'In 1995 we put together a think tank with a remit to look at banking over the next 10 years. Their 10 year view materialised in one year' (Stevenson, 1997). Or as Heller and Spenley (2000: 129) argue, '[i]n revolutionary times the pragmatist is as much a liability as the conservative.' In the Internet Era to be pragmatic is to be branded an enemy of the revolution. Consider the banking sector, which, at least according to corporate folklore, is notorious for both its obdurate pragmatism as well as its cultural conservatism ...

The New e-economy therefore, appears to offer a straightforward Darwinian choice between adaptation and dinosaur-like extinction. As another one of our interlocutors, (a technology manager for a major UK bank) put it:

READING 9.5

Allegories of Creative Destruction: Technology and Organization in Narratives of the E-economy *continued*

By David Knights, Faith Noble, Theo Vurdubakis and Hugh Willmott

I think it was Bill Gates who said that 'the world needs banking but it doesn't need banks' ... we have to adapt. And we have to do it quickly. Or else. (1999)

'E-shock' stories then tell of an ironic reversal in roles, where a bank's material assets – its 'old paradigm infrastructure' – that were formerly sources of its strength are viewed as leaden legacies in an e-Economy able to 'live on thin air' (Leadbeater, 2000). As one of our interviewees in 1998, (a senior executive in the California bank Wells Fargo) put it:

> Even a progressive bank like ours finds it difficult to re-invent itself. I think there is reticence about doing that probably because we have so much infrastructure already committed to the old paradigm, so shifting it you have to be incredibly bold to shift because almost inevitably you are going to take a hit. ...[1]

The Emperor's Virtual Clothes

> Hype is not a business plan. IBM advertisement (*Daily Telegraph*, 24/1/01).

But, how exactly are we to recognize hype when we encounter it? To help clarify what the issue is here, consider the example of Tesco, one of the UK's biggest retail chains ... In November 1996 Tesco launched Internet superstore Tesco Direct. This was one of the first home shopping Websites allowing shoppers to place their orders, and make credit card payments (including a £5 delivery charge) whereupon the items popped into their Superhighway shopping trolley were delivered from a local branch to their home at a specified date and time. The facility was heralded as the dawn of a new era in Internet shopping in the UK ...

While the many were dazzled, some were brave enough to investigate. On closer examination of the Tesco Direct ordering process by a journalist from the *European* newspaper, a more familiar and a more complex picture emerged. Once entered by the customer at the Tesco Website, the order was received at the company offices. There it was first re-typed and then faxed to the customer's local branch where it was picked up and passed on to a shop assistant who assembled the order. The order was then finally handed to the van driver for delivery.

> The leap was not what it seemed. Rather than heralding the arrival of a new era for shoppers where computers and robots merge seamlessly to deliver customers their weekly groceries the site is something of a façade. (Reeve, 1998: 6.)

This is then a version of 'the emperor's new virtual clothes' story. As in the famous scene from the *Wizard of Oz*, the curtain has been drawn back, and the wizard stands exposed in his den. His awe-inspiring powers are cheap tricks produced with the help of a rather ramshackle mechanical apparatus. The Wizard is a merchant of hype. Tesco Direct operation on the ground is then 'revealed' as a *performan*ce of (the image of) Internet retailing. To the apparent surprise of the journalist (also acting as representative of the reader), the transformative influence of the Internet on Tesco's operations amounts to something rather less straightforward than the effortless and unmediated realisation of the grand e-revolutionary narratives.

Performance

> I'll see it when I believe it. (Weick, 1979)

'*Future shock*' stories narrate a misalignment between culture and its technology. Emperor's new clothes stories narrate the misalignment between appearance and reality, words and things (e.g. 'hype'). Both topics have been at the centre of the frequently vociferous arguments between so-called constructivists and their critics. For instance, the degree to which accounts of the social shaping of an artefact can, and should, have recourse to some kind of 'technical bottom line' – itself beyond social analysis – has been the subject of much disputation. A frequently cited example of such controversy, (one might even say an iconic moment), has been the debate between (on the constructivist side) Keith Grint and Steve Woolgar (1992; 1997), and on the realist side,

READING 9.5

Allegories of Creative Destruction: Technology and Organization in Narratives of the E-economy

By David Knights, Faith Noble, Theo Vurdubakis and Hugh Willmott

Rob Kling (1992; See also Ashmore *et al.*, 1994, Latour, 1999: 176–92). Some of the issues raised in this debate are particularly pertinent to our argument here and deserve a closer look. The proposition to affirm or deny, was the claim that 'It is much harder to kill a platoon of soldiers with a dozen roses than with well-placed, high speed bullets' (Kling, op cit.: 362). Grint and Woolgar rise to the challenge by peeling this statement's postulated 'technological core' like an onion arguing that 'with enough ingenuity and effort' any ultimate bottom line argument (shot, injury, death, or even the proverbial hole in the head) can be revealed as a social construction. A succession of false bottoms. 'What counts as technical' they argue 'is precisely a reflection of the effort needed to show it to be social' (Grint and Woolgar, op. cit.: 376).

The abstract epistemological questions of the precise relation between social and technical, representation and object represented, debated by Kling, Grint and Woolgar are certainly interesting. However, such debates always run the danger of being perceived as nothing more than exercises in idle intellectual speculation: Self-declared 'realists' dream up a formulation which turns, so to speak, the 'world upside down'. They then challenge self-described 'constructivists' to show how it can stay that way. This sets off an endless circle in which increasingly preposterous propositions are constructed (by realists) only to be 'de-constructed' (by constructivists) so the whole thing can start all over again – until both sides lose interest. In this light the social study of technology can appear as a rather trivial undertaking ... Rather than remain within a discourse of assertion and counter-assertion, perhaps we can speculate as to the context or circumstances in which a proposition like 'guns do not kill' would be taken seriously. *That is under what conditions could it be understood and intended as guidance to the hearer rather than as a self-evident absurdity?*

In his critique of Grint and Woolgar, McLaughlin (1997: 215–16) argues:

> the [constructivist] approach sidesteps the key question of how grievous bodily harm and murder could be accomplished with roses rather than

guns. It merely asserts that an actor network could turn roses into effective weapons, but does not demonstrate how this might be achieved.

We understand the spirit of the criticism as a challenge to bring Grint and Woolgar's disparate demonstrations of the social construction of technological facts in the debate, together in a coherent plot. In other words, a demand for a narrative in which roses kill but guns do not, *in the course of a single story*. We know of no culture that ever 'enacted' this opposition of roses to guns, it is nevertheless possible to find examples, which are not too far off. That requires a return to the colonial experience for which the *War of the Worlds* constitutes an allegory.

In the summer of 1905, for instance, Kinjikitile Ngwale, medicine man in what was then German East Africa, concocted the *maji* (a war medicine made out of water, millet and castor oil), which rendered the wearer invulnerable to bullets, and proclaimed the rebellion against the Reich. ...

The *maji* (Swahili for water) inspired those who used it. As a village headman told his followers: 'This is not war ... We shall not die. We shall only kill' (cited in Pakenham, 1991: 619). It was not an altogether impossible objective. There were only a few hundred German officered Askari troops in the whole area of the rebellion:

> For the rebels ... August seemed to prove the miraculous truth of all that Kinjikitile had foretold. It was obvious to them that out of the German gun barrels came nothing but water. At a stroke, the Germans were driven from the land of all the peoples protected by the *maji*. (Pakenham, 1991: 619.)

Even the failure of the rebellion[2] in the face of German machine guns and the arrival of General Gotzen's Marines need not *necessarily* constitute a decisive, knockout, argument against the claim that European rifles are ineffective against sufficiently strong magic. True the *maji* had failed but this is not an argument against the whole class of war medicines any more than computer failure (and there are enough of them) is an argument against the functioning of all computers

READING 9.5

Allegories of Creative Destruction: Technology and Organization in Narratives of the E-economy *continued*

By David Knights, Faith Noble, Theo Vurdubakis and Hugh Willmott

(Knights *et al.*, 2000b). Or to put it the other way around, would *success* have proved the veracity of Kinjikitile's claims about the power of the *maji*?

Concluding Remarks

The world of the *maji* appears far removed from that of Active Apparel and the Internet. At the same time it testifies to the transformative power of expectations about, and performances of, technological artefacts in social action. While paying due respect to the transformative role of new technologies, we would nevertheless suggest that notions of 'impact' tend to be rather blunt analytical instruments. There is, we would claim, a need to look more closely at how these impacts are realized in practice. In doing so, it is appropriate to focus more directly on the symbolic importance of new information and communication technologies as representations of efficiency, modernization and progress. We have argued here, that the effects associated with any technology are so to speak 'performed', that is made real or realised, rather than flowing in a straightforward manner from its inherent technical properties (Bloomfield and Vurdubakis, 1997; 2001). This implies that an understanding of the processes through which particular sets of cultural repertoires and expectations are established, is central to all questions concerning the nature of the interdependencies between technologies and the (social) 'context' within which they are embedded and acted upon.

Such issues, we have argued, are at the heart of a wide range of ongoing theoretical and practical debates surrounding current developments in remote trading and micro-electronic communications. Accordingly, this paper has been concerned with how the spectre of virtuality (and of those technologies that are said to make it possible, or even inevitable) is invoked to promote or legitimize particular developments and to justify the expenditure of resources ... The various organizational (re)arrangements and the (often unexpected) technological configurations which firms have set up to interface with the brave new world of all things cyber, should not therefore be viewed simply in terms of profit or instrumental efficiency (or lack thereof). They are simultaneously public demonstrations that an organization or community has as it were 'absorbed' the impact of the new medium ...

[1] We acknowledge Darren McCabe for his involvement with David Knights in conducting the US interviews.

[2] The rebellion and its aftermath would ultimately cost the lives of a quarter of a million Africans.

References

Ashmore, M., Edwards D. and Potter, J., (1994) 'The Bottom Line: The Rhetoric of Reality Demonstrations', *Configurations*, Vol. 2, (1): 1–14.

Bloomfield, B.P. and Vurdubakis, T. (1997) 'The Revenge of the Object? Artificial Intelligence as a Cultural Enterprise', *Social Analysis*, Vol. 4, (11): 29–45.

Bloomfield, B.P. and Vurdubakis, T. (2001) 'The Vision Thing: Constructions of Time and Technology in Management Advice' in Clark, T. and Fincham R. (eds) *Critical Consulting: Perspectives on the Management Advice Industry*, London: Blackwell.

Grint, K. and Woolgar, S., (1992) 'Computers, Guns and Roses: What's Social About Being Shot?', *Science, Technology and Human Values*, Vol. 17, pp. 366–80.

Heller, R. and Spenley, P. (2000) *Riding the Revolution: How Businesses Can and Must Win the E-Wars*, London: HarperCollins.

Kling, R. (1992) 'Audiences, Narratives and Human Values in the Social Studies of Technology', *Science, Technology and Human Values*, Vol. 17, pp. 349–65.

Latour, B. (1999) *Pandora's Hope: Essays on the reality of Science Studies*, Cambridge, MA: Harvard University Press.

Melnicoff, Richard M. (1999) 'The eEconomy: It's later than you think', *Outlook*, http://www.ac.com/overview/Outlook/6.99/over-economy.html. (Date of Access 9/29/99).

McLaughlin, I. (1997) 'Babies, Bathwater, Guns and Roses' in I. McLaughlin and M. Harris (eds.) *Innovation, Organizational Change and Technology*, London: Cengage Learning Business Press: 207–22.

Reeve, S. (1998) 'Net Loss', *The European*, 16–22 February: 26–7.

Stevenson, A. (1997) Barclays Bank Information Strategy, October, quoted by Mike Gibson-Sharpe, Marketing Manager, International Business Division of BT.

Toffler, A. (1971) *Future Shock*, London: Pan.

Weick, K. (1979) *The Social Psychology of Organizing*, Reading, MA: Addison–Wesley.

Wells, H.G. ([1898]1971) *The War of the Worlds*, Harmondsworth: Penguin.

Discussion Questions

1. How does the way that technology is conceptualized or theorized influence how it is understood?
2. Can technology ever be seen merely as a technical or neutral phenomenon?
3. Does new technology have implications for the way that organizations and employees are managed?
4. Why do you think that both positive and negative narratives seek to bring about the very technological outcomes they claim merely to describe?

Introduction References

Schotter, A. (1981) *The Economic Theory of Social Institutions*, Cambridge: Cambridge University Press.

Wells, H.G. ([1898] 1971) *The War of the Worlds*, Harmondsworth: Penguin.

Williamson, O.E. (1975) *Markets and Hierarchies: Analysis and Anti-Trust Implications*, New York: Free Press.

Recommended Further Readings

See references accompanying the Readings plus:

Castells, M. (2001) *The Internet Galaxy: Reflections on the Internet, Business and Society*, Oxford: Oxford University Press.

Guile, B.R. and Quinn, J.B. (1988) *Managing Innovation: Cases from the Services Industries*, New York: National Academy of Engineering, National Academy of Sciences.

Simpson, L.G. (1995) *Technology, Time and the Conversations of Modernity*, New York: Routledge.

Calvert, T.J.M. (1997) *Processed Lives: Gender and Technology in Everyday Life*, New York: Routledge.

METHODOLOGY

CHAPTER 10

READINGS

Silverman, D. (1993) *Interpreting Qualitative Data: Methods for Analysing Talk, Text and Interaction*. London: Sage, pp. 4–7.

Alvesson, M. and Deetz, S. (2000) *Doing Critical Management Research*. London: Sage, pp. 49–79.

Knights, D. (1995) 'Refocusing the Case Study: The Politics of Research and Researching Politics in IT Management' in *Technology Studies*, Vol. 2, No. 2: pp. 230–284.

Morgan, G. (1975) *Beyond Method: Strategies for Social Research*, London: Sage, pp. 332–4.

Rosen, M. (1991) 'Coming to Terms with the Field: Understanding and Doing Organizational Ethnography' in *Journal of Management Studies*, Vol. 28: pp. 1–24.

Law, J. (2004) *After Method*, London and New York: Routledge, pp. 4–6; 7–8; 9.

Jacques, R. (1996) *Manufacturing the Employee: Management knowledge from the 19th to 21st centuries*, London: Sage. Preface pp. x–xii, p. xvii and Introduction p. 7.

INTRODUCTION

Following the intervention of Adorno *et al.* (1976) to challenge positivism (i.e. the assumption that the human world is only different from nature in degree not in kind), large numbers of social scientists reject the ambitions of those who seek to establish laws that have the same level of predictability, validity and reliability as those of the natural sciences. For those unwilling to accept that social life could be studied as if there were no ontological discontinuity between 'natural' and social phenomena, positivism has become a term of abuse. While the approach to methodology in this book takes as given a sceptical view of positivist approaches, we will see that a number of qualitative researchers are quite heavily influenced by precisely those frames of reference. Take our first contribution. Although his preferred method of research is to analyse transcripts to display how talk gets socially organised, **David Silverman** (Reading 10.1) insists on placing methodology and

177

methods within a framework of theory leading to hypotheses that particular methods drawn from either quantitative or qualitative methodologies can test. This is a framework taken straight out of the deductive hypothetico method of Popper (1961) who can be seen as the father of positivist methodology. Rather than becoming preoccupied with a stale debate, **Mats Alvesson and Stan Deetz** (Reading 10.2) follow our own line in taking as given that the critique provided by several philosophers of social science is unanswerable from within the positivist framework. Instead they challenge the distinction between quantitative and qualitative methodology on the basis that they find it neither insightful nor useful. However, they then find themselves relying on the distinction as their argument turns on a belief that qualitative researchers often remain equally as positivist as their quantitative compatriots. **David Knights** (Reading 10.3) takes a similar line of argument but suggests that anti-positivists need not be apologetic for their chosen methodology since it is the positivists that have to defend their continued use of such a methodology against the assault that has been produced over the last three decades. By contrast, **Gareth Morgan** (Reading 10.4) adopts a post- or anti-methods methodology. Rather than adumbrating a range of different methodologies and methods, he simply selects a research orientation that draws on what he calls a dialectical form of structural analysis. Morgan argues that the continuity of social structures (i.e. institutionalized or regularized sets of social relations) is dependent on their being reproduced through the enactments of practices or subjectively and intersubjectively shared meanings, purposes and assumptions. A dialectical approach examines social arrangements concretely within their contexts or the total social formations in which they are embedded but must always remain aware that the context is itself a historically developing social arrangement.

Michael Rosen (Reading 10.5) argues that ethnography is inadequately understood and recognized within administration science. But it is ideal as a method for studying organizational culture. Rosen is concerned to avoid producing a recipe of the necessary ingredients of an ethnographical study on the grounds that there is a diverse range of theoretical approaches, even within the limited scope of organizational ethnography, making a list of conceptual categories or empirical properties impossible. Broadly, however, he follows a social constructionist framework (Berger and Luckmann, 1967) that is compatible with the other methodological approaches adopted by the authors of these selected readings. Organizational ethnographies seek to decode, translate, and interpret the behaviours and attached meaning systems of those occupying and creating the social organizations under investigation. Consequently, the method is largely about making sense of events and translating their meaning from one context to another. It is always a second order construction or account and its strength usually lies in the way that the 'thick descriptions' emanating out of the field research are then developed to form theoretically interesting understandings. Because researchers in ethnographic studies are steeped in the culture that is the object of their investigations, the whole process is recursively self-reflexive such that by the end of the project it is likely that the field workers have been transformed. Self-development goes hand in hand with theoretical advance in the same way that most teachers hope will occur in the learning experience of students. **John Law** (Reading 10.6) begins his analysis by asking rhetorically whether attempting to describe messy realities with less messy accounts would not make a bigger mess of it. Standard rule-based research methods that are found in most social science methodology texts, he argues, are badly adapted to studying what is often ephemeral, indefinite, irregular and indeterminate. But he challenges not so much their hegemony as such but their normative constraints where we are told more or less 'how we must see and what we must do when we investigate' (p. 4 of original text). His objection to this is that it is grounded in an assumption that reality is out there waiting to be discovered as a definite, and more or less stable entity. Firstly, it is rarely definite and stable rather than fluid and dynamic but secondly, the assumption makes no allowance for our participation, whether as researchers or citizens, in producing the reality that we might claim only to describe. We complete the section with an extensive extract from **Jacques'** (Reading 10.7) distinctive approach to studying management and organization. This distinctiveness derives in no small part from his late entry into academic life, having worked as a software designer in industry before deciding to switch careers and take up a doctorate. Having found an MBA degree of little help to him in practical management work, he came to the conclusion that the model of science adopted by a majority of social scientists that work in the field of management and organization was entirely inappropriate. For he subscribes to Foucault's view that a linear, progressive, and testable model of behaviour fails to reflect the discursively problematic and historically discontinuous development of social organization. His experience as a practising manager and his belief that the study of management is probably much more practical when it is also theoretical leads him to resist following a myopic strategy of refining and testing hypotheses and then seeking to quantify everything simply because that is the norm of science. His view is that we have to study where we have been in order to know where we are going. But this is not to argue for exact prediction of the future so much as simply seeking to understand the present from insights that we can derive from studying the past. He argues that common sense assumptions are the enemy and here we might want to challenge the certainty with which he sets up a false dichotomy between common sense and critical reflexivity. It is our view that assumptions should always be challenged but we have to recognize that the challenge itself will be based on some other often hidden assumptions.

READING 10.1	## Interpreting Qualitative Data: Methods for Analysing Talk, Text and Interaction

By David Silverman

This is a text on qualitative methodology. However, any methodology only makes sense if we understand what the research process is all about.

At the outset it helps to clarify our terms. In this chapter, we shall be discussing theories, hypotheses, methods, and methodologies.

As we see from Table 10.1.1, theories provide a set of explanatory concepts. These concepts offer ways of looking at the world which are essential in defining a research problem. As we shall see shortly, without a theory, there is nothing to research. In social research, examples of such theories are *functionalism* (which looks at the functions of social institutions), *behaviourism* (which defines all behaviour in terms of 'stimulus' and 'response') and *symbolic interactionism* (which focuses on how we attach symbolic meanings to interpersonal relations).

READING 10.1	**Interpreting Qualitative Data: Methods for Analysing Talk, Text and Interaction** *continued*

By David Silverman

TABLE 10.1.1 | BASIC CONCEPTS IN RESEARCH

Concept	Meaning	Relevance
Theory	A set of explanatory concepts	Usefulness
Hypothesis	A testable proposition	Validity
Methodology	A general approach to studying research topics	Usefulness
Method	A specific research technique	Good fit with theory, hypothesis and methodology

So theories provide the impetus for research. As living entities, they are also developed and modified by good research. However, as used here, theories are never disproved but only found more or less useful.

This last feature distinguishes theories from hypotheses. Unlike theories, hypotheses are tested in research. Examples of hypotheses, considered later in this book, are:

– that how we receive advice is linked to how advice is given;

– that responses to an illegal drug depend upon what one learns from others;

– that voting in a union election is related to non-work links between union members.

As we shall see, a feature of many qualitative research studies is that there is no specific hypothesis at the outset but that hypotheses are produced (or induced) during the early stages of research. In any event, unlike theories, hypotheses can, and should, be tested. Therefore, we assess a hypothesis by its validity or truth.

A methodology is a general approach to studying a research topic. It establishes how one will go about studying any phenomenon. In social research, examples of methodologies are *positivism* (which seeks to discover laws using quantitative methods) and, of course, *qualitative methodology* (which is often concerned with inducing hypotheses from field research). Like theories, methodologies cannot be true or false, only more or less useful.

Finally, methods are specific research techniques. These include quantitative techniques, like statistical correlations, as well as techniques like observation, interviewing and audio-recording. Once again, in

themselves, techniques are not true or false. They are more or less useful, depending on their fit with the theories and methodologies being used, the hypothesis being tested and/or the research topic that is selected. So, for instance, positivists will favour quantitative methods and interactionists often prefer to gather their data by observation. But, depending upon the hypothesis being tested, positivists may sometimes use qualitative methods – for instance in the exploratory stage of research. Equally, interactionists may sometimes use simple quantitative methods, particularly when they want to find an overall pattern in their data.

The Variety of Qualitative Methods

There are four major methods used by qualitative researchers:

observation;

analysing texts and documents;

interviews;

recording and transcribing.

These methods are often combined. For instance, many case studies combine observation with interviewing. Moreover, each method can be used in either qualitative or quantitative research studies. As Table 10.1.2 shows, the overall nature of the research methodology shapes how each method is used.

Think, for instance, of how much interviews are central to making sense of our lives.

All this means that we need to resist treating research methods as mere *techniques*. This is reflected in the attention paid in this book to the *analysis* of data rather than to methods of data *collection*.

| READING 10.1 | **Interpreting Qualitative Data: Methods for Analysing Talk, Text and Interaction** |

By David Silverman

TABLE 10.1.2 | DIFFERENT USES FOR FOUR METHODS

	Methodology	
Method	Quantitative research	Qualitative research
Observation	Preliminary work, e.g. prior framing questionnaires	Fundamental to understanding another culture
Textual Analysis	Content analysis, i.e. counting in terms of researchers' categories	Understanding participants' categories
Interviews	'Survey research': mainly fixed-choice questions to random samples	'Open-ended' questions to small samples
Transcripts	Used infrequently to check the accuracy of interview records	Used to understand how participants organise their talk

| READING 10.2 | **Doing Critical Management Research** |

By Mats Alvesson and Stanley Deetz

For some time, considerable dissatisfaction has existed with conventional approaches to social research, including management research. Much of this conventional research was dominated by positivistic or neo-positivistic assumptions and methods emphasizing ideals such as objectivity, neutrality, scientific procedure, technique, quantification, replicability, generalization, and discovery of laws. The inadequacies of the dominant quantitative, hypothesis-testing approach has led to an increasing use of qualitative methods (Denzin and Lincoln, 1994; Morgan and Smircich, 1980). Still the popularity, status and use of qualitative methods varies among different social and behavioural sciences and different countries. For example, in the US quantitative approaches still heavily dominate, whereas in British and Swedish management studies qualitative methods take the upper hand. More generally, anthropology is typically as strongly qualitative as psychology is quantitative. In management studies, the study of organizational cultures has been largely anthropological and qualitative while studies of 'organizational behaviour' –

leadership, motivation, stress – frequently draw upon the research ideals dominant in psychology.

Problems with the Qualitative/Quantitative Division

Generally, one can say that qualitative research is increasingly popular in the various fields of social science, including management studies. Arguments for this shift include claims that qualitative research makes possible broader and richer descriptions, sensitivity to the ideas and meanings of the individuals concerned, increased likelihood of developing empirically supported new ideas and theories, together with increased relevance and interest for practitioners (Denzin and Lincoln, 1994; Martin and Turner, 1986). Practitioners in many fields often view questionnaire studies as superficial and the abstractions of quantified material and statistical correlations as very remote from everyday practice and therefore, of little use – at least when dealing with human aspects of organizational life. Apart from the relative merits and claims, the last three decades have been filled

| **Doing Critical Management Research** *continued*

By Mats Alvesson and Stanley Deetz

with debates between quantitative and qualitative researchers and many attempts to form a happy marriage between them.

We do not find the quantitative/qualitative distinction terribly insightful or useful.

Many versions of qualitative method do not deviate radically from nineteenth-century positivist assumptions:

- an objective external reality awaits the discovery and dissection by science;
- scientific methods give privileged access to this reality;
- language is a transparent medium for categorization, measurement and representation;
- the observer-scientist stands outside and above the social reality;
- he or she authoritatively develops or validates robust theories about social reality.

Our sympathy is with qualitative methods, but the conventional understanding of these is far more problematical than most advocates of these methods seem to acknowledge. Recently there has been more awareness, however, regarding these matters. Also qualitative work – even when carried out by people trying to maximize the rationality of the process – has difficulties in claiming good access either to social reality 'out there' or to the level of meanings, ideas, values, cognitions or subjectiveness of people being studied. Rather than searching for a superior methodology solving problems with the interactive, language- and norm-governed nature of interviews, the theory- and language-impregnated nature of observations, and the selectivity and the fictional character of the use of empirical work in all research when 'writing it up', the challenge is to develop a way of thinking which is not overburdening a method with naïve expectations and unrealistic purposes and which tries to interpret all empirical material in terms of multiple meanings and fruitful ways of utilizing it.

Summary

This chapter has provided a critical review of mainstream methodologies. Instead of repeating the well-known critique of positivism on a programmatic level, we have concentrated on illuminating some of the basic problems in relationship to a specific research field: leadership studies. One such problem is

the tendency to suppress variety and impose an essence on a multitude of diverse phenomena; a standardized, abstract concept of leadership imposes unity and 'freezes' parts of what goes on in organization under its label. Another problem is the inherent difficulties with the favoured method: questionnaires. These typically overburden language with demands of clarity of meaning and assume that the ticks or crosses that are put in the choice alternative boxes say something definitive about how people think, feel, relate and act. Arguably, in order to understand 'leadership' one should study the processes in which it may occur rather than questionnaire responses (or interview statements). The same goes for (almost all) other management phenomena.

Despite our preferences for loosely structured interviews and observations of 'naturally occurring' (rather than laboratory) events, we are not happy about some of the ways the differences between qualitative and quantitative research typically are represented. The idea of framing social research in terms of objective and subjective is deeply problematic. Good research acknowledges that there is a researcher making an immense number of choices affecting the research results. Good research also struggles with the problems of personal (and group) bias or idiosyncrasies. The problem becomes elevated when the problematic distinction is equated with the quantitative–qualitative distinction. Much qualitative research is one-sidedly driven by the personal preferences of the researcher concerning the questions that are of interest and what language the research objects should subordinate themselves to. Many (perhaps most) quantitative researchers are struggling to persuade their readers (and perhaps themselves) that their reliance on procedures, techniques, rules and the reliability of their numbers in the data make their research 'objective'.

References

Denzin, N. and Lincoln. (1994) *Handbook of Qualitative Research*, Thousand Oaks: Sage.

Martin, P.Y. and Turner, B.A. (1986) Grounded Theory and Organizational Research, *Journal of Applied Behavioral Science*, Vol. 22, No. (2): 141–157.

Morgan, G. and Smircich, L. (1980) The Case for Qualitative Research, *Academy of Management Review*, 491–500.

READING 10.3

Refocusing the Case Study: The Politics of Research and Researching Politics in IT Management

By David Knights

In recent years the case study approach to research has attracted considerable attention in social science, and particularly within the field of management and organizational studies (Gouldner, 1957; Dalton, 1961; Nichols and Beynon, 1977; Zimblast, 1979; Pettigrew, 1985). Not least this was part of a general trend wherein considerable scepticism, or outright opposition had grown towards 'positivism' – that is, those attempts to emulate what were thought to be the methods of the natural sciences in the study of human behaviour (Lincoln and Guba, 1985; Silverman, 1985). Despite this, case study researchers if not the ethnographers (i.e., those researchers who apply the methods of social anthropology in steeping themselves in the culture of an organization in order to grasp the particularities of its ways of working) from whom they draw their inspiration, have remained sensitive to the charge that their findings are non-generalizable.

It is in response to this and an associated range of criticisms about the rigor and validity of case study research that a number of texts (Becker, 1970; Denzin, 1970; Johnson, 1976; Yin, 1984) have arisen designed to achieve academic credibility for qualitative studies. But the impetus for this defensive literature is a concern to demonstrate that case study research can replicate the representational and generalizable claims of quantitative (usually positivist) research. In effect, the case study has laboured under the legacy of positivism that even when openly dismissed, regularly creeps back in to qualitative research programmes in the form of a claim for scientific legitimacy.

One result of this is that the case study has found itself in a defensive position, being judged against criteria on which it is always disadvantaged vis-à-vis more positivist approaches to research. This pursuit of respect from the mainstream of establishment quantitative social science is perfectly understandable but it is not without its penalties. One of these is a vulnerability to challenges from the other side of the spectrum, where a growing critical, phenomenological, poststructuralist or postmodernist critique of representational modes of analysis pour scorn on the narrative form of much case study research.

While there are variants of this critique, it had its early genesis in misgivings regarding the post-colonialist, western ethnocentric ethnographies (Clifford, 1983; 1988; Clifford and Marcus, 1986) of traditional anthropological research. This variant of the critique could be seen as having its roots in earlier radical political criticisms of the Chicago School and other ethnographies of deviance and the underdog in society (see, for example, Cohen and Taylor, 1971; Gouldner, 1973). In poststructuralist hands, the critique can be said to be informed by a much stronger opposition to universal generalizations and totalizing claims (i.e. those that offer a comprehensive or virtually exhaustive account of a phenomenon) than ever defenders of case study research articulate when they question the decontextualized nature of survey research. Indeed as the critique has developed, it points to the way that the narrative of ethnography often functions as a totalizing knowledge that 'correlates to the subject's own desired wholeness' (Smith, 1989: 162 quoted in Clough, 1992: 3). In this sense, the case study or ethnographic approach shares with its positivist 'arch-enemy' a preoccupation with representation as an *authoritative* account of empirical reality. But, as Clough (1992) argues, the author's own desire for a unified identity remains a hidden agenda, or is denied any acknowledgement in a heroic (masculine) struggle to capture the reality of the empirical world in a totalizing set of scientific depictions. Even when an account addresses divergent and multiple realities (e.g., Dogherty, 1992), insofar as it is unreflective concerning how the pursuit of a comprehensive or exhaustive account relates to the security of an authorial and authoritative self, it can in Clough's sense be a totalizing representation. According to the post-structuralist critique, then, there is nothing to choose between positivism and the case study or ethnographic version of anti-positivism since both share a common concern to provide true and exhaustive *representations* of reality. Neither acknowledge a relationship to authors' own (perhaps unconscious) desires to secure themselves in particular identities and discourses.

READING 10.3 | **Refocusing the Case Study: The Politics of Research and Researching Politics in IT Management** *continued*

By David Knights

In acknowledging our part as researchers in constituting rather than merely recording reality, we also have to recognize that there is an exercise of power and not just over the data but also over those who might be persuaded of the plausibility of our constructions and interpretations. Since this is an exercise of power, there can be no ultimate closure on these processes and the constructions or interpretations of meaning emanating from them. They are always 'open' to being interpreted differently. The case study approach, then, is not to be defended on the basis of its more accurate representation of reality; its value is one of simulating and taking into account the process whereby reality is produced by participants in everyday life and subjecting a researcher's own reality construction to a range of alternatives that render them more critically reflective.

References

Becker, H.S. (1970) *Problems of Method*. Chicago: Aldine.

Clifford, J. (1983) 'On Ethnographic Authority', *Representations*, 1: 118–46.

Clifford, J. (1988) *The Predicament of Culture*. Cambridge: Cambridge University Press.

Clifford, J. and Marcus, G. (1986) *Writing Culture*. Berkeley: University of California Press.

Clough, P.T. (1992) *The End(s) of Ethnography*. Newbury Park, California: Sage.

Cohen, S. and Taylor, L. (1971) *Images of Deviance*. Harmondsworth: Penguin.

Dalton, Melville. (1961) *Men Who Manage*. New York: Wiley.

Denzin, N.K. (1970) *The Research Act*. New York: Wiley.

Dogherty, D. (1992) 'Interpretive barriers to successful product innovation in large firms', *Organization Science*, 13, (2): 179–191

Gouldner, A.W. (1957) *Patterns of Industrial Bureaucracy*. London: Routledge.

Gouldner, A.W. (1973) 'The Sociologist as Partisan' in *For Sociology*, Harmondsworth: Allen Lane.

Johnson, J. (1976) *Doing Field Research*. New York: Free Press.

Lincoln, Y.S. and Guba, E.G. (1985) *Naturalistic Enquiry*. New York: Sage.

Nichols, T. and Beynon, H. (1977) *Living with Capitalism*. London: Heinemann.

Pettigrew, A.M. (1985) *The Awakening Giant*. Oxford: Blackwell.

Silverman, D. (1985) *Qualitative Methodology and Sociology*. Aldershot: Gower.

Yin, R.K. (1984) *Case Study Research: Design and Methods*. London: Sage.

Zimbalist, A. (1979) *Case Studies on the Labor Process*. New York: Monthly Review Press.

READING 10.4 | **Beyond Method: Strategies for Social Research**

By Gareth Morgan

The dialectical method consists of interrelated ontological, epistemological, and axiological commitments (see, for example, Lukács, 1971; Goldmann, 1969, 1976; Gouldner, 1980; Lefebvre, 1968, 1976; Markovic, 1974; Marx, 1973; McLellan, 1977). In developing the view presented here, I have been particularly influenced by Bernstein (1976), Bhaskar (1978, 1979), and Applebaum (1978). These commitments are embedded in a conceptual framework that is capable of guiding inquiry into specific phenomena. The framework provides a basis for a dialectical form of structural analysis, or perhaps 'genetic structuralism' to use Goldmann's (1969) phrase.

The basic ontological commitments stress social production. People produce the social world and are in turn produced by it. The world in which we live and

Source: Reproduced with kind permission of Gareth Morgan from Beyond Method: Strategies for Social Research © *1975 Sage Publications.*

Beyond Method: Strategies for Social Research
By Gareth Morgan

that shapes our development is a produce of prior human activity. Furthermore, it depends on human activity every day for its reproduction; it is reproduced in and through the everyday practices of people.

The process through which people create a social world involves the enactment of practices within the context and under the constraint of previously constructed practices. The constructions are shaped by social locations, interests, and constraints or limits. Practices are not merely objective phenomena (as in a set of externally observable routines), but are enactments involving subjectively and intersubjectively shared meanings, purposes and assumptions. Practices, in this conception, defy classification as either subjective or objective phenomena. As people strive to satisfy their needs (e.g., to overcome scarcity) they generate new forms of social organisation (e.g., new divisions of labour, technologies, and modes of control).

Forms of social organization (ensembles of social relations), once in place, have determinate tendencies. A way of organizing social life, which is at root merely an arrangement of the social practices followed by people, has at its core a tendency to develop in predictable directions, so long as the core practices remain in place. In the Marxian view, the core practices centre on the production of material goods. Changes in the sets of social practices concerned with the production of material goods tend to occasion changes throughout the total social formation.

Caught within a particular way of organizing social life, people lose control of the production and reproduction of their social worlds. In this fundamental sense, they are alienated. Their alienation is ironic in that the determinate force of the social order rests ultimately on their practices, on the orderliness and predictability of the social relationships they create and the re-create each day. Their alienation stems in part from the assumptions they make about the social world (for example, the assumption that it is necessary or inevitable or natural). These are not necessarily the assumptions built into philosophies or theories, but rather the assumptions that govern routine practices of everyday life.

A form of social organization (or ensemble of social relations), as it develops in accord with its own inherent tendencies, eventually creates contradictions; that is, it generates sets of practices that threaten its own essential character or reach beyond its limits. Contradictions, while not determining outcomes exactly, do force continuing reorganizations of the ensemble.

Dialectical analysis must be concerned with the emergence within a social formation of new, incompatible components. The ongoing process of social production, guided by the essential tendencies of a social formation, generates new forms of social organization that contradict the limits of a particular order. These new forms, although generated by the core tendencies of a given order, gradually undermine the bases of that order. An understanding of these contradictions permits an explanation for ongoing events (e.g., conflicts) and a basis for projecting future possibilities.

The dialectical method locates contradictions in social organizations rather than in the confrontation between people and their social arrangements. The arrangements consist of people acting in certain ways, carrying out certain practices. Contradictions are then confrontations between opposing or incompatible ways of arranging social life. The analytical task is to identify the social conjunctures, the combinations of social forces that make change possible or probable. This knowledge may serve an emancipatory function, allowing people to see through the ideological covering of the social order and to understand crises and potentialities for action. People may then act concertedly to contradict the limits of the social order.

Social arrangements must be examined concretely rather than abstractly. This means locating events in their total contexts (totalities) rather than abstracting them from contexts. Since social production always occurs in and is shaped by social contexts, dialectical analysis must always include a totalizing movement. This does not mean that in every study the whole of the social formation must be examined, an impossible dictum anyway. Rather, it means that a prominent feature of the analysis must be the location of observations within total social formations, i.e., in relation to the core structures and tendencies of the social formation. In this totalizing move, the formation itself must be conceived as a historically developing arrangement or ensemble of social relations.

| READING 10.4 | **Beyond Method: Strategies for Social Research**
continued |

By Gareth Morgan

References

Applebaum, R. (1978) 'Marxist Method: Structural Constraint and Social Praxis', *American Sociologist*, 17: 73ff.

Bernstein, R. (1976) *The Restructuring of Social and Political Theory*, Philadelphia: University of Philadelphia Press.

Bhaskar, R. (1978) *A Realist Theory of Science*, Hassocks, England: Harvester.

Bhaskar, R. (1979) *The Possibility of Naturalism*, Hassocks, England: Humanities.

Goldmann, L. (1969) *The Human Sciences of Philosophy*, London: Jonathan Cape.

Goldmann, L. (1976) *Cultural Creation*, St. Louis, MO: Telos.

Gouldner, A. (1980) *The Two Marxisms*, London: Macmillan.

Lefebvre, H. (1968) *Dialectical Materialism*, London: Jonathan Cape.

Lefebvre, G. (1976) *The Survival of Capitalism*, London: Allen & Busby.

Lukács, G. (1971) *History and Class Consciousness*, London: Merlin.

Markovic, M. (1974) *From Affluence to Praxis*, Ann Arbor: University of Michigan Press.

Marx, K. (1973) *Grundrisse: Foundations of the Critique of Political Economy*, New York: Vintage.

McLellan, D., editor (1977) *Karl Marx: Selected Writings*, Oxford: Oxford University Press.

| READING 10.5 | **Coming to Terms with the Field: Understanding and Doing Organizational Ethnography** |

By Michael Rosen

Ethnographic analyses of organizational cultures are largely absent from the administration science literature, primarily because such work derives from a social constructionist understanding of science. The knowledge of organizations thus provided is interpretive, denying the subject–object dichotomy inherent in mainstream empiricist applications of social analysis.

Interpretation is the consummate goal of ethnography because meaning is understood in the social constructionist realm to derive from interpretation, where knowledge is significant only insofar as it is meaningful (Spooner, 1983, p. 3). We accept an ethnographic explanation as meaningful if it appears plausible against our own set of explicit and implicit assumptions about social process and if we can associate the framework and data the ethnographer proposes against the interpretation framework we have systematized throughout our lives.

In ethnographic explanation a framework for producing meaning may be understood to derive ultimately from one or a combination of three fundamental forms. Theses are based in establishing: (1) the appropriateness of the reported data to human needs (functionalism); (2) the tendency of the reported data to reinforce social and cultural equilibrium (structural-functionalism), or (3) the consonance of the data with presumed meta-patterns of thought (structuralism) (Spooner, 1983, p. 3). Our current forms of ethnographic explanation may be understood to derive from one or a combination of these basic approaches.

While an ethnographic report may – and depending upon the writer frequently does – claim interpretive authority, each report is limited insofar as it derives from what is a partial perspective. Any interpretation also is only a second or third order construction. The ethnographer interprets that which he or she observes, experiences, or was told by others, recording this cultural data in field notes and consciously and unconsciously letting it settle against a tableau of meaning structures within his or her own imaginings. The resulting ethnographic interpretations are reworked as time and data accumulate and permit (Van Maanen, 1987, p. 75), mediated by experiences in and out of the field. What appears as written ethnography, therefore, is as much a product of the time and context in which it was written as of any purported truth of interpretation.

Coming to Terms with the Field: Understanding and Doing Organizational Ethnography

By Michael Rosen

However, while the authority of an interpretation is never absolute, its value does not rest on whether an alternative explanation accounts for the data in a plausible manner, or whether we are able to provide our own accountings for the reported data. An ethnographic work is valid even in this latter case, for the goal of generating meaning for the cultural data of another is accomplished. Ethnographers study others to find out more about themselves and others (Spooner, 1983, p. 3). In so doing they change not only their own lives, but also the lives of those studied. In the process they bring the place of epistemology, the place of the meaning of data and enquiry, to the forefront of activity. As Spooner (1983, p. 3) notes, epistemological issues inform:

> How to select the data you [the ethnographer] work with, how you can logically delimit their context or universe, and see the relationship between the data and the purpose for which they were gathered, and – most important of all – their significance or what they will *mean* and how to test that meaning scientifically.

While the place of epistemology is largely overlooked in the mainstream empiricist applications of social science, it cannot be ignored in ethnographic work. A discussion of the epistemological underpinnings of a social constructionist approach is thus included in this work.

Most ethnography, Spooner (1983, p. 4) notes, is written about *general* forms of organization and *general* ways of thinking in particular contexts. By 'general' he intends 'the ways in which particular people behave and think in their everyday lives without being consciously "organized" for a specific objective' (1983, p. 4). Organizational ethnography, on the other hand, is predominantly concerned with those social relations coalesced around a subset of goal-orientated activities. The rules, strategies and meanings operating within such 'structural poses' (Gearing, 1958, p. 1149) are different from those in everyday life, but likely congruent with them (Spooner, 1983, p. 6). People interact with each other according to this action and meaning subset for the duration of the specialized activity.

A group of hunter–gatherers will subconsciously adopt a special set of social rules and behaviours as they set out on a raid (Spooner, 1983, p. 6). These will be in operation, however, for a short period of time relative to the year-by-year, nine-to-five routine of an IBM employee. This is to say that within our complex society structural poses have become formalized and elevated to a central social position; we perceive ourselves to be an 'organizational society' (Galbraith, 1983; Pfeffer, 1981).

While a specific definition of 'rules' will not be proffered here, the centrality of this concept may be approached in a general non-determinist fashion. Rather than being independent of context, following Wittgenstein (1953, pp. 80–1), we may understand the meaning of the rule to be obtained only in context, where rules are consulted to interpret what is perceived as intentional action. Weider (1974) notes this interpretational approach in his study of social process in a halfway house, writing that:

> Instead of predicting behaviour, the rule is actually employed as an interpretive device. It is employed by the observer to render any behaviour he encounters intelligible *i.e.*, as coherent in terms of motivation (1974, p. 179).

There is a fundamental reflexivity here. Members of a social system generate rules through the very interpretive mechanisms used to decide the meaning and applicability of rules, the rules are used to define the meaning of a situation' (Leiter, 1980, p. 234). The understanding of rules here is also embedded in the analogy of social behaviour to one or another form of game. While this analogy has derived from a greater variety of sources in the social (and mathematical) sciences – Wittgenstein's conception of forms of life as language games, von Neumann's and Morgenstern's work on game theory, Goffman's application of game imagery to an amazingly wide slice of American life – underlying them all, as Geertz (1983, p. 25) writes:

> is the view that human beings are less driven by forces than submissive to rules, that the rules are such as to suggest strategies, the strategies are such as to inspire actions, and the actions are such as to be self-rewarding – *pour le sport.*

More so than the culture of a general social group – and particularly those well insulated groups traditionally

READING 10.5

Coming to Terms with the Field: Understanding and Doing Organizational Ethnography *continued*

By Michael Rosen

favoured by anthropologists – organizational culture is likely to be rough-edged and contested (Van Maanen, 1987, p. 109). It is by definition partial and frequently ambiguous. Given that organizations are centred around the interests of at least a segment of their memberships, organizational culture is also palpably political.

Finally, another peculiarity of organizational ethnography concerns the relationship of the ethnographer to the group he or she studies. Ethnographers traditionally invaded foreign cultures to collect their data. Organizational ethnographers, on the other hand, largely study organizations peopled by individuals like themselves. Hayano (1982) terms this 'auto-ethnography', the cultural study of one's own people. Such work provides a special set of concerns that must be addressed by one engaged in it.

References

Galbraith, J.K. (1983) *The Anatomy of Power*. Boston, Mass.: Houghton Miffiin.

Geertz, C. (1983) *Local Knowledge*. New York: Basic Books.

Hayano, D.M. (1982) 'Auto-ethnography'. *Human Organization,* Vol. 38, 99–104.

Leiter, K. (1980) *A Primer on Ethnomethodology*. New York: Oxford University Press.

Pfeffer, J. (1981) *Power in Organizations*. Marshfield, Mass.: Pitman.

Spooner, B. (1983) 'Anthropologists and the people they study, and the significance of anthropology for non-anthropologists'. Unpublished lecture notes. University of Pennsylvania (20 December).

Van Maanen, J. (1987) *Tales of the Field: On Writing Ethnography*. Chicago, Ill.: University of Chicago Press.

Weider, D.L. (1974) 'On meaning by rule'. In Douglas, I. (Ed.), *Understanding Everyday Life*. Chicago, Ill.: Aldine, 107–35.

Wittgenstein, L. (1953) *Philosophical Investigations*. New York: Macmillan.

READING 10.6

After Method

By John Law

... I want to argue that while standard methods are often extremely good at what they do, they are badly adapted to the study of the ephemeral, the indefinite and the irregular. ... This implies that the problem is not so much the standard research methods themselves, but the normativities that are attached to them in discourses about method. If 'research methods' are allowed to claim methodological hegemony or (even worse) monopoly, and I think that there are locations where they try to do this, then when we are put into relation with such methods we are being placed, however rebelliously, in a set of constraining normative blinkers. We are being told how we must see and what we must do when we investigate. And the rules imposed on us carry, we need to note, a set of contingent and historically specific Euro-American assumptions.

Here the problem is not that our research methods (and claims about proper method) have been constructed

in a specific historical context. *Everything* is constructed in a specific historical context and there can be no escape from history. Rather it is that they, or at least their advocates, tend to make excessively general claims about their status. The form of argument is often like this (think, for instance, about rules for statistical sampling, or avoiding leading questions in interviews). 'If you want to understand reality properly then you need to follow the methodological rules. Reality imposes those rules on us. If we fail to follow them then we will end up with substandard knowledge, knowledge that is distorted or does not represent what it purportedly describes.' There are two things I want to say in response to such suggestions about the importance of methodological rule-following. The first is counter-intuitive. It is that methods, their rules, and even more methods' practices, not only describe but also help to *produce* the reality that they understand. I will carefully explore

Source: Reproduced by permission of Taylor & Francis Books UK from the Journal of Management Studies © 2004 Routledge.

After Method

By John Law

the reasons for making this suggestion in due course. However, for the moment let me simply note that there is a fair amount of heavyweight work on the history of science and social science that makes precisely this argument. Perhaps again counter-intuitively, I will also say that if methods tend to produce the reality they describe, then this may be, but is not necessarily, obnoxious. Again I will return to this argument at some length in due course. But what is important now is to note that if these two claims are right then they have profound implications for our understanding of the nature of research.

There is a further and more straightforward point to be made. This is that claims about the general importance of methodological rules also tend to get naturalized in social science debate. *Particular* sets of rules and procedures may be questioned and debated, but the overall need for proper rules and procedures is not. It is taken for granted that these are necessary. And behind the assumption that we need such rules and procedures lies a further range of assumptions that are also naturalized and more or less hidden. These have to do with what is most important in the world, the kinds of facts we need to gather, and the appropriate techniques for gathering and theorizing data. All of these, too, are naturalized in the common sense of research. Yes, things are on the move. Nevertheless, the 'research methods' passed down to us after a century of social science tend to work on the assumption that the world is properly to be understood as *a set of fairly specific, determinate, and more or less identifiable processes.*

Within social science conventions, which are the best methods (and theories) for exploring those somewhat specific processes? This is a matter for endless debate. Neo-Marxists discover world systems, or uneven developments, or they theorize regulation. Foucauldians discover systems of governmentality. Communitarians discover communities and the need for informal association and responsibility. Feminists discover glass ceilings, cultural sexisms, or gendering assumptions built into scientific and social science method. As a part of this, social science common sense also assumes that society changes. But, overall, the social is taken to be fairly definite. Such is the framing assumption: that there are definite processes out there that are waiting to be discovered. Arguments and debates about the character of social reality take place *within* this arena. And this is what

social science is meant to do: to discover the most important of those definite processes. But this is precisely the problem: *this is not necessarily right.* Accordingly, it indexes the broadening shift that I want to make. The task is to imagine methods when they no longer seek the definite, the repeatable, the more or less stable. When they no longer assume that this is what they are after.

So what are those elusive realities? This is for discussion. I have my own sense of what it is that might be important and this informs my argument. However, I do not want to legislate a particular suite of research methods. To do so would be to recommend an alternative set of blinkers. Instead I argue that the kaleidoscope of impressions and textures I mention above reflects and refracts a world that in important ways cannot be fully understood as a specific set of determinate processes. This is the crucial point: what is important in the world including its structures is not simply technically complex. That is, events and processes are not simply complex in the sense that they are technically difficult to grasp (though this is certainly often the case). Rather, they are also complex because they *necessarily exceed our capacity to know them.* No doubt local structures can be identified, but, or so I want to argue, the world in general defies any attempt at overall orderly accounting. The world is not to be understood in general by adopting a methodological version of auditing. Regularities and standardizations are incredibly powerful tools but they set limits. Indeed, that is a part of their (double-edged) power. And they set even firmer limits when they try to orchestrate themselves hegemonically into purported coherence.

- I am not saying that there is no room for conventional research methods. Such is not at all the point of my argument.
- Second, and more generally, I am not saying that there is no point in studying the world. I am not recommending defeatism. On the contrary, the task is to reaffirm a reshaped set of commitments to empirical and theoretical inquiry. The issue is: what might social science inquiry look like in a world that is an unformed but generative producer of realities? What shapes might we imagine for social science inquiry? And, importantly, what might responsibility be in such a world?

READING 10.6

After Method *continued*

By John Law

- Third, I am not recommending political quietism. I shall have a lot more to say about politics below, but the basic point is simple. Since social (and natural) science investigations interfere with the world, in one way or another they always make a difference, politically and otherwise. Things change as a result. The issue, then, is not to seek disengagement but rather with how to engage. It is about how to make good differences in circumstances where reality is both unknowable and generative.

- Finally, what I am arguing is not a version of philosophical idealism. I am not saying that since the world defies any overall attempt to describe and understand it, we can therefore realistically believe anything about it we like. I also discuss this much more fully below, but everything I argue assumes that there is a world out there and that knowledge and our other activities need to respond to its 'out-thereness'. It is a world, as I've suggested, that is complex and generative. I will argue that we and our methods help to generate it. But the bottom line is very simple: believing something is never enough to make it true.

My aim is thus to broaden method, to subvert it, but also to remake it. I would like to divest concern with method of its inheritance of hygiene. I want to move from the moralist idea that if only you do your methods properly you will lead a healthy research life – the idea that you will discover specific truths about which all reasonable people can at least temporarily agree. I want to divest it of what I will call 'singularity': the idea that indeed there are definite and limited sets of processes, single sets of processes, to be discovered if only you lead a healthy research life. I also want to divest it of a commitment to a particular version of politics: the idea that unless you attend to certain more or less determinate phenomena (class, gender or ethnicity would be examples), then your work has no political relevance. I want to subvert method by helping to remake methods: that are not moralist; that imagine and participate in politics and other forms of the good in novel and creative ways; and that start to do this by escaping the postulate of singularity, and responding creatively to a world that is taken to be composed of an excess of generative forces and relations.

To do this we will need to unmake many of our methodological habits, including: the desire for certainty; the expectation that we can usually arrive at more or less stable conclusions about the way things really are; the belief that as social scientists we have special insights that allow us to see further than others into certain parts of social reality; and the expectations of generality that are wrapped up in what is often called 'universalism'. But, first of all we need to unmake our desire and expectation for security.

READING 10.7

Manufacturing the Employee: Management Knowledge from the 19th to 21st Centuries

By Roy Jacques

Background

When I first applied to doctoral programmes a decade ago I saw (and see) myself as a pragmatic person, a practising manager in the field of financial software development. My decision to return to school was motivated by two very concrete questions: (1) why don't organizations work better than they do?; (2) why was my MBA degree of so little use in answering the first question?

When I finally entered my doctoral programme, I quickly learned two things about management education. First, having returned to school with what

Source: Reproduced with permission of Sage Publications, London, Los Angeles, New Delhi and Singapore from Manufacturing the Employee: Management knowledge from the 19th to 21st centuries © 1996 Sage Publications.

Manufacturing the Employee: Management Knowledge from the 19th to 21st Centuries

By Roy Jacques

I considered relatively specific interests and problems for study, I was quite amazed to find that in what I would now call the 'disciplinary' school of business there are no business problems. There are only accounting problems, finance problems, human resource problems, and so forth. Even within the department where I finally got my degree, problems were divided into human resource management (HRM), organizational behaviour (OB), organizational theory (OT) and policy. Thinking like 'the practitioner', I found my interests transected the school's disciplinary boundaries. Nobody in business has 'an OB problem'. There is an OB *aspect* to every problem, but there is also an accounting aspect, a policy aspect and so forth. So my first lesson as an academic was that I must choose between working on the problems of business *people* or those of the business *disciplines* (and we perpetually wonder why 'the practitioner' fails to read our research or come to our conferences!).

The second thing I learned was that, even compared to the relative conservatism of business, the boundaries of business school discourse are surprisingly narrow. As it is with most of the mid-career doctoral students I meet in my current teaching position, issues of organizational power were central to the questions I brought from the business world. I quickly learned that power was a peripheral topic and one the savvy management scholar avoided lest s/he be branded insufficiently soft on Marxism. There was also the question of language. The business world is a pidgin language a polyglot of overlapping dialects. The business school speaks the artificially clarified and semantically impoverished language of hypothesis testing alone. Because of my training in biology, computer information systems and business, and my work background supporting financial forecasting software for hospital budgeting analysts, I find the language of statistics useful – where appropriate – but the paradigmatic insistence that *anything* of value in organizational studies can be expressed as a statistically significant difference struck me (then and now) as unnecessarily limiting, counterproductive and, frankly, somewhat silly. One can produce useful knowledge without being a scientist and one

does not become a scientist simply by adopting the forms of scientific inquiry.

As my socialization as a management scholar continued, I learned that expressing any doubts about the adequacy of probability theory to produce a paradigmatic science of business and any resistance to reshaping problems to fit the disciplinary structure of the academy was 'radical'; lockstep conformity to restrictive norms of inquiry was enforced informally, yet effectively, by The Four Buts. 'You can do that but …' one is told by those presumed to know: '… it won't constitute a dissertation', '… it won't be publishable', '… you won't get a job if you write that', or '… you won't get tenured'. Thus, potentially fresh insights are put on ice for a decade or more, by which time the subject is encrusted like a barnacle in research s/he has been told is 'safe'. Thus, the boundaries of the discipline continue to narrow, solidify and become ever more out of step with the broader society. I am no bolder than my peers, but I had the good fortune to enter a doctoral programme that never enforced conformance to these norms. Even those who thought my studies a bit odd were generally tolerant and often constructive. As a result, I could remain 'pragmatic'; that is, I could follow the interests I had developed as a manager and pursue whatever studies helped me answer the questions I had brought with me from the business world.

As these interests led into comparative literature, philosophy and nursing, even I began to wonder if my studies were turning into an academic shell game. These doubts accumulated as the years passed. The turning point came in 1991 when I was doing field research on a nursing unit in a large teaching hospital. What I saw and how I saw it were profoundly shaped by the detours I had taken into post-analytic thought and feminist theorizing. To paraphrase an overly quoted aphorism, I found there was nothing quite so practical as a good feminist-poststructuralist theory. …

Whether the present time represents the dawn of a post-industrial or postmodern era at all is still a matter for debate. Still more contestable are opinions regarding the meanings such a transition would entail. What the postmodern/post-industrial debates *should*

| **Manufacturing the Employee: Management Knowledge from the 19th to 21st Centuries** *continued*

By Roy Jacques

signal for business people, management professors and consultants is that these are times for thinking carefully about change, for examining the taken-for-granted, and for asking how relevant our habits of practice are to the future we participate in constructing.

This has implications for understanding the ideology embodied in this book. Like the work of Foucault, this ideology advocates questioning the *status quo,* but it does not do so within an established 'radical' context of seeking to replace one system with another. Questioning of disciplinary society cannot be reduced to 'opposition'. That would be simplistic, a nostalgic atavism. If, today, certain aspects of hierarchy and control are becoming less prominent, the social relations that intersected to produce the normalized or 'disciplinary' individual – standardization, massification, interconnection, and so on – continue to exist. In fact, these networks are becoming *more* elaborated in post-industrial society. A view of the future cannot simply announce 'emancipation' from disciplinary relationships. It must be more subtle, articulating different possibilities and implications that exist *within* these relationships.

p. xvii
The Need for Critically Reflective Practice
Management has not been a philosophical discipline. The US business hero, real or fictional, has been the 'man *[sic]* of action'. Getting to 'the bottom line' is highly valued. Even management scholarship has aspired to be eminently pragmatic. In the founding issue of *Administrative Science Quarterly,* Thompson expresses a vision of administrative science as the applied arm of the social sciences 'as engineering stands with respect to the physical sciences, or as medicine to the biological' (1956: 103). During times of incremental change, this pragmatic approach allows one to focus one's efforts on solving concrete problems. Treating the work, the worker and the world as objects of common sense allows one to deal with what Thomas Kuhn (1962/1970) called puzzle-solving science. It facilitates the accumulation of

knowledge within a well-defined domain. During times of transformational change, however, not only do new problems arise; old *ways* of understanding problems become problems *themselves.* To be successful, puzzle-solving must assume a certain structure of assumptions; thus it does not permit examination *of* assumptions. If present times are indeed times of discontinuous change, prudence suggests inquiring how puzzle-solving science may constitute a barrier to dealing with today's central issues.

Paradoxically, during times such as these, 'pragmatic' approaches to problem-solving are *obstacles* to solving concrete problems while questioning basic values and assumptions – philosophy – is pragmatic. Such times of transformation require critically reflective practice, a blending of the poles of the traditional theorist/ practitioner dichotomy. Both practice uninformed by theoretical reflection and theory disconnected from the workplace are sterile and vreinforce the *status quo.* All too often we see this manifested in theory which accepts as 'normal' an assembly-line or hardhat workplace that has been declining in importance since the 1930s. Correspondingly, practising managers often accept, as given, management principles developed in the 1960s or before as well as workplace structures that emerged in response to the needs of industrialization a century ago.

In order to break this cycle of reliance on obsolete expertise, managers, consultants and management scholars must become, in a sense, applied philosophers. These critically reflective practitioners (both theoretical practitioners and practical theorists) must raise issues that were once of central importance to business writing, but have been dormant within mainstream managerial literature for decades: What is 'the organization?' Who is 'the employee?' What is the purpose of the organization in society? What are the rights, responsibilities and values of organization members?

References
Thompson, J.D. (1956) 'On Building an Administrative Science', *Administrative Science Quarterly*, 1: 102–111.

Discussion Questions

1. Can research methods ever escape questions of interpretation and narrative?
2. Does critical management research demand different and more self-reflexive methodologies?
3. Can the case study or ethnographic method be defended or is it always to be seen as inferior to positivist methods?
4. To what extent is it possible to discuss methodologies independently of theory?

Introduction References

Adorno, T.W., Frenkel-Brunswik, E., Levinson, D.J. and Sanford, R.N. (1976) *The Authoritarian Personality*.

Berger, P. and Luckmann, T. (1967) *The Social Construction of Reality*, Harmondsworth: Penguin.

Recommended Further Readings

See references accompanying the Readings plus:

Alvesson, M. and Sköldberg, K. (2009) *Reflexive Methodology: New Vistas in Qualitative Research*, London: Sage.

Clough, P. and Nutbrown, C. (2007) *A Student's Guide to Methodology*, London: Sage.

Dean, M. (1994) *Critical and Effective Histories: Foucault's Methods and Historical Sociology*, London: Routledge.

Gomm, R. (2003) *Social Research Methodology: A Critical Introduction*, London: Palgrave Macmillan.

INEQUALITY AND DIVERSITY

READINGS

Martin, J. (1997) 'Deconstructing Organizational Taboos: The Supression of Gender Conflict in Organizations' in *Post Modern Management Theory.* Edited by M.B. Calas and L. Smircich. London: Ashgate Publishing. pp. 275–291.

Kerfoot, D. and Knights, D. (1996) 'The Best Is Yet to Come?: Searching for Embodiment in Management' in *Men as Managers, Managers as Men.* Edited by D. Collinson and J. Hearn. London: Sage. pp. 78–98.

Nkome, S.M. (1992) 'The Emperor has no Clothes: Rewriting "Race in Organizations"' in *Academy of Management Review*, Vol. 17, No. 3: pp. 487–513.

Sennett, R. and Cobb, J. (1977) *The Hidden Injuries of Class*. Cambridge University Press. pp. 57–8; 73–4; 77–9; 118; 131–4; 219.

INTRODUCTION

Social inequality has traditionally been a focus for organization studies, particularly since the 1970s when legislation in several Western countries outlawed sexual and racial discrimination. Yet despite these laws and their strengthening, women and ethnic minorities continue to experience discrimination and unequal opportunities. In recent times the analysis of social inequality has begun to be studied primarily as an issue of diversity in organizations. This is partly because it has been recognized that in focusing directly on inequality, there is a tendency to be negative rather than positive and this has little or no impact with decision-makers in organizations unless a case in law can be brought against the company. By speaking about diversity, the argument goes, a case can be made to suggest that there is 'value added' in the different benefits that people from diverse backgrounds can contribute to the organization. Because the customer base of most organizations is diverse socially and culturally, a better understanding of the consumer can be established if the organization makes full use of its own internal diversity. Once this is recognized, it is then easier to put forward claims for equal treatment and opportunity, thus reaching the same goals as would have followed from a more direct assault on issues of inequality and discrimination. This fits with the approach to Human Resource Management for which the asset dimension of the human resource is emphasized. We then have a situation in which the diversity of the human resource cannot only be freed from discrimination but there is also an incentive to generate more diversity where such diversity is absent. Of course, the instrumental motive for non-discrimination is of some concern to traditional critics of social inequality. More importantly, though, this shift from a pejorative to a laudatory and valorized view of those previously discriminated against can be seen as a continuation of the binary with limited reversals of the asymmetry. The very act of separating out for attention women, homosexuals, ethnic minorities, and other minorities retains their distinction as Other rather than acknowledging the hybridity of their inclusion. This is part of what Latour (1993) might describe as the demand for purification or a secure identity within modernity wherein despite, but also because of, the proliferation of hybrids, their existence has to be denied. By exposing the purification strategies that protect white, male and homosocial identities from proliferating hybrids, this analysis could be seen to show how and why binary representations remain in place despite much evidence that contradicts them. The current stress on diversity management reflects this exclusionary/inclusionary ambivalence in treating the Other as both a resource for purification and as a distinction that disappears or dissolves in hybrid practices of boundary breakdown.

In our first extract, **Joanne Martin's** paper (Reading 11.1) focuses on a story told by a CEO of a large multinational company that prided itself on being humanitarian and caring about the well-being of its employees. The CEO was telling his story to a conference and was claiming the moral high ground in that he had allowed one of his senior managers to stay at home when launching a new product that she had been instrumental in developing. This was because she had arranged to have a Caesarean operation one week before the launch but the CEO arranged to have a closed-circuit television from her home on the day of the launch. Joanne Martin provides a feminist reading in which she deconstructs this narrative line by line to illustrate the hidden yet insidious gendered content of this CEO's claim to humanitarian practice. In doing so, she wants to demonstrate the value of deconstructive analyses not just for gender research but also with respect to the more dominant logical positivist approach to research in organization and management studies. For it is not just a methodology but has implications for 'the inescapable ambiguities of theory building and research in any field' (340). Having shown that the CEO's short narrative (see introduction of excerpt) is riddled with gendered assumptions and insensitivities, for example, the CEO beginning his story by saying 'we have a young woman' with its propensity to be interpreted in sexual as well possessive terms, Martin produces a parody by reconstructing the story through reversing the terms of its content. Instead of the birth having to be arranged so as not to disrupt the timetable of the launch of the company's new product, it is given priority and the company's product is launched early to enable the birth to take place without the disruption of the mother's bedroom being turned into a temporary television studio. Instead of the company paternalistically *insisting* that the mother stay at home, the mother could insist that she comes into the office and that the company make provision for the baby. The point she is making is that organizations could be transformed to accommodate the demands of human reproduction but she then goes on to argue that the constraints and responsibilities could also be more equally shared between mother and father. Both of these flexibilities are occurring to a limited extent but it is clear that it is difficult for them to become more universal when the gendered assumptions exposed in the paper are so deeply embedded unreflectively in everyday consciousness and discourse.

Deborah Kerfoot and David Knights (Reading 11.2) have a concern to trace both the genesis of management as a practice that only became institutionalized with the rise of the separation of ownership and control within capitalist production and its close association with masculine identity and discourse. Tracing this genesis, however, is only of interest to them insofar as it helps to contextualize contemporary masculine preoccupations and insecurities. These preoccupations revolve around high levels of purposive–rational or instrumental action designed to secure control of relations and events. It is a concern with competence, conquest, superiority, status and success but the pleasure and satisfaction gained is usually fleeting leaving its self-induced victims forever repeating the cycle of instrumental, yet self-defeating, projects to secure their masculine identities. This process of becoming masculine or sustaining a masculine identity involves considerable sacrifice, as the projects of conquest and achievement are unceasing and routinely demanding. Leisure, family, personal life, and even physical and mental health are often at risk in this incessant pursuit of management control and mastery. The authors are less concerned with identifying the numerous psychoanalytic, ontological or social sources of the masculine preoccupation with identity that reflects and reinforces the pursuit of control as with identifying specific forms of its reproduction within managerial and organizational work. One condition of its reproduction is the very uncertainty within which management functions that is a product of the absence of any knowledge that could secure predictable outcomes and thereby deliver on the control that is sought. This is doubly disconcerting because not only does it leave managers bereft of a technology of prediction and control but also it undermines the legitimacy of their privileges of income and status. Because of this managers are vulnerable to offerings from the corporate equivalent of snake oil salesmen that swarmed the Barnum and Bailey world of early twentieth century America. Management gurus selling the latest panacea seem attractive precisely because, while rarely tested, the 'knowledge' is claimed to ensure management competence and control, and organizational performance, productivity and profit. Its price in terms of consultancy and the wealth and status of its messenger created by airport best-selling books render this 'knowledge' exclusive and provides managers with at least the promise, if not always the realization, of control, mastery and legitimacy – the holy grail of masculine-infused management. The chapter ends by raising questions as to whether this highly instrumental, self-estranged and disembodied masculine mode of management is compatible with the new 'entrepreneurialism'. For here there is a demand for flexibility and social relations that can generate commitment from employees and loyalty and satisfaction from customers whose custom is competitively sought after. Compulsive masculinity is fine when managing at a distance through bureaucratic rules, machines and technology or the manipulation of abstract data through micro-electronic media, but it may be less suited to managing social relations so as to enable staff to secure service quality and a distinctive customer image.

Stella Nkomo (Reading 11.3) draws on the European Hans Christian Andersen folktale *The Emperor's New Clothes* to illustrate the way that organization theory denies its own nakedness or silence in failing to examine the importance of race and ethnicity at work. This silence with respect to matters racial is seen as the ethnocentric error of drawing universal generalizations based on the dominant white male in Euro-American culture. It takes for granted this hegemonic image of itself so as to relegate all other racial and ethnic groups to subcategories whose experience cannot contribute to the mainstream knowledge of organizations. Also it reflects and reproduces knowledge that is produced by, and of concern to the values and interests of, Western white males. Based on the idea that race theories invariably reflect the particular condition of race relations at the time of their development, Nkomo suggests that the dominant conceptions of race throughout most of the twentieth century have revolved around the ethnicity paradigm where the focus has been on two diametrically opposed strategies around managing immigration. One was to seek to assimilate immigrants into the main culture such that their difference would be de-emphasized or disregarded. Another was the cultural pluralist alternative strategy that was to allow the separation of ethnic minorities so they could assert their distinctive identities. This became more prominent when the model of assimilation seemed not to be working although explanations for its failure and the consequent ethnic stratification tended to revolve around essentialist arguments about socio-biological or genetic predisposition. Nkomo finds both sets of theories to be grounded in the dominant male white culture – assimilation theory explicitly so but in cultural pluralism it is more implicit. Assimilation theory is predominantly individualistic perceiving non-assimilation to be a function of individual attitudes of prejudice and discriminatory behaviour on the part of both the dominant and minority ethnicities. Because of a belief in an equal opportunity society, failure to succeed is attributed to individual deficiencies not the institutionalization of inequality. While respecting distinct cultural identities, the cultural pluralist model is similarly based on an assumption that the mainstream majority culture is superior and that this superiority is reflected in the superficial tolerance to celebrate difference much like the tourist gazing at, or being entertained by, people from a world way beyond their everyday experience.

In our final extract, **Richard Sennett and Jonathon Cobb** (Reading 11.4) provide a devastating picture of what it is like to fail to secure the material and symbolic success that in contemporary American culture is seen to be your birthright as a citizen. While undoubtedly a myth, the ideology of equal opportunity and the 'American Dream' is so institutionalized that it leaves those who do not enjoy the comfort and privilege of wealth, status and success feeling personally responsible for their failure. Whereas in a traditional class system as in Europe or caste system as in India, it is simply an accident of birth and the social structure that determines whether you secure a reasonable share of the wealth and status produced in society. The apparent existence of equal opportunity means that there is no one to blame but yourself. In extensive interviews with largely white working class men, this became very clear as most would simply attribute their relative poverty and low status to not having tried hard enough at school or having been lacking in ambition, initiative, and hard work when younger. It clearly demonstrates the very real success of the American culture to manufacture and distribute an ideology that is almost totally internalized by its population and is, no doubt, a significant resource in maintaining social order. The cost, however, in terms of damage to the psychological and social well-being of large sectors of the society is considerable. It creates a dramatic polarization between the successful and the unsuccessful because the assumption that success or failure is entirely due to your own personal ability. A lack of ability then generates feelings of superiority and inferiority probably greater than those that are characteristic of more ascribed systems of social and economic inequality. To see yourself as a failure in a society that idealizes success and celebrity is truly demeaning and, in the authors' language, deprives you not only of the benefits and pleasures of material and symbolic affluence but also of your very human dignity. Moreover, in what is seen as the richest country in the world, the US has one of the least generous welfare systems so that the costs of failure are much greater in terms of material well-being than in the less affluent societies of Europe.

| READING 11.1 | **Deconstructing Organizational Taboos: The Suppression of Gender Conflict in Organizations** |

By Joanne Martin

The schools of Business, Law, Education and Medicine at a major university recently sponsored a conference focusing on the ways that individuals, businesses, and other organizations can help solve societal problems. Students and faculty from the university, as well as the press and members of the surrounding community, came to hear an anchor man from NBC Nightly News interview several panellists. One of those panellists was the president and Chief Executive Officer of a very large, multi-national corporation. This company has an unusual reputation for being deeply concerned, in a humanitarian fashion, about the personal well-being of its employees. In response to a question about the company's concern for the well-being of women employees with children, the president told the following story. (The appendix [in the original text] includes excerpts from the official conference proceedings, including events that immediately preceded and followed the telling of this story.)

We have a young woman who is extraordinarily important to the launching of a major new (product). We will be talking about it next Tuesday in its first world wide introduction. She has arranged to have her Caesarean yesterday in or-

der to be prepared for this event. We have insisted that she stay home and this is going to be televised in a closed circuit television so we're having this done by TV for her and she is staying home three months and we are finding ways of filling in to create this void for us because we think it's an important thing for her to do.

In this paper, I deconstruct and reconstruct this story from a feminist viewpoint, examining what it says, what it does not say, and what it might have said. This analysis highlights suppressed gender conflicts implicit in this story and shows how apparently well-intentioned organizational practices can reify, rather than alleviate gender inequalities.

Deconstructing the Story

Dismantling the Public/Private Dichotomy
Deconstruction dismantles a dichotomy by showing it to be a false distinction ...

There is a dichotomy that is central both to the Caesarean story and to many organizational theories and practices, particularly those based on an ostensibly humanitarian philosoxphy of management. This

Source: Reproduced by kind permission of Joanne Martin from 'Deconstructing Organizational Taboos: The Suppression of Gender Conflict in Organizations', in Post Modern Management Theory © 1997 Ashgate Publishing.

Deconstructing Organizational Taboos: The Suppression of Gender Conflict in Organizations *continued*

By Joanne Martin

is the public/private dichotomy that contrasts the public domain of the marketplace, the political arena, and the legal system with the 'closed and exclusive sphere of intimacy, sexuality, and affection characterizing the modem nuclear family'.

This public/private dichotomy is an ideological assumption, not a social fact. Indeed, other eras and other cultures have used different definitions of what is public and what is private ... If this dichotomy is indeed so problematic, why is it ... perpetuated?

Woman is to Private as Man is to Public?

This public/private dichotomy is associated with gender. Supposedly, the public world of politics, economics, and organizations is territory dominated by men, while women watch over the private sphere where children are conceived and family members are nurtured. This gendered characterization of the dichotomy, like the dichotomy itself is oversimplified.

Who is in Control of the Private Domain?

This part of the deconstruction explores what is not said, what is left out of the Caesarean story (for a more general description of this kind of deconstructive move, see Macherey 1978, p. 60). The Caesarean story begins with the phrase, 'We have a young woman ...' rather than 'A young woman works for us'. This phrase situates the text at the juncture between the public and the private domains and offers a redefinition of the usual employment contract. Such a contract is generally conceived of as an exchange. Employees surrender, within some ill-defined limits, control of their behaviour at work. In exchange, the employees are guaranteed pay, benefits, and certain explicit and implicit rights.

This standard conception of an employment contract implicitly attempts to separate an employee's public and private lives, giving the employer extensive control over the employee's behaviour at work. In contrast, the possessive language of the Caesarean text, (e.g., 'having'), suggests that the company has access to the whole of the woman – her health and her homelife – as well as her work. The usual boundaries between the public and the private have been transgressed to an unusual degree – far in excess of

the usual understandings of what is implicitly and explicitly entailed in an employment contract.

The choice and timing of the Caesarean operation is also problematic. A Caesarean operation is painful, its timing can be crucially important, and current medical practice questions its necessity or helpfulness in many cases. The sentence, 'She arranged to have her Caesarean yesterday in order to be prepared for this event', suggests that the employee may have let the choice of this treatment, or its timing, be influenced by the company's product introduction schedule. Since the employee agreed to the Caesarean operation and 'she arranged' its timing, it is not clear whether the company forced her, or encouraged her, to make these choices. Either way, the text implies that the product introduction schedule affected the timing of the baby's birth.

It would be highly unusual if such a serious operation were not followed by some period of recuperation away from work. Such phrases as 'We insisted she stay home ...' indicate that the corporate 'we' took responsibility for making decisions that are usually the responsibility of a doctor and a patient – not an employer. This use of 'we', as in the first sentence of the text, lends the authority of a group to the words of an individual (in this case, the president) while absolving that individual speaker, to some extent, of personal responsibility.

The placement of the closed circuit television in the employee's bedroom was also apparently an initiative of the company: 'so we're having this done by TV for her'. The employee seems to have lost control over decisions about what goes in her bedroom. Of course, she may have appreciated the chance to keep in touch with her work, perhaps as a welcome distraction from pain. It is also possible that she resented the placement of closed-circuit television in her bedroom. Arguably, had she actually chosen to have the television transmissions, the invasion into her privacy could be seen as even greater than if this intrusion occurred against her expressed will. Because the story is not told from the employee's point of view, it includes no mention of how the employee reacted to these events.

| READING 11.1 | **Deconstructing Organizational Taboos: The Suppression of Gender Conflict in Organizations** |

By Joanne Martin

Whether she acquiesced to these decisions with alacrity or felt she had little choice, the silences and absences of this text are eloquent, documenting a corporation that has, to an unusual degree, taken control of aspects of an employee's life usually considered 'private'. Next, I ask who benefits from this attempt to 'help' a working mother.

Who Benefits?

In addition to focusing on what is not said, deconstruction also analyses disruptions. The hidden ideology of a text is revealed at those places where the text is disrupted, where a contradiction or a glimpse of meaninglessness reveals a subtext that may be inconsistent with the text's apparent message:

> How could we ever discover the nature of the ideology that surrounds us if it were entirely consistent, without the slightest contradiction, gap or fissure that might allow us to perceive it in the first place? (1985, p. 124)

The most obvious disruption in the Caesarean text is 'we are finding ways of filling in to create this void for us'. This incoherence surfaces precisely at the point where the text addresses the organizational costs of the arrangements described in the text. The contradiction, evident in simultaneously 'filling' and 'creating' this void, reflects the organization's ambivalence about the extent to which the organization and the employee benefit from this acknowledgement of the interconnections between the public and private spheres.

The text suggests that the employer was willing to invest in having the television brought to the sickroom, so that this important employee could keep up to date concerning her work responsibilities. In this regard, the benefits to the company were clear. The employee's need to take an extended leave of absence, however, was of less obvious direct benefit to the company. When the president jumbled his words and contradicted himself, ambivalence about entailing these latter costs became evident.

To summarize, beneath the surface of the company's apparently benign concern with the employee's well-being are a series of silences, discomforts, and contradictions. These difficulties arise because the Caesarean operation exposes conflicts of interest between the organization (for example, to have the product released on time, to have the employee perform her job) and the individual employee (such as, to rest and let her incision heal). Although the president ostensibly was claiming holistic concern for the employee's well-being, the text's disruptions reveal that concern is expressed, not as an end in itself, but rather as a means of maintaining some level of employee involvement and productivity during a leave. The primary beneficiary of this company's attempt to 'help' a working-woman is the company, not the woman.

At this point, it is essential to acknowledge that none of the observations offered so far are gender-specific. An employee by definition has entered an unequal power relationship with the employer, and in a roughly comparable surgical situation, the interests of a male employee might well be similarly subordinated to those of the employing organization.

For example, the phrase, 'We have a young woman', is a 'double entendre'. The sexual meaning of 'having a woman' enters the text. In the context of the Caesarean story, the disruption of the president's language also has sexual undertones. 'We are finding ways of filling in to create this void for us' carries sexual meanings. In addition to the void at the office created by the employee's absence, there was a void in the woman's body. That void, once filled by a man, and then by the child, was emptied by the Caesarean.

These interpretations have the linguistic effect of making the woman sexually accessible ('filling in' her void, 'having' her). The incest taboo of motherhood has been semantically broken. No wonder, then, that the president's language was disrupted ('filling in to create this void') at this particular point in the text.

The corporate 'we' of the Caesarean text is masculine because it is (usually) a man who has a woman and it is a man who fills the void. To explore what is left out here, the relationship between reproduction and production must be examined. Traditionally, reproductive capacities are the aspects of womanhood that have been associated with the private domain.

READING 11.1

Deconstructing Organizational Taboos: The Suppression of Gender Conflict in Organizations *continued*

By Joanne Martin

Supposedly, a woman provides physical and emotional nurturance for her family, thereby freeing her husband to devote his energies to the workplace and the broader public domain. Because women experience sexual pleasure independently of reproduction and production, this gendered way of attempting to separate public from private effaces – by ignoring – a woman's potential for sexual pleasure (Spivak 1987).

Thus, the sexual double entendres in the Caesarean story presume a masculine perspective which, in effect, supports men's dominance of production in the public arena, reinforces women's responsibilities for reproduction and nurturance in the private domain, and excludes consideration of a woman's need for sexual pleasure. Such attempts to reify a gendered public/private dichotomy mask the ways organizations structure childcare and sexuality by making the birth process, children's needs for nurturance, and some aspects of female sexuality taboo in organizational contexts. These are ways the public/private dichotomy serves as a linchpin of gender discrimination.

Although awareness of the interconnections between work and family life is the first step to dismantling this false dichotomy, a deeper acknowledgment of these interconnections could deeply disrupt and transform the language, premises, and objectives of organizational discourse … [The author then reconstructs the story reversing the priorities that were given above to the corporate interest and with the new child taking centre stage and we recommend students to consult the original article to witness the irony in the text.]

Why Gender Discrimination is so Persistent

In this paper, I have used deconstruction to achieve a specific objective: to reveal gender conflicts suppressed between the lines of a story about a Caesarean operation. This story was told by a corporation president as evidence of his firm's humanitarian concern for the well-being of women employees with children. Deconstruction revealed that the primary beneficiary of this apparently well-intentioned effort to 'help' was the corporation – not the woman or her child. The deconstruction used a comparison of the Caesarean operation with coronary bypass surgery to separate gender-specific difficulties from the problems inherent in other unequal power relationships.

Some of these gender-specific issues included the organizational taboos that make life at work extremely difficult for a pregnant woman. Her visible pregnancy, capacity for sexual pleasure, and involvement with intimate emotions and nurturance all become evident in an organizational context where such aspects of life are considered 'inappropriate'. In this part of the paper, the deconstruction revealed how apparently well-intentioned efforts to alleviate gender inequality can force it into hiding, leaving it free to surface in more subtle and pernicious forms …

Breaking the Taboos of Mainstream Organizational Thinking

It is reasonable to ask at this point if this deconstruction of suppressed gender conflict makes a contribution to organizational research. Previous studies have, for example, measured the extent of gender inequality, documented the unfairness of certain organizational practices, and offered women advice about how to fit into a male-dominated organizational world. Much of this research assumes that public/private boundaries are real and that current structural and institutional arrangements are fixed (cf. Blum and Smith 1988; Calas and Smircich 1989).

Instead of asking how women might fit into existing organizational structures, this paper asks how structures will have to be changed – radically – if women and children are to be genuinely helped. In this respect, this paper fails to offer a direct contribution to mainstream organizational research, in the usual sense that the word 'contribution' is used. Such a contribution would, in effect, be using a feminist perspective as 'a special-interest glamorization of mainstream discourse' (Spivak 1987, p. 130) …

Familiar dichotomies might be abandoned. Some of the most basic categories of organizational theory might need to be rethought. For example, female

READING 11.1	**Deconstructing Organizational Taboos: The Suppression of Gender Conflict in Organizations**

By Joanne Martin

sexual pleasure, the needs of children, emotions of fear, attraction, sadness, and love – such topics would no longer be taboo territory for organizational theory. Organizational researchers might seek viable alternatives to hierarchy and stable divisions of labour ('jobs'), thereby putting into question the correlation of income with occupational status ... If feminist perspectives were fully incorporated, the usual emphases on rationality, hierarchy, competition, efficiency, and productivity would be exposed as only a very small piece of the organizational puzzle.

References

Blum, L. and Smith, V. (1988) 'Women's Mobility in the Coorporation: A Critique of the Politics of Optimism,' *Signs*, 13, (3): 528–545.

Calas, M. and Smircich, L. (1987) 'Post-Culture: Is the Organizational Culture Literature Dominant but Dead?' Paper presented at the third International Conference on Organizational Symbolism and Corporate Culture, Milan, Italy.

Macherey, P. (1978) *A Theory of Literary Production*, Routeledge and Kegan Paul: London, England.

Spivak, G.C. (1987) *In Other Words: Essays in Cultural Politics*, Methuen, New York.

READING 11.2	**'The Best is Yet to Come?': Searching for Embodiment in Management**

By Deborah Kerfoot and David Knights

Management, it may be argued, is a comparatively modern phenomenon, the seeds of its genesis being sown with the transition from domestic to factory production during the industrial revolution in the eighteenth century.

Largely concerned with the co-ordination and control of a diverse range of collectively organized work tasks, modern management becomes necessary once labour is transformed into a formally 'free' agent of production under economically organized systems of corporate capitalism.

The recent decline of manufacturing and expansion of services in Western economies places even more demands upon management at one and the same time as making those demands more difficult to deliver. The demands are greater because the service sector is far more labour intensive than manufacturing, thus increasing the responsibilities of management to provide the requisite levels of co-ordination and control. They are more difficult because service outputs are comparatively less visible and measurable than material goods since they reside

substantially in the amorphous and uncontrollable set of social relations through which they are delivered. This is the background against which, in this chapter, we wish to discuss management as a site for the reproduction of what we refer to as 'masculinity' in contemporary organizations.

It has been argued with some philosophical force that management is precarious and insecure because it lacks the knowledge which could ensure that its decisions and actions had precise and predictable outcomes (MacIntyre, 1981). This uncertainty surrounding its practice also raises questions of managerial legitimacy with those who are delegated to execute the decisions of management. Such philosophical examinations are supported by considerable empirical research (Mintzberg, 1973; Stewart, 1976b; Burns and Stalker, 1961) which also shows that management, in practice, is not the systematic, unambiguous and rational process of planning and control it is often assumed to be by outsiders.

But the continuous necessity to search for, and apply, new knowledge is in itself anxiety-provoking and

READING 11.2	**'The Best is Yet to Come?': Searching for Embodiment in Management** *continued*

By Deborah Kerfoot and David Knights

generative of insecurity (see Anthony, 1994, *passim;* Watson, 1994). There is, then, a double sense in which managers are insecure: first, they are aware that management knowledge does not have the certainty and stability of scientific knowledge even though managerial legitimacy is based upon a specialist 'expertise' that is dependent precisely on such uncertain knowledge. Second, these conditions make it necessary for managers continually to seek new knowledge. This, it may be argued, is one of the main reasons why those offering plausible prescriptions can very soon 'grow' into gurus. From scientific management to business process re-engineering, the history of management is littered with prescriptive knowledges that provide the most convincing response to the demand for solutions to uncertainty. But these solutions themselves promote continuous change that threatens routinized securities, especially given that the solutions often take the form of a fashion to be abandoned almost as speedily as adopted, once a new solution emerges. In combination, these insecurities exacerbate the anxieties that we have already identified as a feature of masculinity.

The instrumental preoccupations of masculinity are directed towards the achievement of goals or projects and the excitement associated with their attainment. But the thrill that such success provides is always fleeting, compelling its self-induced victims continuously to repeat the experience. Moreover, however momentary, the corporeal 'feel' of success that this provides must always be bitter-sweet given that it depends crucially on the approbation of others. Since it is neither self-contained nor self-assured, masculine subjects require the metaphorical 'pat on the back' not only from workplace peers, subordinates or superiors but also from partners, spouses, family and friends. Where masculinity requires constant confirmation from others, its short-lived thrill can only be resuscitated if it is embellished and elaborated in countless freeze-framed dinner table, bar room or clubhouse tellings amongst the middle class or in more direct macho behaviour at football matches, on the street, in pubs, or on the shopfloor within working-class communities. In both sets of situations

the sexist elevation of men and masculinity over women and femininity predominates even though its expression varies. As everyday conversation so clearly reveals, spouses are frequently enrolled as reluctant witnesses to unseen instances of their partners' heroic success. Accounts of organizational encounters become tales of organizational heroism, or targets met, meetings conquered and moments of weakness, failure or despair retold and reconstructed as personal triumphs over adversity, hopelessness or social impotence. Masculine subjects thus constitute the organizational and managerial world as a series of discrete challenges, in order to rise above them. The act of conquest, however fleeting, becomes its own validation. Yet it remains transient, caught up in the necessity to be reflected back by the 'approving other' and made potent in the telling. Masculine subjects are dependent not only on the thrill of conquest but on the need for constant confirmation from onlookers, real or otherwise. But the confirmation can only be maintained if the recipients continue to take on new conquests and struggles.

In sum, this form of masculinity is a disembodied, self-estranged and socially disengaged mode of being wherein alternative relationships with self and others are displaced by the desire to control and to use others instrumentally in its service. Thus, masculine subjects 'know no other' than control and the instrumental use of others to secure that control, however momentary or precarious. In addition, masculine subjects control not least themselves. The self acquires the status of a project to be worked upon, policed for weaknesses, fought against, pushed and honed to meet the refinements of the ideal – this in spite of the often very real sensation of fear, weakness, or failure to live up to the image of the masculine ideal. This then is the dynamic process through which self-estrangement is sustained, and disembodiment produced and reproduced. The question is how compatible is this form of masculinity with the new forms of organization that are being cultivated by the change management gurus? For much of this change is encouraging an emphasis on the productive value of *social* relationships.

| READING 11.2 | 'The Best is Yet to Come?': Searching for Embodiment in Management |

By Deborah Kerfoot and David Knights

Masculinity and 'New Wave' Management Practices

Our interest here is to note a shift in the means of managing organizations and to document some of the practices (for example, service quality, teamworking, flattening hierarchies, the internal market) *vis-à-vis* work-forces that are both their condition and consequence.

Moreover, in delineating some key features of this shift, our objective is to suggest that the increased reliance on social relationships as a means of managing complex organizations and workforces renders masculinity doubly problematic.

In place of the 'old' order then, hierarchically flatter, horizontal structures are to be found which draw on peer networks cemented by greater autonomy and responsibility under the rubric of empowerment, participation and increased involvement (Kerfoot and Knights, 1995). Conventional forms of managerial control and supervision are thus rendered problematic amid the legions of project groups, multi-function work groups and forms of teamworking. But if the 'flexibility' offered by such working practices can render employees more productive in terms of output, a question arises as to the parallel 'success' of the abilities of their management.

What seems to be demanded of new managers is that they have to reveal themselves as human beings with all the associated weaknesses and vulnerabilities which under the conventional managerial practices of more bureaucratic regimes could be hidden.

So what are the implications of this discussion for masculinity as a hitherto predominant discourse in organizations? A number of questions need to be examined. If what we have termed 'management at a distance' is compatible with self-estranged and disembodied masculine modes of being, then these new practices of entrepreneurialism in management may be extremely threatening. This is because in contrast to numbers and files, 'real' human beings are unpredictable, uncertain and not easily controllable. But the threat is not only one of control; it is also a problem of relating to people rather than mere data. For those dominated by masculine discourses, this is not a straightforward task nor simply an act of individual or managerial will. For managers to engage more fully with those under their supervision, they first have to become more comfortable with themselves, no longer hiding from the scrutiny and judgment of others with respect to their social skills. Masculine preoccupations leave individuals ill-equipped to break from the grip of self-estrangement and disembodiment and thus generate a sense of subjective well-being appropriate to the new circumstances.

Because of their overly rational, disembodied and instrumental pursuits, modern management and work organization are particularly important sites for the reproduction of masculine discourses and practices. In one sense management might be seen to legitimize this disembodied instrumentality, making it appear wholly self-evident and unproblematic, such that there is no space for alternatives. However, the extent to which this gender myopia can continue is questionable when, on the one hand, feminist discourses – in the media, leisure, politics – are challenging masculine domination and, on the other, organizations are seduced by management gurus who are peddling 'soft', human-oriented managerial philosophies which are in tension with traditional 'hard' systems of management control.

References

Anthony, P.D. (1994) *Managing Culture*. Milton Keynes: Open University.

Burns, T. and Stalker, G.M. (1961) *The Management of Innovation*. London: Tavistock.

Kerfoot, D. and Knights, D. (1995) 'Empowering the Quality Worker?' The Seduction and Contradiction of the Total Quality Phenomenon', in A. Wilkonson and H.C. Wilmott (eds). *Making Quality Critical*. London: Routledge.

MacIntyre, A. (1981) *After Virtue: A Study in Moral Theory*. London: Duckworth.

Mintzberg, H. (1973) *The Nature of Managerial Work*. New York: Harper & Row.

Stewart, R. (1976b) *The Reality of Management*. Harmondsworth: Penguin.

Watson, T. (1994) *In Search of Management: Culture, Chaos and Control in Managerial Work*. London: Routledge.

READING 11.3

The Emperor has No Clothes: Rewriting 'Race in Organizations'

By Stella M. Nkomo

The children's fairy tale, *The Emperor's New Clothes*, is an excellent allegory for the primary way in which organization scholars have chosen to address race in organizations. For the most part, research has tended to study organization populations as homogeneous entities in which distinctions of race and ethnicity are either 'unstated' or considered irrelevant. A perusal of much of our research would lead one to believe that organizations are race neutral (Cox & Nkomo, 1990).

Although the emperor, his court suitors, and his tailors recognize that he is naked, no one will explicitly acknowledge that nakedness. Even as the innocent child proclaims his nakedness, the emperor and his suitors resolutely continue with the procession. Similarly, the silencing of the importance of race in organizations is mostly subterfuge because of the overwhelming role of race and ethnicity in every aspect of society.

The purpose of this article then is to analyse how race has been written into the study of organizations in incomplete and inadequate ways. It demonstrates how our approaches to the study of race reflect particular historical and social meanings of race, specifically a racial ideology embedded in a Eurocentric view of the world. This view is evident first in the general exclusion of race when organizational theories are developed and, second, in the theoretical and methodological orientation of the limited body of research on race ... The intent is not to provide a specific theory of race but to suggest ways of 're-visioning' the study of race in organizations.

On the Exclusion of Race in the Study of Organizations

Why do we as organizational scholars continue to conceptualize organizations as race neutral? Why has race been silenced in the study of organizations? One way of explaining this exclusion is to examine what Minnich (1990) has called intellectual errors in the production of knowledge. The root error might be labelled faulty generalization or noninclusive universalization. This error occurs when we take a dominant few (white males) as the inclusive group, the norm, and the ideal of humankind (Minnich, 1990). The defining group for specifying the science of organizations has been white males. Only recently have we begun to study the experiences of women in management, and even this body of literature focuses mainly on white women (Nkomo, 1988). We have amassed a great deal of knowledge about the experience of only one group, yet we generalize our theories and concepts to all groups. ...

The faulty generalization error stems mainly from bias in science. The practices of science reflect the values and concerns of dominant societal groups (Harding, 1986). The concepts and approaches used in Western academia help to maintain the political and intellectual superiority of Western cultures and people (Joseph. Reddy, and Searle-Chatterjee, 1990). Kuhn (1962) argued that problem selection and the search for explanations by scholars are influenced by the social and political conditions of the times. To the extent that white males have dominated the production of knowledge, their values and concerns are predominant. The study of race is an especially sensitive issue because scholars must not only be aware of how prevailing societal race relations influence their approach to the study of race but they must also understand the effects of their own racial identity and experiences on their work (Alderfer, 1982).

The dominant racial paradigm in the field of race and ethnic studies for the last half century has been that of ethnicity (Blanton, 1987; Omi and Winant. 1986; Thompson, 1989) ... Ethnicity theorists' main empirical reference point was the study of immigration and the social patterns and experiences of European immigrants (Omi and Winant, 1986).

Research on race emanating from the ethnic-based paradigm centered on questions of why racial minorities were not becoming incorporated or assimilated into mainstream society. Or directly stated, 'What obstructs assimilation?' Much of this research was devoted to problems of prejudice and discrimination and grew out of social psychological approaches to the study of intergroup relations (Oudenhoven and Willemsen, 1989).

The major failure of assimilationists to explain the lack of African-American assimilation spawned a new

The Emperor has No Clothes: Rewriting 'Race in Organizations'

By Stella M. Nkomo

paradigm, which has been called the new ethnicity (Steinberg, 1981; Thompson, 1989; Yinger, 1986). The new in new ethnicity is not so much a significant shift in theory as an attempt by assimilationists to explain the enduring nature of racial stratification (Thompson, 1989). According to Thompson (1989: 91), this paradigm is based on two interrelated positions: (a) that ethnic and racial criteria have become major forms of group-based sociopolitical behaviour because of the changing nature of industrial society and (b) that ethnic and racial groups ought to maintain their separate boundaries and seek their separate interests provided such interests recognize and respect the multitude of other, different ethnic interests (i.e., the cultural pluralism creed).

The theoretical dilemma that existed within the new ethnicity paradigm was how to explain the persistence of racial and ethnic stratification. Two different explanations have been offered. One explanation is that the persistence of racial and ethnic stratification reflects biological tendencies and that people, by nature, have a basic, primordial need for group identification. This explanation is grounded in sociobiology and primordialism.

In a similar vein, van den Berghe (1981: 80l) theorized that ethnic and racial sentiments are extensions of kinship sentiments and, as such, express the sociobiological principle of inclusive fitness. In his analysis, van den Berghe (1981) argued that genetic predisposition for kin selection causes people to behave in racist and ethnocentric ways.

The alternate explanation rejects biological criteria and relies upon social psychological theories that attribute the failure of minority group assimilation to improper attitudes of majority group members or the lack of self-reliance on the part of minorities (Thompson, 1989). The common denominator for all of these explanations is that they stress some essential property of individuals.

Assimilationalism is basically individualistic in its ontology, and in this case, race is largely conceptualized as a problem of prejudiced attitudes or personal and cultural inadequacies of racial and ethnic groups (Thompson, 1989) ... [and] ... is conceptualized as a one-way process that requires non-European, non-English-speaking groups to change to fit the dominant culture (Feagin, 1987). Consequently,

researchers have tended to focus on other groups as having race, and questions of 'why aren't they like us, or how can they become like us' dominate.

Assimilation represents an inadequate model for understanding racial hierarchy in organizations. ...

Successful achievement and mobility reflect a group's willingness and ability to accept the norms and values of the majority group.

The theoretical alternative to assimilation, cultural pluralism, supposedly allows for the possibility that groups do not assimilate but remain distinct in terms of cultural identity. However, similar to users of assimilation theory, proponents of cultural pluralism still maintain the existence of an allegedly 'normal' (understood to mean superior) majority culture, to which other groups are juxtaposed (Omi and Winant, 1986). Further, they suggest that separation of racial and ethnic groups is natural and immutable. ...

Several observations can be drawn from the way race was considered in management studies. Much of the research lies along the prejudice/discrimination axis, with an emphasis on discovering objective evidence of racial discrimination and racial differences in behaviour, primarily between blacks and whites. ...

Conspicuously absent from these articles is any suggestion or recognition of the different sociohistorical experience of African-Americans or other racial minorities in the United States. There was little awareness that racial minorities may have something to contribute to organizations or that perhaps race can inform our understanding of organizations in other ways. For the most part, in this literature, race has been considered an issue or a problem.

Rewriting Race into the Study of Organizations

To rewrite race, we must not continue the emperor's procession by remaining silent about race or studying it within the narrowly defined ethnicity-based paradigm that has dominated much of our research. First, we must acknowledge that the emperor is indeed naked. Organizations are not race-neutral entities. Race is and has been present in organizations, even if this idea has not been explicitly recognized. Second, rewriting race is not a matter of simply clothing the emperor, but the emperor must be dethroned as the universal, the only reality. We need to revise

READING 11.3

The Emperor has No Clothes: Rewriting 'Race in Organizations' *continued*

By Stella M. Nkomo

our understanding of the very concept of race and its historical and political meaning. Only then can race be used as a productive analytical concept for understanding the nature of organizations.

Power–conflict approaches to race and ethnicity emphasize issues of economic power, inequalities in access to material resources and labour markets, and the historical development of racism (Bonacich, 1980; Cox, 1948; Reich, 1981). One of the earliest

proponents of these approaches (Cox, 1948) argued that racial exploitation and race prejudice developed with the rise of capitalism and nationalism. In Cox's analysis, American colonies imported African slaves to fill a particular labour need and simultaneously incorporated the ideology of racism as a justification of slavery. He contended that the idea of racial inferiority didn't precede the use of minority groups as servile labour but that an ideology of racial inferiority

TABLE 11.3.1 | ASKED AND UNASKED QUESTIONS ABOUT RACE

Research questions from ethnicity paradigm

Does discrimination exist in recruitment, selection, etc.?

Can the Afro-American be an effective executive?

Do blacks identify with the traditional American work ethic?

Do blacks' and whites' problem-solving styles differ?

How can blacks/minorities be assimilated into organizations?

How can organizations manage diversity?

How can organizations comply with equal employment opportunity/affirmative action requirements?

Do blacks and whites have the same job expectations?

Are there different levels of motivation between black and white employees?

Is there racial bias in performance ratings?

What is the role of stereotyping in job bias?

Does differential test validity exist?

Silenced research questions from alternative paradigms

How are societal race relations reproduced in the workplace?

How did white males come to dominant management positions?

To what extent is race built into the definition of a 'manager'?

What are the implications of racial identity for organization theories based on individual identity?

How does racial identity affect organizational experiences?

How does the racial identity of white employees influence their status and interaction with other groups?

Why, despite national policies like affirmative action, does inequality still exist in the workplace?

Are assimilation and managing diversity the only two means of removing racial inequality in the workplace?

How do organizational processes contribute to the maintenance of racial domination and stratification?

Are white male-dominated organizations also built on underlying assumptions about gender and class?

What are the patterns of relationships among different racial minorities in organizations?

| **The Emperor has No Clothes: Rewriting 'Race in Organizations'**

By Stella M. Nkomo

developed to maintain Africans and other racial minorities in a servile status. According to Cox, the racial division of labour into white and black workers hindered any positive contact between the white and black masses. Thus, the persistence of racial stratification in society was not a function of atomistic individuals or cultural deficiencies of minorities but was rooted in the class positions of workers.

These and other power–conflict theories attempt to analyse race within the relations of capitalists' production without reducing it to an epiphenomenon (Thompson, 1989; Wilhelm, 1983). Thus, if applied to organizational analysis, power–conflict theories would focus our attention on understanding how organizations have become racially constructed, the power relations that sustain racial divisions and racial domination, and the important role of capitalist modes of production in maintaining these divisions.

Rewriting race also suggests recognizing the limitations of positivist research methods. Research strategies determine the kinds of knowledge produced, and a realistic view of the research process encourages us to use these strategies in different ways (Morgan, 1983). A majority of the organizational studies mentioned in this article relied upon comparative designs in which race was categorized as a two-level variable (i.e., black and white). There are two basic problems with this approach. First, comparative designs too often adopt a position of cultural monism that assumes equivalence of groups across race (Azibo, 1990). In such a case, meaningful and valid interpretations of any observed differences are hindered. An awareness of the appropriate use of emic (within culture) and etic (cross-culture) approaches is critical (Triandis, 1972). Azibo (1990) noted that researchers must seek a balance between the assumption that cultures can best be understood in their own terms and the desire to establish universal theories of human behaviour … Reconceptualizing race not as a simple property of individuals but as an integral dynamic of organizations implies a move toward phenomenological and historical research methods that would contribute toward building theories and knowledge about both how race is produced and how it is a core feature of organizations.

References

Azibo, D.A.Y. (1990) Personality, clinical and social psychological research on blacks: Appropriate & inappropriate research frameworks. In T. Anderson (ed.), *Black studies: Theory, method and cultural perspectives*: 25–41 Pullman: Washington State University Press.

Blanton, M. (1987) *Racial theories*. Cambridge: Cambridge University Press.

Bonacich, E. (1980) Class approaches to ethnicity and race. *Insurgent Sociologist*. 10: 93.

Cox, O.C. (1948) *Caste, class, and race: A study In social dynamics*. New York: Doubleday.

Cox, T. Jr. and Nkomo, S.M. (1990) Invisible Men and Women: A status report on race as a variable in organization behaviour research. *Journal of Organizational Behaviour*, 11: 419–431.

Feagin, J. (1987) Changing black Americans to fit a racist system? *Journal of Social Issues*, 43, (1): 85–89.

Harding, S. (1986) *The science question in feminism*. Ithaca: Cornell University Press.

Joseph, G.G., Reddy, V. and Searle-Chatterjee, M. (1990) Eurocentrism in the social sciences. *Race & Class* 31, (4): 1–26.

Kuhn, T. (1962) *The structure of scientific revolutions*. Chicago: University of Chicago Press.

Morgan, G. (1983) Toward a more reflective social science. In G. Morgan (Ed.) *Beyond method: Strategies for social research*: 368–376. Beverly Hills, CA: Sage.

Omi, M. and Winant, H. (1986) *Racial formation in the United States: from the 1960s to the 1980s*. New York: Routledge & Kegan Paul.

Oudenhoven, J.P.V. and Williemsen, T.M. (Eds.). (1989) *Ethnic minorities: Social psychological perspectives*. Amsterdam: Sivets & Zeitlinger.

Reich, M. (1981) *Racial Inequality*. Princeton, NJ: Princeton University Press.

Steinberg, S. (1981) *The ethnic myth*. New York: Atheneum.

Thompson, R.H. (1989) *Theories of ethnicity: A critical appraisal*. New York: Greenwood Press.

Triandis, H.C. (1972) *The analysis of subjective culture*. New York: Wiley.

Wilhelm, S. (1983) *Black in white America*. Cambridge. MA: Schenkman.

Yinger., J.M. (1986) Intersecting strands in the theorization of race and ethnic relations. In J. Rex & D. Mason (Eds.). *Theories of race and ethnic relations*: 20–41. Cambridge: Cambridge University Press.

READING 11.4 | The Hidden Injuries of Class

By Richard Sennett and Jonathan Cobb

Why then does independence matter so much to people like Frank Rissarro? When he thinks about his entry into the white-collar world, the 'reward' of success for him is that he can act more independently, be more personally in control. Kartides, too, imagines dignity within the confines of manual labour to be the carving out of some social space in which he is alone. To be free for these people living in a corporate, interdependent society is to get on their own: why will such freedom give them dignity? If we can answer these questions, which are about hidden dimensions of individualism in a corporate society, we may be able to uncover the burden of class in that society: the feeling of not getting anywhere despite one's efforts, the feeling of vulnerability in contrasting oneself to others at a higher social level, the buried sense of inadequacy that one resents oneself for feeling.

Carl Dorian, the electrician, James, the college student, Frank Rissarro, the meat-cutter turned bank clerk, are all touched by this conception of the individual as well. Looking up the ladder of social hierarchy from where they stand, they imagine they see fewer and fewer people who have been allowed the freedom to develop personal resources that others will value. They are ambivalent about this image. They resent the fact that society has created a split between the many, who are just ordinary workers, and the few individuals who are members of the professional and upper-middle classes; yet despite this resentment, when they think of themselves personally as lost among the many, they are also afraid that there may be some truth to this image.

Historians know very little about how poor people in cities reacted to the ideologies of class that took form five generations ago. In a way, it would at the time have been nonsensical for a steel worker or garment worker to get emotionally involved in how or whether his abilities had placed him in a certain position in society. At hand were much more terrible material penalties for being a worker: he went hungry, and so did his children; when illness or some other family crisis struck and he could not work, he was a doomed man.

While the lot of many white American manual labourers today remains precarious, the sheer physical degradation of the sweatshops or mills is gone for most. Indeed, in terms of income, amount of taxing physical exertion, and styles of living, the lines are not now sharp between many blue-collar and low-level office workers. To conclude that class differences are therefore disappearing would be wrong, however. What episodes like the hard-hat debate and the writings on authoritarianism suggest is that the lines of class difference are being redrawn.

Freedom is no longer simply the freedom to eat. Now it is a matter of how much choice a person has, and the development of human resources of men and women in a post-scarcity society. Classes of human beings can still be usefully defined by their productive function – but, as shall presently appear, class distinctions in both productive and emotional terms are growing sharper than they were under the old conditions of scarcity. 'Mass', in the sense that the word applies to men like Rissarro or Kartides, refers to the kind of work where people do not feel they express enough that is unique in themselves to win others' respect as individuals; 'elite' refers to people who have become so complex they must be treated as special cases. Overlying these distinctions is a morality of shaming and self-doubt.

Now a badge of ability seems the perfect tool to legitimatize power. This concept of human potential says that the few are more richly endowed than the many. Having gained 'more' dignity by virtue of greater personal power, it is logical that they ought to rule the many. Apply to that simple meritocratic argument the tentative rule about legitimized power: the more inclined are the many, the masses, to a belief that dignity exists in these terms, and the more they surrender their own freedom to the few, the less chance they have of respecting themselves as people with any countervailing rights.

If, however, the people we encountered in the course of writing this book taught us anything, it is that this set of notions is all wrong, because the people who are subject to limits on their freedom do not take the dignity away from themselves that they accord to higher classes – as though dignity were a commodity. They react to power in a much more complicated way: look at Frank Rissarro's attitude toward 'educated' work, for example. Educated men

READING 11.4

The Hidden Injuries of Class

By Richard Sennett and Jonathan Cobb

can control themselves and stand out from the mass of people ruled by passions at the bottom of society; that badge of ability earns the educated dignity in Rissarro's eyes. Yet the content of their power – their ability considered in essence rather than in relation to his personal background and memories – this he finds a sham, and repugnant. Still, the power of the educated to judge him, and more generally, to rule, he does not dispute. He accepts as legitimate what he believes is undignified in itself, and in accepting the power of educated people *he* feels more inadequate, vulnerable, and undignified.

The feelings he, and the other men and women we encountered, have about power in relation to their own freedom and dignity, demand some kind of fresh explanation. All these people feel society has limited their freedom more than it has limited that of middle-class people – by which they mean society has limited their freedom to develop powers inside themselves, not just restricted how much money they can make – but they are not rebellious in the ordinary sense of the word; they are both angry and ambivalent about their right to be angry.

The divided self is like most other kinds of conscious defences human beings erect for themselves; it stills pain in the short run, but does not remove the conditions that made a defence necessary in the first place. If the defence fails finally to make men happy, or even reconciled, the failure is at worst a sign that men do not have within themselves the power to transcend the world like Nietzsche's gods, that despite an extraordinarily subtle rebalancing of their feelings, they cannot escape the influence of a destructive social order.

Discussion Questions

1. Can gender inequality be resolved simply through legal means?
2. To what extent do you think that successful competition and conquest satisfy the pursuit of a secure masculine identity?
3. Can racial inequality be eradicated when theories about it are conducted largely from within the dominant white male Euro-American culture?
4. Do ideologies of equal opportunity have the effect of making the underprivileged guilty about their failure not to have done better?

Introduction Reference

Latour, B. (1993) *We Have Never been Modern*, Harlow, Essex: Pearson Education.

Recommended Further Readings

See references accompanying the Readings plus:

Blackburn, R. (1972) 'The New Capitalism' in Blackburn, R. (editor) *Ideology in Social Science*. London: Fontana.

Collinson, D. (1992) *Managing the Shopfloor: Subjectivity, Masculinity and Workplace Culture*, Berlin: de Gruyter.

Mohanty, C.T. (2004) *Feminism without Borders*, Durham: Duke University Press.

IDENTITY

CHAPTER 12

READINGS

Knights, D. and Willmott, H. (1999) 'Management Lives: Power and Identity in Work Organisations' in *Identity and Insecurity at Work.* London: Sage. pp. 62–84.

Kondo, K. Dorinne (1990) *Crafting Selves: Power, Gender and Discourses of Identity in a Japanese Workplace,* University of Chicago Press. pp. 300–308.

Jermier, John, M. (1985) 'When the Sleeper Wakes: A Short Story Extending Themes in Radical Organization Theory' in *Journal of Management,* Vol. 11, No. 2: 67–80.

INTRODUCTION

Until quite recently the concept of identity was neglected in organization studies largely because it was seen as primarily psychological in character and therefore the preserve of the social psychology of organizations. This was unfortunate, given that psychologists have tended to subscribe to individualistic or *asocial* conceptions of identity and yet it is through identity or the process of identifying with something outside the self that we see the mediation between individual and society. But even this way of understanding identity gives too much credence to a discreteness between the individual and society that leaves us only with mechanistic ways of reintegrating them. The discipline of sociology from where organization analysis derives much of its theorizing is more inclined to see everything in society, including the individual, as social, since both the individual and society are merely abstract concepts and *not* realities in need of reintegration. Identity has become a more widely utilized concept in organizational analysis by virtue of the purchase it gives us in understanding a range of issues such as gender, ethnicity, status, culture and consumption that secure and sustain meaning for people in organizations as a result of their identification with them. But it is also important in seeing how when threatened by organizational innovation and change, new technology and organizational forms, power and control or ethical conflicts, identity might be the source of resistance. Theoretically, identity has been at the centre of interactionist theory with its idea that the self mediates between external stimuli and behavioural responses, but more recently the concept has been given a boost by the impact influence of Foucault on organizational analysis (Knights, 1992; Townley, 1993; McKinley and Starkey, 1998; Alvesson and Willmott, 2002; Knights, 2002; Bergström and Knights, 2006). Although Foucault concentrates on the notion of subjectivity and its formation as an effect of power, it can be argued that the effectiveness of power on subjectivity is partly a function of insecurities about identity or the sense that we all have of the precariousness in which we are seen by others and ultimately ourselves.

Reading 12.1 is taken from **Knights and Willmott** *Management Lives* and provides a critical examination of two of the most prominent base theories – behaviourism and symbolic interactionism – that underlie much social science. In particular the extract focuses on identity or what would be termed the formation of the self and suggests that while both of these fundamental theories help us to understand human behaviour, neither provide an adequate theorizing of identity. In its focus on stimulus and response mechanisms, behaviourism denies the existence of an autonomous self that could be the basis for an identity. By contrast, symbolic interactionism exaggerates the autonomy of the self to a point where the theory has a potential to have self-defeating consequences for individuals that subscribe to its premises. We suggest an alternative approach to identity that sees it as the product of an enlightenment discourse and the dualistic thinking of Descartes. Foucault (1970) has described this differently as the transition from a classical to an era of modernity occurring in the seventeenth century where man (sic) became the objective target as well as the subjective agent of knowledge. Without the Cartesian separation of the mind from the body representing the broader dualism between subject and object, the development of the study of human existence would have remained within the realm of speculative metaphysics, philosophy and theology. However, while the growth of the human and social sciences may be seen as a positive outcome of enlightenment and dualistic thinking, the price has been a preoccupation with identity of almost narcissistic proportions. The authors argument is that this preoccupation reflects and reinforces an anxiety and insecurity that follows from our self-conscious awareness of our separation as subjects from objects (including other subjects) in the world. This sense of separation has both positive and negative consequences. It is positive in the sense that it stimulates us to be active and creative in the belief that this, even if it cannot eradicate the anxiety, will at least divert our attention from the morbidity of thinking about subject–object separation. It is negative in the sense that projects designed to alleviate the anxiety of separation frequently exacerbate, as subjects become preoccupied with alleviating, such anxiety. In short, the myopia surrounding the desire to overcome our anxiety and insecurity is often a major source of its reproduction and thereby a self-defeating contradiction.

The extract from **Dorinne Kondo's** *Crafting Selves* (Reading 12.2) is selected because of the way in which the author makes a virtue of being visible in the writing about the formation, deformation and restoration of identity in Japanese society. As a Sansei, third-generation Japanese American, she produces an oppositional discourse to challenge the stereotypical identities that have been assigned workers in her country of origin. These images of a harmonious, homogeneous workplace where there is guaranteed life-time employment rewarded by employee loyalty and conformity to the corporate goals of profit and productivity were established during the post-war economic miracle that brought Japan close to the top of the world league table of successful economies. Japanization or the attempted export to western economies of this apparent success in corporate management was prefaced precisely on a set of assumptions that provided 'fixed' representations of Japanese identities and the communities from which they were nurtured or she would say disciplined. The stereotypical image of Japan as a country of authoritarian leaders and submissive followers is not so much rejected as critically examined and found problematic as the author experienced first hand how identities were crafted within relations of power whether at work, in the community or within the family. She also readily acknowledges that her oppositional discourse reproduces conventions even as it problematizes them.

John Jermier's extract (Reading 12.3) provides us with a poetic narrative concerning how easy it is to shift between two polarized views of our identity and life in the modern workplace. On the one hand, there is the utopian image of a life full of stimulating diversity and hedonistic pleasure. On the other, we have a dystopian image of endless subjugation to the performative demands of the corporation and its irresponsibility to the environmental dangers and the social-psychological damage of its reckless pursuit of profit. This is an innovative device whereby the author creates a short story to express the ambiguity and ambivalence experienced by many of us in (post)modern workplaces where our moral sensitivities are often weakened by material luxury and hedonistic pleasure. When teaching a course that encourages critical self-reflection, students often say to us why do you want to disturb the comfort of our self-satisfied existence as 'happy robots'? Waking people from the dream is not always easy to justify, especially when we know that such awakening can result in a life of frustration as it becomes clear we are unlikely to divert more than a small minority from the addictive complacency of material affluence.

READING 12.1

Management Lives: Power and Identity in Work Organisations

By David Knights and Hugh Willmott

Behaviourism

The key assumptions underpinning behaviourism can be summarized as follows:

1. Behaviour is lawful. Its laws are amenable to the same methods of investigation used by natural scientists. They are discovered through establishing a set of correlations between environmental stimuli and behavioural responses.
2. Behaviour is determined by environmental as well as genetic factors. Of these, the environmental factors can be observed and changed to ensure that behaviour corresponds with that which is desirable.

3. When applying a scientific approach, it is misleading to identify 'feelings' or other inner states of mind as causes of behaviour.

Symbolic Interactionism

The basic premises of symbolic interactionism can be summarized as follows:

1. People act on the basis of the meanings they ascribe to the objects in their world, not in terms of the stimuli given off by these objects.
2. Communications between people evolve through processes of interaction in which they make

Management Lives: Power and Identity in Work Organisations *continued*

By David Knights and Hugh Willmott

and interpret symbolic indications to one another, in the form of speech and gestures.

3. Social action is accomplished as individuals mobilize meanings to interpret and enact the situations in which they are involved.

Beyond Behaviourism and Symbolic Interactionism

What can be learned from behaviourism, symbolic interactionism and the criticisms that have been levelled against them? To begin with, it is worth noting that their respective perspectives are by no means novel. Consider the example of employees going on strike. When strike action is characterized in terms of a predictable response to a given set of stimuli, assumptions shared by behaviourism are implicitly invoked. Alternatively, assumptions shared by symbolic interactionism are mobilized when strike action is seen as reflecting the 'mood' of the workforce, who interpret their situation as unfair or unreasonable. To this extent, behaviourism and symbolic interaction do not so much challenge common sense as clarify, and make more available to critical reflection, the premises that guide its reasoning.

For behaviourists, the heart of the difference between behaviourism and symbolic interactionism, we have argued, is a disagreement about human autonomy. For behaviourists, this autonomy is a myth that obstructs the development of a more rational society. In such a rational society, environments would be redesigned to produce the stimuli that elicit socially desired responses. For symbolic interactionists, in contrast, autonomy is at the very centre of what it is to be human. Autonomy enables human beings to interpret stimuli in novel, imaginative ways that elude or defy behaviourist control.

It is unlikely, and perhaps undesirable, that the debate will ever be settled between those who believe in human autonomy or 'free will' and those who deny its existence. This is because both accounts are based upon metaphysical assumptions, which cannot be conclusively falsified. Such 'undecidability' can invite despair. But only if there is a (naïve and scientistic) expectation that social science will deliver absolute

answers rather than provide fuel for continuing debate. The value of social science can be understood to reside in its capacity to clarify, and press to their limits, common sense understandings of everyday life. Then tolerance of any inconclusive investigations helps keep alive debate upon the moral and political legitimacy of the various competing frameworks which have been developed to guide our actions in the world.

The way this chapter has been structured in a linear developmental fashion may suggest a 'progressive' history of ideas approach. While that is not intended, we do see the theory of identity that we are now about to develop as an amalgamation of social psychological and sociological ideas about, or theories, of human behaviour. Whilst it captures elements of both behaviourism and symbolic interaction theory, it should not be regarded as superior but simply different and equally open to critique. Indeed were it not likely to generate more confusion for our readers, we would be critical of the implicit masculinity of identity theory.

In other words, our own inclination is to emphasize how both behaviourists and symbolic interactionists assume human nature to be plastic. How people behave depends upon the design of the reinforcement schedules or (re)construction of interpretive frameworks. Building upon their shared assumption about the plasticity of human nature, we now outline a theory of identity that builds upon our critical reflections on behaviourism and symbolic interactionism. In particular, we draw upon behaviourism to expose the limits of humanistic formulations, which assume the centrality of human autonomy in a way that exaggerates its power. But equally we are sympathetic to the symbolic interactionist emphasis upon the mediation of human action and self-formation through processes of interpretation.

The Precariousness of Identity in the Context of Work and Society

The Limits of Rational Control

It is in the world of management and formal work where we expect to find the most refined form of

Management Lives: Power and Identity in Work Organisations

By David Knights and Hugh Willmott

rational, planned action. Yet empirical research repeatedly reveals a more chaotic scenario (Knights and Murray, 1994; Hearn *et al.*, 1989). Even the best-laid plans cannot anticipate all conceivable contingencies or take full account of the interactive and contingent quality of relationships. As a consequence of unanticipated events, personal and corporate plans are often discredited. They fall into disuse or assume a purely formal ceremonial quality. Having been commended as the key to successful business in the 1970s and 80s, elaborate, detailed planning has fallen into disrepute in an age where increased importance is attached to general strategic intent and direction, corporate agility and incremental progress (Mintzberg, 1994). Arising out of the development of 'flexible specialisation' (Piorre and Sabel, 1984), the 'flexible firm' (Atkinson, 1984) and other systems of corporate responsiveness to changing markets and more demanding customers, management have been at pains to demonstrate intra- and entrepreneurial skills in the pursuit of customer service. In Kundera's (1984) novel the *Unbearable Lightness of Being* (ULB), the pendulum has swung away from the 'heaviness' of grand strategic planning to the comparative 'lightness' of husbanding competencies and, in Tom Peters' (1989) words, 'thriving on chaos'. Such injunctions invite managers to construct their sense of identity and to direct their actions in a specific manner, albeit one that is less wedded to the formulation and implementation of bureaucratic procedures.

Compared to the corporate arena, the private world of sex is widely assumed to be less amenable to planning on account of the volatility of human emotions. Nonetheless, Tomas's fear of women fuelled his desire to possess them in a way that was purely physical, devoid of any human significance or responsibility. He therefore developed a working plan or method:

> He considered (t)his method flawless: The important thing is to abide by the rule of the threes. Either you see a woman three times in quick succession and then never again, or you maintain relations over the years but make sure that the rendezvous are at least three weeks apart. The rule of threes enabled Tomas to keep intact his liaisons with some women while continuing to engage in short-term affairs with many others. (Kundera, 1984: 12)

He planned his sex life to conform with a self-consciously designed strategy.

Identity Formation in Conditions of Uncertainty

We have illustrated how behaviour is facilitated and constrained by routines or methodical ways of organizing human affairs. Self-consciousness allows, yet also demands, that human behaviour be purposive. For this reason, self-consciousness is a condition of anxiety and insecurity. Under conditions of material scarcity (e.g. lack of food), the desire to survive directs our purposiveness towards the production or the appropriation of the means of remedying this scarcity. Precisely how this desire is fulfilled depends upon the cultural (e.g. ethical, religious, regulatory) practices within which processes of production or appropriation are embedded (see Figure 12.1.1). Except in the most extreme of circumstances, meanings – such as customs and moral and religious beliefs – mediate

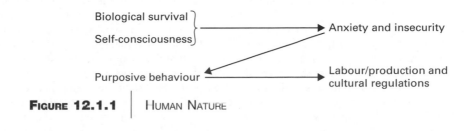

FIGURE 12.1.1 | HUMAN NATURE

Management Lives: Power and Identity in Work Organisations *continued*

By David Knights and Hugh Willmott

desire and its satisfaction. For it is impossible to separate out material or biological survival from the concerns that human beings have with symbolic meaning and identity as mediated through language.[1]

Feelings of insecurity about physical survival can be aroused when material scarcity is identified. Of equal if not greater importance, especially in materially affluent societies, anxieties are aroused by threats to symbolic survival in the form of social encounters that unsettle a stable or secure sense of self. For our sense of self is endangered by situations where we perceive ourselves to be vulnerable to social or interpersonal rejection or denial. Whereas (other) animals tend to react instinctively to stimuli in the environment, human beings interpret every situation through a self-conscious perception of what it means for symbolic as well as material security. The formation of a sense of identity within social institutions means that the 'appropriateness' of behaviour can be challenged or may shift unpredictably from one moment or situation and context to another. This is what makes for the 'lightness of being' – a lightness that can be experienced as 'unbearable'. Perversely, it is precisely this experience, or its anticipation, that strengthens our commitment, or attachment, to established routines and obligations ("Es muss sein").

In ULB, Teresa was always uncertain about how to behave in response to Tomas's promiscuity. At first, she simply complained about it in a passive way. Later, becoming more assertive, she left him temporarily and also experimented with adultery. Finally, though perhaps only because Tomas himself came to regard womanizing as a form of enslavement, there was an agreement to move to the countryside. There, she anticipated that there would be a 'harmonious world' (ibid.: 128) in which 'everyone came together in one big happy family with common interests and routines' (ibid.), such as dancing in the local tavern on Saturdays and attending church on Sundays.

What she found, in contrast, was a suspension of the traditional way of life by a communist state that had turned the tavern into offices, shut down the local church and forbidden religious holidays. There was nowhere for the villagers to 'come together'. Their evenings were now spent watching television

and (ironically) dreaming of moving into town to escape the boredom. Yet, unlike those living in the urban areas of Czechoslovakia, the villagers were not overseen or directly controlled by state officials, precisely because their passivity posed little threat to the state. The authorities were willing to allow the workers a degree of 'self-determination' so that they were able, for example, to elect the chairman of the collective farm (ibid: 283) – a move that has its parallels in the empowerment programmes imposed upon employees by the managers of capitalist enterprises ...

The response of the villagers to the loss of 'the old-age pattern' of country life (ibid. 283) was not one of rebellion or an active quest to re-establish their traditions. Instead, they retreated into their private worlds and fantasies of leaving the place that 'offered them nothing in the way of even a minimally interesting life' (ibid. 283). They adapted by willingly surrendering their identity as members of a rural community. Instead of resisting the authorities, they emulated the lives of city people, even in the way that they furnished their homes ...

Identity and Consumption

Marx (1867) was critical of the divisive, exploitative and destructive consequences of capitalism. But he also stressed its superior productive efficiency relative to previous economic regimes. This understanding leads Marx to identify a contradiction in the capacity of capitalism to produce a quantity of goods far in excess of the (unstimulated) demand for their use or the disposable income available for their purchase. This contradiction has been addressed by the growth of credit and the advent of mass advertising. People are encouraged to identify consumption as a meaningful, pleasurable activity through which they can establish themselves as rational autonomous agents. This they do by making choices between a proliferating range of products, services and diverse lifestyles. Demand is stimulated so as to absorb supply.

Building a unique, style-sensitive brand image is also regarded as a more effective means of securing profitable growth than engaging in price wars. Unless price cuts succeed in increasing market share by pushing smaller players out of the market, price-based

READING 12.1

Management Lives: Power and Identity in Work Organisations

By David Knights and Hugh Willmott

competition risks reductions in margins that, once lost, can be difficult to regain. Also price wars are a possible self-defeating outcome of price competition. But the degree of price competition is exaggerated by 'free market' rhetoric; by inducing imperfect knowledge where it does not already exist, price competition can be avoided. Because of the contradictory nature of price competition, companies much prefer to seek customer loyalty through service quality. Again this helps to account for the proliferation and seductive nature of initiatives intended to secure or enhance 'quality'. Advertising is deployed to boost demand, often by associating a product with 'lifestyles' (i.e. identities) to which potential consumers are believed to aspire and with which they are encouraged to identify.

Advertising appeals to and contrives to stimulate a multiplicity of human 'needs' that would otherwise not exist or be disregarded. These 'needs' are constructed or elaborated through symbols and images that arouse concerns about status and self-esteem. This observation echoes the central claim of symbolic interactionism that self-consciousness is at the centre of human life. As aspirations are raised and anxieties are amplified by advertising, individuals are seduced and their energies directed narcissistically toward the acquisition of the symbols or attributes that signify a successful (self) image. In the context of capitalist society, the most compelling and legitimate means of

relieving anxieties about social position and self-identity is through an individualistic pursuit of the material and symbolic indicators of success. This narcissistic project takes the form of domination and control in the spheres both of production and consumption (see Figure 12.1.2).

Coveted positions in organizations and society – from playing for Manchester United to being appointed as Chief Executive of a major corporation – are socially acclaimed and respected, at least in formal (i.e. hierarchical) terms. These positions promise to provide material and symbolic privileges that enable their occupants to cope with anxiety and insecurity. Such privileges serve as generic institutional substitutes for those interpersonal confirmations of self that traditionally have bestowed upon identities a degree of stability and security. Yet the presence of these privileges rarely eradicates existing anxieties and insecurities. Indeed, they invariably engender new and even more intense preoccupations with securing material and symbolic success. For example, in *Nice Work* (Lodge, 1989) Vic Wilcox lies awake in the small hours as 'worries streak towards him like enemy spaceships'. Sherman McCoy, the self-appointed Master of the Universe, is anxious lest his wife discovers his adulterous deception (Wolfe, 1988).

Like Vic and Sherman we find ourselves searching for, or striving to protect, a valued set of meanings

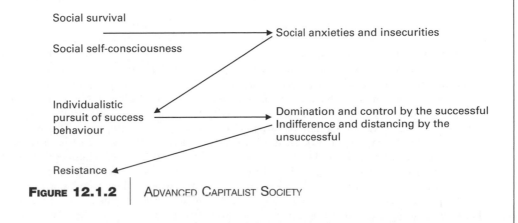

FIGURE 12.1.2 | ADVANCED CAPITALIST SOCIETY

| READING 12.1 | **Management Lives: Power and Identity in Work Organisations** *continued* |

By David Knights and Hugh Willmott

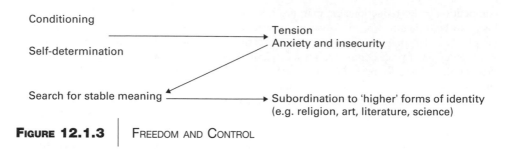

FIGURE 12.1.3 | FREEDOM AND CONTROL

(e.g. a job or a marriage) that make us feel wanted, superior or seem somehow to transcend the ephemeral character of such ambitions. This requires us routinely and recurrently to contrive ways of neutralising or eliminating eventualities that pose a threat to these meanings and thus of the sense of self-identity derived from them.

Conclusion

In this chapter, we have explored 'identity at work' in a multiplicity of ways, how identity 'works' and, more importantly, how identity has to be 'worked at' in contemporary organizations and everyday life. Drawing principally on Kundera's *The Unbearable Lightness of Being*, we have deployed his metaphor of 'lightness' and 'weight' to frame our reflections upon the 'openness' of human existence, the conditional quality of autonomy, the centrality of self-consciousness, the virtue and necessity of interpretation, and the operation of power/knowledge within institutional and economic life.

Weight is added to our being by responsibilities and obligations that attend the development of a sense of purpose or mission, however grandiose or prosaic. In moments of reflection we may be relieved of some or all of this weight. Certain philosophies or religions (e.g. Buddhism) inspire us to shed the weight of our attachments to material and symbolic existence so as to enter a world where the grasping of ego and the anxious preoccupation with making reality comply with its demands is dissolved (see Figure 12.1.3).

However, the lightness of being can become unbearable when the jettisoning of attachments render

life meaningless and individuals find themselves floundering in a directionless void. When this happens there can be a breakdown of established routines as people lose a sense of control and even escape into a world void of everyday meaning and normalized expectations that is conventionally understood as mental illness. Alternatively, and more commonly, an encounter with the void manifests itself in a compulsive and self-defeating desire to escape. For Theresa, the void took the form of intense and completely debilitating jealousy caused by Thomas's repeated infidelities. For many years she was overwhelmed by a preoccupation with this problem as it destroyed her identity as a married woman. At the end of her tether, the intensity of her suffering drove Theresa to engage in a casual extra-marital sexual encounter. She fully expected that sex without intimacy would be suffused with a lightness that would ease the burden of her compulsive preoccupation with Thomas's promiscuity. Instead, it produced a weight of such proportions that she had the immediate urge to void her bowels. In the context of advanced capitalist societies, a consumerist orientation generates a comparable experience of temporary gratification followed by a sense of continuing, oppressive emptiness. This is addressed through a variety of stratagems, such as workaholism, indifference and renewed consumption. Both in the novel and our theoretical deliberations, we have emphasised the awesome but also inspiring ambivalence of human existence where we are caught between, and struggle to reconcile, the lightness of irresponsible autonomy, on the one hand, and the burdensome desire

Management Lives: Power and Identity in Work Organisations

By David Knights and Hugh Willmott

for a secure identity with its attendant responsibilities, on the other.

[1] The focus on language is somewhat neglected or perhaps taken-for-granted by both behaviourists and symbolic interactionists and yet it is through rational reflections or rationalizations of behaviour that behavioural reinforcement and identity construction take place.

References

Hearn, J., Sheppard, D.L., Tancred-Smith, P. and Burrell, G. (1989) editors, *The Sexuality of Organisation*, London: Sage.

Knights, D. and Murray, F. (1984) *Managers Divided*, London: Wiley.

Kundera, M. (1984) *The Unbearable Lightness of Being*, London: Faber & Faber.

Lodge, D. (1989) *Nice Work*, Harmondsworth: Penguin.

Marx, K. (1867/1976) *Capital: A Critical Analysis of Capitalist Production*, Trans. By S. Moore and E. Aveling and edited by F. Engels, London: George Allen & Unwin Ltd.

Mintzberg, H. (1994) *The Rise and Fall of Strategic Planning*, Englewood Cliffs, New Jersey: Prentice-Hall.

Peters, T. (1989) *Thriving on Chaos*, London: Pan

Piore, M. and Sabel, C. (1984) *The Second Industrial Divide*, New York: Basic Books

Wolfe, T. (1988) *The Bonfire of the Vanities*, London: Pan Books.

The Stakes

By Dorinne K. Kondo

I have argued throughout this book that selves are crafted in processes of work and within matrices of power, and that categories such as personal and political, experiential and theoretical, personal and social are persistent North American narrative conventions unable to fully account for the complexities and ambiguities of everyday life. In the introductory chapter, I made and attempted to enact an argument that "experience" and "theory" cannot be neatly separated from one another.[1] To recapitulate my "theoretical" emphasis on the importance of understanding selves as "subject-positions" crafted within relations of power, let me end by briefly making explicit my stakes in presenting and thematizing the material as I have.

Meaningful axes of identity, such as race and gender, loom large in American society as they do in Japan, and my shifting positionings as a Japanese American woman crafting a self within a particular historical and cultural matrix have informed this work subtly but unmistakably. Certain modes of explanation and exposition seem especially comfortable or strategically important in light of these shifting positions. More specifically, "experience" leads me to a "theoretical" concern with the place of meaning and power in social life.

Culture and meaning, though for many years I had no name for these abstractions, lay in an awareness of assumptions, deeply felt, that shaped everyday life in the Japanese American community where I grew up. Mostly these assumptions had to do with the proper conduct of human relationships: the eloquence of silence, the significance of reciprocity, the need to attend closely to nuance, subtlety, ellipsis. Such deeply held orientations, imbued with moral, emotional, and intellectual significance, were sometimes at sharp variance with dominant cultural modes of action, and thus radically cast into relief the socially constituted nature of both "their" assumptions and "ours." Culture, from this standpoint, is no reified thing or system, but a meaningful way of being in the world, inseparable from the "deepest" aspects of one's "self"—the trope of depth and interior space itself a product of our own cultural conventions. These

READING 12.2 | **The Stakes** *continued*

By Dorinne K. Kondo

cultural meanings are themselves multiple and contradictory, and though they cannot be understood without reference to historical, political, and economic discourses, the experience of culture cannot be reduced to these nor related to them in any simple, isomorphic way.

Moreover, these meanings could never be disentangled from relations of power. For some ways of being in the world were and are more legitimate, more rewarded, more recognized than others—as anyone in a marginal or minority position will attest. My attempts to emphasize the nexus of power and meaning, then, are conditioned by my subject-positionings as a Japanese American woman.[2] The Japanese economy has spawned a plethora of works replaying a tired ostinato of harmony, homogeneity, lifetime employment, and flattened, unidimensional portrayals of automaton-like workers happily singing the company song, burning with enthusiasm for their quality control circles, and driven by the Confucian ethic. Clearly, there is some superficial truth to these images, at least for the full-time, regular male employees in large firms. But people I knew did not belong to that much-celebrated sector of Japanese industry, and their work lives controvert many of these familiar stereotypes. My intention in choosing to work with people like the Satōs was precisely to complement/criticize images derived from the Japanese mainstream.

Furthermore, my writing strategies are deployed as an oppositional discourse to other insidiously persistent tropes that constitute the phantasm "Japan" in the contemporary United States: not only Organization Man and automaton, but submissive, subjugated Japanese Woman, domineering, sexist Japanese Man, Japanese despot, or perhaps most basically, "the (undifferentiated) Japanese." And I am in the paradoxical position of deploying what is conventionally known as an antihumanist discourse for humanist ends. That is, my emphasis on complexity, power, contradiction, discursive production, and ambiguity is invoked in part to demonstrate complexity and irony in the lives of the people I knew, in order to complicate and dismantle the ready stereotypes that erase complexity in favor of simple, unitary images. My friends and co-workers at the Satō factory, like

us, forge their lives in the midst of ambivalences and contradictions, using the idioms at their disposal.

My general stance, in short, is opposed to a body of literature that would reinscribe familiar narrative conventions of fixed identity and a realm of meaning beyond the reach of power, and to the stereotyped portrayals of "the Japanese" which emerge when those conventions remain unproblematized. And like all oppositional discourse, the opposition can never be pristine or transcendent, but it is always already situated within other discourses, reproducing conventions even as it problematizes them.

These points emerge clearly in my use of the first-person voice in the introduction and here, at the end. My intent is antiromantic and anti-nostalgic, but by invoking my "experience" as a Japanese American, or more specifically, as a Sansei, third-generation Japanese American, moments of a nostalgic rediscovery of aspects of my identity may inevitably intrude. Moreover, arguing for the complex humanity of my Japanese friends and co-workers is—within the context of a not-always-welcoming American Society and an historical economic climate in which martial metaphors of Japanese invasion and trade wars abound—an argument for my own humanity. In this text, the deployment of the first-person is strategic, indended to show the ways my experiences as a Sansei woman were different from those of a white ethnographer and to argue that those differences were not insert—either for the Japanese people I encountered or in the crafting of this text. Of course these differences are not the only ones that matter. But invoking that important difference, that positioning, is a way of arguing for the inevitable locatedness and partiality of any understanding and for a voice acknowledging that partiality. For most third-generation returnees to the "mother land," the temptations of romanticism or apologism are great, but our different positionings could at the very least create the *possibility* for accounts written from perspectives different from dominant perspectives in mainstream social science.

In its writing strategies and its explicit theoretical message, *Crafting Selves* is an attempt to reconsider definitions of the self, at levels we would call collective and individual. There can be no radical rupture with the fixity and essentialism of our narrative

READING 12.2

The Stakes

By Dorinne K. Kondo

conventions, but emphases on potential conflict, ambiguity, irony, and the workings of power in the very process of constructing identities could yield other insights and other rhetorical strategies to explore. Rather than bounded, essential entities, replete with a unitary substance and consciousness, identities become nodal points repositioned in different contexts. Selves, in this view, can be seen as rhetorical figures and performative assertions enacted in specific situations within fields of power, history, and culture.

The intertwinings of power and identity in the disciplinary production of selves in the particular Japanese contexts I described led me to confront dilemmas of representation. Is it possible to avoid the otherness of exoticism and ineffable strangeness, on the one hand, and the cultural imperialism of appropriation—"They are just like us" or "What is so Japanese about that?"—on the other? The ethics retreat is a prime example. In its vivid and exaggerated form, it is a highly culturally and historically specific phenomenon, considered extreme even in Japan. But it is a pastiche of both profoundly "Japanese" and profoundly "Western" elements, and as such it plays out in an extreme way the contradictions, ironies, and creative, coercive deployments of power at work in any crafting of identity. While plunging into icy baths, running marathons, and shouting greetings at Mount Fuji seem initially ridiculous and exotic, these extreme practices both recombine elements from a particular historical/cultural repertoire (including allusions to Gestalt therapy and the use of English to lend an exotic, contemporary flavor to the proceedings) and point us toward our everyday lives. And they do so in ways that should take us beyond stereotypes of authoritarian/submissive Japanese (or worse, "Orientals"), surpassing comparisons to EST, Outward Bound, boot camp, or even other company training programs, though these might provide instructive parallels. Rather, this experience would, I hope, occasion reflection on the ways our institutions, languages, and social formations—schools, corporations, families, and meaningful cleavages such as class, race, gender, and age—are vehicles for the disciplinary production of selves. Selves everywhere are crafted through coercions and disciplines, which offer culturally,

historically specific pathways to self-realization as well as to domination.

For my friends, neighbors, and co-workers showed me that there is no place beyond power or beyond "the law." Love in the *uchi* is not separable from authority, from guilt and the weight of obligation, and from self-realization. The wrenching dilemma Masao faced threw into relief these contradictions and ironies. We saw how different people forged their lives within *ie* and *uchi*, and how these idioms offered specific—if changing and contestable—possibilities for happiness and for coercion. Obāchan, tied down to her "shitty old man," eventually became a "merry widow." Minako-san, suffering the hardships of recreating herself as a bride of the Sakamoto household, both adjusted with difficulty and set up boundaries of resistance, refusing to perfectly enact her expected role. Her life points the way toward change. The Satōs, finally, embody the cultural ideal of disciplined subjects finding fulfillment in that discipline. Life in households and family firms draw on this discourse of participatory belonging and self-fulfillment. But seeing in "the Japanese" a utopian model of human connectedness and belonging fails to see that for my neighbors—or, I would argue, for anyone else in any other setting—this belonging and connectedness is never beyond power. In this light, any idealization of family or communitarian sentiments in family firms seems highly suspect.[3]

Shifting, contradictory, multiple discourses constructed the identities of *uchi*, and once again, this collective identity is both compelling and coercive, fluid and constraining. People mobilize and deploy the idiom, but their acts are shaded by ironies and unintended consequences. Indeed, a major argument in this book is that no action has a single effect. For example, the Satōs on many levels enact in their own lives the notion that *uchi* and *kaisha* are one, but collisions with other discourses, the hierarchies of belonging to the company, and the obvious apparatuses of surveillance, create contradictions and possibilities for ironic distance and for change. Even the most successful attempts to "add the family flavor" cannot be said to work in an unproblematic way for all the employees. Oft-cited benefits such as the company trip sometimes backfire, provoking

READING 12.2 | **The Stakes** *continued*

By Dorinne K. Kondo

more resentment and complaint than loyal gratitude. Still, *uchi no kaisha* is far from completely undermined. Workers could use *uchi no kaisha* as an idiom through which resistance could be structured, as when they took the *shachō* to task for being inadequately familial. Pride in *uchi no kaisha*, especially a prosperous firm like the Satōs', could alternate with criticism, complaints, satire, and parody.

The meanings of *uchi no kaisha* are in turn constructed by a changing political/economic context. "Company as family" meant quite different things to apprentices in a *noren uchi* during the late Tokugawa period, to the mill girls in the factories during Meiji, and to the employees of a Satō company in the 1970s and 1980s. The Meiji revolution and the deployment of household-state metaphors, the growth of capitalism, changing kinship relations, dramatic legal changes, global configurations of power— including the perceived threat from "the West"—and the out-comes of war, among other factors, indelibly mark *uchi no kaisha* and the possibilities for constructing its meaning. Moreover, the specificity of the Satō company's location—a prosperous company of problematic size, where fact-to-face paternalism was desired, yet only sporadically realized, where union organization was absent, as it is in virtually all small firms—further constrained and created possibilities for the deployments of *uchi no kaisha*. The fluidity and complexities of these deployments far exceed the strictures of some Confucian ethic or unchanging cultural legacy from the Tokugawa past, and they subvert and undermine any notion of romanticized solidarity or unmitigated coercion.

At the level of what we would conventionally call "collective" identity, we see that identities are multiple, fraught with tension and contradiction, and asserted in specific performative contexts. The same is true of identities we would call "individual," as we saw in the cases of Ohara-san, Ikatura-san, Satō-san, Iida-san, and Teramura-san, and in my own case. Taking cues from the linguistic ideologies underlying spoken Japanese, I have argued for a view of identities as constructed oppositionally and relationally. Selves are not referential symbols, the Transcendental Signified, but strategically deployed signifiers. Rather than universal essences, selves are rhetorical assertions, produced by our linguistic conventions, which we narrate and perform for each other.

Identities on the individual level resist closure and reveal complicated, shifting, multiple facets. And selves were never separable from context: that is from the situations in which they were performed, the audience to whom the narrative production of self was addressed, the exclusions implicit in any construction of "self", the historical and political/economic discourses, and the culturally shaped narrative conventions that constructed "the self."

If analyzing the lives of my informants leads us to a reconceptualization of the self, it also leads us to reconsider the nature of power. Again, my argument is not that there is some essential substance, power, which some people have and some people do not. Rather, power must be seen as creative, coercive, and coextensive with meaning, so that we might begin by examining the specificity of the workings of power in a given context, in the process searching out potential points of resistance. In such a view, even those who "have power"—the *shachō* and Ohara-san, for instance—are themselves dominated in the context of a changing political economy. Acts of caprice and exclusion both consolidate and undermine the power of these men in the context of the factory. Further, those conventionally defined as "without power," including the ultimate structural marginals, the part-time women workers at the Satō factory, are both marginal and central to factory life. Conventional enactments of identity provide a way for these to assert positive strengths, just as the constitutive histories constructing idioms of gender limit possibilities for subversion.

Finally, to underline the location and partiality of this and every account, this text should be seen as the product of particular encounters among particular people with particular agendas in particular historical moments. In our efforts to understand each other, my friends, neighbors, co-workers and I asserted our own identities and attempted to force each other into comprehensible categories: to craft each other. Contradiction, multiplicity, and ambiguity emerged through my unforgettable experiences with the complicated and wonderful people who allowed me to intrude on their lives, For my relatives, neighbors, friends, and above all, my co-workers in the Satō factory showed me that my implicit, unconscious assumptions about a "concept of self," based on a notion of referential meaning, of "authentic resistance," and of the neat

READING 12.2 | # The Stakes

By Dorinne K. Kondo

separability of "personal" from "political" or theoretical," were discursively produced, the sediments of my own culture and history. Hatanaka-san, Satō-san, Itakura-san, Ohara-san, Obāchan, Minako-san, and Masao-kun, among others, helped me to realize that quests for utopian spaces of communitarianism or resistance, a bounded, essential whole subject, or neatly separable categories like "personal" and "political" are likely to prove fruitless and self-deceiving. Their lives point us toward investigations of identity which follow out the multiple ways people launch and deploy meanings within culturally and historically specific narrative fields. Above all, my Japanese friends, co-workers, and neighbors helped me to see and to appreciate the complicated tangle of ironies and ambiguities we create for ourselves, and that are created for us, as we craft our selves and our lives within shifting fields of power.

[1] A handful of anthropologists have explicitly discussed these issues. Notable among them are moving works by R. Rosaldo (1984) and Taylor (1988).

[2] I am not arguing here that all Japanese American women embrace the same point of view. Even given similar histories, mine is only one of a variety of possible stances. But given certain subject-positionings, it is a predictable stance.

[3] One such idealization occurs in Piore and Sabel (1984). Arguing against teleological explanations of industrialization which privilege large firms and mass production, they make a case for "flexible specialization" in smaller firms as a solution to contemporary capitalism's dilemmas. The choice now facing late capitalism they label the "second industrial divide." But in putting forth their case for flexible specialization, they romanticize communitarianism, solidarity, and familialism, citing Japanese family enterprise and other familial styles of management in approving terms. As I have argued, this solidarity, harmony, and communitarianism is a far more ambiguous and complicated matter for the people who actually work in these small firms.

References

Haraway, Donna (1988) Situated Knowledges: The Science Question in Feminism and the Privilege of the Partial Perspective, *Feminist Studies*, 14/3 575–600.

Piore, Michael J. and Charles F. Sabel (1984) The Second Industrial Divide, New York: Basic Books.

Rosaldo, Renato (1984) Grief and a Headhunter's Rage: On the Cultural Force of Emotions, in Edward Bruner (editor) *Text, Play and Story: The Construction and Reconstruction of Self and Society*, Washington DC: The American Ethnological Society.

Taylor, Julie (1988) Elite Socialization as Sequence and Collage: The Gaucho and Europe in Argentina, Paper presented at the panel, Elite socialization, American Anthropological Association, Meetings, Phoenix, Arizona.

READING 12.3 | # When the Sleeper Wakes: A Short Story Extending Themes in Radical Organization Theory

By John M. Jermier

"Turn up the radio – I like this song." Charlie did so.

On a dark desert highway, cool wind in my hair, warm smell of coleus, Rising up through the air … Mirrors on the ceiling, pink champagne On ice, and she said: "We are all just prisoners here, of our own device" … "Relax," said the night-man, "we are programmed to receive – you can check out any time you like, but you can never leave."

In his dream, Mike Armstrong had simply said … "'Hotel California'! What a classic! The guitars

sound awesome through those speakers." Mike drifted back to the song's lyrics:

Mirrors on the ceiling, pink champagne on ice, and she said – "we are all just prisoners of our won device." … Last thing I remember I was running for the door. I had to find the passage back to the place I was before. "Relax," said the night-man, "we are programmed to receive – you can check out anytime you like, but you can never leave."

READING 12.3

When the Sleeper Wakes: A Short Story Extending Themes in Radical Organization Theory *continued*

By John M. Jermier

Immediately, the screaming guitars captured Mike's attention and drove the lyrics from his mind …

When he awakes, however, he sees it as: "The perfect description of Thomas Industries," Mike exclaimed. "We help lay the traps. We punch out, but don't stop working. It shows on our faces. Our minds are *crippled!*" Charlie and Randy nodded. "The noise from the control room, that Thomas Industries sign, the gyp mountain, smokestacks … every night this mess is with me before I go to sleep." Charlie and Randy were silent.

They arrived just in time to punch in before the 7 o'clock whistle. "Goddamn whistles," Mike grumbled. "Remind me of grade school." As he grabbed his time card, he thought of the Woody Guthrie cartoon poster of the worker punching out, with a punishing right, the horrified face on a time clock. He smirked.

Ever since whistles were installed, Mike tried to avoid his workstation until at least 7:15. As he entered the sulphuric acid reactor complex, he heard Phil say: "… if God intended us to live without fertilizer, he wouldn't have given us the brains and machinery to mine the wet rock and mix it with acid." Mike noticed Phil glancing at him disapprovingly.

Indignation always gripped Mike when Phil used religion to defend the industry. He thought: "Phil, you, I, Barkley, and every other employee here knows that gypsum pile is hot. Do we need a Karen Silkwood scene to shake it up? There's too much fluoride gas in the plant. There aren't enough safety checks made on the power and steam lines, heavy machinery, or storage bins. Every year there's less money for product testing, safety and environmental stuff. Who do you think you're kidding?"

Mike knew it was a mistake to openly challenge Phil. He walked away resolutely. The group began moving towards the Personnel Auditorium. Mike motioned to his coworkers to pick up the slack while he was gone and followed the group.

Following a short speech by Byron Johannsen from OSHA on safety violations in the plant, Jack Barkley began talking: "We're cooperating with the OSHA 100% on this … Any of you with beards or hair that keep those masks from fitting right have to clean up your act, right away. Any questions?"

Mike probed: "Does that mean nothing can be done about the dust and vapors, or …" Before Mike could finish, Barkley began the answer Mike knew his question would provoke: "… We can't tinker with the process – it's the most rational way to make triple … Engineers have studied this … There's a very delicate natural balance among parts."

Mike whispered acrimoniously to Charlie: "Why do we have to make all the adjustments? They should clean this warzone up – spray the dry-side more, get rid of the vapor leaks, check the uranium dumps! Man! We shouldn't have to take this."

Barkley looked directly at Mike and said calmly: "If you have a problem with that, it's because you're not thinking straight. Talk to a technician if I don't make sense to you. All this benefits you! Besides, it's OSHA that forced these issues.

Ask Johannsen!"

"Men," said Johannsen reluctantly as everyone's eyes turned toward him, "our job is to protect your health. At this point, we can't make the company eliminate dust and fumes. We know the face masks are uncomfortable, but they will fit. It's the best we can do, now. We think they will protect you."

Mike's sense of frustration multiplied as Johannsen spoke, but he knew it was unwise to provoke Barkley further. He nodded his head in mock acquiescence.

"Being rational doesn't just mean following production logic," thought Mike, as he walked back to his station. "These guys may look easy, but I bet they'll find a way to get back at the company for this. I sure have!"

Phil unexpectedly walked into the control room. Mike was beginning final checks before shift change. "Bad news, Mike, I had to bust Larry Jones and Randy Markus in Granulating … We'll probably have to let them go."

Mike viewed drug-taking as a crutch, never accepting it as a liberating act, but was furious on principle: "Phil! That rule hasn't been enforced in over three years. Why the hell now? And why in Granulating? The work there is the worst in the plant – it's hot

When the Sleeper Wakes: A Short Story Extending Themes in Radical Organization Theory

By John M. Jermier

and dirty and boring! Everybody on nights is high or low.

The work gets done. You're trying to get back at Randy for filing against you!"

Phil stared mutely at Mike and then started to walk away. He turned, and angrily, but deliberately, responded: "Mike, if the rules are too tough here, I'm sure you can find other work."

Mike called the threat: "Don't push me, Phil. That's on my mind every day – and everyone else's too."

Phil shouted as he left the room: "Let me know when!"

Mike recalled all the layoffs last year and thought: "I'm an idiot! I let him get to me. I should know better than to go one-on-one with a supervisor. There are so many other ways to fight back."

Mike left the control room to find Randy and met him and Charlie walking toward the time clock. Randy looked ragged and resigned. Mike embraced him compassionately and said: "The whole plant's in an uproar. We'll find a way for you to keep your job – you can count on that. Let's go to the sunset and have a drink."

In the parking lot, Mike glanced back at the plant and thought resentfully: "You can check out any time you like, but you can never leave …"

Reprise

Like Graham, the central character in H.G. Wells' anti-utopian novel, *When the Sleeper Wakes,* this story's main figure, Mike Armstrong, encountered a nightmare world upon awakening from a deep sleep. However, it was not the dramatically inhuman, mechanical-urban world of the 22nd century which Armstrong encountered. This was not a story about dark, dusty, subterranean factories, blue-uniformed workers pale and disfigured from their labour but automatically punctual, or brutal state police who coerce labourers. Instead, it was a story about alienated life in and around a modern, urban factory where the mechanisms of administrative control are subtle, complicated and not encompassed by the plant gates.

Armstrong experienced these events first during a dream state and then again while awake. This literary device was used to compare and contrast two radical descriptions of subjective alienation, reified consciousness, and reflective militancy, and to illustrate the power of mythical forces in organizational settings. The main character's dual states of mind and action dramatize the existential moments of personal alienation (Laing, 1965) and symbolize the self-contradictory aspects of capitalist systems.

This study is primarily a theoretical analysis which uses typical cases to illustrate positions. The method is subjectivist (Morgan and Smicich, 1980; Poole, 1972) because the realities probed are psychic, and differs from purely fictional expression in that the characters' lives are created from actual field work and theoretical description.

The sections below briefly recast the theoretical issues and concepts relevant to the study and develop some of its implications.

Worker Cognitions and Organization Theory

Most contemporary theories of organization contain descriptions of worker characteristics that mediate organizational events and worker reactions. Included are those which are relatively objective, such as age, sex, race, or need states, and those which are relatively subjective, such as preferences, values, and belief systems. In fusing cognitive theory and organization theory, Weick (1979) extended inquiry on employee cognitions into the deeply subjective, into the inner frameworks through which people select, organize, and interpret sensory impressions to make meaning to their world. The concept of schema is crucial in understanding these cognitive processes. Schemata are abstract, psychic frameworks of organized past experiences which establish relations among specific events and entities (cf. Bartlett, 1932; Hastie, 1981).

Worker Consciousness and Organization Theory

With the emergence of Radical Organization Theory, many traditional and neo-Marxist concepts have been applied in studies of workplace dynamics (see Goldman, 1985, for review). However, a specific type of schema, studied extensively in Marxist analyses of the worker, remains unfamiliar to most organization theorists. One of the purposes of this study

When the Sleeper Wakes: A Short Story Extending Themes in Radical Organization Theory *continued*

By John M. Jermier

was to integrate concepts of class-consciousness, defined as the extent of workers' awareness of their emancipatory role in history (cf. Mann, 1973), into the writings on organizations. These concepts are developed in terms of the subjective alienation literature and are proposed as active, psychic forces, which serve the worker in selecting, organizing and making meaning from impressions associated with capitalist power dynamics.

Moments of Subjective Alienation

In Marx's (1932/1964) early philosophical writing, worker alienation is presented as an historically necessary result of the tension generated between the contradictory social forces of production and the private appropriation of capital. Workers are legally separated from ownership of the means and product of their labour (objective alienation) and comprehend, in a shared way, their position in oppressive, class-based production systems (cf. Bramel and Friend, 1981; Nord, 1977). Thus, while objectively alienated, awareness of class oppression and the transformative historical mission prevents separation from true self.

Neo-Marxist formulations of alienation, originating with Lukacs' (1923/1971) classic essay, attempted to describe and explain the lack of awareness of class-based oppression on the part of workers. Concepts of subjective alienation were developed to represent mystified psychic states where workers misconstrue the reality of class-based oppression for freedom (Jermier, 1982).

Table 1 presents elements of two prominent humanistic Marxist theories of subjective alienation. Critical Theory and dialectical Marxism, and contrasts these with humanistic organization theory's self-actualizing worker. The table was constructed to summarize differences in perspectives on subjective alienation illustrated in the story and discussed below.

Central to Critical Theory formulations of worker consciousness and alienation (represented in 'The Dream') is the concept of reification. In capitalist market systems, workers must sell their labour power and thus become semi-human objects of ex-

change, commodities, things (Israel, 1975). Reification is the "moment in the process of alienation in which the characteristic of thinghood becomes the standard of objective reality" (Berger and Pullman, 1965, p. 198). Reified consciousness is characterized by a *deprivation of awareness* which prevents realization that the world is socially constructed and can be remade. There is a concretizing and *naturalizing* (or *supernaturalizing*) of existing technical processes, social relations, concepts of reason, meanings of time, and definitions of adjustment (see Horkheimer, 1947/1974; Horkheimer and Adorno, 1944/1972). Only those not momentarily not under "the spell" (Adorno, 1966/1973, p. 312) resist absolute integration or reject the benefits of the status quo.

The power of reification in rationalizing existing conditions of employment for workers is supplemented by the "culture industry" (Horkheimer and Adorno, 1944/1972) which is at once ideological and diversionary. Marx used the term "camera obscura" in *The German Ideology* to refer to the process whereby a distorted upside-down version of the world (propagated by the privileged classes) becomes the standard of objective reality. The major institutions in society (schools, churches, the family, advertising and entertainment, etc.) act in harmony to present a version of the worker in society which denies oppressive realities. Cultural domination is completed when consumption is manipulated so thoroughly that consumers feel compelled to frenetically buy and use the culture industry's latest products, even though they see through them (Horkheimer and Adorno, 1944/1972). Workers are anaesthetized by the persuasive rationalizations readily accessible in mythical structures and by manipulated, diversionary consumption, such that the injuries of class are neither perceived nor felt. Workers are viewed as eternal dreamers. Partly due to their programmed atomization, they are unable to transcend their entrancement.

The contemporary worker's subjective experience of alienation has also been addressed in the writings of New Left Marxists (e.g. Marcuse, 1969) and Existential Marxists (e.g., Sartre, 1960/1963, 1960/1976). They are referred to here as dialectical Marxists

When the Sleeper Wakes: A Short Story Extending Themes in Radical Organization Theory

By John M. Jermier

(represented in "The Nightmare") because of their emphasis upon the central role of the ultimately free individual in resisting class based structures of domination. In rejecting both the class-conscious, collective subject of traditional Marxism and the totally dominated, individual subject of Critical Theory, Dialectical Marxists characterize the ordinary worker as subjectively alienated (falsely conscious), but engaged in responsible, meaningful protest and new forms of class radicalism. Thus, workers are capable of understanding the actual operation of the system (Best and Connolly, 1979) and there is an awareness of deprivation and disadvantage, even though this awareness rarely fosters revolutionary motives. Individual workers are not psychologically dominated by property-based power dynamics to the point of mystification or resignation. They experience workplace events from reflectively militant schemata, usually rejecting simplistic and exploitive definitions of situations. Although the worker's world is full of oppressive realities, it is at the same time rich in critical resources; reflective interpretation mobilizes these resources. Each day, the worker resists domination; sometimes with overt and dramatic actions, more frequently with sensible, subterranean forms of sabotage (Ehrenreich and Ehrenreich, 1976). The injuries of class are internalized, cumulative, and latently explosive (Lefebvre, 1970).

The theoretical viewpoints on alienated consciousness illustrated here depict the effects of problematical organizational events on workers quite differently. The anesthetized Critical Theory worker is so skilled at programmed rationalization and diversionary consumption that he or she barely notices the recurring surgery that separates and subjugates true self (cf. Laing, 1965). There is no counterforce or retaliation since this worker mistakes even capricious and surplus repression as natural and inevitable; there is no noticeable injury, hence no reprisal. The effects on the reflectively militant worker are poignant and potentially explosive. This worker cannot live at the level of ideology and therefore openly experiences the "buried features of working class life" (Matza and Wellman, 1980, p. 1). This creates feelings of incredulity, indignation, anger, horror, dread, fear, and loathing. The injuries are usually internationalized, but their comprehension in a broader system of meaning creates an unexpected resiliency. It is the carefully timed and varied reprisals, which generate managerial transformations and crises (cf. Morgan, 1984).

Concepts of humanistic management that are radically different from traditional organization theory derive from Critical Theory and Dialectical Marxism. They emphasize the importance of the political-economic context in analysing subjective states and propose macrolevel change strategies to eliminate alienation and humanize work (e.g., Jacoby, 1975; Nord, 1977).

In this study, class-based workplace dynamics have been dramatized in relation to divergent forms of alienated consciousness to illustrate the importance of human meaning-making processes in understanding organizational behaviour. Further theoretical analysis and research will clarify and assess the realism of these alternative viewpoints on the meaning of alienation at work.

References

Adorno, T.W. (1973) *Negative dialectics*. New York: Seabury Press. (Original work published 1966.)

Bartlett, F.C. (1932) *Remembering*. Cambridge: Cambridge University Press.

Berger, P. and Pullman, S. (1965) Reification and the sociological critique of consciousness. *History and Theory,* 4: 195–208.

Best, M.H. and Connolly, W.E. (1979) Politics and subjects: The limits of structural Marxism. *Socialist Review,* 9: 75–99.

Bramel, D. and Friend, R. (1981) Hawthorne, the myth of the docile worker, and the class bias in psychology. *American Psychologist,* 36: 867–878.

Ehrenreich, J. and Ehrenreich, B. (1976) Work and consciousness. *Monthly Review,* 28: 10–18.

Hastie, R. (1981) Schematic principles in human memory. In E.T. Higgins, C.P. Herman, and M.P. Zanna (Eds.), *Social cognition: The Ontario symposium* (pp. 39–88). Hillsdale, NJ: Lawrence Erlbaum.

Horkheimer, M. (1974) *Eclipse of reason.* New York Continuum. (Original work published 1947.)

Horkheimer, M. and Adorno, T.W. (1972) *Dialectic of enlightenment.* New York: Seabury Press. (Original work published 1944.)

READING 12.3

When the Sleeper Wakes: A Short Story Extending Themes in Radical Organization Theory *continued*

By John M. Jermier

Israel, J. (1975) Alienation and reification. *Social Praxis,* 3: 40–57.

Jacoby, R. (1975) *Social amnesia.* Boston: Beacon Press.

Jermier, J.M. (1982) Infusion of critical social theory into organizational analysis: Implications for studies of work adjustment. In D. Dunkerley & G. Salaman (Eds.), *The international yearbook of organization studies 1981* (pp. 195–211). London: Routlege & Kegan Paul.

Laing, R.D. (1965) *The divided self.* Harmondsworth: Penguin Books.

Lefèbvre, H. (1970) *The explosion.* New York: Monthly Review Press.

Lukács, G. (1971) *History and class consciousness.* Cambridge: MIT Press. (Original work published 1923.)

Marcuse, H. (1969) *An essay on liberation.* Boston: Beacon Press.

Marx, K. (1964) *The economic and philosophical manuscripts of 1844.* New York: International Publishers. (Original work published 1932.)

Matza, D. and Wellman, D. (1980) The ordeal of consciousness. *Theory and Society,* 9: 1–28.

Morgan, G. (1984) Opportunities arising from paradigm diversity. *Administration and Society,* 16: 306–327.

Morgan, G. and Smircich, L. (1980) The case for qualitative research. *Academy of Management Review,* 5: 491–500.

Nord, W. (1977) A Marxist critique of humanistic psychology. *Journal of Humanistic Psychology,* 17: 75–83.

Poole, R. (1972) *Towards deep subjectivity.* New York: Harper Torchbooks.

Sartre, J-P. (1963) *Search for a method.* New York: Knopf. (Original work published 1960.)

Sartre, J-P. (1976) *Critique of dialectical reason.* London: NLB. (Original work published 1960.)

Weick, K.E. (1979) Cognitive processes in organizations. In B.M. Staw (Ed.), *Research in organizational behavior:* 1: 41–74. Greenwich, CT: JAI Press.

Discussion Questions

1. Why is identity so important to human beings but also of significance for organizations?
2. Is the search for a secure identity never ending?
3. Why are industrial workers always seeking to escape from work?
4. Do you think that a concern for identity and belonging is one of the more effective tools in managing change and innovation?

Introduction References

Alvesson, M. and Willmott, H.C. (2002) 'Identity regulation as organizational control: producing the appropriate individual' *Journal of Management Studies,* Vol. 39, No. 5: 619–44.

Bergström, O. and Knights, D. (2006) Organizational discourse and subjectivity: subjectification during processes of recruitment, *Human Relations,* Vol. 59, No. 3: 351–377.

Foucault, M. (1973) *The Order of Things: An Archaeology of the Human Sciences,* New York: Vintage Books.

Knights, D. (1992) 'Changing spaces: the disruptive power of epistemological location for the management and organisational sciences', *Academy of Management Review,* Vol. 17, No. 3: 514–36.

Knights, D. (2002) 'Writing organization analysis into Foucault', *Organization,* Vol. 9, No. 4: 575–93.

McKinley, A. and Starkey, K. (editors) (1998) *Foucault, Management and Organization Theory,* London: Sage.

Townley, B. and Foucalt, M. (1993) 'Power/knowledge, and its relevance to human resource management', *Academy of Management Review,* Vol. 18, No. 3: 518–45.

Recommended Further Readings

See references for Knights and Willmott, and Jermier above plus:

Ainsworth, S. and Hardy, C. (2004) 'Critical discourse analysis and identity: why bother?', *Critical Discourse Studies* Vol. 1, No. 2: 225–59.

Alvesson, M. and Willmott, H. (2002) Identity regulation as organizational control: producing the appropriate individual, *Journal of Management Studies* Vol. 39, No. 5: 619–44.

Casey, C. (1995) *Work, Self and Society: After Industrialism*, London and New York: Routledge.

Fineman, S. (1993) *Emotion in Organisations*, London: Sage.

Dorinne, K. (1990) *Crafting Selves*, Chicago: University of Chicago Press.

Pullen, A., Beech, N. and Sims, D. (2007) *Exploring Identity*, London: Palgrave Macmillan.

CONSUMPTION

CHAPTER **13**

READINGS

Bauman, Z. (1998) 'From the Work Ethic to the Aesthetic of Consumption' in *Work, Consumerism and the New Poor.* Maidenhead: Open University Press. pp. 23–6, 30–2.

Knights, D. and Morgan, G. (1994) 'Organisation Theory, Consumption and the Service Sector' in *Towards a New Theory of Organizations.* Edited by J. Hassard, and M. Parker. London: Sage. pp. 134–9.

Du Gay, P. (1996) *Consumption and Identity at Work.* London: Sage. pp. 80–82; 87–8; 191–2.

INTRODUCTION

There is little question that our contemporary society is preoccupied with consumption but the significance of this for the critical study of organizations is not always clear. The literature displays a very wide range of theoretical ideas and criticisms of consumer society. Critiques of mass consumption see it as little more than the manipulation of an industrial labour force looking for some meaningful escape from the drudgery of their work. Cultural theorists especially of the postmodern variety, on the other hand, are just as likely to celebrate consumption as evidence of an everyday popular aesthetic. Some of the literature focuses primarily on the consumer, discussing whether she or he is sovereign or victim, hedonist or addicted. Each of these stereotypes of the consumer is of course linked to political or social theories about our consumer society. The consumer is king thesis reflects and reinforces the competition model of neo-classical economics. Consumers here are rational and utilitarian in their consumerism and their power in conditions of competition is expected to stimulate economic efficiency on the part of suppliers of goods and services. Both hedonist and addictive conceptions of consumers are largely indicative of a Freudian influence. For the hedonist, consumption is seen to be the outcome of a battle in which Eros and the pleasure loving and sexual desires of the id are victorious against the repressive constraints of social conscience, morality and civilization represented by the super-ego. For the addictive, whether it takes the form of shopping binges, kleptomania or merely keeping up with the Joneses, consumption is seen to be the distorted outcome of repressed desires, usually sexual ones. However, more recently a range of postmodern theories have colonized this perspective as they have stressed the symbolic significance of consumption as a system of signs and signifiers in perpetual circulation, and attached and detached from individuals as they seek or discard particular identities. It is clear that we construct and sustain our identities out of the products we consume, although such identity work has to be seen as less to do with the product itself than the fact that certain other people with whom we identify also consume such products. Consumption, whether it is of a style of music, leisure, sport or material artefacts such as cars, homes or clothes is then a statement of who we are and whether or not we can claim membership of this or that social circle, club, status group, or class. Describing our current consumerism as a way of life, Miles (1998: 151) follows Bauman (1988) in seeing consumption as forging a new concept of freedom. Those who are 'seduced' by consumption experience their ability to choose among a vast range of products liberating and for a large number of people this contrasts sharply with the world of work, where they are often subjected to super-ordinate controls. This liberation, however, is restricted to those with the material resources to participate in the consumer society. It can equally be seen as 'repressive' for those whose limited resources exclude them from consuming as a way of life. These people find themselves not only marginalized by the preoccupation with consumption but also dependent for their limited resources on basic 'handouts' from the state.

An alternative to the view of consumption as liberation is to see the consumer as a victim of the manipulations of corporate capitalism that depends for its unceasing demand for profit on ever increasing levels of consumption. This argument derives largely from a neo-Marxist perception wherein consumption is seen simply as conformity with the social controls of the capitalist machine or as an illusory substitute for the lost relationship between labourers and their products perpetrated by the commodity system of production.

It is the influence of Marxism that has perhaps kept subordinated discourses of consumption to a marginal role in organization theory. As simply a part of the cultural superstructure that is determined by the economic infrastructure, consumption is of interest only insofar as it fulfils the demands of production to realize surplus value. To some extent, this perception was easier to sustain when manufacturing was dominant and more importantly when effective demand exceeded supply. Marx was aware of the reversal of this supply–demand relationship as the productive capacity of capitalism increased exponentially with the growth of new technology and mass production facilities. But it was not until service industries and the service side of manufacturing way exceeded material production in terms of economic value and levels of employment that the importance of consumption for organizations could no longer be ignored. For what this phenomenon revealed was the close relationship between production and consumption because in the service industries, it could be claimed, production invariably only takes place at the point of consumption. This immediately blurs the boundary between organization and the market and it is clear that to analyse an organization independently of the market, or as if the consumer were entirely 'other' would be highly misleading.

In the first extract (Reading 13.1), **Zygmunt Bauman** provides us with an elaboration of the development of what we now call our 'consumer society'. He contrasts this with what he believes was during its industrial phase a 'producer society' where people were engaged primarily in production and almost everything that was important was dictated by the need to produce. By contrast, in the consumer society people's lives are much more dictated by the need to consume and to secure their identities through this process (see the Jermier extract in the Identity section, Chapter 12). Bauman makes it clear that living in a consumer society does not mean the demise of production for after all we could not consume unless 'things' were produced. It is just a matter of emphasis wherein the central focus attached to production in the previous era is now displaced by the importance of consumption. Two features about this emphasis on consumption are distinctive, according to Bauman. One is the transitory, impermanent and volatile nature of consumption such that there is an almost insatiable appetite of serially promiscuous proportions for consuming different goods. Second is the individual or solitary character of consumption compared with the more collective nature of production. Bauman goes as far as to claim that consumers are even alone when they consume together. Consumer choice has become the measure of all values and differentiations in a consumer society and, in contrast to the ethical norms of the producer society, the driving force is aesthetic interests. The consumer world is an 'immense matrix of possibilities', of new albeit transitory sensations and pleasures.

David Knights and Glenn Morgan (Reading 13.2) argue that although throughout its history organization analysis has generally been parasitic on social theory, by focusing on consumption and subjectivity, it could make a significant contribution to debates about the changing nature of modern consumer society. They begin by providing a sympathetic yet critical examination of the analysis of how subjectivities are constituted in organizational life by the social theorists Miller and Rose. Their conclusion is that these authors firstly concentrate too heavily on theoretical or systematized bodies of knowledge rather than informal knowledge. It is often through knowledge that is not formally represented in the career or authority structures of an organization that both localized constitutions of subjectivity and resistance to particular identities take place. Secondly, Miller and Rose focus largely on the construction of subjectivity within the organization, thus ignoring the relationship between producers and consumers of goods and services. Yet it is through their market research that organizations are heavily involved in constructing the subjectivity of those that consume their products and services. Moreover, in our consumer society, commodities are consumed not merely for their material use but also for their symbolic value in creating and sustaining identities. Thirdly, Knights and Morgan argue that informal knowledge and consumption are not entirely distinct in practice. This is particularly so in the service industries and especially some financial services such as insurance where production only really takes place at the point of consumption. Consequently, in the fastest-growing sector of the economy, it is argued, there is a complex interpenetration of subjectivity, knowledge and consumption.

Paul du Gay (Reading 13.3) follows a similar line to the previous reading in arguing that the traditional distinction between production and consumption has broken down largely as a result of what he calls a new political rhetoric of entrepreneurialism, workplace reform and organizational innovation. The extract begins with an account of traditional representations of consumption within organizational analysis or industrial sociology. He describes the Marxist subordination of consumption to production with its depiction of consumers simply seeking to compensate for their 'alienated' conditions of work by consuming the products from which they have been alienated. He then turns to the Frankfurt school of critical theory and their mass culture thesis where consumers are treated as cultural dopes whose meaning constructions are wholly vulnerable to the exploit(ations) of capitalist determination. Du Gay draws on cultural theorists and postmodernists to critique these Marxian inspired views. Both sets of theory are based on the philosophical anthropology that identifies human creativity and self-expression as residing first and foremost in material production within the workplace. Even were that a plausible thesis to hold at the time of its assertion and there are obvious criticisms of its essentialism (i.e. a fundamental of human nature regardless of social and historical context), contemporary life renders it exceedingly outdated. Many have objected to the Marxian portrayal of the worker as a passive victim but it was Foucault (1982) who highlighted a central contradiction when he pointed to the distinction between power and domination. If the behaviour of the target of power could be determined, he argues, there would be no need for power since the latter is only exercised upon 'free' subjects whether in production or consumption. Recalcitrance and resistance on the part of labour and consumers is what makes management and marketing an expensive and knowledge-intensive business. Cultural theorists have tended to object more to the portrayal of the consumer as passive but, as du Gay points out, their activating of the consumer is at the expense of a continuing attachment to the Marxist view of the alienated worker. Finally our extract draws from the conclusion of the book where du Gay criticizes the ideology of the entrepreneurial forms of government and of the self that has begun to dominate contemporary life.

| READING 13.1 | ## From the Work Ethic to the Aesthetic of Consumption |

By Zygmunt Bauman

Ours is a consumer society. We all know, more or less, what it means to be a 'consumer'. A consumer is a person who consumes, and to consume means using things up: eating them, wearing them, playing with them and otherwise causing them to satisfy one's needs or desires. Since in our part of the world it is money which in most cases 'mediates' between desire and its satisfaction, being a consumer also means – normally means – appropriating most of the things destined to be consumed: buying them, paying for

them and so making them one's exclusive property, barring everybody else from using them without one's permission.

To consume also means to destroy. In the course of consumption, the consumed things cease to exist, literally or spiritually. Either they are 'used up' physically to the point of complete annihilation, such as when things are eaten or worn out, or they are stripped of their allure, no longer arouse and attract desire, and forfeit their capacity to satisfy one's

READING 13.1 | # From the Work Ethic to the Aesthetic of Consumption

By Zygmunt Bauman

needs and wishes – for example, an overused toy or an overplayed record – and so become unfit for consumption.

This is what being a consumer means, but what do we mean when we speak of a consumer society. Is there something special about being a consumer in a consumer society? And besides, is not every known society a society of consumers, to a greater or lesser extent? All the features listed in the preceding paragraph, except perhaps the need to pay money for things meant to be consumed, are surely present in any kind of society. Of course, what sort of objects we see as the potential stuff of consumption, and how we consume them, may differ from time to time and from one place to another, but no human being anywhere or at any time can stay alive without consuming.

And so when we say that ours is a 'consumer society' we must have in mind something more than the trivial, ordinary and not particularly illuminating fact that all members of that society consume. Ours is a 'consumer society' in a similarly profound and fundamental sense in which the society of our predecessors (modern society in its industrial phase described in the previous chapter) used to deserve the name of a 'producer society' in spite of the fact that people have produced since the beginning of the human species and will go on producing until the species' demise. The reason for calling that older type of modern society a 'producer society' was that it engaged its members primarily as producers; the way in which that society shaped up its members was dictated by the need to play this role and the norm that society held up to its members was the ability and the willingness to play it.

In its present late-modern, second-modern or post-modern stage, society engages its members – again primarily – in their capacity as consumers. The way present-day society shapes up its members is dictated first and foremost by the need to play the role of the consumer, and the norm our society holds up to its members is that of the ability and willingness to play it. The difference between then and now is not as radical as abandoning one role and replacing it with another. Neither of the two societies could do without at least some of its members taking charge of producing things to be consumed, and all members

of both societies do, of course, consume. The difference is one of emphasis, but that shift of emphasis does make an enormous difference to virtually every aspect of society, culture and individual life. The differences are so deep and ubiquitous that they fully justify speaking of our society as a society of a separate and distinct kind – a consumer society.

The passage from producer to consumer society has entailed many profound changes; arguably the most decisive among them is, however, the fashion in which people are groomed and trained to meet the demands of their social identities (that is, the fashion in which men and women are 'integrated' into the social order and given a place in it). Panoptical institutions, once crucial in that respect, have fallen progressively out of use. With mass industrial employment fast shrinking and universal military duty replaced with small, voluntary and professional armies, the bulk of the population is unlikely ever to come under their direct influence. Technological progress has reached the point where productivity grows together with the tapering of employment; factory crews get leaner and slimmer; 'downsizing' is the new principle of modernization. As the editor of the *Financial Times*, Martin Wolf calculates between 1970 and 1994 the proportion of people employed in industry fell from 30 per cent to 20 per cent in the European Union and from 28 per cent to 16 per cent in the USA, while industrial productivity progressed on average by 2.5 per cent per annum.[1]

The kind of drill in which the panoptical institutions excelled is hardly suitable for the training of consumers. Those institutions were good at training people in routine, monotonous behaviour, and reached that effect through the limitation or complete elimination of choice; but it is precisely the absence of routine and the state of constant choice that are the virtues (indeed, the 'role prerequisites') of a consumer. And so, in addition to being much reduced in the post-industrial and post-conscription world, the panoptical drill is also irreconcilable with the needs of a consumer society. The qualities of temperament and life attitudes which the panoptical drill excels in cultivating are counter-productive in the production of ideal consumers.

From the Work Ethic to the Aesthetic of Consumption *continued*

By Zygmunt Bauman

Ideally, acquired habits should lie on the shoulders of the consumers just like the religiously/ethically inspired vocational and acquisitive passions used to lie, as Max Weber repeated after Baxter, on the shoulders of the protestant saint: 'like a light cloak, ready to be thrown aside at any moment'.[2] And habits are indeed continually, daily, at the first opportunity thrown aside, never given the chance to solidify into the iron bars of a cage. Ideally, nothing should be embraced by a consumer firmly, nothing should command a commitment forever, no needs should be ever seen as fully satisfied, no desires considered ultimate. There ought to be a proviso 'until further notice' attached to any oath of loyalty and any commitment. It is the volatility, the in-built temporariness of all engagement that counts; it counts more than the engagement itself, which should not outlast the time necessary for consuming the object of desire (or for the desirability of that object to wane).

That all consumption takes time is in fact the bane of a consumer society and a major worry of the merchandisers of consumer goods. Ideally, the consumer's satisfaction ought to be instant, and this in a double sense. Consumed goods should bring satisfaction immediately, requiring no delay, no protracted learning of skills and no lengthy groundwork; but the satisfaction should end the moment the time needed for their consumption is up, and that time ought to be reduced to a bare minimum. This reduction is best achieved if the consumers cannot hold their attention nor focus their desire on any object for long; if they are impatient, impetuous and restive, and above all easily excitable and equally susceptible to losing interest.

When waiting is taken out of wanting and wanting out of waiting, the consumptive capacity of consumers may be stretched far beyond the limits set by any natural or acquired needs or determined by the physical endurability of the objects of desire. The traditional relationship between needs and their satisfaction will then be reversed: the promise and hope of satisfaction will precede the need and will be always greater than the extant need, yet not too great to preclude the desire for the goods which carry that promise. As a matter of fact, the promise is all the more attractive the less the need in question is familiar; there is a lot of fun in living through an experience one did not even know existed and was available. The excitement of the new and unprecedented sensation is the name of the consumer game. As Mark C. Taylor and Esa Saarinen put it, 'desire does not desire satisfaction. To the contrary, desire desires desire';[3] the desire of an ideal consumer at any rate. The prospect of the desire fading off, dissipating and having nothing in sight to resurrect it, or the prospect of a world with nothing left in it to be desired, must be the most sinister of the ideal consumer's horrors.

To increase their capacity for consumption, consumers must never be given rest. They need to be constantly exposed to new temptations in order to be kept in a state of a constantly seething, never wilting excitation and, indeed, in a state of suspicion and disaffection. The baits commanding them to shift attention need to confirm such suspicion while offering a way out of disaffection: 'You reckon you've seen it all. You ain't seen nothing yet!' It is often said that the consumer market seduces its customers. But in order to do so it needs customers who are ready and keen to be seduced (just as, in order to command his labourers, the factory boss needed a crew with the habits of discipline and command-following firmly entrenched). In a properly working consumer society consumers seek actively to be seduced. They live from attraction to attraction, from temptation to temptation, from swallowing one bait to fishing for another, each new attraction, temptation and bait being somewhat different and perhaps stronger than those that preceded them; just as their ancestors, the producers, lived from one turn of the conveyer belt to an identical next.

To act like that is, for the fully-fledged, mature consumer, a compulsion, a must; yet that 'must', that internalized pressure, that impossibility of living one's life in any other way, reveals itself to them in the form of a free exercise of will. The market might have already picked them up and groomed them as consumers, and so deprived them of their freedom to ignore its temptations, but on every successive visit to a market place, consumers have every reason to feel in command. They are the judges, the critics and the choosers. They can, after all, refuse their allegiance to

READING 13.1

From the Work Ethic to the Aesthetic of Consumption

By Zygmunt Bauman

any one of the infinite choices on display – except the choice of choosing between them, that is. The roads to self-identity, to a place in society, to life lived in a form recognizable as that of meaningful living, all require daily visits to the market place.

In the industrial phase of modernity one fact was beyond all questioning: that everyone must be a producer first, before being anything else. In 'modernity mark two', the consumers' modernity, the brute unquestionable fact is that one needs to be consumer first, before one can think of becoming anything in particular. ...

Work as Judged by Aesthetics

Producers can fulfil their vocation only collectively; production is a collective endeavour, it presumes the division of tasks, cooperation of actors and coordination of their activities. Certain partial actions can be performed on occasion singly and in solitude, but even then dovetailing them with other actions, which converge on the creation of the final product remains the crucial part of the task and stays high on the performer's mind. Producers are together even when they act apart. The work of each one can only gain from more inter-individual communication, harmony and integration.

Consumers are just the opposite. Consumption is a thoroughly individual, solitary and, in the end, lonely activity; an activity which is fulfilled by quenching and arousing, assuaging and whipping up a desire which is always a private, and not easily communicable sensation. There is no such thing as 'collective consumption'. True, consumers may get together in the course of consumption, but even then the actual consumption remains a thoroughly lonely, individually lived-through experience. Getting together only underlies the privacy of the consuming act and enhances its pleasures.

Choosing is more satisfying when performed in the company of other choosers, preferably inside a temple dedicated to the cult of choosing and filled to the brim with worshippers of choice; this is one of the foremost pleasures of going out to dinner in a heavily booked-up restaurant, of milling around a crowded shopping mall or amusement park, of group sex. But what is jointly celebrated in all these and similar cases is the individuality of choice and

consumption. The individuality of each choice is restated and reconfirmed through being replicated by the copy-cat actions of the crowd of choosers. Were this not so, there would be nothing to be gained by the consumer from consuming in company. The activity of consumption is a natural enemy of all coordination and integration. It is also immune to their influence, rendering all efforts of bonding impotent in overcoming the endemic loneliness of the consuming act. Consumers are alone even when they act together.

Freedom to choose sets the stratification ladder of consumer society and so also the frame in which its members, the consumers, inscribe their life aspirations – a frame that denies the direction of efforts towards self-improvement and encloses the image of a 'good life'. The more freedom of choice one has, and above all the more choice one freely exercises, the higher up one is placed in the social hierarchy, the more public deference and self-esteem one can count on and the closer one comes to the 'good life' ideal. Wealth and income do count, of course; without them, choice is limited or altogether denied. But the role of wealth and income as capital – that is, money which serves first and foremost to turn out more money – recedes to a second and inferior place if it does not disappear from view (and from the pool of motivations) altogether. The prime significance of wealth and income is in the stretching of the range of consumer choice.

Hoarding, saving or investing would make sense solely for the promise they hold for the future widening of consumer choice. They are not, however, the options intended for the bulk of ordinary consumers, and were they embraced by a majority of consumers, they would spell disaster. Rising savings and shrinking credit purchases are bad news; the swelling of consumer credit is welcomed as the sure sign of 'things moving in the right direction'. A consumer society would not take lightly a call to delay gratification. A consumer society is a society of credit cards, not savings books. It is a 'now' society. A wanting society, not a waiting society.

Again, there is no need for 'normative regulation' with its attendant disciplining drill and ubiquitous policing to make sure that human wants are harnessed to

READING 13.1

From the Work Ethic to the Aesthetic of Consumption *continued*

By Zygmunt Bauman

the market-operators' profits, or any need to reforge the 'needs of economy', the consumer-goods economy, to match the desires of consumers. Seduction, display of untested wonders, promise of sensations yet untried but dwarfing and overshadowing everything tried before, will do nicely. Providing of course, that the message falls on receptive ears and that all eyes are focused on thrill-presaging things when scanning the signals. Consumption, ever more varied and rich consumption, must appear to the consumers as a right to enjoy, not a duty to suffer. The consumers must be guided by aesthetic interests, not ethical norms.

It is aesthetics, not ethics, that is deployed to integrate the society of consumers, keep it on course, and time and again salvage it from crises. If ethics accord supreme value to duty well done, aesthetics put a premium on sublime experience. Fulfilment of duty has its inner, time-extensive logic and so it structures time, gives it a direction, makes sense of such notions as gradual accumulation or delay of fulfilment. The search for experience, however, has no good reason to be postponed, since nothing but 'waste of opportunity' may follow the delay. Opportunity of experience does not need nor justify groundwork, since it comes unannounced and vanishes if not instantly grasped (waning, to be sure, shortly after having been grasped).

Opportunity of experience is something to be caught in full flight. There is no peculiar moment especially suitable for doing this. One moment does not differ in this respect from another, each moment is equally good – 'ripe' – for the purpose. Besides, the choice of the moment is the one choice not available to those who have chosen choice-making as their mode of life. It is not for the consumer to decide when the opportunity of a mind-boggling experience may arise, and so she or he must be ever ready to open the door and welcome it. He or she must be constantly on the alert, permanently capable of appreciating the chance when it comes and doing whatever is needed to make the best of it. If the producer society is Platonian by heart, seeking unbreakable rules and the ultimate patterns of things, the consumer society is Aristotelian – pragmatic, flexi-

ble, abiding by the principle that one worries about crossing the bridge no earlier (but no later either) than one comes to it. The sole initiative left to a sensible consumer is to be on that spot where opportunities are known to be thick on the ground, and be there at the time when they are known to be particularly dense. Such initiative can accommodate only wisdom of a 'phronesis' kind, a collection of rules of thumb, not foolproof recipes and algorithmic commands. Hence it requires a lot of trust, and above all it needs safe havens where that trust can be securely anchored. No wonder a consumer society is also a counselling and advertising paradise, as well as a fertile soil for prophets, fortune-tellers or pedlars of magic potions and distillers of philosophical stones.

To sum up: it is the aesthetics of consumption that now rules where the work ethic once ruled. For the successful alumni of consumer training the world is an immense matrix of possibilities, of intense and ever more intense sensations, of deep and deeper still experiences (in the sense conveyed by the German notion of Erlebnis, as distinct from Erfahrung; both German terms translate into English as 'experience'. Roughly speaking, Erlebnis is 'what I live through', while Erfahrung is 'what happens to me'). The world and all its fragments are judged by their capacity to occasion sensations and Erlebnisse – the capacity to arouse desire, the most pleasurable phase of the consumer's life pursuits, more satisfying than the satisfaction itself. It is by the varying volumes of that capacity that objects, events and people are plotted on the map; the world map in most frequent use is aesthetic, rather than cognitive or moral.[4]

[1] M. Wolf. (1997) Mais pourquoi cette haine des marchés, *Le Monde Diplomatique*, June, p. 15.

[2] M. Weber. (1976) *The Protestant Ethic and the Spirit of Capitalism*, trans. T. Parsons. London: George Allen & Unwin, p. 181.

[3] M.C. Taylor and E. Saarinen (n.d.) *Imagologies: Media Philosophy*. London: Routledge, Telerotics, p. 11.

[4] For the distinction between cognitive, aesthetic and moral spacings, see Z. Bauman (1993) *Postmodern Ethics*. Oxford: Blackwell.

| READING 13.2 | **Organisation Theory, Consumption and the Service Sector** |

By David Knights and Glenn Morgan

The paper is divided into three sections. First we develop our argument concerning the inter-relationship between organizations, consumption and subjectivity. Second, we seek to show that the issues we have uncovered are very pertinent to understanding how organizations are changing. We therefore present some of our research on financial services as a means of illustrating the argument. Informed by this analysis, the third section considers the implications of this approach for contemporary organizational research.

Organizations, Consumption and Subjectivity

Traditionally, the field of organization theory has been concerned with how organizations are internally organized in order to produce goods and services. From this perspective, a range of problems can arise depending on the particular approach taken. Thus, systems models develop ideas concerning the need to match structure to certain objectively determined characteristics of the internal and external environment. Power-based models analyse the role of domination and exploitation in the operation of management and the labour process. (The models and their many associated variants have been analysed *ad nauseam* in the textbooks e.g. Burrell and Morgan 1979, Gareth Morgan 1986). It would not be difficult to show how closely related the popularity of these models *within* organization theory has been to their popularity in the wider area of the social sciences.

However, over the last decade, there have emerged new perspectives on social relations which offer significant alternatives. In particular, there has been increased interest in the concept of subjectivity and its relation to concrete historical and social practices. In this view, we cannot talk of a 'transcendental subject', which possesses characteristics that are 'innately' human and beyond social and historical determination. Rather we have to understand discourses of 'subjectivity' as historical products and 'the subject as the constitutive product of a plurality of disciplinary mechanisms, techniques of surveillance and power-knowledge strategies' (Knights 1989: 319). Although this approach is predominantly associated with the writings of Foucault (especially Foucault 1979, 1980,

1982), there are strong resonances in the writings of Norbert Elias and Max Weber (see Elias 1978, on the relationship between Foucault and Weber, see O'Neill 1986, Dandeker 1990 ch. 1; see also Abercrombie, Hill and Turner 1986 for a sustained attempt to create an approach which synthesizes a number of these insights). In all these authors, it can be argued that a central concern is the way in which the 'modern subject' becomes constituted; whilst the emphasis is laid on different elements of this process, there is a shared concern with concrete historical discourses and practices, together with a recognition that organizations play a central role in these developments.

One of the most sustained attempts to use these ideas within the general sphere of organizational analysis has been that of Miller and Rose in a series of books and articles (Miller, 1987; Rose, 1990; Miller and Rose 1988). Through examining their arguments, it is possible to develop a more general approach to organizations and subjectivity. Miller and Rose examine management in terms of the creation of power–knowledge discourses and show how these processes develop in particular professional settings. In this view, the organization is crucially a sphere for the construction of subjectivities. So, for example, Miller indicates the importance that knowledge plays in Foucault's concern to account for the emergence of subjectivity. As he puts it, it is important first:

> to chart the structure of those knowledges, which seek to produce a knowledge of the subject. This is a question of those concepts central to a particular body of knowledge, and also of those mechanisms through which it operates (the doctor–patient relation for example). Secondly, a concern with the institutional framework through which such knowledges operate ... all institutions exist, one can argue, in intimate association with a complex body of theoretical knowledge ... Thirdly, there is what one might refer to as administrative or governmental programmes for the regulation of society as a whole.
> (Miller 1987: 216)

READING 13.2 | Organisation Theory, Consumption and the Service Sector *continued*

By David Knights and Glenn Morgan

While sympathetic to the general orientation of this approach to subjectivity and knowledge, our own view is that it only begins to be meaningful when related to '*particular* socio-historical contexts and localities' (Knights and Vurdubakis, 1991/3). It is difficult to speak about power, knowledge and subjectivity in a purely theoretical and abstract way as Miller attempts here, although elsewhere he does direct his analysis to concrete historical knowledges such as psychiatric practice (Miller 1986) and accounting technologies (Miller and O'Leary 1987). Although seeking to link more directly with specific, organizations, Rose follows a similar path:

> The management of subjectivity has become a central task for the modern organization ... To a greater or lesser extent, bosses, military commanders, educationalists and so on are now obliged to attend to the subjectivity of the employee, soldier or pupil in achieving their objectives.
> (Rose 1989: 2)

Rose goes on to associate this with the 'birth of a new form of expertise, an expertise of subjectivity'. He continues:

> The new languages for construing, understanding and evaluating ourselves and others have transformed the ways in which we interact with our bosses, employees, workmates, husbands, wives, lovers, mothers, fathers, children and friends. Our thought worlds have been reconstructed, our ways of thinking about and talking about our personal feelings, our secret hopes, our ambitions and disappointments. Our techniques for managing our emotions have been reshaped. Our very sense of ourselves has been revolutionized. We have become intensely subjective beings.
> (Rose 1989: 3)

In this approach, the study of organizations is no longer about the way in which commodities are produced; it is about how subjectivity is produced. Organizations do not so much produce 'things' as 'people'.

At present, this approach is still in its infancy in organization theory (see also Knights and Morgan 1991). In order to develop it, however, we need to make a number of amendments to Miller and Rose's presentation. First, as can be seen from the above quotations, Miller and Rose focus principally on theoretical or systematized bodies of knowledge (e.g. scientific management, the Tavistock programme, cost accounting, etc.). Thus they seek to show how particular constructions of subjectivity are embedded within or constituted through these discursive formations and practices. Consequently, they tend to ignore the development of 'informal knowledges' which, in our view, are particularly significant to the constitution of and resistance to any given subjectivity in specific localized settings. So, as we shall show in our presentation of empirical case study material below, 'informal knowledges' relating to gender 'competencies', selling and management styles grounded in conflicting masculinist cultures and the view that insurance is sold not bought, for example, have considerable effects upon relations and subjectivities both among staff and between them and their customers.

This relates directly to our second major concern with Miller and Rose's work. Notwithstanding Miller's reference to the doctor–patient relation above, they tend to concentrate on the subjects constructed *within* the organization. However, we would argue that just as important is how organizations construct the subjectivity of those who consume their products. Here, our argument draws on those analysts of consumption who have examined how we utilize commodities as signs of what and who we are.

Commodities and services are exchanged not merely because they contribute to our material existence; in a consumer society like our own, symbolic value is equally (if not more) important. This is a complex process which involves active participation on the part of the consumer *but* it is generated principally by discourses and knowledges produced inside the organization. The sale and marketing of commodities and services is constructed in ways which embody particular ideas about who is the 'normal consumer'. By buying particular commodities and services, we buy into these ideas. We are constituted as particular subjects

READING 13.2	**Organisation Theory, Consumption and the Service Sector**

By David Knights and Glenn Morgan

by our consumption of the products of the organization (for an extended review of literature which develops this point, see Morgan and Knights 1991).

Thirdly, we would want to argue that these informal knowledges and consumption processes are not distinct. Here, our argument draws on those analyses of the modern economy which note the importance of the shift from manufacturing to service industries. In service industries, production actually takes place at the point of consumption when the service consumed is provided by another person(s). As Urry puts it, 'the production of services involves some interaction between producers and consumers at the point of production' (Urry 1990: 68). As a result, the subjectivities of the producers and consumers are inevitably interdependent. The employees work directly under the gaze and inspection of their customers, whilst the experience of the customers is directly dependent on the activity of those serving them. In other words, not only must we develop an understanding of the subjectivities of employees *and* consumers, but as far as the service sector is concerned, we must focus on the interpenetration of the two – the simultaneous moment of production and consumption which constitutes the service (see Urry 1990: 68).

To summarize our argument, then, we agree with Miller and Rose that it is fruitful to consider how subjectivities are constituted within organizational settings. This involves us considering how power–knowledge practices operate to construct normal modes of behaviour that are subject to governmentality. Where we would seek to expand the model is in first defining 'knowledges' more widely to include the 'informal knowledges' that are developed within organizations about normality and deviance; in then considering how subjectivities are constituted through all the practices associated with the consumption of commodities and, finally, through focusing on the point of interaction between producers and consumers.

One of the dangers of this sort of analysis of subjects is its potential crudity and totalizing nature, so we have to put in a big caveat at this point. To say that organizations constitute subjectivity, whether of their employees or of their consumers, is not to say that the subjective identity of any one individual can be 'read' off from the organization in which that individual

works or the objects he or she consumes. Rather, the constitution of subjectivity through organizations is better understood as referring to fields of power and discipline that are generated within certain contexts. Thus, particular forms of subjectivity are the power effects of knowledge and practice generated in these specific contexts. Since there are many such fields of power, none of which overrides or acts as a 'totalizing' influence on the rest, the subjective identity of distinct individuals is a much more complex construction than is the constitution of particular forms of subjectivity or categories of subject such as bank clerk, manager, sales representative or bank customer. From the organizational point of view, what is of interest is the nature of the subjectivities which are constituted both within the organization and through the sale and/or exchange of the organization's products.

In the discussion so far we have tried to show how organization theory can develop a new agenda for research that is parasitic on key themes emerging in other social and cultural sciences. We have emphasized in particular the need to consider the role of organizations in the construction of subjectivities. We have shown how this is linked to the need for increased attention to the sphere of consumption and how both of these features enable us to be more sensitive to the issues of an emerging service economy.

References

Abercrombie, N., Hill, S. and Turner, B. (1986) *Sovereign Individuals of Capitalism*, London: Allen & Unwin.

Burrell, G. and Morgan, G. (1979) *Sociological Paradigms and Organizational Analysis*, London: Heinemann.

Dandeker, C. (1990) *Surveillance Power and Modernity*, Cambridge: Polity Press.

Elias, N. (1978) *The Civilizing Process* Vol. 1, Oxford: Blackwell.

Foucault, M. (1979) *Discipline and Punish*, Harmondsworth, UK: Penguin.

Foucault, M. (1980) *Power/Knowledge: Selected Interviews and other Writings 1972–77*, translated and edited by C. Gordon, London: Tavistock

Foucault, M. (1982) 'The Subject and Power' in H.L. Dreyfus and P. Rabinow, *Beyond Structuralism and Hermeneutics*, Brighton: Sussex Harvester Press, pp. 208–226.

| READING 13.2 | **Organisation Theory, Consumption and the Service Sector** *continued* |

By David Knights and Glenn Morgan

Knights, D. (1989) 'Intervention and Change' in M.C. Jackson, P. Keys and S.A. Cropper, eds., *Operational Research and the Social Sciences*, New York: Plenum Press, (1989), pp. 287–293.

Knights, D. and Morgan G. (1991) 'Subjectivity and the Labour Process in Selling Life Insurance' in C. Smith, D. Knights and H. Willmott, editors, *The Non-manual Labour Process*, London: Macmillan, pp. 217–240.

Knights, D. and Vurdubakis, T. (1991) 'Calculations of Risk: Towards an Understanding of Insurance as a Moral and Political Technology', Unpublished paper later published in *Accounting, Organisations and Society*, Vol. 19, No. 7/8 1993, pp. 729–764.

Miller, P. (1986) 'Psychotherapy of Work and Unemployment', in P. Miller and N. Rose (eds) *The Power of Psychiatry*, Cambridge: Polity Press.

Miller, P. (1987) *Power and Domination*, London: Routledge & Kegan Paul.

Miller, P. and O'Leary, T. (1987) 'On the Role of Governmentality in Accounting', *Accounting, Organizations and Society*.

Miller, P. and Rose, N. (1988) 'The Tavistock Programme: The Government of Subjectivity and Social Life', *Sociology* 22, (2): 179–92.

Morgan, G. (1983) *Beyond Method: Strategies for Social Research*, Beverly Hills, California: Sage.

Morgan, G. (1986) *Images of Organization*, London: Sage.

Morgan, G. and Knights, D. (1991) 'Constructing Consumer Protection: The Case of the Life Insurance Industry', in R. Burrows and C. Marsh (eds) *Consumption and Class: Divisions and Change*, London: Macmillan.

O'Neill, J. (1986) 'The Disciplinary Society: From Weber to Foucault', *British Journal of Sociology* 37, (1): 42–60.

Rose, M. (1975) *Industrial Behaviour: Theoretical Developments Since Taylor*, London: Allan Lane.

Rose, M. (1988) *Industrial Behaviour: Research and Control*, London: Penguin.

Rose, N. (1988) 'Calculate Minds and Manageable Individuals', *History of the Human Sciences*, 1, (2): 179–200.

Rose, N. (1990) *Governing the Soul: The Shaping of the Private Self*, London: Routledge.

Rose, N. (1990a) 'Psychology as "Social" Science', in I. Parker and J. Shotter (eds) *Deconstructing Social Psychology*, London: Routledge.

Urry, J. (1990) *The Tourist Gaze*, London: Sage.

| READING 13.3 | **Extract from *Consumption and Identity at Work*** |

By Paul du Gay, Journal of Management Studies, 29/4: 616–33.

Traditional Representations of Consumption

For what seems like an inordinate length of time, sociologists in general, and industrial sociologists in particular, have observed that work is not 'the central life interest' of the majority of men and women in paid employment in modern Western societies (Mills, 1953; Dubin, 1962; Goldthorpe *et al.*, 1969; Fox, 1980). However, while this observation has achieved a somewhat normative status within the social sciences, it has not led to any significant changes in the central research interests of industrial sociologists. On the whole, the sociology of work and employment has remained firmly wedded to a 'productionist' orientation whereby the 'public' realm of paid work is represented as *the* vital existential sphere in contrast to the 'private' sphere of the domestic, of consumption and leisure. Once again, the influence of 'alienation' can be detected in the marginalization of consumption from the research agenda.

As various commentators have argued (Goldthorpe *et al.*, 1969; Moorhouse, 1989; Pateman, 1989), the continued attachment of many sociologists to an old philosophical anthropology of production to a devaluation in all forms of 'self-creation' that take place outside the workplace. In other words, while many sociologists point to the growing importance of consumption to people's sense of who they are, because they have incorporated a Marxist emphasis

READING 13.3

Extract from *Consumption and Identity at Work*

By Paul du Gay, Journal of Management Studies, 29/4: 616–33.

on labour as the only 'real' site of human self-constitution, they tend to view consumption simply as an arena where 'alienated' workers attain derisory compensations for their lack of self-actualization in work; an overriding concern with consumption is thereby seen to reflect the subject's fundamental 'alienation' in work.

In this type of critique – articulated most famously perhaps in the work of critical theorists such as Marcuse (1964) – it is because the worker is 'not at home' in 'his' work, because 'work is a calamity', that 'he' can only find satisfaction in the sphere of non-work, in the 'false', 'passive needs of personal consumption and domestic life' (Gorz, 1965: 16–17). Furthermore, consumers are regarded as fully determined by capital. Consumer desires and needs are 'created' by producers through the medium of advertising and market research and then 'satisfied' by the goods and services provided by those same producers. There is no sign of 'dislocation' here; consumers simply follow to the letter of the law a script pre-written by capital. Their very 'needs' and 'wants' are created by the market and through the manipulation of 'public opinion' by the mass media controlled by capital. In the emergent homogeneous mass culture, therefore, all material culture is reduced to the status of 'commodity', while the people that live in and through that object-world are constituted as alienated, 'passive' consumers.

Because consumption is completely determined by production in this account, there is no room for 'human agency'. 'Structure' predominates to such an extent that the universe appears to be nothing more than a self-regulating totality (Laclau, 1990: 51–2). However, it is with just such a conception of a self-regulating totality that the logic of dislocation breaks. If the category of 'production' only has meaning in relation to the category of 'consumption', if it can only constitute itself in relation to an 'outside', then production cannot fully determine consumption in the manner suggested in the mass culture critique. Rather consumption both denies the identity of production and provides its condition of possibility at one and the same time. After all, if production saturated consumption there would be no need for the term 'manipulation' in the language of the mass culture critique (Miller, 1987: 166). As Foucault (1982)

argued, 'power' can only be exercised where there is freedom; to be successful in making others act in accordance with one's own wishes one requires knowledge of their motives. The fact that producers do not completely dominate consumers but must ceaselessly attempt to exercise power over them is attested by the development of motivation research as a part of modern marketing and advertising techniques (Mort, 1989). Activity under this heading is largely directed towards delineating the dreams, desires and aspirations of consumers. In other words, the cultural intermediaries of advertising, design and market research don't attempt to manipulate 'consumers' *per se*, but rather the *symbolic meanings* which are attached to products.

In his early work, for example, Baudrillard (1988: 45) exposed the essentialist conception of human nature underlying the mass culture critique by indicating ways in which the products of human labour are not aimed at the fulfilment of 'fundamental', transparent, 'needs' which lie at the basis of the materiality of humanity, but constitute a system of signs that differentiate the population:

> if we acknowledge that a need is not a need for a particular object as much as it is a 'need' for difference (the desire for social meaning), only then will we understand that satisfaction can never be *fuelled,* and consequently that there can never be *a definition* of needs.

Similarly, Campbell (1987: 48) argues that the mass culture critique rests upon an assumption that consumption is and must always be a rational process. Therefore, in so far as 'emotion', 'imagination' and 'desire' enter into the processes through which objects are consumed by individuals then ideological 'mystification' and 'exploitation' must be at work. By projecting a unidimensional evaluation of consumption in terms of the rational calculation of 'needs', the mass culture critique is unable to delineate the dynamic cultural logic at the heart of modem consumerism. For if 'consumerism' is founded on 'desire', as Baudrillard suggests, and 'desire' can never be realized because it fulfils no possibility and has no content, then it is impossibility which 'drives' modern consumption; consumption is dynamic because

READING 13.3   **Extract from *Consumption and Identity at Work***
continued

By Paul du Gay, Journal of Management Studies, 29/4: 616–33.

disillusionment is the necessary concomitant of the acquisition of goods longed for in fantasy.

The traditional critique cannot grasp this fundamental tension. Rather than being unproblematically focused and directed at the object and the intrinsic satisfaction it might bring, 'consumer behaviour' in fact 'responds to quite different objectives: the metaphoric or displaced expression of desire, and the production of a code of social values through the use of differentiating signs' (Baudrillard, 1988: 46) …

Both subcultural analysis and the more recent 'pleasures of consumption' thesis have involved not inconsiderable gains over both the 'structural pessimism' of the mass culture critique and over those theories that conceptualize consumption simply in terms of social differentiation. They have done this through, for example, insisting on seeing social subjects as active agents in the process of their own self-constitution and in indicating how *bricolage* cuts across given social divisions to produce hybrid identities. However, and unsurprisingly, both these explorations of consumption also bear interpretive costs. In particular, as a number of critics have argued (Williamson, 1986; Morris, 1988; Clarke, 1991), from the quite plausible (if increasingly banal) premise that consumption practices cannot be derived from or reduced to a mirror of production – that consumers make meanings in reception and do not simply 'receive' and 'ingest' sent messages – many studies appear to end up disconnecting consumption entirely from the forces and relations of production.

Having rescued consumption from the pessimism of the mass culture critique, certain forms of cultural analysis end up inverting the errors of earlier accounts. Instead of representing consumer behaviour through an exclusively productionist frame, these accounts project a vision of consumption practices as inherently democratic and implicitly 'subversive'. As Williamson (1986: 14–15) has argued, the blatant populism of the 'pleasures of consumption' thesis leads to the virtual abandonment of any form of critical distance: all consumer behaviour becomes imbued with a romantic glow of creativity leaving no room for questions of textual quality and the 'privileged creativity necessary for the production of cultural texts and artefacts' (Willis, 1990: 153).

In effect, through attempting to indicate that the cultural forms and meanings of consumption are not reducible to class and the economic – 'that consumerism doesn't simply mirror production' (Nava, 1987: 209) – cultural analysis ends up treating consumption 'as a quasi-autonomous reality diverging from another "reality" called "production" – which after Marxism, we are supposed to know quite enough about for the time being' (Morris, 1988: 21). However, if, for example, the 'economic' itself is not reducible to 'class and the economic' as traditionally conceived; if 'economic activity' is itself 'cultural', as suggested in Chapters 2 and 3, then such a division between production and consumption cannot be maintained. Rather, the relationship between production and consumption is one of dislocation. In other words, instead of representing production and consumption as two fully constituted objectivities, they should be conceptualized in terms of mutual constitution, or as Laclau (1990: 24) puts it, as 'relational semi-identities' involved in 'unstable relations of imbrication'.

In some forms of contemporary cultural analysis 'imbrication' loses out to binary opposition as a de-alienated sphere of consumption is counterposed to an alienated, deskilled and already determined world of paid employment. While exploding the myth of the 'passive consumer', cultural analysis institutes in its place the myth of the totally determined, deskilled worker. A routinized, impoverished world of paid work becomes the 'other' against which the 'pleasures of consumption thesis' constitutes its identity (du Gay and Negus, 1994) …

While their advocates may believe that emerging entrepreneurial forms of government and the blurring of spheres that they engender are the source of an increasing egalitarianism and a deepening pluralism, I have tried to indicate that the conceptions of equality and pluralism that they deploy are remarkably thin.

The equality they promote is, in Walzer's terminology, simple not complex, being premised upon the triumph of one good over all others: enterprise. As Walzer (1994: 38) himself has argued, simple equality is the hallmark of unjust societies. Justice

READING 13.3	**Extract from *Consumption and Identity at Work***

By Paul du Gay, Journal of Management Studies, 29/4: 616–33.

requires the defence of difference – different goods distributed for different reasons among different groups of people – and enterprise, as we have seen, flattens difference by making distinct spheres commensurable through the medium of the market mechanism.

Similarly, their pluralism is premised upon a vision of human wholeness. The pluralization of the centre that Donzelot (1991) refers to, for example, involves the devolution of the problems of the state so that individuals and collectivities become implicated in the task of solving them. However, as we have seen, the price of this involvement is the requirement that they conduct themselves in accordance with a particular model of action – that of the enterprise form. This latter mode of action obviously draws upon certain human capacities but it certainly does not exhaust them. Indeed, what sort of 'pluralization' process is it which presupposes a single ethical hierarchy with the entrepreneur at its apex? Such a process seems remarkably one-dimensional and frighteningly thin.

The pluralism and equality that enterprise promises and delivers can seem like an unalloyed good when seen in a certain light. By traversing established barriers between different spheres of existence, levelling the hierarchies of value they incorporate and by redefining individuals as entrepreneurs of their own lives, enterprise appears to offer the possibility of spreading the satisfaction of ruling more widely throughout the social This has ensured it some contemporary popularity on both the Right and the Left of the political spectrum. For the Right, 'spheres' means unnecessary regulation: that which inhibits individual freedom and responsibility as well as economic efficiency. On the Left, particularly the cultural Left, talk of barriers and boundaries is inimical to cherished romantic values such as freedom from normative compulsion. No wonder then that the simple egalitarian and pluralist claims of enterprise have met with continuing success, chiming as they do with crucial elements of contemporary Right- and Left-wing populism.

The possibility that different spheres of life give rise to different conceptions and comportments of the person is anathema to those predisposed to think that a common form of ethical life exists in the capacities of the individual human subject, whether as

neo-conservatives we identify this figure with the 'entrepreneur of the self' as cultural radicals we project these capacities onto 'embracing multiplicity and provisionality'. In their different ways they urge us to the same course of action: we should reject the 'exclusionary' discourses and practices that presently delimit our perceptions and abrogate our freedom of action. On the other hand, this is advocated in order to that we can better become what we are – responsible, autonomous, risk-taking, free-choosing individual entrepreneurs of ourselves ...

On the other hand, boundary crossing is advocated by the cultural Left in order that we might become more flexible and multidirectional in our mode of being and thus do justice to everything we have recently leaned about the historicity of our situatedness; we should classify less and be forever open as befits a creature 'always in process'.

At least with the former conception of personhood one always knows where one is because everything is amenable to one singular rationale – enterprise. The latter conception is, however, simply impossible. As Stanley Fish (1994: 251) has argued, this form of 'indeterminate negativity' – understood as a refusal to be pinned down in any context – cannot be lived, and it cannot be lived because it

> demands from a wholly situated creature a mode of action or thought ... that is free from the entanglements of situations and the lines of demarcation they declare; it demands that a consciousness that has shape only by virtue of the distinctions and boundary lines that are its content float free of these lines and boundaries and remain forever unsettled.

References

Baudrillard, J. (1988) *Selected Writings*, ed. M. Poster Cambridge: Polity Press.

Campbell, C. (1987) *The Romantic Ethic and the Spirit of Modern Consumerism*, Oxford: Blackwell.

de Certeau, M. (1984) *The Practice of Everyday Life*, London: University of California Press.

Chambers, I. (1986) *Popular Culture: the Metropolitan Express*, London: Methuen.

READING 13.3 | **Extract from *Consumption and Identity at Work***
continued

By Paul du Gay, Journal of Management Studies, 29/4: 616–33.

Clarke, J. (1991) *New Times and Old Enemies*, London: Harper Collins.

Donzelot, J. (1991) 'The mobililzation of society' in G. Burchellet al. (eds.) *The Foucault Effect*, Brighton: Harvester Wheatsheaf.

Dubin, R. (1962) 'Industrial workers' worlds' in A. Rose (ed) *Human Behaviour and Social Processes*, London: Routledge and Kegan Paul.

Featherstone, M. (1990) *Consumer Culture and Post-modernism*, London: Sage.

Fish, S. (1994) *There's No Such Thing as Free Speech … and it's a Good Thing Too*, Oxford University Press.

Fiske, J. (1989) *Understanding Popular Culture,* London: Unwin Hyman.

Foucault, M. (1982) 'The subject and power', in H.L. Dreyfus and P. Rabinow, *Beyond Structuralism and Hermeneutics*, Brighton: Sussex Harvester Press, pp. 208–226.

Fox, A. (1980) 'The meaning of work' in G. Esland and G. Salaman (eds.) *The Politics of Work and Occupations*, Milton Keynes: Open University Press.

du Gay, P. and Negus, K. (1994) 'The changing site of sound: music retailing and the composition of consumers', *Media, Culture Society*, Vol. 16, No. 3: 395–413.

Goldthorpe, J.H., Lockwood, D., Bechoffer, F. and Platt, J. (1969) *The Affluent Worker in the Class Structure*, Cambridge University Press.

Gorz, A. (1965) 'Work and consumption' in P. Anderson and R. Blackburn (eds.) *Towards Socialism*, Harmondworth: Penguin.

Laclau, E. (1990) *New Reflections on the Revolution of our Time*, London: Verso.

Marcuse, H. (1964) *One-dimensional Man*, Harmondsworth: Penguin.

Miller, D. (1987) *Material Culture and Mass Consumption*, Oxford: Blackwell.

Mills, C.W. (1953) *White Collar*, New York: Oxford University Press.

Morris, M. (1988) 'Banality in cultural studies', *Discourse*, 10: 2–29.

Mort, F. (1989) The writing on the wall, *New Statesman and Society*, 12 May: 40–41.

Nava, M. (1987) Consumerism and its contradictions', *Cultural Studies*, 1/2: 204–10.

Peters, T. (1987) *Thriving on Chaos*, Basingstoke: Macmillan.

Rose, N. (1990) *Governing the Soul*, London: Routledge.

Walzer, M. (1994) *Thick and Thin: Moral Argument at Home and Abroad*, Notre Dame, Indiana: University of Notre Dame Press.

Warde, A. (1992) 'Notes on the relationship between production and consumption', in R. Burrows and C. Marsh (eds) *Consumption and Class: Divisions and Change*, Basingstoke: Macmillan.

Williamson, J. (1986) 'The problems of being popular', *New Socialist*, 41: 14–15.

Willis, P. (1990) *Common Culture*, Milton Keyes: Open University Press.

Discussion Questions

1. Why do you think that consumption has become more important than production?
2. To what extent do organizations construct the identities of their customers?

3. Is it the case that the idea of enterprise has invaded all aspects of social life?

Introduction References

Bauman, Z. (1998) 'From the work ethic to the aesthetic of consumption' in *Work, consumerism and the new poor*. Maidenhead: Open University Press. pp. 23–6, 30–2.

Foucault, M. (1982) 'The subject and power' in Dreyfus, H.F and Rabinow P., *Michel Foucault:*

Beyond Structuralism and Hermeneutics. Brighton: Harvester, pp. 208–26.

Miles, S. (1998) *Consumerism as a Way of Life*. London: Sage.

Recommended Further Readings

See references accompanying the Readings plus:

Brewer, J. and Trentmann, F. (eds) (2006) *Consuming Cultures, Global Perspectives: Historical Trajectories, Transnational Exchanges*, Oxford: Berg Publishers.

Edgell, S. Hetherington, K. and Warde, A. (eds) (1996) 'Consumption Matters: the production and experience of consumption', *Sociological Review Monograph*, Oxford: Blackwell.

Lee, N. and Munro, R. (eds) (2001) 'The Consumption of Mass', *Sociological Review Monograph*, Oxford: Blackwell.

Paterson, M. (2007) *Consumption and Everyday Life*, London: Taylor & Francis.

Trentmann, F. (ed.) (2006) *The Making of the Consumer: Knowledge, Power and Identity in the Modern World*, Oxford: Berg Publishers.

Featherstone, M. (1991) *Consumer Culture and Postmodernism*, London: Sage.

POSTMODERNISM

CHAPTER **14**

READINGS

Cooper, R. and Burrell, G. (1988) 'Modernism, Postmodernism and Organizational Analysis: An Introduction' in *Organization Studies*, Vol. 9, No. 1: pp. 95–96, 97–98, 99–100, 101–102.

Kildruff, M. (1993) 'Deconstructing Organisations' in *Academy of Management Review*, Vol. 18, No. 1: pp. 13–16, 19–20, 21, 294–25, 26–27, 27–28, 28–29.

Knights, D. (1997) 'Organization Theory in the Age of Deconstruction: Dualism, Gender and Postmodernism Revisited' in *Organization Studies*, Vol. 18: pp. 1: 3–4, 14–15, 16.

INTRODUCTION

If any term serves to remind us that the meaning of terms is contested, it is postmodernism (Alvesson, 1995). Efforts to pin down or specify a universally accepted definition of postmodernism directly contradict a distinctive feature of postmodernism as a movement/argument. Namely, that the modernist project of regulating or controlling meaning and actions, epitomized in bureaucratic procedures and a positivist conception of science, no longer enjoys the magnetic appeal that it once had. Using the modernist device of a table (see 14.1) to polarize what are mutually dependent oppositions can, paradoxically, indicate how the 'modernism'/'postmodernism' distinction projects a change of mood. This change is apparent in organizational practice where there is increasing interest in emotionally charged ways of organizing and rewarding employees that, from a modernist perspective, seem irrational; and also in organization theory where there is increasing use of metaphors and methodologies – such as play and the use of focus groups – that, from a modernist standpoint, appear to elevate style over substance.

Postmodernism challenges and disrupts the modernist aspiration to secure control by eliminating unpredictability. It recognizes and celebrates the presence and value of diverse, multiple rationalities in opposition to the search for an authoritative grand narrative favoured by modernism. Instead of assuming 'organization' to

TABLE 14.1 | MODERNISM/POSTMODERNISM

Modernism	Postmodernism
Purpose	Play
Design	Chance
Literalism	Irony
Determinacy	Indeterminacy

be an entity amenable to study, it is recognized as an integral part of an organizing process in which reality is carved up or configured in a particular but precarious way. Instead of regarding established concepts, such as structure or hierarchy, as descriptive of a given entity, they are understood to be effects of established, yet largely unexamined, organizing processes that privilege a particular way of accounting for the world. The turn to postmodernism articulates a return, and positive valuation, of what is repressed in the rationalist vision of modernism. In this respect, there is a degree of affinity with the reflexive concerns of ethnomethodology (see Organization theory section, Reading 1.2) where students of organization are urged to adopt taken-for-granted resources of analysis, such as 'structure', as topics of analysis.

As Parker (1992: 3) summarizes the differences distilled in the polarization of modernism and postmodernism, in modernism:

> The world is seen as a system which comes increasingly under human control as our knowledge of it increases. The common terms of this kind of belief system are positivism, empiricism and science ... In contrast, the postmodernist suggests that this is a form of intellectual imperialism that ignores the fundamental uncontrollability of meaning. The 'out there' is constructed by our discursive conceptions of it and these conceptions are collectively sustained and continually renegotiated in the process of making sense.

To the committed modernist, the implication of breaching the bastions of modernism is anarchy and chaos. Overlooked or dismissed is the possibility that playfulness may be a less self-defeating way of addressing uncertainties than modernist efforts to control and eliminate it. There is no consideration of the possibility that a postmodern sensibility offers a 'light' aesthetic of fun, improvization and absurdity as an alternative to the heavy aesthetic of modernism's investments in repetition, predictability and clarity. As the totalizing authority of modernist knowledge claims is problematized, space for irony and playfulness is opened up. It is, of course, precisely these 'unserious' qualities and inclinations, dubbed as 'subjectivist', 'hedonistic', etc., that modernists find objectionable.

Nonetheless, 'postmodernism' has been adopted or appropriated as a label to distinguish ostensibly novel features of contemporary organizations – such as empowerment, increased flexibility (Clegg, 1990) or increasing use of cultural and ideological control (Heydebrand, 1989). Without denying that organizations are changing, and that certain techniques (e.g. teamworking, outsourcing, etc.) are becoming more widespread, other terms – such as post-Fordism – continue to offer an alternative, and arguably less confusing, lexicon for characterizing these developments. For this reason, in our choice of readings postmodernism is conceived as a distinctive way of analysing organizing practices rather than as a way of describing changes in these practices.

Robert Cooper and Gibson Burrell (Reading 14.1) provide a broad overview of modernist and postmodernist discourses in which they make a useful distinction between critical and systemic versions of modernism. Systemic modernism assumes that progress is a matter of advancing scientific knowledge to direct innovation and change. Critical modernism stresses the importance of placing scientific and technological development under genuinely democratic control in which the path and contribution of knowledge can be subjected to critical scrutiny in terms of enhancement of the quality of life. Systemic modernists regard science and technology as neutral or even inherently progressive, whereas critical modernists are more sceptical of its claims and consequences and, are disparaging of its capacity to dominate and suppress thought or activity that deviates from its totalizing vision. What systematic and critical modernisms share nonetheless, Cooper and Burrell argue, is a presupposition that reason – in the form of scientific knowledge or debate through a democratic process – is the key to developing a more rational society. Postmodernism, in contrast, commends an acceptance of indeterminacy and instability that defies rational resolution or control. All forms of authority are seen to be contingent, and to rest upon foundations that are vulnerable to deconstruction (see Readings 14.2 and 14.3). Only through the (rational, systemic) exclusion or suppression of this contingency is its vulnerability denied. It is by problematizing this power-invested closure that postmodernists seek to disclose the precariousness of the claims, and associated ambitions, of systemic and critical versions of modernism. In the context of organization studies, the point is illustrated by efforts – theoretical (e.g. Human Relations) as well as practical (e.g. the Excellence literature) – to subject the 'informal' in organizations to systematic control in an effort to render it predictable and functional. Postmodernist analysis involves the problematizing of these ventures – by recalling how they rely upon seemingly stable distinctions whose conditions of possibility are contingent and whose consequences are unexpected.

The extracts by **Martin Kilduff** (Reading 14.2) **and David Knights** (Reading 14.3) illustrate how deconstructive analyses serve to problematize received wisdoms within organization studies. Martin Kilduff offers a deconstructive analysis of March and Simon's (1958) landmark text *Organizations*. He shows how the sense of authority and objectivity, displayed in its use of standardized propositions, standardized variables, testable hypotheses and the like is constructed in particular ways to produce this effect – an effect that relies upon the active exclusion of features that might otherwise disrupt this appearance. Kilduff demonstrates how a text that is widely regarded as a model of objective and dispassionate enquiry attains its 'objectivity and persuasiveness' by making 'a series of strategic exclusions'. *Organizations*, he shows, is founded upon a dichotomy between the (outmoded) conception of the employee as machine v. the employee as decision-maker, a model advocated by March and Simon (MS). Through a close reading of the text, Kilduff argues that the latter model is no less mechanical as it also assumes that 'human machines can be programmed to perform precise iterations'. Kilduff's discussion of *Organizations* is usefully complemented by some reflections upon his own stake in deconstructive analysis where he acknowledges that the status of his claims could themselves be subjected to a deconstructive analysis. It is also noted that much deconstructive work has been confined to the analysis of texts and urges its application to the world as text (see, for example, Learmonth, 1999; Chia, 1994).

David Knights concentrates upon deconstructing the tendency for analysis to rely upon dualisms – such as those between action/structure, reason/emotion, objective/subjective, modernism/postmodernism, etc. Such analyses are challenged on the grounds that they tend to assume and reproduce an 'episteme of representation' in which knowledge is thought to reflect or capture its object, rather than to frame and constitute it in a particular, politically charged way. Instead of deploying dualisms to elevate one side by negating its 'other', Knights commends resistance to such practices. The inescapability of distinctions is accepted but their use to inhibit awareness of their contingent conditions and unforeseen consequences is rejected. For example, Knights notes how social sciences are distinguished from natural sciences on the basis of a representation that privileges differences in their objects of inquiry, yet also presumes that standards of 'scientificity' developed in the natural sciences are equally applicable to the social sciences. As Knights suggests, a key to challenging this presumption is to problematize the epistemology upon which it is based – a project that has been vigorously pursued by sociologists of (natural) scientific knowledge (e.g. Galison and Stump, 1996). Knights illustrates his argument through a sympathetic interpretation of Doreen Kondo's (1990) study of lives in work in modern Japan. He shows how postmodern, feminist conceptions of the self serve to disrupt established binary oppositions between management and labour, power and resistance, and so on.

READING 14.1 | **Modernism, Postmodernism and Organizational Analysis: An Introduction**

By Robert Cooper and Gibson Burrell

Modernism has two versions: *critical modernism,* a reanimation of Kant's programme of enlightenment, and *systemic modernism,* the instrumentalization of reason envisioned by Saint-Simon and Comte.

Systemic modernism is currently seen to be the dominant form of reason, now more usually expressed as 'instrumental rationality'. This is well brought out in Bell's (1974) thesis that modern (or post-industrial) society differs from previous societies in relying on knowledge that is essentially theoretical. Bell cites the chemical industry as the first of the truly modern industries because its origin lies in the intimate linkage between science and technology: it is necessary to have a theoretical knowledge of the macro molecules being manipulated in order to create chemical synthesis (the recombination and transformation of compounds). Bell's vision of how theoretical knowledge is used in the post-industrial era reveals its technocratic and systemic character. 'Post-industrial society is organized around knowledge for the purpose of social control and the directing of innovation and change ...' (Bell, 1974: 20). The point is further elaborated in the argument that theoretical knowledge offers a 'methodological promise' for the management of the complex, large-scale systems which distinguish the modern world. The major social, economic and political questions of the post-industrial era centre around the problem of 'organized complexity': large-scale systems with many interacting variables, 'which have to be co-ordinated to achieve specific goals'. The new intellectual technologies now available for this endeavour are: information theory, cybernetics, decision theory, game theory, utility theory, etc. The distinctive function of this technical armoury is the definition of rational action and the identification of the means for achieving it.

| READING 14.1 | **Modernism, Postmodernism and Organizational Analysis: An Introduction** |

By Robert Cooper and Gibson Burrell

Problems are formally defined in terms of certainty/uncertainty, of constraints and contrasting alternatives.

> Certainty exists when the constraints are fixed and known. Risk means that a set of possible outcomes is known and the probabilities for each outcome can be stated. Uncertainty is the case when the set of possible outcomes can be stipulated, but the probabilities are completely unknown.
>
> *(Bell 1974: 30).*

In this context, rationality is that action which can yield the preferred outcome, given several competing alternatives ...

Critical modernism stands opposed to the cybernetic-like monolithism of systemic modernism. Its chief exponent in contemporary social science is Jürgen Habermas whose project has been to reclaim the spirit of enlightened rationalism for late modernism. Again, discourse is the object of analysis. For Habermas, language is the medium of reason: 'All ordinary language allows reflexive allusions to what has remained unstated' (Habermas 1972: 168). This sets ordinary language, with its origins in the spontaneous activities of the common life-world, against the instrumental-calculative language of organized systems. Hidden but still active in ordinary language is a 'natural' kind of reason which speaks to us with the instinctive wisdom of an ancient oracle, thus guiding our communal works. The contemporary fate of this 'communicative rationality' has been its repression by the discourse of systemic modernism. For Habermas, the discourse of the ordinary life-world is the basis of his critical modernism and it is through the 'language of the community' that we may refind that lost sense of enlightenment which Kant first revealed to us. Moreover, the need for such critical reason is now more urgent than ever precisely because of the colonization of the life-world by systemic reason. Kantian reason takes on an added significance; it is no longer a measure of human 'maturity' but has become a *sine qua non* for emancipating individuals from the totalising control of systemic logic.

Despite the difference between the systemic and critical forms of modernism – the one bent on the mechanization of social order; the other, on the liberation of the life-world – they share the belief in an intrinsically logical and meaningful world constituted by Reason or the universal firm foundation. This takes two forms: (1) that discourse mirrors the reason and order already 'out there' in the world, and (2) that there is a thinking agent, a subject, which can make itself conscious of this external order. In the case of systemic modernism, the rational subject is the system itself which works according to the cybernetic discourse of 'control and communication in the animal and the machine' (Wiener 1948); this discourse has its own laws which can be discovered through the application of scientific and mathematical techniques. In this context, reason is a privileged property of the system as distinct from its parts. For critical modernism, the thinking subject is the human individual or, more precisely, a network of interacting individuals who, through the common sense of ordinary discourse, can reach a 'universal consensus' of human experience. There is thus a presupposition of unity which legitimates (i.e. provides an authoritative 'logic') to the critical position, so that what is critiqued are the forces that fragment the ideal of this unity or prevent its emergence as a possibility. It is such legitimating meta-positions to which postmodernism objects.

Postmodernism

The key to understanding the discourse of postmodernism is the concept of *difference*: a form of self-reference in which terms contain their own opposites and thus refuse any *singular* grasp of their meanings, e.g., the paradox of the 'global village' in which the enlargement of the world through modern communication techniques actually makes it smaller. Difference is thus a unity which is at the same time divided from itself, and, since it is that which actually constitutes human discourse (Derrida, 1973), it is intrinsic to all social forms. At the very centre of discourse, therefore, the human agent is faced with a condition of irreducible indeterminacy and it is this endless and unstoppable demurrage which postmodern thought explicitly recognizes and places in the vanguard of its endeavours. In this context, Lyotard has defined postmodern discourse as 'the search for instabilities' (Lyotard, 1984: 53). Lyotard notes that modern science is based on indeterminacy: quantum theory and microphysics demand a redefinition of our

Modernism, Postmodernism and Organizational Analysis: An Introduction *continued*

By Robert Cooper and Gibson Burrell

ideas of determinate, predictable systems because their data reveal the world as a network of self-referential structures, e.g., it is found that far from uncertainty decreasing with more precise knowledge (i.e., greater control), the reverse is the case: uncertainty increases with precision. ...

Starting from the position that meaning and understanding are not naturally intrinsic to the world and that they have to be constructed, Derrida develops a *deconstructive* method which, in reversing the process of construction, shows precisely how artificial are the ordinary, taken-for-granted structures of our social world. Derrida's purpose is to show that rationality and rationalization are really processes that seek to hide the contradictions at the heart of human existence. What motivates the call to organize is the recognition of a discursive 'gap' which organization serves to cover up.

Derrida's analysis is focussed on the processual, as opposed to structural, character of human institutions. He wants to show that the world of common sense structures is the active product of a process that continually privileges unity, identity, and immediacy over the differential properties of absence and separation; in this active privileging there emerges the element of contestation in which the logic of unity and identity is pitted against the forces of difference and undecidability. Modernist reason now becomes more like Lyotard's conception of a contest in which reason is aligned against unreason, truth against error, etc. ...

For Foucault, enlightenment is the experience of sudden and spontaneous insight when one is seized by a power beyond rational, conscious thought, i.e., by the auratic. Foucault reveals the experience of estranging enlightenment most notably through his adaptation of Nietzsche's method of genealogy (Foucault, 1977: 139–164). Genealogy is opposed to the search for pure and ideal forms which pre-exist our profane, everyday world. Instead, the genealogist finds that ideal essences, essential truths, are fabrications taken from 'alien forms'. What we find at the so-called origin of things is not a reassuring state of perfection, now lost but still reclaimable; instead there is disparity, difference, indeterminacy. Foucault's genealogical method is therefore similar to Lyotard's agonistics and Derrida's deconstruction: all deny the concept of a perfect origin and substitute for it a process of differential contestation.

For this reason, Habermas criticizes Foucault (and the postmodernists in general) for being 'irrational'. Habermas (1984) considers reason to be conditional on a concept of the perfect origin; his 'communicative rationality' presupposes just such an ideal state. But the logic of postmodern thought starts from a different understanding of reason, one that appears at times more veraciously argued than that of rival positions. It is a rationality that is based not on finding answers to problems but of 'problemizing' answers. This is entirely consistent with the genealogical position which says that disparity (and not parity) is the source of human structures: answers are merely temporary inversions of problems. Whereas Habermas is looking for *the* answer (or at least an approach to it), Foucault can only see answers as ways of short-circuiting problems, as expressions of the 'haste of wanting to know'. His analysis always proceeds from the complex process of how thoughts are structured so as to give a solution. In the human world, this is always subject to the work of power, inevitably because power is intrinsic to the agonistic logic of disparity. Discourse is the expression of power that is centred on problems. Power precedes the answer through its subtle and covert prior structuring of the problem. This is why Foucault is so concerned with 'problematizing', since the proper understanding of a solution can only be got from seeing how the problem was structured in the first place. ...

References

Bell, D. (1974) *The coming of post-industrial society*. London: Heinemann.

Derrida, J. (1973) *Speech and phenomena*. Evanston: Northwestern University Press.

Foucault, M. (1977) *Language, counter-memory, practice*. Ithica, N.Y.: Cornell University Press.

Foucault, M. (1980) *Power/Knowledge*. Brighton: Harvester Press.

Habermas, J. (1972) *Knowledge and human interests*. London: Heinemann.

Habermas, J. (1984) *The theory of communicative action. I: reason and the rationalization of society*. Boston: Beacon Press.

Lyotard, J.F. (1984) *The postmodern condition: a report on knowledge*. Manchester: Manchester University Press.

Wiener, N. (1948) *Cybernetics, or communication in the animal and the machine*. New York: Wiley.

READING 14.2

Deconstructing Organizations

By Martin Kildruff

In the field of organizational studies, few texts are as foundational as March and Simon's (1958) contribution simply titled *Organizations*. This text is listed in every major survey of the classics that have shaped the field (e.g. Lawrence, 1987). Far from fading away as a piece of outmoded science, *Organizations* continues to be frequently cited in the organizational studies journals. Yet interpretive commentaries about this book are strangely absent, despite occasional criticisms by *Organizations'* admirers concerning textual discrepancies and self-contradictions (e.g. Perrow, 1986: 125).

Interpretive scholars have issued calls for the textual analysis of foundational texts across the social sciences (e.g., Van Maanen, 1988: 141), and such analyses have begun to appear in print (e.g., Calas, 1987; Ditton, 1981; Edmondson, 1984; Green, 1988). Part of the reason why *Organizations* has escaped such fine-grained literary analysis is that the text conforms to positivist conventions and, therefore, gives the appearance of straightforward objectivity. The text is couched in terms of standard propositions, operationalized variables, and testable hypotheses. The power of *Organizations* appears to reside in its embodiment of logic, rationality, and truth, rather than in its literary qualities.

The authors of *Organizations,* in fact, explicitly claim to sacrifice literary style for the sake of scientific format (1958: 7). The text has been praised for its self-proclaimed restriction on the use of metaphorical language (Keeley, 1980: 337; Pinder and Bourgeois, 1982: 647). March and Simon's (1958) readiness to devalue the importance of style and metaphor is quite consistent with the Western metaphysical tradition, which, from Plato to Heidegger, has regarded writing as merely 'an unfortunate necessity' (Rorty, 1978: 145). From this logocentric perspective, scientific and philosophical texts are representations of ideas. Writing, as a medium of expression, cannot add anything of value to such representations and could possibly 'infect the meaning it is supposed to represent' (Culler, 1982: 91).

A dissenting perspective is provided by Jacques Derrida (1976; 1978; 1988) who, in a series of critiques of philosophical texts, has drawn attention to textual production itself. The power of the text for Derrida derives in large part from what he calls *difference:* the play of meaning between textual levels. In exposing the metaphysical and metaphorical dependencies of philosophical texts, Derrida has opened up all writing to textual analysis. He has shown that philosophical writing depends upon the very techniques it condemns and that philosophy thereby fails to achieve the ideal of merely expressing the logic of ideas.

In this [extract], Derrida's perspective is used to re-evaluate the appearance of progress in organizational theory. A deconstructive analysis of an exemplary foundational text – *Organizations* – reveals a simultaneous rejection and acceptance of the tradition the authors sought to surpass. This double movement of rejection and replication is fully consistent with a hermeneutic approach to organizational studies, but it is discrepant with the positivist philosophy of scientific progress that *Organizations* itself embraces. A deconstruction of *Organizations* shows that it replicates the moves of the predecessors it condemns. But first, what is deconstruction?

Deconstruction

Jacques Derrida has emerged as perhaps the most influential post-structuralist philosopher (Agger, 1991: 112). He has succeeded in exposing the metaphysical and rhetorical dependencies of canonical texts and has thereby implicated all writing as inherently literary. Thus, Derrida has directly confronted positivist pretensions, which are characteristic, for example, of structuralism (see Dews, 1987), with evidence that rigorous objectivity in writing has never been possible. Derrida's own writing style often has become 'extravagantly convoluted' (Agger, 1991: 106) as he has worked to change the reader's understanding of a text without himself indulging in the oversimplification and the declarations of certainty that characterize the metaphysical tradition under critique.

For Derrida, there is literally 'nothing outside the text' (1976: 158). Deconstruction offers a way of examining human behaviour as a textual production, a kind of writing. For Derrida, writing includes not only language but 'before all that gives rise to inscription in general' (1976: 9), namely, all those rule-based aspects of people's lives that involve the reproduction of behaviour. The world is not a stage. According to Derrida, it is a text, and the dynamics of this text can

Deconstructing Organizations *continued*

By Martin Kildruff

be studied as a series of relationships between textual levels. Derrida's readings focus on literary and philosophical texts, but other authors have extended deconstruction to such differing contexts as bureaucracy (Frug, 1984), the language of organizations (Martin, 1990), and the practice of psychology (Parker and Shotter, 1990; Sampson, 1983).

By questioning the organizing principles of canonical texts, Derrida aims to place these principles in a new relation to each other, suggesting the possibility that complications can be debated rather than suppressed. Thus, deconstruction is used, not to abolish truth, science, logic, and philosophy, but to question how these concepts are present in texts and how they are employed to systematically exclude certain categories of thought and communication. The implications of a deconstructive reading are, therefore, not limited to the language of the text itself but can be extended to the political and social context in which the text is placed. For example, Derrida's debate with Searle on the subject of speech act theory has implications for the practice and politics of academic discourse itself (Derrida, 1988: 111–154).

One of the symptoms of an undeclared metaphysics is the dependence of the text on hierarchically ordered binary oppositions (e.g., mind/body, mechanistic/organic, male/female). Derrida brings the reader's attention to the play of meaning between the two terms, one of which is often suppressed or marginalized. As a first step, Derrida focuses on that which is suppressed. As a second step, he displaces the binary system itself so that it no longer controls the reader's response to the text. By calling attention to the way in which the power of the text derives from the suppression of one half of a binary opposition, deconstruction works to leave a permanent 'trace' in the text, that is, a shift in the way the reader responds to the language used. (See Martin, 1990, for an example of how the deconstruction of corporate language in terms of a masculine/feminine opposition can permanently alter the received meaning of such language.)

A deconstruction of a text also can reveal the dependence of the text on an idealism that seeks to exclude deviations, mistakes, marginalia, and trivia. The deconstructive gesture is used to explore precisely what the text has neglected and to show that what is excluded is necessarily implied in the categories the text includes. Thus, the concept 'normal' must include the existence of the 'abnormal', in order for the concept to make any sense. The claim that the abnormal is a later development,

or is a parasite upon the normal, cannot, therefore, be supported by appeals to logic (Derrida, 1988).

A deconstructive reading opens up the text to renewed debate concerning the limits of the text and the relationship between explicit and hidden textual levels. In investigating the limits of the text, the critic asks: Why are certain authors, topics, or schools excluded from the text? Why are certain themes never questioned, whereas other themes are condemned? Why, given a set of premises, are certain conclusions not reached? The aim of such questions is not to point out textual errors but to help the reader understand the extent to which the text's objectivity and persuasiveness depend on a series of strategic exclusions. ...

According to March and Simon [hereafter MS], the employee is a subjectively rational information processor (*Organizations*, Chapters 6 and 7). From this perspective, 'Most behaviour and particularly most behaviour in organizations, is governed by performance programs' (p. 142). These performances programs are activated as follows: 'an environmental stimulus may evoke immediately from the organisation a highly complex and organized set of responses' (p. 141). Human beings, according to MS, can be programmed in much the same way that computing machines are programmed. The following quotation is one of many that make explicit the assumption that humans and machines are functional equivalents.

> The extent to which many human activities, both manual and clerical, can be programmed is shown by the continuing spread of automation to encompass a wider and wider range of tasks. In order to substitute automatic processes for human operatives, it is necessary to describe the task in minute detail, and to provide for the performance of each step of it. The decomposition of tasks into their elementary program steps is most spectacularly illustrated in modem computing machines which may carry out programs involving thousands of such steps. (p. 144)

Particularly striking in this quotation is the apparent assumption that the same programs for controlling behaviour can be written for human or computing machines. From March and Simon's perspective, therefore, humans and machines are identical in their ability to be programmed. This idea is made even more explicit in the following passage, which compares programming a person with programming a machine:

Deconstructing Organizations

By Martin Kildruff

To develop in a person the capacity to carry out a particular program requires an investment in training. In automatic operations, there is an analogous capital investment in machinery capable of carrying out the program. In the case of a computing machine, a substantial part of this investment actually consists of the cost of programming the machine for the particular operations in question. (p. 158)

Programs, then, can either be 'built into machines or acquired by humans' (p. 158). The allocation of the programmed task to the human or the machine is a matter to be decided by the economics of the situation, and as MS stated: 'There are economies to be derived, *ceteris paribus*, from assigning the work so as to minimize this investment cost per unit of program execution' (p. 158). The organization as a whole, from this perspective, 'has available a repertory of programs, so that once the event has been classified the appropriate program can be executed without further ado' (p. 163). ...

What is important to the present discussion is the tension in *Organizations* between the denunciation and the celebration of the machine model of the employee. MS both accuse their predecessors of treating the employee as a machine and fill the absence they claim to have found in the literature with an updated machine model. MS propose a programming that will be inscribed, not in the physical movements of the workers, but in the workers' cognitions, a programming directed not to the body but to the mind. Such programming will control not the physiological response, but the decision-making process. By simultaneously denouncing and glorifying the employee as machine, MS succeed in building on the works of the predecessors they repeatedly condemn. Their own distinctive contribution, the emphasis they give to programmed cognition, is presented not as the direct application of scientific management to decision making, but as the arrival of scientific method to an area dominated by engineering techniques (p. 21). ...

The Ideology of Programming

The MS model of the programmed employee is presented as a scientific, neutral explanation of employee behaviour. The repetition of activity day after day in organizations is so self-evident that it can be compared, in its predictability, to the repetition of lines 'uttered by a Hamlet on the stage'. (p. 143). But from where does this programmed behaviour come?

Programmed behaviour, the reader is told, is inevitable in organizations because human beings have limited intellectual capacity and must therefore rely on repertoires of programs to deal with the multitude of situations that arise. Thus, the structure of the modern bureaucratic organization is derived directly from inherent aspects of human decision-making. This is not an oversimplification; consider a direct quote from *Organizations*:

> It has been the central theme of this chapter that the basic features of organization structure and function derive from the characteristics of human problem-solving processes and rational human choice. Because of the limits of human intellective capacities in comparison with the complexities of the problems that individuals and organizations face, rational behaviour calls for simplified models that capture the main features of a problem without capturing all its complexities. (p. 169)

MS also summarize these ideas:

> The 'boundaries of rationality' that have been the source of our propositions have consisted primarily of the properties of human beings as organisms capable of evoking and executing relatively well-defined programs but able to handle programs only of limited complexity. (p. 171)

The employee, then, is described in this model as a relatively simple computing device who must, because of cognitive limits, rely on prewritten programs to complete organizational work. The employee performs routinized, repetitive work because he or she is literally incapable of doing anything else.

This model is the source and the centre of MS's contribution, but it remains outside the positivist philosophy to which the text so strongly adheres. The assertion that a certain type of bureaucratic structure is an inevitable consequence of the inherent features of human decision making is neither operationalized nor subjected to empirical testing. Such an assertion

Deconstructing Organizations *continued*

By Martin Kildruff

must be accepted, if it is accepted at all, on faith, as ideology rather than science. According to this ideology, repetitive, programmed work is an inevitable, not-to-be-questioned feature of organizational life because it derives from cognitive limits over which organizational designers have no control. ...

A Confessional Tale

What is my own stake in this debate? Can I continue to play the role of the neutral analyst while insisting on the pervasiveness of ideology in organisational writing? Why, in fact, am I conducting this deconstruction? Perhaps I can borrow from the conventions of the confessional tale (Van Maanen, 1988: 73–100) to reveal my own motives.

As an academic researcher I already have a stake in the outcome of the debate initiated by the deconstruction of *Organization*. Previously, I have tried to undermine the claims of the information-processing model as applied to job design (Kilduff and Regan, 1988). In that earlier piece, the argument in the present article was prefigured: My co-author and I tried to show empirically that the model of the employee as a passive, easily programmed automaton was a fiction sustained only within the bounds of an experimental paradigm that ignored the behaviour of the subjects being studied. By first replicating the information processing attitudinal results and then extending the experiment so that freely chosen behaviour reversed the established results, we sought to deconstruct the taken for granted claims of the information-processing model. Rebutting empirical work, however, leaves untouched the ideology of programming as it is expressed in foundational texts.

Therefore my motive for this deconstruction is not only to expose textual limitations, but also to permanently change the way the text is used in management education and research. To the extent that ideology of programming as embedded in *Organizations* continues to legitimate fractionation of work and restriction of innovation, I believe the text must bear some responsibility for the prevalence of these problems in industry. The deconstruction of the text, then, focuses attention on an ideology that extends from the text – to the Academy – to the world of work. ...

At this point, I should caution the reader about the epistemological status of the deconstruction of *Organizations*: Is it the only one possible? Can I claim that the analysis performed here is simply the application of a method to a problem that is independent of my own agenda? Clearly, such a claim cannot be sustained. Different readers can potentially unlock different narratives from the same text. All of these narratives may be present in the text, especially if the text is complex.

A deconstruction of a text involves a close reading of one such narrative that has been absent from scrutiny, absent because the narrative contradicts or undermines the apparent message the text is thought to impart. Bringing together absence and presence in this way, deconstruction exposes the play of meaning between textual levels. It is from this *différance* that the text derives its rhetorical power, a power often hidden behind claims of scientific objectivity and disavowals of literary tricks. ...

Deconstruction, as an approach to texts, also has its limits. Derrida's difficult language serves as the first limiting factor: Many social scientists are impatient with an elusive, parenthetical style that avoids the simplification of ideas. Derrida's refusal to offer a clear definition of the deconstructive process and its implications, for example, is consistent with his overall suspicion of abstraction and generalization. Those who dare to deconstruct a text must rely on their own understanding of the gestures of deconstruction as practised by Derrida: There is no programmatic summary of the techniques of a deconstructive reading. The challenge, as Fischer (1986: 229) pointed out, is to use Derrida's deconstructions as examples while moving toward more accessible analyses.

A second limiting factor concerns the difficulty of relating textual analysis to institutions. Derrida has limited himself to canonical texts and has largely avoided extensive commentary on the structures of society. If the "potentially enormous" (Agger, 1991: 114) relevance of Derrida's work for social science is to be realized, deconstruction must be extended to the analysis of social, political and organizational contexts. (See Dorst, 1989; Martin, 1990, for very different examples of extending deconstruction.) Deconstruction, in other words, must go beyond the limits practised by Derrida.

| # Deconstructing Organizations

By Martin Kildruff

References

Agger, B. (1991) Critical theory, poststructuralism, postmodernism: Their sociological relevance. *Annual Review of Sociology*, 17: 105–131.

Calas, M.B. (1987) Organization science/fiction: The postmodern in the management disciplines. Unpublished doctoral dissertation, Amherst, MA: University of Massachussetts.

Culler, J. (1982) *On deconstruction: Theory and criticism after structuralism*. Ithica, NY: Cornell University Press.

Derrida, J. (1976) *Of grammatology*. Baltimore, MD: John Hopkins University Press.

Derrida, J. (1978) *Writing and difference*. Chicago, IL: University of Chicago Press.

Derrida, J. (1988) *Limited Inc.* Evanston, IL: Northwestern University Press.

Dews. P. (1987) *Logics of disintegration: Post-structuralist thought and the claims of critical theory*. New York: Verso.

Ditton, J. (1981) *The view from Goffman*. London: Macmillan.

Edmondson, R. (1984) *Rhetoric in sociology*. London: Macmillan.

Fischer, M. (1986) Ethnicity and the post-modern arts of memory. In J. Clifford and G.E. Marcus (Eds.), *Writing culture: The poetics and politics of ethnography*: 194–233. Berkeley, CA: University of California Press.

Frug, G.E. (1984) The ideology of bureaucracy in American Law. *Harvard Law Review*, 97: 1277–1388.

Green, B.S. (1988) *Literary methods and sociology theory: Case studies of Simmel and Weber*. Chicago, IL: University of Chicago Press.

Keeley, M. (1980) Organizational analogy: A comparison of organismic and social contract models. *Administrative Science Quarterly*, 25: 337–362.

Kildruff, M. and Regan, D.T. (1988) What people say and what they do: The differential effects of informational cues and task design. *Organizational Behaviour and Human Decision Processes*, 41: 83–97.

Lawrence, P.R. (1987) Historical development of organizational behavior. In J.W. Lorsch (Ed.), *Handbook of organizational behaviour*: 1–9. Englewood Cliffs, NJ: Prentice-Hall.

March, J.G. and Simon, H.A. (1958) *Organizations*. New York: Wiley.

Martin, J. (1990) 'Deconstructing organizational taboos: The suppression of gender conflict in organizations', *Organization Science*, 1, 4: 399–359.

Parker, I. and Shotter, J. (eds.) (1990) *Deconstructing social psychology*. London: Routledge.

Perrow, C. (1986) *Complex organizations: A critical essay* (3rd ed.). New York: Vintage (Original work published in 1867).

Pinder, C.C. and Bourgeois, V.W. (1982) Controlling tropes in administrative science. *Administrative Science Quarterly*, 27: 641–652.

Rorty, R. (1978) Philosophy as a kind of writing: An essay on Derrida. *New Literary History*, 10: 141–160.

Sampson, E.E. (1983) Deconstructing psychology's subject. *The Journal of Mind and Behaviour*, 4: 135–164.

Van Maanen, J. (1988) *Tales of the field: On writing ethnography*. Chicago, IL: University of Chicago Press.

| # Organization Theory in the Age of Deconstruction: Dualism, Gender and Postmodernism Revisited

By David Knights

Since its very formation, organization studies has been plagued by a polarization of theoretical positions that revolve around the problematic nature of the relationship between 'action' and 'structure'. This, it may be argued, was inherited from the social sciences more generally although it is only perhaps in social, philosophical and feminist theory that attention has been seriously focused on the problems, or concerned with challenging the preconceptions, of what has come to be defined as dualistic thinking and theorizing (e.g. Giddens 1979; Derrida 1978; Foucault 1980; Fraser 1989; Game 1991; Hekman 1992; Layder 1994). Although the separation of 'action' and 'structure' is perhaps the most prevalent dualism in organizational analysis, different dualisms predominate in the other social sciences. To take

Source: Reproduced with permission of Sage Publications, London, Los Angeles, New Delhi and Singapore from 'Organization Theory in the Age of Deconstruction: Dualism, Gender and Postmodernism Revisited', in Organization Studies © 1997 Sage Publications.

READING 14.3

Organization Theory in the Age of Deconstruction: Dualism, Gender and Postmodernism Revisited

continued

By David Knights

just a few examples, dualisms take the form of the individual and society in sociology, micro and macro phenomena in economics, the mind and body in psychology, men and women in liberal feminism, individualism and holism in methodology, and ideal in contrast to material reality in philosophy. As there are some within organization studies (e.g. Thompson and Ackroyd 1995; Reed 1995) who seem currently to want to defend dualism, perhaps the first task is to justify a perception of such theorizing as problematic.

There are many reasons why dualistic forms of analysis in general may be rejected, but here I will focus on only three of them. First there is the argument that dualistic thinking privileges those forms of knowledge that appear most compatible with the episteme of representation and consequently the physical sciences over the social sciences. This 'hierarchy in the epistemological status of knowledge' (Chia 1996: 40) renders the social sciences and humanities always inferior, marginal or 'subjective' compared to the 'objective' and certain knowledge produced by the natural sciences. Moreover, what is interesting in regard to this dualism between natural and social science is that the hierarchy cannot be eradicated without a deconstruction of the representational epistemology upon which the former constructs its superior claims to truth. Positivist emulation of the natural sciences always leaves the social sciences in a position of inferiority, marginality or subordination to the positive ideal they can never quite fulfill (Knights 1996).

Second, and associated with the privileging of certain knowledge, is the way in which dualisms are constructed almost always as a way of privileging one side over the other ... This privileging process can readily be seen in the following antinomies: reason/emotion; rationality/irrationality; objective/subjective; and masculine/feminine. In each case, the former is privileged but the condition of such elevation is only made possible by a 'closure of meaning' around what is privileged and by reference to that which it is not – its opposite. Dualistic theorizing has been described by Derrida (1978, 1982) as 'logocentricsm' where any narrative that does not comply with the dominant logic is marginalized or rendered absent.

This takes us to the third reason for rejecting dualistic analysis. At the root of dualistic theorizing is what Derrida identifies as a logocentric and phallocentric reason that legislates the form in which we are to think in terms of a binary opposition between what is present and what is absent or marginal. Hekman (1992) and other feminists (e.g. Kristeva, Irigaray – see Marks and de Courtivron 1980; Moi 1985) draw upon Derrida's thesis on the dominance of a masculine legislative reason that reduces the 'feminine' to an absent 'other' on the margins of 'reality' into an argument for 'displacing the play' ... [of binary] '... oppositions that has informed not only western thought but also the inferior status of women' (Hekman 1992: 26).

A central argument for seeking a deconstruction of the binary oppositions and dualistic thought processes of enlightenment epistemology, then, is to displace the mode of reasoning that reproduces the subordination of women in western society. As Hekman (ibid.) makes clear, this is not a project for reversing the oppositions so as to elevate femininity over masculinity or to create a new orthodoxy, but rather to eradicate the epistemological grounds that make possible these dualisms in the first place. However, this process of eradication may already be underway for Derrida (1978) has already detected a 'rupture' beginning to occur through the decentring and deconstruction of the 'closure of meaning' surrounding the conceptual polarities that constitute the various types of dualism (Hekman 1992). This rupture is part of what is characterized as postmodernism, but, so far, only traces of it can be found in organization studies (cf. Cooper and Burrell 1988; Martin 1990; Calas and Smircich 1991; Cooper 1992; Hassard and Parker 1993; Chia 1996; Newton 1996). An important qualification needs to be made here, for while a concern of this paper is to eradicate dualisms, it does not imply the illegitimacy of distinctions *per se*. Clearly, communication, knowledge and language are dependent on distinctions and the classificatory schemes or typologies that are their social science counterparts. It is only when distinctions are transformed from heuristic devices into reified ontological realities that they become dualistic. What has come to be defined as the problem of dualism occurs

Organization Theory in the Age of Deconstruction: Dualism, Gender and Postmodernism Revisited

By David Knights

when polarized distinctions are combined with an episteme of representation, wherein what is distinguished as 'this' or 'that' is reified as an ontological reality rather than merely a provisional, subjectively significant, and hence contestable, ordering of 'things'. Dualistic theorizing, then, commits the fallacy of misplaced concreteness since it believes that the distinctions made as part of ordering 'reality' or organizing the world are accurate or true representations of a reality beyond, and as if it were independent of, the theorist ...

... [The deconstructionist perspective] is thereby more 'open' to what is advertently or inadvertently hidden within modernist analyses since it focuses upon that which is 'other', marginalized or disavowed in any construction or representation of reality. Kondo (1990) generates a research account that counters representations of the Japanese economy as providing life-time employment, consensus and harmony and an ethic of teamwork that has pushed it to world pre-eminence. The largest corporations may resemble this state of affairs, she argues (ibid.: 50), but they are an 'infinitesimal, though powerful, sector'. Through fully participant observation, Kondo (ibid.) researched a small family-owned business and its surrounding community and sensitively theorized the self-formation of gendered subjectivity and directly exposed the myth of Japanese workplace relations as characterized by homogeneity, consensus and employee docility. Whereas many ethnographies (e.g. Willis 1977; Burawoy 1979; Collinson 1992) seek to display how conflict and contradictions at work can be managed or reconciled, Kondo's aim is to illustrate how diversity and discontinuity in Japanese work relations undermine the Western manufactured myth of consensus and homogeneity.

Theoretically, Kondo draws upon certain postmodern feminist conceptions of the self (e.g. Butler 1990) to support her empirical findings that the Japanese eschew Western humanistic beliefs in self-autonomy and sovereignty. Through, for example, an examination of the language that individuals use to refer to themselves and one another, Kondo (1990: 33) displays how the conventional treatment of the self as a bounded and fixed unity which is 'spatially and ontologically distinct' from the 'world' or

'society' does not resonate with the way that her research subjects live their lives. In this sense, in her empirical field at least, there is no problem of dualism because Kondo's research respondents do not apparently reflect and reproduce the enlightenment conception of themselves as autonomous subjects. They may not therefore be expected to experience the tensions and contradictions suffered by many Western industrial workers. However, in carrying out her research not in the primary sector of the economy where conditions of work are supposed to reflect some community of respect for, and paternal care of, the employee, Kondo and her subjects experienced 'uncaring and exploitative practices' (e.g. low wages, long hours, breaches of the Labor Standards Law, coercive and unpredictable bursts of management power, etc.) trading on a 'family-like past' (ibid.: 204). Kondo finds it impossible to understand this and the responses of her research subjects within the narratives of consent and 'resistance provided in the social science literature' (ibid.: 218). Drawing on a postmodern literature, she suggests that it may be inappropriate to articulate 'the problematic of power in terms of resistance'. This is because modern narratives of resistance 'operate within a metaphysics of closure and presence, presuming that human lives can be seen in terms of neat, closed, monolithic, internally coherent categories' (ibid.: 219). While it is possible to project onto the research field the conventional binary oppositions between management and labour, or between power and resistance, Kondo demonstrates the difficulty of such orderings, suggesting that 'no single category, meaning, motivation or aspect of selfhood can be sifted out from its shifting placement in matrices of power' (ibid.: 221). While there is much in Kondo's ethnography that reflects her earlier modern perspective,[1] this is an excellent example of the direction that a postmodern approach to empirical studies of organizations might go ...

... The implication ... for organization analysis is one of exploring more closely what insights postmodernism and deconstructionism have to offer rather than dismissing them simply because they are incompatible with unitary, dualist or pluralist perspectives. As already indicated, these perspectives are suffering disruption as a result of the decentring and deconstruction of the 'closure of meaning'

READING 14.3

Organization Theory in the Age of Deconstruction: Dualism, Gender and Postmodernism Revisited

continued

By David Knights

(Derrida 1987) surrounding the conceptual polarities that constitute the various types of dualism (Hekman 1990). If meaning cannot be rendered unproblematic, then encapsulating the world in terms of a dualism between, for example, 'actor' and 'structure' is no longer viable and its continued attempt can only be seen as reflecting a hidden desire for order and stability. Recently, the absurdity of hierarchical or present/absent dichotomies within dualistic thinking has been recognized, but instead of dismantling the dualistic edifice, attempts have been made to reconcile the terms of the polarity by generating some kind of balance between them (Knights and Willmott 1983; Collinson 1992; Reed, this issue). Deconstruction theory, however, does not simply mean an overturning or reversal of the hierarchy of dualistic categories or a reconciling of the presence/absence dichotomy, but their complete eradication (Derrida 1982: 329).

---

[1] It would appear that Kondo may have been influenced by postmodern feminism some time after collecting and perhaps working on her field data, for tension surfaces at times between discrepant theoretical assumptions informing the pre- and post-data collection period of the research. This could perhaps have been drawn upon to some advantage had it been a topic of the research report for it is an illuminating illustration of the discontinuity of self and subject matter.

References

Burawoy, M. (1979) *The manufacture of consent*. Chicago: Chicago University Press.

Butler, J. (1990) *Gender trouble: Feminism and the subversion of identity*. London: Routledge.

Calas, M. and L. Smircich (1991) '**Voicing seduction to silence leadership**'. *Organization Studies*, 12, 4: 567–602.

Chia, R. (1996) '**The problem of reflexivity in organizational research: Towards a postmodern science of organization**', *Organization*, 3, 1: 31–59.

Collinson, D.L. (1992) *Managing the shopfloor: Subjectivity, masculinity and workplace culture*. Berlin: de Gruyter.

Cooper, R. (1992) '**Formal organization and representation: Remote control, displacement, abbreviation**' in *Rethinking organization: New directions in organization theory and analysis*. M. Reed and M. Hughes (eds.), 254–272. London: Sage.

Cooper, R. and G. Burrell (1988) '**Modernism, postmodernism and organization analysis: an introduction**'. *Organization Studies*, 9, 1: 91–112.

Derrida, J. (1978) *Writing and difference*, trans. By A. Bass. Chicago: University of Chicago Press

Derrida, J. (1987) *Margins of philosophy*, trans. By A. Bass. Chicago: University of Chicago Press.

Foucault, M. (1980) *Power/Knowledge*, trans. and edited by M. Gordon. London: Tavistock.

Fraser, N. (1989) '*Unruly Practices': Power, discourse and gender in contemporary social theory*. Cambridge: Polity Press.

Game, A. (1991) *Undoing the social: Toward a deconstruction of sociology*. Milton Keynes: Open University Press.

Giddens, A. (1979) *Central problems of social theory*. London: Macmillan.

Hassard, J. and M. Parker (1993) *Postmoderism and organizations*. London: Sage.

Hekman, S.J. (1992) *Gender and knowledge*. Oxford: Polity Press.

Knights, D. (1996) '**Refocusing the case study: researching politics in IT and the politics of IT research**', *Technology Studies*, 2, 2: 230–254.

Knights, D. and H. Willmott (1983) '**Dualism and domination: A critical examination of Marx, Weber and the existentialist**'. *Australian and New Zealand Journal of Sociological*, 19, 1: 33–49.

Kondo, D.K. (1990) *Crafting selves: Power, gender and discourse of identity in a Japanese workplace*. Chicago: University of Chicago Press.

Layder, D. (1994) *Understanding social theory*. London: Sage.

Marks, E. and I. de Courtivron, *editors* (1980) *New French feminism*. Amherst, MA: University of Massachusetts Press.

Martin, J. (1990) '**Deconstructing organizational taboos: The suppression of gender conflict in organizations**', *Organization Science*, 1, 4: 399–359.

Moi, T. (1985) *Sexual/textual politics: Feminist literary theory*. New York: Methuen.

Newton, T. (1996) '**Postmodernism and action**'. *Organization*, 3, 1: 7–29.

Reed, M. (1995) '**In praise of duality: Reconnecting the 'local' and the 'global' in organization analysis**'. Paper presented at the workshop on 'Action, Structure and Organizations', Paris: ESSEC IMD, May 11–12th.

Thompson, P. and S. Ackroyd (1995) '**All quiet on the workplace front? A critique of recent trends in British industrial sociology**'. *Sociology*, 29, 4: 615–633.

Willis, P.E. (1977) *Learning to labour*. London: Saxon House.

Discussion Questions

1. What is distinctive about 'postmodernism' and what contribution does it make the study of organizations?
2. What is the claim of 'deconstruction' and what does it add to our knowledge of organizing and organizations?
3. Postmodernist analysis exhibits a degree of scepticism about science and rationalism. What is the nature of this scepticism and how might it be countered or supported?
4. Kilduff invites us to deconstruct his analysis of *Organizations*. How might you take up such an invitation?

Introduction References

Alvesson, M. (1995) 'The Meaning and Meaninglessness of Postmodernism : Some Ironic Remarks' *Organization Studies* 16(6):1047–75.

Chia, R. (1994) 'The Concept of Decision: A Deconstructive Analysis' *Journal of Management Studies* 31(6):781–806.

Clegg, S. (1990) *Modern Organizations: Organization Studies in the Postmodern World*, London: Sage.

Galison, P. and Stump, D.J. (eds) (1996) *The Disunity of Science: Boundaries, Contexts and Power*, Stanford University Press.

Heydebrand, W. (1989) 'New Organizational Forms' *Work and Occupations* 16(3): 323–57.

Kondo, D. (1990) *Crafting Selves: Power, Gender, and Discourses of Identity in a Japanese Factory*, Berkeley: University of California Press.

Learmonth, M. (1999) 'The NHS Manager: Engineer and Father? A Deconstruction' *Journal of Management Studies* 36(7):999–1012.

March, J.G. and Simon, H.A. (1958) *Organizations*, New York: Wiley.

Parker, M. (1992) 'Post-Modern Organizations or Postmodern Organization Theory' *Organization Studies* 13(1): 1–17.

Recommended Further Reading

See references above to Alvesson (1995), Clegg (1990) and Parker (1992) plus:

Boje, D.M. (1995) 'Stories of the Storytelling Organization: A Postmodern Analysis of Disney as "Tamara-Land"', *Academy of Management Journal*, 38(4): 997–1035.

Boje, D.M., Gephart, R.P. and Thatchenkery, T.J. (eds.) (1996) *Postmodern management and organization theory*, Thousand Oaks, CA: Sage.

Calas, M.B. and Smircich, L. (1999) 'Past Postmodernism? Reflections and Tentative Directions', *Academy of Management Review*, 24(4): 649–671.

Chia, R. (1996) *Organizational Analysis as Deconstructive Practice*, Berlin: de Gruyter.

Deetz, S., (1996) 'Describing Differences in Approaches to Organization Science: Rethinking Burrell and Morgan and Their Legacy', *Organization Science*, 7(2): 191–207.

Gergen, K.J. and Thatchenkery, T.J. (2004) 'Organization Science as Social Construction', *Journal of Applied Behavioral Science* 40(2): 228–49.

Hancock, P. (2001) Work, postmodernism and organization: a critical introduction, London: Sage.

Hassard, J. (1994) 'Postmodern Organizational Analysis: Towards a Conceptual Framework', *Journal of Management Studies*, 31(3): 303–24.

Hassard, J. and Parker, M. (1993) Postmodernism and organizations, London: Sage.

Kilduff. M. and Mehra, A. (1997) 'Postmodernism and Organizational Research, *Academy of Management Review*, 22(2): 453–481.

Lawrence, T.B. and Phillips, N. (1998) Commentary: Separating Play and Critique – Postmodern and Critical Perspectives on TQM/BPR', *Journal of Management Inquiry*, 7(2): 154–160.

Willmott, H. (1992) 'Postmodernism and Excellence: The De-differentiation of Economy and Culture', *Journal of Organizational Change Management*, 5 (1): 58–68.

ETHICS AND ENVIRONMENT

CHAPTER **15**

READINGS

Parker, M. (2003) 'Business, Ethics and Business Ethics: Critical Theory and Negative Dialectics' in Alvesson, M. and Willmott, H.C. (eds) *Studying Management Critically*. London: Sage, pp. 199–201.

Purser, R.E., Park, C. and Montuori, A. (1995) 'Limits to Anthropocentrism: Toward an Ecocentric Organization Paradigm?' in *Academy of Management Review*, Vol. 20, No. 4: 1053–54, 1062–63, 1080–83.

Gladwin, T.N., Kennelly, J.J. and Krause, T.S. (1995) 'Shifting Paradigms for Sustainable Development: Implications for Management Theory and Research' in *Academy of Management Review*, Vol. 20, No. 4: 876–787, 896–900.

INTRODUCTION

Ethics and environment are intertwined topics that have increased in prominence over the past decade or so. In an era where concerns have been raised about the erosion of ethics as a source of moral regulation, the province of ethics has extended from the management of people to a focus upon wider relationships with the environment and ecological sustainability. When concerned with the management of people in businesses (e.g. customers and suppliers as well as employees), it has been widely assumed that the strengthening of ethics is compatible with, and indeed functional for, improved economic performance. Rarely is there an acknowledgement of how business practice and ethical principle co-exist in a relation of some tension. In general, the relevance of 'business ethics' for securing goodwill and cooperation is emphasized as what counts as 'ethical' is moulded and subordinated to business-as-usual. The already institutionalized ethics of business are taken as given and the pragmatic emphasis is upon identifying an ethically acceptable means of accommodating to the status quo. Notably, codes of ethics are drawn up with which employees are supposed to comply.

Whether such codes actively encourage more ethical forms of action or simply add to existing organizational rules that are introduced to control behaviour is a moot point. More generally, does such responsiveness to an ethical deficit directly enable employees to wrestle with moral dilemmas or to resist pressures to equate ethical action with passive, instrumental conformity to the letter, at least, of ethical codes. The possibility that a credible and defensible ethics might redefine and challenge the organization of modern business practice – as exploitative, divisive and inhumanly pressurized – is not contemplated. Instead, modern business organization is routinely naturalized and then sustained by the introduction of codes which serve to legitimize it. These codes may operate to inhibit some of the worst excesses of corporate behaviour but they do little to change institutionalized forms of exploitation and coercion. The limits of a business-centric formulation of ethics is more directly revealed and placed in doubt when attention is turned to the ethics of the environment. It is in relation to the environment that, as investors, employees or customers, our ethics are perhaps readily recognized as rapacious, as evident in the unsustainable degradation of biodiversity, deforestation, pollution, ozone depletion and so on. In this respect, there is a growing convergence between a less business-centric sense of ethics and an attentiveness to issues of globalization, governance and corporate social responsibility examined in Chapter 16.

Martin Parker (Reading 15.1) notes how the contemporary emphasis upon ethics at once responds and contributes to a 'moral panic' about business malpractice and unintended negative consequences for which it is offered up as a relevant remedy. Ethics, it is suggested, has become something that companies must be seen to address and display – to investors but also to customers and employees – in order to demonstrate their credentials as a bona fide business. But, as Parker notes, the intellectual sources used to specify the ethics are highly selective – the liberalism of Bentham and Mill rather than the radicalism of Marx or Foucault. Consideration of debates in political philosophy around topics such as democracy, justice and human rights are marginalized in discussions of business ethics: 'politics' are effectively disassociated from 'ethics'. This marginalization of politics is congruent with the moulding and subordination of ethics to business-as-usual. Acting 'ethically' is conceived primarily, and often exclusively, as a personal matter for individual deliberation and choice. It is not as something that is also deeply embedded in our everyday practices and institutions, for which we bear collective responsibility. Contemporary ethics of business are, as a consequence, shallow in conception, narrow in scope and unambitious in direction. These limits become very clear when consideration is given to the bigger picture of sustainability and the formation of a radically different ethics as a condition of its possibility.

The degradation of the environment is related, in Reading 15.2 by **Ronald Purser, Changkil Park and Alfonso Montouri**, to an ethic of anthropocentricism in which *Homo sapiens* is placed at the apex and centre of life and assumes the priority of human values and demands. Typically, other life forms and the wider environment are regarded as instruments for the realization of those values and demands, without regard for the intimate connectedness of humankind and nature. This 'egocentric' orientation is legitimized by a widely held belief that pursuing self-interest is collectively beneficial. Without dwelling upon its detrimental effects for the quality of life and its connivance in nationalism, it is doubtful whether the dictum of 'ethical egoism' (Reading 15.2, p. 273) can be reconciled with environmental preservation. It is perhaps no coincidence that the society that has embraced so-called 'ethical egoism' for longest is also the society that, assisted by the global reach of its major corporations, currently makes the biggest per capita contribution to global warming and environmental degradation.

This disregard for the environment is reflected in management and organization theory. Until recently there has been minimal consideration of the dependence and impact of corporations upon the ecosystem. Exploitation of natural resources has been regarded as the prerogative of their owners, with minimal regard to their consequences for the biosphere and hence for all life forms. Even today, attention is given to legal compliance and the calculation of business risks associated with the probabilities of detection and prosecution. Attentiveness to, and care of, the environment tends to be limited to what is assessed to be least costly or most beneficial for the business, and not what is most sustainable or of greatest value to future generations. An alternative, 'ecocentric' approach commended by Purser *et al.*, anticipates the development of a democratic mode of governance where businesses are held more directly accountable to their stakeholders, and no longer driven by the pursuit of profits appropriated primarily by a privileged elite. The basis for this, it is suggested, is a 'new moral ecology' (Reading 15.2, p. 273) in which the bottom-up emphasis is upon mutual preservation rather than heavy reliance upon top-down, technocratic efforts to mitigate the most damaging or embarrassing consequences of corporate egocentrism. The challenge is to engage citizens in an alternative 'moral ecology' where we become active participants, rather than reluctantly compliant adjuncts, in the challenging process of developing an ecologically sustainable global economy.

What sustainable development might mean is taken up by **Thomas Gladwin, James Kennelly and Tara-Shlomith Krause** (Reading 15.3). Their conception of development incorporates social as well as ecological sustainability; and it is defined in relation to ideas of inclusiveness, equity, prudence and so on. Conversely, an activity is unsustainable if it operates to exclude, disconnect, increase inequality, accommodate recklessness or increase insecurity. Here once again, the realization of sustainable development is related to, and largely conditional upon, the emergence of a new ethics where an emphasis upon social and ecological development takes priority over the relentless pursuit of (profitable) growth. The study and attainment of sustainable development is seen to involve an extensive and radical agenda that includes, for example, critical scrutiny of whether the mobility of financial capital works against the idea of organization-in-community, and whether the shift to sustainable development requires a renationalization of capital. It is acknowledged that this agenda resonates with ethical concerns as its fulfilment requires 'profound value change' (Reading 15.3, p. 278) and a preparedness to engage 'ideas dangerous to greed, shortsightedness, indulgence, exploitation, apathy' (Reading 15.3, p. 278) and so on. It is envisaged that the creation and refinement metrics and models which embrace the value of sustainability can assist the process of transformation But it is also emphasized that the 'tools of "greening"' (Reading 15.3, p. 278) used to reduce pollution, for example, must not be a substitute for a more radical and extensive commitment to preserving and enabling biodiversity and developing institutions that more completely integrate and articulate an ethos of sustainability.

Business, Ethics and Business Ethics: Critical Theory and Negative Dialectics

By Martin Parker

A very common opening gambit in texts on Business Ethics is to suggest, implicitly or explicitly, that there is some kind of crisis of ethics. Put simply, this is a diagnosis of the present age which compares it unfavourably with the past. It is suggested that people don't trust businesses anymore, that negative images of organizations are common in the media, that hyper-competition is making employees and organizations perform whatever the costs, that globalization is causing competing belief systems to collide, or that the environment can no longer sustain unbridled capitalism (Cannon, 1994: 1; Hoffman and Frederick, 1995: 2). Now if this is the case, then managers are in a different and potentially dangerous world and are sorely in need of guidance. As is clear, this is a diagnosis that essentially relies on a narrative of ethical decline. I have elsewhere written about this as a version of the long-standing tension between nostalgia and modernization which can be located in many accounts of the transition to modernity, perhaps most notably Durkheim's version of anomie and the division of labour (Parker, 1998: 29). This kind of story suggests that modernization involves the loss of community and traditional forms of moral regulation. The small-scale, high-trust and face-to-face interactions that once constrained market exchanges have now been replaced with anonymous and huge corporate structures. The players in global marketplaces now have no meaningful responsibilities to people or places. Indeed, to even admit such responsibilities is seemingly to court disaster because capital, like a nervous bird, can flee so rapidly at the slightest sign of conscience.

In a sense, the empirical accuracy of this kind of history is unimportant, what seems to matter is that it helps to legitimize the need for Business Ethics. In practice, sustained historical analyses of capitalism over the last few hundred years are rare in the Business Ethics literature. Indeed, the very notion of a 'new' ethical crisis often requires that historical continuities are denied by, for example, dismissing Marx by claiming that he was writing about bad old nineteenth-century capitalism (Stewart, 1996: 22). Whatever the accuracy of the history, what is important is that the story provides a space for Business Ethics to step into. Ethical analysis, education and regulation is now needed, when previously it was not. Importantly, this is a history that is also very often used to legitimize management and the business school in general with talk about 'hyper-competition', 'globalization', and change being the only constant. More effective business and management then becomes the answer. This is rather like being told that we 'need' estate agents, or pet psychologists, or better deodorants. The creation of the need is an essential move in legitimizing the product. Businesses, and busy-people, now 'need' ethics, when presumably they did not before. And if the abstractions of this argument are not enough to persuade, then they can be supported by a simple assertion that it is important for all businesses to think hard about ethics because state legislation and heightened public awareness demand it (Clutterbuck *et al.*, 1992: 15; Drummond and Bain, 1994: 2). This is what Griseri calls the 'compliance function' (1998: 216) – which is akin to saying that ethics is a part of contemporary business practice, and whether you like it or not, it is something you must know about. In a strangely performative way, the fact that people talk about Business Ethics proves that it is needed.

And so, the need created, the question that then arises is who is to fill it. Or, as Jackson puts it in the introduction to her text – 'I have to show that

Business, Ethics and Business Ethics: Critical Theory and Negative Dialectics

By Martin Parker

business people ... have something to learn that they do not know already and that they need to know' (1996: 1). Business Ethicists have two cards to play here. The first is a body of ethical knowledge which it largely inherits from moral philosophy. This is a substantial piece of cultural capital, stretching back to Plato and Aristotle, and incorporating big words (utilitarianism, deontology) and big names (Immanuel Kant, John Stuart Mill). The usefulness of such language should not be underestimated, since it is sufficiently arcane to impress, and allows the putative business ethicist to be a gatekeeper to the knowledges that are the province of the academy. To put it simply, without moral philosophy, it would have been more difficult to legitimate Business Ethics as a discrete and credible domain of enquiry. Virtually all Business Ethics texts hence contain references to Kantian conceptions of duty, particularly the implications of the categorical imperative – 'do as you would be done by'. Such arguments are then usually counterposed to utilitarian notions of the greatest good for the greatest number, often connecting these to their contemporary formulations in stakeholder theory. Often there is also reference to virtue theory and discussions of the importance of individual or organizational character. However, there are also some interesting blind spots in what counts as the relevant intellectual capital. The moral philosophies which are incorporated largely comprise the classics of the analytical cannon, and it is rare to find references to twentieth-century 'continental' philosophy here. Nietzsche, Heidegger, Gadamer, Sartre, Foucault, Derrida, Lyotard and so on, are largely absent from the Business Ethics text, as are many references to the various forms of twentieth-century Marxism (of which much more below). In addition, there are also some clear absences in terms of the intersections between moral philosophy and political theory. Detailed interrogations of law, the state, power, justice, equality, liberty, democracy, human rights and so on are also absent from the centre of Business Ethics. Rather ominously, 'politics' does not seem to be part of 'ethics'.

The second card that Business Ethicists have to play is in stressing the application and relevance of

their knowledges. Tactically, this is important in order to avoid accusations of irrelevance by a busy, practically minded audience, or what Sorell has called the 'alienation problem' (1998: 17). This issue largely boils down to stressing the role of Business Ethics as a form of mediation between the intellectual capital of the academy and the pragmatism of management decision-making in the real world. This is clearly a delicate balancing act between 'ethics' and 'business' which answers the question 'why business needs ethics' (Stewart, 1996: 5). Too far in the direction of ethics and there is little connection to the lifeworld of business; too far in the direction of business and the discipline becomes a rehearsal of management common sense with no 'unique selling proposition', as the marketers put it. As a result, most Business Ethics texts stress their applied and practical nature – 'straight talk about how to do it right' (Trevino and Nelson, 1999; see also Jackson, 1996; Ottensmeyer and McCarthy, 1996); the experience of their authors in business or running an ethics consultancy (Drummond and Bain, 1994); or even contain inspiring photographs of (and quotes from) CEOs at the start of every chapter (Stewart, 1996).

Perhaps most importantly though, virtually all of these texts use the usual repertoire of case studies and discussion questions that are common in management teaching texts. Such cases, often copyrighted as being 'owned' by a particular person or institution, are almost always framed as a personalization of the issue concerned. 'What would *you* do in this situation? Give reasons for your decisions.' I suppose this stress on the agency of the individual is hardly surprising, given the absence of consideration of what is normally termed 'politics'. That is to say, an emphasis on individualism seems to obviate consideration of structural constraints, even to the extent of filling in questionnaires to determine 'your cynicism quotient' and an exercise on 'walking my talk' (Tevino and Nelson, 1999: 18, 169). Indeed, the philosophical resources most commonly deployed – deontology, utilitarianism, and a curiously de-socialized version of virtue ethics – encourage precisely these kind of individualized thought experiments. Whether interrogating one's moral

| READING 15.1 | **Business, Ethics and Business Ethics: Critical Theory and Negative Dialectics** *continued* |

By Martin Parker

duties; evaluating potential means and ends; or considering traits of character such as wisdom, fidelity and so on, the emphasis is on active consciousness-informing personal choices. The management decision-maker collects the evidence, models a set of potential algorithms, and then makes a decision on what actions should be taken. Further, these decisions are also often then framed within chapters on key business issues – sexual harassment and diversity, health and safety, whistleblowing, intellectual property, the environment, and so on. This is, of course, both eminently 'practical' by definition, but it also succeeds in excluding many matters which are then deemed beyond the remit of the case in point. Rather like the *ceteris paribus* of economics, only certain matters are defined as relevant, and everything else becomes a form of background noise. Everything else is somehow 'outside' Business Ethics.

Finally, and perhaps most importantly, there is the question of whether Business Ethics will actually make businesses more ethical. Do the means – studying Business Ethics – have any demonstrable effect on the desired ends – more ethical businesses? Here, the texts are generally more cautious, and justifiably so. For a start, since the ends very rarely include the overthrow of managerial capitalism, or even radical state intervention, the centre of the project is amelioration rather than revolutionary change. It is rare to find analyses that suggest alternative understandings of markets, of hierarchical organization, or the work–effort bargain. Instead the emphasis is on working within contemporary business organizations in order that their worst excesses can be tempered. Indeed, since the vast majority of ethics texts tend to assert that ethics makes for better business, or at least that there is no contradiction between ethics and business, sometimes even amelioration seems irrelevant. Ethics becomes a specific part of a business and marketing strategy. Second, and as I discussed above, the personalization of ethical problems leads to an emphasis on individual rationality within a satisficing mode of decision-making. The reader of these texts is assumed to be an individual who will meet, or

has met, everyday dilemmas and might have to make decisions that they are not completely comfortable with. Different stakeholders have 'rights' that need to be balanced (Ottensmeyer and McCarthy, 1996), and people in business must operate within the rules of the game. The rhetorical mode of the practical and personalized case study is hence to position a set of unmovable assumptions, and then ask the reader to work within these. This means that Business Ethics is rarely utopian, or even moderately ambitious, in its aims. Its mode of address is to suggest personal development, or perhaps sensible reform, as reasonable ends. Such modesty is laudable in the often breathless arena of management in general, but if so little is expected, then little is likely to be achieved.

References

Cannon, T. (1994) *Corporate Responsibility*. London: Pitman.

Clutterbuck, D., Dearlove, D. and Snow, D. (1992) *Actions Speak Louder. A Management Guide to Social Responsibility*. London: Kogan Page.

Drummond, J. and Bain, B. (eds) (1994) *Managing Business Ethics*. Oxford: Butterworth-Heinemann.

Griseri, P. (1998) *Managing Values*. Basingstoke: Macmillan.

Hoffman, W. and Frederick, R. (1995) *Business Ethics: Readings and Cases in Corporate Morality*. New York: McGraw-Hill.

Jackson, J. (1996) *An Introduction to Business Ethics*. Oxford: Blackwell.

Ottensmeyer, E. and McCarthy, G. (1996) *Ethics in the Workplace*. New York: McGraw-Hill.

Parker, M. (1998) Business Ethics and social theory: Post-modernizing the ethical. *British Journal of Management*. 9: 27–36.

Sorell, T. (1998) Beyond the fringe? The strange state of Business Ethics. In M. Parker (ed.), *Ethics and Organisations*. London: Sage.

Stewart, D. (1996) *Business Ethics*. New York: McGraw-Hill.

Trevino, L. and Nelson, K. (1999) *Managing Business Ethics*. New York: Wiley.

READING 15.2	**Limits to Anthropocentrism: Toward an Ecocentric Organization Paradigm?**

By Ronald E. Purser, Changkil Park and Alfonso Montuori

Over the course of three decades, modern organizations have been the target of escalating criticism from environmentalists (Carson, 1962; Commoner, 1990; Devall and Sessions, 1985; McKibben, 1989; Orr, 1992; Rozak, 1979). Industry continues to face a media backlash that has heightened public concern over toxic wastes, exposures to environmental disasters and pollution, loss of biodiversity, ozone depletion, and greenhouse warming. Despite the increasing public concern over environmental degradation, the field of business and management studies 'betrays little evidence of the influence of environmentalism on business' (Shrivastava, 1994b: 236). Within the universe of management and organization discourse, Shrivastava (1994b) estimated that only a mere 10% of the studies have been concerned with social issues in management or relations between business and the natural environment. Similarly, in the field of American sociology, research on the sociological causes of environmental degradation has been ignored. As Dunlap and Catton (1993) pointed out, between 1970 and 1990 not one article on environmental problems was published in either the *American Sociological Review* or the *American Journal of Sociology* – the two mainstream sociological journals.

Our statements should not be interpreted as a grand indictment of organization sciences. On the contrary, we are encouraged by the growing number of scholars whose efforts are now focused on ecologically sustainable organization research as evidenced by the recent formation of the 'Organization and Natural Environment' interest group in the Academy of Management and the appearance of this Special Topic Forum. Despite these encouraging developments, it is important to understand why there has been a paucity of research in this area. One of the major reasons for this lack of articles can be attributed to an anthropocentric bias in the field of organization science. For example, based on their review of the major theories of strategic management, Pauchant and Fortier (1990) concluded that such theories were all based on the underpinnings of an anthropocentric ethic. In a similar vein, Shrivastava and Hart (1992) claimed that the central limitation of

organizational studies has to do with its narrow, ideological, 'de-natured' view of organizational environments. Understandably, Shrivastava (1994a) decries the fact that organizational theorists continue to spin off theories as if nature were an infinitely renewable resource or external commodity.

Anthropocentrism is based on the perception of a fundamental dualism between organizations and the natural environment (Buchholz, 1993; Pauchant and Fortier, 1990; Shrivastava, 1995). According to ecophilosophers, anthropocentrism is an ontological position that influences the code of ethics toward nature. Eckersley (1992: 51) defined anthropocentrism as 'the belief that there is a clear and morally relevant dividing line between humankind and the rest of nature, that humankind is the only principal source of value or meaning in the world'. However, the problematic issue is not so much one of human centeredness, for it seems perfectly natural for human beings to place themselves at the center of their concerns. Even the Rio Declaration at the Earth Summit asserted the claim: 'Human beings are at the centre of concerns' (United Nations Conference on Environment and Development [UNCED], 1992). What is problematic is humankind's structure of values as they are deeply rooted in a human-nature dualism. Anthropocentrism must be recognized and eradicated before fundamental changes can take place in people's attitudes and actions toward the nonhuman world (Oelschlaeger, 1991). This fundamental perceptual and attitudinal change is difficult but necessary, for a 'revolution in ethics' cannot occur until there is a 'revolution in perception' (Rodman, 1980) ...

Egocentric Orientation

The anthropocentric agenda has provided the legitimacy for a focus that is egocentrically oriented toward finding the means whereby rational, self-interested agents can optimize and exploit the social and natural environment for their 'competitive advantage'. Recognizing the limitations of the egocentric orientation, Trist (1981: 43) insightfully observed: 'Traditional organizations serve only their own ends. They are, and indeed are supposed to be, selfish.' Adherents to an egoistic value orientation

Limits to Anthropocentrism: Toward an Ecocentric Organization Paradigm? *continued*

By Ronald E. Purser, Changkil Park and Alfonso Montuori

are likely to consider that enlightened self-interest will guide society to a sustainable future. The moral source of this position is 'ethical egoism' (Olsen, 1965; Rand, 1967). With ethical egoism and self-interest as dominant value orientations, egocentric actors – whether they be individuals or organizations – are more likely to pursue an economically advantageous course of action when confronted with a choice between environmental preservation or economic development (Axlerod, 1994: 101; Merchant, 1992). The most cost-effective solution to dump toxic waste chemicals into a watershed may benefit the individual firm, but places the surrounding ecosystem at risk, as toxic chemicals find their way into the biological food chain (Carson, 1962).

Different theoretical models of organization–environment relationships share a common egocentric orientation. This is ironic, given the fact that organization theorists turned to the life sciences and imported organismic metaphors to help explain organization–environment transactions (Katz and Kahn, 1966; Morgan, 1986; von Bertlanffy, 1950). However, the application of these organismic theories in modern corporations has managed to ignore the existence of the natural environment. This occurred as a result of a reductionistic interpretation of organismic theories through the world hypothesis of mechanism (Pepper, 1942; Purser, 1993). Emery (1995) noted that the mechanization of open systems theory occurred as sociotechnical systems practitioners in the United States narrowly defined the concept of directive correlation as a limited problem of adaptation to the *task* environment. Similarly, contingency theory offered a means of identifying patterns of 'good fit' (Lawrence and Lorsch, 1967) between organizational structure and the complexity of the *business* environment. The resource-dependence model viewed organizations as actively seeking *resources* from the environment (Pfeffer and Salancik, 1978), focusing on how organizations can optimize their capacities for resource acquisition, in order 'to manipulate the environment to their own advantage' (Hall, 1987: 303). Taking a population ecology view (Hannan and Freeman, 1977), other organizational theorists placed more emphasis on the economic and *institutional* environment as a force in organizational survival.

Implicit in these egocentric organization theories is a Lockean view of the environment; the land, or nature, is seen as potential 'real estate,' an idle resource that is without value until it is used by humans. The issue here has to do with the locus of value, or 'value ownership' (Roiston, 1994). Although it may be true that only humans are capable of bestowing value upon things in nature, this truism has been distorted to mean that value is exclusively located in humans. This misconception also implies that value in the environment does not exist objectively, unless value is ascribed by humans (Martell, 1994). This is a fallacy of misplaced location (Roiston, 1994), a fundamental cognitive distortion of the anthropocentric view.

Organizations with an egocentric orientation, if they pursued environmental reforms at all, would do so only if it was in their self-interest. The pursuit of environmental protection by egocentric organizations is perceived in terms of how organizational constituents would benefit or be affected. Egocentric organizations are concerned with problems related to depletion of resources that are required for production processes, compliance with environmental legislation and alleviation of health hazards to avoid litigation, and image enhancement of the corporation to retain shareholder value (Post and Altman, 1994). These reforms fall under the rubric of corporate environmentalism. Corporate environmentalism addresses these issues quite effectively, but for anthropocentric reasons. Which types of environmental problems, the scope of care, and range of ethical extension to different parts of the environment will be limited to a narrow domain that incurs immediate benefits to egocentric organizational concerns? Even the current practice of sociotechnical systems design (Pasmore, 1988; Taylor and Felten, 1993) defines the unit of survival in the environment as a single focal organization. Discourse involving environmental decision making is confined to issues and positions that maintain the egocentric identity of the firm (Boje and Dennehy, 1993) ...

Ecological Democracy

In an ecological democracy, employees and nonhuman lifeforms would not be subjected to being managed, exploited, controlled, or dominated by an elite

Limits to Anthropocentrism: Toward an Ecocentric Organization Paradigm?

By Ronald E. Purser, Changkil Park and Alfonso Montuori

group (i.e., supervisors or planetary managers) that presumes to occupy a superior position above the systems to which it belongs. This is the mechanistic view of power, or the Cartesian notion that one substance can exert its dominion over another substance. In contrast, power in an ecological democracy derives from systems maintaining open energy exchanges with other systems and, in fact, is based on the systems theory concept of synergy. In this schema, power is not something one substance does to another substance, but rather, it is something that is gained through the emergence of collaborative assemblies, interdependent domains, and cooperative networks. This action is in concurrence with the negotiated order strategy, based on a mutual acceptance that resources must be shared and objectives must be linked if any of the parts are to survive (Emery & Trist, 1973). This new ecological sensibility emphasizes democratic coexistence, what Gitlin (1989: 57) referred to as 'a new moral ecology – that in the preservation of the other is a condition for the preservation of the self'.

This ecological approach to democratic organizations is oriented toward reversing the patterns of exploitation and increasing the attentiveness of employees and managers to concerns that are significant to the long-term survival of the biosphere – which includes the emancipation of humans. Thus, the target of ecological critique is not management per se, but managerial egotism and human arrogance. It is a move away from the philosophical immaturity that concedes that exploitation of the natural environment is simply a managerial prerogative.

Advances in theory and practice should focus on the design and development of ecologically democratic organizational forms. Ecologically democratic organizations should (a) be designed in accordance with the highest ideals of their members; (b) disperse the power to participate to employees, involving them in policy decisions that normally have been the purview of management; (c) democratize planning processes that affect strategic decisions regarding choices of product design, resource use, production methods, and marketing plans; (d) be able to shift from an orientation of control to the exploration of the potentials for collaboration,

whether among employees, employees and management, or organizations and environment.

As Trist (1981) pointed out, this democratic future will largely depend upon organizations aligning their purposes with the purposes of the wider society and also with the purposes of their members. By doing so, organizations become both 'environmentalized' and 'humanized' (and, thus, more truly purposeful), rather than remaining impersonal and mindless forces that increase environmental turbulence and degradation. This is a crucial point because of the emergence of public support and pressure for collective responses to environmental problems. The majority of Americans consider protection of the environment and fighting pollution as urgent and serious concerns. This is true for the majority of Europcans (Eurobarometer, 1992), and the concern is just as high among people in developing countries in the South as it is for the North American public (Dunlap, Gallup, and Gallup, 1993). In addition, recent surveys show that for the younger generation, environmental problems are the number-one topic of concern (Stern and Dietz, 1994).

One probable future that these trends point to is that new and unexpected coalitions may form in and across sectors of society mobilized around ecological agendas. For example, up to this point, organized labor has been subsumed under the dominant social paradigm, viewing the agenda of fundamentalist environmentalists as contradictory to their economic interests. However, Beck (1992) has suggested that as conflicts between environmental 'risk-winning' and 'risk-losing' sectors increase, workers may become mobilized by a greened labour movement.

Ecological democracy will require forms of social change that are alternatives to social engineering and authoritarian technocratic solutions. Elden (1986) has demonstrated that a top-down, 'empowerment-as-structure' approach to sociotechnical systems design usually results in massive employee resistance and passivity. Likewise, a 'sustainability-as-structure' approach to solving global environmental problems – where, in this case, the state or governmental technocrats introduce a grand design for global planetary management – is also likely to lead to compliance rather than a fundamental change in the consciousness

Limits to Anthropocentrism: Toward an Ecocentric Organization Paradigm? *continued*

By Ronald E. Purser, Changkil Park and Alfonso Montuori

within organizational ecologies and local communities. Ecological democracy will require new forms of self-management, where the responsibility for the control and coordination of environmental strategies is located at the domain level, where organizations belonging to that domain can maximize collaboration, lower resistance to change, and undertake innovative approaches toward ecocentric organization development.

Conclusion

Theory developers of an ecocentric organization paradigm must pay greater attention to understanding how concepts are modulated by different concepts of space, time, and knowledge. The more extreme, Arcadian-ecocentric natural history perspective harks back to a time before industrialization, before automobiles, highways, and toxic wastes and, in some cases, before the appearance of humans. That image of the past – of an untrammeled wilderness world, in some ways – has also been projected as a desirable prospect for the planet. Clearly, in this case, the 'long' view of time is taken, drawing far back into Nature's unspoiled history, coupled with a spatially 'large' view of the planet. Along with this broad sweep of time and space, a major change in human knowledge is also called for – a veritable paradigm shift. The environmental management perspective, on the other hand, is limited to a short time perspective, focused on developing some form of immediate but temporary solutions to environmental problems within the limited radius of egocentric organizations. Although this perspective calls attention to the significance and importance of environmental problems, triggering a reassessment of technological knowledge as it relates to the efficient management of them, the shift is not truly dramatic.

Both of these perspectives, and indeed, any discussions of environmental problems must confront the issue of the future. That the famous Club of Rome *Limits to Growth* (Meadows, Meadows, and Behrens, 1983) study was a piece of futurism should remind us of the close connection between ecology and future studies. Future studies typically have involved extrapolation of emerging present technological breakthroughs into the future, without researchers

seriously questioning the direction of the future. More of the same meant progress. Despite its flawed methodological assumptions, if there is anything *Limits to Growth* has taught – along with the ensuing onslaught from environmentalists and postmodernists alike – it is that the future is not what it used to be. Humankind's notion of progress – if by progress one means more technology, more industry, more urbanization, more agribusiness, more control over Nature, and so forth – will also change.

Competing ecological paradigms add to the confusion already existing in organizational studies (Pfeffer, 1993) coupled with the erosion of a secure sense of the future and clear notion of progress. We believe that there is no single paradigm or theory that can promise to offer unfailing solutions or clear guidance to organizations for resolving current and future ecological dilemmas. Further, we could argue that the Arcadian ecocentric paradigm is a nostalgic dream, which, although perhaps philosophically tenable and aesthetically attractive, is simply 'unrealistic' in the context of socioeconomic realities. There seems to be little consensus as to what constitutes 'ecosystem sustainability' or 'beauty,' 'integrity,' 'health,' and so forth. However, we argue that the environmental management approach simply doesn't go far enough, that it really amounts to an incremental strategy, and that it does not highlight how deep-seated the ecological crisis really is. Thus, there are limits to anthropocentrism.

However, movement toward an ecocentric organization paradigm is not inevitable; it will require a serious debate regarding how different organization–environment relationships should be organized. This debate will involve difficult choices, new types of learning, and a diffusion of democratization processes both within and across organizations at both local and global levels of society. Now is a crucial juncture in human and natural history, and as some researchers suggest, the planetary ecosystem may be heading toward a point of irreversible destruction (McKibben, 1989). It is apparent that new approaches and new organizational–environment configurations must be invented. Indeed, if the future is a human creation, driven by human choices, the process of learning

READING 15.2 | # Limits to Anthropocentrism: Toward an Ecocentric Organization Paradigm?

By Ronald E. Purser, Changkil Park and Alfonso Montuori

how to learn about the future and the ecology will require a great deal of social creativity.

References

Allerod, L.J. (1994) Balancing personal needs with environmental preservation: Identifying value that guide decisions in ecological dilemmas. *Journal of Social Issues*, 50(3): 85–104.

Beck. (1992) *The risk society: Towards a new modernity*. Newbury Park, CA: Sage.

Boje, D. and Dennehu, R. (1993) *Management in a postmodern world*. Dubuque, LA: Kendall-Hunt.

Buchholz, R. (1993) *Principles of environmental management: The greening of business*. Englewood Cliffs, NJ: Prentice Hall.

Carson, R. (1962) *Silent spring*. Boston, MA: Houghton Mifflin.

Commoner, B. (1990) *Making peace with the planet*. New York: Bantam.

Devall, B. and Sessions, G. (1985) Deep ecology: *Living as if nature mattered*. Layton, UT: Gibbs-Smith.

Dunlap, R.E. and Catton, W.R. (1993) The development, current status, and probable future of environmental sociology: Toward an ecological sociology. *Annals of the International Institute of Sociology*: 3.

Dunlap, R.E. Gallup, G.H. and Gallup. A.M. (1993) Of global concern: Results of the health of the planet survey. *Environment*, 35(9): 7–15, 33–39.

Eckersley, B. (1992) *Environmentalism and political theory*. Albany: State University of New York Press.

Elden, M. (1986) Sociotechnical systems ideas as public policy in Norway: Empowering participation through worker-managed change. *Journal of Applied Behavioral Science*, 22: 239–255.

Emery, M. (1995) *Searching* (New Ed.). Amsterdam: Van Gorcum.

Emery, F.E. and Trist, E. (1973) *Towards a social ecology: Contextual appreciations of the future in the present*. New York: Plenum Press.

Eurobarometer. (1992) *Europeans and the environment in 1992*. Brussels, Belgium: Author.

Gitlin, T. (1989) Post-modernism: The stenography of surfaces. *New Perspectives Quarterly*, 6: 55–66.

Hall, B.H. (1987) *Organizations: Structures. processes and outcomes*. Englewood Cliffs, NJ: Prentice Hall.

Hannan, M. and Freeman, I. (1977) The population ecology of organizations. *American Journal of Sociology*, 82: 929–964.

Katz, D. and Kahn, R. (1966) *The social psychology of organizations*. New York: Wiley.

Lawrence, G. and Lorsch, J. (1967) *Organization and environment*. Cambridge. MA: Harvard Business School.

Martell, L. (1994) *Ecology and society*. Amherst, MA: University of Massachusetts Press.

McKibben, W. (1989) *The end of nature*. New York: Anchor Books.

Meadows, D.H., Meadows, D.L. and Behrens. W. (1983) *The limits to growth: The Club of Rome's project on the predicament of mankind*. London: Pan.

Merchant, C. (1992) *Radical ecology: The search for a livable world*. New York: Routledge, Chapman & Hall.

Morgan, G. (1986) *Images of organization*. Newbury Park, CA: Sage.

Oelschlaeger, M. (1991) *The idea of wilderness: From prehistory to the age of ecology*, New Haven, CT: Yale University Press.

Olsen, R.G. (1965) *The morality of self-interest*. New York: Harcourt.

Orr, D. (1992) *Ecological literacy: Education and the transition to a postmodern world*. Albany, NY: State University of New York Press.

Pasmore, W.A. (1888) *Designing effective organizations: The sociotechnical systems perspective*. New York: Wiley.

Pauchant, T. and Fortier, L. (1990) Anthropocentric ethics in organizations, strategic management and the environment. In P. Shrivastava, and R. Lamb (Eds.). *Advances in Strategic Management*, vol 6: 99–114. Greenwich, CT: JAI Press.

Pepper, S. (1942) *World hypotheses*. Berkeley, CA: University of California Press.

Pfeffer, J. (1993) Barriers to the advance of organization science: Paradigm development as a dependent variable. *Academy of Management Review*, 18: 599–620.

Pfeffer, J. and Salancik, G.R. (1978) *The external control of organizations: A resource dependence perspective*. New York: Harper & Row.

Post, J. and Altman, B. (1994) Managing the environmental change process: Barriers and opportunities. *Journal of Organizational Change Management*, 7: 64–81.

Purser, H.E. (1993) 'Opening up' open systems theory: Towards a socio-ecological understanding of organizational-environments. In T. Tulku (Ed.), *Mastery of mind: Perspectives on time, space and knowledge*. Berkeley, CA: Dharma Publishing.

Rand, A. (1967) *The virtue of selfishness: A new concept of egoism*. New York: American Library.

Rodman, I. (1980) Paradigm change in political science: An ecological perspective. *American Behavioral Scientist*, 24: 49 78.

Roiston, H. (1994) *Conserving natural value*. New York: Columbia University Press.

Limits to Anthropocentrism: Toward an Ecocentric Organization Paradigm? *continued*

By Ronald E. Purser, Changkil Park and Alfonso Montuori

Roszak, T. (1979) *Person–planet: The creative disintegration of industrial society.* New York: Anchor Books.

Shrivastava, P. (1994a) Castrated environment: Greening organizational science. *Organization Studies*, 20: 705–726.

Shrivastava, P. (1994b) Greening business education: Toward an ecocentric pedagogy. *Journal of Management Inquiry*, 3: 235–243.

Shrivastava, P. and Hart, S. (1992) Greening organizations: 2000. *International Journal of Public Administration*, 17: 607–635.

Shrivastava, P. (1995) Ecocentric management for a risk society. *Academy of Management Review*, 20: 118–137.

Stern, P. and Dietz, T. (1994) The value basis of environmental concerns. *Journal of Social Issues*, 50(3): 65–84.

Taylor, I. and Felten, D. (1993) *Performance by design: Sociotechnical systems in North America.* Englewood Cliffs, NJ: Prentice Hall.

Trist, E.L. (1981) The sociotechnical perspective: the evolution of sociotechnical systems as a conceptual framework and an action research program. In A.H. Van de Ven and W.F. Joyce (Eds.), *Perspective on organization design and behavior*, 19–75. New York: Wiley.

United Nations Conference on Environment and Development (UNCED). (1992) *The Rio declaration.* New York: United Nations.

Von Bertalanffy, L. (1950) The theory of open systems in physics and biology. *Science*, 111: 23–29.

Shifting Paradigms for Sustainable Development: Implications for Management Theory and Research

By Thomas N. Gladwin, James J. Kennelly and Tara-Shelomith Krause

Toward a Meaning of Sustainable Development

Sustainable development has been variously conceived in terms of vision expression (Lee, 1993), value change (Clark, 1989), moral development (Rolston, 1994), social reorganization (Gore, 1992) or transformational process (Viederman, 1994) toward a desired future or better world. The core idea was defined most influentially by The World Commission on Environment and Development (i.e. The Brundtland Commission) as 'development which meets the needs of the present without compromising the ability of future generations to meet their own needs' (1987: 8). In its broadest sense, this normative abstraction has been widely accepted and endorsed by thousands of governmental, corporate, and other organizations worldwide (Gladwin and Krause, In press).

Definitions of Sustainable Development

Since the time of the Commission report, scores of alternative definitions of sustainable development, sustainable economies, and sustainable societies have been proposed. See Table 15.3.1 for an abbreviated gallery of some of the more detailed and/or leading conceptions in recent years.

A perusal of Table 15.3.1 (along with a content analysis of many other definitions of sustainable development catalogued in Gladwin, 1992; Pearce, Markandya, and Barbier. 1989; Pezzey, 1992) indicates that the construct is fundamentally infused with multiple objectives and ingredients, complex interdependencies and considerable 'moral thickness' (Williams, 1985). As a consequence, some observers forecast that the notion of sustainable development will remain fuzzy, elusive, contestable, or ideologically controversial for some time to come (Beckerman, 1994; Dowie, 1995; Levin, 1993). Yet definitional diversity is to be expected during the emergent phase of any potentially big idea of general usefulness; sustainability is akin to democracy, liberty, equality, or security in this regard. As Kuhn noted, new paradigms tend to emerge from entirely new fundamentals and, at first, without a full set of concrete rules or standards (1962). Rather than

Source: Reproduced with permission (via Copyright Clearance Center) from 'Shifting Paradigms for Sustainable Development: Implications for Management Theory and Research', in the Academy of Management Review © 1995 Academy of Management Review.

Shifting Paradigms for Sustainable Development: Implications for Management Theory and Research

By Thomas N. Gladwin, James J. Kennelly and Tara-Shelomith Krause

TABLE 15.3.1 | REPRESENTATIVE CONCEPTIONS OF SUSTAINABLE DEVELOPMENT

To maximize simultaneously the biological system goals (genetic diversity, resilience, biological productivity), economic system goals (satisfaction of basic needs, enhancement of equity, increasing useful goods and services), and social system goals (cultural diversity, institutional sustainability, social justice, participation) (Barbier. 1987: 103).

Improving the quality of human life while living within the carrying capacity of supporting ecosystems (The World Conservation Union, United Nations Environment Programme and Worldwide Fund for Nature. 1991: 10).

Sustainability is a relationship between dynamic human economic systems and larger dynamic, but normally slower-changing ecological systems, in which (a) human life can continue indefinitely, (b) human individuals can flourish, and (c) human cultures can develop; but in which effects of human activities remain within bounds, so as not to destroy the diversity, complexity, and function of the ecological life support system (Costanza, Daly, and Bartholomew, 1991: 8).

A sustainable society is one that can persist over generations, one that is far-seeing enough, flexible enough, and wise enough not to undermine either its physical or its social systems of support (Meadows, Mcadows, and Randers, 1992: 209).

Sustainability is an economic state where the demands placed upon the environment by people and commerce can be met without reducing the capacity of the environment to provide for future generations. It can also be expressed as … leave the world better than you found it, take no more than you need, try not to harm life or the environment, and make amends if you do (Hawken, 1993: 139).

Our vision is of a life-sustaining earth. We are committed to the achievement of a dignified, peaceful, and equitable existence. We believe a sustainable United States will have an economy that equitably provides opportunities for satisfying livelihoods and a safe, healthy, high quality of life for current and future generations. Our nation will protect its environment, its natural resource base, and the functions and viability of natural systems on which all life depends (U.S. President's Council on Sustainable Development, 1994: 1).

Sustainability is a participatory process that creates and pursues a vision of community that respects and makes prudent use of all its resources—natural, human, human-created, social, cultural, scientific, etc. Sustainability seeks to ensure, to the degree possible, that present generations attain a high degree of economic security and can realise democracy and popular participation in control of their communities, while maintaining the integrity of the ecological systems upon which all life and all production depends, and while assuming responsibility to future generations to provide them with the where-with-all for their vision, hoping that they have the wisdom and intelligence to use what is provided in an appropriate manner (Viederman, 1994: 5).

lament or withdraw from this embryonic state of affairs, we hope that management scholars will proactively embrace the unfolding process of paradigmatic debate, for the advance of all sciences requires conflict between competing schools of thought (Kuhn, 1970).

Components of Sustainable Development

Scholars dealing with sustainability, we believe, must accept the interpenetration of observable fact and humanly assigned value, the hazy lines between description and prescription, and the twin filters of scientific viability and policy usefulness inherent in this value-laden topic. Sustainability, in the end, may lie beyond

or after the fact, in what Clifford Geertz might call the realm of 'unabsolute truths' (Berreby, 1995). For now, we are forced to deal with the topic at a rather high level of abstraction. It surely will be some time before the technical characteristics, operational indicators and moral injunctions of sustainable development enjoy widespread consensus.

It is however possible to deduce some principal components of the ideas that are generally shared by a majority of recently published conceptions such as those presented in Table 15.3.1. Our own content analysis suggests that sustainable development is a process of achieving *human development* (widening

READING 15.3	**Shifting Paradigms for Sustainable Development: Implications for Management Theory and Research** *continued*

By Thomas N. Gladwin, James J. Kennelly and Tara-Shelomith Krause

or enlarging the range of people's choices: United Nations Development Programme, 1994) in an *inclusive, connected, equitable, prudent,* and *secure* manner. *Inclusiveness* implies human development over time and space. *Connectivity* entails an embrace of ecological, social, and economic interdependence. *Equity* suggests intergenerational. intragenerational and interspecies fairness. *Prudence* connotes duties of care and prevention: technologically, scientifically, and politically. *Security* demands safety from chronic threats and protection from harmful disruption.

We accept that debate over the meaning of sustainable development will go on, and *should* go on, for a long time, and that our chosen abstract conception is but one of many that might be offered at this time. The formula is very simple, in that human development is subjected to five constraints. In this view, development is unsustainable when an enlargement of human choice excludes, disconnects, promotes inequity, reflects imprudence or raises insecurity. We recognize that all of these terms are challenging to define, with notions such as security or prudence more easily identified by their absence than their presence. Yet if the reader contemplates the representative definitions in Table 15.3.1 we believe she or he will agree that these constraints on the range of human choice represent a reasonable basis upon which to move the debate forward ...

The conception of sustainable development as inclusive, connected, equitable, prudent, and secure human development suggests implications that are applicable to a broad range of management theory. Sustainability shifts boundary constraints from plenitude to limitation and from efficiency to equity. It suggests that management theories must be framed as if the world is relatively full, rather than empty. Organizations collectively confront limits, both social and biophysical. Both regenerative (source) services and absorptive (sink) services of natural systems are limited (Goodland, 1992). Organizations confront social and physical carrying capacities in any region of operation; scale is bounded by finitude (Ehrlich, 1994).

Because the world is no longer empty, strategies for reducing economic inequality cannot depend on expanding the scale of human activity. Sustainable development imposes a constraint of distributive justice (i.e., fair distribution of benefits and burdens) upon the efficient allocation of resources as determined by the market. Theories of management, which, when implemented, serve to redistribute wealth from the poor to the rich, or from the future to the present, would thus be inconsistent with sustainable development. Sustainability may represent an emergent hypernorm under which a range of ethical belief systems will converge to limit the moral 'free space' of organizations (Donaldson and Dunfee, 1994; Taylor. 1989).

As constraints of optimal ecological scale are approached and rules of fair distribution are enforced, societal goals are likely to shift from *growth* to *development*. Societies that shift from growth to development must find ways (now only dimly perceived) to have organizations operating within them to do the same. Thus it can be expected that organizational incentive systems will shift in emphasis from *quantity* to *quality*. Organizations in harmony with sustainability will increase the quality of life in equitable ways that maintain or reduce energy/matter throughput. Such organizations cannot grow indefinitely, but they can develop indefinitely. This idea implies removing assumptions of infinite growth from theories of strategy and organization. It is based on theorizing about qualitative improvement in the absence of quantitative expansion.

Sustainable development suggests shifts in how management scholars conceptualize organizations. It includes translating the *organismic metaphor,* which is so prevalent in organizational theory, into actual reality. Restricting the metaphor to only human elements of the environment and to only human-related exchanges across organization–environment boundaries has unduly restricted the conceptualization of organizations. Advocates of the sustainability paradigm demand a complete notion of the external environment, an acknowledgement of the full range of material exchanges with the physiosphere, ecological exchanges with the biosphere, and nonmarket exchanges with the broader sociosphere.

Sustainability also demands fuller acceptance of *systemic interconnection.* Such a view would see organizations both partially causing and being affected by biodiversity loss, climate change, freshwater scarcity, food insecurity, population growth, persistent

READING 15.3

Shifting Paradigms for Sustainable Development: Implications for Management Theory and Research

By Thomas N. Gladwin, James J. Kennelly and Tara-Shelomith Krause

poverty, gender bias, and explosion of megacities. Its believers would suggest ways in which organizations could thrive by helping to resolve these global problems. New insights about system dynamics and predictability emerging from the study of complex systems may become critical in making these connections (Costanza *et al.*, 1993).

The idea of sustainable development pushes management research toward interdisciplinary and *transdisciplinary* modes of inquiry. Although management theorists have established strong links with many social sciences, there is little evidence of cross-fertilization with natural and physical science. Indeed, transdisciplinary approaches will be difficult to achieve, given the social organization and incentive systems of academia. Significant contributions toward understanding ecologically and socially sustainable economies, societies, and organizations, however, will arise only from new fundamentals, new languages, and new lenses. Ultimately, the study of sustainability may draw researchers beyond the puzzle-solving exercises of normal science (Kuhn, 1970) toward the realm of postnormal science (Funtowicz and Ravetz, 1993).

Along with these general shifts of emphasis, we see a need for three central transformations if management theory and research, in which sustainability matters, are to develop.

Agency to Communion

Futurist Willis Harman argued that 'business has become, in the last century, the most powerful institution on the planet. The dominant institution in any society needs to take responsibility for the whole' (Harman, cited in Hawken, 1992: 100). However, we sense that large corporations are increasingly becoming merely transient members of communities, embracing only parts of the world that happen to be useful to them, and cocooning themselves in contented pockets of the planet, while the larger biosphere and full human community atrophy (Gladwin, 1993b). Has the body of management theory inadvertently encouraged this diminishment of communion and enlargement of hyperagency (i.e., excessive concern with autonomy and self-preservation)? Do theories emphasize organizational freedom over union, rights over responsibilities, independence over interdependence, and what works (efficiency) over what is worth pursuing? Have management theories, when implemented, pushed organizations into a pathological agency, where severance from communities (both human and ecological) sets forces in motion that eventually destroy the conditions upon which organizations ultimately depend?

Admittedly, the suggested research agenda is extensive and radical. Does sustainability require organizations to develop a sense of place, to become rooted in communities? Do forces of globalization and the mobility of financial capital systematically work against the idea of organization-in-community? Does free trade work to the benefit of all or only serve a narrow range of established interests (Bhagwati, 1993; Daly, 1993; Lang and Hines, 1993)? Does sustainable development require a new protectionism or a renationalization of capital?

Indeed, what are an organization's social contract with society and natural contract with the biosphere? Do charters of incorporation imply duties of sustainable corporate citizenship and accountability (Grossman and Adams, 1993)? Can stakeholder models be extended to be more spatially and temporally inclusive (Chappell, 1993; Donaldson and Dunfee, 1994; Roddick, 1991; Starik, 1995)? Are positive contributions to sustainability more likely to arise from organizations that are more female versus male in their values spheres (Merchant, 1990; Shiva, 1989; Warren, 1994)? Behind all of these questions is the larger question: What is the purpose of organizations (Handy, 1993)?

Exterior to Interior

Future researchers may need to focus on whether sustainability requires shifts in human thinking (from linear to cyclical, analytic to synthetic, reductive to integrative) and whether it is possible to increase the rate of people's evolutionary consciousness toward a 'new mind' appropriate for a sustainable world (Ornstein and Ehrlich, 1991). Researchers will need to confront, in this regard, the possibility that humans and their organizations have been programmed by evolutionary forces to instinctively discount over both time

READING 15.3

Shifting Paradigms for Sustainable Development: Implications for Management Theory and Research *continued*

By Thomas N. Gladwin, James J. Kennelly and Tara-Shelomith Krause

and space, such that the extended mental and moral embrace required in sustainedcentralism may be difficult to obtain.

Along with cognitive transformation, sustaincentrism also requires profound value change toward stewardship, equity, humility, permanence, precaution, and sufficiency. Are members of the organizational science community willing to seriously entertain ethical and value-laden questions? Sustainability, like human medicine, mixes both descriptive and normative or action-guiding content. Has our domain become devoid of ideas dangerous to greed, shortsightedness, indulgence, exploitation, apathy, narrowness, and other values inconsistent with sustainability (Orr, 1994)? In short, the study of sustainability must shift from objective to subjective, from exterior nuts and bolts to interior hearts and minds.

Concept to Implementation

Although a broad, overlapping consensus is forming around the goal of sustainable development, progress depends on greater attention to issues of transformational change and operationalization. Some theorists argue that business is the only institution in the modern world powerful enough to foster the changes necessary for ecological and social sustainability (Hawken, 1993). However, in order to harness this power, sustainable behavior must become a source of competitive advantage (Collins and Porras, 1994; Makower, 1994; Scott and Rothman, 1994; Shrivastava, In press). There will also need to be major shifts in public policies to provide appropriate signals for pushing and pulling organizations toward sustainability (Schmidheiny, 1992). Creative institutional or cultural reforms may be needed to overcome the problems of collective action, limits of altruism, prisoners' dilemmas and social traps that so pervasively affect human and organizational behavior (Cross and Guyer. 1980; Fox, 1985; Hardin, 1982).

Operationalization and measurement of sustainability along the lines of the principles remains in their infancy, and many difficult technical and conceptual questions have not yet been addressed (Cernea, 1993; Serageldin, 1994). Practical decision-support tools are needed to systematically include sustainability criteria

in evaluating the design and selection of products, processes, and projects. Further development of tools such as design for environment, life-cycle analysis, full-cost pricing, and industrial ecology models may be useful in this quest (Allenby and Richards, 1994). These tools of 'greening', however, which focus on instrumental or process objectives such as pollution reduction or continuous improvement, must be transformed into tools of 'sustaining' that focus on ultimate or outcome objectives such as assuring ecosystem and sociosystem health and integrity. Tools of greening, in other words, move organizations in the right direction, but fail to inform them about the distance from or variance with the ultimate destination of sustainability. Management must shift from the prevailing metaphor of greening (Walley and Whitehead, 1994), which merely 'reduces the bads' to that of sustaining or 'realizing the goods.'

References

Allenby, B.R. and Richards, D.I. (Eds.). (1994) *The greening of industrial ecosystems*. Washington, DC: National Academy Press.

Barbier, E. (1987) The concept of sustainable economic development. *Environmental Conservation*. 14(2): 101–110.

Beckerman, W. (1994) Sustainable development: Is it a useful concept? *Environmental Values*. 3(3): 191–209.

Berreby, D. (1995) Unabsolute truths: Clifford Geertz. *New York Times Magazine*. April 9: 44–47.

Bhagwati, J. (1993) The case for free trade. *Scientific American*. 270(11): 42–49.

Cernea, M. (1993) The sociologist's approach to sustainable development. *Finance and Development*. 30(4): 6–10.

Chappell, T. (1993) *The soul of a business: Managing for profit*. New York: Bantam.

Clark, W.C. (1989) Managing planet earth. *Scientific American*. 261(3): 47–54.

Collins, J.C. and Porras, 1.I. (1994) *Built to last: Successful habits of visionary companies*. New York: Harper Business.

Costanza, R., Daly, H.E. and Bartholomew, J.A. (1991) Goals, agenda and policy recommendations for ecological economics. In R. Costanza (Ed.). *Ecological economics; The science and management of sustainability*: 1–20. New York: Columbia University Press.

Costanza, R. Wainger, L., Folke, C. and Maler, K.G. (1993) Modeling complex ecological- economic systems. *Bioscience*. 43(8): 545–555.

READING 15.3

Shifting Paradigms for Sustainable Development: Implications for Management Theory and Research

By Thomas N. Gladwin, James J. Kennelly and Tara-Shelomith Krause

Cross, J.G. and Guyer, M.I. (1980) *Social traps*. Ann Arbor: University of Michigan Press.

Daly, H.E. (1993) The perils of free trade. *Scientific American*. 270(11): 50–57.

Donaldson, T. and Dunfee, T.W. (1994) Toward a unified conception of business ethics: Integrative social contract theory. *Academy of Management Review*. 19: 252–284.

Dowie, M. (1995) *Losing ground: American environmentalism at the close of the twentieth century*. Cambridge. MA: The MIT Press.

Ehrlich, P. (1994) Ecological economics and the carrying capacity of earth. In A. Tansson, M. Hammer, C. Folke, & B. Costanza (Eds.), *Investing in natural capital: The ecological economics approach to sustainability*: 38–56. Washington. DC: Island Press.

Fox, D.R. (1985) Psychology, ideology, utopia, and the commons. *American Psychologist*. 40; 48–58.

Funtowicz, S.O. and Ravetz, J.R. (1993) Science for the post-normal age. *Science*, 25(7): 739–755.

Gladwin, T.N. and Krause, T. (In press). *Business, nature and society: Toward sustainable enterprise*. Burr Ridge, IL: Irwin.

Gladwin, T.N. (1992) *Building the sustainable corporation: Creating environmental sustainability and competitive advantage*. Washington, DC: National Wildlife Federation.

Gladwin, T.N. (1993b) The global environmental crisis and management education. *Total Quality Environmental Management*. 3(1): 109–114.

Goodland, R. (1992) The case that the world has reached limits. In R. Goodland, H.E. Daly, & S.E. Serafy (Eds.). *Population, technology and lifestyle: The transition to sustainability*: 3–22. Washington, DC: Island Press.

Gore, A. (1992) *Earth in balance: Ecology and the human spirit*. New York: Houghton Mifflin.

Grossman, R.L. and Adams, F.T. (1993) Citizenship and the charter of incorporation. *World Business Academy Perspectives*. 7(4): 17–31.

Handy, C. (1993) What is a company for?, *Corporate Governance*. 1(1): 14–17.

Hardin, R. (1982) *Collective action*. Baltimore: Johns Hopkins University Press.

Hawken, P. (1992) The ecology of commerce. *Inc*. April: 93–100.

Hawken, P. (1993) *The ecology of commerce: A declaration of sustainability*. New York: Harper Business.

Kuhn, T.S. (1962) *The structure of scientific revolutions*. Chicago: University of Chicago Press.

Kuhn, T.S. (1970) *The structure of scientific revolutions* (2nd ed) Chicago: University of Chicago Press.

Lang, T. and Hines, C. (1993) *The new protectionism: Protecting the future against free trade*. London: Earthscan. 904 *Academy of Management Review* October.

Lee, K.N. (1993) Greed, scale mismatch and learning. *Ecological Applications*. 3(4): 560–564.

Levin S.A. (1993) Science and sustainability. *Ecological Applications*. 3(4): 1–2.

Makower, L. (1994) *Beyond the bottom line: Putting social responsibility to work for your business and the world*. New York: Simon & Schuster.

Meadows, D.H., Meadows, D.L. and Randers, J. (1992) *Beyond the limits: Confronting global collapse–envisioning a sustainable future*. Post Mills, VT: Chelsea Green.

Merchant, C. (1990) *Radical ecology: The search for a livable world*. New York: Routledge.

Ornstein, R. and Ehrlich, P. (1991) *New world new mind*. London: Paladin.

Orr, D.W. (1994) *Earth in mind: On education, environment, and the human prospect*. Washington, DC: Island Press.

Pearce, D.W. Markandya, A. and Barbier, E.B. (1989) *Blueprint for a green economy*. London: EarthScan.

Pezzey, I. (1992) Sustainability: An interdisciplinary guide. *Environmental Values*. 1 21–2.

Roddick, A. (1991) *Body and soul: Profits with principles*. New York: Crown Publishing.

Rolston, H. (1994) *Conserving natural value*. New York: Columbia University Press.

Scott, M. and Rothman, H. (1994) *Companies with a conscience*. New York: Citadel Press.

Schmidheiny, S. (1992) *Changing course: A global business perspective on development and the environment*. Cambridge. MA: MIT Press.

Serageldin, I. (Ed.). (1994) *Making development sustainable: From concepts to action*. Washington, DC: World Bank.

Shiva, V. (1989) *Staying alive*. London: Zed Books.

Shrivastava, P. In press. *Greening business: Profiting the corporation and the environment*. Cincinnati. OH: Thompson Executive Press.

Starik, M. (1995) Should trees have managerial standing? Toward stakeholder status for non-human nature. *Journal of Business Ethics*. 14(3): 207–218.

Taylor, C. (1989) *Sources of the self: The making of the modern identity*. Cambridge, MA: Harvard University Press.

United Nations Development Programme. (1994) *Human development report 1994*. New York: Author.

U.S. President's Council on Sustainable Development. (1994) *A vision for a sustainable U.S. and principles of sustainable development*. Washington. DC: Author.

| **Shifting Paradigms for Sustainable Development: Implications for Management Theory and Research** *continued*

By Thomas N. Gladwin, James J. Kennelly and Tara-Shelomith Krause

Viederman, S. (1994) The economics of sustainability: Challenges. Paper presented at the workshop, *The Economics of Sustainability*. Recite, Brazil: Fundacao Joaquirri Nabuco.

Warren, K.J. (Ed.). (1994) *Ecological feminism: Environmental philosophies*. London: Routledge.

World Commission on Environment and Development. (1987) *Our common future*. Oxford, England: Oxford University Press.

World Conservation Union. United Nations Environment Programme, and World Wide Fund for Nature. (1991) *Caring for the earth: A strategy for sustainable living*. Gland, Switzerland: Author.

Walley, N. and Whitehead, B. (1994) It's not easy being green. *Harvard Business Review*. 72(3): 46–53.

Williams, B. (1985) *Ethics and the limits of philosophy*. Cambridge, MA: Harvard University Press.

Discussion Questions

1. What are the strengths and limitations of established conceptions of business ethics?
2. What are the difficulties of reconciling 'ethical egoism' with environmental protection?
3. Is an ethos of sustainability compatible with continuing capitalist development?

Recommended Further Readings

See references to all the above texts plus:

Benson, J. (2000) *Environmental Ethics: An Introduction with Readings*, London: Routledge.

Brennan, A. and Lo, Y.S. (2008) 'Environmental Ethics', Stanford Encyclopedia of philosophy, available at http://plato.stanford.edu/entries/ethics-environmental/

Clegg, S., Kornberger, M. and Rhodes, C. (2007) 'Organizational Ethics, Decision Making, Undecidability' *Sociological Review* 55(2): 393–409.

Crane, A. and Matten, D. (2006) *Business Ethics: Managing Corporate Citizenship and Sustainability in the Age of Globalization*, Oxford University Press.

Davidson, J. (2000) 'Sustainable Development: Business as Usual or a New Way Of Living?' *Environmental Ethics* 22(1): 45–71.

Jamieson, D. (2008) *Ethics and the Environment: An Introduction*, Cambridge University Press.

Hoffman, W.H. (1991) 'Business and Environmental Ethics' *Business Ethics Quarterly* 1(2): 169–184.

Jones, C. (2003) 'As if Business Ethics were Possible, "within Such Limits"…' *Organization* 10(2): 223–48.

Jones, C., Parker, M. and Ten Bos, R. (2005) *For Business Ethics*, London: Routledge.

Kronstad, B. and Willmott, H.C. (1995) 'Business Ethics: Restrictive or Empowering?' *Journal of Business Ethics* 14: 445–64.

Levy, D.L. and Kolk, A. (2002) 'Strategic Responses to Global Climate Change: Conflicting Pressures on Multinationals in the Oil Industry' *Business and Politics* 4(3): 275–300.

Light, A. and Holmes, R. (2003) *Environmental Ethics: An Anthology*, Oxford: WileyBlackwell.

Roberts, J.T. and Parks, B.C. (2007) *A Climate of Injustice: Global Inequality, North-South Politics and Climate Policy*, MIT Press.

Livesey, S.M. (2001) 'Eco-Identity as Discursive Struggle: Royal Dutch/Shell, Brent Spar, and Nigeria' *Journal of Business Communication* 38(1): 58–91.

Shrivastava, P. (1995) 'Ecocentric Management for a Risk Society' *Academy of Management Review* 20(1): 118–37.

Werhane, P.H. (1999) *Moral Imagination and Management Decision-Making*, Oxford University Press.

Westley, F. and Vrenderburg, H. (1996) 'Sustainability and the Corporation: Criteria for Aligning Economic Practice with Environmental Protection' *Journal of Management Inquiry* 5(2): 104–119.

GLOBALIZATION, GOVERNANCE AND CORPORATE SOCIAL RESPONSIBILITY

CHAPTER 16

READINGS

Scholte, J.A. (2005) *Globalization: A Critical Introduction* 2nd ed., Basingstoke: Palgrave Macmillan. pp. 185–223.

Scherer, A.G. and Palazzo, G. (2007) 'Towards a Political Conception of Corporate Responsibility: Business and Society seen from a Habermasian Perspectives' in *Academy of Management Review*. Vol. 32, No. 4: 1096, 1098–1099, 1106–07, 1108–1110.

Edward, P. and Willmott, H. (2008) 'Structures, Identities and Politics: Bringing Corporate Citizenship into the Corporation' in A. Scherer and G. Palazzo (eds) *Handbook of Research on Global Corporate Citizenship*, London: Edward Elgar. pp. 415–416, 419–421, 425.

INTRODUCTION

One way to conceive of 'globalization' is as a means of signalling and appreciating the increased interconnectedness and time–space compression of the contemporary world facilitated by the use of information and communication technologies (see Guellén, 2001 for a comprehensive overview of debates). It is manifest in increasing flows of goods, services, capital, people, lifestyles and aspirations across national borders. It is also evident in planetary climate change, pandemics, human migrations to more prosperous regions, and so on. Increasing interconnectedness extends to the interrelationships between governments and corporations and is reflected in concerns about 'governance' and 'social responsibility' that are directed at corporations and not only at states (see Chapter 15). There is a growing sense in which pressing issues and mounting problems – economic, environmental and ideological – are global in scope. There is also an emergent understanding of how corporations are deeply implicated in these problems, as well as an increasing expectation that the operation and influence of companies must be interrogated as part of their solution. When understood as a process involving criss-crossing, interactive flows between diverse and increasingly transnational institutions, attentiveness to 'globalization' is accompanied by an intensified focus upon corporate governance and the social responsibility of corporations. In many cases, large corporations are more influential for geo-political development than many nation-states; and – assisted by the IMF, the World Bank and the World Trade Organization – corporations routinely lend their support to diverse forms of legalized dispossession as well as to neo-imperialist military and intelligence adventures led by states. The rise of a global justice movement is symptomatic of a shift in which nations have become increasingly dependent upon corporations for their development, and the supporters of this movement directly question such means of capital accumulation (for discussions of these developments, see contributions to Appelbaum and Robinson, 2005).

In Reading 16.1, **Jan Scholte** notes how processes of globalization are associated with a shift in which state-based regulation is supplemented and to a degree eclipsed by transterritorial forms of regulation, such as the European Union and numerous other organizations of regional governance. A feature of globalization, then, is not only a 'multilayering' of governance arrangements but also a growth of 'private' forms of regulation – for example, corporate reporting that is compliant with international accounting standards – that are 'devised and regulated through nongovernmental arrangements' (Reading 16.1, p. 288), and which may have the tacit or active support of states. The rise of neoliberalism from the 1980s has favoured a smaller core of state regulation accompanied by an expansion of self-regulation in areas, for example, of corporate social responsibility where companies have either developed individual codes of conduct with regard to employment practices and environmental stewardship or have formed industry-wide codes and standards. Increasingly, non-governmental organizations (NGOs), such as the Forestry Stewardship Council (FSC), have exposed and sought to remedy regulatory deficits by providing monitoring and certification of corporate practices. Another manifestation of globalization has been the formation of a so-called anti-globalization movement which has prioritized justice rather than capitalist expansion, pressing for radical forces of globalization to be mobilized to cancel crippling debts, abandon destructive 'modernization' programmes and projects, and champion sustainable forms of development. Underpinning these demands for global justice is a rejection of top-down technocratic governance by elites in favour of increased civil society engagement, especially through bottom-up grass-roots activism, and a struggle for more democratic control of decisions that directly affect (global) citizens' life-chances and the quality of life.

Andreas Georg Scherer and Guido Palazzo's 'Toward a political conception of corporate responsibility' (Reading 16.2) questions the adequacy of the dominant, 'positivist' approaches to researching corporate responsibility. Their effect, it is argued, is to reproduce the status quo as they attempt to map existing expectations, processes and consequences of corporate social responsibility (CSR) programmes without considering how these are shaped and delivered through processes of political struggle and negotiation. So long as the actions of companies match expectations, they are understood to be acting responsibly. Critical scrutiny of norms is deemed to lie beyond the sphere of scientific inquiry; and yet by, by default, existing norms are tacitly endorsed and legitimized.

To enable critical scrutiny of norms, such as what is counted as 'corporate social responsibility', Scherer and Palazzo recommend a process of deliberative democracy in which the emphasis is upon the quality of processes of discussion and reflection that precede the making of decisions or the casting of votes. In principle, this process should aspire to open dialogue that is accessible to all citizens, with the expectation that the outcome will be more widely accepted as well as more broadly and rigorously determined. So, instead of the instrumental development of CSR initiatives and programmes to ensure that corporations are responsive to public expectations, the suggestion is that the meaning and import of CSR should be rationally deliberated (and not simply derived from established norms propagated or promoted by elites). Taking their lead from the thinking of Jürgen Habermas, a leading contemporary social theorist, the idea of deliberative democracy is inspired by an ideal of equality of participation and absence of coercion in processes of decision-making. But deliberative democracy is also pragmatic in striving to move in the direction of greater involvement in the processes that result in the formation of preferences and their continuing re-evaluation.

With regard to CSR, Scherer and Palazzo contrast more established, 'postivist' approaches that focus upon how corporations endeavour to respond effectively to stakeholder pressures with their focus on how corporations participate in processes of public will formation. More specifically, their interest is in the role of corporations in processes that address 'global environmental and social challenges' (Reading 16.2, p. 293). As they note, this is a departure from the understanding that the role of business is to create wealth, and it is for the state to ensure that this is done in a socially acceptable manner. It is a departure justified in part by the realization that corporations are already engaged in forms of regulation and provision with regard *inter alia* to public health, education, social security, the protection of human rights, forms of self-regulation and so on. From this perspective, corporations are not simply 'complying with societal standards in legal and moral terms' but are active participants in deliberations that 'aim at *setting* and *redefining* those standards and expectations' (see Reading 16.2, p. 293). To illustrate how corporations can be seen to engage in 'political co-responsibility' – in which an established approach to stakeholder management is not merely enhanced but embedded in 'an ongoing process of observing and participating in public discourses' – Scherer and Palazzo offer the example of the FSC, an NGO, that has established principles of sustainable forest management and certifies timber – a task that companies and governments have hesitated to address.

In Reading 16.3, **Peter Edward and Hugh Willmott** agree with Scherer and Palazzo that what has provided corporate legitimacy in the past is under increasing strain resulting in 'the politicization of the corporation' and efforts – including programmes of corporate responsibility and reforms of corporate governance – to regain legitimacy. But they also advocate an alternative conception of 'corporate citizenship' based upon a social theory of hegemony (Laclau and Mouffe, 1985). Key to this theory is the understanding that 'deliberative democracy' tends to conceal or silence as much as it strives to expose and discuss. By taking as given the undemocratic nature of the 'private sphere' of a market economy, it is seen to paper over its precarious formulation in a way that largely escapes collective regulation and accountability.

Edward and Willmott begin by returning to the Habermasian thinking that underpins the deliberative approach before examining more closely the specific example of the FSC. They note that the pragmatic shift from an ideal, counter-factual situation of undistorted communication and open dialogue to one of deliberation relies upon, but then discards, its initial presuppositions. At the heart of the issue is whether the idea of deliberative democracy is sufficiently potent to accomplish any meaningful sense of corporate citizenship – in the sense of corporations being responsive to, as well as being participants within, democratic processes. For this to occur, the incommensurability of deliberative democracy with the (undeliberated) preservation of a market economy has to be acknowledged and addressed. Otherwise, there is every likelihood that, in the public sphere, 'life-world' values, such as those of fairness and democracy, will be displaced or appropriated by 'system' priorities and logics that are exemplified by the dominant key performance measures (of productivity, profitability and growth) applied in modern organizations. A close examination of FSC practices presented in a report by the Rainforest Foundation supports this assessment as it details a lack of accountability and reveals how the FSC 'privileged certification bodies and commercial clients as it marginalized the voice of local communities and indigenous people' (Reading 16.3, p. 299). At the very least, this raises some questions about the transformative potential of deliberative democracy when the FSC is held up as a shining example of 'corporate embeddedness in processes of democratic will-formation and problem solving in a transnational context of political governance' (Reading 16.2, p. 293, also cited in Reading 16.3, p. 299). It suggests that advocacy of deliberative democracy as a basis for global corporate governance might too readily accept a substitution of a system mentality drawn to auditing formal principles and procedures rather than to attending to their practical implementation in everyday organizing practices.

READING 16.1 | Globalization and Governance: From Statism to Polycentrism

By J.A. Scholte

Alongside, and often in close relation with, shifts in the social structure of production, contemporary globalization – and the rise of supraterritoriality more particularly – has also encouraged a number of changes in the organization of governance in the contemporary world. Territorialism as the previously prevailing framework of social space was closely interlinked with statism as the previously prevailing mode of regulation. Hence a move away from territorialism in geography has, not surprisingly, unfolded together with a move away from statism in governance. As a result, society in today's more global world is regulated in what can be termed a polycentric manner.

READING 16.1	**Globalization and Governance: From Statism to Polycentrism**

By J.A. Scholte

'Statism' refers here to a condition where societal governance is more or less equivalent to the regulatory operations of territorial bureaucratic national governments. In statist circumstances, all formulation, implementation, monitoring and enforcement of societal rules occurs more or less directly through the state and inter-state relations. Under statist governance, macro-regional and global regulatory mechanisms are small in scale, if present at all, and fall more or less completely under the thumb of country governments. Likewise, in a statist mode of governance local governments have no significant autonomy from central governments regarding national policy questions. Moreover, local authorities in a statist situation lack substantial possibilities to engage directly with the wider world outside their state. In short, as the term suggests, statism entails governance that is for all intents and purposes reducible to the state.

Following – and spurred on by – half a century of accelerated globalization and growing supraterritorial connections, statist conditions no longer mark governance today. To be sure, country governments remain major and indispensable sites of regulation in the contemporary more global world. The end of statism in no way entails the end of the state itself. However, governance now also involves suprastate (regional and transworld) regimes that operate with some autonomy from the state. In addition, many substate (municipal and provincial) governments today engage directly with spheres beyond their country.

In other words, governance in the more global world of the twenty-first century has become distinctly multi-layered and trans-scalar. Regulation occurs at – and through interconnections among – municipal, provincial, national, macro-regional and global sites. No single 'level' reigns over the others, as occurred with the primacy of the state over suprastate and substate institutions in territorialist circumstances. Instead, governance tends to be diffuse, emanating from multiple locales at once, with points and lines of authority that are not always clear.

The dispersal of governance in contemporary history has occurred not only across different layers and scales of social relations from the local to the global, but also with the emergence of various regulatory mechanisms in private quarters alongside those in the public sector. Many rules for global companies, global finance, global communications, global ecology and other global matters have been devised and administered through nongovernmental arrangements. Although this private governance has generally depended on support, or at least tolerance, from government agencies, it too has maintained substantial autonomy from the state. ...

Privatized governance

Governance has become polycentric under the influence of globalization not only with the diffusion of regulation across multiple layers of the public sector, but also by the spread of private, non-statutory frameworks of rules (cf. Cutler *et al.*, 1999; Ronit and Schneider, 2000; Brühl, 2001; Haufler, 2001; Knill and Lehmkuhl, 2002; Hall and Biersteker, 2003). Given statist conditions of the past, one might easily assume that governance is by definition a public operation through governmental and intergovernmental agencies. However, the formulation, implementation, monitoring and enforcement of societal rules could in principle also occur through nonofficial channels like market-based agencies and civil society organizations.

Contemporary globalization has encouraged a substantial privatization of governance in two main ways. First, a number of private regulatory arrangements have arisen to fill regulatory gaps in suprastate governance. Although transworld and macro-regional regimes have undergone unprecedented degrees and rates of expansion in recent history, this growth has often still lagged well behind the regulatory needs of expanded global relations. Various areas – including global markets and global finance – have suffered major governance deficits as a result. In a number of cases non-governmental actors have stepped in where public regulatory frameworks have been deficient or absent. The private agencies have then constructed the necessary standards and norms that enable increased global relations to develop.

Second, the prevailing neoliberalist approach to contemporary globalization has also promoted the rise of private regulation. The logic of neoliberalism can easily move from prescribing the privatization of production to advocating the privatization of

Globalization and Governance: From Statism to Polycentrism *continued*

By J.A. Scholte

governance. At an extreme, neoliberalists might affirm that the global private sector can – together with consumer and other stakeholder pressure in the marketplace – adequately regulate itself.

Like most phenomena connected with contemporary globalization, private global governance is not completely new to recent history. For example, in the second half of the nineteenth century a number of business associations created standard forms of contract to govern cross-border trade in commodities such as corn and cotton (Wiener, 1999: 165). However, the scale of current private regulation far outstrips anything seen in the past.

Moreover, private global governance of earlier times tended to be sanctioned by intergovernmental treaty, so that states retained considerable initiative and control of the overall process. To be sure, approval or at least tolerance of states (especially big states) remains necessary for the operation of today's private regulatory arrangements. Yet much recent private governance has arisen with little direct involvement of governments.

One major contemporary growth area of private governance of globalization are schemes of so-called 'corporate social responsibility', sometimes also termed 'corporate citizenship' (Zadek *et al.*, 1997; Zadek 2001; Andriof and McIntosh, 2001). Official suprastate measures to regulate transborder companies have remained either moribund (like the UN Centre for Transnational Corporations code of 1979), or weak (like the UN Global Compact launched in 2000), or unratified (like the draft UN Norms on the Responsibilities of Transnational Corporations of 2003), or highly general in terms (like the OECD Guidelines for Multinational Enterprises, first issued in 1976 and subsequently revised), or very narrow in focus (like the 2003 WHO Framework Convention on Tobacco Control). However, nonstatutory rules for transborder enterprises have proliferated since the 1990s, especially regarding labour, environmental and human rights practices (cf. Hopkins, 1999; Richter, 2001; Jenkins *et al.*, 2002; Abrahams, 2004; Bendell, 2004). By 2002 around 4,000 of the 65,000 transnational corporations were promising social and environmental reports (Utting, 2006).

Private CSR frameworks have taken several forms. Some of these voluntary codes for transborder firms are self-regulatory arrangements. That is, the schemes are operated either by a single company over its own activities or by a group of companies over their own sector. For example, Nike and Unilever have developed company-based codes (which notionally also cover their subcontractors and suppliers), while the International Council of Toy Industries has overseen an umbrella code for the sector. Outside consultants have devised other CSR arrangements like the Global Reporting Initiative (GRI), started in 1997, and the Social Accountability Standard SA8000, operational since 1998. Some civil society groups have also promulgated CSR standards. For example, Amnesty International issued its Human Rights Principles for Companies in 1998, while scores of Christian associations have used the Interfaith Center on Global Corporate Responsibility to screen firms for investment. Recent years have also seen the emergence of so-called 'multi-stakeholder initiatives' involving firms, labour unions and NGOs in jointly pursued nonofficial regulatory arrangements for global business. Like the consultancy schemes, multi-stakeholder initiatives involve standard setting, independent monitoring, certification and reporting. Examples include the Forest Stewardship Council (FSC), which has since 1993 linked timber companies, workers, environmentalists and indigenous peoples in efforts to promote sustainable logging (Humphreys, 1996, 2003).

Other significant private global governance has expanded since the 1970s in respect of commercial adjudication. Whereas states have submitted their trade conflicts to a public body, the GATT/WTO, global companies have tended to handle their disputes through private arbitration, thus avoiding litigation in state or suprastate courts (Dezalay and Garth, 1996; Mattli, 2001; Lehmkuhl, 2003). The available mechanisms include the International Court of Arbitration of the International Chamber of Commerce, the London Court of Arbitration (LCA), and the China International Economic Trade Arbitration Commission (CIETAC). The New York Convention on the Recognition and Enforcement of Foreign Arbitral Awards (1958) stipulates that national courts

Globalization and Governance: From Statism to Polycentrism

By J.A. Scholte

cannot review the judgements of arbitrators on core issues. To give one indication of the scale of this private governance practice, the Secretariat of the ICC had received 10,000 requests for arbitration by 1998, more than two-thirds of them since 1976 (Craig *et al.*, 1998: 2).

In addition to global production and trade, much private governance has also applied to transplanetary finance (Porter and Coleman, 2002). The many relevant sites include the International Chamber of Commerce Commission on Banking Technique and Practice, the World Federation of Exchanges (for securities markets), and the Derivatives Policy Group (with members drawn from academics and investment bankers). Bodies like the International Accounting Standards Board and the International Federation of Accountants have respectively developed the main global accountancy and auditing norms currently in use. Rating agencies like Moody's and Standard & Poors have also played something of an unofficial policing role in the contemporary global economy, rewarding governments and companies that score well and punishing those that rate poorly (Levich, 2002; Sinclair, 2005).

Considerable additional privatized governance has emerged in relation to global information and communications. For example, the International Telecommunication Union has moved from being an intergovernmental organization to a hybrid construction with 600 affiliated companies as well as 189 member states (Salter, 1999). Titles and addresses in cyberspace are regulated through the Internet Corporation for Assigned Names and Numbers, created in 1998 with operations that involve business, technical, academic and user inputs (Franda, 2001: ch 2).

Multiple further instances of private governance of globalization can be found across other sectors. The International Organization for Standardization, formally a nongovernmental body, has often agreed its measures together with the major companies involved (Clapp, 1998). The ICC's Uniform Customs and Practice for Documentary Credits have been accepted by banking associations in 175 countries (Wiener, 1999: 183). The International Air Transport Associa-

tion (IATA) has standardized airline documentation. The Rome-based Codex Alimentarius Commission has set global food standards with considerable inputs from industry. The World Tourism Organization ('the other WTO') has a Business Council that includes representatives of different facets of the industry in 70 countries. The Bill and Melinda Gates Foundation has donated more for health care programmes in Africa than WHO has had available from governmental contributions. Between 1974 and 2004 some 90 so-called 'public–private partnerships' were established to combat global diseases. The vast majority of these 'PPPs' have emerged since the mid-1990s (IPPPH, 2004; also Reich, 2002).

Finally, substantial privatization of governance has occurred in the course of contemporary globalization in the form of 'contracting out' the delivery of public services to private providers. For instance, non-profit organizations have come to figure prominently in the supply of humanitarian relief. The mid-1990s annual budgets of the giants in this field included $586 million for CARE International, $419 million for World Vision International, and $350 million each for Oxfam and Save the Children (Smillie, 1999: 17–18). By comparison, the operating budget for the UN High Commissioner for Refugees (UNHCR) has run at about $1,000 million per annum. Not surprisingly, in view of these resource constraints, UNHCR in 1998 maintained connections with more than 500 non-profit organizations as 'Partners in Action' (UNHCR, 1999). Likewise, bilateral and multilateral donor organizations have since the 1970s made far more use of non-profit bodies (rather than official agencies) to execute development assistance projects.

Outsourcing has even extended to military operations. Mercenaries more or less vacated the world scene by the late eighteenth century, but these soldiers-for-hire have reappeared (usually on a small scale) in recent decades in various armed conflicts, for example, in Angola, Chechnya, former Yugoslavia, and elsewhere. Moreover, the 1990s saw the rise for the first time of private military companies. Examples include South Africa-based Executive Outcomes and US-based Military Professional Resources, Inc. These

Globalization and Governance: From Statism to Polycentrism *continued*

By J.A. Scholte

firms have mainly provided logistical support for state armies or protection for business premises, but they can also offer direct combat capacities. For example, Executive Outcomes was contracted to undertake humanitarian operations in Sierra Leone in the mid-1990s (Shearer, 1998; Zarate, 1998; Brayton, 2002; Mandel, 2002; Singer, 2003). ...

(Global) civil society

Given all of the developments reviewed above, globalization has fostered a considerable dispersal of regulatory competences across substate, state, suprastate and private sites of governance. This shift from statism to poly-centrism has in turn had important implications for civil society activity.

The concept 'civil society' has meant many things since it appeared in sixteenth-century English political thought (Chambers and Kymlicka, 2002; Cohen and Arato, 1992). In today's context we might conceive of civil society as a political space, or arena, where self-generated associations of citizens seek, from outside political parties, to shape the rules that govern social life. Civil society groups bring citizens together non-coercively in deliberate attempts to mould the formal laws and informal norms that regulate social relations.

Civil society associations assemble people who share concerns about a particular policy issue. The many examples of civil society activity include anti-poverty campaigns, business forums, consumer advocates, criminal syndicates, pro-democracy groups, development cooperation initiatives, environmental movements, ethnic lobbies, faith-based associations, human rights promoters, labour unions, local community groups, peace advocates, peasant movements, philanthropic foundations, professional bodies, relief organizations, think tanks, women's networks, youth associations, and more. Civil society therefore includes – but also ranges far wider than – NGOs. The huge diversity of civil society groups is evident not only in their broad range of focal issues, but also in their multifarious organizational forms, constituencies, capacity levels, geographical scopes, ideological persuasions, strategic visions, and campaign tactics.

With its concern to shape the rules of social life, civil society activity unfolds in relation to a governance apparatus. In former circumstances of statism, when governance came down to government, civil society functioned in relation to the state. However, when the framework of governance changes – as it has done with contemporary globalization – the character of civil society may be expected to alter in tandem (Scholte, 2002a). In today's more polycentric condition, civil society associations have redirected some of their attention from states to other sites and networks of governance, including global regulatory arrangements. An unofficial 'new multilateralism' of civil society associations has arisen alongside the official multilateralism of global governance agencies (Schechter, 1999b; O'Brien *et al.*, 2000). ...

Of course civil society interventions have also sometimes blocked global governance initiatives, prompting some observers to speak of an '*anti-globalization* movement'. For example, NGOs played an important role in thwarting negotiations in the OECD toward a Multilateral Agreement on Investment in 1998 (Kobrin, 1998b; Henderson, 1999; Goodman, 2000; Smythe, 2000). Civil society opposition to neoliberalist globalization has also played a part in frustrating WTO Ministerial Conferences at Seattle in 1999 and Cancún in 2003 as well as cancelling a World Bank meeting in Barcelona in 2001 (Cockburn and St Clair, 2000; Kaldor *et al.*, 2000; Yuen *et al.*, 2001). Coalitions of NGOs and grass-roots groups have halted several World Bank-funded dam constructions or obtained better compensation arrangements for people adversely affected by these projects (Udall, 1998; Khagram, 2000).

Civil society engagement with global governance has sometimes also reverberated back on state regulation. Employing a so-called 'boomerang effect', civil society groups have worked through global arenas in pursuit of changes to state policy (Keck and Sikkink, 1998). For example, civil society associations in Kuwait have utilized global events and measures to press their government to change budget allocations, economic planning, and environmental laws. Some women's associations in Eastern Europe and Central Asia did not meet their country authorities until both sides attended UN meetings on gender issues.

READING 16.1

Globalization and Governance: From Statism to Polycentrism

By J.A. Scholte

With such a dispersion of regulatory activities, polycentric governance involves major challenges of producing coherent and effective policy. No single actor or committee of actors plays an overall coordinating role in, say, the regulation of climate change, epidemics, intellectual property, the Internet, or refugee flows. The possibilities of gaps, overlaps, confusions and contradictions between agencies are considerable. Moreover, with no final site of adjudication, people in a situation of polycentrism can always appeal their case to another authority.

To take one prominent example, regulation of a global financial crisis involves governments of the countries directly affected, as well as transstate networks like the G7, G20 and G24, as well as global agencies such as the BIS and the IMF, as well as macro-regional institutions like the European Central Bank, as well as private bodies with regulatory functions such as the IASB and the International Securities Market Association, as well as civil society associations like the IIF and Friends of the Earth (Scholte, 2002c). Nothing like a World Financial Authority exists to provide general oversight and coordination. In this situation, responses to global financial crises – like in Asia in 1997–8 – have tended to be rather ad hoc and muddled. Similar comment could be made about the governance of many other global problems.

References

Abrahams, D. (2004) *Regulating Corporations: A Resource Guide*. Geneva: United Nations Research Institute for Social Development.

Andriof, J. and McIntosh, M. (eds.) (2001) *Perspectives on Corporate Citizenship*. Sheffield: Greenleaf.

Bendell, J. (2004) *Barricades and Boardrooms: A Contemporary History of the Corporate Accountability Movement*. Geneva: United Nations Research Institute for Social Development, Technology, Business and Society Programme Paper No. 13.

Brayton, S. (2002) 'Outsourcing War: Mercenaries and the Privatization of Peacekeeping', *Journal of International Affairs*, vol. 55, no. 2 (Spring), pp. 303–29.

Brühl, T. *et al.* (eds.) (2001) *Die Privatisierung der Weltpolitik. Entstaatlichung und Kommerzialisierung im Globalisierungsprozeß*. Bonn: Dietz.

Chambers, S. and Kymlicka, W. (eds.) (2002) *Alternative Conceptions of Civil Society*. Princeton, NJ: Princeton University Press.

Clapp, J. (1998) 'The Privatization of Global Environmental Governance: ISO 14000 and the Developing World', *Global Governance*, vol. 4, no. 3 (July-September), pp. 295–316.

Craig, W. L. *et al.* (1998) *International Chamber of Commerce Arbitration*. Dobbs Ferry, NY: Oceana Publications, 3rd edn.

Cockburn, A. and St. Clair, J. (2000) *Five Days that Shook the World: Seattle and Beyond*. London: Verso.

Cohen, J. L. And Arato, A. (1992) *Civil Society and Political Theory*. Cambridge, MA: MIT Press.

Cutler, A.C. *et al.* (eds.) (1999) *Private Authority in International Affairs*. Albany: State University of New York Press.

Dezalay, Y. and Garth, B. G. (1996) *Dealing in Virtue: international Commercial Arbitration and the Construction of a Transnational Legal Order*. Chicago: University of Chicago Press.

Franda, M. (2001) *Governing the Internet: The Emergence of an International Economy*. Chicago: University of Chicago Press.

Goodman, J. (2000) 'Stopping a Juggernaut: *the Anti-MAI Campaign*', in J. Goodman and P. Ranald (eds.), Stopping the Juggernaut. Annandale, NSW: Pluto Press, pp. 33–52.

Hall, R. B. and Biersteker, T. J. (eds.) (2003) *The Emergence of Private Authority in Global Governance*. Cambridge: Cambridge University Press.

Haufler, V. (2001) *The Public Role of the Private Sector: Industry Self-Regulation in a Global Economy*. Washington, DC: Carnegie Endowment for International Peace.

Henderson, D. (1999) *The MAI Affair: A Story and its Lessons*. London: Royal Institute of International Affairs.

Hopkins, M. (1999) *The Planetary Bargain: Corporate Social Responsibility Comes of Age*. Basingstoke: Palgrave Macmillan.

Humphreys, D. (1996) *Forest Politics: The Evolution of International Cooperation*. London: Earthscan.

IPPPH (2004) Website of the Initiative on Public-Private Partnerships for Health: www.ippph.org, accessed on 31 August.

Jenkins, R. *et al.* (eds.) (2002) *Corporate Responsibility and Labour Rights: Codes of Conduct in the Global Economy*. London: Earthscan.

Kaldor, M. *et al.* (2000) 'Seattle: December '99?' *Millennium: Journal of International Studies*, vol. 29, no. 1, pp. 103–40.

READING 16.1　| **Globalization and Governance: From Statism to Polycentrism** *continued*

By J.A. Scholte

Keck, M. and Sikkink, K. (1998) *Activists beyond Borders: Transnational Advocacy Networks in International Politics*. Ithaca, NY: Cornell University Press.

Khagram, S. (2000) 'Toward Democratic Governance for Sustainable Development: Transnational Civil Society Organizing around Big Dams', in A. M. Florini (ed.), *The Third Force: The Rise of Transnational Civil Society*. Tokyo/Washington, DC: Japan Centre for International Exchange/Carnegie Endowment for International Peace, pp. 83–114.

Knill, C. and Lehmkuhl, D. (2002) 'Private Actors and the State: Internationalization and Changing Patterns of Governance', *Governance: An International Journal of Public Policy*, vol. 15, no. 1 (January), pp. 41–64.

Kobrin, S. J. (1998) 'The MAI and the Clash of Globalizations', *Foreign Policy*, no. 112 (Autumn), pp. 97–109.

Lehmkuhl, D. (2003) 'Resolving Transnational Disputes: Commercial Arbitration and the Multiple Providers of Governance Services'. Paper for the 2003 ECPR Joint Sessions, 28 March-2 April.

Levich, R. M. *et al.* (eds.) (2002) *Ratings, Ratings Agencies and the Global Financial System*. Norwell, MA: Kluwer Academic.

Mandel, R. (2002) *Armies without States: The Privatization of Security*. Boulder, CO: Rienner.

Mattli, W. (2001) 'Private Justice in a Global Economy: From Litigation to Arbitration', *International Organization*, vol. 55, no. 4 (Autumn), pp. 919–48.

O'Brien, R. *et al.* (2000) *Contesting Global Governance: Multilateral Economic Institutions and Global Social Movements*. Cambridge: Cambridge University Press.

Potter, T. and Coleman, W. (2002) 'Transformations in the Private Governance of Global Finance', Paper presented at the International Studies Association Annual Convention, March.

Reich, M. R. (ed.) (2002) *Public-Private Partnerships for Public Health*. Cambridge, MA: Harvard University Press.

Richter, J. (2001) *Holding Corporations Accountable: Corporate Conduct, International Economy, and Citizen Action*. London: Zed.

Ronit, K. and Schneider, V. (eds.) (2000) *Private Organizations in Global Politics*. London: Rouledge.

Salter, L. (1999) 'The Standard Regime for Communication and Information Technologies', in A. C. Cutler *et al.* (eds.), *Private Authority in international Affair*, Albany, NY: State university of New York Press, pp. 97–127.

Schechter, M. G. (1999) *Innovation in Multilateralism*. Tokyo: United Nations University Press.

Scholte, J. A. (2002a) 'Civil Society and Governance in the Global Polity', in M. Ougaard and R. Higgott (eds.), *Towards a Global Polity*. London: Routledge, pp. 145–65.

Scholte, J. A. (2002b) 'Governing Global Finance', in D. Held and A. McGrew (eds.) *Governing Globalization: Power, Authority and Global Governance*. Cambridge: Polity, pp. 189–208.

Shearer, D. (1998) 'Outsourcing War', *Foreign Policy*, no. 112 (Fall), pp. 68–81.

Sinclair, T. J. (2005) *The New Masters of Capital: American Bond Rating Agencies and the Global Economy*. Ithaca, NY: Cornell University Press.

Singer, P. W. (2003) *Corporate Warriors: The Rise of the Privatized Military Industry*. Ithaca, NY: Cornell University Press.

Smillie, I. (1999) 'At Sea in a Sieve? Trends and Issues in the Relationship between Northern NGOs and Northern Governments', in I. Smillie and H. Helmich (eds.), *Stakeholders: Government-NGO Partnerships for International Development*. London: Earthscan.

Smythe, E. (2000) 'State Authority and Investment Security: Non-State Actors and the Negotiation of the Multilateral Agreement on investment at the OECD', in R. A. Higgott *et al.* (eds.), *Nonstate Actors and Authority in the Global System*. London: Routledge, pp. 74–90.

Udall, L. (1998) 'The World Bank and Public Accountability: Has Anything Changed?' in J. A. Fox and L. D. Brown (eds.), *The Struggle for Accountability: The World Bank, NGOs and Grassroots Movements*. Cambridge, MA: MIT Press, pp. 391–436.

UNHCR (1999) *1998 Global Report*. Geneva: united Nations High Commissioner for Refugees.

Utting, P. (2006) 'Corporate Social Responsibility', in R. Robertson and J. A. Scholte (eds.), *Encyclopaedia of Globalization*. London: Routlede.

Wiener, J. (1999) *Globalization and the Harmonization of Law*. London: Pinter.

Yuen, E. *et al.* (eds.) (2001) *The Battle of Seattle: The New Challenge to Capitalist Globalization*. New York: Soft Skull.

Zadek, S. (2001) 'The Rise of Liberal Democracy', *Foreign Affairs*, vol. 76, no. 6 (Novemeber/December), pp. 22–43

Zadek, S. *et al.* (eds.) (1997) *Building Corporate Account Ability: Emerging Practices in Social and Ethical Accounting, Auditing and Reporting*. London: Earthscan.

Zarate, J. C. (1998) 'The Emergence of a new Dog of War: Private International Security Companies, International Law, and the New World Disorder', *Stanford Journal of International Law*, vol. 34, no. 1 (Winter), pp. 75–162.

READING 16.2

Towards a Political Conception of Corporate Responsibility: Business and Society Seen From a Habermasian Perspective

By Andreas Georg Scherer and Guido Palazzo

Many CSR studies comply with the positivist research paradigm in management (e.g., Bacharach, 1989; Seth & Zinkham, 1991). By *positivist* we mean a paradigm that tries to uncover correlations and causal relationships in the social world by using the empirical methods of (natural) science (Donaldson, 1996). Research interest is directed toward the description and explanation of observable social phenomena. Once the cause–effect relationships are identified, this knowledge can be applied in managerial practice to achieve certain outcomes. We argue that the positivist framework of CSR leads to a merely instrumental interpretation of corporate responsibility (see Jones, 1995) that fits into an economic theory of the firm (see, critically, Margolis and Walsh, 2003). We show that positivist CSR does not provide a good moral grounding for the issue of CSR. ...

It is the goal of positivist CSR researchers 'to provide a distinctive view of a corporation's overall efforts toward satisfying its obligations to society' (Wartick and Cochran, 1985: 758). Three types of issues are addressed (Strand, 1983): (1) the societal expectations toward companies ('social responsibility'), (2) the processes that companies generate to meet these expectations ('social responsiveness'; Epstein, 1987), and (3) the effects – or, rather, the measurable results – that follow the processes ('social responses'). These problem areas are integrated within the so-called corporate social performance models (CSP models), which are designed to explain the social efforts of companies (Carroll, 1979; Strand, 1983; Wartick and Cochran, 1985; Wood, 1991). CSP models stipulate that the societal expectations that define the role of a company in society will align the processes of strategy formulation and implementation with the social aspects of management. Thus, the results will be socially tolerable consequences.

Some scholars formulate hypotheses and empirically examine the *causal* relationship between CSP and the explaining variables (e.g., Christmann, 2004; Frooman, 1999; Hocevar and Bhambri, 1989). Their research efforts are oriented toward the empirical sciences and the associated positivist methodology (Bacharach, 1989). As a result, CSR and mainstream management research share the same positivist concept of theory:

> A theory is a *systematically related* set of statements, including some *lawlike generalizations,* that is *empirically testable*. The purpose of theory is to increase scientific understanding through a systematized structure capable of both explaining and predicting phenomena (Seth and Zinkhan, 1991: 75).

Obviously, the CSP models are meant to be conceptual representations of reality. Thus, the validity of a particular CSP model depends on the correspondence of its assertions with empirical observations. These models are created to explain the status quo common to social systems, with their elements and causal relationships. The implicit goal is to produce *technical knowledge* about how organizations work and how their survival in a competitive environment can be achieved (Burrell and Morgan, 1979). This can be described as a technical research interest (Habermas, 1971) – one that also dominates research in strategic management (see, critically, Alvesson and Willmott, 1996; Shrivastava, 1986). Such a technical research interest is made explicit in the 'instrumentalist view' of stake-holder research (Berman, Wicks, Kotha, and Jones, 1999; Jones, 1995; Jones and Wicks, 1999). The positivist paradigm does not attempt a justification of norms: only the description and explanation of norms and expectations are allowed, not a critical questioning of those norms (Wicks and Freeman, 1998). Therefore, 'the [CSP] models fail to effectively integrate normative perspectives into their descriptive focus' (Whetten *et al.*, 2002: 384). ...

Towards a Political Conception of Corporate Responsibility: Business and Society Seen From a Habermasian Perspective *continued*

By Andreas Georg Scherer and Guido Palazzo

A Theory of Deliberative Democracy

The liberal approach to democracy conceptualizes the citizen in his or her role as a private (and mainly economic) actor who has fixed preferences and follows self-interested goals (Elster, 1986). A liberal citizen is able to *bargain* over preferences in order to find a compromise. However, the fixed preferences cannot be *transformed* during the process of bargaining. Therefore, societies need institutions for channeling conflicts between citizens that result from competing and incompatible interests in limited resources or colliding values. To resolve the problem of coordination of the activities of a large number of people, *voluntary exchange* on free and open markets is considered the best measure to guarantee the freedom of individuals. However, the market cannot establish the conditions of its own existence. Rather, these conditions have to be erected by the state apparatus that defines the rules of the game (Friedman, 1962).

As a third-party enforcer, the state interferes in private affairs and constrains individual freedom only if it is unavoidable. Such a liberal model draws a clear line between private economic activities on the one hand and public political activities on the other. The political order aims at guaranteeing the stability of the legal context of the private actor so that individual freedom is protected both vis-à-vis the state and the fellow citizen. The citizen expresses preferences over public concerns and tries to program the state system toward his or her respective causes in a system of elections, vote aggregation, and representation (Elster, 1986). The legitimacy of political decisions is controlled simply by the output of the elections and a – more or less – closed bureaucratic process *within* the political system. Despite its suspicion regarding a strong state, liberal theory rests on the assumption that the state system is more or less capable of regulating the economic system so that its output contributes to the common good (Friedman, 1962).

The liberal conception of democracy seeks political legitimacy simply in the output of elections but neglects the *procedural input* that precedes the decisions. This is challenged by the deliberative approach, which starts with the assumption that the legitimacy of a political decision rests on the discursive quality of the decision-making process (democratic legitimacy; Gutmann and Thompson, 2004; Habermas, 1998). Deliberative democracy casts doubt on the idea of fixed preferences and exclusive self-interest. The discourse can lead to a transformation of preferences. Citizens may share the interest in a common good beyond the aggregation of their economic interests (Zey, 1998). Therefore, political decision making 'on the basis of dialogue and public justification accessible to all citizens' (Parker, 2002: 37) will lead to more informed and rational results, will increase the acceptability of the decisions, will broaden the horizon of the decision maker, will promote mutual respect, and will make it easier to correct wrong decisions that have been made in the past (Fung, 2005; Gutmann and Thompson, 2004; Habermas, 1996).

Habermas argues that it is difficult, if not impossible, to implement concepts of radical democracy (i.e., all citizens participate in all public decisions) in modern societies (Habermas, 1998). Therefore, he shifts attention toward the associations citizens form, such as NGOs, movements, or civil society networks (e.g., see Boli and Thomas, 1999; Keck and Sikkink, 1998), in order to advocate their causes in a broader public context. Seen from this perspective, these spontaneously emerging civil society associations and movements that map, filter, amplify, bundle, and transmit private problems, needs, and values are the core actors in the process of democratic will formation (Habermas, 1996).

As we have shown, Habermasian discourse ethics (Habermas) analyzes the ethical quality of a specific desicion via a list of demanding discourse criteria (ideal speech situation). In contrast, the concept of deliberative democracy (Habermas) shifts the analytical focus to the macro level of the procedural design of political institutions (Habermas, 1996). However, the idea is not a (utopian) attempt at a large-scale application of the criteria of the ideal speech situation as it was envisioned by the critical strategy approach. Nor is it based on the idea that all political decision making can be or must be exposed to public deliberation (see Elster, 1986) – nor does it advocate consensual

| READING 16.2 | **Towards a Political Conception of Corporate Responsibility: Business and Society Seen From a Habermasian Perspective** |

By Andreas Georg Scherer and Guido Palazzo

solutions for all kinds of political disputes or the participation of each single citizen (Habermas, 1998). Rather, it builds on the (more modest) conviction that, in a pluralizing society, the existing democratic institutions need a much stronger link to civil society. And such a deliberative embeddedness of political decision making can be achieved by 'making the routines of bargaining, campaigning, voting, and other important political activities more public-spirited in both process and outcome' (Gutmann and Thompson, 2004: 56). Of course, in real societies deliberative democrats 'act in a wide range of suboptimal circumstances' (Fung, 2005: 400) …

The Corporation as a Politicized Actor

We propose a deliberative concept of CSR that mirrors the discursive link between civil society and the state. This concept aims at the democratic integration of the corporate use of power, especially in the transnational context of incomplete legal and moral regulation. Our interpretation of CSR shifts the focus from an analysis of corporate reaction to stakeholder pressure to an analysis of the corporation's role in the overarching processes of (national and transnational) public will formation and these processes' contribution to solving global environmental and social challenges. Corporate responsibilities are analyzed as resulting from the corporation's embeddedness in a context of changing societal institutions (Dubbink, 2004), and the corporation is understood as a political actor (Matten, Crane, and Chapple, 2003; Scherer, Palazzo, and Baumann, 2006).

As indicated above, the discussion on Habermas in the management literature (Habermas) still has not embraced the pragmatic turn from discourse ethics to deliberative democracy. However, we believe that deliberative democracy delivers a better starting point for a communicative interpretation of CSR than Habermas because it lessens the problem of utopianism and, furthermore, takes the *direct practice of life* (Dewey, 1925) as the starting and reference point of theoretical efforts, thus advocating the *primacy of democracy to philosophy* (Habermas, 1996). What then prevails is not the purity of the philosophical

argument but its link to the established context of democratic procedures and the problems and interests of the citizens. A deliberative concept of CSR embeds corporate decision making in processes of democratic will formation. These processes, driven by civil society actors and spanning a broad field of public arenas, establish a *democratic control on the public use of corporate power* (Dryzek, 1999).

Some have argued in the literature that the growing importance of civil society engagement as conceptualized in the deliberative model does not solve legitimacy problems but, rather, creates new ones. NGOs as the main actors of a vibrant civil society suffer from the same legitimacy problems as corporations. They try to influence corporate and political decision making without being democratically legitimate representatives of the citizens (Rugman, 2000). This problem is mitigated, to a certain degree, by the multiplicity and diversity of civil society engagement. However, given the radicalism of some activists' positions, the danger of an unbridled influence of some civil society actors on corporate decision making should not be underestimated. The oversimplified antagonistic opposition of the corporation as the 'bad guy' representing economic interests and the NGO as the 'good guy' representing moral interests does not consider the fact that, in the deliberative concept of CSR, discourse quality derives from the analysis of arguments, not actors. It is not the quantity of NGO positions adopted that leads to political embeddedness but the willingness and capacity of the corporation to participate in the public process of exchanging arguments its engagement in solving broader societal challenges, and its accountability and transparency in any process of CSR implementation …

The New Political Responsibility of the Business Firm

As already described, scholars in management theory have often understood political and economic responsibilities as descriptions of opposed domains. As Levitt and others argue, the role of business is to earn profit, and social responsibility is the task of the state (Levitt, 1970; see also Friedman, 1970; Jensen, 2002;

READING 16.2

Towards a Political Conception of Corporate Responsibility: Business and Society Seen From a Habermasian Perspective *continued*

By Andreas Georg Scherer and Guido Palazzo

Sundaram and Inkpen, 2004). However, the changing conditions of corporate responsibility in a transnational context do not only appear in theoretical debates. Anecdotal evidence shows that corporations already have started to assume enlarged responsibilities in their globally expanded business environments – responsibilities once regarded as genuine governmental responsibilities (Walsh, Weber, and Margolis, 2003). They engage in public health, education, social security, and protection of human rights in countries with repressive regimes (Kinley and Tadaki, 2004; Matten and Crane, 2005); address social ills such as AIDS, malnutrition, and illiteracy (Margolis and Walsh, 2003); engage in self-regulation to fill global gaps in legal regulation and moral orientation (Scherer and Smid, 2000); and promote societal peace and stability (Fort and Schipani, 2004). Those activities go beyond the common understanding of stakeholder responsibility and CSR as conceptualized in the positivist tradition (see, critically, Crane, Matten, and Moon, 2004). Some corporations do not simply follow powerful external expectations by complying with societal standards in legal and moral terms; they engage in discourses that aim at *setting* or *redefining* those standards and expectations in a changing, globalizing world and assume an enlarged political coresponsibility (Scherer *et al.*, 2006).

Such a collaborative approach helps to preempt potential conflicts between a corporation and its societal environment. Indeed, stakeholder conflicts do not vanish, but we expect that the practice of political coresponsibility leads to an improved contextual sensitivity of the embedded corporation in comparison with those 'just-in-time tactical responses' (Schrage, 2004: 20) that might result from a merely instrumental approach to CSR. As Fung argues in his analysis of labor conditions, 'Deliberative engagement of this sort will not silence the most strident or skeptical advocates, but it will differentiate firms that are responsive and proactive from the ones that are defensive or that fail to adopt workplace conditions as a priority' (2003: 61). A deliberative concept of CSR changes the modus of responsibility from the reactive model

of the positivist approach to a proactive concept of societal involvement. The corporation, within the network of civil society communication, does not replace the idea of stakeholder management but enhances it and frames it in an ongoing process of observing and participating in public discourses.

In order to illustrate the idea of a deliberative concept of CSR, we cite the example of the Forest Stewardship Council (FSC). This example demonstrates the corporate embeddedness in processes of democratic will formation and problem solving in a transnational context of political governance (see www.fsc.org; see also Hollenhorst and Johnson, 2005). After the failure of governments at the 1992 United Nations Conference on Environment and Development (UNCED) to develop shared standards and activities for the protection of forests worldwide, the obvious global governance gap was addressed by a group of NGOs and corporations. The FSC was founded in 1993 as a result of that cooperation.

The FSC developed a set of principles and criteria for sustainable global forest management. Today, the organization includes a wide range of members interacting in a governance structure that aims at a broad level of equal participation and deliberation. It includes corporations such as IKEA, Home Depot, and OBI, along with human rights activists, development aid agencies, indigenous peoples groups, and environmental NGOs. The General Assembly, as the highest decision-making body of the FSC, is organized into three membership chambers – environmental, social, and economic – for balancing the voting power of its diverse members. On the basis of its principles and criteria, the FSC has developed a certification for timber and timber products that is approved by independent bodies. The certification process itself contains rigorous standards and independent monitoring procedures, which lead to a broad acceptance of the council among critical civil society organizations.

Of course, the FSC has been criticized. Some, for instance, have argued that the council's fast growth strategy has led to the certification of noncomplying

READING 16.2

Towards a Political Conception of Corporate Responsibility: Business and Society Seen From a Habermasian Perspective

By Andreas Georg Scherer and Guido Palazzo

corporations that cannot be controlled sufficiently (Counsell & Terje Loraas, 2002). However, we suggest that the FSC can be considered one of the most advanced concepts in the sense of our proposed political CSR. It illustrates some of the key aspects of a politically embedded corporation we unfolded in the discussion above: one of the main environmental challenges that national governments are not able or willing to tackle is addressed. Self-regulation takes place in a broad process of democratic will formation in collaboration with civil society actors. The independent third-party certification of corporate sustainability performance enforces a democratic control of corporate activities. The FSC is designed around deliberative criteria such as broad participation, the attempt to exclude corporate power as a decision criterion, and a constant process of improvement based on critical feedback about the council's performance or form of organization. The FSC does not represent a form of stakeholder dialogue, in which corporations invite stakeholders into their internal decision-making processes. Rather, it represents a corporate move into the political processes of public policy making through the creation of and collaboration with global institutions of political governance.

This example of corporate engagement goes beyond passive normative compliance and the simple support of causes, and it goes beyond the management of stakeholder pressure. We do not argue that the described case is an example of power-free discourses of political will formation. In real societies suboptimal circumstances are unavoidable. What we want to demonstrate is that CSR is increasingly displayed in corporate involvement in the political process of solving societal problems, often on a global scale. ...

References

Alvesson, M. and Willmott, H. (1996) *Making sense of management*. London: Sage.

Bacharach, S. (1989) Organizational theories: Some criteria for evaluation. *Academy of Management Review*. 14: 496–515.

Berman, S.L., Wicks, A.C., Kotha, S. and Jones, T.M. (1999) Does stakeholder orientation matter? The relationship between stakeholder management models and firm financial performance. *Academy of Management Journal*. 42: 488–506.

Boli, J. and Thomas, G.M. (Eds.) (1999) *Constructing world culture*. Stanford, CA: Stanford University Press.

Burrell, G. and Morgan, G. (1979) *Sociological paradigms and organisational analysis*. London: Heinemann.

Carroll, A.B. (1979) A three-dimensional conceptual model of corporate social performance. *Academy of Management Review*. 4: 497–505.

Christmann, P. (2004) Multinational companies and the national environment: Determinants of global environmental policy standardization. *Academy of Management Journal*. 47: 747–760.

Counsell, S., and Terje Loraas, K. (2002) *Trading in credibility*. London: Rainforest Foundation.

Crane, A., Matten, D. and Moon, J. (2004) Stakeholders as citizens? Rethinking rights, participation, and democracy. *Journal of Business Ethics*. 53: 107–122.

Dewey, J. (1925) Existence, value and criticism. In J.A. Boydston (Ed.), *Experience and nature: The later works, 1925–1952*, vol. 1: 295–326. Carbondale, IL: Carbondale University Press.

Donaldson, L. (1996) *For positivist organization theory*. London: Sage.

Dryzek, J.S. (1999) Transnational democracy. *Journal of Political Philosophy*. 7(1): 30–51.

Dubbink, W. (2004) The fragile structure of free-market society. *Business Ethics Quarterly*. 14: 23–46.

Elster, J. (1986) The market and the forum: Three varieties of political theory. In J. Elster and A. Hylland (Eds.), *Foundations of social choice theory*: 103–132. Cambridge: Cambridge University Press.

Epstein, E.M. (1987) The corporate social policy process: Beyond business ethics, corporate social responsibility, and corporate social responsiveness. *California Management Review*. 29(3): 99–114.

Fort, T.L. and Schipani, C.A. (2004) *The role of business in fostering peaceful societies*. Cambridge: Cambridge University Press.

Friedman, M. (1962) Capitalism and freedom. Chicago: University of Chicago Press.

Friedman, M. (1970). The social responsibility of business is to increase its profit. *New York Times Magazine*, September 13. Reprinted in Donaldson, T., and Werhane, P.H.

| **Towards a Political Conception of Corporate Responsibility: Business and Society Seen From a Habermasian Perspective** *continued*

By Andreas Georg Scherer and Guido Palazzo

(Eds.). (1970) *Ethical issues in business:* 217–223. Englewood Cliffs, NJ: Prentice-Hall.

Frooman, J. (1999) Stakeholder influence strategies. *Academy of Management Review.* 24:19 1–205.

Fung, A. (2003) Deliberative democracy and international labor standards. *Governance.* 16(1): 51–71.

Fung, A. (2005) Deliberation before the revolution. *Political Theory,* 33: 397–419.

Gutmann, A. and Thompson, F. (2004) *Why deliberative democracy?* Princeton, NJ: Princeton University Press.

Habermas, J. (1971) *Knowledge and human interests.* Boston: Beacon Press.

Habermas, J. (1996) *Between facts and norms.* Cambridge, MA: MIT Press.

Habermas, J. (1998) Three normative models of democracy. In *The inclusion of the other:* 239–252. Cambridge, MA: MIT Press.

Hocevar, S.P. and Bhambri, A. (1989) Corporate social performance: A model of assessment criteria. *Research in Corporate Social Performance and Policy.* 11: 1–20.

Hollenhorst, T. and Johnson, C. (2005) *Tools for corporate social responsibility: Forest Stewardship Council.* http://www.ifpeople.net/resources/downloads/tools/fscen.pdf, accessed May 5.

Jensen, M.C. (2002) Value maximization, stakeholder theory, and the corporate objective function. *Business Ethics Quarterly.* 12: 235–256.

Jones, T.M. (1995) Instrumental stakeholder theory: A synthesis of ethics and economics. *Academy of Management Review.* 20: 404–437.

Jones, T.M. and Wicks, A.C. (1999) Convergent stakeholder theory. *Academy of Management Review.* 24: 206–221.

Keck, M.E. and Sikkink, K. (1998) *Activists beyond borders.* New York: Cornell University Press.

Kinley, D. and Tadaki, J. (2004) From talk to walk: The emergence of human rights responsibilities for corporations at international law. *Virginia Journal of International Law.* 44: 931–1022.

Levitt, T. (1970) The dangers of social responsibility. In T. Meloan, S. Smith, and J. Wheatly (Eds.), *Managerial marketing policies and decisions:* 461–475. Boston: Houghton Mifflin.

Margolis, J.D. and Walsh, J.P. (2003) Misery loves companies: Rethinking social initiatives by business. *Administrative Science Quarterly.* 48: 268–305.

Matten, D. and Crane, A. (2005) Corporate citizenship: Toward an extended theoretical conceptualization. *Academy of Management Review.* 30: 166–179.

Matten, D., Crane, A. and Chapple, W. (2003) Behind the mask: Revealing the true face of corporate citizenship. *Journal of Business Ethics.* 45: 109–120.

Parker, C. (2002) *The open corporation.* Cambridge: Cambridge University Press.

Rugman, A. (2000) *The end of globalization.* London: Random House.

Scherer, A.G. and Smid, M. (2000) The downward spiral and the U.S. model principles. Why MNEs should take responsibility for the improvement of world-wide social and environmental conditions. *Management International Review.* 40: 351–371.

Scherer, A.G., Palazzo, G. and Baumann, D. (2006) Global rules and private actors. Toward a new role of the TNC in global governance. *Business Ethics Quarterly.* 16: 505–532.

Schrage, E. (2004) Supply and the brand. *Harvard Business Review.* 82(6): 20–21.

Seth, A., and Zinkham, G. (1991) Strategy and the Research process: A comment. *Strategic Management Journal.* 12: 75–82.

Shrivastava, P. (1986) Is strategic management ideological? *Journal of Management.* 12: 363–377.

Strand, R. (1983) A systems paradigm of organizational adaptations to the social environment. *Academy of Management Review.* 8: 90–96.

Sundaram, A.K. and Inkpen, A.C. (2004) The corporate objective revisited. *Organization Science.* 15: 350–363.

Walsh, J.P., Weber, K., & Margolis, J.D. (2003) Social issues and management: Our lost cause found. *Journal of Management.* 29: 859–881.

Wartick, S.L. and Cochran, P.L. (1985) The evolution of the corporate social performance model. *Academy of Management Review.* 4: 758–769.

Whetton, D.A., Rands, G. and Godfrey, P. (2002) What are the responsibilities of business to society? In A. Pettigrew, H. Thomas, and R. Whittington (Eds.), *Handbook of strategy and management:* 373–408. London: Sage.

Wicks, A.C. and Freeman, R.E. (1998) Organization studies and the new pragmatism: Positivism, antipositivism, and the search for ethics. *Organization Science.* 9: 123–140.

Wood, D.J. (1991) Corporate social performance revisited. *Academy of Management Review.* 16: 691–718.

Zey, M. (1998) *Rational choice theory and organizational theory: A critique.* London: Sage.

READING 16.3 | # Structures, Identities and Politics: Bringing Corporate Citizenship into the Corporation

By Peter Edward and Hugh Willmott

Habermas's notion of deliberative democracy is predicated on two key dualities. The first of these is lifeworld–system: lifeworld as symbolic reproduction in socially integrated action; system as material reproduction in system integrated action (Habermas 1987, pp. 319–320). The second duality is morals–ethics: morals are considered universally valid norms while (discourse) ethics are productive of contingent values (Habermas, 1990). However, Habermas conceives of these dualities not as comprising absolute, separable entities but as differences in degree (Fraser, 1989; Habermas, 1990, p. 211). In his more recent work on deliberative democracy, the 'melding' of the theorized dualities is taken even further – particularly in the elision of the public sphere of the lifeworld into civil society. A fundamental issue, then, is whether this de-differentiation of the grounding dualities in Habermas's work can legitimately be made while maintaining the essential insights that derive from theorising these social phenomena as dualities. In other words, can we assume that principles derived from an idealized decoupling of lifeworld and system can still be invoked when that decoupling is denied in the name of pragmatism? At issue here is a possible weakening of Habermas's resolve to preserve the centrality of 'lifeworld' priorities in the face of its colonization by system logics and demands.

With regard to corporations, Palazzo and Scherer, (2006) point to the weakening ability of national law to control transnational corporate activities, combined with increasingly heterogeneous and changing societal expectations, which are seen to undermine the cognitive and pragmatic foundations that, in the past, have provided corporate legitimacy. These developments are understood to foster a politicization of the corporation as 'an unavoidable result of the changing interplay of economy, government and civil society in a globalising world' (ibid., p. 76). In this respect, Scherer and Palazzo echo and considerably broaden and deepen the 'extended' view of corporate citizenship advanced by Matten and Crane as they commend Habermas's notion of deliberative

democracy as a relevant response to the politicization of the corporation (Palazzo and Scherer, 2006, Scherer and Palazzo, 2007) …

From the perspective of the social theory of hegemony 'communicative power' works in the theory of deliberative democracy as a signifier that operates inadvertently to occlude and silence its own constitutive dislocation. Noonan, (2005) identifies the same dislocation, though in different language, when he says that 'because Habermas argues that the economy must be left to function according to endogenous market dynamics, he accepts as a condition of democracy … a social structure that is in fact anti-democratic.' (p. 101). Our view is that if deliberative democracy is to become a preferred articulation (to achieve grip) for corporate citizenship then it must be complemented by a radical democratic element. This move can be seen as an attempt to ensure that the dislocation remains visible, unable to become fully sedimented into accepted 'commonsense'. To support this view, we now illustrate what can happen when this occlusion of ambiguity occurs in corporate citizenship.

The Forestry Stewardship Council

Following Habermas's thinking on deliberative democracy, Scherer and Palazzo, (2007, p. 1105; Habermas, 1996) state that, 'it [now] seems naïve to assume that all coordination problems in the context of economic activities can be solved in processes of argumentation that are oriented toward mutual understanding and agreement'. According to them, this 'less idealistic and more pragmatic approach' (Scherer and Palazzo 2007, p. 1107) singles out collective actors such as non-governmental organizations (NGOs), citizen movements and networks as 'actors in the process of will-formation' who can 'map, filter, amplify, bundle, and transmit private problems, needs, and values' (ibid.). In other words, 'civil society' here predominantly signifies instrumental processes that exist, for Habermas, at the system level; and the 'collective actors' form part of 'the

READING 16.3

Structures, Identities and Politics: Bringing Corporate Citizenship into the Corporation *continued*

By Peter Edward and Hugh Willmott

procedural design of political institutions' (Scherer and Palazzo 2007, p.1107, referencing Habermas, 1996). In this process, it seems to us that the original significance and value of the lifeworld, as the locus where processes and objects of identification take shape, and as the site of the emancipatory force in *all* human beings, risks dilution and marginalisation. In the name of non-naïve pragmatism, we are invited to occlude, or to circumvent, the inescapable presence of dislocation in the social realm. To the extent to which this occurs, the critical edge of Habermas's thinking becomes softened by a 'realistic' readiness to accommodate the demands of the system. As we shall now argue, this translates, in Scherer and Palazzo's thinking, to a combination of issuing appeals to corporations to be public spirited combined with lending encouragement to NGOs (which lack any democratic mandate) and other collective actors to pressure and collaborate with corporations in order to get them to 'participate in the public process of exchanging arguments' (ibid., p. 1109) and facilitating forms of self-regulation that mitigate social and ecological destructiveness.

The example used by Scherer and Palazzo, (2007) to support and illustrate their argument is the case of the Forest Stewardship Council (FSC) which was established in 1993 as a collaborative venture between NGOs and major corporations such as IKEA, Home Depot and B&Q (see also Scherer *et al.*, 2006). We will argue that this example highlights the dangers of focusing upon procedures rather than effective political action and/or the vulnerability of Habermas's ideas to a reading that identifies the operation of the FSC with even their partial actualization.

Ten years after the establishment of the FSC, the Rainforest Foundation (RF) (2002) conducted a detailed (160 page) report on the FSC's activities. Scherer and Palazzo, (2007, p. 1110) refer to the FSC report, but despite its pertinence for their thesis, mention only the report's criticism of the Council's fast growth strategy that is linked to the certification of non-complying companies. The full RF report makes uncomfortable reading for advocates of deliberative democracy as it illustrates the vulnerability of its principles to capture and

subversion. The report is highly critical of the transparency of the FSC and the lack of democratic accountability. A flavour of the problems is given in the executive summary where it is noted:

> Key stakeholders are effectively excluded from many FSC processes ... Whilst legitimate forest stakeholders, such as local communities and indigenous people, remain marginalized in FSC's decision-making processes, the influence of other stakeholders – such as certification bodies and their commercial clients – has grown ... The FSC's complaints procedures concerning certifiers and their certifications are essentially non-functioning. They are cumbersome and onerous, discriminatory against weaker stakeholders, and biased in favour of the certifiers and their commercial clients. There is therefore no effective means of redress for many stakeholders in the event of dispute ... There has been a serious lack of transparency or 'democracy of knowledge'. Key FSC processes have been undertaken without proper information being available to the membership and the wider public. This has undermined accountability of the organization ... (Rainforest Foundation, 2002, p. 7).

In short, according to the RF, the operation of the FSC privileged certification bodies and commercial clients as it marginalized the voice of local communities and indigenous people who were unable to obtain redress from the FSC as a consequence of a cumbersome complaints procedure ...

Silence on the RF findings allows Scherer and Palazzo to offer the unqualified view that 'the FSC can be considered one of the most advanced concepts in the sense of our proposed political CSR' (Scherer and Palazzo, 2007, p. 1110). Of course, no organization is going to be without significant imperfections. But to identify the FSC as a model of 'political CSR' and to claim that the FSC 'demonstrates the corporate embeddedness in processes of democratic will-formation and problem solving in a transnational context of political governance' (ibid., p. 1110) does

READING 16.3

Structures, Identities and Politics: Bringing Corporate Citizenship into the Corporation

By Peter Edward and Hugh Willmott

fuel some concern about the value and/or application of Habermas's deliberative democracy. What the RF report communicates to us is a triumph of system over lifeworld legitimized by a discourse of deliberative democracy where it is claimed, for example, that 'The FSC is designed around deliberative criteria such as broad participation, the attempt to exclude corporate power as a decision criterion ...' (ibid.).

If the findings of the RF report are accepted as a reliable indicator of the operation of 'corporate citizenship' at the FSC, then it illustrates the importance of 'buy in' to the principles of citizenship and, more specifically, the likely consequences if mere lip-service is paid to commitments to develop skilful processes that transform and democratize corporate practices. More specifically, there is a risk that formal principles and structures are established that approximate to ideals of deliberative democracy but that the everyday practices of organizing fail to embody and nurture such lofty ideals. While a superficial tick-box audit might show that the relevant procedures are 'in place', it is only when attention is given to the outcomes of specific practices that significant doubt is cast, for example, upon the claim that the FSC 'demonstrates the corporate embeddedness in processes of democratic will-formation and problem solving in a transnational context of political governance' (ibid., p. 1110) ...

We anticipate that some readers may associate the stance of radical democracy with being overly 'romantic' or insufficiently pragmatic. Our response has been to show how the advocacy and pursuit of deliberative democracy *per se* can be excessively pragmatic and conservative. From a radical democratic standpoint, traversing the tensions – learning to live with them and to appreciate them as constitutive necessities of the social world – is considered to be

endemic to the puzzles and possibilities of citizenship. While we support the intent of deliberative democracy, our support is qualified by a concern to highlight and correct what we assess to be the vulnerability of deliberative democracy to cooption and formalization ...

References

Fraser, N. (1989) *Unruly Practices: Power, Discourse and Gender in Contemporary Social Theory*, Minneapolis: University of Minnesota Press.

Habermas, J. (1987) *The Theory of Communicative Action. Volume 2: Lifeworld and System: The Critique of Functionalist Reason*, Cambridge, UK: Polity Press.

Habermas, J. (1990) *Moral Consciousness and Communicative Action*, translated by C. Lenhardt and S.W. Nicholsen, Cambridge, UK: Polity Press.

Habermas, J. (1996) *Between Facts and Norms: Contributions to a Discourse Theory of Law and Democracy*, translated by W. Rehg, Cambridge: Polity Press.

Noonan, J. (2005) 'Modernization, Rights, and Democratic Society: The Limits of Habermas's Democratic Theory', *Res Publica*, 11: 101–123.

Palazzo, G. and Scherer, A.G. (2006) 'Corporate Legitimacy as Deliberation: A Communicative Framework', *Journal of Business Ethics*, 66: 71–88.

Scherer, A.G., Palazzo, G. and Baumann, D. (2006) 'Global Rules and Private Actors: Toward a New Role of the Transnational Corporation in Global Governance', *Business Ethics Quarterly*, 16(4): 505–532.

Scherer, A.G. and Palazzo, G. (2007) 'Towards a Political Conception of Corporate Responsibility – Business and Society Seen from a Habermasian Perspective', *Academy of Management Review*, 32(4): 1096–1120.

The Rainforest Foundation (2002) 'Trading in Credibility: The Myth and Reality of the Forest Stewardship Council', http://www.rainforestfoundationuk.org/files/Trading%20in%20Credibility%20full%20report.pdf, accessed 24 October 2007.

Discussion Questions

1. Why is it relevant to consider 'globalization' when studying management and organization?
2. Why do Scherer and Palazzo believe that it is necessary to introduce the concept of 'deliberative democracy' into considerations of corporate governance and, more specifically, corporate social responsibility?
3. What do Edward and Willmott regard as the main shortcoming of 'deliberative democracy' as a means of enabling responsible corporate citizenship?

Introduction References

Appelbaum, R.P. and Robinson, W.I. (eds) (2005) *Critical Global Studies*, London: Routledge.
Guellén, M.F. (2001) 'Is Globalization Civilizing, Destructive or Feeble? A Critique of Five Key Debates in the Social Science Literature', *Annual Review of Sociology*, 27: 235–60.
Laclau, E. and Mouffe, C. (1985) *Hegemony and Socialist Strategy*, London: Verso.

Recommended Further Readings

See references to all the above texts plus:

Bannerjee, S.B. (2007) *Corporate Social Responsibility: The Good, the Bad and the Ugly*, London: Edward Elgar.
Becht, M., Bolton, P. and Röell, A. (2005) *Corporate Governance and Control* available at http://bordeure.files.wordpress.com/2008/09/ssrn-id343461.pdf
Blowfield, M. and Murray, A. (2008) *Corporate Responsibility: A Critical Introduction*, Oxford University Press.
Burchell, J. (ed.) (2007) *The Corporate Social Responsibility Reader: Context and Perspectives*, London: Routledge.
Carroll, A.B. (1999) 'Corporate Social Responsibility: Evolution of a Definitional Construct' *Business & Society*, 38(3): 268–95.
Crane, A., McWilliams, A., Matten, D., Moon, J. and Siegel, D.S. (eds), *The Oxford Handbook of Corporate Social Responsibility*, Oxford University Press.
Freeman, R.E. and Liedtka, J. (1991) 'Corporate social responsibility: a critical approach', *Business Horizons*, 34(4): 92–8.
Held, D. ed., (2003) *The Global Transformations Reader: An Introduction to the Globalization Debate*, 2nd ed., Oxford: Polity Press.
Hirst, P., Thompson, G. and Bromley, S. (2000) *Globalization in Question*, 3rd edition, Oxford: Polity Press.
Kolk, A., van Tulder, R. and Welters, C. (1999) 'International Codes of Conduct and Corporate Social Responsibility: Can Transnational Corporations Regulate Themselves?' *Transnational Corporations* 8(1): 143–180 also available at http://www.unctad.org/en/docs/iteiit12v8n1_en.pdf#page=151
Lazonick, W. and O'sullivan, M. (2000) 'Maximizing Shareholder Value: A New Ideology for Corporate Governance', *Economy and Society*, 29(1): 13–35.
Roberts, J. (2001) 'Corporate Governance and the Ethics of Narcissus', *Business Ethics Quarterly*, 11(1): 109–127.
Scholte, J.A. (2005) *Globalization: A Critical Introduction*, 2nd ed., Basingstoke: Palgrave Macmillan.
Stiglitz, J. (2003) *Globalization and its Discontents*, Harmondsworth: Penguin.
Windsor, D. (2001) 'The Future of Corporate Social Responsibility', *International Journal of Organizational Analysis*, 9(3): 225–56.

INDEX

abbreviation principle 169
Abercrombie, N. *et al* 74
Adorno, T. 177
alienation 228, 236
Althusser, L. 101
American Dream 198–9, 210–11
Anthony, P. 54
anthropocentrism 273–7
Argyris, C. and Schon, D.A. 42, 52
Armstrong, P. 80
Azibo, D.A.Y. 209

Bachrach, P. and Baratz, M. 143
Baudrillard, J. 97, 245–6
Bauman, Z. 97, 98
Beck, U. 275
Behaviourism 179, 215, 216
Bell, D. 254
belonging 85–6, 96–7
    consumption thesis 97–101
Bentham, J. 169–70, 268
Berger, P. and Luckmann, T. 128–9
Bittner, E. 9–10
Blackler, F. *et al* 65
Bonfire of the Vanities (T.Wolfe) 147, 148–50
Booth, C. 73
Bourdieu, P. 67
Braverman, H. 40, 54, 88, 142
Bryman, A. 124
Burawoy, M. 55
bureaucracy 8–9, 41–2, 47–9
Burris, B. 44

Campbell, C. 245
capital 40

change management 83, 85–6, 163
Child, J. 43, 44
China International Economic Trade
    Arbitration Commission (CIETAC)
    290
civil society 292
class 210–11
Clegg, S. 76
Clough, P.T. 183
Codex Alimentarius Commission 291
cognitive interest 11
    emancipatory 11, 13–14
    practical 11, 12–13
    reflection on 14–15
    technical 11, 12
Cohen, A.P. 98, 100
Comay, R. 155
commonsense thinking 9–11
consumer society 235, 236–40
consumption 97–8, 101, 231
    addictive 231, 234
    aesthetics 240
    ambiguities 100
    boundary crossing 247
    democratic/subversive 246
    hedonist 231–2
    identity and 218–19
    inclusion/exclusion 99–100
    individual/solitary 235, 239
    liberating/repressive 234
    market logic 98–9
    Marxist influence 234, 236, 244–5
    mass culture critique 245–6
    needs/wants 245
    pluralism/equality 246–7
    production/consumption distinction
        235–6, 244–7

social conduct 99
subjectivities 235, 241–3
subversive 246
temporal 238
traditional representations 244–7
transitory, impermanent, volatile
    235, 236–7
control 197
    bureaucratic 142, 146
    elements 142
    rational 216–17
    self-managing teams 89–91
    simple 142, 145
    structural 142
    technical 142, 145–6
    TQM 92–6
Cook, S.D.N. and Brown, J.S. 27
corporate citizenship 301–3
corporate culture 45–6
corporate social performance (CSP)
    295
corporate social responsibility (CSR)
    286–7, 295
    corporation as politicized actor
        297
    deliberative democracy 287–8,
        296–7
    global 290
    new political responsibility 297–9
    positivist approach 287
Cress, D.M. and Snow, D.A. 75
Critical Theory 11–15, 43–6
    Marxist 228–9
    reification 228
    strategic management 71–6
Crozier, M. 88
cultural theory 231–4, 244–7

305